Beatrice

Beatrice

A Genealogy of Fellows, Stegall, and Cardwell

KENNETH E. BURCHETT

Amity America
Branson, Missouri

Library of Congress Control Number: 2021909081

ISBN: 978-1-7350442-1-7

On the cover: Asher Brown Durand, *The Beeches.*
Scene from the Catskill Mountains.
1845. Oil on canvas, 60 3/8" x 48 1/8".
Metropolitan Museum of Art.

Title page: *Three Generations.*
Belle Fellows, Tom Cardwell,
Beatrice and son.
1942.

Amity America, Publishers
One Seventeen Westwood Drive
Branson, Missouri 65616

For Sharron and Sharleen
In Memory of Belle

Contents

Acknowledgements

A debt of gratitude goes to the family historians who preserved the memory of past Fellows and Cardwell generations. A special thank you to the scholars who shared their work and to the archives that opened their research collections. I wish to acknowledge those both past and present whose work inspired my own. Rand Cardwell, Marjorie Daum Columbus, David Fellows, Dennis Fellows, Edwin Wilcox Fellows, George Marshall Fellows, Jerry Fellows, Mark D. Fellows, Willie Ira Fellows, Sharleen Hobson, Mabel Fellows Murphy, Sharron O'Connor, Allen Pendergraft, Helen Peyton, Effie Fellows Ready, Louis Dow Sisco, Jean Nips Swaim, Dawn Watts Westfall, and a very special thank you to Beatrice Richardson who good-naturedly consented to long interviews.

This book will undoubtedly fall short in many respects. Although every effort went into rendering an accurate account of the ancestry of Beatrice and true descriptions of events that shaped each generation, I take full responsibility for any errors of fact or interpretation, and confess the same shortcomings that historian Richard A. Wheeler acknowleded in his *History of the Town of Stonington.* "For reasons not now generally understood the graves of many of our early settlers have no headstones to mark their last earthly resting places, and in many instances their names do not appear on our town or church records, which have greatly embarrassed me in my work and with all its imperfection."

With apologies to anyone who I may have missed, I wish to acknowledge the special assistance of the staffs of the institutions and organizations that contributed to my research; namely, Connecticut Historical Society, Essex Institute, Family History Library, Green County Archives and Records Center, Greene County Library Center, Ipswich Historical Society, Library of

Congress, Library of Virginia, Missouri State Archives, National Archives and Records Administration, and Sumner County Archives.

Finally, I deeply appreciate the forbearance and encouragement of family members who patiently indulged my preoccupation with a seemingly endless project.

Preface

The life of Beatrice Cardwell was much like that of many Americans in the early 20th century. She grew up in rural southwest Missouri, went to a one-room school through the eighth grade, married, and raised a family. Curiosity about her family tree never went much beyond two generations. However, like many Americans she had a rich heritage. There were men and women of great prominence and renown in her past, which every genealogist hopes to discover. Her tenth great grandfather was the colonist Roger Williams, the Puritan founder of the State of Rhode Island; she shared a distant relationship with Judy Garland; and had the same ancestors as Presidents George H.W. Bush and George W. Bush. Notwithstanding these examples, her people were mostly farmers of modest means who made up the core of the American story. They lived at pivotal times in the history of the country and joined in the call for American Independence before it became a reality. The sons of her ancestors fought in every war from the French and Indian War, through the American Revolution, to the Civil War, and both World Wars.

The Fellows and Cardwells were part of the Great Migration that brought the English to the New World. Each generation pressed further westward to settle the wilderness frontiers. The presence of her ancestors is in the documents of courthouses from Massachusetts to New York, North Carolina to Tennessee and Kentucky, and in California, Illinois, Kansas, and Missouri.

This book is in two parts.

Part 1 traces the Fellows family form William Fellows of Ipswich, Essex County, Massachusetts, in 1635, to Maude Belle Fellows who married Thomas Edward Cardwell in 1904 in Cedar County, Missouri.

Part 2 covers the history of the Cardwell family from Thomas Cardwell of Granville, North Carolina, to Beatrice Cardwell, with an introduction to the life of Thomas Cardwell of Virginia in 1636, and his descendants.

Each chapter covers one family group. There is no attempt to extend the genealogy beyond the immediate family household of an ancestor. The list of descendants of a generation seldom goes beyond naming the children of the forbearer. Each household is one link in the chain of descendants. Coverage proceeds from a specific individual to the next in a linear line of descent to the most recent family member included in the genealogy. Therefore, the usual genealogical reference numbers do not apply. Each generation includes a biographical sketch of the ancestor and a family group. The + symbol beside a name in a family group means that person is next in line and is the subject of a biographical sketch. Where the record of an individual is incomplete or unsubstantiated, the qualifiers of *possible* and *probable* denote a level of interpretation. Discursive endnotes contain alternative interpretations of disputed documents and sources.

A genealogy is a reasonable interpretation of available information at a specific point in time. New documents will no doubt surface in the future, adding to the genealogical record, clarifying, and correcting present knowledge. This is the expected outcome of the evolution of genealogy and the reason new researchers and writers add to family history. If the present book creates a foundation upon which to build a more complete history of the Fellows, Stegall, and Cardwell families, it has attained its purpose.

ANCESTRY

1609 -1958

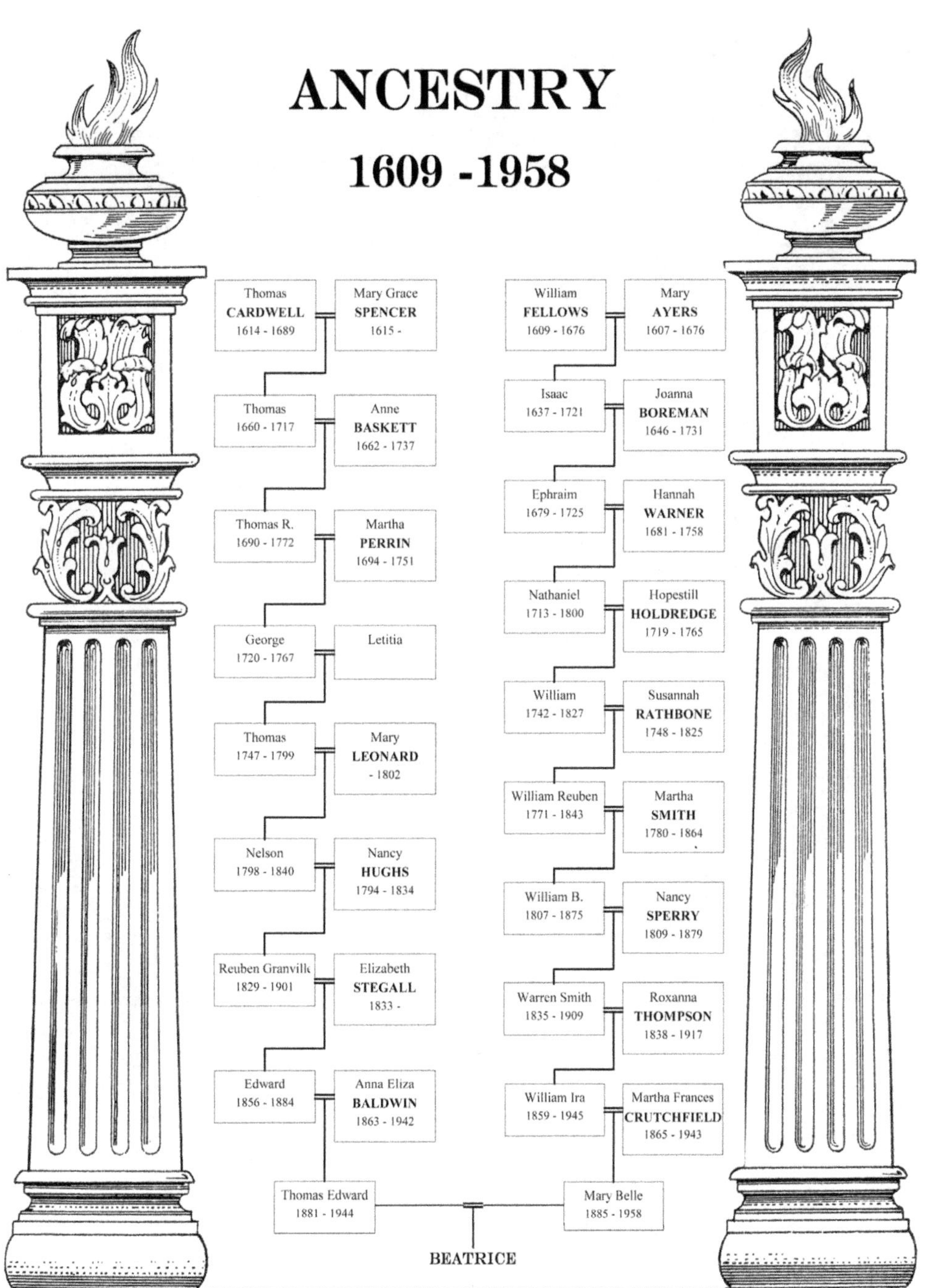
Thomas CARDWELL 1614 - 1689
Mary Grace SPENCER 1615 -
Thomas 1660 - 1717
Anne BASKETT 1662 - 1737
Thomas R. 1690 - 1772
Martha PERRIN 1694 - 1751
George 1720 - 1767
Letitia
Thomas 1747 - 1799
Mary LEONARD - 1802
Nelson 1798 - 1840
Nancy HUGHS 1794 - 1834
Reuben Granvill
1829 - 1901
Elizabeth STEGALL 1833 -
Edward 1856 - 1884
Anna Eliza BALDWIN 1863 - 1942
William FELLOWS 1609 - 1676
Mary AYERS 1607 - 1676
Isaac 1637 - 1721
Joanna BOREMAN 1646 - 1731
Ephraim 1679 - 1725
Hannah WARNER 1681 - 1758
Nathaniel 1713 - 1800
Hopestill HOLDREDGE 1719 - 1765
William 1742 - 1827
Susannah RATHBONE 1748 - 1825
William Reuben 1771 - 1843
Martha SMITH 1780 - 1864
William B. 1807 - 1875
Nancy SPERRY 1809 - 1879
Warren Smith 1835 - 1909
Roxanna THOMPSON 1838 - 1917
William Ira 1859 - 1945
Martha Frances CRUTCHFIELD 1865 - 1943
Thomas Edward 1881 - 1944
Mary Belle 1885 - 1958
BEATRICE

1

Fellows Genealogy Introduction

The Fellows family in America begins in 1635 with William Israel Fellows of Ipswich, Essex County, Massachusetts. As late as 1896, history knew little about his branch of the Fellows family. Historian Henry A. Baker wrote, "William Fellowes came to this country from England before 1641, and settled at Ipswich, Mass., and became an inhabitant of that town. It does not appear from which portion of England he came, nor the exact time of his arrival here. He was married before he left England, but the name of his wife is not known, nor when or where they were married. The names of his children are found in the last will."[1] The history of the Fellows family is more complete now than when Baker published in 1896. New discoveries have added to an aleady robust genealogy of the Fellows ancestry. Nevertheless, genealogical research is sometimes open to dispute. Historical information is frequently lacking or difficult to decipher. Common first names recur repeatedly within the same families and between generations. Ancestors tended to name children after themselves and close family relatives causing researchers sometimes to make mistakes in lineage. For example, three successive generations of the Fellows family had at the head of the household William Fellows, and there were many associated kin of the same first name William. Mistakes committed by one genealogist trying to sort out the various identities passed to the next researcher who picked up and duplicated the errors. Despite extensive study of the Fellows genealogy by several historians, there are still areas in the Fellows' family history where genealogists disagree on exact lineage.[2] However, enough primary source records survive to make Fellows one of the more reliable lineages in American family history.

The origin of the Fellows name is English. The name in antiquity meant "dweller at, or near the newly cultivated land." More commonly spelled in England as Fellowes; the word 'Fellow' in some dialects signified a young unmarried man—a servant engaged in agriculture. The name dates at least to the twelfth century on the Hundred Rolls, appearing as Le Felove, Le Felawes, and Fellowe.[3] Spelling of the name varies greatly but most often appears as Fellows, Fellowes, Felagh, Felaghs, and Fellow. Variations in spelling occurred often because of the high degree of illiteracy that was prevalent in earlier times, as well as plain carelessness and language differences found between localities. As late as the 19th century in the United States, many people did not know how to spell their own names, leaving civil officials to spell the name as it sounded to them when recording people and events in local town and county records.[4]

Alonzo B. Fellows, a descendant of the immigrant William Fellows and a leading farmer and foremost citizen of Essex County, Massachusetts—the seat of the Fellows family in America—claimed in 1898 that he was of English Colonial stock; said, however, to have originated in Holland; the name in very early times having been spelled 'Felles.'[5] Meanwhile, Willie Ira Fellows, likewise a descendant of William of Ipswich, wrote in his autobiography in 1940, "My folks told me that the first Fellows came from England on the *Mayflower* in 1620. There is a man in Springfield, Missouri, who was raised in New York, by the name of Fellows. He had his branch of the family traced back to England and it says that the first Fellows who came over from England was Frank Fellows. I suppose he is our branch of the family."[6] Unfortunately, there were no men of the name Fellows onboard the *Mayflower*, nor among the 19 *Mayflower* men who left descendants.[7]

Notwithstanding the undecided variances of English heritage, the present genealogy begins with William Fellows of Ipswich, Massachusetts. Competing theories of his English origin have yet to be resolved. Nevertheless, there is clear evidence that he was the progenitor of the present line of Fellows descendants in America.

Genealogy research is like a walk through American history. Descendants of William Fellows fought in every American conflict, starting with the War of King Philip in 1676, the French and Indian Wars, the American Revolution, the War of 1812, the Civil War, and both World Wars, not to mention Korea, Vietnam, and recent conflicts. They immigrated from coast to coast, border to border and stretched through the entire social structure of the country. The descendants of William Fellows included American presidents, U.S. Supreme Court justices, and captains of industry.[8] They were doctors, lawyers, and farmers, and occasional societal misfits of less desirable character, even a few out-and-out criminals.[9]

2

The Great Migration

The Great Puritan Migration to America took place between the years 1620 and 1640, when thousands of Europeans crossed the Atlantic Ocean to settle in the New World. Robert C. Anderson chronicled these early pioneers in a multi-volume set of works titled *The Great Migration Begins* and *The Great Migration.*[1] An estimated fifteen percent of the immigrants to New England arrived in the fourteen years from 1620 to 1633. There was a steep increase in migration beginning in 1634. Two thousand to 2,500 immigrants arrived in 1634, and new arrivals remained at that level each year for the rest of the decade.[2] Eighty-five percent came over in half as many years during the six years from 1634 to 1640 than arrived in the previous fourteen years from 1620 to 1633. Of these, about thirteen hundred came to New England between 1634 and 1635, amounting to approximately 25 percent of the entire Great Migration. Fortunately, for those years—1634 to 1640—there are more surviving passenger lists than for any other part of the Great Migration. It was in 1635 that William Fellows arrived in Massachusetts.

The history of the first of the Fellows name to arrive in America began with three brothers allegedly from southern Leicestershire, England.[3] Richard Fellows was at Hartford, Connecticut in 1643; removed to Springfield, Massachusetts in 1659; soon after to Northampton, Massachusetts; and in 1661 settled in Hatfield, Massachusetts. Samuel Fellows, born in England in 1619, settled at Salisbury, Massachusetts, in 1639.[4] William Fellows, the subject of the present genealogy and the older brother of Richard and Samuel, came to Ipswich, Massachusetts, in 1635.[5] On March 26, 1639, he purchased a house, a one-acre house lot, and a planting lot of six acres in Ipswich, which had belonged to Humphrey Wise of Ipswich, deceased.[6] This inaugural presence of the Fellows family in the early history of Massachusetts enjoys broad agreement among genealogists.[7]

William had two brothers and two sisters. His arrival in America preceded that of his brothers, Richard and Samuel, according to Mark D. Fellows who documented the ancestral family. "Samuel Fellows arrived in 1641 settling in Salisbury, Massachusetts. Although Samuel had only two children, his son Samuel Jr. became the ancestor of Fellows family stock that spread throughout New Hampshire and Northern Massachusetts. Richard Fellows, William's second brother, came to Hartford, Connecticut, in 1643, bringing his wife and three children with him. He appears to have been a frontier trader dealing in horses and cattle. He died in 1663. His only son Richard died at the hands of Indians in 1675, thus ending his line. Elizabeth Fellows, the first of William's sisters came to America, married John Moricke, and settled in Roxbury, Massachusetts, near Boston. She died in 1660. Grace Fellows, the last sister, remained in England her entire life, marrying Mr. Allam."[8] Notwithstanding the Mark Fellows detailed account, historians do not fully agree on the roots of William Fellows, except to agree that he came from England in 1635.

Evidence suggests that he was the son of Noble Fellows of London and the grandson of Willyam [*sic*] Noble Fellowes of Northampton in the East Midlands of England.[9] His great grandfather may have been Robert Marerres Fellowes born about 1520 in Nottinghamshire, England, the setting of the legendary Robin Hood of Sherwood Forest.[10] Robert Marerres Fellowes was allegedly born in Selston, Nottinghamshire, the son of Richard Fellowes and Phoebe Elizabeth Barton.[11] He married Elizabeth Moroke in October 1542, in Selston. They had seven children. He died December 19, 1558, in Selston at the age of 38.[12] He had a son, Willyam Noble Fellowes born June 15, 1546, who married Alice Alton Boyle. They in turn had a son, Noble Fellowes born February 1, 1578, in Selston. According to this interpretation of the genealogical record, William Fellows of Nottinghamshire, later of Ipswich, Massachusetts, descended from this Fellows line.

Meanwhile, Anderson makes a case for Leicestershire, England, as the origin of William Fellows of Ipswich. He writes, "In her will, dated 14 March 1649/50 and 'deposed' 5 September 1650, Elizabeth Moricke, widow of John Moricke of Hingham, near Boston, 'but now dwelling in Roxbury,' mentioned numerous people and made many bequests. She appointed 'Leonard Fellowes of Great Bowden in Old England' [Leicestershire] to be one of the executors, and left sums of money to 'William Fellowes of Ipswich,' £10; 'Richard Fellowes of Connecticut,' £10; and 'Samuell Fellowes of Salisbury' £10. She also left £5 to her 'sister' Grace Allam in Lincolnshire."[13] This, of course, suggests a connection among the men named Fellows and probably also between them and the testatrix, Elizabeth Moricke.[14] The above-mentioned Leonard Fellows and his wife Jane Morbey had children from 1626 through 1641 (including a son Samuel) baptized in Great Bowden.[15] The burial of Jane (Morbey) Fellows was in Great Bowden on 15 January 1680/81. No probates are extant for Leonard Fellows or Jane. However, estimated dates suggest that Leonard was born say 1601 and was perhaps a decade older than William Fellows of Ipswich.

Anderson also appears to agree with the family tradition of three Fellows brothers who first settled in America. He continues, "Richard Fellows was in Hartford, [Connecticut] by 1643, and had a child as early as 1646, and so was born perhaps about 1621.[16] Samuel Fellows was in Salisbury in 1641, deposed on 11 November 1679, 'aged about sixty-one years,' and so was born about 1618.[17] These two men were clearly of an age to be of the same generation as William Fellows. Note that both Richard and William named sons Samuel."[18]

In the course of his research on the Fellows family, Erwin W. Fellows discovered the 1630 Will of Willyam Fellows of Foxton, Leicestershire. Based on names mentioned in his will, that man could have been the grandfather of the immigrant, William Fellows of Ipswich, and the Fellows brothers.[19]

Notwithstanding the differing opinions on the origin of William Fellows of Ipswich, according to the general theory, he was born in 1609 in England based on the baptism of a William Fellows November 22, 1609, in Selston, a village twelve miles north of Nottingham, England.[20] However, this date, too, is problematic when compared to other records alleged to name this William Fellows.[21] For example, the ship register that recorded his passage to America listed him as age 24 in 1635, which calculates to a birth year of 1611.[22] On the other hand, the 1609 date appears to match a deposition filed in court papers on September 27, 1659, when he was "about age 50."[23]

William Fellows married Mary Ayers about 1637.[24] Historians cite a petition filed in the Essex County Court of Massachusetts on March 29, 1659, and another in November 1661 as proof of her identity.[25] John Ayers and William Fellows jointly petitioned the court on behalf of the minor children of "our brother William Lampson" and Widow Sarah Lampson who they described as "our sister Sarah Lampson." Sarah married William Lampson, who died

February 1, 1658. She then wanted to marry Thomas Hartshorne, which presented a problem for the Lampson children who inherited half of their father's estate. William Fellows and John Ayers, Sarah's "brothers," opposed the marriage and petitioned the court to protect the children's rights. Moreover, they complained that the William Lampson property had not been valued high enough, and his children's rights not properly secured. An interpolation of the record infers that John Ayers was a true brother of Sarah and that William Fellows married the sister of Sarah and John Ayers; thus the maiden name of Ayers for Mary, William's wife.[26] John Ayers was the brother of Sarah (Ayers) Lampson who was, in turn, the sister-in-law ("sister") of William Fellows.[27] In response to the court petition of John and William, Thomas Hartshorne offered his own property as security for payment of several of the Lampson children's claims.[28]

The record reveals little about Mary (Ayers) Fellows. Genealogists estimate she was born about 1607 in England.[29] Some say she was the daughter of John Ayers and Hannah Everid.[30] Family historian Erwin W. Fellows pointed to the possibility that Mary was the daughter of Humphrey Eyre [*sic*] of Foxton, England. He died in 1628. He had two children: Goodithe born September 9, 1607, and John born January 7, 1609. Mr. Fellows assumed Goodithe to be Mary and linked the two Eyre children to John and Mary Ayers of Ipswich. He concluded that Mary (Ayers) Fellows died about 1702 in Ipswich, Essex County, Massachusetts.[31] However, the theory seems implausible given that she would have been age 95 at the time of her death. Moreover, historians disagree on whether William and Mary married in England or in Massachusetts. They had eight children, the eldest of whom, a son, Isaac, was allegedly born in England.[32]

William Fellows sailed out of London sometime after April 11, 1635, registered as "William Felloe," destined for America aboard the ship *Planter*, captained by Nicholas Travice [Trerice].[33] He had a certificate of transport from St. Albans Parish in Hertfordshire.[34] The ship manifest listed him as age 24 with the vocation of shoemaker.[35] He arrived in Boston on June 7, 1635, and soon settled in Ipswich, Massachusetts.[36] Some genealogists assume William traveled with his wife Mary and son Isaac.[37] However, the ship manifest did not list them, which has led others to assume that he married and began his family not in England but in America.[38] It would have been highly unusual for the passenger list to omit anyone from the ship maifest, especially family members, because of the strict rules that London required ship captains to follow in accounting for their human cargos. Meanwhile, the *Planter's* voyage of two months was in keeping with the length of Atlantic crossings in the 1600s, which rarely was inside of six weeks.[39]

William settled in Ipswich, Essex County, Massachusetts. His occupation of shoemaker, or cordwainer, coincided with the early historic interest at Ipswich in the trade of tanning and leatherwork.[40] Whether William influenced the craft, or immigrated to Ipswich because of it, is speculative. In any event, he put aside that occupation to pursue husbandry and farming.[41]

Of the 118 persons listed on the passenger list of the *Planter,* at least eight settled in Ipswich.[42] The village of Ipswich was hardly a year old when William arrived. First called Agawam after the native Indian village that occupied the site, colonists occupied it in 1633. In March 1633, John Winthrop, Jr., son of Governor Winthrop, "arrived up river" with a group of 12 pioneers to begin the first settlement. With him were "gentlemen" bearing the title of Mister. Historians like to point to this as the start to Ipswich that caused this remote little frontier village to become a cultural center in 17th century America.[43]

The village incorporated on August 4, 1634, with the name Ipswich, named for the town in Suffolk County, East Anglia [England], the locale from which most of the first settlers of Ipswich originated.[44] Ipswich sat in a hilly region of the Massachusetts coast surrounded by a topographical landscape of marshes, dunes, beaches, uplands, forests, fields, and farmland. The Ipswich River originated 40 miles to the west and ran through the town on its way to the Atlantic Ocean. The freshwater river turned into tidal brine in the ebb and flow of its coastal tributaries.[45] In his book, *Candlewood,* Thomas F. Waters described the founding of Ipswich and mentioned William Fellows. One of the landmarks of Ipswich is a stone bridge said to be the first stone bridge in the country. According to Waters, William Fellows was one of the men who built it. There are today still a Fellows Lane and Fellows Road running next to the ancient Fellow's property. An estate house that once belonged to William Fellows and his descendants passed into other hands long ago.[46]

County map of England and Wales. The area of England most often associated with the origin of the Fellows family was in a 40-mile long region of the Midlands in Leicestershire, Nottinghamshire, and Northamptonshire Counties. Gray's *New Book of Roads*, 1824.

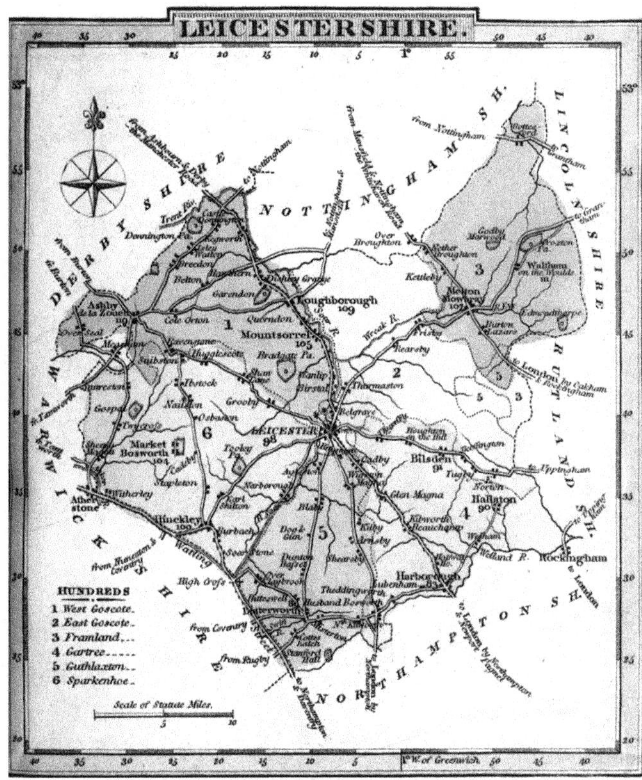

Map of Leicestershire County, England. The will of Willyam Fellowes, dated 1630 and found in Foxton, Leicestershire County, England, identified the seat of the Fellows family in southern Leicestershire, in the Midlands of England. Foxton was in the Gartree Hundred (No. 4 on the map) about 10 miles north of Market Harborough, and east of Great Bowden. Each was a town associated with the Fellows name and situated on the Leicestershire border across from Northamptonshire County, another sometimes mentioned location of Fellows ancestors. *Gray's New Book of Roads*, 1824, Plate 30.

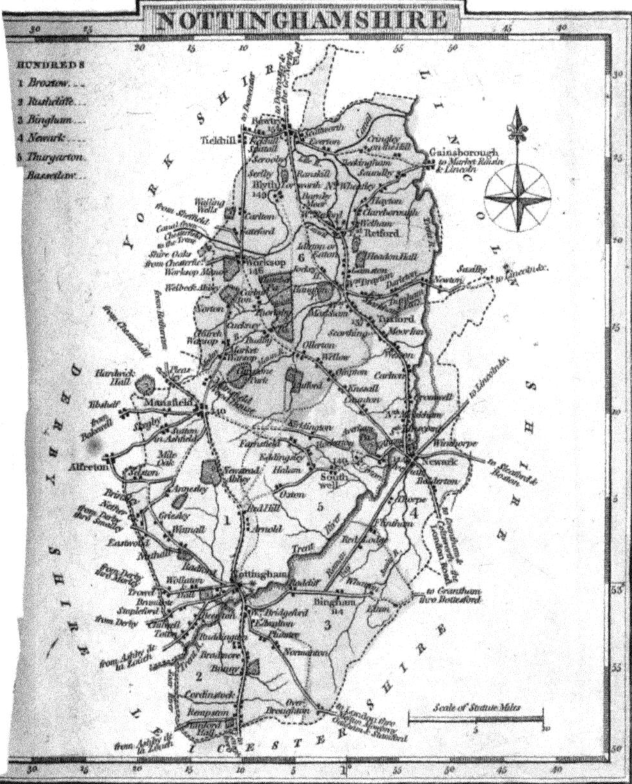

Map of Nottinghamshire County, England. Historians identify Selston, about 12 miles north of Nottingham on the county's western border, as the birthplace of William Fellows of Ipswich. Situated in the Broxtow Hundred (No. 1 on the map), Selston was approximately 40 miles north of Foxton, in Leicestershire County. *Gray's New Book of Roads*, 1824, Plate 26.

3

Candlewood

The neighborhood that William and Mary Fellows called home was the community of Candlewood. The following is from *Candlewood, An Ancient Neighborhood in Ipswich,* written by Thomas Franklin Waters. The culture and geography of Ipswich has changed since its publication in 1909. Nevertheless, Mr. Waters wrote a timeless picture of colonial life in this little Massachusetts village.[1]

"A long series of wills, inventories, and conveyances reveals many interesting secrets of the life of this little community [Candlewood]. It was wonderfully self-sufficient. These farmers cultivated only a few acres. Their farm stock was limited and their 'utensils of husbandry,' as they are styled in one ancient inventory, were few and simple. Despite the fact that all the farm labor was done by hand, they had opportunity and necessity, no doubt, to turn to other employments, to complete the round of their activities. So, we find few men, who are styled yeomen or farmers and many who tilled their lands, but added to their yeomanry the trades of the house carpenter, glazier, brick maker and blacksmith, of the cordwainer, weaver and tailor, and by these trades they were known.

"Hence the community had little need of help from without. When a new house was required, the noble oaks and pines were felled on their own wood lots, the great beams were fashioned with the axe, and the neighboring sawmill of Major Samuel Appleton on Mile River converted the great logs into boards and smaller timber, shingles and clapboards. The brick maker supplied the bricks, the blacksmith, nails, hinges and latches, and the carpenter and glazier did the rest.

"The individual household was likewise an economic unit. Its food supplies were almost entirely derived from the Indian corn and rye, the beef, pork, and poultry. The milk and eggs, butter and cheese, raised on the farm, while from their barley, malted at the Rogers malt house, they made their home brewed beer. Every family had its flock of sheep and a field was always sown with flax. Then the tireless and ingenious women of the household with deft touch spun and wove and bleached, provided table and bed linen and made the beautiful bed quilts, which are prized still for their splendid handiwork, cut and fashioned garments, knit stockings, and mittens. Happily, William Brown, the professional weaver, could help in the production of the heavier fabrics and the neighborhood tailor could fashion the more elaborate overcoats and fine dress coats, which the wealthier men needed. The cordwainers made the shoes. The wood lots at Chebacco and the great peat meadow, close at hand, provided fuel for the huge fireplaces. Homemade candles and smoky 'betty lamps,' or smokier pitch pine strips gave a feeble light.

"All of these old farmhouses were comfortably furnished and some inventories give evidence of luxury. There were neighborhood aristocrats... Clad in his velvet coat and short clothes, with wig and silver buckles and buttons, the Candlewood gentleman made a brave appearance.[2] Some traces of the oldest houses remain in the cellars of the present dwellings, where the ancient oaks still support the hearths of the fireplaces. The beveled edges indicate well-finished dwellings.

"In the great social necessities of life the old neighborhood proved adequate to its own needs as well. A study of the genealogies makes it plain that in the large proportion of marriages, both bride and groom were from this group of houses. Playmates and schoolmates, these Browns and Fellowses and Kinsmans and the Appletons, a little farther removed, finally became partners for life. Frequently they spent their lives in the same dwelling in which they were born, and never went far enough afield to lose sight of the smoke from the chimneys or the smell of the peat reek of the old neighborhood. This passion for home has descended to the present generation and in thirteen of the comfortable dwellings of today [1909], either husband or wife was born and bred on Candlewood soil.

"Children came into these old homes in glad profusion, and it rarely happened that the first-born son did not bear his father's name. Some names were loved so well that they passed from generation to generation, and in one case, John Brown of the hamlet in Revolutionary times was enrolled as John Brown 7th. In the very beginning of our town, there were three John Browns, distinguished as Senior, the Farmer, and the Glazier, and in a land lawsuit, the John Brown in possession based his defense in part, upon the fact that the writ did not specify which John Brown he was, as there were several of the name in the town.

"Numerous as their children were, the parents were never at a loss for names. The Bible furnished an inexhaustible series of noble and significant names, and beginning with Adam and righteous Abel, the names of the patriarchs and prophets, the soldiers and sages of the Hebrew Word, the evangelists and apostles of later times, and of the holy women of Bible story, were given to their offspring.

"The families themselves were patriarchal. Ten and twelve children were not unusual, and sometimes the numbers swelled to heroic proportions… No wonder Sabbath day congregations were large in those good old days, when church going was the rule and whole families were found in the family pew, though the meetinghouse was cold and cheerless.

"The ability to bear the burden which was put upon the mothers of these old families passes our comprehension. The mere clothing of her household from husband to the babe, never absent from the cradle, when few fabrics were bought, and everything was made by hand, the providing of the daily food with the primitive conveniences of the fireplace, the butter and cheese making, the manufacture of the household linen, the endless anxieties, were too much for flesh and blood, as we think it. Sometimes dreadful epidemics caused terror in every home… The great white plague was always claiming its victims. Scarlet fever was regarded as unavoidable and of no great significance.

"The housemother's care for her own was always increased by her readiness to minister to her neighbor's family in every critical hour. All modern rules for mothers and babes were habitually violated. Modern remedies and modern nursing was alike unknown. Yet they lived and reached a ripe old age."[3]

"Under such circumstances, it might be imagined that the lot of the children was as hard as that of their mothers, and that they must have suffered much from neglect. It is a fact that they were not dressed according to Paris fashions. They had less school privilege than the law demands for children today. But those children were taught diligently in the Bible and the catechism and the great hymns of the church. They learned to read and write, and sew and knit.

The crowning glory of the girl's education was the sampler, cleverly wrought on the homespun canvas. The alphabet, in capitals and small letters, was generally followed by some genealogical record or by a mournful verse. One sampler, preserved in the collection of the Historical Society, bears the lugubrious sentiment: *When I am dead and in my grave*
And all my bones are rotten,
When this you see remember me
That I mayn't be forgotten.[4]

"Happily, the little maid who wrought that sampler was accustomed to these painful moralizings and all her playmates shared her dismal experience. Nevertheless, her education prepared her well on the whole for her prospective cares and responsibilities. No doubt, the joys of Thanks giving, the excitements of the frequent weddings and the common home pleasures offset the dullness and straightness of child life in very satisfactory fashion.

"The ancient neighborhood had its days of darkness and fear. John Brown Senior's inventory in 1677 contains the item, 'axes, sithes, sawes and other utensells of husbandry with some Armor'...The dread of Indian assault was always with them and when night settled down upon those scattered farm houses and the wolves howled in the forests, many a brave heart trembled at some unusual sound. When King Philip's war at last broke out, Ephraim Fellows was a trooper with Captain Paige and then with our Ipswich soldier, Captain John Whipple; Isaac Fellows was in Captain Willard's Company. Joseph Fellows and John Brown were also enrolled.

"While the love of home has been the conspicuous trait of the neighborhood life, in all these generations, there have been many migrations elsewhere. Capt. Jonathan Fellows long ago removed to Gloucester, and from him has descended a conspicuous line of merchants and wealthy and prominent citizens in Boston and New York. Fellows Athenaeum in Roxbury, now used by the Boston Public Library, was built and endowed by Caleb Fellows of this family line... Multitudes of worthy and lovable men and women have gone far and wide, and through these sons and daughters, the fathers and the mothers who lived their simple and hard lives so well, are handing on their stalwart virtues, their love of toil, their broad and sympathetic good neighborliness to the generations that are to come."

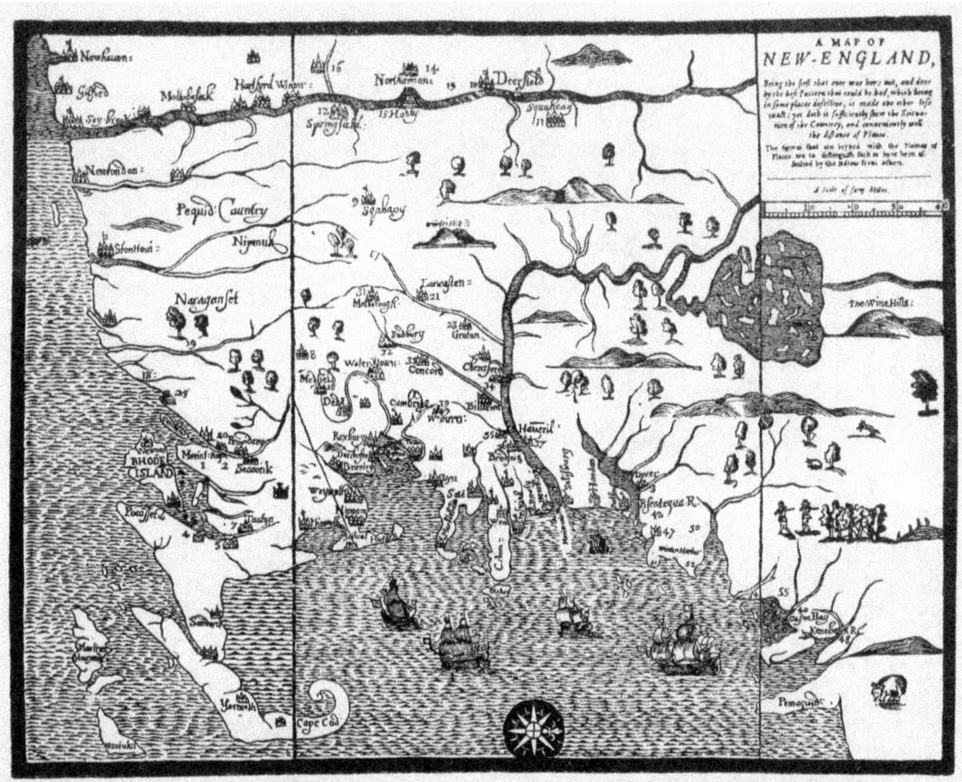

Ipswich and Massachusetts Bay. English colonists established the village of Ipswich on Massachusetts Bay in 1633. This period map of 1677 depicts Cape of Ipswich, Rowly, Newbury, and Salisbury, all coastal towns associated with the colonial settlement of the Fellows brothers in America in 1635. The large stream depicted is the Merrimack River. Map of New England from Hubbard's *History of the Indian Wars in New England*, 1677.

Stone Bridge. Candlewood and its adjoining neighborhoods were places of many bridges. The coastal town of Ipswich features numerous stream crossings, many of them built in colonial times. According to family tradition, William Fellows helped to build one such stone bridge like the one pictured here over Gould's Creek (originally Labor in Vain Creek). Photo by Arthur Wesley Dow 1904.

4

William Fellows of Ipswich

William Fellows first appeared in the colonial records on January 26, 1639, at a court-ordered estate sale of the late Humphrey Wisse of Ipswich where William Fellows bought "the house and house-lot of one acre and a planting lot of six acres, with appurtenances."[1] At about the same time, "during the first day of the first month," records indicated that he engaged in tending the Ipswich village herd of cows.[2] His contract read, "To drive them out to feed before sunne be half an hour high and not bring them home before half an hour before sunset." The date on the contract was September 1639, and it ran through the grazing season from April 20 to November 20.[3] The pay was in either corn or money, a total of fifteen pounds.[4] His job was to keep the herd of cows on the south side of the river and to drive the cattle, "coming over the River back over the River at night," and to take charge of them "as soon as they are put over the River in the morning." He was liable for any harm coming to the heard and was to receive 12 pence for each cow before he took them; a shilling and six pence fourteen days after mid-summer; and the rest of his pay at the end of the contract term in corn or money, a total of £15.[5]

A few things are evident from William's first appearance in the records of Ipswich. First, he was not necessarily a wealthy man but of sufficient means to afford a house and some land. Secondly, he does not appear to have been an indentured servant, which means he had sufficient resources to pay for his own passage from England to America. The length of time from 1635 when he arrived until 1639, when he appeared to be a freeman able to purchase real estate, was less than the normal indenture term of seven years. Thirdly, he was working in Ipswich as a trusted member of the community, which infers that he was not a new arrival and probably came straight from Boston to Ipswich, placing him there as early as 1635 as one of the earliest residents of the town. His job as south-side cow herder associated him with Mark Quilter and Simon Thompson in 1640, the cow keepers on the north side of the river.[6]

By the year 1641, William achieved the status of Commoner in Ipswich, and on June 2, 1641, took the freeman's oath, listed on the register as "Willi ff".[7] Commoner referred to the protective agreement among a community of citizens to arrange their homes next to a meadow or "common" usually consisting of a tract of land of sufficient size to harbor and mutually protect all their livestock. Residents of each community had to establish their own local defenses and were required to become members of a militia providing for the defense of the town against Indians.[8] Each settler had to bring his own rifle, but could draw upon town supplies of gunpowder and lead for use if needed. In October 1643, authorities fined William and 26 other townsmen for not returning their gunpowder supply to the town. The experience did not dent William's loyalty to the militia because one year later he subscribed to a fund for Daniel Dennison as head of the town militia of Ipswich.[9]

William reached a milestone of community involvement on March 28, 1654, when the Essex County Court admitted him to the Court as a "Freeman of the Colony," the second man listed in a sequence of five Ipswich men.[10] Colonial Freeman was a social and legal position achieved through a combination of land ownership and Orthodox Church membership implied by his Freeman status.[11] It meant he could vote and participate in all matters related to the Massachusetts Colony.

It was also about this time that he joined with Captain John Ayers of Ipswich to petition the court on behalf of Mr. Ayer's sister Sarah in the case of the estate of William Lampson, Sarah's deceased husband. As previously noted, after Mr. Lampson died in 1658, Sarah wanted to marry Thomas Hartshorne, a marriage that threatened to disinherit the Lampson children. Her "brothers" objected to the marriage. Genealogists interpret "brothers" to mean that John was a true brother of Sarah, and William was her brother-in-law, husband of her sister Mary Ayers; thus, the maiden name of Ayers for Mary Fellows.[12]

William Fellows became owner of considerable property in the Ipswich area. His name appeared on numerous real estate transactions. [13] For example, on November 15, 1649, he sold fifteen acres on the Great Brook towards the north to John Pierpont. [14] On February 7, 1658, he took ownership of a farm on the south side of the river, bounded by the Mill Brook West.[15] At the same time in September 1659, he and his son were also leaseholders of 15 acres of meadow near the land of Deputy Governor Symonds.[16]

The real estate transactions of William are of particular interest. He owned and rented substantial amounts of land in and around Ipswich. He bought the John Andrews farm and took up residence in the ancient Candlewood neighborhood, of Ipswich.[17] On 16 February 1659/60, John Andrews of Ipswich, yeoman, and wife Sarah sold to "William Fellows of the same town and county aforesaid, husbandman, that my farm containing all my right & interest to & in both upland & meadow on the south side of the river of Ipswich... with all the houses, barns, stables, orchards, fences, timber, wood, waters, watercourses & all other privileges & appurtenances thereunto belonging (moveables excepted), also a parcel of meadow containing twenty acres, be it more or less, in Chebacco in Ipswich... also a parcel of marsh lying in Hogg Island Marsh containing about six or eight acres more or less."[18]

Here in Candlewood in the town of Ipswich, William lived out the remainder of his life as a farmer and keeper of livestock, overseeing the large, ever-growing expanse of acreage under his care. In 1664, when Richard Saltonstall conveyed the title in several lots to his son upon his son's marriage, Saltonstall included in his gift a farm of 150 acres at Chebacco, "now in the occupation of William and Isaac Fellows.[19] Soon thereafter on August 23, 1666, with John Proctor, Sr., William jointly acquired a four-rod lot with a house on the west corner of Green Street and the Meeting House Green.[20] That partnership with Proctor continued until his death.[21] It was an interesting property that stood on the northeast side of the Green almost as far as the Great Rock behind the Town House. The Great Rock was a lofty pinnacle, since blasted away.[22]

William Fellows was an active member of town affairs. From about 1651 going forward, his name appeared frequently in land and court transactions. He served on the Ipswich petit jury in the years 1651, 1656, and 1664.[23] The confirmation of his birthdate of 1609 is in part from September 27, 1659, when he participated in a court hearing during a trial over the boundary line between the farms of Mr. Richard Saltonstall and Mr. Wade. The court deposed William to testify and identified him as "William Fellows, aged about fifty years."[24]

He remained an active citizen of Ipswich and Essex County well into his advanced years, including selection for duty on a Grand Jury September 24, 1667, on a committee to "take care of the commons" on the south side of the river. He signed a petition on March 21, 1669, for restricting tree cutting on town lands.[25] He served a second term on the Grand Jury in the fall of 1672.[26]

The King Philip War broke out in 1675, underlining the dread of Indian assault that always threatened the ancient neighborhoods of colonial America and their scattered farm houses open to the peril of attack. The war began on June 19, 1675, when Indians attacked the house of Plymouth, Massachusetts, Governor Josiah Winslow. The uprising took the name of King Philip, the Wampanoag chief, Metacomet who answered to the English name King Philip. When the war broke out, three of William's sons enrolled in the force to put down the rebellion.[27] All three of them returned safely. The war ended in August of 1676 with the killing of King Philip and the capture of his wife and son, coincidentally in the year of the death of William Fellows.

William Fellows died sometime between the time he wrote his will on November 27, 1676, and December 21, 1676, when a land transaction spoke of him as deceased.[28] The exact date of his death remains unsubstantiated.[29] However, he died before December 21 because that was the date that his heirs bought from the heirs of John Proctor the Proctor interest in the house William and Mr. Proctor had jointly purchased a decade earlier, and declared him deceased.[30] His burial was in the Parish of St. Michael, Ipswich, Essex County, Massachusetts.[31]

William signed his will with a shaky hand, which added to speculation among genealogists as to his level of literacy. He had signed his name as a witness on August 20, 1664, but made his mark on a petition on November 24, 1668.[32] Nevertheless, an inventory of his estate inferred that he was an educated man because his holdings included "books, a pillion and a riding cloth" valued at £17.[33] The inventory of the estate of "William Fellows of Ipswich deceased" taken December 27, 1676, totaled £581 17s. 11d. (against which were debts of £83 11s. 7d.), of which £350 was real estate: "38 acres of upland at home and 26 acres of marsh," valued at £250; and "all the housing," valued at £100. The inventory did not place a value on the "four rods of ground on the Meeting House Hill where the old house stood."[34]

William did not name an executor of his will. On March 27, 1677, the court granted administration to "the three sons, Ephraim, Samuell, & Joseph." They were "to order the division of the estate according to the mind of their father, according to the intent he hath expressed in this paper called his will."[35] The final disposition of the property of William Fellows stood unresolved for several years. The family shared its occupation until March 30, 1702, when his heirs filed an agreement to partition the land. "Isaac Fellows, Ephraim Fellows, Ruth Fellows, widow administratrix to the estate of her husband Joseph Fellows deceased, all of Ipswich..., & Samuel Ayers [husband of Abigail Fellows] of Newbury assign our attorney to Samuel Fellows of the same town." They agreed to "settle & divide the real estate of their father William Fellowes formerly of Ipswich according to his donation in his last will & testament."[36] Isaac Fellows was part of this agreement, although his name did not appear in the will. Historian Robert Anderson deduced from this that "since Isaac is consistently mentioned separately from the other three sons, and since he is not included in the injunction to make the sons' portions equal with those of the daughters, Isaac must have been the eldest son." As such, he would have previously benefitted from William's favor.[37]

William Fellows of Ipswich, Massachusetts, was a formative presence in the earliest days of colonial America. He died before the famous "taxation without representation" issue came up in 1687, which hastened the colonies toward eventual independence from the British Crown. That task he left to his children and their descendants who in the course of time became part of the colonial resistance and the founding of the United States.[38]

Mary (Ayers) Fellows survived her husband, as did all of their seven children.[39] The date of her death remains unknown. The children of William and Mary were Isaac, Ephraim, Elizabeth, Mary, Samuel, Joseph, Abigail, and Sarah. [40] The genealogy continued from William and Mary (Ayers) Fellows to their eldest son Isaac Fellows.[41]

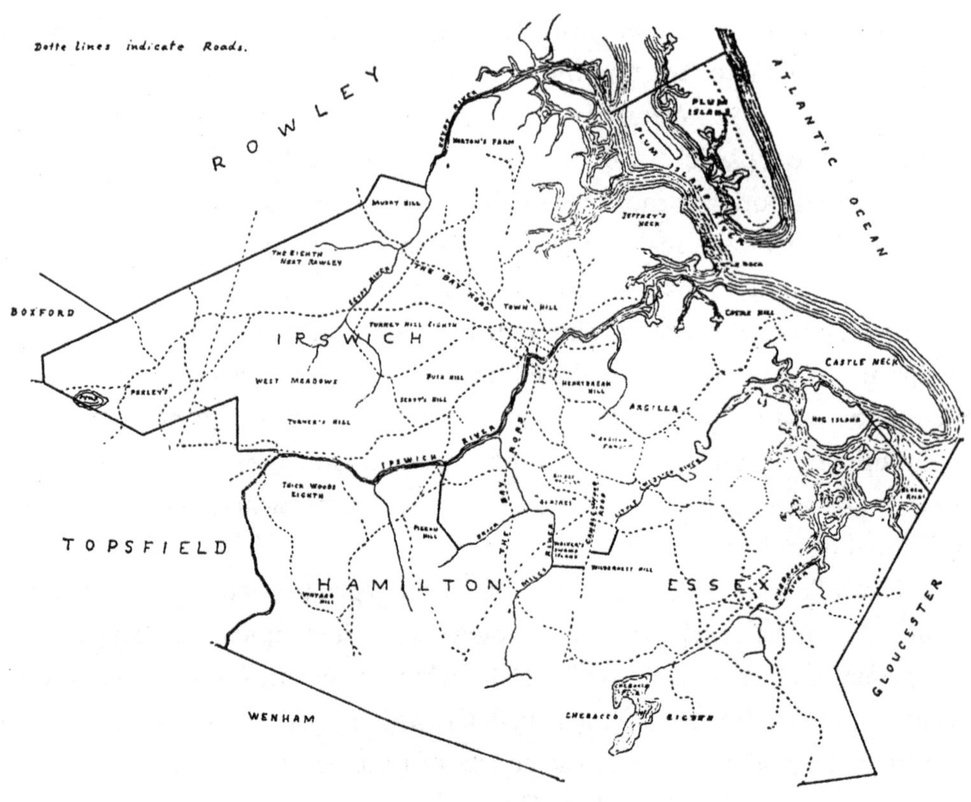

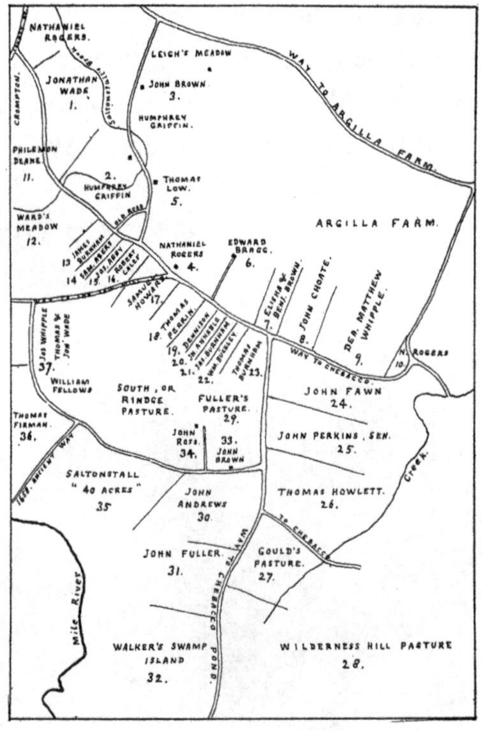

Map of Ipswich, Essex County, Massachusetts.

Map of Candlewood, Ipswich, Massachusetts, known as "The South Eighth."

Waters, *Candlewood, An Ancient Neighborhood in Ipswich: with genealogies of John Brown, William Fellows, Robert Kinsman,* 1909.

Swasey Tavern, Ipswich, Massachusetts. Many of the houses of the First Colonial Period architecture style survive today in Ipswich, some of them built during the lifetime of William Fellows. John Ayres built this "house" in 1693. He was a descendant of the Ayres family that intermarried with the Fellows family. The wife of William Fellows was Mary Ayres. Their daughter married Samuel Ayres. The first houses in Ipswich were relatively small but comfortable. However, there were examples of often spacious and elegant homes. This Ayres house sold in 1705, and the new owner converted it into an inn. In 1789, George Washington addressed the citizenry from its steps. Photo by George Dexter, c. 1900.

The Ruth Fellows House at No. 16 Fellows Road in Ipswich, Massachusetts. Ruth Fellows was the widow of Joseph Fellows, son of William Fellows of Ipswich. Her house in Ipswich dates to 1714. She died April 14, 1729. *Historic Ipswich*, Ipswich Historical Commission.

Fellows First Generation Family Group

William Israel FELLOWS was born in 1609 in England. He died between 29 Nov and 21 Dec 1676 in Ipswich, Essex County, Massachusetts. His burial was in 1676 in the Parish of St. Michael, Ipswich, Essex County, Mass.

William married **Mary AYERS**, daughter of John Ayers and Hannah (Webb) Evered, about 1635. Mary was born about 1607. She died after 1676 in Ipswich, Essex County, Massachusetts.

They had the following children.

+ 1. **Isaac FELLOWS** was born in 1637. He died on 6 Apr 1721 in Ipswich, Essex County, Massachusetts. His burial was in Essex County. Isaac married **Joanna BOREMAN**, daughter of Thomas Boreman and Margaret Offing, on 29 Jan 1672/73 in Ipswich, Essex County, Mass. Joanna was born in 1646 in Ipswich, Essex County. She died on 22 Mar 1731/32 in Ipswich.

2. **Ephraim Fellows** was born in March 1640/41 in Ipswich, Essex County, Massachusetts, based on depositions filed 31 Mar 1668 when he was "aged twenty-seven years," and 5 May 1674 when he was "aged about thirty-three years."[42] He was the second son of William and Mary (Ayers) Fellows.[43] He died in 1713 in Plainfield, Windham County, Connecticut.[44] His burial was in Connecticut. Ephraim married **Mary** (last name unspecified).[45] They married about 1660 and began their family in Ipswich, Essex County.[46] They had at least two children, William and John born in 1666 and 1668 respectively.[47] Ephraim became a surveyor of highways and was in that line of work between the years 1669, working on roads between Windmill Hill and Haefield's Bridge, and 1678 surveying from the location of Goodwife Fellows to Chebacco Falls.[48] Goodwife Fellows was likely Ephraim's mother, Widow Mary (Ayers) Fellows.

Ephraim appeared in several court cases that were typical of early colonial life. For example, in 1668, he gave testimony in court substantiating a complaint that someone was illegally hunting wild pigs on Hog Island. Court records stated, "Ephraim Fellows, aged twenty seven years, deposed that when he was coming home from Castle Neck in a canoe, he heard a great hunting of dogs at the island in the marsh behind the round island. Standing up in the canoe, he could not see where they were, but saw a spotted hog come from Hog Island to the marsh and then go inside again. Further, that Goodman Wood's canoe lay near the place where the hunting was."[49]

Another incident occurred in the early fall of 1670 on the highway between Wenham and Ipswich that involved Ephram and four other men. According to this story, "Ephraim [Fellows] and Nathaniel Wade were riding their horses following two other men, Obadiah Bridges and Andrew Peters, on their way to Ipswich. Bridges and Peters first accosted the young Mr. Thomas Stevens when they came upon and challenged him, wanting to know who he was and what he was doing. They kept after him until they saw Ephraim and Nathaniel approaching. As Ephraim and Wade passed the group, they were cordial to Mr. Stevens and bid him a good evening, whereupon both Bridges and Peters grabbed Nathaniel's horse's reins, demanding that he stay put and stated that, 'they would make him stay and light his pipe in the Brook before they would let him go.' A fight broke out with Ephraim resisting from being pulled off his horse."[50] The court fined Bridges and Peters 40 shillings damage for stopping Mr. Stevens, for stopping Mr. Wade, and for abusing Mr. Ephraim Fellows. The court further required the defendants to swear oaths and bound them by their good behavior. Later, Bridges sued Ephraim for abuse in the fight. There was no record of the outcome, except that Ephraim paid his own court costs.[51]

Another episode concerned an incident in May 1674 at the town meeting house when "Ephraim Fellows, aged about thirty-three years, deposed that he often saw John Pearce playing at the meeting in the time of exercise, spitting on other boy's hats and clothing, etc."[52]

In the year 1670/71, the court granted Ephraim a permit to fell trees for a log house 16 feet square.[53] A house in Ipswich was, for the most part, modest and plain but generally above the simple log cabins of the southern colonies. Waters wrote, "We should find that it was not only habitable, but comfortable, and the furnishings much beyond our anticipation."[54] Unfortunately, Mary Fellows, Ephraim's wife, died that year on 23 Feb 1670/71 in Ipswich.[55]

Ephraim Fellows served in King Philip's War. He was a trooper in the service of the command of Captain Nicholas Paige's Company on 3 Sep 1675 when he participated in an expedition to Mount Hope and Narraganset. He was also credited three pounds nine shillings for services with Captain Whipple's Company of Ipswich, Massachusetts, on 24 Aug 1676. [56]

Meanwhile, in 1676, the patriarch William Fellows died, and the family divided his estate. Ephraim and his brother Joseph lived together with their families on the old Fellows homestead inherited from their father.[57] The year 1676 was also the year he and his siblings purchased the John Procter property from Joseph and Benjamin Proctor, which had long been a partnership between their father and Mr. Procter. In January 1694/95, Ephraim and his siblings sold the property to a relative also named William Fellows who then sold it out of the Fellows family in 1708.[58]

Ephraim held the status of Commoner in 1678, an indication of his good standing in the Ipswich community.[59] Nevertheless, he and his neighbor Mr. Jacobs had an ongoing dislike for each other that finally spilled over in court. Mr. Jacobs' swine crossed a bridge built by Jacobs and got into Ephraim's grain, causing considerable damage that cost Ephraim approximately twenty bushels of Indian corn. The next day, Ephraim missed training with the militia, which cost him a fine. When he eventually showed up and complained about the fine, he stated that he had urgent business at home. An investigation found that a neighbor had seen Ephraim putting an axe to Jacobs' bridge. The court fined Ephraim 20 shillings and 26 shillings court costs for the damage. [60]

On another occasion, Ephraim complained that William Chapman had spoiled a valuable cow of his.[61] The court ordered that Chapman "serve Daniell Hovey one year after his time is out, said Hovey having paid Fellows for it."[62] This verdict suggested that Chapman was an indentured servant who had an extra year added to his term of service for the damages caused to Ephraim's cow. Since Chapman's indenture was to Mr. Hovey, Hovey paid Ephraim for the damage, and then recovered his cost with the extra year of service from Mr. Chapman.

In 1683, Ephraim married secondly **Anna Hannah (Cross) Marshall**, widow of Thomas Marshall, Jr. and daughter of Robert Cross and Anna Jordan, at Ipswich, Essex County, Massachusetts.[63] Anna (aka Ann) was born in 1651 in Ipswich.[64] She was the widow of Thomas Marshall, Jr. whom she married between 1671 and 1679. The dates of her marriages come from Essex County records that show she was aged 21 and unmarried as Anna Cross in her father's house in 1671, and then Anna Marshall at her father's house in 1679. Her last Marshall child was born in 1682 and her first Fellows child in 1685.[65] On 25 Mar 1684, Thomas Marshall, Sr. of Chebacco, Ipswich, for unspecified reasons sued "Ephraim Fellowes and Ann his wife, relict and administratrix of the estate of Thomas Marshall, deceased."[66] The court did not file a resolution of the case.

In 1681, Ephraim sold his land on Fellows Lane to his brother, Joseph.[67] He remained in Ipswich, Massachusetts, at least through 1687.[68] Sometime afterwards, he removed with his family to western Massachusetts, and then to Plainfield, Connecticut.[69] A deed dated in 1694 stated that his occupation at the time was as a locksmith.[70] He had a seat appointed to him in the meetinghouse in 1700. He remained in Plainfield, Connecticut, until his death in 1713. Records show that the Fellows family property sold in Ipswich that same year.[71]

Conflicting claims about the death of Anna list dates of 1693 and 1710.[72] The latter appears to be accurate. She was living in Plainfield, New London County, Connecticut, in 1710, according to a record dated 4 Dec of that year.[73] "Stephen Herrick of Beverly, allowing to Mary Herrick of Preston, Connec'tt, Ephraim Fellows, and Anna his wife of Plainfield, Connec'tt, both daughters of Robert Cross late of Ipswich: in consideration of twenty-three pounds money of N-England, acquit to William Butler of Ipswich all claims on their father's estate."[74]

Ephraim and Anna (Cross) Fellows had five children.[75] Family historian Anderson pointed out that the long gap between the death of Ephraim's first wife Mary and the first evidence of marriage to Anna suggests the possibility of an unrecorded marriage between the two documented marriages. Ephraim and Anna (Cross) Fellows were the ancestors of U.S. Presidents George H.W. and George W. Bush.[76]

3. **Samuel Fellows** was born about 1643 probably in Ipswich, Mass.[77] He died between 14 Apr and 11 Dec 1713 in Rowley, Essex County, Mass. His burial was in Massachusetts. Samuel Fellows, son of William and Mary (Ayers) Fellows, lived a quiet life with little mention of him in the records. He was one of the court-appointed family administrators of his father's will in 1677. A deed of 1676 listed him with his siblings in the purchase of the John Proctor property, and its subsequent sale in 1694.[78] In 1701, he was living in Newbury, Massachusetts, probably with his sister Abigail Ayers.[79] It is possible that some genealogists confused Samuel with his Uncle Samuel Fellows, his father's brother who also lived in Salisbury.[80]

Samuel of Ipswich never married, but lived with his sister Abigail and her husband Samuel Ayers, Sr. who agreed to keep Samuel throughout his life. Samuel Fellows, late of Ipswich, made a conveyance of his property to Samuel Ayers, Sr. of Newbury on 23 May 1701 in consideration of the many and "great kindnesses his loving brother-in-law" had shown him. He wrote, "having for many years living with him & have been provided for by him as also for & in consideration of an obligation, that he hath this day with his two sons Samuel, Jr. and John [conveyed to Samuel Ayers, Sr.] all my housing and land, upland and meadow which were given to me by my father William, 1/3 of 1/2 of his farm, 1/3 of the buildings." When the elder William Fellows of Ipswich died in 1676, each of his three sons, Ephraim, Joseph, and Samuel divided one-half of William's farm and buildings. Isaac, the eldest son of William, had already received one-half of the Fellows' property before William died.[81] For many years, the provisions of William's will lay unexecuted. The Fellows children lived amicably on the land. On 30 Mar 1702, they filed an agreement to partition the inheritance from their father, and gave power of attorney to Samuel of Newbury. They agreed to "settle & divide the real estate of their father William Fellowes formerly of Ipswich according to his donation in his last will & testament."[82] Samuel oversaw the task.

Samuel Fellows died in 1713 in Rowley, Essex County, Mass.[83] In his will, dated 14 Apr 1712 and proved 14 Dec 1713, "Samuell Fellows of Rowly" bequeathed his entire estate to "my loving sister Abigaill Ayers & Sam'l Ayers & John Ayers my cousins [nephews]."[84] On 11 Dec 1713, Samuel Ayers and John Ayers allowed their mother Abigail Ayers the full use and benefit of the estate "of our uncle Sam'l Fellows."[85]

4. **Mary Fellows** was born about 1645 in Massachusetts. She died between 1690 and 1699 probably in Reading, Middlesex County, Massachusetts.[86] Mary married **Josiah Brown**, son of Nicholas Brown and Elizabeth Leids, on 23 Feb 1665/66 in Reading, Middlesex County, Massachusetts.[87] Josiah was born in 1630 in Lynn, Essex County, Massachusetts. He died on 29 Jan 1690 in Reading, Middlesex County, Mass.[88] The genealogical record is mostly silent on Mary Fellows, daughter of William and Mary (Ayers) Fellows.[89] She and

Josiah lived first in Marblehead, Essex County, Massachusetts, in 1668-69 and in 1677-78.[90] The couple joined the church at Reading, Massachusetts, 12 May 1670. Her father made Mary a legatee in his will in 1676.[91] Josiah became a Freeman of the Massachusetts Colony in 1684.[92] Mary was living in Reading as late as 1688.[93] Sources place her death in 1691, about the same year in which her husband Josiah Brown died.[94] The Fellows and Brown genealogies converged again in 1767 when Susannah Rathbone, daughter of Tabitha (Brown) Rathbone, a descendent of Thomas Browne, Josiah Brown's brother, married William Fellows of Stonington, Connecticut, later of Stephentown, New York, and great-great-grandson of William Fellows of Ipswich.[95]

5. **Joseph Fellows**, the youngest son of William and Mary (Ayers) Fellows, was born about 1650 in Ipswich, Essex County, Massachusetts, and died 1 Oct 1693, in Ipswich.[96] He appears to have been a tailor, a trade that was in abundance in Ipswich. Some tailors went from house to house, making new garments and making over the old ones.[97] On 19 Apr 1675, Joseph married **Ruth Fraile** in Ipswich, Essex County, Massachusetts.[98] She was born on an unknown date, and died 14 Apr 1729, in Ipswich.[99] Records mention her as Mrs. Ruth Fellows an "ancient widow."[100] She was the daughter of George Fraile.[101] Known as a woman of uncommon energy, she had an addition built on to the Fellows homestead, with rooms that were to be specifically hers even after her husband died, as specified in his will.

As a young man, Joseph Fellows obtained certain rights of commonage in 1664. He served in King Philip's War in 1676, fighting in the Great Swamp Fight near Kingston Station (present South Kingston), Rhode Island, under the command of Captain Samuel Borcklebanks and the Marlborough Garrison. Officials assigned his wages to Ipswich in 1675/76. Joseph participated in the battle of the Swamp Fort of the Narraganset Indians on 19 Dec 1675, listed as a Soldier Grantee in the 1733 allocation of lands to soldiers of the Narraganset Campaign. The government promised land for services in the war. However, Joseph never personally received his land. His son Joseph, Jr. received the land after his father's death.[102]

Joseph, Sr. was a co-administrator of his father William's estate in Ipswich in 1677. He received of his father's will 1/3 of 1/2 of his father's land.[103] He subsequently purchased additional land on Fellows Lane in 1681 from his brother Ephraim. He also acquired the Saltonstall and Firman pastures, and land owned by Nathaniel Jacobs.[104] Both he and his brother Ephraim lived together for many years with their families on the old homestead. Joseph remained on the Ipswich farm until his death in 1693, making his home on the farm that he had acquired by inheritance and purchase.[105]

He was a voter in town affairs in 1679, recorded as a Freeman of the Colony on 26 May 1682. The inventories of his estate when he died in 1693 amounted to £791 15s. His wife Ruth rendered the inventory of his estate on 7 Nov 1693.

His assets included real estate valued at £451, and personal property worth £235 15s. It was distributed one-third part to Ruth his widow of real estate £150 6s. 8d. and personal property of £85 11s. 8d. The estate settled on Joseph, Jr. the eldest son was real estate £85 18s. and personal property of £48 8s. Each of the other children received, real property of £42 19s. and personal property of £24 8s. The Widow Ruth "charged April 15, 1697, to keeping three children 3 and 1/2 years to this time, £15."[106]

In January of 1694, Ruth Fellows joined the remaining Fellows brothers on behalf of her deceased husband Joseph to sell the old John Proctor property—the four-rod lot and house. It was the property that Proctor and William Fellows had owned together for a decade and purchased by his heirs from Proctor's sons. It remained jointly in Fellows hands for many years until the family sold it to William Fellows, the son of Ephraim, thus it passed to the next generation. William sold it out of the family in 1708.[107]

Of the six children born to Joseph and Ruth (Fraile) Fellows, Joseph, Jr. was the eldest son, born in 1678, and the next in line of descent.[108] On 17 Dec 1701, he married Sarah Kimball who was born 19 May 1680 and died 2 Sep 1720, leaving Joseph, Jr. with five sons. He married for his second wife Widow Mary Story, by whom he had one daughter. He claimed his father's grant for service in the King Philip War, and later acquired additional land until the Fellows family owned land on both sides of the road in Ipswich.[109]

6. **Elizabeth Fellows** was born about 1653 probably in Ipswich, Essex County, Mass. She resided in Portsmouth, New Hampshire, but later returned to Ipswich.[110] She died after 1676. History remembers little about Elizabeth Fellows, except that she was the daughter of William and Mary (Ayers) Fellows.[111] Family historian Mark Fellows cited sources placing the undated birth of Elizabeth Fellows in Bristol, Grafton County, New Hampshire.[112] However, this seems unlikely. Elizabeth was a legatee of her father's will written at Ipswich on 29 Nov 1676, and unmarried at the time.[113] She apparently died before 1702 when the final disposition of the Fellows estate occurred because her name did not appear among the other siblings in the agreement to partition the estate.[114]

7. **Abigail Sarah Fellows** was born about 1655 probably in Ipswich, Essex County, Massachusetts.[115] She died after 1722 in Rowley or Ipswich, Essex County, Mass. Abigail married **Samuel Ayers** son of Capt. John Ayers and Susannah Symonds on 16 Apr 1677 in Ipswich, Essex County, Mass.[116] Samuel Ayers died after 7 Feb 1695/96. Mark Fellows provided extensive documentation of Abigail Fellows and Samuel Ayers, citing "The Hammett Papers," and *Candlewood* by Thomas Waters, among other sources.[117] Louis Dow Sisco stated that Abigail Fellows was a legatee in 1676 and married her cousin Samuel Ayers in 1677. In later years, they removed to Newbury, Mass. Abigail

was still living there as a widow in 1723. The couple had several children.[118] Her brother Samuel Fellows lived with her family."[119]

The genealogical record appears to support the existence of two different Abigail Fellows.[120] However, family historians generally agree that she married Samuel Ayers, 16 Apr 1677.[121] Capt. John Ayers, Samuel's father, who lived in Quaboag (later Brookfield), Massachusetts, died at the hands of Indians at Squakeag, now Northfield, in the Massacre of 2 Aug 1675, during King Philip's War. Samuel's mother Susannah then moved to Ipswich, Massachusetts, with her six boys and one daughter following John's death.

It is possible that Samuel and Abigail Ayers resided in a part of Rowley, Massachusetts, now known as Byfield Parish, in Newbury, Essex County, Massachusetts. The Rowley Church admitted Abigail and Samuel Ayers to the Church 13 Oct 1700. James Tenney of Rowley by deed dated 22 Feb 1703/04 conveyed to Samuel Ayers, Sr. and Samuel Ayers, Jr. both of Rowley, a right in Rowley that the town previously granted to his father Thomas Tenney, deceased.[122]

According to Lodgette, citing Connecticut records, Indians killed Samuel Ayers in 1710, at Winter Harbor, Maine, during Queen Anne's War, also known as the Third Indian War. Opinions vary concerning the disposition of his estate. Mark Fellows claimed he wrote his will dated 3 Feb 1696/97. In it, he bequeathed to his son Samuel, Jr. "Homestead and six acres pasturage land at Heart Break Hill and a three-acre lot at Plum Island, he to maintain his mother." He gave his son Joseph Ayers, "land where his house stands."[123] On the other hand, Lodgette claimed that Samuel died intestate (no will) and no one took administration of his estate. On complaint of a creditor, the court issued a citation on 28 Nov 1713, to his Widow Abigail and her sons, Samuel and John. On 30 Nov 1713, Abigail Ayers, Samuel Ayers, and John Ayers refused to take administration of the estate.[124]

On 13 Feb 1722/23, Abigail and her sister Sarah communicated to the probate court their desire to have "Cousin Jonathan Fellows" administer the residual estate of "our father William Fellows." Jonathan Fellows was the grandson of the immigrant William of Ipswich and probable son of Isaac Fellows. Abigail and Sarah chose to use their maiden name Fellows in this instance probably to confirm their relationship, although Abigail had married Samuel Ayers nearly half a century earlier, and Sarah was the wife of John Potter.[125]

8. **Sarah Fellows** was born 26 Jul 1657 in Ipswich, Essex County, Mass., the youngest child of William and Mary (Ayers) Fellows, and the only one of their children whose birth is in town records. She was a legatee in William's will in 1676, and unmarried. She was living in Ipswich, Mass., in 1723. She died on 13 Jun 1724 in Ipswich, Essex County. Family historians generally agree that she married **John Potter** in 1677 in Ipswich, Essex, Massachusetts,

and had many descendants.[126] John Potter of Ipswich was the son of Anthony Potter and Elizabeth Whipple.[127] He subscribed six shillings towards "the bigger bell" in 1700. His mother Elizabeth Potter subscribed three shillings.[128] Nevertheless, conflicting sources exist on Sarah's marriage to Potter. Torrey called the marriage to John Potter "possible/probable."[129] Meanwhile, other genealogists dispute her marriage to Potter. Some claim that she did not marry Potter but instead married **John Rust**. George Marshall Fellows listed her marriage date as 1686 to Rust. Frank T. Waters claimed she married Rust, and was living unmarried and a probable widow 3 Feb 1722.[130] Louis Dow Sisco documented Sarah Fellows' marriage to Potter.[131] However, Anderson argued that she did not marry John Potter and that Potter's wife was the daughter of John Kimball.[132] It appears that Anderson may have been correct. On 13 Feb 1722/23, Sarah Fellows and her sister Abigail Fellows signified to the probate court their desire to have "Cousin Jonathan Fellows" administer on the residual estate of "our father William Fellows." Both used the surname Fellows, although Abigail had been married to Samuel Ayers for many years.[133] It is possible that the same applied to Sarah. Some genealogists characterize her alleged marriage to John Rust as her second marriage.[134] Sarah had five children.[135]

5

Isaac Fellows and King Philip's War

On August 4, 1634, Massachusetts colonists incorporated the village of Ipswich, a town named for the locale in Suffolk County, England, where many of the first settlers originated. Commerce and community building soon followed. Tanning and shoemaking, shipbuilding and fishing became dominant business activities of Ipswich in the 17th Century. Adventurers were able to secret machines out of England in pots of Yorkshire butter in defiance of English export laws to make Ipswich, among its many vocations, the birthplace of American lacemaking and hosiery.

In 1635, William Fellows came ashore in Boston and quickly made his way to the enterprising village of Ipswich. For more than four decades, he was a leader in colonial Massachusetts and a rising figure in the birth of American independence. At the end of his life in 1676, one hundred years before the hopes of the visionaries of Ipswich took form in the Declaration of Independence; his descendants took up the charge of building a future in the New World.[1]

Isaac Fellows, the eldest son of William and Mary (Ayers) Fellows, and progenitor of the present branch of the Fellows Family Tree, was born about 1637 in Ipswich, Massachusetts, a date based on a court document filed April 6, 1721, when he was "upwards of 84 years."[2] Claims that he was born in London, England, prior to 1635 have gone unproven.[3] The best arguments for the date of his birth make him the first of the Fellows name born in America.[4] He grew up in Ipswich on the shore of the Atlantic Ocean.

He maintained an active presence in the community affairs of Ipswich. He was associated with his father in the lease of the Saltonstall farm in the Argilla neighborhood, and other land. Argilla lay east of Ipswich near Castle Hill, on the Massachusetts coast. He owned and rented substantial amounts of land in and around Ipswich. In 1664, when Richard Saltonstall conveyed the title in several lots to his son upon his son's marriage, he included in his gift a farm of 150 acres at Chebacco, "now in the occupation of William and Isaac Fellows."[5]

On January 29, 1672/73, Isaac married Joanna Boreman who was born in 1646 in Ipswich.[6] Her name appears in records variously transcribed as Boreman, Boardman, Bourne, Born, and Brown.[7] The record of her marriage recorded her as "Bonn" or "Born" believed to be a contraction of Boreman.[8] Genealogists generally agree that she was the daughter of Margaret Offing and Thomas Boreman of Oxfordshire, England.[9] Historian Abraham Hammatt stated that Thomas Boreman had an unmarried daughter named Joanna. The will of Boreman's wife Margaret Borman, written August 8 1679, mentioned her daughters and included a bequest to "my daughter Fellowes."[10] In a marriage agreement between William Fellows, the father of Isaac, and Thomas Boreman, the father of Joanna, William pledged that a portion of his estate upon his death would go to Isaac and the remainder would go to Thomas Boreman, an indication of a dowry arrangement for the marriage of Isaac and Joanna.[11]

History remembers Isaac best for his participation in King Philip's War, the bloodiest war ever fought on American soil in which more people died per capita than in any war before or since. The conflict occurred in 1675–1678 between New England colonists and the indigenous inhabitants of New England seeking to reclaim Indian lands. Historian Charles Hudson wrote, "The horrors and devastation of Philip's war have no parallel in our history. The revolution was a struggle for freedom; the contest with Philip was for existence. The war lasted only about fourteen months; and yet the towns of Brookfield, Lancaster, Marlborough, Middlefield, Sudbury, Groton, Deerfield, Hatfield, Hadley, Northfield, Springfield, Weymouth, Chelmsford, Andover, Scituate, Bridgewater, and several other places were wholly or partially destroyed, and many of the inhabitants were massacred or carried into captivity." Hudson went on to say, "During this short period, six hundred of our brave men, the flower and strength of the Colony, had fallen, and six hundred dwelling houses were consumed. Every eleventh family was houseless, and every eleventh soldier had sunk to his grave."[12]

The War of King Philip was a predictable Indian rebellion against continuing Puritan incursions into Native American lands. Edward Randolph, emissary of King James II sent to the colonies to investigate the overall state of colonial affairs, wrote of the causes of the war. "Various are the reports and conjectures of the causes of the present Indian war. Some impute it to an imprudent zeal in the magistrates of Boston to Christianize those heathen before they were civilized and injoying them the strict observation of their lawes, which, to a people so rude and licentious, hath proved even intolerable, and that the more, for that while the magistrates, for their profit, put the lawes severely in execution against the Indians, the people, on the other side, for lucre and gain, entice and provoke the Indians to the breach thereof, especially to drunkenness, to which those people are so generally addicted that they will strip themselves to the skin to have their fill of rum and brandy."[13] The English assumed the government of the country, and followed their course of settlement with small regard for the rights of the natives. By 1670, New England's European population was about 50,000 inhabitants and the colonies were thriving. Conversely, European-borne diseases had decimated the Indian population, and every passing year found them with less game and less land.

The chief of the Wampanoag Indians was Metacomet, the son of Massasoit who ironically had fifty years earlier befriended and saved the original Plymouth Colony from starvation. Chief Massasoit died in 1661, and his son succeeded him. The colonists knew the son Metacomet by his English name Philip, called King Philip by the colonists. Impatient with colonial laws and humiliations, King Philip (Metacomet) began plans to wage war against the colonies. His goal was no less than to clear the Connecticut Valley of all English settlers.

Isaac Fellows and two of his brothers, Ephraim and Joseph, answered the call to defend the colonies. Isaac Fellows enlisted in the service of Major Willard's Company of the Massachusetts Regiment that engaged in the Narragansett campaign. The story of the action of that campaign is a chronicle of the survival of the English colonialization of America.

The colonists had few standing military units to respond, and passed America's first draft laws that called for the enrollment of all males between 16 and 60. Isaac Fellows was about age 38. In February of 1675, Massachusetts ordered a levy on Norfolk and Essex Counties. Forty-eight men were sent from Essex County, among them most likely was Isaac Fellows who served with Captain Willard's Company.[14] The levy was a hasty response to King Philip's threats on Groton and other nearby Massachusetts towns. Under Major Simon Willard of Groton, the force arrived at the town on March 14; unfortunately, a day after the Indians had destroyed all the houses in town except the garrison houses to which most of the people had escaped. The Indians were elated with their success at Groton, and threatened to attack and destroy all the towns in the region, including even Boston. Major Willard, after applying the Essex and Norfolk men to assist in the relief of the besieged towns, released some of the men, while ordering a remainder "to scout abroad untill they heare from me agayne." Many believe that Isaac Fellows was among this small band of scouts—21 men in all—who continued to serve Major Willard.

On June 20, 1675, a band of Pokanokets attacked several isolated homesteads in the small Plymouth colony settlement of Swansea, Massachusetts. The attackers laid siege to the town, destroyed it five days later, and killed several people. They were emboldened by their conquest, which came just a week before a full eclipse of the moon in the New England area, an event interpreted by various tribes in New England as an omen to attack the colonists.

Another Indian divulged King Philip's plans to wipe out the English colonies of New England, and Philip had the traitor murdered. When English authorities captured the murderers and subsequently executed them under colonial law, King Philip was incensed and began renewed attacks the next day on Plymouth Colony villages. In early autumn, the Wampanoag sought to build an alliance with the Nipmuc of southwestern Massachusetts and the Narragansett of Rhode Island. By November, the entire upper Connecticut Valley threatened to be once again Indian Territory. The Indian attacks were rapid and ferocious, often killing men, women, and children in their homes and fields where they were at work. Historians estimate that over the course of the war, 3,000 colonists died compared with 2,500 casualties on the Indian side.[15]

In October, the Indians struck again, this time in the interior of the colony with raids against Hatfield, Northampton, and Springfield, Massachusetts, almost burning the settlement at Springfield to the ground.

In the autumn of 1675, after the campaign in the western parts of the colony of Massachusetts, the United Colonies decided to carry the war against the powerful tribe of the Narragansett who, although not yet directly aligned with King Philip, had shown themselves to be hostile against the colonists.

Isaac Fellows and his brothers, Ephraim and Joseph, responded for service when the call went out for the veteran troops of earlier campaigns to reorganize. On November 2, 1675, the United Colonies declared war against the Narragansett and mounted an offensive in a combined force of about 1,000 militia against the Narragansett tribe. Their objective was the great Swamp Fort of the Narragansett located in present day Rhode Island.

The Narragansett campaign consisted of three regiments: Massachusetts, Plymouth, and Connecticut. The full quota of Massachusetts was 527 men who enrolled on December 9, 1675. The Massachusetts Council issued a proclamation to the soldiers, "If they played the man, took the Fort, & Drove the Enemy out of the Narragansett Country, which was their great Seat, that they should have a gratuity in land besides their wages."[16]

Coming by land and sea, they mustered on December 18, 1675, at Pettisquamscot (Tower Hill, South Kingston, Rhode Island), and prepared to begin the assault on the fort about 10 miles distant. The weather was bitter cold. Historian George Madison Bodge wrote, "In a severe snow-storm, the whole force, about one thousand men [half from Massachusetts], encamped in the open field through that bitter cold night. Sunday, Dec. 19th, before daybreak—around 5 o'clock—the whole force marched away towards the enemy's great rendezvous."

The Swamp Fort occupied an island of four or five acres in the midst of a cedar swamp, which was impassable except to the Indians by their accustomed paths, and now made passable only by the frozen ground from the severe cold of the previous day and night. Historians say the fort would have been almost impregnable to the colonial troops had not the swamp been frozen. The fort was of palisaded construction, built of upright logs set in the ground. Within this wall was a clay wall. A 'hedge' of trees some ten feet deep surrounded the entire fort. However, the inhabitants had not quite finished the fort at the time of the assault, and it was through an unfinished opening that the colonial forces moved in around one o'clock in the afternoon, the Massachusetts regiment leading the assault.

The First Company of Massachusetts was under the command of Major Samuel Appleton, of Ipswich, home of the Fellows brothers, and it is probable that they were in his company. In any event, they were no doubt a part of this initial attack on the fort. Bodge says, "We are assured that all took part in the engagement, coming on in turn as needed." The Fourth and Fifth Massachusetts led the charge but were eventually forced to withdraw after severe losses at enemy hands. Major Appleton then massed his entire Ipswich Company as a storming column and carried the entrance to the fort, followed closely by the rest of the force. Fierce hand-to-hand combat followed, eventually forcing the Indians, said to be above 5,000 in number, to flee into the swamp after about three hours of battle.

Fearing a counterattack from the enemy against their now exhausted and depleted force, the army of the United Colonies decided to retreat to their camp at Tower Hill. Bodge reconstructed the march back to the camp. "They marched through a bitter cold winter's night, in a blinding snow-storm, carrying two hundred and ten of their wounded and dead; these soldiers, who had marched from dawn till high noon, had engaged in a desperate life-and-death struggle from noon till sunset, now plodded sturdily back to their quarters of the day before, through deepening snows and over unbroken roads." Fearing ambush from the Indians, they took unbroken trails to avoid contact with the enemy.

Many historians believe that in terms of heroism, stubborn patience, and intrepidity, the achievement of these men remains unexcelled in American warfare. Some historians go even further, crediting these few brave soldiers, their officers, and the victory at the Swamp Fort with breaking the resolve of the Indians to annihilate the colonies. Retribution fueled the ferocity of the soldiers in the engagement for atrocities remembered from earlier campaigns of King Philip's raids on the colonists, in which hundreds of colonists died or fell into captivity. Bodge stated, "The soldiers knew that the very life of the colonies was threatened by this war; many thriving hamlets were already in ashes; hundreds of families were broken up and scattered up and down, with loss of all; fathers, husbands, and brothers slain or in captivity, farms and homes laid waste, whole communities huddled in wretched block-houses, while the 'reign of terror' swept about them." Consequently, the sack of the Narragansett Fort spared no one. The invading colonial troops killed Indian warriors, women, and children, anyone in their path. Indian prisoners later reported that about 700 Indians died at Narragansett.

Soon, the colonial regiments effectively resisted other Indian attacks. When the United Colonial armies came together to destroy the great Swamp Fort, the loss of shelter and supplies in the midst of winter increased the desperation of King Philip's cause. Indian raids continued through the spring and summer of 1676 but by smaller, less-coordinated bands of marauders. Although colonists continued to die and towns fell into ruin, better-prepared and determined residents often repulsed the Indians. Friendly Indians in increasing numbers began to assist the colonists. Pushed out of their native lands, disease and famine began to undermine support for Philip's War. When the Mohawks, potentially strong allies of King Philip, refused to join him, it sent a signal in the spring of 1776 that Philip's strongest supporters saw his cause was hopeless. In April 1776, soldiers captured Canonchet, Chief of the Narragansett, and the real leader of all active operations of the Indians by now. His execution dealt a deathblow to the war. The Colonial militias continued to search out and destroy marauding bands of Indians. The tribes became divided and demoralized. A friendly Indian killed King Philip on August 12, 1676, essentially ending the war.

At the end of their service, the Massachusetts soldiers received credit on the rolls of their respective towns and the amount of pay due them. Bodge chronicled the soldiers of the conflict. "The troops that went up from Norfolk and Essex were credited under their special officers. The following are those who received credit under Major Willard, and are those probably who were employed in scouting with him in the early part of the winter: July 24th, [1676]." On the list of credit was Isaac Fellows £1 5s. 6d. The towns assumed the payment of the wages of their own soldiers to their families left at home. The families thus received sure and immediate aid. The towns, in return, received credit in that amount for their colonial 'rates,' or taxes. It was doubtless a means of great help to the families and of savings to the towns because it secured at once the support of the families without public charge, and at the same time the prompt payment of colonial taxes. Bodge concluded that where a man assigned his wages to a town, he considered that his place of residence, thus Isaac Fellows received credit to the town of Ipswich. Credits for service were at the close of such service, or at regular monthly or bi-monthly settlements. However, many who were in the Narragansett campaign did not receive payment until the general settlement on June 24, 1676, or in Isaac's case August 24, 1676, when "Ipswich-Towne Cr by Sundry accpts; viz. £67 15s. 09d" of which credit went to Joseph Fellows £1 15s 0d; Isaac Fellows £1 5s 6d."[17] Ever after, Isaac answered to the title of Corporal Fellows.[18]

Meanwhile, "It will be remembered," Bodge wrote, "that when, on December 10th, 1675, the forces of Massachusetts Colony were mustered on Dedham Plain, to march against the Narragansett fort, a proclamation was made to the soldiers, in the name of the Governor, that, 'if they played the man, took the fort, and drove the enemy out of the Narragansett country, which is their great seat, they should have a gratuity of land, besides their wages.' We find that after they had so valiantly performed the service, and the war was long past, the soldiers were not forgetful of their claim, nor the colony unmindful of its obligations."[19] The name of Isaac Fellows does not appear on surviving company rolls for the Narragansett campaign. The proof of his participation comes from the land grant records which list him as one entitled to the land grant benefit, which he only earned if he was a soldier in the Narragansett expedition. [20] After years of petitions and political wrangling, the government finally fulfilled its promise to give land to the soldiers in 1733. By this time, many of those entitled to grants had died or removed from the region, and few of those entitled ever settled.

Isaac Fellows was not active in the politics of colonial Massachusetts, although he held minor offices as a "Tything man." Nevertheless, his presence in Ipswich helped to earn for the town the sobriquet of "The Birthplace of American Independence."[21] The title arises from a protest, led by Reverend John Wise in 1687, when angry townsfolk refused to submit to "taxation without representation" promoted by the oppressive "Taxation Edict" of notorious royal governor, Sir Edmund Andros. [22]

Isaac Fellows lived out his long life at Ipswich, Massachusetts.[23] The records contain ample evidence of his presence. In 1678, he was one of the surveyors of highways along with his brother Ephraim. He purchased from Henry Bennett a house and marsh lots on Wigwam Hill in 1680, and he may have moved there but sold it in 1694.[24] In 1707, he conveyed to his son, Jonathan, another farm, mentioning that William Durgey then occupied it. Waters mentioned in his book on *Candlewood*, "Isaac Fellows, son of William, conveyed to his son, Jonathan, 'my farm, lately in the tenure and occupation of William Durgey, excepting 5 acres, about 50 acres, dwelling etc., reserving the use of the premises during his life,' [dated] March 31, 1705."[25]

On the east side of the Bay Road, in Candlewood, the great tract of pasture, tillage land, meadow and swamp, bounded in part by Fellows Lane, was part of the Common Land of the Town. In 1709, the citizens of Ipswich divided this great area of Common lands into Eighths. The Fellows property became part of the division known as the South Eighth, and later known as the Inner Common of the South Eighth. Around the year 1726, the proprietors of the Inner Common apportioned individual shares. Thus, Fellows descendants benefitted from the foresight of William Fellows who first established himself on the Commons in 1659.[26]

In Isaac's day and before, as early as the first settlement of William Fellows, the center of Ipswich was the Meeting House Green. It stood on Town Hill and was the center of early Ipswich. The first building went up in 1636, surrounded by a high wall to protect town citizens from the danger of Indian attacks. Dwellings had to be within one-half mile of the Meeting House. Local ordinance required inhabitants to attend a yearly meeting under threat of fine if they did not attend. During the seventeenth century, the complex consisted of a meetinghouse, jail, fort, town pound, and stocks. Near the first meetinghouse stood First Church on Meeting House Green, rivaling the town seat of government.

Long Sabbath meetings at First Church required special accommodations, including for horses. A special Committee approved select parishioners to erect sheds on Meeting House Green near the church. In due time, prominent citizens were able to build pews. Nevertheless, over time, the congregation outgrew general seating patterns. In March 1719/20, the church appointed the Committee for Assigned Seating according to social standing, wealth, or official station. A new church house went up, but it, too, soon became overburdened and the Committee doubled down on its duties to apportion seating, especially in the most dignified portions of the building. A group of distinguished elders had seats at the communion table directly in front of the pulpit. The next rows went to more of the elderly in the form of the Men's Short fore seat in the front and the Women's front seat on the other side of the aisle. Among the assignees to this special seating was Mrs. Fellows who absent her first name in the records may have been the Widow Mary (Ayers) Fellows, widow of William. Although, it seems more likely that she was Johanna (Boreman) Fellows, wife of Isaac because the Men's third seat included Mr. Isaac Fellows seated among the "important and prosperous" citizens of Ipswich. The people of Ipswich strictly adhered to the seating rules. In a vote of the town on May 25, 1724, residents adopted the editc that "all persons shall be obliged to Observe the Order of the Committee…and shall not sit in an higher seat than that which shall be ordered for him, under a forfeiture of five shillings for each offence."[27]

Corporal Isaac Fellows died April 6, 1721 "upwards of 84" in Ipswich, Massachusetts. His Widow Joanna (Boreman) Fellows died March 22, 1731/32, in Ipswich.[28] Their burials were in the Old Burying Ground of Ipswich.[29] The Old Burying Ground—referred to in the records as Old Burying Hill—lies immediately south of present Highland Cemetery on the north edge of Ipswich.

For many years, historians believed that Isaac never personally received his promised lands for his service in King Philip's War.[30] However, a deed discovered in York, Maine, included him among several grantees named in the legalese of colonial business. "Mr. Harlackenden Symonds, Gentleman of Ipswich, Have Given, Granted, bargained, sold, Infeoffeed and Confirmed and by these presents Doe fully, Clearly and absolutely Give, Grant, bargain, sell, Alienate, and Infeoff and confirm unto Isack [*sic*] Fellows [and thirty two others so listed] to them and their heires and Assignes forever, a certaine Tract of land, six miles in length and foure miles in breadth, known by the name of Cokshall in the County of Yorkshiere, in the Province of Maine."[31] Isaac died before the apportionment of the land, and his son Jonathan claimed his grant. Joseph Fellows, Isaac's brother, also received a grant of land, which his son Joseph, Jr. claimed after his death. Whether Isaac personally benefited from the large parcel of land in Maine, it passed to his son, Jonathan. In his will, Jonathan passed the property on to his children, "Whereas I have a tract of land which I have not disposed of lying in the province of Maine, commonly known as Cock's Hill, I do hereby bequeath it to all my children, sons, and daughters equally to have shares and rights therein."[32] Cock's Hill was near Buxton, Maine, later known as Coxhall. It was the land promised by the government to Jonathan's father Isaac for Isaac's service in the King Philip War of 1675-1676.[33]

The six children of Isaac and Joanna (Boreman) Fellows recorded in the Isaac Fellows Bible were Isaac, Jr., Samuel, Ephraim, Jonathan, David, and Joanna.[34] Isaac's two eldest sons preceded him in death, leaving his third son Ephraim as his heir. The line of genealogical descent continued with Ephraim Fellows.

Metacomet of Pokanoket (aka Philip). This period engraving pictures the leader of King Philip's War against the English colonies in 1775. His portrait is from an account of the war written by Captain Benjamin Church, a participant in the conflict. A militia led by Church tracked down and killed Philip at Mount Hope in Bristol, Rhode Island. Engraving by Paul Revere, in *The Entertaining History of King Philip's War* by Church, 1716.

Meeting House Green of Ipswich. This was the hub of colonial Ipswich from the earliest date of its founding until well into the nineteenth century. Once a fortified complex built to defend against Indians, the Green was the center of town business and the location of the first churches in the village. Woodcut, 1838, attributed to S.E. Brown. *Historic Ipswich*, Ipswich Historical Commission.

Fellows Second Generation Family Group

Isaac FELLOWS was born in 1637 in Ipswich, Essex County, Massachusetts. He died on 6 Apr 1721 in Ipswich, Essex County, Massachusetts. His burial was in Old Burying Ground, Ipswich, Essex County. He was the son of **William Israel FELLOWS** and **Mary AYERS.**

Isaac married **Joanna BOREMAN**, daughter of **Thomas BOREMAN** and **Margaret OFFING**, on 29 Jan 1672/73 in Ipswich, Essex County, Mass. Joanna was born in 1646 in Ipswich, Essex County, Massachusetts. She died on 22 Mar 1731/32 in Ipswich, Essex County. Her burial was in Old Burying Ground, Ipswich.

They had the following children.

1. **Isaac Fellows, Jr.** was born on 27 Nov 1673 in Ipswich, Essex County, Massachusetts. He died before 8 Mar 1707/08.[35] Isaac did not marry. The genealogical record refers to him as Isaac Fellows, Jr. He purchased the Samuel Younglove house and land on South Main Street in Ipswich on 16 Jun 1694. His brother Ephraim Fellows presented Isaac Jr.'s estate to the court in Ipswich on 3 May 1708. Ephraim then sold the Younglove property to Dr. Samuel Wallis 20 Nov 1713.

2. **Samuel Fellows** was born on 8 Feb 1676 in Ipswich, Essex County, Massachusetts. He died in 1707 in Hampton, Rockingham County, New Hampshire.[36] Samuel married **Deborah Sanborn** on 15 Nov 1698 in Hamton Falls, Rockingham County, New Hampshire. Deborah was born in 1681. She died in 1725 in Hamton Falls, Rockingham, New Hampshire. Samuel was a Sadler by trade. He moved from Ipswich, Massachusetts, to Hampton, New Hampshire, sometime before 1689. He joined the Church of Hampton in 1689. He granted administration of his estate to his wife Debora Fellows 2 Sep 1707. There is disagreement among family historians regarding his marriage. Frank T. Waters and others claimed Samuel married Sarah Fuller 5 Jan 1731 and had one daughter. Another researcher listed six children all born in Hampton, New Hampshire. Genealogists appear to confuse him with his son Samuel Fellows, Jr. born 3 Oct 1707, who married Sarah Fuller. The Bible of Isaac Fellows—Samuel, Sr.'s father—did not show a marriage or children for him. Nevertheless, historian Mark Fellows claimed Samuel married Deborah Sanborn. She was administrator of the estate of her husband Samuel on 5 Sep 1708, according to Fellows, "to bring up six children, one eight year old called Isaac, John six years

old, Hannah five years old, Isaiah four years old, Rach two years old, and Samuel born two months after his father's decease. Deborah married Benjamin Shaw after Samuel's death."[37] Children of Samuel Fellows and Debora Sanborn: 1) Isaac Fellows b. 20 Jan 1699/70 in Hampton, Rockingham County, New Hampshire, d. 1773 in Exeter, Rockingham County; 2) John Fellows b. 23 May 1701 in Hampton, Rocking-ham County, d. Oct 1723 in Kingston, New Hampshire, m. Elizabeth Towle b. Kensington, New Hampshire; 3) Joanna Fellows b. 29 Sep 1702 in Hampton, Rockingham County, New Hampshire; 4) Sarah Fellows b. 9 Apr 1704 in Hampton, Rockingham, d. 2 Sep 1720 in Ipswich, Massachusetts; 5) Rachel Fellows b. 10 Mar 1705/06 in Hampton, Rockingham County; and 6) Samuel Fellows, Jr. b. 3 Oct 1707 in Hampton, Rockingham County, d. 25 Aug 1735 in Ipswich, Essex County, Massachusetts.[38]

\+ 3. **Ephraim FELLOWS** was born on 3 Sep 1679 in Ipswich, Essex County, Massachusetts. He died on 12 Mar 1725/26 in Stonington, New London, Connecticut. He was buried in Great Plain Cemetery, North Stonington, New London County, Connecticut. Ephraim married **Hannah WARNER**, daughter of **Nathaniel WARNER** and **Hannah BOYNTON**, on 19 May 1703 in Ipswich, Essex County, Mass. Hannah was born on 13 Feb 1681 in Ipswich. She died 19 Mar 1758 in North Stonington, New London County, Connecticut. She was buried in Great Plain Cemetery, North Stonington, New London County.

4. **Jonathan Fellows** was born on 28 Sep 1682 in Ipswich, Essex County, Massachusetts. He died on 21 Jan 1753 in Kensington, Rockingham County, New Hampshire.[39] Jonathan married **Hannah Dutch** on 17 May 1704 in Ipswich, Essex County, Massachusetts. Hannah was born about 1685 in Ipswich, Essex County. She died on 28 Jan 1709/10 in Ipswich, Essex County. Town records showing Jonathan Fellows first married Elizabeth [*sic*] Dutch on 7 Mar 1704/05 may have been a clerical error because he married first not Elizabeth but Hannah Dutch, 17 May 1705.[40] Jonathan married secondly **Sarah Day**, daughter of John Day and Sarah Wells, about 13 Dec 1712 in Ipswich, Essex County, Massachusetts. Sarah was born on 9 Jan 1691/92 in Ipswich. She died on 1 May 1716 in Ipswich, Essex County. Jonathan married thirdly **Sarah Potter**, daughter of John Potter and Sarah (Fellows) Potter, about 29 Dec 1716 in Ipswich, Essex County, Mass. Sarah Potter was born on 11 Dec 1685 in Ipswich, Essex, Massachusetts. She died on 30 May 1725 in Ipswich, Essex County. Sarah (Fellows) Potter was the aunt of Jonathan Fellows. Some

researchers have questioned the Jonathan Fellows-Sarah Potter marriage.[41] Jonathan married fourthly **Deborah (Batchelder) Hilton**, daughter of Nathanial Batchelder and Elizabeth Foss, on 8 Jun 1733 in Ipswich, Essex County, Massachusetts. Deborah was born on 9 Apr 1686. She first married David Hilton.[42] Researchers have not recorded children for Jonathan Fellows and Deborah (Batchelder) Hilton-Fellows.

Jonathan Fellows succeeded to his father Isaac's farm and retained it from 1705 to 1742. Records refer to him as 'Sergeant' and 'Deacon.' He was a Deacon of the First Church in Ipswich, Massachusetts. In 1742, he sold all his Ipswich property and moved with his family to Kensington, New Hampshire, where he died in 1753. In his will, he passed his property in Maine on to his children. "Whereas I have a tract of land which I have not disposed of lying in the province of Maine, commonly known as Cock's Hill, I do hereby bequeath it to all my children, sons, and daughters equally to have shares and rights therein." His will bore the date of 3 Feb 1752, proved at Portsmouth, Maine. Cock's Hill was near Buxton, Maine, and known as Coxhall after 1780. In 1803, it was Lyman, Maine. The land was land promised by the government to Jonathan's father Isaac for Isaac's service in "the French and Indian War." A reference in the record to the French and Indian War was King Philip's War of 1675/76.[43]

Jonathan had 10 children by three of his four wives. Children of Jonathan Fellows and Hannah Dutch were 1) Hannah Fellows b. 30 Mar 1706 in Ipswich, Essex County, Massachusetts; 2) Jonathan Fellows, Jr. b. 15 Jun 1707 in Ipswich, d. 20 Jun 1759 in Gloucester, Essex County, Massachusetts; and 3) Elizabeth Fellows b. 22 Oct 1709 in Ipswich, Essex County.[44]

Children of Jonathan Fellows and Sarah Day were 4) Isaac Fellows b. bef. 6 May 1714 in Ipswich, Essex County, Massachusetts, d. 20 May 1717 in Ipswich, at age three; and 5) John Fellows b. bef. 25 Apr 1716 in Ipswich, d. 18 May 1716 in Ipswich, at one month of age. The death date of infant John's mother on 1 May 1716 suggests that both mother and child died of complications of childbirth.[45]

Children of Jonathan Fellows and Sarah Potter were 6) Sarah Fellows b. 18 Dec 1717 in Ipswich, Essex County, Massachusetts; 7) Isaac Fellows b. 12 May 1719 in Ipswich, d. 8 May 1791 in Hopkinton, Merrimack County, New Hampshire; 8) Abner Fellows b. bef. 4 Dec 1720 in Ipswich, d. 1786; 9) Mary Fellows b. 28 Nov 1722 in Ipswich, m. 1-Nathan Smith, 2-Richard Tucker; and

10) Jeremiah Fellows b. 2 Apr 1724 in Ipswich, d. 5 Mar 1797 in Kensington, Rockingham County, New Hampshire.[46]

5. **David Fellows** was born on 7 Apr 1687 in Ipswich, Essex County, Massachusetts. David did not marry.[47]

6. **Joanna Fellows** was born on 19 Nov 1689 in Ipswich, Essex County, Massachusetts. She died on 25 Sep 1781 in East Sudbury, Middlesex County, Massachusetts.[48] Joanna Fellows was the only known child not listed in the Bible of her father Isaac. Nevertheless, Ipswich vital records list her as his daughter. Joanna married **Joseph Smith**, son of Richard Smith and Hannah Cheney, about 9 Feb 1710 in Ipswich, Essex County, Massachusetts. Joseph was born in Jul 1685 in Ipswich, Essex County. He died on 3 May 1754 in East Sudbury, Middlesex County, Massachusetts. Captain Joseph Smith served in the Revolutionary War and commanded a Sudbury company in Col. Jas. Barrett's Regiment, which marched on the alarm at the Battle of Lexington and Concord 19 Apr 1775.[49] Children of Joanna Fellows and Joseph Smith were 1) Joanna Smith b. bef. 22 Apr 1711 in Ipswich, Massachusetts; 2) Jemina Smith b. bef. 17 Aug 1718 in Ipswich; 3) Isaac Smith b. bef. 7 May 1721; 4) Ephraim Smith b. bef. 2 Apr 1727; 5) Hannah Smith b. unknown; and 6) Joseph Smith b. unknown.[50]

6

Ephraim Fellows

Ephraim Fellows was born September 3, 1679, in Ipswich, Essex County, Massachusetts.[1] He was the third of six children born to Isaac Fellows and Joanna (Boreman) Fellows.[2] He died March 12, 1725/26, in Stonington, New London County, Connecticut.[3] His burial was in Great Plain Cemetery, North Stonington, New London County.[4]

Ephraim first married Hannah Warner, daughter of the late Nathaniel Warner and Hannah Boynton on May 19, 1703, in Ipswich, Massachusetts.[5] Hannah was born August 28, 1684, in Ipswich.[6] She died March 19, 1758, in North Stonington Connecticut.[7] Her burial was in Great Plain Cemetery, North Stonington, New London County.[8]

Ephraim Fellows grew up in Ipswich, Massachusetts, on the shore of Massachusetts Bay. Ephraim and Hannah lived in Ipswich until about 1706 when for unknown reasons they removed to upper Stonington Township in New London County, Connecticut.[9] The time of their move to Stonington occurred between the birth of their daughter Hannah in 1705 recorded in Ipswich, and the birth of Ephraim, Jr. in 1707 in Stonington, Connecticut.

Stonington is a town in New London County in the southeastern corner of Connecticut, The ancient records describe it as "a township at four miles wide on the east side of the river Thames, and six miles from the sea northwardly."[10] Its first settlement dates to 1649 when European colonists established a trading post in what was once Pequot Indian land. The village took the name of Souther [*sic*] Towne because it occupied a location that was at the time part of South Massachusetts. In 1658, the Commissioners of the United Colonies rendered a decision that all the Pequot territory west of Mystic River belonged to Connecticut, and all the territory east of it, including Stonington, North

Stonington, and part of the town of Westerly, belonged to Massachusetts.[11] A meetinghouse went up in 1661 as a place of worship. Small and uncomfortable, the people did not use it in cold weather but held their meetings at a resident's house situated nearby.[12]

The political climate shifted, and the Massachusetts lands received a royal charter as part of Connecticut in 1662. In 1665, the name of Souther Towne was by the General Court changed to that of Mystic; according to Wheeler, "in memory of that victory God was pleased to give this people of Connecticut over the Pequot Indians." In May 1666, an act passed as follows, "The town of Mystic is by this court named Stonington, the Court doth grant to the plantation to extend the bounds thereof ten miles from the sea up into the country northward and eastward to the river called Pawcatuck."[13] It is today the point on a map where the present states of New York, Connecticut, and Rhode Island converge.

Ephraim Fellows settled first at Plainfield, Connecticut, probably in the company of his uncle and namesake Ephraim, son of William Fellows of Ipswich. In 1709, Ephraim Fellows was an inhabitant of Plainfield village, in Windham County, Connecticut, about 20 miles north of Stonington.[14]

Ephraim the younger kept up his interests in Ipswich, although it lay a hundred miles distant from Stonington as the crow flies. His older brother Isaac Fellows, Jr. died, and he returned to Essex County, Massachusetts, to present his brother's estate to the court in Ipswich on May 3, 1708. He sold land owned by Isaac, Jr. in the fall of 1713. [15] Meanwhile, his next oldest brother Samuel Fellows died leaving Ephraim the heir apparent of his father Isaac's estate. The elder Isaac died in 1721.

On December 19, 1722, Rev. Ebenezer Rosseter became Pastor of the Church of Christ, in Stonington, after which time he admitted several persons to the church, including Hannah Fellows on December 22, 1722, and Ephraim on November 1, 1724.[16] The First Congregation Church of Stonington had a storied history. Historian Richard Wheeler wrote, "From the earliest settlement of the town, and the formation of the Church in 1674, several of the inhabitants residing on the east side of Groton, attended meeting at Agreement Hill. They, too, as well as the inhabitants of the Mystic Valley, were opposed to the erection of a new house, because it carried their place of worship farther away from the meeting house." The church had met at a resident's house on Palmer Hill before agreeing to build the first churchhouse on appropriately named Agreement Hill.[17]

North Stonington Township split off from Stonington in 1724, and Ephraim and his family were thereafter associated with North Stonington. The Congregational Church at North Stonington organized in 1727, being then the second church of Stonington.[18] Unfortunately, Ephraim did not live to see a new churchhouse built. He died from an accident on March 12, 1725/26, at the age of 47.[19] He died as the result of a hunting accident from a gunshot wound to the head.[20]

Following his death, Widow Hannah moved to North Stonington, Connecticut. On May 7, 1727, the Congregational Church of Stonington dismissed the "widow Fellowes" and recommended her "to ye communion of ye Church of Christ in North Stonington."[21]

The unexpected premature death of Ephraim left his estate planning in an unfinished state.[22] His oldest son was not yet age 21, and it fell to his widow to settle his property and considerable business affairs, which she did. In May 1728, Hannah appealed to the General Assembly of Connecticut for relief. "Upon the prayer of Hannah Fellows, administratrix on the estate of her deceas'd husband Ephraim Fellows, late of Stonington, deceas'd, representing to this Assembly that the said deceas'd dyed indebted the sum of forty pounds eight shillings and nine pence more than his chattels are sufficient to answer: This Assembly grants power to the administratrix of said estate, with the advice of the court of probate of the county of New London, to sell and dispose so much of the real estate of said deceas'd as shall suffice to pay the said sum of forty pounds eight shillings and nine pence and the charges of selling and all things relating thereunto."[23]

Hannah lived to a good age. On May 25, 1754, she appeared in court with her son Ephraim, Jr. as witness to the will of William Avery.[24] She died March 19, 1758, at the age of 73, in North Stonington, Connecticut.[25] Her burial was beside Ephraim in Great Plain Cemetery of North Stonington.

Ephraim and Hannah Fellows had eight children: Hannah, Ephraim, Sarah, Nathaniel, Isaac, John, Johanna, and Mary. Hannah Fellows, the eldest child, was born in Ipswich August 12, 1705; all others except her were born in Stonington, Connecticut.[26] John and Mary preceded their father Ephraim in death.

The genealogical line of descent continued from Ephraim and Hannah (Warner) Fellows to their fourth-born child and second son, Nathaniel Fellows.

DEACON FELLOWS HOUSE.

Deacon Fellows House. Deacon Elnathan Fellows was the grandson on Ephraim Fellows. He built this house of a quaint-shaped, gambrel-roofed style with an underground room and lean-to at the back. The house stood against a little rise of land in Stonington, Connecticut, near the place where he kept his carpenter shop. Wheeler, *The Homes of Our Ancestors in Stonington.*

First Congregational Church of Stonington, Connecticut. Erected in 1829, this church replaced the old meetinghouse destroyed by fire. Patterned after the original architecture, it incorporated materials salvaged from the old church. Part of the worshippers left the First Congregational Church to attend a new church in North Stonington. The two congregations reunited a century later in 1827. Photo before 1875 from Wheeler, *History of the First Congregational Church.*

Fellows Third Generation Family Group

Ephraim FELLOWS was born on 3 Sep 1679 in Ipswich, Essex County, Massachusetts. He died on 12 Mar 1725/26 in Stonington, New London County, Connecticut. His burial was in Great Plain Cemetery, North Stonington, New London County, Connecticut.[27] He was the son of **Isaac FELLOWS** and **Joanna BOREMAN**.

Ephraim married **Hannah WARNER**, daughter of **Nathaniel WARNER** and **Hannah BOYNTON**, on 19 May 1703 in Ipswich, Essex County, Massachusetts. Hannah was born on 28 Aug 1684 in Ipswich, Essex County. She died on 19 Mar 1758 in North Stonington, New London County, Connecticut.[28] Her burial was in Great Plain Cemetery, North Stonington, New London County.[29]

They had the following children.

1. **Hannah Fellows** was born in Ipswich, Essex County, Massachusetts. Her christening was on 12 Aug 1705.[30] Hannah first married **Samuel Ingalls** on 29 Feb 1723.[31] She married secondly **Thomas Hall** on 10 Jul 1730 in Stonington, New London County, Connecticut.[32] Thomas died on 20 Feb 1777. His burial was in Robinson Burial Ground, Stonington, New London, Connecticut. Hannah was the eldest child of Ephraim and Hannah (Warner) Fellows born in Ipswich, Massachusetts, which places the date of the migration of the family from Ipswich to Stonington, Connecticut, between her birth in 1705 and the birth of Ephraim, Jr. in 1707, in Stonington. Her marriage was in the Congregational Church of Stonington by Rev. James Noyes. The citizens of Stonington organized the Congregational Church in 1727, it being then the second church of Stonington. Records of the church are complete through 1781. Genealogists have questioned the accuracy of the marriage of Hannah to Thomas Hall claiming that it was a different Hannah Fellows who married Hall, and that Hannah actually married Samuel Ingalls instead.[33] However, Hannah married Thomas Hall in the same church where the marriage ceremony took place for the wedding of her sister, Sarah to Samuel Holdredge.[34] Given the dates of Hannah's two marriages, it is likely that she was married twice, first to Ingalls in 1723 and then to Hall in 1730.

Children of Hannah Fellows and Thomas Hall: 1) Amie Hall b. 15 May 1731 in Westerly, Rhode Island; 2) Jeremiah Hall b. 22 Mar 1732/33 in Westerly; 3) Nathaniel Hall b. 1 Mar 1734/35 in Westerly; 4) Abigail Hall b. 12 Sep 1736 in

Westerly, Rhode Island; 5) Sara Hall b. 26 Oct 1738 in Westerly; 6) Anna Hall b. 6 Mar 1740/41; 7) Eunice Hall b. 31 Aug 1743 in Westerly; 8) Hannah Hall b. 2 Jul 1745 in Westerly; and 9) Lucy Hall b. 7 Jun 1748 in Westerly, Rhode Island.[35]

2. **Ephraim Fellows, Jr.** was born on 5 Apr 1707 in Stonington, New London County, Connecticut.[36] He died on 24 Apr 1780 in North Stonington, New London, Connecticut. His burial was in Great Plain Cemetery, Stonington.[37] Ephraim married **Prudence Plumb**, daughter of George Plumb and Prudence Richardson, on 13 May 1731 in Stonington, New London County, Connecticut.[38] Prudence was born on 18 Nov 1709 in Stonington, New London. She died on 11 Jun 1796 in North Stonington, New London County, Connecticut.[39] Her burial was in Great Plain Cemetery, North Stonington.[40] Ephraim and Prudence Plumb married before the Rev. Ebenezer Russell. Witnesses were Samuel Holdredge and Sarah Fellows. Sarah was the sister of Ephraim Fellows, Jr. She would marry Samuel Holdredge later that year in the same church.[41] Ephraim, Jr. was a Deacon of the First Congregational Church of Stonington, Conn. Records refer to him as Deacon Ephraim Fellows.[42] Children of Ephraim Fellows and Prudence Plumb were 1) Hannah Fellows b. 28 Dec 1731 in Stonington, New London County, Connecticut, d. 10 Nov 1798 in North Stonington, New London. *Vital Records of Stonington* gives her death date as 9 Mar 1758. Her gravestone at the Great Plain Cemetery, North Stonigton says, "Hannah Fellows, daughter of Deacon Ephraim, died Nov. 10, 1798, age 66."[43] 2) Ephraim Fellows, [III] b. 2 Oct 1733 in Stonington, d. 31 Mar 1818 in Stonington. He married Rhoda Smith 24 Apr 1766 in North Stonington, Connecticut.[44] *Vital Records of Stonington* confirm his birth, "Ephraim, son Ephraim b. Oct 2, 1733." 3) George Fellows b. 15 Aug 1735 in Stonington, d. 10 Dec 1736 in Stonington. George was instrumental in the defense of Stonington Borough during the War of 1812. He commanded the fire from the battery that repulsed the enemy;[45] 4) Samuel Fellows b. 4 Oct 1737 in Stonington, m. Mary Udal 7 Mar 1765 in North Stonington, Conn., d. 1829 in Wheelock, Caldonia County, Vermont;[46] 5) Warner Fellows b. 13 Oct 1739 in Stonington, d. in infancy 3 Nov 1739 in Stonington. *Vital Records of Stonington* confirm his birth and death, "Warner, son Deacon Ephraim b Oct 13, 1739, died Nov 3, 1739." 6) John Fellows b. 7 Nov 1740 in Stonington, d. 16 Oct 1760. John was a soldier who died in the French and Indian War. He never married. *Vital Records of Stonington* confirm his birth, "John, son Deacon Ephraim b. Nov 7, 1740;" 7)

Prudence Fellows b. 2 Nov 1742 in Stonington, m. Ebenezer Williams 5 Sep 1776 in North Stonington, New London County, Connecticut.[47] *Vital Records of Stonington* confirm her birth, "Prudence, dau. Deacon Ephraim b. Nov 2, 1742;" 8) Sarah Fellows b. 28 Sep 1744 in Stonington. *Vital Records of Stonington* confirm her birth, "Sarah, dau. Deacon Ephraim b Sept 28, 1744;" 9) and Joseph Fellows b. 7 Oct 1746 in Stonington, d. 30 Jun 1752 in Stonington, at the age of six. *Vital Records of Stonington* confirm his birth and death, "Joseph, son Deacon Ephraim b Oct 7, 1746, died June 30, 1752."[48]

3. **Sarah Fellows** was born on 3 Jan 1710/11 in Stonington, New London County, Conn.[49] Her christening was on 19 Mar 1711 in First Congregational Church, Stonington.[50] She died on 17 May 1803 in Stonington, New London County, Connecticut.[51] Sarah married **Samuel Holdredge**, son of William Holdredge and Deborah Elliott, on 23 Sep 1731 in First Congregational Church, Stonington, Connecticut.[52] Samuel was born on 17 May 1705 in Stonington, New London County, Connecticut.[53] The Fellows and Holdredge families connected again in 1767 through Tabitha Holdredge, the sister of Samuel Holdredge, who married Humphrey Brown, ancestor of Susannah Rathbone, wife of William Fellows of Stephentown, New York. William Fellows was the grandson of Ephraim Fellows who was the brother of Sarah Fellows. Moreover, Nathaniel Fellows, other brother of Sarah, married Hopestill Holdredge, sister of Samuel Holdredge and the mother of William Fellows of Stephentown. William Fellows married Susannah Rathbone, Samuel's cousin.

Children of Sarah Fellows and Samuel Holdredge: 1) Samuel Holdredge b. 17 May 1734; 2) Unidentified Infant b. 1736; 3) Unidentified Infant b. 1736; 4) Unidentified Infant b. 1736; 5) Desire Holdredge b. 29 Jun 1737 in Stonington, New London, Connecticut; 6) Isaac Holdredge b. 10 Oct 1741 in Stonington; 7) Content Holdredge b. 14 Aug 1743 in Stonington; 8) William Holdredge b. 28 Feb 1745/46 in Stonington; 9) Thomas Holdredge b. 30 Nov 1748 in Stonington; 10) Unidentified son b. 1749; 11) Hannah Holdredge b. 10 Mar 1750/51 in Stonington; 12) Phebe Holdredge b. 7 Aug 1753 in Stonington, d. May 1754; and 13) Ephraim Holdredge b. 7 Jul 1755 in Stonington, Connecticut.[54] Three of the children born to Sarah (Fellows) Holdredge and Samuel Holdredge were reportedly born in 1736. This may be an error of transcription of the records, or may represent the birth of triplets. Meanwhile, records of the Holdredge Cemetery, Ledyard, New London, Connecticut, show a son, Phineas Holdredge b. 1741, d. 1 Jan 1815 in Groton, New London, Connecticut. Phineas married

Mary Thompson of Stonington. He may have been a twin of Isaac born 10 Oct 1741.

+ 4. **Nathaniel FELLOWS** was born on 22 Jun 1713 in Stonington, New London County, Connecticut. His christening was on 6 Sep 1713 in First Congregational Church, Stonington, New London, Connecticut.[55] He died on 25 Aug 1800 in Stonington, New London County, Connecticut. Nathaniel married **Hopestill HOLDREDGE**, daughter of **William HOLDREDGE** and **Deborah ELLIOTT**, on 2 Mar 1736/37 in North Stonington, New London County, Connecticut.[56] Hopestill was born on 18 Feb 1719/20 in Stonington, New London, Connecticut. She died on 3 Jul 1765 in Stonington, New London County, Connecticut. Nathaniel married secondly **Sarah Watson**. Sarah died on 17 May 1803 in Stonington, New London, Connecticut. Records refer to Nathaniel and his brother Ephraim Fellows as Deacon Ephraim Fellows and Deacon Nathaniel fellows.

5. **Isaac Fellows** was born on 19 Feb 1718/19 in Stonington, New London County, Connecticut.[57] His christening was on 16 Aug 1719 in First Congregational Church, Stonington, Connecticut.[58] He died on 22 Mar 1806 in Stonington, New London County, Connecticut. Isaac married **Margaret Want** on 30 Sep 1742 in Stonington, New London County, Connecticut. Margaret was born on 26 Oct 1723 in Stonington, New London, Connecticut. She died in Apr 1809 in New London, Connecticut. Isaac was born and died in Connecticut. He was a good friend of Joshua Hempstead of New London, Conn., who was one of the original founders of the town. Isaac helped build the Hempstead house, which is now a historical landmark of New London. Joshua Hempstead kept a meticulous diary for over 47 years in which he detailed daily events in New London. Specific entries of the *Hempstead Diary* talk about Isaac Fellows. Some genealogists claim that this Isaac Fellows was the man from Bolton who mustered for the alarm at Lexington. However, Mark D. Fellows showed that a different Isaac Fellows answered the alarm.[59]

Children of Isaac Fellows and Margaret Want were 1) Mary Fellows b. 7 Jul 1743 in New London, New London County, Connecticut, d. 9 Feb 1836; 2) Isaac Fellows b. abt. 13 Oct 1745 in New London, d. 9 Aug 1773 in New London. Isaac did not marry; 3) William Fellows b. 6 Oct 1747 in New London, Conn.; 4) Pryington Fellows b. 7 Jan 1749/50 in New London, d. 9 Aug 1771 in New London. Pryington did not marry; 5) Thomas Fellows b. 11 Mar 1751/52, New London, d. 4 Aug 1753 in New London, at age one and one-half years. The

Hempstead Diary recorded his death; 6) Joseph Fellows b. 1 May 1754 in New London, d. 14 Jul 1815 in New London, m. Polly Ward in New London; 7) Elizabeth Fellows b. 2 Jul 1756 in New London, d. 25 Jul 1757 in New London. The *Hempstead Diary*, page 689, says "Monday, Jul 25, 1757, Foggy morning. A child of Isaac Fellows died at night-about 1 year old." 8) Elizabeth Fellows b. 8 Apr 1759 in New London; 9) Lucretia Fellows b. 13 Feb 1761 in New London, d. 6 Sep 1845 in New London, age 83; 10) Hannah Fellows b. 26 Aug 1763 in New London, d. 17 Oct 1834 in New London, age 70; and 11) Sarah Fellows b. 13 Jul 1766 in New London, d. 24 Sep 1767 in New London, at about age one.[60]

6. **John Fellows** was born on 8 Oct 1722 in Stonington, New London County, Connecticut. He died in infancy on 22 Apr 1723 in Stonington, New London, Connecticut.[61]

7. **Joannah Fellows** was born on 4 Apr 1724 in Stonington, New London County, Conn.[62] Her christening was on 19 Jul 1724 in First Congregational Church, Stonington, Connecticut.[63] Joannah married **William Brown** on 1 Jul 1742 in First Congregational Church, Stonington, Connecticut. William was born in Stonington, New London County, Connecticut.[64] In Colonial New England, the New Year Started on March 25. It was 2 July 1742 when Joannah and William married and still 1742 eight months and three days later when their first child was born 5 Mar 1742/43. Children of Joanna Fellows and William Brown were 1) Sylvanus Brown b. 5 Mar 1742/43 in Stonington, New London County, Connecticut; 2) Gilbert Brown b. 5 Jul 1744 in Stonington; 3) William Brown b. 2 Feb 1745/46, Stonington; 4) Thomas Brown b. 25 Dec 1747, in Stongington; 5) Martha Brown b. 29 Apr 1749 in Stonington; 6) Isaac Brown b. 22 Oct 1750 in Stonington, d. 1752 in Stonington, age two; 7) Isaac Brown b. 13 Feb 1751/52 in Stonington; 8) Euphrasia Brown b. 20 Mar 1751/52 in Stonington; 9) Thomas Brown b. 28 Apr 1755 in Stonington; 10) Joseph Brown b. 9 Sep 1757 in Stonington; 11) Hannah Brown b. 26 Jun 1759 in Stonington; 12) Lydia Brown b. 20 May 1765 in Stonington; and 13) Nancy Brown b. 8 Oct 1767 in Stonington, Connecticut.[65]

8. **Mary Fellows** was born on 16 Aug 1726 in Stonington, New London County, Connecticut. She died on 16 Sep 1726 in Stonington, New London. The *Vital Records of Stonington, Connecticut*, listed her as the daughter of Ephraim Fellows.[66]

7

Deacon Nathaniel Fellows

athaniel Fellows was born June 22, 1713, in Stonington, New London County, Connecticut. His christening was on September 6, 1713, at the First Congregational Church in Stonington.[1] He was the fourth child of Ephraim and Hannah (Warner) Fellows.[2]

He grew up on a farm in the upper region of Stonington Township, near the villages of Milltown and North Stonington, about five miles northwest of the town of Westerly, Connecticut, and some seven miles north of Stonington situated on Little Narragansett Bay. The larger towns of Norwich and New London, Connecticut, were ten to twelve miles distant, and Hartford, the seat of government of the Connecticut Colony, was a good day's ride to the west.

He was eleven years old when his father died. The task of looking after family affairs fell mostly to him and his older brother, Ephraim, Jr. who was not yet 18. Nathaniel grew up attending the First Congregational Church in Stonington. On April 7, 1734, when he turned 21, he "owned the covenant," meaning he accepted the tenets of the church on his own account as an adult.[3] The following year on April 20, 1735, the church admitted him as a member of the congregation.[4] He was an active member and leader of the church. The baptisms of his children were there, and records refer to him as Deacon Nathaniel Fellows, although he did not enjoy that title to the extent that history remembers his older brother, Deacon Ephraim Fellows, often cited as deacon in Stonington affairs.

Nathaniel married Hopestill Holdredge, daughter of William Holdredge and Deborah Elliott on March 2, 1736/37, in North Stonington, Connecticut.[5] Hope was born February 18, 1719/20, in Stonington.[6] Their marriage was by Rev. Joseph Fish, Harvard graduate and respected writer who became famous for his journals on the Pequot and Narragansett indigenous Indian people.[7] His sermons were widely read.[8] The First Congregational Church admitted Hopestill (Holdredge) Fellows to the church on July 26, 1741.[9]

The first Nathaniel Fellows house was at Stonington, near the end of the point where the old windmill stood.[10] Wheeler described the setting looking north out of Stonington. "To the north are the dense woods, which are ever varying in their hue and beauty, while at the south lies the village of Stonington, the harbor with its shipping, the many farm and summer houses, and nearer by, the various lower peaks of rock and land, where with no great stretch of imagination, we can see in the near future, more new houses for the city people, who continually find in our town, that which delights the eye and brings rest to the world weary ones."[11]

Documents suggest that Nathaniel held property in both Stonington and North Stonington. He owned a tract of 5 acres on Stony Brook in Stonington, and likely kept an interest in land in North Stonington where his parents lived in the latter years of their lives. Mention is often made of the Road to Mt. Pleasant upon which the First Congregational Church—the "Road Church"—stood, which served as a main thoroughfare between Stonington and North Stonington townships.

As time went by, unrest in the colonies pointed toward ominous events. In 1755, the Connecticut General Assembly ordered the mustering of colony men to fight in what became the French and Indian War. The rolls of the muster included "Fellows, Nath'l." of the Third Connecticut Regiment under the Command of Eleazer Fitch. This was Nathaniel Fellows, Jr., eldest son of Nathaniel and Hope. He was age 19. He joined the Twelfth Company of the Third Regiment commanded by Captain John Denison. The young Nathaniel served through the campaign year of 1758.

On July 3, 1765, Hope Fellows died, in Stonington.[12] She left behind a large family of eight surviving children—five of her thirteen children preceded her in death, including her firstborn, Deborah, who died at birth. At the time of Hope's passing, her youngest son was five years old.

Nathaniel, Sr. married secondly Sarah (Watson) Miner, widow of Thomas Miner. Thomas Miner had died in 1760.[13] Sarah was born in 1719, in Massachusetts. She had four young children of her own from her previous marriage to Miner, the oldest child being eleven. The blended family of Fellows and Miner caused some genealogists to conclude for many years that Nathaniel Fellows fathered 17 children instead of 13.

Nathaniel Fellows built the first gristmill in Stonington, on Stony Brook and for many years, locals called it the Fellow's Mill.[14] Wheeler described it. "Coming down the driveway again, we cross the road [Church Road] and follow a deep rutted cart path through a gate and into a pasture where wending our way for some distance beneath the drooping boughs of forest trees, we come to a most picturesque spot which was once one of the business centers of the town, for here was the old grist mill, built by Mr. Nathaniel Fellows who married in 1737, Hopestill Holdredge and put up his house and mill here. Mr. Fellows had a family of thirteen children, one of whom, Lydia, married Mr. Nathan Noyes, and their son Nathan used to tell about the mill there, which was run by an immense overshot wheel that stood nearly as high as the house beside it. A long wooden trough led from the dam, a few rods north, to the wheel and Mr. Noyes, when a boy, used to run up this flume and open the gate at the dam and then, turning, would race with the water, running the length of the flume, and jumping off before the water caught up with him, which was an hairbreadth escape."[15] Nathaniel disposed of the mill, and it became the property of Dr. William Lord.[16]

Going into the decade of the 1770s, events were moving rapidly toward a declaration of independence from the British Crown. The citizens of Stonington presaged what was to come. In the spring of 1776, the British presence at Stonington became untenable. Nathaniel and his son Nathaniel, Jr. joined a committee of about 100 other colonists in a petition to urge authorities to keep a protective force at Stonington. A previous communication had earlier made a similar plea to the General Assembly.

The petition read, "In May 1776, Rev. Nathaniel Eells of Long Point, Stonington, Conn., was appointed Chaplain of the regiment stationed at New London. There was much delay in providing the means of defence, and the dissatisfaction caused the following memorial to be presented to the General Assembly: 'Your Honors may remember that this town is the only one in this State that has received any damages from those sons of tyranny and despotism, sent by that more savage tyrant, George the Third, to deprive us of those unalienable rights that the Supreme Governor of Heaven and Earth has invested us with.' Your memorialists therefore pray that the number of men ordered here may remain; and that the two eighteen pounders and four twelve pounders, and shot, &c., that were previously ordered here may be delivered as soon as possible, as the harbor is perhaps more used by coasters, and vessels bound to sea than any other harbor in the state; and is a place of great consequence, not only to this, but to other states. We therefore beg leave to inform your Honors that several vessels have been chased into this harbor by the King's Ships, and have been protected. Your memorialists further pray that the three large cannon (now at New London) belonging to this town be likewise ordered to this place; and the two field pieces lent to the town of New London, by this town, be ordered back to Stonington. And your memorialists will ever pray, &c."[17]

Nathaniel, Sr. was in his sixties when the Revolutionary War started and did not serve in combat. However, his sons William and Nathaniel, Jr. did, as did his grandson, Nathaniel, III.[18] Wheeler noted, "There is no perfect roll or list of the men of Stonington who served in the army of the Revolution." Nevertheless, on his list he included the names of Nathaniel [Jr.] Fellows and William Fellows.[19] Nathaniel, Jr. was a corporal in the Connecticut militia in 1775, and enlisted in the Continental Army in 1777, in Capt. James Eldridge's Company, serving honorably until 1780. In his three years of service, he fought in many battles.[20] The people of Stonington furnished men and means to Boston to enable them to maintain their liberties. Soldiers of the Fellows name were at Bunker Hill.[21]

Despite being one of the smallest colonies to participate in the American Revolutionary War, Connecticut fielded a large number of soldiers. Connecticut war records listed "Fellows, Nath'l" First Connecticut Regiment of Foot, commanded by Col. Josiah Starr. He was also in Capt. Enoch Reed's Company, which passed to the command of First Regiment Commander, Col. Huntington. Meanwhile, Ephraim Fellows also enlisted in Col. Starr's company.[22]

Nathaniel Fellows, Sr. had a habit of issuing promissory notes, which somehow he never got around to paying. On multiple occasions, his creditors took him to court to secure payment of their notes. For example, Robert and Peleg Chesebrough, important men in Stonington, made a complaint against him on May 27, 1779, and filed it with the court a year later on June 12, 1780. The court ordered the sheriff of New London County to attach Nathaniel's estate to the tune of £10,000 for debts owed them, and to arrest Nathaniel if they could find him. In a follow up order dated June 12, 1780, the plaintiffs demanded attachment against his house and 5 acres on Stony Brook.[23] They extended their complaint to include attachment of the estate of Nathaniel and his son Joseph, "both of Stonington." The standard language of colonial attachment orders, which called for attachment of the "estate and Body of the defendant" to ensure their appearance in court at Norwich to answer the complaint, caused genealogists to assume Nathaniel died about 1779. However, he did not. He lived on another 20 years. Meanwhile, the writs against him continued. The above case was still active in 1781; another promissory note in default became known in 1787; and cases pended in court as late as 1789. Court documents do not record the dispositions of the various cases against Nathaniel. Nevertheless, one may assume that out-of-court settlements occurred because Nathaniel continued to go actively about his affairs in Stonington. His legal court difficulties did not slow him, nor did it interfere with his standing in the community. The church reaffirmed him as a Communicant entitled to receive Communion in May 1780.[24] Neighbors continued to refer to him as Deacon Nathaniel.[25]

For the first time, in 1790, the United States Census took place. Nathaniel was the first of the Fellows generations to appear in the new U.S. census. The 1790 census recorded him living in New London County, in the Connecticut community that included four of his sons: Nathaniel, Elnathan, Ephraim, and Joseph.[26]

The first United States census schedules differed in format from later census material. Each enumerator made his own copies on whatever paper he could find. The census gave only the name of the head of the household, enumerating other household members only as male or female. Nathaniel appeared in New London County living with two females, probably his second wife Sarah, and an unidentified second person. The 1790 Census recorded three generations of Nathaniel Fellows each marked on the tally as Nathaniel 1, Nathaniel 2, and Nathaniel 3, along with three of his other sons living in the same community of New London County. Nearby were the families of Chesebrough and Noyes, descendants of the first founders of Stonington and prominent men in town affairs. Nathaniel's daughter Lydia married Nathan Noyes.

Nathaniel Fellows died August 25, 1800 in Stonington, New London, Connecticut, after a long life of 87 years.[27] His final resting place remains unknown. His burial and that of his long-deceased wife Hopestill was likely in North Stonington, New London County, near the burials of his parents in Great Plain Cemetery.

Sarah (Watson) Miner-Fellows, second wife of Nathaniel, continued to live in Stonington. In the 1800 census, the census-taker listed her as Sarah Watson, head of a large household.[28] She lived but a brief time after Nathaniel's death, and died May 17, 1803, in Stonington. Her burial was in Miner Cemetery at Stonington.[29] Upon her death, her gravestone identified her cryptically as "Sarah Fellows, wife of Thomas Miner."

Nathaniel and Hopestill (Holdredge) Fellows had a very large family of 13 children.[30] They were with birthdates 1) Deborah 1738, 2) Nathaniel, Jr. 1738/39, 3) Warner 1740/41, 4) William 1742/43, 5) Hopestill 1744/45, 6) Lydia 1746/47, 7) Mercy 1749, 8) Elnathan 1751, 9) Ephraim 1753, 10) Priscilla 1755, 11) Mary 1757, 12) Joseph 1757, and 13) David, 1760. For reasons never disclosed, four of their first seven kids were born in the month of February.

The genealogy continued from Nathaniel and Hopestill (Holdredge) Fellows to their third-born son, William Fellows.

Opposite page. Maps of Fellows Resettlement from Massachusetts to Connecticut. A vintage map of the New England Colonies dated 1780 shows the movement of Ephraim Fellows from Ipswich, Massachusetts, to Stonington, Connecticut, about 1706. Outline maps depict the state of Connecticut with a graphic overlay of New London County enlarged in the inset. Stonington and North Stonington Townships lie in the southeastern corner of New London County. Dots on the 1854 map-insert show 1) the location in Stonington Township where Nathaniel Fellows owned property on Stony Brook; and 2) Great Plain Cemetery in North Stonington Township, the gravesite of Ephraim and Hannah (Warner) Fellows. Map credits: John Hinton, 1780 and William E. Baker, 1854; courtesy of the Library of Congress.

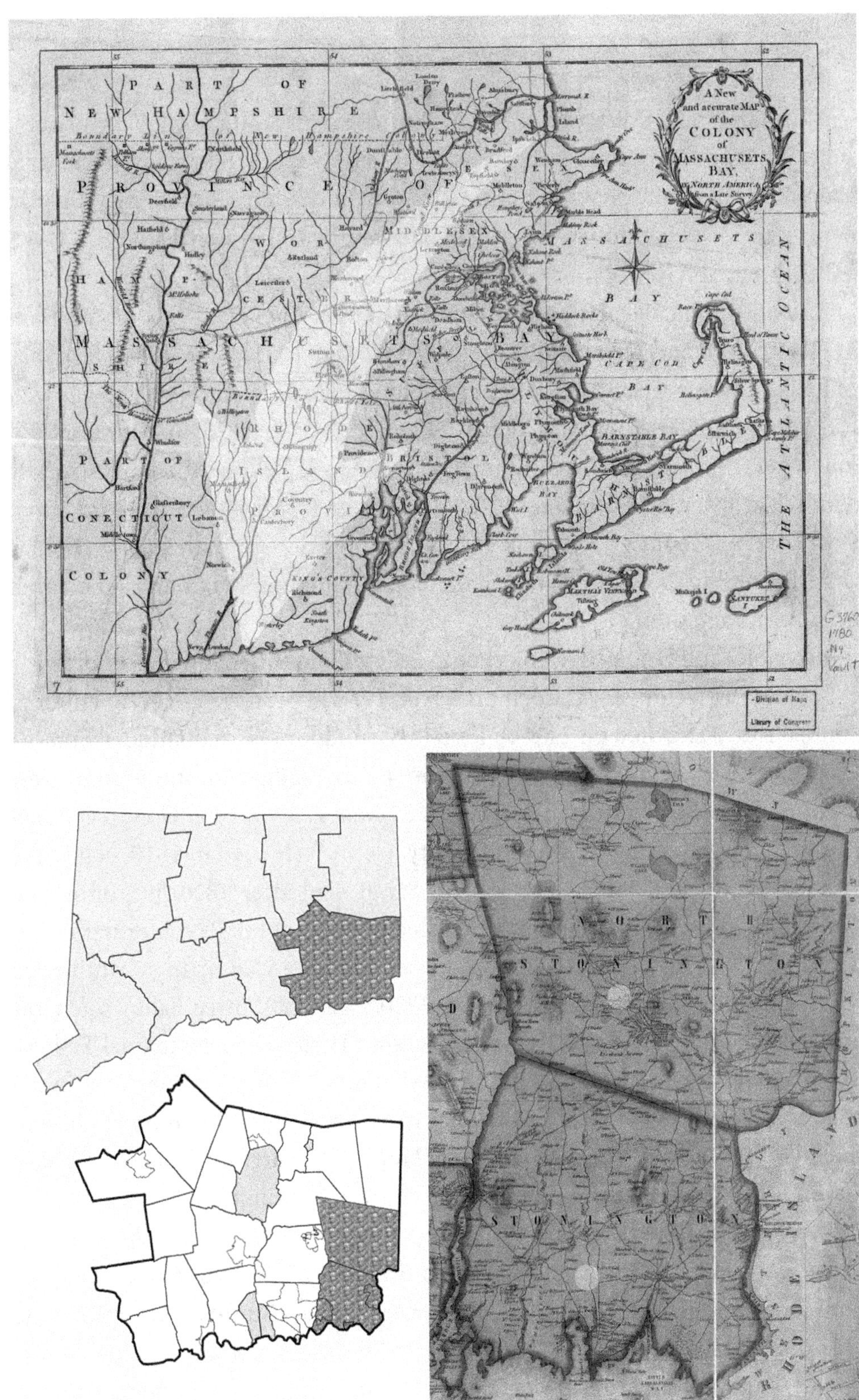
A New
and accurate MAP
of the
COLONY
of
MASSACHUSETS
BAY,
IN NORTH AMERICA,
from a Late Survey.
PART OF NEW HAMPSHIRE
PROVINCE OF
MASSACHUSETS BAY
MIDDLESEX
WORCESTER
HAMPSHIRE
RHODE ISLAND
PROVIDENCE
BRISTOL
KING'S COUNTY
PART OF CONECTICUT COLONY
BARNSTABLE
CAPE COD BAY
BARNSTABLE BAY
BUZZARDS BAY
MARTHAS VINEYARD
NANTUCKET
THE ATLANTIC OCEAN
Boston
Providence
Division of Maps
Library of Congress
NORTH STONINGTON
STONINGTON
RHODE ISLAND

Fellows Fourth Generation Family Group

Nathaniel FELLOWS was born on 22 Jun 1713 in Stonington, New London County, Conn. His christening was on 6 Sep 1713 in First Congregational Church, Stonington, New London, Connecticut. He died on 25 Aug 1800 in Stonington, New London, Connecticut. He was the son of **Ephraim FELLOWS** and **Hannah WARNER.**

Nathaniel married **Hopestill HOLDREDGE**, the daughter of **William HOLDREDGE** and **Deborah ELLIOTT**, on 2 Mar 1736/37, in North Stonington, New London County, Connecticut. Hopestill was born on 18 Feb 1719/20 in Stonington, New London County. She died on 3 Jul 1765 in Stonington.[31] Following the death of Hopestill in 1765, Nathaniel Fellows married secondly Widow **Sarah (Watson) Miner.**[32] Sarah died on 17 May 1803 in Stonington, New London County, Connecticut. She was previously married to Thomas Miner.[33] Her burial was in Miner Cemetery, Stonington.[34] Nathaniel and Sarah did not have children.

Nathaniel and Hopestill (Holdredge) Fellows had the following children.

1. **Deborah Fellows** was born on 4 Apr 1738 in Stonington, New London, Connecticut.[35] She died on 11 Apr 1738 in Stonington, New London, Conn.[36]

2. **Nathaniel Fellows, Jr.** was born on 4 Feb 1738/39 in Stonington, New London, Conn.[37] His christening was on 25 Mar 1739 in First Congregational Church, Stonington, New London County, Conn.[38] He died in 1810. Nathaniel married **Sarah** (last name unspecified). Sarah died after 1820 in Stonington, New London, Conn.[39] Nathaniel, Jr. enlisted in 1777 for the Revolutionary War. He was a Lt. in Preston's Company and Capt. Eldridge's Company, Continental Army. His honorable discharge was in 1780.[40] In 1790, three Fellows generations—Nathaniel Fellows I, Nathaniel Fellows II [Jr.], and Nathaniel Fellows III—lived next door to each other in New London County, Connecticut, in the same community as the elder Nathaniel's younger brothers, Elnathan, Ephraim, and Joseph.[41] Nathaniel, Jr.'s daughter, Hopestill, married Zebulon Ward, a descendant of the wealthy Chesebrough family of Stonington, Connecticut.[42]

3. **Warner Fellows** was born on 15 Feb 1740/41 in Stonington, New London County, Conn.[43] His christening was on 5 Apr 1741 in First Congregational Church, Stonington, Connecticut.[44] Warner married **Eunice Hall** on 25 Nov 1762 in First Congregational Church, North Stonington, New London County, Conn.[45] Eunice was born about 1743 in Stonington, New London County.

Eunice may have been previously married. Warner moved his family to Norwich, Connecticut.[46] Children of Warner Fellows and Eunice hall were 1) Eunice Fellows b. 27 Dec 1764 in Norwich, New London County, Connecticut; 2) Hopestill Fellows b. 23 May 1766 in Norwich; 3) Warner Fellows b. 16 May 1768 in Norwich; and 4) Lovicy Warner Fellows b. 2 Jul 1769 in Norwich, New London County, Connecticut.[47]

+ 4. **William FELLOWS** was born on 19 Jan 1742/43 in Stonington, New London County, Connecticut. His christening was on 12 Jun 1743 in First Congregational Church, Stonington, New London, Connecticut.[48] He died on 24 Jul 1827 in Stephentown, Rensselaer, New York. His burial was in Fellows Cemetery, Stephentown, Rensselaer County, New York. William married **Susanna RATHBONE**, daughter of **Rev. Valentine Wightman RATHBONE** and **Tabitha BROWN**, on 8 Nov 1767 in First Congregational Church, Stonington, New London County, Connecticut.[49] Susanna was born on 15 May 1748 in Groton, New London, Connecticut. She died on 15 Jul 1825 in Stephentown, Rensselaer County, New York. Her burial was in Fellows Cemetery, Stephentown, Rensselaer, New York.

5. **Hopestill Fellows** was born on 8 Feb 1744/45 in Stonington, New London County, Conn.[50] Her christening was on 7 Apr 1745 in First Congregational Church, Stonington.[51] Hopestill married **John Belcher** on 1 May 1763 in First Congregational Church, Stonington, Connecticut.[52] John was born in Westerly, Washington County, Rhode Island,[53]

6. **Lydia Fellows** was born on 20 Feb 1746/47 in Stonington, New London County, Conn.[54] Her christening was on 10 May 1747 in First Congregational Church, Stonington, New London, Conn.[55] Lydia married **Nathan Noyes** son of Thomas Noyes and Mary Thompson on 23 Sep 1770 in First Congregational Church, Stonington, New London County, Connecticut.[56] Nathan was born about 1738. He died in 1831.[57] Children of Nathan and Lydia (Fellows) Noyes: 1) Nathan Noyes, 2) John Noyes, 3) Lydia Noyes, 4) Prudence Noyes, and 5) David Noyes. Known records do not show birthdates of the children, assumed to have been born in Stonington, New London County, Connecticut.

7. **Mercy Fellows** was born on 10 Aug 1749 in Stonington, New London County, Connecticut.[58] Her christening was on 8 Oct 1749.[59] She died on 16 May 1757.[60]

8. **Elnathan Fellows** was born on 13 Aug 1751 in Stonington, New London, Connecticut.[61] His christening was on 29 Sep 1751 in First Congregational

Church, Stonington, Connecticut.[62] He died on 31 Jan 1837 in Stonington, New London, Connecticut.[63] His burial was in Robinson Burying Ground, Stonington, New London County.[64] Elnathan married **Hannah Packer** on 24 Nov 1774 in Stonington, New London, Connecticut.[65] Hannah was born in 1758. She died on 16 Aug 1845 in Stonington, New London, Connecticut. Her burial was in Robinson Burying Ground, Stonington, New London County, Connecticut.[66] The records refer to Elnathan as Deacon Elnathan Fellows. In 1776, he was Captain of the ships *Bradley* and *Greenfield*. He moved the effects of war refugees from the Battle of Long Island, New York, after the Continental Army's defeat in August 1776. The 1800 Connecticut Census showed Elnathan Fellows living in Stonington, New London County, Connecticut. He was pastor of the First Baptist Church until 1810. He owned and ran a shipyard, building whaling ships. He had 13 children.[67] A sketch of his house in Stonington appeared in Wheeler, *The Homes of Our Ancestors in Stonington*.[68]

Children of Elnathan Fellows and Hannah Packer were 1) Hannah Fellows b. 1776 in Stonington, New London County, Connecticut, d. 1829,[69] m. Capt. Stephen Brewster 5 May 1799;[70] 2) Polly Fellows b. 3 Jan 1777, d. August 1778; 3) Nathan Fellows b. 30 Dec 1779 in Stonington, d. 1810, m. Lucy Eldridge;[71] 4) Elizabeth Betsey Fellows b. 19 Dec 1783, d 1818 in Stonington, New London. Conn.;[72] 5) Joseph Fellows b. 18 Nov 1784 in Stonington, d 1833, m. Sophia Farnham;[73] 6) Mary Fellows b. 1 Jan 1786 in Stonington, New London, d. 1813 in Stonington;[74] 7) Lydia F. Fellows b. 5 Mar 1790 in Stonington, d. 1882 in Stonington, m. Chesebro [*sic*], also m. Deacon Samuel Langworthy of Stonington.[75] The number of children attributed to Elnathan and Hannah (Packer) Fellows differs from five to 13, depending on various published genealogies.[76]

9. **Ephraim Fellows** was born on 19 Nov 1753 in Stonington, New London, Connecticut.[77] He died on 22 Dec 1753 in Stonington.[78] An Ephraim Fellows married Rhoda Smith, both of Stonington, on 24 Apr 1766 [*sic*].[79] However, the date of marriage of 1766 conflicts with his dates of birth and death in 1753, suggesting this was a different Ephraim Fellows or his life dates are incorrect.

10. **Priscilla Fellows** was born on 14 Apr 1755 in Stonington, New London County, Connecticut.[80] She married **John Devol** on 15 Dec 1774 in First Congregational Church, Stonington, New London County, Connecticut.[81] John Devol was born about 1765. He died before 1792.[82] Priscilla married secondly **John Haley** on 4 Oct 1792 in Stonington, New London, Connecticut. John Haley was born about 1769.[83]

11. **Mary Fellows** was born on 16 May 1757 in Stonington, New London County, Connecticut.[84] She died at birth.[85]

12. **Joseph Fellows** was born in 1757 in Stonington, New London County, Connecticut. His reported birthdate of 1757 suggests that he was a twin of Mary Fellows. His christening was in First Congregational Church on 29 Sep 1757 in Stonington, New London, Conn.[86] He died in 1778. Joseph married **Mary Hewitt** on 11 May 1777 in First Congregational Church, North Stonington, New London County, Conn.[87] Mary was born on 25 Jan 1759 in Stonington, New London. Joseph Fellows fought with the Continental army at the Siege of Boston during the Revolutionary War. He served in Capt. Titus Slater's Company, Maj. Hacketts' Battalion. He was an Ensign in Preston's Company. He died on a prison ship in New York harbor. The following information concerning a Joseph Fellows found in *Public Records of the Colony of Connecticut* states, "Upon the memorial of Joseph Fellows of New London, owner of the slooop 'Two brothers,' burden about 18 tons, well found, and that in Jan 1780, he was on a trip to New York City as a cartel for the exchange of prisoners by the order of Commissary Ledyard, in an unfortunate storm, he lost his sloop and company."[88] The government paid him 120 pounds for his loss. This was likely Joseph of Stonington because his brother Elnathan was also a ship captain who was moving refugees from the New York area about the same time. The name of Joseph's ship, "Two Brothers," seems to support the connection.[89]

13. **David Fellows** was born on 16 Mar 1760 in Stonington, New London County, Connecticut.[90] His christening was in Stonington, New London, Connecticut. Marshall says that David Fellows died in 1786 at sea. No details are given.[91]

8

William Fellows of Stonington

William Fellows was the fourth child of Nathaniel and Hopestill (Holdredge) Fellows.[1] He was born January 19, 1742/43, in Stonington, New London County, Connecticut.[2] His christening was June 12, 1743, in the First Congregational Church of Stonington.[3] He died July 24, 1827, in Stephentown Township, Rensselaer County, New York. His burial was in the Fellows Cemetery at Stephentown.[4]

On November 8, 1767, he married Susannah Rathbone (aka Rathbun), daughter of Valentine Rathbone and Tabitha (Brown) Rathbone.[5] Susannah was born May 15, 1748, in Groton, New London County, Connecticut.[6] The couple married in the First Congregational Church of Stonington.[7] Susannah died July 15, 1825, in Stephentown, Rensselaer County, New York.[8] Her burial was in Fellows Cemetery, Stephentown Township, Rensselaer County.[9] She was a 7th generation descendant of Richard Rathbone who came to America in the 1600s and settled in Ipswich, Essex County, Massachusetts, where he died in 1717.[10] Coincidentally, Ipswich was also the home of William Israel Fellows, second great-grandfather of William Fellows of Stonington.

The most significant historical event to occur during the lives of William and Susannah Fellows was the Revolutionary War. William supported the movement for American independence, and signed a petition to the General Assembly urging the defense of Stonington on May 10, 1774. Some think he went on to serve in the Revolutionary War with brothers Nathaniel and Elnathan.[11] However, genealogists divide on the question of his service in the war because there were two William Fellows of the same name, approximately the same age, and living in the same general area of Connecticut. A soldier, or soldiers, of the name William Fellows served in different units from the first days of the war to its conclusion. The most complete record is that of Corporal William Fellows who served in the company of Capt. Titus Watson, in the Seventh Connecticut Regiment commanded by Col. Heman Swift from 1777 to 1780.[12] Col. Swift was a Revolutionary War hero known to Gen. Washington. He carried the wounded Lafayette off the Brandywine battlefield.[13] His Seventh Connecticut Regiment was at Valley Forge. The muster roll of Valley Forge included Corporal William Fellows of Connecticut. [14] The Seventh Connecticut saw battle at Brandywine, Germantown, and Monmouth, all pivotal fights in the War of Independence.

On the other hand, he may have been the William Fellows of the Fourth Connecticut Regiment of light horse under the command of Maj. Ebenezer Backus of New London County and later Windham County, Connecticut, in 1776. Among its campaigns, the Fourth Regiment served as reinforcements for George Washington's army. The William Fellows of the Fourth Regiment served in Capt. Rogers Company from Cornwall, in Col. Gay's Second Battalion of Wadsworth's Brigade.[15] Prior to that, William Fellows was a private in the 9th company of Col. Henman's Fourth Regiment in the spring of 1775. That unit dissolved in late 1775, and Henman became commander of the Seventh Regiment of Connecticut.[16] The Seventh Regiment formed out of the Connecticut counties of Litchfield, Fairfield, New Haven, and New London. [17] Therefore, the subject of the war records could be either William of Stonington, New London County, or William of Canaan, Litchfield County. The consensus settles on the William Fellows of Canaan, Litchfield, and not William of New London, for being the corporal in Henman's Seventh Connecticut.

Just as there is no full agreement on which William Fellows served in the Revolutionary War, there is uncertainty about the origin of William of Litchfield. He was the son of Thomas and Sarah (Lawrence) Fellows of Canaan, Connecticut, born April 30, 1757.[18] Some say he was the descendant of the immigrant William Fellows of Ipswich while others trace him to Samuel Fellows brother of William of Ipswich and one of the three immigrant brothers who came from England. In either case, William of Stonington and William of Canaan were distant cousins. There was a very large contingent of Fellows in Litchfield County, all with names similar to the known descendants of William of Ipswich; viz., Ephraim, Joseph, Jonathan, and William. The William Fellows of Litchfield died in Canaan in 1782. Connecticut records sometimes confuse him with his uncle, also named William Fellows, who died in Canaan in 1771.[19]

The issue of the service of William Fellows in the Revolutionary War is of less interest perhaps than that of his father-in-law, Valentine Wightman Rathbone. Descendants who aspire to join the Sons of the American Revolution fraternity do not cite kinship to William Fellows as qualification for membership, but rather to his wife, Susannah Rathbone, Daughter of the American Revolution. During the Revolution, her father, Valentine Rathbone, was prominent in the affairs of state.[20]

Valentine Rathbone was born in Stonington, New London County, Connecticut, in 1724. He was a deeply religious person and became a Baptist preacher at a time when a split from the Congregational Church drew the ire of governing officials. The Congregational Church was the official church of the colonies akin to the Anglican Church of England. Baptists suffered arrest for not supporting the Congregational churches. People regularly received fines, and even jail time, for refusing to pay the church tax.[21] Nevertheless, there were three Baptist churches at Stonington, belonging to the Stonington Association. The first one organized in 1743; the second one, which was at Waverly but met regularly at Stonington, was the one that sent Valentine Rathbone into the ministry; and the third church welcomed him as its first preacher.[22]

Around the year 1767, he answered a call to serve as a Baptist preacher at Bellingham, Massachusetts.[23] He was the last of a series of pastors called to the Bellingham pulpit. Bellingham, Norfolk County, Massachusetts, was a center for the Baptist church in the region and led the struggle for religious freedom. Rev. Rathbone did not receive the full support of the congregation at Bellingham, and left to accept a call in Bridgewater in Plymouth County, Massachusetts.[24]

By 1769, he had settled in Pittsfield, Berkshire County, with his brothers in western Massachusetts. He owned a fulling-mill, or clothier's shop, in Pittsfield and worked as a local preacher. In 1772, he formed a Baptist church at Pittsfield and became its minister.[25] He incorporated the Baptist Religious Society of Pittsfield, with the rights and immunities enjoyed by dissenting parishes; but the society eventually died out.[26]

He became active in politics. In late May of 1775, the citizens at Pittsfield instructed "Valentine Rathbun [*sic*] to use his influence with the Assembly to notify the Continental Congress. You shall, on no pretense whatever, favour a union with Great Britain, as to our becoming in any sense dependent on her ever hereafter; and use your influence with the honourable House to notify the honourable Continental Congress that this whole Province are waiting for the important moment which they in their great wisdom shall appoint for the declaration of Independence and a free Republic."[27] The citizens of Pittsfield drafted the first pleas of the colonies for a declaration of independence from Great Britain, and sent Valentine Rathbone as their messenger. In 1776, Berkshire County elected him as a delegate to the General Court and member of the Council of Safety from Berkshire County, Massachusetts.[28] He did not serve in any military capacity during the war but played a leading role in the drive for independence. In 1779, he was a delegate from Pittsfield to the Massachusetts Constitutional Convention.

Despite his fervent patriotism, he did not support the U.S. Constitution as written. The constitution, as framed by the convention of 1787, was not in all its provisions acceptable to either the progressive or the conservative elements in the proposed union. In the state conventions, the radical democrats—then known as anti-federalists—continued unconditionally to oppose ratification. In the case of Massachusetts, the representation of Pittsfield was by Valentine Rathbone, an ultra-democrat who feared the constitution was a "cunningly-prepared stepping-stone towards a monarchical or an aristocratic state." On the final vote, Rev. Rathbone gave the voice of the town against its ratification.[29] Nevertheless, Massachusetts ratified the constitution on February 5, 1788, albeit by a margin of 187 to 168.

Rev. Valentine Rathbone filled many preaching pastorates in his lifetime, living in many different places. In 1802, he purchased 300 acres, including a lot, in Marcellus, Onondaga County, New York. It was his last assignment location. He died there on April 10, 1813.[30] He was a complex person—Valentine Rathbone—a minister, mill operator, and Revolutionary War leader.[31] Family historian, John Cooley wrote, "The temperament of the man suggests that it was fiery and vehement and nervous."[32] Rathbone left numerous writings. Among them were two treatises laced with diatribes against the Shaking Quakers. He wrote, "It is as impossible to fully set forth the power and effects of this new religion as to trace the airy road of the meteor."[33]

The prominence of Valentine Rathbone in the Baptist Church did not appear to persuade his daughter. William Fellows and Susannah (Rathbone) Fellows continued to embrace the Congregational Church. Fellows' descendants eventually gravitated to the Episcopal Methodist Church and kept to the Methodist faith in each succeeding generation.

William and Susannah Fellows had a large family of 11 children. The Robinson Burying Ground monument in Stonington includes the death of their infant daughter, Content Fellows, January 17, 1770. However, at least five of their children lived well into their eighties.

About 1784, William removed from Stonington, Connecticut, to Stephentown, Rensselaer County, New York.[34] The births of the youngest children, Ruby and Pamela, were in Stephentown after 1787. Therefore, William moved his family to Stephentown sometime between 1770 and 1787.[35] The record is silent on why William left Stonington for Stephentown. He was a ships carpenter at Stonington, a shipbuilder that may have worked with his brother, Elnathan, who supposedly owned a shipyard in Stonington.[36] Years later, the Stonington shipyard launched a ship christened the *Deacon Fellows* in memorial of the Fellows family.[37] William possibly moved to Stephentown because of its shipbuilding trade, although family historians think he abandoned shipbuilding for the livelihood of farming because most of the Fellows of his line were farmers.[38]

In any event, the 1790 census recorded William Fellows in Stephen Town [*sic*], Albany County, New York, with Susannah and their eight children.[39] This first United States census schedule of 1790 did not include household member names, and enumerators counted all females as a single category, regardless of age. Nevertheless, the 1790 documents provide valuable insight into early American life. When the territory of New York divided into 10 counties in 1683, Albany County was one of them with a very large territory. Out of it came the counties of Tyron and Charlotte in 1772, Columbia in 1786, Rensselaer and Saratoga in 1791, a part of Schoharie in 1795, a part of Greene in 1800, and Schenectady in 1809. At the time of the first census in 1790, Rensselaer County did not yet exist, and Stephentown, New York, was in Albany County. The following year, in 1791, New York created Rensselaer out of Albany.

Stephentown was a relatively new town, established in 1784 in Rensselaer County, in the southeastern part of the county bounded on the east by Massachusetts. A picturesque town of hills and rocky terrain, blanketed with sections of forest, settlers found the soil best adapted to grazing. The Taghkanic Mountains ran along the eastern part of the town and the Petersburgh Mountains along the western part. Through the narrow valley between them, the Black and Kinderhook creeks flowed south. One visitor wrote, "The entire district is wild and rugged, an ideal resort for a lover of the grander forms of nature."[40] William Fellows was in a wave of pioneers entering Stephentown from Connecticut and locating on the high hills in the southeastern part of the town. Notwithstanding the challenges of cultivating the rocky land, the major occupation around Stephentown was farming. Census records show most citizens were either farmers or farm laborers. After the Revolution, the area became an important dairy district. Meanwhile, Stephentown had a number of other businesses, among them shipbuilding.

William Fellows lived mostly as a farmer, affirmed by the Rensselaer County tax rolls.[41] Meanwhile, the census records from 1800 to 1820 depict a steadily decreasing Fellows household, as the children married and moved to their own homes.[42] In 1810, the census listed William and a family of four living in Stephentown, New York. The census of 1810 did not give names of household members either. However, age categories corresponded to the ages of William as 67 and Hopestill as age 62. The other four persons in William's household were probably their son David Fellows and his family. When other members of the Fellows family went separate ways, David remained in Stephentown and was William's heir.[43] By 1820, William and Susannah were living alone, except for their daughter Polly and a couple of grandchildren helping with chores. William was still trying to farm at age 77. David had settled into his own place nearby, and Jeremiah had done likewise. The oldest boys, William and Warner had left Stephentown for Otsego County, New York.[44]

Susannah (Rathbone) Fellows died July 15, 1825, and shortly thereafter William wrote his will on October 8, 1825.[45] In it, he left legacies to his children as his heirs. He named sons William, Joshua, Isaac, Jeremiah, and David Fellows; and daughters Susannah, wife of William Hunt; Parmela, wife of Moses Cowe, Jr.; Ruby, wife of Daniel Wright; and Polly Fellows; and his granddaughter Eliza Ann Fellows. His executors were David and Polly Fellows.[46]

Two years after Susannah's death almost to the day, and 21 months and 18 days after he wrote his will, William Fellows died July 24, 1827, at the age of 84. The family laid him to rest beside Susannah in the Fellows Cemetery of Stephentown.[47] William was the fourth generation to be born in America. He pioneered the further journey westward of the Fellows family, which started from Ipswich, Massachusetts, to Stonington, Connecticut, and then to Stephentown, New York. The genealogy continued from William and Susannah (Rathbone) Fellows of Stephentown to their son, William Reuben Fellows.[48]

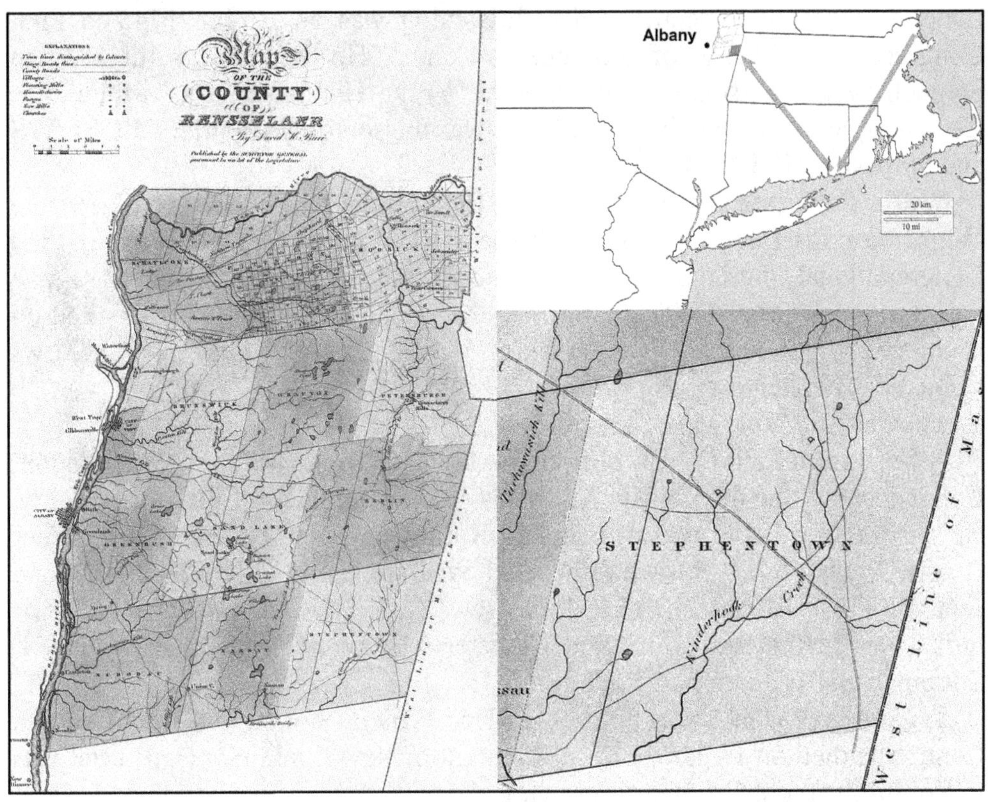

Map of Rensselaer County, New York. The founding of Rensselaer County dates to 1791. The upper right diagram shows the migration path of the Fellows family from 1635 to 1785, beginning at Ipswich, Massachusetts, proceeding to Stonington, Connecticut, and then to Stephentown, New York. Bottom right inset shows the location of Kinderhook Creek in Stephentown Township. The village of Stephentown was on Kinderhook Creek. *An Atlas of the State of New York*, 1829.

Fellows Fifth Generation Family Group

William FELLOWS was born on 19 Jan 1742/43 in Stonington, New London County, Connecticut. His christening was on 12 Jun 1743 in First Congregational Church of Stonington, Conn.[49] He died on 24 Jul 1827 in Stephentown, Rensselaer County, New York. His burial was in Fellows Cemetery, Stephentown, New York. He was the son of **Nathaniel FELLOWS** and **Hopestill HOLDREDGE**.

William married **Susannah RATHBONE**, daughter of **Rev. Valentine Wightman RATHBONE** and **Tabitha BROWN**, on 8 Nov 1767 in First Congregational Church of Stonington, New London County, Conn.[50] Susannah was born on 15 May 1748 in Groton, New London, Connecticut. She died on 15 Jul 1825 in Stephentown, Rensselaer, New York. Her burial was in Fellows Cemetery, Stephentown, New York.[51]

They had the following children.[52]

1. **Susannah Fellows** was born on 6 May 1768 in Stonington, New London, Connecticut.[53] She died on 18 Aug 1854 in New Lebanon, Columbia County, New York. Her burial was in Brainard Rural Cemetery, Brainard, Rensselaer County, New York.[54] Susannah married **William Hunt** son of Ziba Hunt and Johanna Clark Blount in Rensselaer, New York.[55] He died 8 Oct 1852. His burial was in the Brainard Rural Cemetery, Brainard, Rensselaer County.[56] Susannah and William had 10 children.

2. **Content Fellows** was born on 24 Dec 1769 in Stonington, New London, Conn. She died on 17 Jan 1770 in Stonington, New London.[57] Her burial was in Robinson Burial Ground, Stonington, Conn.[58]

\+ 3. **William Reuben FELLOWS** was born on 5 Apr 1771 in Stonington, New London County, Connecticut.[59] He died on 6 Dec 1843 in the hamlet of Schenevus, in the town of Maryland, Otsego County, New York. William married **Martha SMITH** on 29 Dec 1796 in Stephentown, Rensselaer County, New York. Martha was born on 3 Mar 1780 in Stephentown. She died on 12 Apr 1864 in the hamlet of Schenevus, in the town of Maryland, Otsego County, New York.

4. **Warner Fellows** was born on 9 Apr 1773 in Stonington, New London, Connecticut. He died on 5 Apr 1853 in Westfield, Chautauqua County, New York.[60] His burial was in Westford Cemetery, Westford, Otsego County, New York.[61] Warner married **Lucinda Winslow**, daughter of Job Winslow, on 8 Nov 1797 in New Lebanon, Columbia County, New York.[62] Lucinda was born about 1780 in Connecticut.

Family historians disagree on whether Warner was the son of William and Susannah (Rathbone) Fellows. He is absent from earlier genealogies. For example, Cooley, in his *Rathbone Genealogy* did not include Warner as a son of William and Susannah. Erwin W. Fellows repeated Cooley and likewise omitted Warner. Mark D. Fellows, citing Erwin W. Fellows, made Warner of Otsego County and husband of Lucinda a distant cousin of William Fellows of Otsego. Others repeat this claim.

Nontheless, the name Warner traces back to Hannah Warner wife of Ephraim Fellows, who lived in Stonington, Connecticut. Hannah (Warner) Fellows was the great-grandmother of William Fellows and probably Warner Fellows. It is true that William Fellows of Stonington did not include a Warner in his will. He included only four of his alleged six sons attributed to him by some genealogists. The 1790 census accounted for four sons but the categories of their ages do not match the known ages of the four sons named in his will.

Erwin Fellows listed Warner Fellows from Norwich, Connecticut, as the son of Warner Fellows and Eunice Hall, and grandson of Nathaniel. This was the Warner that Mark Fellows identified as the Warner who settled in Otsego County. He was born 16 May 1768, according to his genealogy. However, his gravestone in Westford Cemetery, Otsego, County, New York, records a birthdate of 9 Apr 1773, which matches his age of 77 recorded in the 1850 census. The gravestone also says he died at the age of 79, which calculates to a birth year of 1774, a near match to the census birthdate and not the 1768 date for the Warner of Norwich.[63]

With the caveat that he may not have been the son of William and Susannah (Rathbone) Fellows, a sketch of his life is nevertheless included. Whether he was brother or cousin to William Reuben Fellows, he was a pioneer in the settlement of the Fellows family in Otsego County, New York, and a close neighbor of William Reuben and Martha (Smith) Fellows, son of William and Susannah. The 1800 census showed him living in Otsego County, New York.

Warner Fellows was Westford's first post rider. He regularly carried mail to Cherry Valley, Otsego, New York.[64] He carried the mail on horseback, some say as far as Albany, New York. He "made a trip from Cherry Valley every two weeks without fail. The mail came from Albany by stagecoach it is said. There were not many letters, and few papers to be read. Mail was brought from Cooperstown by wagon in a later day."[65]

Warner was one of the first trustees of the Methodist Episcopal Church of Westford, New York, along with four other men. The date of his trusteeship is not specific. However, the church organized in 1790, and the congregation erected the first church building in 1823. Therefore, Warner was a trustee after 1790 and probably before 1823.[66] He appeared in every U.S. Census beginning in 1800. Census records provide reliable data about his location and family life. In 1800, he was age 27 living in Worcester, Otsego County, New York. The census did not list the names of household members before 1850.[67]

Worcester Township divided in 1808. Therefore, in 1810, he was in Westford, Otsego, New York, because of the geography change.[68] However, he never left the farm where he originally settled. In 1820, he was living in

Westford, Otsego County, New York. He was about age 47 and a farmer. The census listed nine children as of 1820. Reuben Fellows, a possible nephew of Warner, was 19 in 1820 and thought to be among those listed in Warner's household. Like his kin, Warner Fellows was never a slave owner, a status regularly acknowledged in succeeding U.S. censuses.[69]

As the town grew, Warner played an active role in the community. At a meeting in March 1844, he moderated a meeting where the town resolved to build a new schoolhouse.[70] In 1850, the census finally identified household members. By that time, the children of Warner and Lucinda were on their own and no longer part of the Fellows household. Warner and Lucinda lived their entire lives in Westford, New York. In the summer of 1850, Warner was age 77 and Lucinda age 70. Warner retired in his advanced age and listed no occupation on the census in 1850. The value of his real estate was a modest $600.[71]

Warner died in the spring of 1853 in Westford, followed six years later by his wife Lucinda in the fall of 1859. Warner Fellows and Lucinda (Winslow) Fellows raised a large family of 13 children, including 1) Mary Fellows b. 18 Nov 1798 in Westford, Otsego County, New York, m. Daniel Kelley of Maryland, Otsego County, New York, on 11 Mar 1822; 2) Susannah D. Fellows b. 25 Sep 1800, m. William Darling; 3) Warner Fellows (II) b. 3 Jul 1802, m. Charlotte Howe; 4) Amos Fellows b. 19 Feb 1804, and died 16 Mar 1886 in Walworth, Wisconsin.[72] Genealogists sometimes mistakenly list Amos as a son of William Reuben Fellows, the brother/cousin of Warner. Amos married **Anna Cook**, daughter of Henry Cook and Betsey Buell. Anna was born on 17 Mar 1806. She died on 31 Jan 1849 in Lysander, Onondaga County, New York. Her burial was in Warner Cemetery.[73] Amos married secondly **Louisa Coffin** on 15 May 1849 in Lysander, Onondaga County. Amos was a farmer and moved to Onondaga, New York, around 1827.[74] Amos and Anna (Cook) Fellows had 13 children.[75]

5. **Joshua Fellows** was born on 22 Aug 1775 in Stonington, New London, Connecticut.[76] William did not name Joshua in his will.

6. **Jeremiah Fellows** was born on 3 Dec 1777 in Stonington, New London County, Conn.[77] He died in May 1860 in Stephentown, Rensselaer County, New York.[78] His burial was in Fellows Cemetery, Stephentown, New York.[79] The name of Jeremiah Fellows appeared on an index of claims presented by residents of Rensselaer County to the State of New York for payment of military clothing and equipment provided by individuals who volunteered, or the governor drafted, for service in the Militia of the State of New York during the War of 1812. Information included the order or claim number, name of applicant, residence of applicant and amount allowed.[80] In Jeremiah Fellows' case, the amount was $58.

7. **Isaac Fellows** was born on 16 Jun 1780 in Stonington, New London, Connecticut.[81]

8. **Polly Fellows** was born on 21 Jan 1783 in Stonington, New London, Connecticut.[82] Polly married **John Gardner** in 1823.

9. **David Fellows** was born on 16 Mar 1785 in Stonington, New London County, Connecticut.[83] He died on 19 May 1865 in Stephentown, Rensselaer, New York.[84] His burial was in Fellows Cemetery, Stephentown, New York.[85] David married **Chloe Turner**, daughter of John and Katherine Turner on 8 Oct 1812 in Nassau, Rensselaer, New York.[86] Chloe was born on 13 Jun 1794 at Middleton, Middlesex County, Connecticut. She died on 13 May 1878 in West Lebanon, Columbia County, New York. Her burial was in Fellows Cemetery, Stephentown, New York.[87] Children of David and Chloe Fellows were 1) Amanda Melvina Fellows b. 11 Oct 1815. The 1880 census listed Amanda Fellows, age 64, living in 1880 with her brother, Lorenzo, age 57, in Stephentown, Rensselaer, New York, with two other families. The census listed both Amanda Fellows and Lorenzo Fellows as single; both were born in New York; their father was born in Connecticut; and their mother was born in New York. Lorenzo listed an occupation of farmer; Amanda was keeping house. The Fellows Cemetery in Stephentown, New York, lists "Fellows, Amanda M. 11 Apr 1886 70y 6m d/o David and Chloe Fellows."[88] 2) David H. Fellows b. abt. 1822, d. Aug 1903; 3) Lorenzo D. Fellows b. 2 Dec 1823 in Stephentown, New York. Fellows Cemetery, Stephentown, Rensselaer County, New York, lists "Lorenzo Fellows 2 Dec 1823 - 20 Nov 1904." 4) Chloe J. Fellows b. 4 Jul 1829. Fellows Cemetery, Stephentown, Rensselaer County, N.Y., lists "Chloe J. 21 Nov 1867 38y 4m 17d d/o David and Chloe Fellows." 5) Mary Laurietta Fellows b. 1836, NewYork, d. 1906, m. 1-Daniel M. Beers, 2-David Beers; 6) Jane N. Fellows b. unknown, d. 26 Nov 1887 in West Point, Wis., and 7) Catherine S. Fellows b. abt. 1834.[89] While some names overlap between this listing and one compiled by Mark D. Fellows, genealogists consider this a more complete list of the children of David Fellows and Chloe Turner.[90]

10. **Ruby Fellows** was born on 3 Mar 1787 in Stephentown, Rensselaer County, New York. She died on 25 Oct 1873 in Lake Geneva, Walworth County, Wisconsin.[91] Ruby married **Daniel Wright** on 10 Jul 1820 in Stephentown, Rensselaer, New York. Daniel was born on 9 Mar 1793 in Maryland, Otsego County, New York. He died on 14 Aug 1879 in Lake Geneva, Walworth County, Wisconsin.

11. **Parmela Fellows** was born on 23 Sep 1790 in Stephentown, Rensselaer County, New York. She died 22 May 1826 in New Lebanon, Columbia County, New York.[92] Her burial was in West Lebanon Cemetery, West Lebanon, Columbia County, New York.[93] Parmela married **Moses Cowles, Jr.** on 1 May 1809 in New Lebanon, Columbia County, New York. Moses was born 10 Aug 1775 in Canaan, Columbia County, New York. He died 1 Nov 1848 in Lyons,

Walworth County, Wisconsin. His burial was in Lyons Quaker Cemetery, Lyons, Walworth County.[94] Parmela and Moses had six children.

9

William Reuben Fellows

William Reuben Fellows was the son of William Fellows and Susanna (Rathbone) Fellows. He was born April 5, 1771, in Stonington, Connecticut, the third son in a family of four brothers and one sister.[1] He died December 6, 1843, at the age of 72, in Maryland Township, Otsego County, New York.[2] His burial was in Schenevus Cemetery, Otsego County.[3] He was among the earliest settlers of east central New York, arriving in eastern New York sometime around 1785. He left his birthplace of Stonington, Connecticut, when he was about age 14, traveling first with his parents to Stephentown, New York, where his parents settled.[4]

An influx of immigrants to New York followed the end of the Revolution to settle the fertile regions taken recently from the Iroquois and other American Indian tribes once indigenous to the area. The Fellows were part of this migration that came toward the end of the 18th century, pushing out of New England and eastern New York and creating a new American geography. According to Hurd, the very large county of Albany, New York—formed November 1, 1683—at one time included the state of Vermont. Tyron County was set off from Albany in 1772 (the name was changed to Montgomery County in 1784). Otsego County, in turn, derived from Montgomery in 1791. The Otsego County seat of Cooperstown, named after its founder Judge William Cooper, father of famed author James Fennimore Cooper, sat on the edge of Otsego Lake. Cooper's classic book, *The Pioneers,* was a fictional account of the lives of the early settlers in Otsego County.[5] The county originally consisted only of Otsego and Cherry Valley subdivisions.

Around 1795, Warner Fellows, said to be a cousin or possible brother of William Reuben Fellows, bought 250 acres of land and appurtenances in Cherry

Valley Township in Otsego County, in central New York, in the hill-and-valley country northwest of the Catskill Mountains.[6] Much of the land along the creeks and rivers was rich bottomland; most was tree-covered. Here would be the home of Fellows ancestors for at least the next two generations.

The new Otsego County embraced the two original townships of Otsego and Cherry Valley, perched upon the highlands at the head of the Susquehanna River, southeast of the center of the state and 66 miles east of the state capital at Albany, New York. The topography of the county was mainly hilly upland, divided into several ridges, each separated by deep, broad valleys. Cherry Valley, in the northeast corner of the county, was a hilly and mountainous upland, crowned by Mount Independence, the highest summit in the county. The high and rocky upland extended into the southeast corner of the county terminating upon Schenevus Creek in a bluff some 300 to 500 feet high. Otsego Lake lay in the northeast part of the county and formed the source of the Susquehanna River where Cooperstown stood at the foot of the lake. Smaller Schuyler Lake was a few miles northeast of the village of Otsego. Otsego County was stock-raising and dairying country, both principal employments of the region.[7]

There were no families of the name Fellows in Otsego County in 1791 when the county formed. When Warner Fellows bought land in Cherry Valley in 1795, he began the westward movement of the Fellows family. William Reuben Fellows had not yet left Stephentown in recently formed Rensselaer County, New York. Rensselaer formed out of Albany County in 1791.

On December 22, 1796, William married Martha Smith of Stephentown. She was not yet age 17 at the time. Born March 3, 1780, probably in Stephentown, New York, she was the daughter of Ebenezer Smith, late of Stephentown.[8] There was many of the name Ebenezer Smith in Albany County in this period. Her most likely ancestor was the Ebenezer Smith who appeared on the tax rolls of Stephentown, Rensselaer County from 1799 to 1802, and then in Worcester Township, Otsego County in 1803, and who died in Stephentown in 1812.[9] Meanwhile, her relationship to the Revolutionary War veteran, Gideon Smith, remains uncertain. Like Ebenezer Smith, there were many of the name Gideon Smith in Albany and Rensselaer Counties, including in Stephentown in 1790.[10] A Gideon Smith removed from Stephentown to Oneonta, Otsego County, New York, in Maryland Township, about 10 miles from where Martha and William Fellows settled.[11] However, it is unknown if he was the Gideon Smith of the

Revolution. The circumstantial evidence of Martha's connection to these Smith families was in the name of her son, Gideon Ebenezer Smith Fellows.

After the formation of Otsego County in 1791, Worcester Township organized in 1797. William and Martha removed from Stephentown to Worcester, Otsego County, around 1798.[12] Enumerators of the 1800 census found them in Worcester Township in the summer of 1800. The census listed William as Reuben Fellows who matched William's age and included a female of the age of his wife Martha. The middle name of William was thereafter Reuben, which was also the name of his eldest son Reuben R. Fellows.[13]

Worcester Township, as it was originally drawn, was a region of fertile soil, particularly along the valley of Schenevus Creek and the Charlotte River. Hurd characterized it as "some of the finest farming lands in the country."[14] It saw its first settlements about 1788, and by the dawn of 1800, Worcester was one of the most prosperous localities in the country. Nevertheless, the New York frontier was an isolated place. It took a week to ten days to make a round trip to Albany, New York, the marketplace for the potash produced in the Worcester region. When Worcester divided in 1808 into the townships of Westford, Maryland, and Decatur, it was in response to the growing settlements that began in 1790. Although the region settled later than other areas and towns in eastern New York, by 1793 the area had witnessed the arrival of many settlers anxious to locate their homes in this fertile region. William and Warner Fellows were among these early arrivals, William in Maryland Township and his cousin/brother Warner across the township line in Westford where each lived respectively the rest of their lives.[15]

William Reuben Fellows first lived near Warner Fellows in Worcester Township, Otsego County.[16] The Tax Rolls of Worcester listed both William and Warner Fellows from 1799 to 1804.[17] They settled originally in Worcester Township. In 1808, when the Townships of Maryland, Westford, and Decatur spun off parts of Worcester, Warner's farm became part of Westford and William's farm became part of the creek-fed valleys and hilly uplands of Maryland Township where he farmed and raised cattle.[18]

The changing geography of New York in the early 19th century added a degree of difficulty in tracing the movements of William Reuben Fellows. In 1808, when the Otsego County townships were set off from Worcester Township, it appeared that William and Warner moved to different townships when actually they only obtained new geographic addresses for their previously established farms in old Worcester Township. The township line divided the two farms. Warner's place in Westford, like that of William in Maryland, was in a fertile agricultural area that became largely devoted to dairying. Both had successful albeit small farming operations. In William's case, he started with a house and farm in 1799 with a tax value of $380 and by 1801 saw his real estate taxable value nearly double to $750.[19]

D. Hamilton Hurd in his *History of Otsego County* wrote about the Fellows family in Otsego County.[20] He did not mention William Reuben Fellows specifically by name as being a settler of Otsego County. However, there is little doubt that William was among the very earliest to reach that region of New York. Hurd singled out William's son, Reuben, in his book in connection with his marriage to Betsy Goddard, daughter of Edward Goddard, who also garnered attention by Hurd as an early pioneer. Hurd also mentioned Warner Fellows.

Maryland Township was on the south line of Otsego County where the surface is hilly upland, broken by the deep ravines of the streams feeding into Schenevus Creek flowing southwesterly on its way to a juncture with the Susquehanna River. South Hill, part of the 500 feet high bluff that towered above the valley, extended along the south bank of Schenevus Creek flowing through the town of Schenevus. William Fellows lived on Elk Creek a few miles north of its convergence with the Susquehanna. The village of Westford was about four miles further up Elk Creek.[21] It was along Elk Creek that William Reuben Fellows and subsequent generations of Fellows farmed for many years.[22]

William was a charter member of the Elk Creek community. In 1809, his name appeared on the list of Path Masters for the ensuing year, assigned to Road Ward No. 28.[23] Communities provided their own road maintenance, and appointed local residents to oversee the task. Beyond William's engagement in farming and civic work, little information about the family survives. They were members of the Methodist Episcopal Church, and William supposedly inclined toward the Whig Party in politics.[24]

By 1810, William had settled comfortably into Maryland Township.[25] The 1810 census described a young growing family. It also introduced minor genealogical questions about his early life. The enumerations in the various age categories corresponded to William, age 39, Martha, age 30; sons, Reuben age nine; William, three; Gideon, two; and David, one. The one female under age ten on the census did not correlate with the known age of William and Martha's daughter, Affia, and may be an unknown child who died. Affia was not born until 1812. This suggests a daughter who did not survive, or Affia's birthdate preceded the generally accepted date of 1812. Living across the township line as a neighbor to William in 1810 was a "W. Fellows" and his family. This was Warner Fellows, age 37 at the time, the other half of the two Fellows pioneers who moved westward to the new frontier of New York.[26] In 1814, Warner Fellows and Lucinda his wife sold 143 ½ acres of land to William and Martha.[27]

The 1820 census again located William and his family in Maryland Township.[28] In the summer of 1820, he was engaged in agriculture, along with his sons, except for one son working in a manufacturing job in the adjoining Township of Westford where Warner resided with his family. Some genealogists claim that William Reuben lived first in Westford Township and then removed to Maryland Township between 1812 and 1820. However, records indicate that he lived his entire life in Maryland Township.

The Fellows presence in Maryland Township grew larger as the children of William and Martha married and started families of their own. However, none moved far from the seat of the family in Maryland Township. By 1830, William was age 59, Martha was 50, and their sons were all adults working on the family farm, or in son Reuben's case married and keeping his own place nearby. Son William B. Fellows had married in 1829. He and his new wife Nancy (Sperry) Fellows were living in William's household. Meanwhile, Warner Fellows farmed a place across the township line not far from William.[29] Another decade rolled over to 1840 and the children were out of the house. William and Martha lived alone for the next few years near their sons William B. and Gideon Fellows in Maryland Township.[30]

In his will, written October 23, 1843, and proved May 27, 1845, in Otsego County, William mentioned all of his children. On May 27, 1845, his heirs petitioned the Surrogate Court of Otsego County at Cooperstown to prove his will. The petition listed his survivors, including his widow Martha and their five children.[31] In his will, he divided the major remaining portion of his farmlands among his three sons and daughter who were farming adjacent lands. To his oldest son Reuben, he bequeathed 37 acres; to William, 18 acres plus all his "Book Accounts proper, that is, all debts due and owing to me...and all of my farming utensils now in his possession;" to Gideon, 18 acres and "the father's farming tools then possessed by him," and to Affia (Fellows) Sperry, 18 acres.

To his son David, who had moved to Van Buren, in Onondaga County, New York, he gave $500. "In the sixth place, I give and bequeath unto my beloved wife Martha all of my household furniture and wearing apparel, household goods, bedsteads & bedding, and other furniture," He named sons William B. and Gideon Fellows co-executors.[32]

William Reuben Fellows died at the age of 77 in December of 1843.[33] Warner Fellows died in 1853. Their families then each went separate ways. William B. Fellows, son of William Reuben, remained in Otsego County, but son Gideon removed to Wisconsin in 1855.[34] After William's death, Martha lived with her son David and family in Van Buren, Onondaga County, New York, recorded there in the 1850 census.[35] She then moved 750 miles to Lake Geneva, Walworth County, Wisconsin, to reside with Gideon and his family. She was there in 1860 at age 82, living with Gideon in Geneva Township, Walworth County, Wisconsin, near the town of Elkhorn.[36] Following the tragic deaths of Gideon's wife Rachel and three of his adult children during the time of the Civil War, Martha left Wisconsin and returned to New York. She lived for a couple of years alternately with the family of her daughter Affia (Fellows) Sperry and husband Matthew Sperry, and with her son William B. and Nancy (Sperry) Fellows who remained in the Schenevus and Elk Creek hamlets of Maryland Township, Otsego County. Martha died there on April 12, 1864, at the age of 84.[37] Her burial was near her husband William Reuben Fellows in Schenevus Cemetery, Schenevus, New York.[38]

The Children of William and Martha (Smith) Fellows were Reuben, William B., Gideon E.S., David, and Affia Fellows.[39] The genealogy continued from William Reuben Fellows and Martha (Smith) Fellows to William B. Fellows.

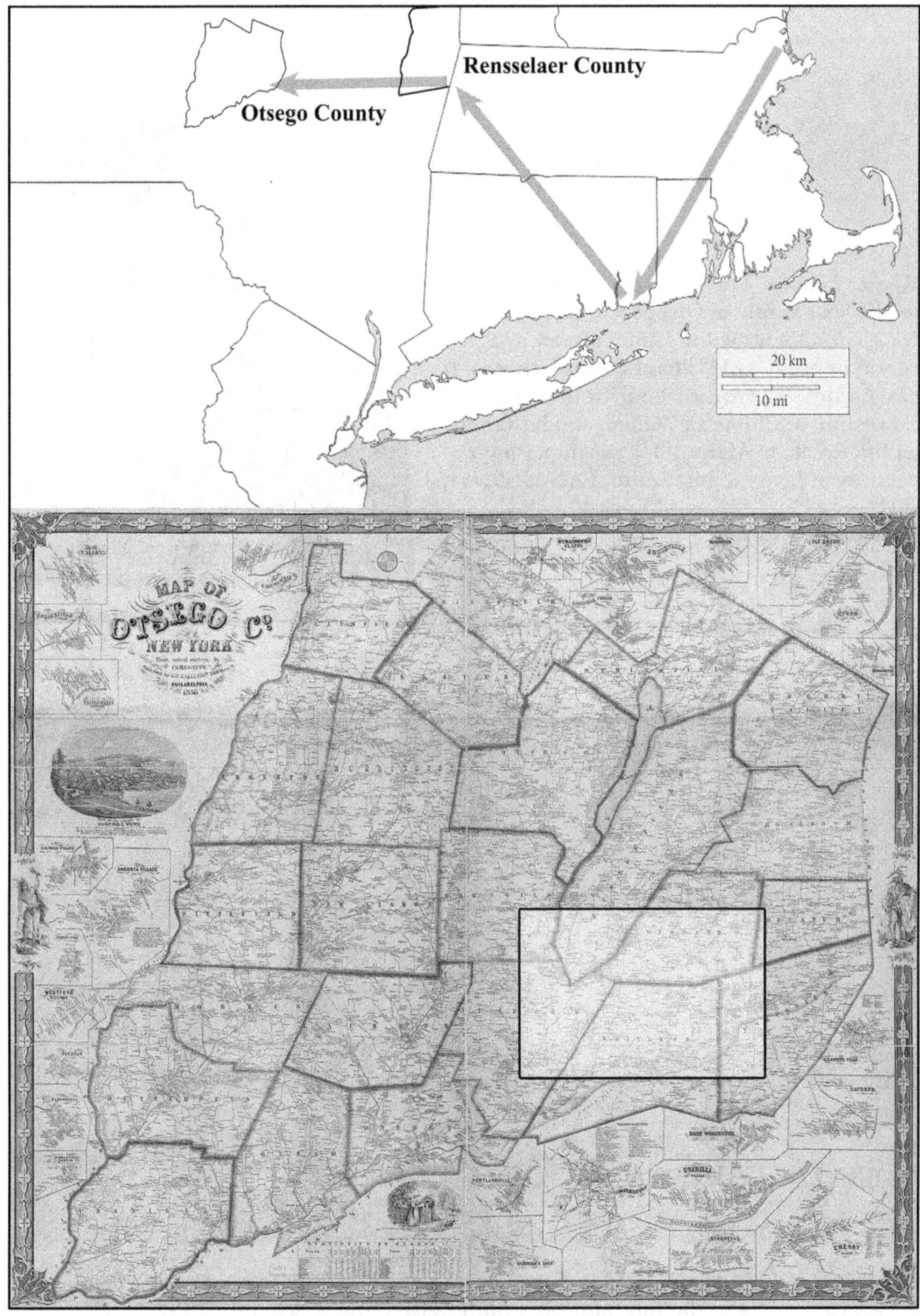

Fellows Migration Route. William Reuben Fellows left Stephentown, Rensselaer County, New York, about 1798, migrating west to Otsego County. He settled in Maryland Township on Elk Creek in the area highlighted on the map. Library of Congress.

Warner Fellows. He pioneered the settlement of the Fellows family in Otsego County, in eastern New York. Identified in family history as a cousin or brother of William Fellows, he was a postal rider and farmer who lived in Worcester Township, next door to William and his family on Elk Creek, in Maryland Township. Photo courtesy of Joan Stewart Smith, FAG 161191453, 2017.

Schenevus, New York. Situated in the mountainous upland of Otsego County, the town of Schenevus stands at the foot of a high bluff poised above Schenevus Creek. The creek parallels the road running horizontally across the middle of the photo. William and Warner Fellows settled near Schenevus. This postcard pictures the town as it appeared in 1908 looking sourh toard South Hill. Private collection.

Fellows Sixth Generation Family Group

William Reuben FELLOWS was born on 5 Apr 1771 in Stonington, New London, Connecticut. He died on 6 Dec 1843 in Schenevus, Maryland Township, Otsego County, New York.[40] His burial was in Schenevus Cemetery, Schenevus, Otsego County.[41] He was the son of **William FELLOWS** and **Susannah RATHBONE.**

William married **Martha SMITH** on 22 Dec 1796 in Stephentown, Rensselaer County, New York. Martha was born on 3 Mar 1780 probably in Stephentown, New York. She died on 12 Apr 1864 in Schenevus, Maryland Township, Otsego County, New York.[42] Her burial was in Schenevus Cemetery, Schenevus, Otsego County.[43]

They had the following children.[44]

1. **Reuben R. Fellows** was born on 21 Jun 1801 in Otsego County, New York. He died on 1 Oct 1847 in Maryland Township, Otsego County, New York.[45] His burial was in Schenevus Cemetery, Maryland, Otsego County.[46] Reuben married **Betsy Goddard**, daughter of Edward Goddard and Hannah Mann, on 17 Feb 1825 in Maryland, Otsego County, New York.[47] Betsy was born in 1797. She died on 10 Aug 1881 in Maryland, Otsego, New York. Her burial was in Schenevus Cemetery, Maryland, Otsego.[48] Reuben was the eldest son of William and Martha (Smith) Fellows.[49] In 1810, he was living with his parents and siblings in Westford, Otsego, New York. He did not appear in the 1820 census but at age 19 was possibly in another household. He married in 1825, and the 1830 census found him and his wife Betsy living not far from his father, William Reuben Fellows, in Maryland, Otsego County. *The Biographical Review* published an article in 1893 about his daughter Mary (Fellows) Dunham, which mentioned Reuben Fellows and his family. "He [Reuben] was a farmer, and a man well known for many miles around. He died October 1, 1847, his wife dying August 10, 1881, aged eighty-three. They were the parents of four children, viz: Edward R., Affia M., Diana E., and Mary. Edward R. Fellows is a farmer of Montgomery County, Pennsylvania. Mrs. Dunham's grandfather, William Fellows, was one of the earliest settlers in the town of Maryland, and her maternal grandfather, Edward Goddard, was a very early settler in the same town. He was born April 25, 1767, and lived to a great age, dying October 6, 1846. Mrs. Dunham above being Mary Fellows, d/o Reuben who m. Samuel Dunham. Reuben R. Fellows (William 2, William 1) was born June 1801 in

Westford, Otsego Co., N.Y., and died October 1847 in Maryland, Otsego Co., N.Y. He married Betsy Goddard February 1825 in Cherry Valley, Otsego Co., N.Y., daughter of Edward Goddard. Reuben's mother was Martha Smith."[50]

In the 1840 Census for Maryland, Otsego County, New York, Reuben Fellows was living among a group of Goddard households (including that of Betsy's father, Edward Goddard).[51] Edward Goddard came into the area in about the year 1793, and located on lands north of Schenevus. He was an active and influential pioneer; was the first supervisor of the town, and officiated in that capacity successively until 1816, and at various times for fourteen years.[52]

Enumerators of the 1850 census for the first time recorded the names of every person in the household. Added to this, enumerators had instructions that resulted in a greater degree of accuracy compared with earlier censuses. The official enumeration day of the 1850 census was 1 Jun 1850. Unfortunately, it came too late to include Reuben Fellows. He died in 1847 at the early age of 46, three years before the 1850 census. The census recorded Betsy, age 52, living in Maryland Township, Otsego County, New York, with the four Fellows children, ranging in age from 14 to 24. She was living near her brother William Goddard. Her nephew Samuel Hubbard was living in her household and helping work the farm.[53] Betsy lived on to a long life, and died in her 83rd year on 10 Aug 1881. Her burial was in Schenevus Cemetery, the site of the 1861 Civil War Soldiers Memorial and Fellows family burials.[54]

Children of Ruben Fellows and Betsy Goddard were 1) Diana E. Fellows b. 29 Dec 1826 in Maryland Township, Otsego County, New York, d 20 June 1891 in Maryland, Otsego, New York, buried at Schenevus Cemetery, Maryland, Otsego, New York.[55] She married Woodbury R. Cook. 2) Mary Fellows b. 3 Jul 1829 in Maryland, Otsego, New York, d. 26 May 1905 in Maryland, Otsego, m. Samuel [H.] Dunham 1 Oct 1851 in Maryland, Otsego, New York. He was b. 22 Dec 1823 in Worcester Township, Otsego, N.Y., d. abt. 24 Mar 1890 in Maryland, Otsego, New York. A memorial of the life of Samuel Dunham is in *The Biographical Review, Biographies of The Leading Citizens of Otsego County, New York*, c.1893. The article also mentions his wife, Mary Fellows.[56] Their burial was in Schenevus Cemetery, Maryland, Otsego, New York.[57] 3) Affia M. Fellows b. 31 Jan 1831, d. 20 Dec 1856, m. Riley Pierce 16 Jan 1855; and 4) William [Edward] R. Fellows b. 4 Oct 1835, m. Eliza Alexander. Probably this Edward R. Fellows, son of Reuben and Betsy, was the one who served in the Civil War.[58]

+ 2. **William B. FELLOWS** was born on 22 Apr 1807 in Westford, Otsego County, New York. He died on 9 Jan 1875 in Maryland, Otsego, New York. His burial was in Elk Creek Cemetery, Maryland Township, Otsego County. William married **Nancy SPERRY**, daughter of **Ansel SPERRY** and **Olive TYLER**, on 26 Nov 1829. Nancy was born on 5 Aug 1809 in Alford, Berkshire County, Massachusetts. She died on 1 Mar 1879 in Otsego County, New York. Her burial was in Elk Creek Cemetery, Maryland Township, Otsego, New York.

3. **Gideon Ebenezer Smith (E.S.) Fellows** was born on 7 Sep 1808 in Maryland, Otsego County, New York. He died on 31 May 1884 in Allison, Butler County, Iowa.[59] His burial was in Allison Cemetery, Butler County.[60] Gideon married **Rachel Cook**, daughter of Henry Cook and Betsey Buell, on 26 Feb 1835 in Van Buren, Onondaga County, New York. Rachel was born on 9 Nov 1807 in Pompey, Onondaga County. Rachel was a direct line descendant from Francis Cook and Stephen Hopkins of the Ship *Mayflower*.[61] She died on 24 Aug 1861 in Geneva, Walworth County, Wisconsin.[62] Her burial was in North Geneva Cemetery, Como, Walworth County.[63] Gideon married secondly **Laura (Benson) Martin** in Aug 1863. Laura was born 9 Jan 1820 in Vermont.[64] She previously married Milton Martin of Spring Prairie.[65] She died 4 Oct 1902. Her burial was in Burlington Cemetery, Racine County, Wisconsin.[66]

In 1840, Gideon and Rachel were living in Maryland Township, Otsego County, New York. At the time, they had three daughters: Susanna, Betsey, and Clarissa. Their homeplace lay situated between the homes of Gideon's brother William B. Fellows and their father William Reuben Fellows.[67] By 1850, Gideon's family had grown to six in number; the Fellows enclave had enlarged to include not only his brother William but also William's daughter Amanda (Fellows) Webster and their younger sister Affia. A number of relatives and in-laws of the Fellows families spread across Maryland Township.[68] In 1855, Gideon removed to southern Wisconsin, to Geneva Township, Walworth County, Wisconsin.[69] He bought a farm near Elkhorn, Wisconsin, and was a successful farmer in that community for several years.[70] Rachel died in 1861, and Gideon married Laura (Benson) Martin in 1863, widow of Milton Martin, and a woman 12 years Gideon's junior. About 1864, he and Laura moved to Burlington, in Racine County, Wisconsin. Gideon spent his remaining years in that community. His biography in the *History of Racine and Kenosha Counties, Wisconsin* traced his movements. "He went to Geneva, Walworth County, Wisconsin, in 1855, and remained there ten years. When he first went to

Geneva in 1855, he bought 140 acres of land, and improved it and built a residence. In 1863, he moved to Spring Prairie, and, in 1866, sold the property in Geneva; his second wife owned seventy-eight acres of land in Spring Prairie, and, in 1868, he bought forty acres more in the same place… In 1869, he moved to Burlington village, where he lived three years. In March 1872, he bought 87-3/4 acres in Sec. 31, Burlington, with residence on it, and now occupies it [in 1879]… His son Elnathan enlisted in the 22nd Wisconsin, and died of fever in Murfreesboro, Tennessee, Aug. 19, 1863. His son Amos enlisted in the same regiment, and was wounded at the battle of Resaca Woods, near Atlanta, Georgia, and died, June 18, 1864, at Kingston, Georgia, where he was sent when wounded."[71] Gideon lost five family members during the time of the Civil War, his mother and four of his six children: two daughters, and two sons who died because of the war.

The 1880 census found Gideon, Laura, and Laura's son Fred Martin living at Burlington, Racine, Wisconsin, where the family kept a farm. Gideon was in his seventies but with his stepson's help worked the land.[72] Gideon died on May 31, 1884, while visiting his only surviving son Arthur in Allison, Butler County, Iowa. The *Burlington Free Press* published his obituary. "We are pained to learn that Mr. G.E.S. Fellows, who was stricken with paralysis at Allison, Iowa, a week ago last Sunday, at one o'clock in the afternoon, died last Saturday afternoon, May 31st, 1884 at one o'clock p.m. His remains will probably be brought to Elkhorn Prairie for burial. Mr. Fellows was called to Iowa by the illness of his son, Arthur G. Fellows, who died soon after his father's arrival. The excitement, anxiety and exhaustion of the trip and weariness of watching, prostrated him and one week ago last Sunday, as before stated, he was prostrated with paralysis, which ended his life on last Saturday. Mr. Fellows was an old and highly respected citizen, having been a resident of Burlington about twenty years, and for many years previous to his locating in this town he had been a resident of Elkhorn Prairie. His age was 74 years and he had always enjoyed good health until a year or two past, when he began to show signs of failing health. His death will cast a gloom over this community in which he was so highly esteemed for many virtues of head and heart. He leaves a wife and one daughter, five children having preceded him to the great beyond." The one surviving daughter mentioned in Gideon's obituary was Betsey Fellows who died in 1923.[73] Betsey lived to the age of 85. Gideon Fellows was a Fellows family historian. He obtained access to the ancestry records of Elnathan Fellows of Stonington,

Connecticut, and copied largely from them. He added his own research to them over many years. He never published his material, and after his death in 1884, his widow put his work into storage and it passed into obscurity, lost to subsequent generations.[74]

Children of Gideon Fellows and Rachel Cook were 1) Susanna Fellows b. 15 Feb 1836 in Maryland Township, Otsego County, New York, d. 23 Jan 1864, m. Olney R. Perry 30 Apr 1856 in Geneva, Walworth County, Wisconsin; 2) Betsey Fellows b. 9 Apr 1838 in Maryland, Otsego County, New York, d. 1 Sep 1923 in Fort Atkinson, Jefferson County, Wisconsin, m. Stephen Edward Bright 28 Feb 1854 in Geneva, Walworth County, Wisconsin. He died Nov 6, 1899; 3) Clarissa Fellows b. 9 Jul 1839 in Maryland, Otsego County, d. Feb 1880, m. Schuyler Hadden 19 Nov 1862 in Geneva, Walworth County, Wis.; 4) Elnathan Fellows b. 3 Aug 1840 in Maryland, Otsego County, d. 19 Aug 1863 in Murfreesboro, Hertford County, Tennessee. Elnathan fought in the Civil War and was a prisoner in Libby Prison, Richmond, Va., in Mar 1863. 5) Amos Fellows b. 7 Jul 1842 in Otsego County, New York, d. 18 Jun 1864 in Kingston, Bartow County, Georgia. Amos fought with General Sherman in Dallas Woods in the Civil War. Captured during the war, he was a prisoner in Resaka, Georgia. He died during the war, in Kingston, Georgia. 6) Arthur G. Fellows b. 20 Jul 1846 in Maryland, Otsego, New York, d. 22 May 1884 in Allison, Butler County, Iowa. Arthur was a farmer. He died of Typho-malarial fever.[75]

4. **David Fellows** was born on 26 Apr 1810 in Maryland Township, Otsego, New York. He died 9 Mar 1889 in Coldwater, Branch County, Michigan.[76] His burial was in Belvidere Cemetery, Boone County, Illinois.[77] David married **Harriet Lobdell**, daughter of Abraham Lobdell, in 1831. Harriet was born on 29 Aug 1813 in Coxsakie, Green County, New York. She died 13 Jan 1897. Her burial was in Belvidere Cemetery, Boone County, Illinois.[78] David removed to Van Buren, Onondaga County, New York, in 1834, and then to Belvidere, Illinois, in 1856, and on to Coldwater, Branch County, Michigan, in 1866.[79] In 1880, David Fellows, age 70, was living in Coldwater, Branch County, Michigan, with his wife Harriet, age 67, and daughter, Lydia A. Fellows, age 46. He listed his occupation as a farmer, Harriet as keeping house, and Lydia as housekeeper. All were born in the state of New York.[80] Children of David Fellows and Harriet Lobdell: 1) Joseph Hiram Fellows b. 9 Jun 1832 in Otsego County, New York, d. 1911; 2) Lydia Ann Fellows b. 21 Oct 1833 in Otsego; 3) Emily M. Fellows b. 27 Aug 1836 in Van Buren, New York, d. 27 Jun 1900; 4) Isaac C. Fellows b. 18

Sep 1837 in Van Buren, m. Mary Silkworth in 1860; 5) Sabrina J. Fellows b. 30 Mar 1839, m. Sylvanus Hauser. Sabrina (Fellows) Hauser lived in Franklin Grove, Illinois; 6) Rose (aka Rosanna) Ellen Fellows b. 28 Jun 1847, d. 2 Mar 1856; and 7) William Fellows b. 8 Jan 1850 in Van Buren, New York.[81]

5. **Affia M. Fellows** was born on 30 Oct 1812 in Maryland, Otsego County, New York. She died on 17 Aug 1892 in Maryland, Otsego County. Her burial was in Schenevus Cemetery, Otsego County.[82] Affia married **Matthew Sperry**, son of Elisha Sperry and Rhoda Boardman, on 6 Oct 1831. Matthew was born on 6 Nov 1807 in Westford, Otsego, New York. He died on 23 Aug 1883 in Maryland, Otsego County. His burial was in Schenevus Cemetery.[83] The marriage of Affia to Matthew Sperry was an example of the sometimes-complex relationships that often occurred in the sparsely populated frontier of colonial America. Affia's sister-in-law was Nancy (Sperry) Fellows who was also Matthew Sperry's cousin. Matthew and Nancy's grandparents were Anslen and Olive (Tyler) Sperry. Although Affia and her brother William B. Fellows both married into the Sperry family, Affia Fellows and Matthew Sperry were not blood related. The 1850 census listed Affia M. and Mathew Sperry and their three children in the Township of Maryland, Otsego County, New York.[84] Living with them, or nearby, were members of the extended Sperry family. Children of Affia Fellows and Matthew Sperry were 1) Gideon Fellows Sperry b. 4 Oct 1832 in Maryland Township, Otsego County, New York; 2) Henrietta Emogene Sperry b. 22 May 1839, d. 23 Sep 1862; and 3) Betsy Ann Sperry b. 18 Apr 1840 in Maryland, Otsego County.[85]

10

William B. Fellows

William B. Fellows was born April 27, 1807, in Westford (later Maryland Township), Otsego County, New York, the third child, and third son of William and Martha (Smith) Fellows.[1] He died on January 7, 1875.[2]

William B. Fellows grew up on a farm in Maryland Township, Otsego County with the education available in the rural settlements of the New York frontier. He spent most of his life in and around the villages of Maryland and Elk Creek, and the nearby towns of Schenevus and Westford. Like his father before him, William was a farmer. Historian Hamilton Hurd described Westford as a "pleasant village, located northeast of the centre of the Town [Township], on Elk Creek [that] contained four churches, Episcopal, Presbyterian, Methodist, and Baptist."[3] Elk Creek abutted Sperry Hollow in Maryland Township. It was in Sperry Hollow that Ansel Sperry settled with his four brothers, arriving from New England about 1820, all early settlers of Maryland Township, Otsego County. On November 26, 1839, William B. Fellows married Ansel's daughter, Nancy Sperry.[4] She was born August 5, 1809, in Alford, Berkshire County, Massachusetts, the daughter of Ansel and Olive (Tyler) Sperry. The 1840 census found William and Nancy Fellows living on a farm in Otsego County. They lived in the same Maryland Township community as their parents.[5]

By 1850, the Fellows clan had grown. William and Nancy's oldest daughter, Amanda, married Dow Webster and lived in the house next door. William's brother, Gideon, lived in the same neighborhood with his wife and family of six children. William and Gideon's sister, Affia, lived nearby with her husband, Matthew Sperry, their three children, Affia's Grandmother Olive Sperry, and

Olive's daughter, Naomi. Naomi was Nancy (Sperry) Fellows' youngest sister. In the Town of Maryland also in 1850 lived Samuel J. Thompson, his wife Sarah, and their four children, including Roxanne, age 11. Roxanne would become the wife of Warren S. Fellows, son of William B. and Nancy (Sperry) Fellows. It was common to find families living together in the same household or clustered in close-knit communities. Children often grew up to marry the girl or boy next door. There were several other Fellows, Sperry, and Thompson households in the Town of Maryland. For example, when Reuben Fellows, the oldest brother of William B., died in 1847 at the early age of 46, his widow, Betsey continued to live in the same Maryland community as William B. Fellows and the other Fellows family members.[6]

By the time he was in his early forties, William B. had acquired real estate valued at $2,000; his daughter Amanda Rosetta had married well and lived next door with her newly acquired husband, Dow Webster. All of the Fellows school-age children were in school, including two of the oldest, Ansel and Warren who were teenagers in the 1850 census, suggesting that they acquired a high school education. Uncle Gideon lived next to Amanda on a farm valued at $3,000. Likewise, Gideon's school-age children were in school, taken as good evidence that the Fellows families placed a high value on education.[7]

The accumulation of land came as the result of several years of inheritance and purchase. Ansel Sperry, Nancy (Sperry) Fellows' father, died in 1831 and left acreage in Sperry Hollow to his daughter. In 1835, William B. Fellows and his brother Gideon each bought farmland from their father who died in 1843 and gifted his sons more land. Between purchases and inheritance, investment in farmland amounted to a healthy estate.[8]

William B. Fellows did well in farming, a trade he engaged in for his entire life. In 1860, his real estate values had increased to $4,000, with personal property of $800, according to the 1860 census. The children stayed close to home. Russell and Austin helped with the farming; Ansel had a house next door and worked as a carpenter. Warren married and set up his own farming operation a short distance away in another part of the township.[9] Amanda and Dow Webster started their own family next door to William and Nancy, on a farm valued at $3,000 and property of $800, sums interpreted to mean that Dow was about as prosperous as his father-in-law was. Aunt Affia and her husband, Matthew Sperry, lived nearby in Sperry Hollow, doing equally well in the farming business.[10] It was a close community, although a relatively small one.

Schenevus, the largest settlement in Maryland Township, had about 50 houses and probably 200 inhabitants. An isolated locality, it was 16 miles from any place exceeding its size.[11]

The American Civil War erupted in 1861. The election of Abraham Lincoln as president ignited the flames of an already longstanding divide in the country over slavery. States began to secede from the Union even before the inauguration of Lincoln. A call went out for volunteers to put down the rebellion. William and Nancy sent three of their five sons to fight in the Civil War on the Union side, the youngest only nineteen at the time. All three survived some of the hardest fought battles of the War. At the same time, their son-in-law, Dow Webster, paused his work as a general farmer, stock raiser, and dairyman, to serve in the 1st New York Engineers and was said to have been present at the surrender of General Lee.[12] The slavery issue may have motivated the Fellows' strong enlistment in the Union cause. Throughout the Fellows'generations, there is no record that any of them ever owned slaves.

After the war, three of William's sons left the old home place on Elk Creek to pursue a new frontier west of the Mississippi River in Missouri. The two youngest sons remained to work on their father's farm, including Austin recently returned from the war in 1865,[13]

William and Nancy lived out the rest of their lives on Elk Creek near Schenevus. In the summer of 1870, William B. was age 63, and Nancy age 61, sharing their home with their son Aaron Olin at the family farm on Elk Creek. William had sold off some property and invested the money. Nevertheless, the 1870 census showed him to be a moderately wealthy landowner. He owned real estate valued at $2,000; and personal property worth $3,000, an indication of his investments.[14] By 1872, at the age of 65, William B. Fellows retired to a small farm at Schenevus. The 1872-1873 *Gazetteer and Business Directory of Otsego County* listed him as a farmer living on 16-acres about a mile from Schenevus.[15] His name appeared listed as one of the prominent farmers of the township of Maryland. He became a gentleman farmer. He kept a horse, two milk cows, and a hog. He raised mostly oats, Indian corn, and hay on his small acreage. Like most of his neighbors, he kept a nice orchard.[16]

The Fellows was a churchgoing family. They were Methodists. The Methodist church at Elk Creek organized about 1830, the year following the marriage of William and Nancy.[17] However, the first building did not go up until 1857. Dow M. Webster, William's son-in-law, served as a Steward of the church.[18]

Meanwhile, there was another Methodist Episcopal Church situated just west of Schenevus, within easy distance of the Fellows' home.

William B. Fellows wrote his will June 13, 1874. In it, he indicated his six children.[19] There were, in fact, seven children but only six living. A seventh child, Nancy Caroline, had died in infancy in 1841. The petition on the probated estate referred to Olin Fellows as legal heir and next of kin. This was the same person as Aaron O. in the list of children, living at the time with William and Nancy.[20] William's will was a carefully scripted set of instructions about what to do with his estate after his death. He divided cash of $1,450 according to his perception of each child's need, but not equal. Amanda, wife of Dow Webster, got the smallest share. He gave his real estate and investment properties to his wife Nancy with the caveat that the investments should continue to accrue interest, and nothing should sell as long as she lived. He gave $5 to each of his grandchildren.

His will revealed the heart of a caring father. In a carefully worded section of his will, he withheld his youngest son Aaron's legacy. He wrote, "It having been a source of much regret that my son Aaron has not in times past had sufficient control over his appetite to abstain from the too frequent use of intoxicating liquors and showing that when he is so addicted to their use he is liable to make bad use of money entrusted to him. Therefore, I desire for his benefit solely that his portion of my said property shall be retained in the custody of my executors as invested securely in land and mortgages or other lands that shall be safe and secure; and that the interest only be paid to him as he shall need the same unless in the opinion of my said executors he shall be in need of some portion of the principal for his support in which case they shall give it to him."[21] William directed that Aaron's inheritance remain invested, and left to the executors the decision as to when he might be trusted to spend it. If he beat his disease and took care of his mother, William said he was to have an additional sum for their living expenses above the amounts provided to the other children. After William and Nancy died, Aaron Olin moved to Missouri to live with his brother, Warren S. Fellows. There is no further record of the details of his alcoholism, or the outcome of his inheritance, except he never married, and died in 1880 at the age of 34.

William B. Fellows died January 9, 1875, of stomach cancer at the age of 67, at Elk Creek, Maryland Township, Otsego County, New York.[22] His final resting place was in Elk Creek Cemetery in a part of the cemetery first used by the death of his infant daughter Nancy Caroline in 1841 and grandson Ira S. Webster in 1856.[23] Nancy (Sperry) Fellows died on March 1, 1879, and went to rest beside her husband.

Willie Ira Fellows wrote a history of the Fellows family with the lengthy title, *A Short History of W.I. Fellows and the Fellows Family as Far Back as He Can Remember.* He remembered his grandparents, William B. and Nancy (Sperry) Fellows. Although he was a small child at the time, Otsego County left an impression on him. He mentioned Schenevus, Elk Creek, and other area landmarks in Otsego County. He described the fertile countryside and told stories he remembered from his childhood in Maryland Township, Otsego County, New York, including how. William B. Fellows farmed in Otsego County all his life.[24] He wrote, "William [B] Fellows had one brother, Gid Fellows [Gideon E.S.]. I can remember being at his house. Grandmother Fellows had two sisters, one married Warren Smith [Olive Caroline Sperry] and the other, Ira Hanor [Abigail Sperry]. I can remember being at both their homes. Grandfather Fellows and grandmother Fellows raised six children, one girl, and four [*sic*] boys. Their names were Rosetta, Warren, Ansel, Russell, Austen, and Olen. All were married but the youngest, Olen [Aaron Olin]. Aunt Rosetta [Amanda Rosetta] married Dow Webster, Warren married Roxanna [*sic*] Thompson; Ansel and Russell were married, but I don't remember the names of their wives. Austen married Kate Wilson in Missouri in 1875. She died about the year 1879 and then he married Roxanna Pipes in 1882."[25] In his listing of the children of William B. and Nancy (Sperry) Fellows, Willie Ira miscounted "four" and omitted the name of Nancy Caroline Fellows who died in infancy.[26]

The Fellows genealogy continued from William B. and Nancy (Sperry) Fellows to their son Warren Smith Fellows.

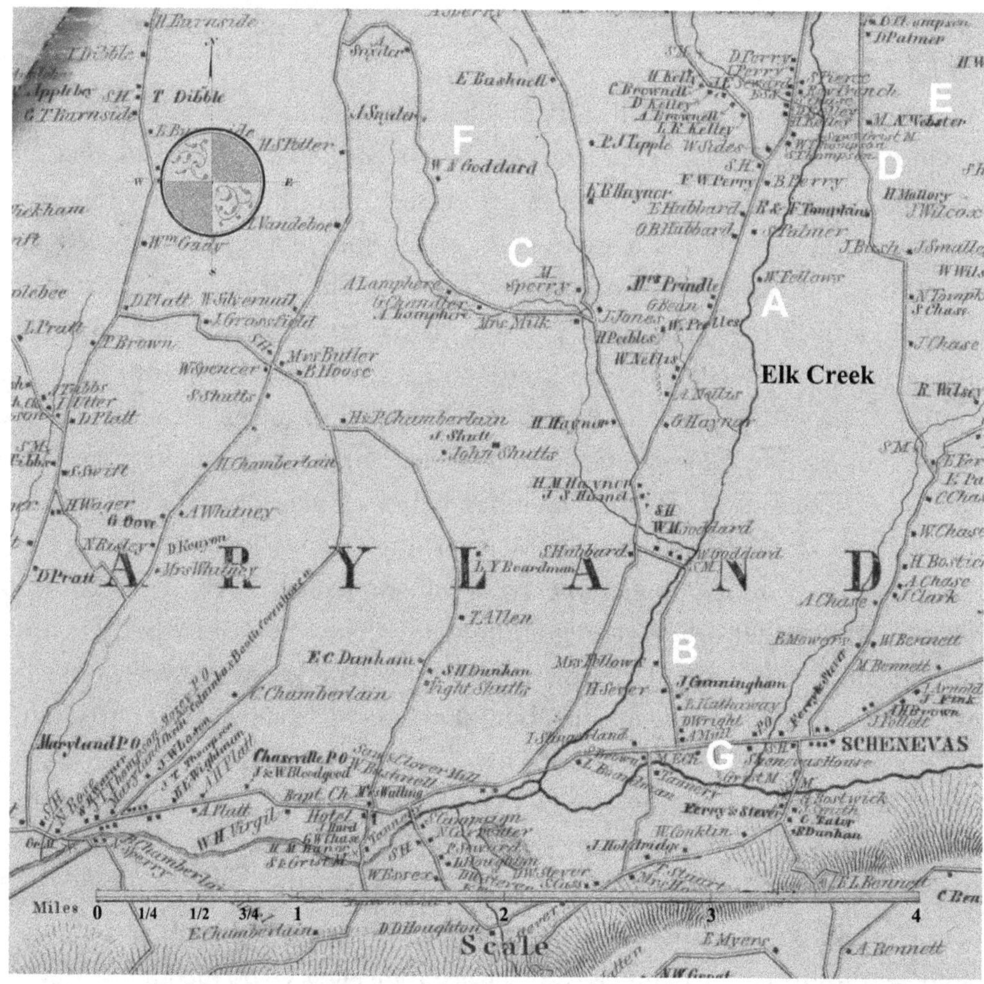

Map of Maryland, Otsego County, New York. This 1856 map shows towns and landowners associated with the Fellows family on Elk Creek in Maryland Township. Charted on the map are (A) William B. Fellows and (B) Mrs. (Martha) Fellows, his mother and widow of William Reuben Fellows. Also charted is Matthew Sperry (C) who married Affia Fellows in 1831. William B. Fellows married Nancy Sperry of this same Sperry family in 1829. A third child of William Reuben and Martha, Reuben R. Fellows, married into the Goddard family (F) in 1825. The letter (D) locates the residence of Samuel Thompson, father of Roxanne Thompson who married Warren Smith Fellows in 1855, the son of William B. Fellows and grandson of William Reuben. Amanda Fellows, eldest daughter of William B. married the son of Miron Noah Webster (E) in 1846. The Methodist Episcopal Church (G) where the Fellows attended services was at Schenevus, spelled 'Schenevas' on the map. Elk Creek converged with Schenevus Creek to become the Susquehanna River below the high ridge that ran across the southern part of Maryland Township. Adapetd from a *Map of Otsego County, New York*, Library of Congress.

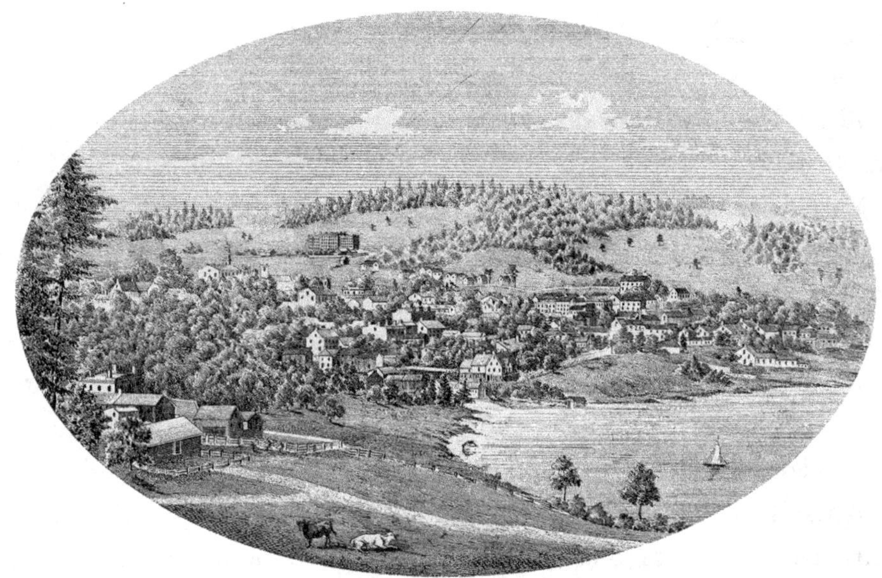

View of the Village of Cooperstown, New York. The county seat of Otsego County was a frequent destination of the Fellows family for three generations. Seen here from the east side of Lake Otsego near the base of Mount Vision, the buildings of the Cooperstown Seminary and Female Collegiate Institute appear in the distance. Adapted from a *Map of Otsego County, New York*, Library of Congress.

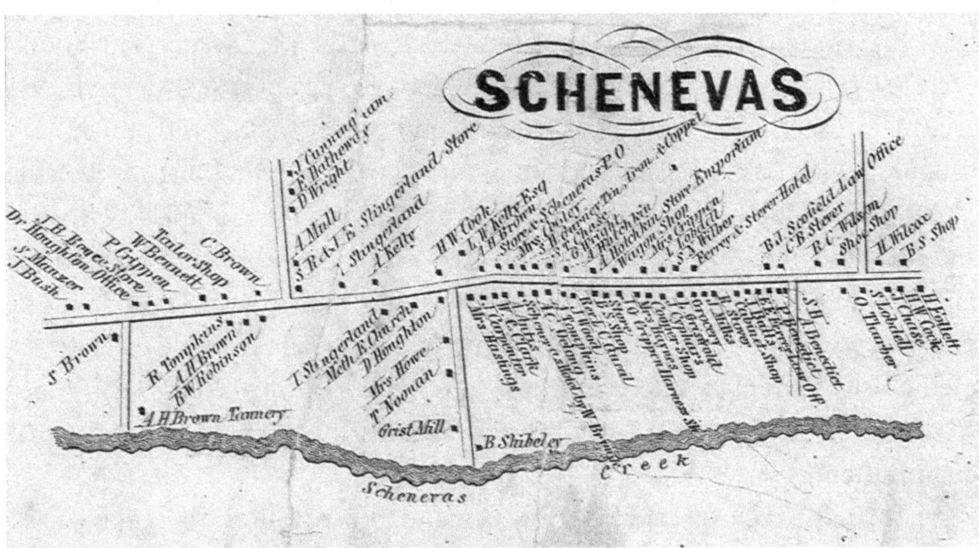

Map Showing the Residents of Schenevus, New York. Families depicted on the map intermarried with members of the Fellows family, including Lobdell, Cook, and Wilson. The Fellows clan lived at Elk Creek and did not live in Schenevus. However, they were the farmers who patronized the stores and shops of Schenevus in what was the only town of any size for several miles. Library of Congress, c.1856

Fellows Seventh Generation Family Group

William B. FELLOWS was born on 22 Apr 1807 in Westford, Otsego, New York. He died on 9 Jan 1875 in Elk Creek, Maryland Township, Otsego County, New York. His burial was in Elk Creek Cemetery, Maryland Township, Otsego County.[27] He was the son of **William Reuben FELLOWS** and **Martha SMITH.**

William married **Nancy SPERRY**, daughter of **Ansel SPERRY** and **Olive TYLER**, on 26 Nov 1829. Nancy was born on 5 Aug 1809 in Alford, Berkshire, Massachusetts. She died on 1 Mar 1879 in Elk Creek, Otsego, New York. Her burial was in Elk Creek Cemetery, Maryland, Otsego, New York.[28]

They had the following children.

1. **Amanda Rosetta Fellows** was born on 18 Apr 1831 in Elk Creek, Otsego County, New York. She died on 15 Feb 1910 at the home of her daughter in Cortland, Cortland County, New York. Her burial was in Elk Creek Cemetery, Maryland Township, Otsego County, New York.[29] Amanda married **Dow Miron Squires Webster**, son of Miron Noah Webster and Armenia (Bivens) Adams, on 19 Aug 1846 in Westford, Otsego County, New York.[30] Dow was born on 9 Mar 1827 in Sharon, Schoharie County, New York. He died on 15 Feb 1904. His burial was in Elk Creek Cemetery, Maryland, Otsego, New York.[31] The 1850 census recorded Dow M. and Amanda R. (Fellows) Webster living on a farm in Maryland Township, Otsego County, New York, with their baby daughter Eleanor.[32] Amanda later went by her middle name Rosetta. Biographer Willie Ira Fellows mentioned her in his autobiography as Rosetta and her husband Dow Webster.[33] Dow M. Webster served as a private in the First New York Engineers, Company E during the Civil War. He rose to the rank of corporal.[34] He was later active in community affairs as a trustee of the Methodist Church at Elk Creek and a director of the Schenevus Valley Agricultural Society in 1865, serving also as Superintendent of Sheep for that organization.[35]

In 1880, the Webster family—Dow, Amanda Rosetta, and son Ralph age 15 and in school—were still farming at their place in Maryland Township. Historian Child wrote in 1893, "He [Dow Webster] and his wife are excellent members of society. They have a pleasant home, and are noted for their generous hospitality, Mr. Webster being a gentleman of the old school, so few of whom are to be met with in these modern days [1893]."[36] Dow died in 1904, and the family laid him to rest in the Fellows family plot at Elks Creek Cemetery.[37]

After her husband died, Amanda Rosetta lived with her daughter Ella (Webster) Seward in Cortland, New York. Amanda Rosetta died in Cortland. The *Otsego Farmer* published a short notice of her passing. "The body of Mrs. Rosetta Webster, a native and for many years a resident of Elk Creek, was brought here on Thursday from Cortland where she made her home with her daughter, Mrs. Ella Seward, for burial in the family lot in the Elk Creek Cemetery."[38]

Rosetta and Dow Webster had three children: 1) a daughter Eleanor A. Webster, born about 1850; and two sons 2) Ira S. Webster, born July 7, 1855, who died in infancy September 14, 1856, and 3) Ralph D. Webster born about 1865.[39]

2. **William Ansel Fellows** was born on 25 Apr 1833 in Elk Creek, Otsego County, New York. He died on 18 Feb 1889 in Newark Valley, Tioga County, New York. His burial was in Hope Cemetery, Newark Valley. William married **Hannah Mary Chamberlain**, the daughter of Deigh Chamberlain and Hannah St. John, on 25 Dec 1854 in Emmons [Oneonta], Otsego County, New York. Hannah was born about 1837 in Elk Creek, Otsego County, New York. She died on 13 Sep 1897 in Oneonta, Otsego, New York. Her burial was in Hope Cemetery, Newark Valley, Tioga County, New York.[40] William Ansel Fellows enlisted in the Union Army in August 1864 and served in Company E of the 1st New York Engineers during the Civil War.[41] His discharge was 1 Jul 1865.[42] He removed to Newark Valley, Tioga County, New York. Willie Ira Fellows mentioned him in his autobiography as Uncle Ansel.[43] The 1880 census listed Ansel and his wife Mary in Newark Valley, Tioga County, New York.[44] At age 46, he gave his occupation as farm laborer. Ansel lived in the same Tioga community as his brother Russell Fellows. According to a family historian, Ansel and Mary had two children: 1) Florence Amelia born 5 Oct 1855, in Westford, Otsego County, New York, and 2) William (Willis) Henry Fellows born May 16, 1859. In 1880, Willis lived with his parents and later married Delta Sheldon in September of 1880.[45]

+ 3. **Warren Smith FELLOWS** was born on 22 Jun 1835 in Elk Creek, Maryland, Otsego, New York. He died on 4 Apr 1909 in Neosho, Newton County, Missouri. His burial was in the Independent Order of Odd Fellows Cemetery, Neosho, Newton County, Missouri. Warren married **Roxanne**

THOMPSON, daughter of **Samuel S. THOMPSON** and **Sarah BELL**, on 16 Mar 1855 in Maryland, Otsego County, New York.[46] Roxanne was born in Oct 1838 in Maryland, Otsego, New York. She died on 6 Dec 1917 in Neosho, Newton County, Missouri. Her burial was in I.O.O.F. Cemetery, Neosho, Newton County, Missouri.

4. **Russell Sylvester Fellows** was born on 28 Aug 1837 in Elk Creek, Otsego County, New York. He died 18 Jan 1905 in Tioga County, New York.[47] His burial was in Hope Cemetery, Newark Valley, Tioga County.[48] Russell married **Mary Ellen Smith** in 1861 in Westford Township, Otsego County, New York. She was born in 1843 probably in Maryland Township, Otsego County. She died 24 Sep 1920 in Tioga County, New York. Her burial was in Hope Cemetery, Newark Valley.[49] R.S. (Russell Sylvester) Fellows was a dentist who settled first in Maine, Broome County, New York, and then in Newark Valley, Tioga County, New York, along with his brother Ansel Fellows who lived in the same community.[50] Willie Ira Fellows mentioned both in his autobiography.[51] The 1880 census located Russell in Newark Valley with his wife Mary and a son Dor S. Fellows, age 10.[52]

5. **Nancy Caroline Fellows** was born on 26 Jul 1840 in Elk Creek, Otsego, New York. She died in infancy on 23 Feb 1841 at the age of 7 months in Elk Creek, Maryland Township, Otsego County, New York. Her burial was in Elk Creek Cemetery, Maryland Township, Otsego County.[53]

6. **Austin Morrell Fellows** was born on 2 May 1843 in Elk Creek, Otsego, New York. He died 21 Feb 1912 in Salisbury, Chariton County, Missouri. His burial was in Salisbury Cemetery, Salisbury, Chariton County.[54] Austin married **Kate Wilson** 16 May 1875 in Howard County, Missouri. Kate was born 14 Dec 1855. She died on 27 Feb 1879 in Howard County, Missouri. Her burial was in Sartain Family Cemetery, Howard County.[55] Austin married secondly **Roxanna J. Pipes** 24 Dec 1882. She was the daughter of Quintus J. and Charlotte M. (Adkins) Pipes. She was born 16 Oct 1866 in Chariton County, Missouri, and died 31 May 1947 in Chariton County. Her burial was in Salisbury Cemetery, Salisbury, Chariton County.[56]

Austin Fellows served three years in the Civil War, from his muster on August 13, 1862, until June 24, 1865. He enrolled at the age of 19. He was a private from Maryland Township in Captain Nelson O. Wendell's Company F of the 121st Regiment of New York State Infantry Volunteers, commanded by Colonel B. Franchot.[57] The unit organized at the village of Herkimer, in

Herkimer County, New York, and left New York on September 2, 1862, bound for Washington, D.C. The 121st became part of the Second Brigade, First Division, Sixth Army Corps of the Army of the Potomac and the Army of the Shenandoah. The 121st Regiment Infantry saw some of the hardest fighting of the Civil War. They fought in 25 battles, among them some recognized as pivotal to the outcome of the war. For example, Austin and the 121st saw action at the battles of Fredericksburg, Chancellorsville, Gettysburg, Wilderness, Spotsylvania Court House, Cold Harbor, Siege of Petersburg, and the Appomattox Campaign. He was at Appomattox to see the surrender of Lee.[58] He suffered a wound at the battle of the Wilderness. At Chancellorsville, the 121st Regiment lost 287 out of 540 men who entered the engagement. The 121st lost during service 14 officers and 212 enlisted men killed and mortally wounded and four officers and 117 enlisted by disease, a total of 347 casualties. A monument at Gettysburg marks the spot held by the New York 121st from July 2, 1862, until the close of the battle.[59] Another Civil War Memorial at Schenevus Cemetery, Maryland Township, Otsego County, New York, includes the name of Austin Fellows along with his brothers William Ansel Fellows, Warren Smith Fellows, and Warren's brother-in-law Beckwith Thompson, all of whom served as Union volunteers from the State of New York.[60] Shortly after the war ended, Austin's brother Warren left his family in New York in 1867 to establish a place to resettle in Missouri. Willie Ira Fellows, only a small boy at the time remembered that Austin accompanied Warren's wife Roxanne and her children from New York, on the train ride to rejoin Warren.[61]

Austin returned to north Missouri, married and settled in Fayette, Howard County, Missouri.[62] He married Kate Wilson in 1875, and they had a son Claud. Kate died in childbirth at the age of 23. Baby Claud passed away less than a month later on March 28, 1879. The 1880 census located Austin at Boones Lick in Howard County, a 33-year-old widower working as a carpenter.[63] He married a second time to Roxanna "Roxie" Pipes on Christmas Eve 1882 in Chariton County, a young woman barely 16 years old and 23 years his junior. Austin and Roxie had three sons: 1) Aubrey P. Fellows, 2) Ralph Manos Fellows, and 3) William W. Fellows.

7. **Aaron Olin Fellows** was born on 20 Nov 1846 in Elk Creek, Otsego County, New York. He died on 15 Dec 1880 in Salisbury, Chariton County, Missouri. His burial was in Salisbury Cemetery, Chariton County, Missouri.[64] Aaron did not marry. He lived in Maryland, Otsego County, with his parents

until their deaths, when he then removed from New York to Missouri to live with his brother Warren S. Fellows. The 1880 census recorded Olin A. Fellows living with Warren S. and Warren's family at Salisbury, Chariton County, Missouri.[65] Olin was an alcoholic, an addiction that caused his father out of concern to make special provisions in his will to delay Olin's inheritance until he was well. The 1880 census listed no occupation for him, suggesting he still suffered from his disability. He died in 1880 at the age of 34 shortly after the enumeration of the census. His nephew, Willie Ira Fellows, mentioned him in his autobiography as Olen [*sic*], but gave no details of his life.[66]

11

Warren Smith Fellows Early Years

Warren Smith Fellows was born on June 22, 1835, in Elk Creek, (Township of Maryland), Otsego County, New York.[1] He was the second son and third of seven children born to William B. and Nancy (Sperry) Fellows.[2] His name Smith came from his Grandmother Martha (Smith) Fellows and Uncle Warren C. Smith, husband of Olive Caroline (Sperry) Smith, his mother's closest sister.[3]

He grew up on the Fellows farm on Elk Creek, in Otsego County.[4] The closest town of any size was Schenevus, a settlement on Schenevus Creek of a few stores and houses situated along the main road (present New York State Route 7) about a mile south of the Fellows farm. Local inhabitants originally called the town Jacksonboro, which changed to Schenevus (pronounced skuh-NEE-vus) in 1848, supposedly named for an Indian Chief of that name.[5] After Schenevus, the nearest urban town was at least 11 miles distant at Cooperstown. Nevertheless, Schenevus was the center of activity for youth growing up in Maryland Township. Schenevus had a wide reputation as a center of excellent education. From an early date, according to Otsego County historian Hamilton Hurd, "The citizens of Schenevus have ever manifested a laudable interest in educational matters, and their graded school ranks among the best educational institutions in the county."[6]

Schenevus Creek flowed southwest through Maryland Township like a ribbon connecting the isolated farmsteads. Elk Creek and several smaller streams were its tributaries. Along these streams as early as 1790 towns and villages sprang up. The hamlet of Elk Creek in the northern part of Maryland Township had one church—Methodist Episcopal—and a store.[7] It was in this community that Warren Smith Fellows called home, living on a farm not far from the village of Elk Creek, which was the closest post office. Elk Creek was rural in every sense. The closest town was Schenevus about three miles away. An isolated locality, Schenevus was 16 miles from any place exceeding its size.[8]

Warren started working on the family farm at the age of ten, going to school in the summer and three months during the winter.[9] The 1850 census recorded him in the William B. Fellows household as a boy of 14, going to school.[10] At age 15, he broke his thighbone in a riding accident, which, according to family historian Marjorie Daum Columbus, he thought was the only notable thing that ever happened to him in his growing up years.[11] He was relatively small in stature, standing five feet six inches tall but handsome with brown hair, grey eyes, and fair complexion. [12] On March 16, 1855, at the age of 19, he married a neighbor girl named Roxanne (aka Roxanna and Roxie) Thompson.[13] She was 16, and three years younger than Warren.[14] She was from a large family of 12 children, the oldest daughter born to Samuel S. and Sarah "Sally" (Bell) Thompson.[15] Her father was one of Otsego County's first residents.[16] His family was among the original settlers of the territory that became Maryland Township. Roxanne's ancestor, John Thompson, came to Otsego in 1794.

Warren and Roxanne grew up in the same community in Otsego County. They were Methodists. Nevertheless, family tradition is that the couple married at the M.E. Church in Westford because that was the location of Roxanne's church. She lived near the Maryland-Westford township border; the M.E. church at the village of Westford was a good distance further from the Thompson home than the church at Elk Creek. However, Elk Creek was a congregation in name only for several years, meeting for church services in the local school building. The people of Elk Creek later built a church, and Warren committed his faith to the Methodist Church there when he was twenty-five.[17]

Warren worked on his father's farm the summer after he and Roxanne married. With the help of Roxanne's father, they bought a few acres close to Schenevus, and the couple set up housekeeping to follow the Fellows tradition as farmers. By 1860, they had two children and everything pointed to a good future for the next generation of the Fellows family. He had $400 in property, on his way to owning his own place.[18] Soon, they sold the small farm and rented a larger place.[19] However, things did not go well in the farming business. Warren sowed about one hundred acres of oats, and the price dropped fifty cents a bushel between his seed price and his harvest. The following year, he rented a dairy farm where he kept 22 cows to sell cheese to the New York markets at eight cents a pound.[20]

Meanwhile, the national political scene grew ominous. Warren cast his first vote in a presidential election in 1856 for the Republican candidate John S. Fremont. Fremont lost to Democrat James Buchanan, ushering in four years of political unease. In 1860, he voted again, this time for Abraham Lincoln. The Civil War soon followed. Warren wrote in a brief autobiography that in 1863 he rented his father's farm and got well into his work when the call of President Lincoln for more men became so urgent that he arranged with his father to look after the farm and enlisted in the Union Army in August 1864.[21] He left Roxanne and their three small children in the care of Roxanne's parents and enlisted as a private in Company D of the 3rd New York Cavalry.[22] Roxanne divided her time between her parents and Warren's.[23]

The 3rd New York Cavalry had a storied service in the war from the beginning. The regiment organized by company. Company D organized at Albany, New York, August 12, 1861. The regiment proceeded to Washington, D.C., on September 9, 1861, where it attached to Banks' Division, Army of the Potomac at Meridian Hill. They served in the defenses of Washington on the Upper Potomac to April 1862. They were at Malvern Hill in 1862. The regiment served throughout North and South Carolina before joining the Cavalry Brigade of the 18th Army Corps in the defenses of New Berne, North Carolina, attached to the Department of Virginia until October 1863. Company D occupied Trenton and Kinston Road, and was instrumental in holding Thompson's Bridge and Goldsboro in the winter of 1863. The company was in operations around New Berne and in the Raid on Wilmington and Weldon Railroad in the summer of 1864. Warren joined the 3rd New York Cavalry in Virginia in September 1864. His company went immediately into combat as part of the siege of Richmond. He wrote in his autobiography that he "was dismounted and went into the breastworks, and in the fight, Company D lost three killed and seven wounded. [We] then did picket duty on the Darby-town road six miles from Richmond. This was the outside line and a dangerous place every night. Some of the men were fired upon, and in the regiment the loss was considerable."[24] In November 1864, Company D went to Portsmouth, West Virginia, to guard the landing at Portsmouth. Here they went into camp for the winter. It was here, too, that Warren contracted "southern fever," which soldiers understood to be typhoid fever, but was more like malaria. He became very ill. Company Morning Reports showed him in the hospital at Portsmouth from late December 1864 to February 1865.[25] He returned briefly to Company D, the war ended May 19, 1865, and he mustered out of the service on June 7, 1865, at Norfolk, Virginia, having served less than a year. The 3rd New York Cavalry served with distinction throughout the war. During the course of the war, the Regiment lost 8 officers and 45 enlisted men killed and mortally wounded and one officer and 150 enlisted men by disease, a total of 199.

Warren's illness in the service was a turning point in his life.[26] He never fully recovered from the experiences of the war. One of his granddaughters later remembered a story told to her by her mother Rose (Fellows) Daum, Warren's daughter. She said, "He had typhoid fever and was very sick and as my mother told it, he was given the job of carrying out amputated limbs and all the suffering and agony was a severe shock to his nervous system and he never entirely recovered."[27] Willie Ira Fellows wrote in his autobiography, "My father, and two of his brothers and one of my mother's brothers served three years [*sic*] in the Union Army during the Civil War. Two of my uncles were in the battle of Gettysburg and the battle of the Wilderness, two of the hardest fought battles during the war. One was wounded. They all came home but my father's health was ruined. He had the southern fever and was in a hospital for some time and he says they ruined his health by giving too much quinine." Willie Ira, who was five years old at the time, remembered, "When my father came home in 1865, we did not know him. He took us all to Cooperstown on the Otsego Lake, and had our pictures taken.[28] Cooperstown was the county seat of Otsego County."[29] Willie Ira also noted, "My father carried a small testament through the Civil War, and Jack Fellows, his grandson, carried the same testament through the war in France. I still have it [1940] and it is in very good shape."[30]

Unfortunately, not everyone came home from the Civil War. Three of Warren's cousins died in the war. His Uncle Gideon lost two of his three sons to the war, as did his Uncle David who lost a son.[31] Located in the Schenevus Cemetery, (Township of Maryland), Otsego County, New York, is a Civil War Memorial, erected to honor those men from Otsego County who served the Union during the war. On the memorial is the name of Warren Fellows and his brothers Austin M. and Wm. Ansel Fellows, along with their cousin Edward R. Fellows. Also on the memorial is the name of Beckwith Thompson, Warren's brother-in-law, and others of the Thompson family related to Roxanne.[32] The memorial stands in the same cemetery as the graves of Warren's parents and members of the Fellows family who for many years made Otsego County their home. Two hundred seven men enrolled in the Civil War from Maryland Township, compared with 30 enlistees from neighboring Westford Township. The difference was even greater than stated because the names of both Warren and his older brother Ansel appeared on the memorial credited to Westford Township and not Maryland.[33]

In the summer of 1865, Warren, Roxanne, and their children were at home with Roxanne's parents in Maryland Township. The New York State Census recorded Warren as still officially in the army, although he had mustered out by that time.[34] Soon, they moved onto a farm of Roxanne's Uncle and Aunt Peter and Mary Ann Strail, about a day's ride north from Warren's parents, and close to the little village of Cherry Valley, (Township of Cherry Valley), in the north part of Otsego County.[35]

Warren ran his own sawmill there when he was not farming.[36] Mills of all sorts sprung up all along the creeks in Otsego County to supply the needs of the ever-increasing population. Powered by a large overshot water wheel, a small creek dammed up to create the millpond fed the Fellows mill. Most of the logs were hemlock, a course pine growing on the mountains. Willie Ira described the logging scene, "On the farm was a large pond, made by building a dam across a small creek. Below the dam was a sawmill run by a large overshot water wheel. The saw was a sash saw; that is, a straight saw that ran up and down. It was a little slow, but it was all they had. The saw was built in a frame attached to the water wheel. All mills and factories were run that way then. The farm was in the valley and the house was a short distance from the mountains. They would cut the logs in the winter and drag them to a chute that had been made down the mountain. They would go down this chute to the valley and then they would haul them to the mill where they were sawed into lumber."[37]

Roxanne and Warren Fellows lived at Cherry Valley for about a year, and then moved back to Elk Creek. In the spring of 1866, Warren decided to leave New York. The Albany and Susquehanna railroad had reached Schenevus in 1865, connecting the community to distant destinations. Warren left Roxanne and the children at Elk Creek and took the train out of Otsego County to Albany, destined for Missouri with the intention to send for his family as soon as he found a place to live.[38] He settled in Linn County, Missouri, near the town of Brookfield, a town in 1866 about the size of Schenevus. Linn County was mostly prairie and many of the settlers lived in the timber along the creeks.

Warren bought some prairie land, rented a farm in the timber close to the prairie, and raised a crop. He opted not to acquire land through the Homestead Act of 1861, probably because the law required a five-year residency on the property and improvements to include a house. His family was in New York, and there was no certainty that he would stay in Missouri. Instead, he purchased government land that was cheap at about $1.25 an acre, and which had only a six-month residency requirement. Owning land and trying to raise a crop on the prairie of Linn County posed its problems. "The trouble with buying that land was the fencing," wrote Willie Ira. "Nothing but rails to fence it with, and they didn't last long when the [prairie] fires came through in the fall."[39] Nevertheless, there were lots of deer, wild turkey, and thousands of prairie chickens and quail to provide food for a frontier family.

After a year of living alone, Warren sent for Roxanne and the kids in the spring of 1867. Roxanne and the four children, Flora, Willie, Belle, and Rosie started west, accompanied at Warren's request by his brother Austen.[40] Willie Ira, a child of six at the time, vividly recalled the trip. ""I can remember well the trip from New York. Our greatest sights were when we went through Illinois. We were used to living in the Catskill Mountains of New York state and the level prairies were a new sight to us. We were riding in the hind coach and we could look back up the track for miles. We carried our grub with us and bought as we needed it along the road.[41] Rosie was a very young baby and I can remember carrying a bottle of Paregoric and a spoon in my pocket all the way through, to give her when she cried. Father's brother, Austen Fellows came with us and we took the train at a little town on Elk Creek, one mile from grandfather Fellows, called Schenevus, and ran to Albany, sixty miles. We lived southeast of Albany. From Albany, we went to Buffalo and along the lakes to Chicago and crossed the Mississippi river at Quincy, Illinois, [and] then on to Brookfield where father met us. He had bought a large team of bay horses called Mike and Charlie and the next day we drove out to the farm where he had raised a crop. The house was of logs and not very good. He had killed a large wild turkey and had it hanging in the smoke house."[42]

They lived there through the winter of 1867. The prairie-land farm in Linn County proved unsatisfactory to Warren, and he traded it in on an improved farm in Howard County, about six miles from Glasgow, on the Missouri River. Heavily timbered, the rolling land was great tobacco country. The farmers would chop down trees and clear land in the winter and in the spring would have a "log rolling." All the neighbors would help each other to roll or carry the logs, put them in large piles, and burn them. In February, they would dig up the ground beneath the burned logs and sow tobacco seed. About May, they transplanted the seedlings into rows set off in the cleared ground and raised a tobacco crop.[43]

Warren's farm contained 120 acres of open land and an eighty in timber that cornered with it. It was rough land and heavily timbered. Two small limestone branches ran through the property, and along the branches were large sugar maple trees. Ever the entrepreneur, Warren leased out part of the maple grove and tapped the rest to make maple syrup. They collected the sap in black walnut troughs about three feet long; some of the troughs were very old. They hauled the sap by wagon to the house where they boiled it down. Willie Ira described his youthful participation. "We had a large fireplace in the kitchen and would put a large kettle in the fireplace and boil it down to thin syrup and finish it up on the cook stove. We made part of it into syrup and part into sugar. In sugaring it off was where one got good eating."[44]

G. E. S. FELLOWS

Uncle Gideon E.S. (Ebenezer Smith) Fellows. He was the son of William Reuben Fellows and Martha (Smith) Fellows and the younger brother of William B. Fellows. He farmed in Maryland, Otsego County, New York, on land located next to William B. He removed to Walworth County, Wisconsin, in 1855. He lost five family members during the time of the Civil War, including two sons who died in the war. Mr. Fellows died in 1884 while visiting his last remaining son in Allison, Iowa. Burlington Historical Society, Racine County, Iowa.

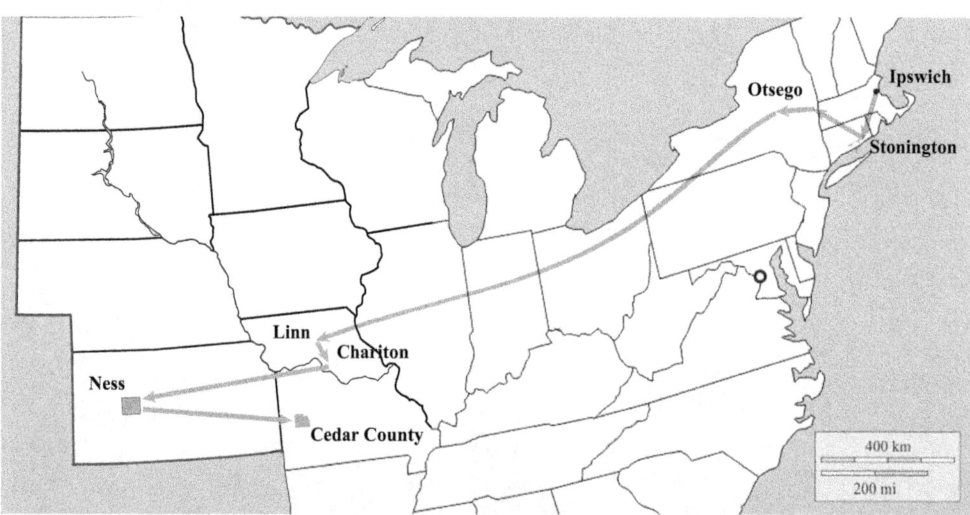

Fellows Migration 1635-1888. Beginning in Ipswich, Massachusetts, generations of the Fellows family settled in Stonington, Connecticut; Otsego, New York; and northern Missouri before removing briefly to Ness, Kansas, and then back to Cedar County in southwest Missouri. The migration journey spanned nine generations over a period of 253 years.

12

Warren Smith Fellows Later Years

In the summer of 1870, the 1870 census found Warren at age 35 and his family living on their farm in Howard County, Chariton Township, north of the Missouri River, close to Glasgow and convenient to the post office at Fayette due east.[1] Warren had a respectable stake in the county with his land valued at $5,000 and personal property of $800. He and Roxanne had five children by now: Flora, Willie, Isabel (aka Belle), Rose, and Ernest, all born in New York except Ernest, born the previous year in Fayette, Missouri. The three oldest were in school, and a sixth child, Katie Caldonia, would come along in a couple of years to complete the family. Warren's younger brother Austin J. Fellows was living in the household and helping with the farming.[2] After accompanying Roxanne and the children from New York, Austen elected to settle in Missouri.

The Howard County farm was an idyllic setting for a young family unused to the abundance of rural north Missouri. Willie Ira described the plethora of wild fruit that grew there. "The first wild fruit in the spring was the sarvisberry. They grew on small crooked trees and the berries were bright red and good to eat. The next fruit was the mulberry; very sweet and large and then the wild plums, large red, and yellow, sweet as sugar. Wild grapes, large and sweet, then came the pawpaws, growing on the ridges everywhere. Then the possum fruit, the persimmon."[3]

Willie told how, "After the first frost, father would take the wagon and he and Flora and myself would go down on the Missouri River and stay all night. In the morning, we would get up early and start gathering nuts and would soon have our wagon full. We would take them home and hull them and put them away for the winter. We would get ridge scaly-bark hickory nuts, not so large as the river nuts, but very thin hulls and very rich. We would go out on the branches and gather walnuts, butternuts, and hazel nuts."[4]

The demands of farming made it a difficult vocation in the 1870s. There was none of the modern methods and equipment that later came in the agrarian revolution of the early 20th century. All the fences were made of ten foot rails made eight rails high, "staked and double ridered," in Willie Ira's words. "The rails were made of fine timber and would last years. Father made thousands of them."[5] Blacksmiths with shops in the country and the little towns made the wagons and plows. Willie Ira said, "The first plow that I plowed with was made in Boones-borough by a blacksmith named John Fisher. The town was in the Boone's Lick hills, close to Salt Springs, where Daniel Boone and the early settlers would go and take their kettles and boil down the water and make their salt. The wagons were linchpin wagons—wooden axels with a strip of iron on the bottom and top of the axel where the wheel ran. A pin through the axel held on the wheel.[6] Corn was cultivated with wooden double shovels made in the neighborhood. They plowed the corn with one horse or mule and drove it with a jerk line for a line. It was tied not quite in the middle of the bridle rein and put in between the hames. One would pull on the line for haw and give it a little quick jerk for gee. All the harness was chains."[7]

Harvest time came in the fall. The thrashing machines were small and run with horsepower. These were treadmill machines, slightly inclined, on which a horse or multiple horses, depending on the size of the treadmill, walked to power a pulley attached by a belt to the thrashing machine. Men removed the horsepower machine from the wagon, set it on the ground, and staked it down. "If the wind changed and blew in the back end of the separator," said Willie Ira, "they would have to turn the separator around and also the horsepower. It took twelve to fifteen horses and mules to run it. It was a great improvement over the old ways of tromping out the grain with stock."[8]

Warren was a successful farmer, raising mostly grain crops like his father before him in New York. An inventory of his holdings in 1876 illustrated the breadth and scale of his farming operation. He owned two horses and a mule, four head of cattle, 13 sheep, and 10 hogs. Grain on hand amounted to 50 bushels of wheat, 1,250 bushels of corn, and 100 bushels of oats. On hand as well were 2,000 pounds of tobacco, 60 pounds of wool, and two tons of hay.[9]

After a decade of farming in Howard County, clearing and improving the land, Warren sold the Howard County property in 1878 and bought 100 acres for $300 in neighboring Chariton County.[10] It was a short move; Chariton County abutted Howard County on the north. He moved his family across the county line to Salisbury Township in the southeast corner of Chariton County.[11] Much had happened in the years before he moved. Over the decade of the '70s, Warren farmed, Roxanne kept house, and the children got their educations. Flora became a teacher, Willie Ira and Ernest worked on the farm, and the other kids stayed busy with the daily duties of farm chores. Austin Fellows moved to Boones Lick and became a carpenter. Olin A. Fellows, Warren's brother, left New York and joined Warren in Missouri, living in the household and helping to attend the farm.[12] Unfortunately, he died in 1880 at the early age of 34.

Meanwhile, the elder William B. Fellows died in 1875 at Elk Creek, New York. Most of the succeeding generations of the New York Fellows family did not stay in Otsego County. Warren and his brothers moved west; some of the family removed to other parts of New York and the Midwest. A few Fellows' kin continued to live in the state of New York; however, in 1879, Nancy (Sperry) Fellows, the last Otsego County, New York, Fellows ancestor, died. The records do not tell us how many times, if any, Warren visited his parents in New York during the 12 years that passed in Missouri.[13] William B. Fellows remembered Warren in his will, and the Fellows siblings kept in contact with each other. Nevertheless, Warren established himself as a successful farmer in Chariton County, Missouri, started a new generation of the Fellows line, and left behind forever the environs of Otsego County, New York.

The illness that Warren contracted in the Civil War took a toll over the years on his ability to do manual labor. It grew worse with each year. In August 1883, he applied to the War Department Pension Office for an invalid pension based on his Civil War-caused disability.[14] The Pension Office required under the 1862 Pension Act that to obtain a pension a soldier had to provide proof of time spent in the military, and that a disability incurred while in service. Thus began a long-running battle with the U.S. War Department over an adequate disability pension. His brother-in-law, Dow Webster, wrote an affidavit from Maryland, New York, in 1884, attesting to Warren's general good health before he served in the army.[15] Warren's eldest daughter, Flora, wrote anonymously describing what it was like to live with an ill father.[16] However, neither proved that the disability resulted from military service. In the spring of 1887, in poor health and in his mid-fifties, Warren quit farming, sold the Chariton County property, and moved to Ness City, Kansas.[17] He and Roxanne would spend the next 20 years of their lives in Ness City.[18] They bought a nice place in town in Center Township, paid for it with cash, and opened a boarding house.[19] They celebrated their fiftieth wedding anniversary in 1905, having raised all six of their children to adulthood.

The quest to convince the Pension Office that his failing health was war-related continued. In 1888, Austin Fellows wrote, "I am a brother of W.S. Fellows. I was with him most all the time from June 1865 until 1878. I remember that he was treated by a physician soon after his discharge from the service for a nervous disease. I did not at the time know the name of the disease, but since know it to be Locomotor Ataxia. I have lived with W.S. Fellows, worked for him, and with him, and lived near him since his discharge in June 1865 until 1878. I came to Missouri with him and have every reason to know that he has not been a well man since his discharge. We all thought when he first came to Missouri that his health was better, but a few months here, he became the same in health, dragging along, and always worn out with a little work. I know that the same disease that he came out of the army with is the same that he has now. For the last nine or ten years he has been a great deal of the time under medical treatment. He has never been able to do hard labor since his discharge. Before enlisting in the army, he was a very stout and healthy man."[20]

On June 27, 1890, President Benjamin Harrison signed the Dependent and Disability Pension Act. The generous new law provided pensions for all veterans who had served at least ninety days in the Union military or naval forces, had an honorable discharge from service, and were unable to perform manual labor, regardless of when the disability occurred. Despite the new more liberal rules, more than a decade passed before the Pension Office acted on Warren's application. In 1895, Dr. Hawkins wrote to the Office that he had known Warren for more than six years, and that he had never been able to do any hard manual labor.[21] "He is lame all the time and has spells of nervous exhaustion. There is but little feeling in his left leg, the muscles are atrophied, and the limb crooked and small due to injury to [his] hip…the left side all the way down is weak. He is agitated with the least exertion and very nervous and trembly…the diseases are permanent. Neurasthenia causes weak heart and poor digestion. He is poorly nourished."[22] Neurasthenia, cited by Dr. Hawkins in his letter, is a disease of the nervous system popularly called nervous prostration. Locomotor Ataxia, another term Austin Fellows used to describe Warren's condition, is an affliction of the spinal cord. The combined symptoms of these diseases are inability to walk, liable to tumble, or be unable to maneuver up steps. Trembling, weakness, and irritability with bouts of depression are likely to occur. The disease is degenerative over time and incurable. Still, the Pension Office refused to grant a pension to Warren.

He took on work as a rural mail carrier, and busied himself as a gardener. Roxanne handled the business of operating the boarding house. Their granddaughter Bessie Daum, Rosie's daughter, remembered her visits to Ness City. "[Warren] had a big irrigating pond on his place in town and raised all the vegetables they used and stored quantities in the cellar for winter. When the ponds froze in the winter, Grandpa would mark the ice for cutting, and neighbors would do the cutting and heavy lifting on shelves. Grandpa stored his ice in sawdust for the summer. Grandmother had a boarding house. Teachers and bankers had rooms there and also their meals and would spoil the grandchildren. Grandmother also had a wonderful flower garden and had cows and they made their own butter. Needless to say, we adored visiting them."[23] Warren and Roxanne sold the boarding house in 1906 and retired to Newton County, Missouri, to the town of Neosho, its county seat. [24] They bought a nice house and property in town intending to live out their remaining years. [25] However, Warren's health did not improve. In March 1906, he wrote his will, leaving all his goods to Roxanne.[26] Finally, in 1907, after 25 years of fruitless effort, the government finally granted Warren a pension of $15 per month, beginning February 18, 1907.[27] However, it was too late to be of much help. His health continued to fail. He died of cancer at the age of 73 on April 4, 1909, in Neosho. His burial was in the Independent Order of Odd Fellows Cemetery, Neosho, Newton County, Missouri.[28]

Roxanne applied for, and immediately received a widows Civil War pension based on Warren's service.[29] In 1910, she was living alone in Neosho, Missouri, at 314 Grant Street, a widow at the age of 71. The census recorded her as the mother of six children, four of them surviving in 1910. Belle and Rosie preceded her in death. She declared on the census form that she lived on her "own income," and she owned the house she was living in free of mortgage.[30] Roxanne died at home of heart failure on December 3, 1917, as the sun was setting about 6 o'clock in the evening.[31] Her death certificate cited "old age."[32] Her burial was in the I.O.O.F. Cemetery of Neosho beside Warren.[33]

The six children of Warren Smith Fellows and Roxanne (Thompson) Fellows were 1) Flora Amanda Fellows (1857–1935), 2) Willie Ira Fellows

(1859–1945), 3) Isabella S. (aka Belle) Fellows (1863–1905), 4) Rosetta (aka Rosie) Fellows (1866–1901), 5) Ernest Samuel Fellows (1869–1941), and 6) Katie Caldonia Fellows (1872–1945).[34] The surviving children of the next Fellows generation came to Roxanne's funeral if they could. Belle (Fellows) Reid and Rose (Fellows) Daum preceded her in death. Katie (Fellows) Cowles could not come from her home in Jacksonville, Florida, because of illness. Flora (Fellows) Rutledge and her husband were there from Pittsburgh, Kansas; Ernest Fellows and his wife Jacqueline came from Sapulpa, Missouri, and Willie Ira came from his home at Jerico Springs, Missouri.[35]

The Fellows genealogy continued from Warren Smith Fellows and Roxanne (Thompson) Fellows to their oldest son Willie Ira Fellows.

Warren Smith Fellows (1835-1909) and Roxanne (Thompson) Fellows (1838-1917)

Fellows Home in Otsego County, New York. Flora Amanda (Fellows) Rutledge, daughter of Warren Smith Fellows, remembered staying in this house and going to school about 1865 when she was eight years old. Pictured at right are Flora and her husband, Rev. Johnson Keith Rutledge. Photo courtesy of Motta/Fulmer Family Tree 2011 and FAG 2015.

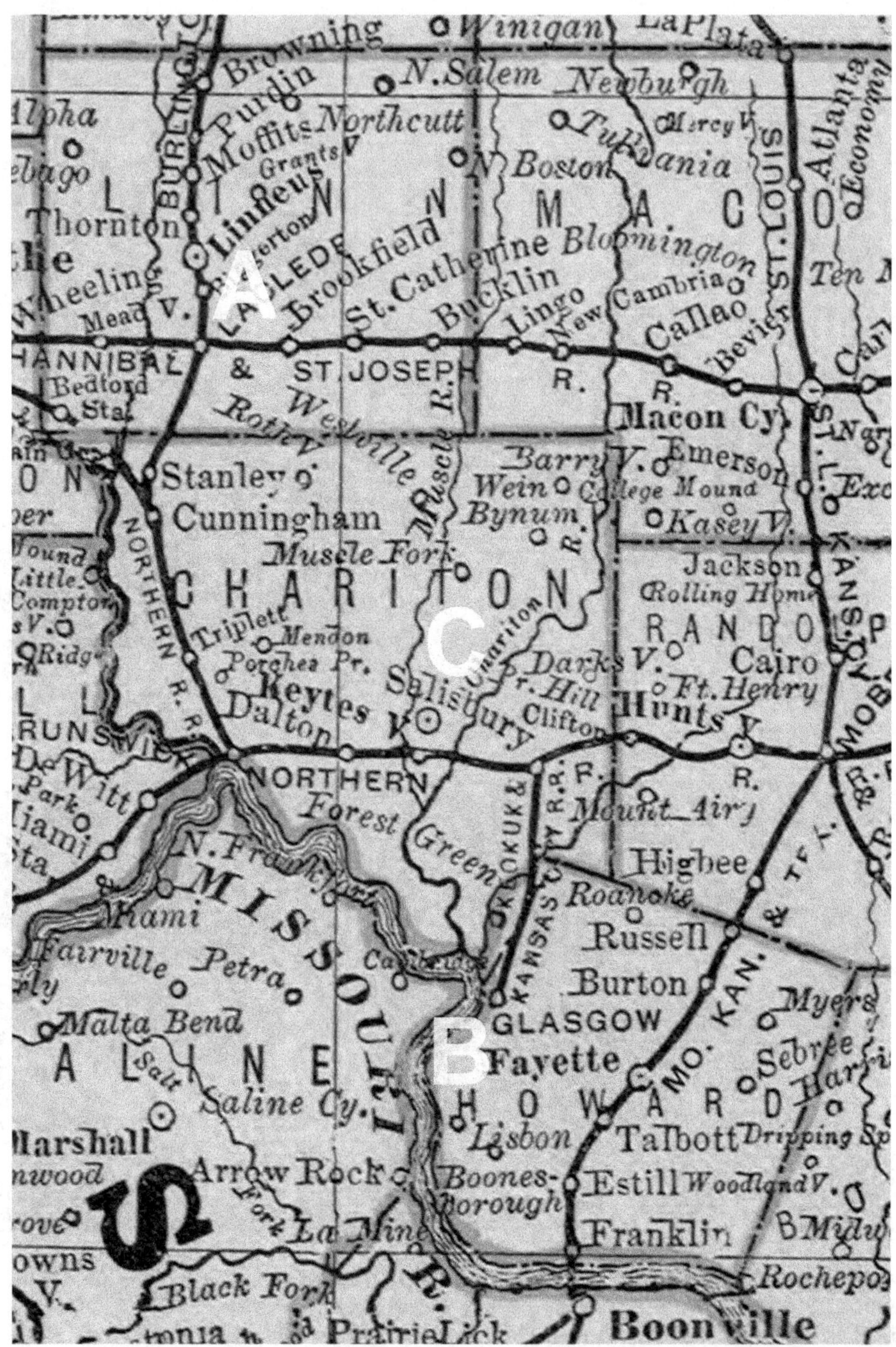

Map of Missouri Counties Linn, Chariton, and Howard. Warren S. Fellows settled in Missouri first at (A) Linn County, at Brookfield, in 1866; removing to (B) Howard County, in 1867, and then to (C) Salisbury, in Chariton County, in 1878. Dark lines on the map represent the railroads that served the region in 1878. Rand, McNally, 1878-79. Library of Congress.

Fellows Eighth Generation Family Group

Warren Smith FELLOWS was born on 22 Jun 1835 in Elk Creek, (Township of Maryland), Otsego County, New York. He died on 4 Apr 1909 in Neosho, Newton County, Missouri. His burial was in the Independent Order of Odd Fellows Cemetery, Neosho, Missouri. He was the son of **William B. FELLOWS** and **Nancy SPERRY**.

Warren married **Roxanne THOMPSON**, the daughter of **Samuel S. THOMPSON** and **Sarah BELL**, on 16 Mar 1855 in Otsego County, New York. Roxanne was born 6 Oct 1838 in Otsego County. She died on 3 Dec 1917 in Neosho, Newton County, Missouri. Her burial was in the I.O.O.F. Cemetery, Neosho, Missouri.

They had the following children.

1. **Flora Amanda Fellows** was born 6 Sep 1857 in Elk Creek, (Township of Maryland), Otsego County, New York. She died in 1935 in Ashdown, Little River County, Arkansas. Her burial was in Fairland Cemetery, Ottawa County, Oklahoma.[36] Flora married **Rev. Johnson Keith Rutledge** 21 Feb 1883. He was born 4 Oct 1856 in McDonough County, Illinois, the son of Richard William Rutledge and Emily Kerby. Rev. Rutledge died 21 Feb 1937 in Hinton, Caddo County, Oklahoma. His burial was in Fairland Cemetery, Ottawa County, Oklahoma.[37] Flora was a teacher and Johnson was a Methodist minister.[38]

\+ 2. **Willie (aka William) Ira FELLOWS** was born on 22 Jun 1859 in Elk Creek, (Township of Maryland), Otsego County, New York. He died on 1 Mar 1945 at home in Cedar County, Missouri. His burial was on 2 Mar 1945 in Brasher Cemetery, Jerico Springs, Cedar County, Missouri.[39] William married **Martha Frances CRUTCHFIELD**, daughter of **John James (Jack) CRUTCHFIELD** and **Frances HENDERSON**, on 27 Dec 1882 in Chariton County, Missouri. Martha was born on 27 Mar 1865 in Salisbury, Chariton County, Missouri. She died on 22 Jan 1943 in Sheldon, Barton County, Missouri. Her burial was in Brasher Cemetery, Cedar County, Missouri.

3. **Isabella S. (Belle) Fellows** was born 16 Apr 1863 in Elk Creek, (Township of Maryland), Otsego County, New York. She died 10 Dec 1905. Her burial was in Salisbury Cemetery, Salisbury, Chariton County, Missouri.[40] She married **Arthur W. Reid**, son of John J. Reid and Emily Springer, on 14 Mar 1888 in Lincoln, Nebraska. Arthur was born 3 Oct 1863, in Kalamazoo County,

Michigan. He died 1 Jan 1947 at Hannibal, Marion County, Missouri. His burial was in Salisbury Cemetery, Salisbury, Chariton County, Missouri.[41]

4. **Rosetta (Rosie) Ella Fellows** was born 2 Dec 1866 in Elk Creek, (Township of Maryland), Otsego County, New York, while her father was in Missouri.[42] She died 24 Apr 1901 at the age of 34 in Lawrence, Kansas. Her burial was in Oak Hill Cemetery, Lawrence, Douglas County, Kansas.[43] She married **Nicholas Freeland Daum** in 1887. He was the son of John and Susanna Daum, born in 1855. He died in 1935. His burial was in Oak Hill Cemetery, Lawrence, Douglas County, Kansas.[44] At various different times, the couple lived in Kansas, Nebraska, and Missouri.[45] Rosie worked as a dressmaker in Lawrence, Kansas.[46] Family tradition says she wrote a book but copies appear no longer to be extant. Her obituary appeared in the Ness City, Kansas, newspaper where her parents resided at the time of her death.[47]

5. **Ernest Samuel Fellows** was born 5 Jun 1869 in Fayette, Howard County, Missouri. He died in 1941 at Newburg, Phelps County, Missouri. His burial was in Maple Park Cemetery, Springfield, Greene County, Missouri.[48] He married **Jacqueline Barnd** of Ness City, Kansas. She was born in 1873 and died in 1969. Her burial was in Maple Park Cemetery, Springfield, Missouri.[49] The 1880 census listed Ernest Fellows as being born in New York. However, he was the first of the Fellows to be born in Missouri. The census also erroneously listed his sister Katie C. Fellows as being the same age as Ernest and born in Missouri.

6. **Katie (aka Kay) Caldonia Fellows** was born in 1872 in Salisbury, Chariton County, Missouri. She died 1 Mar 1945 in Miami Beach, Florida. Ironically, her death preceded that of her older brother Willie Ira by only a few hours.[50] Katie married **Harry Mills Cowles** 23 Jun 1894 in Pueblo, Colorado. He was the son of Mills Glenville Cowles and Annette Eigmey, born 10 Dec 1871 in Chicago, Cook County, Illinois. He died May 1960 in Miami, Dade County, Florida.

13

Willie Ira Fellows

Willie (aka William and Will) Ira Fellows was born on June 22, 1859, at Elk Creek, (Town of Maryland), Otsego County, New York. He was one of seven children and the oldest son born to Warren Smith and Roxanne (Thompson) Fellows.[1] He started school at Cherry Valley in Otsego County with his older sister Flora Amanda while the family lived on the Strail property in 1865, the year their father returned from the Civil War. Willie's first grade teacher was Miss Lizzie Western who began his journey through the one-room rural public schools.[2]

Willie Ira was seven years old when his mother took the family by train out of Schenevus, Otsego County, New York, to Missouri, a journey of more than twelve hundred miles into the Midwest, to Linn County, Missouri, where they joined his father in 1867. Warren Fellows had settled there the year before to prepare a place for his family. They lived on a farm near Brookfield, Missouri, a small town of about 400 residents on the Hannibal and St. Joseph Railroad, a town roughly the size of Schenevus, New York. Flora Amanda and Willie Ira enrolled in a country school outside Brookfield. He wrote in his autobiography, "The teacher was a young man by the name of George R. Huffacre, a fine young man. The schoolhouse was a log building and we had split logs for seats. They took logs about twelve inches through and halved them, hewed off part of the splinters (not all of them) and bored holes in them and put in wooden legs. We didn't do much sliding along the seats. There were no churches closer than town, the Hard-shelled Baptists held meetings in some of the houses."[3]

Life in the Missouri countryside left indelible memories for a young child. For example, Willie Ira recalled, "We made sorghum molasses by grinding the cane with a wooden cane mill and boiled it down in iron kettles. The molasses was about the color of tar and about as good to eat. We gathered wild crabapples and put them in a kettle of molasses before it was done, and cooked them until the apples were soft and called it apple butter, but we had another name for it."[4]

In 1868, his father sold the Linn County farm and moved the family to a place a few miles from the towns of Glasgow and Fayette, in Howard County, Missouri, near the Missouri River. It was superb tobacco-growing country. Growers prepped the land and planted tobacco seeds in late winter to early spring to plant a crop in mid-spring. Willie Ira described the process, "The plants would be large enough to set out in May, and the new ground was plowed and put in fine shape, laid off in rows with a single shovel plow and then hills were made about three feet apart and the plants set in them. That was a backbreaking job. After the tobacco got ripe, they cut it, hung it on four-foot hickory sticks, and hung it in the barns. When it was thoroughly cured, they would take it down and put it in large bulks. Generally, in February, when the weather was damp, they would cover the bulks with old quilts to keep it dry, so that they could strip it. When it was stripped, they would put it in hands about what you could hold between your thumb and middle finger and then take a leaf of tobacco and fold it up and tie it around the bulk and put it down in the bulks again. The neighbors would all go to some ones place called a tobacco stripping and strip the crop in one day. The women would all go and have a big dinner, and generally, the young people would have a dance at night. Those were the good times.

"After the tobacco was stripped, it was put down in bulk and covered up to keep until buyers would come around in March and buy the tobacco. There were tobacco factories in all the towns and the farmers would haul the tobacco to the factories where it was put in bulk and then the tobacco was sorted, generally by Negro men and women. After it was sorted and tied up in hands, it would be put in bulk again and kept there until ready to ship. When ready to ship, it was put in large hogsheads, about 2,000 pounds in each one. It was then put on a riverboat and taken to market. All shipping was done on the river."[5]

The flatland watershed of the Missouri River was dramatically different from the rolling hills of Otsego County, New York, and Elk Creek. One of Willie Ira's best memories as a boy was going down to Boones Lick Park in Glasgow to pick hickory nuts. Glasgow straddled the county line between Howard and Chariton counties on the bank of the Missouri River. Boones Lick Park was one of many such sites in the valley of Salt Creek in southwestern Howard County known for its early 19th century salt manufacturing industry. Here, several saline springs seeped to the surface. Animals such as deer, elk, and bison once gathered at the springs literally to lick the ground to obtain the salt. Nathan and Daniel Morgan Boone, sons of famed frontiersman Daniel Boone, began making salt here in 1805.

There were many stories about growing up in Howard County, living and working on the farm. "When we moved there in 1868," wrote Willie Ira, "they cut all the grain with cradles and bound it by hand. I was nine years old then, and I carried the bundles and father shocked them. There were three cradles and three bundles. The thrashing machines were small and run with horsepower… It took twelve to fifteen horses and mules to run it. It was a great improvement over the old ways of tromping out the grain with stock."[6] Looking back, he said, "I started plowing when I was ten, plowed sixty years, and never missed a season."[7] In 1870, the census recorded Willie Ira and the Fellows family in Chariton Township, in Howard County.[8] He filled in details of life at the time in his autobiography. "The people all rode horse-back or mule-back and the women sideways with long black riding skirts. There was a Baptist church in the community called the Old Mount Marin Church and if standing now [1940] it would be about 126 years old… It was built of brick and the seats were of black walnut, handmade. I went to Sunday school there in the early 1870's."[9] The Fellows going back generations were lifelong members of the Methodist Episcopal Church. However, not all communities had nearby Methodist congregations, and the Baptists were especially prevalent in Missouri.

In 1878, when Willie Ira was 19, and about grown, his father sold the Howard County farm and moved across the county line north to Salisbury Township, in Chariton County, where he bought land and where Willie Ira continued to work on the Fellows family farm.[10] The 1880 census listed him and all his siblings living in the Warren and Roxanne Fellows household. Listed, too, was Olin A. Fellows, Warren's brother, who recently arrived from New York following the death of Nancy (Sperry) Fellows, matriarch of the family in 1879.[11]

Willie Ira cast his first vote in 1880 for Republican candidate James A. Garfield, voting as Fellows voters had voted since the inauguration of the Republican Party, and ever thereafter.

On December 27, 1882, he married a local Salisbury girl named Martha Frances Crutchfield. Of Virginia roots, she was the 16-year-old daughter of John James (Jack) Crutchfield and Frances (Henderson) Crutchfield.[12] A family story told about Martha Frances said that she weighed only three pounds at birth. "You could put a teacup over her head," so the story went. Martha was a religious person, and grew up with strong ties to the Pleasant Woods Methodist Church near her home.[13] Martha was the granddaughter of William Blane Crutchfield. He was born April 14, 1814, in North Carolina and removed to northern Missouri in 1838 soon after his marriage to Martha Matlock in North Carolina.[14] They had 10 children, all born in Missouri including John James Crutchfield, father of Martha Frances (Crutchfield) Fellows.[15]

The newlywed couple lived for three years on the Warren Fellows family farm while Willie Ira continued to work as a farmhand. In the spring of 1886, Martha and Willie Ira homesteaded 160 acres of land in Ness County, Kansas, and with their two small children, they removed to western Kansas.[16] He wrote about the difficulty of the move. "We unloaded our car at Wakeeney, Kansas. Our claim was thirty-five miles due south of Wakeeney, and that was the closest railroad. The Union Pacific at Wakeeney and the old Santa Fe railroad on the Arkansas River were the only railroads in that country. Our homestead was in Ness County, eight miles north of Ness City. We lived in a sod house, burned cow chips, fought fleas and bed bugs, centipedes and rattlesnakes." They lived for about two years in Kansas before moving back to Missouri and settling in Cedar County, in southwest Missouri, in 1888. Ironically, Willie Ira's father Warren Fellows retired from farming in Chariton County, Missouri, and had opened a boarding house in Ness City, Kansas, in 1887, perhaps with the thought of living near his eldest son, who at that time lived near Ness City. However, Willie Ira wrote, "We then proved up on the claim and got a deed for it, put a $600 mortgage on it and traded it off for a three-year-old bull, sight unseen. We sold the bull for $25.00 and started back to Missouri. My wife and baby [John Roscoe "Jack" Fellows] came back on the train and visited with her folks until I drove through and bought a place. That was in the fall of 1888. I made the trip in a covered wagon and arrived a few days before election. I lost my vote and that was the year Cleveland ran for the second term and was beaten by Harrison."[17]

Willie Ira and Martha bought land on Horse Creek, in Benton Township, Cedar County, Missouri, near the newly established post office of Osiris. One of the first items of business was to join the Fairview Methodist Church. The closest town of any size was the village of Jerico Springs but there was a good school across the road from Osiris and within walking distance of the Fellows farm. The 1900 census found the Fellows children, those of school age, enrolled in school. By 1900, the Fellows family included seven children, ages two to 15. Regrettably, baby Charlie Fellows died in January 1897 when he was not yet five months old. They laid him to rest on a cold winter's day in rural Brasher Cemetery a few miles from the family farm.[18]

By 1910, Willie and Martha had a strong presence in rural Cedar County. Their family was complete, eight children living—five boys and three girls; Claude and Belle had married and started their own families; others were finishing school at Fairview School a short distance from the Fellows farmstead. Willie Ira paid off the mortgage on the farm, and he and Martha looked ahead to retirement.[19] Claude moved in with them and took over the duties of looking after the farm. The children married and moved off to other places. Jack and Lee enlisted for World War I and served in France; both returned safely home but like their grandfather before them in the Civil War, their health was ruined.[20] In 1920, only two of the Fellows siblings, Lester and Jack, remained at home on the family farm.[21]

In 1932, because of diabetes, gangrene set in and Willie Ira lost his right leg, amputated at the hip. He spent his final years in a wheelchair. He kept an optimistic outlook on life. He wrote in his autobiography in 1940, "I bought some land on Horse Creek in Cedar County and have lived on the 210 acres most of the time for the past fifty-two years. We raised a family of eight children: Claude, Belle, Jack, Lee, Maud, Irl, Effie, and Lester. Most of them are married and live close to us and are the best children in the world, always ready to help us. I lost my right leg in 1932 and was 72 years old then and am spending my last days in a wheel chair. I was 81 years old the 22nd of June, 1940, My wife was 75 years old last March 27th, 1940. She is blind and bedridden so our last days are not very pleasant, but we know our children will not let us suffer. The 27th day of next December 1940, we will have been married 58 years."[22] Although blind, Martha, so the story goes, retained a keen sense of awareness. Her children would come to her bed, touch her toes, and she could tell which one it was.[23]

Only two of Willie Ira's siblings were still living in 1940: Ernest and Katie. Toward the end of his life, Willie returned to the memories of his childhood, lovingly writing in his autobiography, "Mother and the girls would dry apples and peaches, and father built a drying house in a log shed in the yard where the fruit was dried. They would work all fall drying the fruit. The apples were peeled on paring machines and then quartered and the core taken out. The cull apples were made into cider for vinegar. They would dry a large wagonload of apples, sell them, and get us children clothes, shoes, and books for winter. When it got cold, we would pick our winter apples and put them in bins made of rails and lined with straw to keep them dry and the fruit from freezing. There was not much fruit canned. Some peaches were put up in earthen jars with earthen lids and hot sealing wax run around the lid.[24]

"When winter came the neighbors would come in the evenings to stay until bedtime and we would gather around the large fireplace in the sitting room. The first thing to pass around was a large basket of apples. When they grew tired of eating apples, we would bring in a basket of all kinds of nuts. One would crack and the rest would eat, using horseshoe nails to pick out the nutmeats. When they got tired of eating nuts and apples, the girls would shell popcorn, rake out some coals from the fireplace, and pop corn until we were all full. We would rest awhile, then someone would go down in the cellar and get a pitcher of cider, and we would drink cider until they went home. Everyone went home feeling good. That was the happiest time of my life."[25]

The good times of youth gave way to the infirmaries of old age. Blind for several years, suffering from heart disease, and after many months of illness, Martha died of Pneumonia January 22, 1943, at the age of 77, at Doylesport Hospital in Sheldon, in northeast Barton County, Missouri.[26] She spent the last two years of her life at Sheldon where her sons lived.[27] Her son Jack informed authorities of her passing. Martha went to rest in Brasher Cemetery beside the grave of her infant son.[28] Her death ended a marriage with Willie Ira Fellows of 60 years.

Willie Ira died at the age of 85 of a brain hemorrhage on March 2, 1945, at 9:45 in the evening, at home on the family farm in rural South Benton Township, Cedar County, where he had lived for more than 56 years.[29] They buried him in Brasher Cemetery, beside Martha and Charlie.[30] He was the last of the Fellows children to pass. Ernest had died in 1941, and his sister Katie preceded Willie Ira in death by only a few hours, dying in Miami Beach, Florida, on March 1, 1945.[31]

Newspaper clippings and records of family reunions remembered a family tradition that Willie Ira was a great writer and scribe. Education was always central to his life. He was a member of the school board, the roads commission, and a popular and highly respected figure in the community. People knew him as someone who "was interested in everything that went toward making his community a better place in which to live." When the Fairview Church burned, he was among the first to step forward to help rebuild it. He had a longtime interest in family history. In 1940, probably between the months of July and November, he applied his writing skills to produce his memoir of the Fellows family.[32]

Willie was a patriotic man, and especially proud of the military service of his offspring. Two of his sons served in World War I, and seven of his grandsons enlisted in World War II.[33] The Bible mentioned by Willie Ira and carried by his father in the Civil War, and by his son Jack Fellows in World War I, went through World War II and the Korean War in the possession of Wayne Fellows, son of Claude Fellows, grandson of Willie Ira, and great grandson of Warren Smith Fellows, the Civil War veteran.[34]

Willie Ira and Martha had nine children. All survived their parents, except Charley.[35] The Fellows genealogy continued from Willie Ira and Martha (Crutchfield) Fellows to their daughter, Mary Belle Fellows who married Thomas Edward Cardwell.

Four of the Six Children of Warren Smith Fellows and Roxanne (Thompson) Fellows. Pictured are Ernest, Willie Ira, Flora Amanda, and Kate Caldonia. Not shown are Rose Fellows and Belle Fellows. Rose died in 1901 and Belle died in 1905. Photo private collection, dated circa 1906.

Willie Ira and Martha Frances (Crutchfield) Fellows Family. Rear, left to right standing: Claude Arthur Fellows, Maude (Shepherd) Fellows, Ray Potter, Katie Maude Fellows, Effie Jane Fellows, Mary Belle (Fellows) Cardwell, Thomas Edward Cardwell, John Roscoe "Jack" Fellows, and Lee Crutchfield Fellows. Front, left to right seated: William Irl Fellows, Lester Smith Fellows, Willie Ira Fellows, Martha Frances (Crutchfield) Fellows and an unidentified girl. Photo circa late fall 1914 taken at the family farm in South Benton Township, Cedar County, Missouri. The estimated date of this undated photograph is from the marriage date of Katie Maude Fellows to Ray Potter in 1915.

Willie Ira Fellows (1859–1945) Martha (Crutchfield) Fellows (1865-1943)

Cedar County. Willie Ira Fellows owned a farm (circle) in Section 19 of Twp. 34-N Range 28-W, popularly known as Benton Township, in southwest Cedar County. The closest population centers were Jerico Springs, four miles southeast; and Montevallo, about five miles northwest in Vernon County (not shown on this map). The village of Wagoner in Linn Township was about 6.5 miles west on the Wagoner Road. It was 14 miles from the Fellows farm to Stockton, the county seat of Cedar County. *Standard Atlas of Cedar County*, 1908. Library of Congress.

The Fellows Family. Left to right: John Roscoe "Jack" Fellows, Lee Crutchfield Fellows, Lester Smith Fellows, Claude Arthur Fellows, William Irl Fellows, Willie Ira Fellows, Mary Belle (Fellows) Cardwell, Martha Frances (Crutchfield) Fellows, Effie Jane (Fellows) Ready, and Katie Maude (Fellows) Potter. Photograph c.1940,

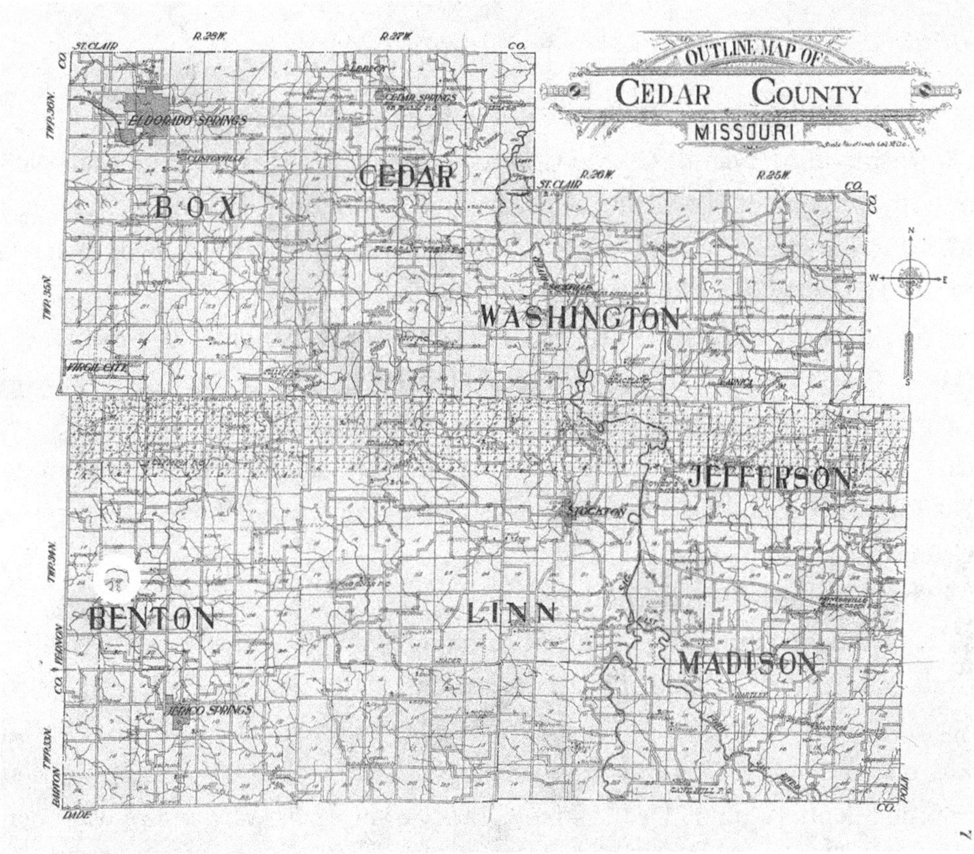

OUTLINE MAP OF
CEDAR COUNTY
MISSOURI
ST. CLAIR
R.28W.
R.27W.
CO.
R.26W.
R.25W.
EL DORADO SPRINGS
CEDAR SPRINGS
VIRGIL CITY
STOCKTON
JERICO SPRINGS
BOX
CEDAR
WASHINGTON
JEFFERSON
LINN
BENTON
MADISON
DADE

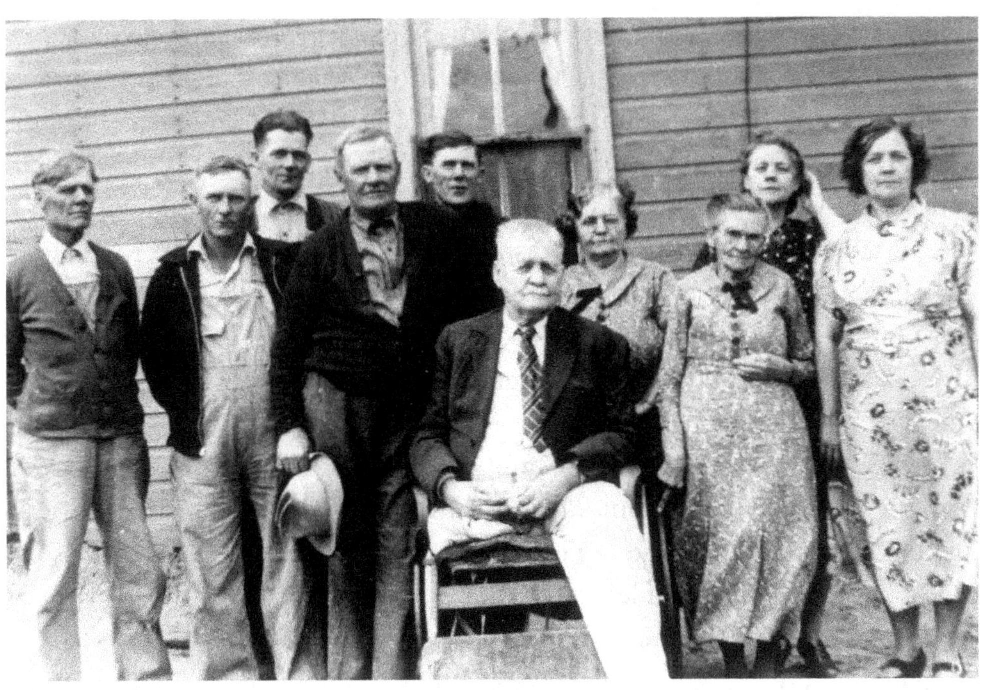

Fellows Ninth Generation Family Group

Willie (William) Ira FELLOWS was born on 22 Jun 1859 in Elk Creek, (Township of Maryland) Otsego County, New York.[36] He died on 1 Mar 1945 at home, in Benton Township, Cedar County, Missouri. His burial was on 2 Mar 1945 in Brasher Cemetery, Cedar County.[37] He was the son of **Warren Smith FELLOWS** and **Roxanne THOMPSON**.

Willie married **Martha Frances CRUTCHFIELD**, daughter of **John James (Jack) CRUTCHFIELD** and **Frances HENDERSON**, on 27 Dec 1882 in Chariton County, Missouri. Martha was born on 27 Mar 1865 in Salisbury, Chariton County, Missouri. She died on 22 Jan 1943 at Sheridan, (Township of Doylesport), Barton County, Missouri. Her burial was in Brasher Cemetery, Cedar County, Missouri.

They had the following children.

1. **Claude Arthur Fellows** was born on 30 Sep 1884 in Salisbury, Chariton County, Missouri. He died of heart disease on 11 Aug 1956 at home, near Jerico Springs, rural South Benton Township, Cedar County, Missouri.[38] His burial was on 13 Aug 1956 in Brasher Cemetery, Cedar County.[39] Claude married **Maude Shepherd** on 25 Dec 1908 in Cedar County, Missouri. Maud was born Sep 1889, the daughter of Jefferson Davis Shepherd and Elisa Jane McClease. Maude was from Walker, Vernon County, Missouri. The marriage ended in divorce. Claude married secondly **Gladys Hope Lester**, daughter of Joseph Lester and Flora (last name unspecified), on 21 Oct 1941.[40] Hope was born on 3 Mar 1903 in Kingston, Caldwell County, Missouri. She died on 11 Oct 1976 in the Medi-Center, Springfield, Greene County, Missouri, after a long illness. Her burial was on 13 Oct 1976 in Brasher Cemetery, Cedar County, Missouri.[41]

Claude Fellows came with his parents to Cedar County when he was about four years old. He spent most of his life farming in Cedar County. Soon after their marriage, Claude and Maude rented a farm in Benton Township, near other members of the Fellows family. He and his brother Jack began as grain farmers.[42] He remained in Cedar County his entire life, except for about eight years in Bartlesville, Oklahoma. It was during this time that his marriage to Maude Shepherd ended in divorce between 1920 and 1930. Their sons continued to live with Claude.[43]

Claude was portly in late middle age, about 5 feet 7 inches tall, 190 pounds, light complexioned, and prematurely gray with blue eyes.[44] He married secondly to Gladys Hope Lester who came to Jerico Springs from Caldwell County, in north Missouri in 1937. She was a schoolteacher before entering business as a private secretary. In later years, the couple lived with Claude's aging parents on the farm northwest of Osiris, Missouri. After Martha and Willie Ira died in 1943 and 1945 respectively, Claude and Hope occupied the old Home Place. After Claude died in 1956, Hope continued to live on the farm until 1974 when she moved into Jerico Springs. Claude and Maude had two sons: Elmo Fellows who lived at De Queen, Arkansas, and Wayne A. Fellows of Neosho, Missouri. Wayne served in World War II and went by the name "Sarge." He was born 4 Oct 1911 and died 6 Jun 1979. His burial was in Brasher Cemetery near his father Claud and grandfather Willie Ira Fellows. He married firstly Marie S. Jackson in Colorado Springs, Colorado. The marriage ended in divorce. He married secondly Ellen Louise (Oliver) Newton in Noblesville, Indiana, 25 Dec 1972. She died 16 Jul 2003 at Stockton Nursing Home, Cedar County, Missouri. Her burial was in Brashear Cemetery.[45]

\+ 2. **Mary Belle FELLOWS** was born on 29 Sep 1885 near Salisbury, Chariton County, Missouri. She died on 1 Aug 1958 at the home of her daughter Beatrice (Cardwell) Richardson, in Cedar County, Missouri, from Stroke. Her burial was on 4 Aug 1958 in Brasher Cemetery, Cedar County, Missouri. Belle married **Thomas Edward CARDWELL**, son of **Edward CARDWELL** and **Anna Eliza BALDWIN**, on 10 Apr 1904 in the home of Linsa Ward, Osiris, Cedar County, Missouri. The marriage ended in divorce. Thomas Cardwell was born in Feb 1881. He died on 25 Jan 1944 in Ozark Hospital, Springfield, Greene County, Missouri, from a wood saw accident. His burial was in Gum Springs Cemetery, Linn Township, Cedar County, Missouri.

3. **John Roscoe (Jack) Fellows** was born on 28 Jun 1887 in Ness County, Kansas. He died on 25 Apr 1947 in Milford, Vernon County, Missouri.[46] His burial was on 26 Apr 1947 in Sheldon Cemetery, Sheldon, Vernon County. Jack did not marry. In 1910, Jack lived with his brother Claude and later with his brother Irl on the farm outside Montevallo, Missouri.[47] Jack drowned in 1947 at the age of 59. The local paper carried the news of the accident. "The body of John (Jack) Roscoe Fellows, fifty nine, was discovered in the well at the home place north of Milford by the deceased's brother, Irl, about seven o'clock Friday morning. Jack and Irl batched together on the farm. The former arose Friday morning and left the house to do the chores. The latter remained in the house to prepare breakfast. When the meal was ready and Jack had not returned, Irl

went out to call him. He searched in the barn and all about the place but to no avail. Later he noted that the well rope was broken and that a board in the platform was broken through. The tragic signals immediately indicated the fate of his missing brother. Apparently, Jack had first started in to water the stock when he left the house. There was evidence that he had drawn one bucket of water from the well. In the act of lifting the second bucket of water from the well, the rope snapped. This threw the deceased off balance and a rotten board in the platform let him down into the well. Although the victim's brother discovered the body not a great while later, when the body was gotten out of the well with the help of neighbors, it was apparent that no efforts at resuscitation would be of any use."[48] A rumor that persisted among family members told that Jack might have drowned himself in the well. However, no mention of suicide is in any of the public records.

4. **Lee Crutchfield Fellows** was born on 26 Oct 1888 in Salisbury, Chariton County, Missouri.[49] He died on 22 Nov 1970 in Community Nursing Home, Eldorado Springs, Cedar County, Missouri, from Stroke.[50] His burial was on 24 Nov 1970 in Dunnegan Grove Cemetery, Sheldon, Vernon County, Missouri.[51] As a veteran of World War I, Lee received burial with full military honors. Lee married **Pauline Richey**, daughter of William Bert Richey and Louisa Lutie Hall, on 29 Feb 1920.[52] The marriage ended in divorce. Pauline was born on 17 Feb 1902 in Bona, Dade County, Missouri. She died on 31 Jul 1974 in Nevada City Hospital, Nevada, Vernon County, Missouri, following a long illness. Her burial was on 3 Aug 1974 in Dunnegan Grove Cemetery, Sheldon, Vernon County, Missouri.[53] Lee spent his early childhood in Chariton County, Missouri. He served in World War I, became ill during the war, and spent time recovering at the Veterans Hospital in Wadsworth, Kansas.[54] He was of slender build about 135 pounds, medium height, and light complexion with brown hair and blue eyes.[55] When Lee and Pauline first married in 1920, they bought a farm in Benton Township, Cedar County, near Lee's parents and other members of the Fellows family.[56] After the couple divorced, Lee was a longtime resident of Jerico Springs, Missouri, and spent several years living at Nevada, Missouri, where his son Merle lived, except for a short time when he lived in Idaho.[57] Pauline lived most of her live in Vernon County where she worked many years at Nevada State Hospital as a Psychiatric Aide, LPN. Lee and Pauline had four children: 1) William Everett, 2) Charles Warren who died in infancy, 3) Merle D. Fellows, and 4) Frances Maxine (Fellows) Cross.[58]

5. **Katie Maude Fellows** was born on 12 Dec 1890 in Cedar County, Missouri. She died on 5 Jan 1983 in Community Nursing Home, El Dorado Springs, Cedar County, Missouri.[59] Her burial was on 8 Jan 1983 in Wagoner Cemetery, Cedar County, Missouri.[60] Katie married **Ray Potter**, son of Daniel Louis Potter and Marcella I. Cox on 17 Feb 1915. Ray was born on 14 Dec 1893 in Cedar County, Missouri. He died on 3 Sep 1979 in Cedar County Memorial Hospital, El Dorado Springs, Cedar County, Missouri.[61] His burial was on 5 Sep 1979 in Wagoner Cemetery, Cedar County, Missouri.[62] Maude lived to the age of 92, living most of her life southeast of Montevallo, near Olympia in Cedar County where she and Ray owned a farm. Some genealogists list her first name as Kathryn. Her namesake was an aunt named Katie Caledonia. Maude did not go by the name Kathryn. Her middle name appears in records as both Maud and Maude. Maude and Ray had one son, Lloyd Preston Potter.

6. **William (Willie) Irl Fellows** was born on 7 Sep 1893 in Jerico Springs, Cedar County, Missouri. He died on 22 Jan 1973 in Lakeside Hospital, Kansas City, Jackson County, Missouri, following a prolonged illness. His burial was on 27 Jan 1973 in Sheldon Cemetery, Vernon County, Missouri.[63] William married **Wanda Horrocks** 28 Sep 1916 in Jerico Springs, Cedar County, Missouri, the daughter of David B. and Minnie Horrocks.[64] The marriage ended in divorce. Wanda was born 23 Apr 1900 in Missouri. She died 23 May 1985 in Yerington, Lyon County, Nevada. Irl rented a farm in 1920 near his parents and siblings in Benton Township, Cedar County, Missouri.[65] He lived and farmed for most of his adult life in the Milford, Missouri, area before moving to Kansas City to live with his daughter.[66] He became blind toward the end of his life and died in Kansas City.[67] Irl and Wanda had one daughter, Lila (Fellows) Halterman. Wanda married secondly to James David Maloney.

7. **Charlie P. Fellows** was born on 5 Sep 1896 in Jerico Springs, Cedar County, Missouri. He died in infancy on 29 Jan 1897 at the age of four months in Cedar County, Missouri. [68] His burial was in Brasher Cemetery, Jerico Springs, Cedar County.[69]

8. **Effie Jane Fellows** was born on 13 Feb 1898 in Jerico Springs, Cedar County, Missouri.[70] She died on 15 Apr 1988 in Heartland Nursing Home, Fulton, Callaway County, Missouri.[71] Her burial was on 17 Apr 1988 in Hillcrest Cemetery, Fulton, Callaway County.[72] Effie married **Joseph Pearl Ready** on 7 Apr 1914 in the family home at Jerico Springs, Cedar County, Missouri.[73] The marriage ended in divorce. Joseph was born on 27 Oct 1893 in Wise, Vernon

County, Missouri. He died on 7 Oct 1971 at University Place, Tacoma, Pierce County, Washington. His burial was in Mountain View Memorial Park, Lakewood, Pierce County, Washington.[74] Effie Jane Fellows lived in Fulton, Missouri, for more than 30 years, except for a brief time when she lived at Kansas City, Missouri. Effie and Joseph had three sons: 1) Delbert, 2) Cleve, and 3) Archie Ready. Effie wrote a brief biography of the Fellows family for her son Archie.

9. **Lester Smith Fellows** was born on 26 Apr 1901 in Jerico Springs, Cedar County, Missouri. He died on 15 Feb 1975 in Barton County memorial Hospital, Lamar, Barton County, Missouri. His burial was on 18 Feb 1975 in Howell Cemetery, near Milford, Barton County.[75] Lester married **Mary Etta Crites** daughter of Perry M. Crites and Mary Jane Faubion 12 April 1944 in Milford, Barton County, Missouri. Etta was born 12 Mar 1906. She died 13 Sep 1997. Her burial was in Howell Cemetery, Barton County, Missouri.[76] Lester was the youngest of the Fellows children. He made his home at Milford near Sheldon, Missouri, for more than 30 years. He kept a store and was an avid croquet player. He built a croquet court next to the store that was a center of entertainment for the Milford community.[77] He died at the age of 73 following a long illness.[78] Etta lived to be 91. Lester and Etta did not have children.[79]

14

Cardwell Genealogy Introduction

Cardwell genealogy is a work in progress. It lacks the documentation needed to establish reliably connected branches of the family. Unlike the Fellows family and other family histories that enjoy broad agreement among historians, the present history of the Cardwell family is less universally accepted. Family historians have tried for years to piece together a coherent story of the Cardwell family but with generally inconclusive and often frustrating results. A Cardwell genealogist learns quickly to forgive wasted time, and be willing to start over again. Nevertheless, the number of Cardwell genealogies available shows the allure of the Cardwell name.

While many genealogies duplicate past efforts and add little that is new, a few historians stand out as significant contributors to the lineage of the Cardwell family. Ina Cardwell, Helen Hart Peyton, Allen Pendergraft, Charlie Bourland, and Rand Cardwell are among the contemporary historians who have added important research to family lore. In each case, they acknowledged unproven assumptions about their particular branch of the family tree. New research has updated parts of their work, but they remain nevertheless foremost among grassroots genealogists of the Cardwell name.

The advent of the Internet introduced a new wave of interest in the Cardwell family. Unfortunately, along with access to documents and records via available data collections in libraries and elsewhere, computerized genealogy enshrined many of the errors of past genealogists, and created endless lists of unproven relationships. Fortunately, among the modernists a few scholars see in technology a new opportunity to set the record straight. Foremost among them is Rand Cardwell. He started researching the Cardwell family in America in 1985, established the Cardwell Family Website, and began the Cardwell DNA Project, which seeks to identify the various distinct branches of the Cardwell Tree.

A dizzying array of surnames intended to broaden the base of Cardwell ancestry have added to the difficulty of sorting out the various pedigrees, most of which purport to descend from Thomas Cordell the Immigrant in 1636. While his story is part of the present genealogy, there is no proof that he was the progenitor of the Cardwell line that settled in Cedar County, Missouri.

It is certain that the Cardwells of true Cardwell lineage descended from a common ancestor, although skeptics believe that any attempt to identify the oldest patron father of the Cardwell family is doomed to failure because of so many variations of the Cardwell name. A common but unverified theory is that the name Cardwell is of Norman origin, derived from the Cardeville family of Normandy. This often-repeated notion assumes a connection to William the Conqueror in 1066, which established the family in England and Wales. Historians point to Richard de Cardeville of Southampton Shire and William de Cardeville of Wiltshire who lived about the year 1273, as being among the earliest recorded Cardwell ancestors.[1] A Thomas Cardville of Yorkshire, England, appeared on a list of the Yorkshire Poll Tax of 1379.

Over the course of time, and suffering the phonetic interpretations of countless scribes, variations of the Cardwell name appeared. The ancient English records contain many such variations: Cardeville, Cardevile, Cardevill, Cardewelle, Cardewell, Cardewille, Cardewill, Cardwill, Cardell, Cardill, Cardwelle, and Cardwell, to name some.[2] Derivations of the Cardwell name experienced additional iterations in America. For example, genealogists assumed the first Cardwell immigrant to America was an Englishman recorded on the ship's passenger list as Thomas Cordell. His descendants spelled the name as Cordell, Cordwell, and Cardwell, often of different spellings within the same generation. A family that began as Cordell or Cordwell became Cardwell depending on which clerk wrote the public record.

The genealogical record must also distinguish among immigrants of different vintages, further complicating the distinction of a clear line of descent for a particular Cardwell branch. For instance, in the 17th century alone, James Cordell immigrated to America in 1654; William Cardwell, Jr., and William Cordwell, Sr. came in 1664, along with Nicholas Cartwell and John Cordwell in the same year.[3] Thomas Cordewell came in 1673/74, just to name a few, all destined for the British Colony of Virginia. It is unlikely that these immigrants were of the same immediate family as Thomas Cordell the Immigrant of 1636, not to mention the many Cardwells and those of related surnames who came later during the waves of immigration in the eighteenth and nineteenth centuries.[4]

Meanwhile, there are many anecdotes about Cardwell ancestors, none more charming perhaps than the story of the Cardwell triplets, Faith, Hope, and Charity. The triplets were born May 18, 1899, to Elza Cardwell and Eliza (Cartwright) Cardwell, in Elmore, Texas. They went without a name for six months, so the story goes, because their parents could not think of suitable names for them. They became something of a cause célèbre. President Grover Cleveland heard of them and suggested the names Faith, Hope, and Charity. They lived to be the oldest living triplets in the world at age 95, so recognized by the *Guinness Book of Records*.[5] This story and more like it present a glimpse of the sometimes-colorful lives that Cardwells lived from the colonial roots of America to the pioneer days of succeeding generations.

15

Thomas Cardwell the Immigrant

Historian William Smith Bryan wrote in 1876, "Thomas R. Cardwell, of England, (hereafter referred to as Thomas the Immigrant), came to America in 1636 and settled in present Richmond, Virginia. His children were John, Perrin, and George. John married Keziah Low, and they had John, Jr., Thomas, William, James, Wiltshire, George, Elizabeth, Nancy, Martha, Lucy, and Mary. George, son of Thomas Cardwell, Sr. (some name him as the son of John Jr.), married Anna Hamilton, and they had John, Elizabeth, William, Keziah, Martha, Mary, George, Jr., Jane, Rebecca, Wyatt, and James. George, Jr., married Ida Vansdoll, and settled in Missouri in 1832. Martha married William Shelley. Wyatt married May Woods and settled in Audrain County in 1834. Jane married William Woods. William married Barbara Sanford and settled in Audrain County in 1837. He was married a second time to Elizabeth Watts."[1] Notwithstanding inaccuracies in Bryan's 1876 Cardwell pedigree, the name of Elizabeth Watts of Audrain County is of particular interest in the present genealogy because a Cardwell descendant in Cedar County, Missouri, married another descendant of the Watts family. Samuel Watts, of Halifax County, Virginia, who was born in England, married Sally Burchett, and they had Rebecca, Daniel, Lizzie, Gillum, John, Roland, Joseph, Berry, Brackett, and Sally.[2] Lizzy (Elizabeth) Watts married Henry Strange of Halifax County, Virginia. Their Daughter Irene Strange married Henry Stegall, and their daughter Elizabeth Stegall married Reuben Granville Cardwell of Kentucky, probable descendant of Thomas Cardwell the Immigrant of Virginia. Reuben and Elizabeth settled in Cedar County, Missouri in 1857.

Cardwell family historian Allen Pendergraft realigned and expanded Bryan's 1876 genealogy to assign a birthdate of 1614 to Thomas the Immigrant, traced his arrival in America, and suggested the place of his origin in England. Pendergraft wrote, "Thomas Cordell [*sic*] emigrated from London to Virginia in 1636 on the ship *Tristram and Jane.*[3] Born by 1614 (assuming he was 21 when he emigrated) in Wiltshire, England. Judge George Cardwell of Hanover [Virginia] Court House recounted in 1942 a family tradition that the first Cardwell came from Wiltshire, England, via Wales in the early 1600s and settled on the south side of the Mattaponi River in what is now King William County 25 miles north of the colonial capital of Williamsburg."[4]

The genealogical record becomes less certain after Thomas the Immigrant. The Bryan genealogy of 1876 listed three sons: John, Perrin, and George. Pendergraft substituted a different list, viz.: William, Richard, Nathaniel, and Thomas, Sr. as probable descendants of Thomas the Immigrant. He also added a subsequent generation of Thomas Cardwell, Jr. who was the possible ancestor of Thomas Cardwell of Granville, North Carolina, and the Cardwell branch that settled in Cedar County, Missouri. Recent research of this Cardwell pedigree traces a line from Thomas the Immigrant, to Thomas Sr., to Thomas, Jr., to George, to John who married Keziah Low, to George, Jr., and finally to Thomas Cardwell of Granville.[5] However, this lineage awaits further proof and does not appear to match the lifedates of the different generations.

Notwithstanding the tenuous nature of much of Cardwell family history, genealogists generally agree that Thomas Cardwell the Immigrant was the first of the Cardwell name to immigrate to the New World. He was an indentured servant who came to Virginia at the age of 21 aboard the ship *Tristram and Jane*, which sailed from London in the spring of 1636. He listed his trade on the ship manifest as "barrel maker." Historians disagree on the origin of his English roots and the details of his movements in America, although he appears to have been the son of William Cardwell (1590-1660) and Mary Wiltshire (1592-1662) of Kirkham, Lancashire, England, who later moved to Thornhill Parish, Yorkshire, England. He landed at present Strawberry Banks, Hampton Roads, Virginia, in the fall of 1636, after passing through the Caribbean, and then up to Virginia where it was customary for ships to pick up the season's load of tobacco for transport back across the Atlantic.[6]

When Thomas Cardwell the Immigrant arrived in Virginia in 1636, the colony was only thirty years old, and only three years since England decreed it numerically large enough to justify division into shires. The colony survived the "Starving Time" during the Jamestown winter of 1609-1610 that took the colony to the brink of failure, and endured the Indian massacre of 1622 that wiped out nearly one-third of the white inhabitants. By 1636, tobacco planting had become a profitable trade, making Virginia a lucrative destination for London merchants wishing to capitalize on the growing colony.[7] It was on one such trade venture that Thomas the Immigrant arrived in Virginia aboard the London ship *Tristram and Jane.*

Historian Martha W. Hiden wrote a description of the ship's journey based on a log of accounts kept by the ship's master.[8] She wrote, "The *Tristram and Jane* probably left England in late summer or early fall of 1636, arriving in Virginia in time to take on the tobacco, which was ready for market by December. On the homeward voyage, the vessel probably reached London the latter part of March 1637. The ship took back to England 99 hogsheads of tobacco totaling 31,800 pounds."[9]

This voyage was typical of the many such trips that merchant ships made crisscrossing the Atlantic. Entrepreneurs brought goods and commodities from England to sell to the colonists, who in turn paid for such goods in tobacco, and sold the rest to the merchants who carried it back to London. The ships also transported the indentured servants of the headright labor system, a system necessary to sustain the labor-intensive routine of tobacco farming. Planters purchased the right to a servant by paying the cost of transport from England, and in return received a parcel of land for each servant, as well as the servant's services for an agreed period of time, usually a term of seven years, after which the servant became a free citizen able to have his own land and servants. Thomas Cardwell the Immigrant was one such indentured servant, a 21-year-old Englishman willing to enter indentured service in return for the cost of his voyage on the *Tristram and Jane.*

Historian Hiden stated in her analysis of the ship's cargo, "There were two paying passengers on the ship and 74 others who were sold as indentured servants for a term of years, the purchaser paying the cost of their transportation.[10] The purchaser, who acquired the immigrant's rights to patent fifty acres of land each, took the names of those persons whose rights he had bought to the court of the county where he lived and made oath that he had paid their transportation charges. Entry of this was made in the order book of the county, the acreage due him and the names of these persons (commonly called his 'headrights') were recorded, and he was given a certificate to this effect. On presentation of the certificate, the Secretary of the Colony issued a patent for the land."[11] The indentured servant headright system also applied to other trades in addition to tobacco farming.

The indenture assignment of Thomas the Immigrant was to John Neale, a merchant. Neale paid 1,000 pounds for his right, which was on the high side of the fees paid for other indentures on the *Tristram and Jane*.[12] His assignment to Master Neale does not mention a term of service nor his trade as a servant, except that he registered on the ship's manifest as a "barrel maker." There is reason to think that he may have been other than a tobacco farmer, although in later years that was his occupation. His association with John Neale also establishes a foothold in the geography of Tidewater Virginia where he landed in 1636. We learn that John Neale—merchant—on February 12, 1632, had taken a 21-year lease on 50 acres lying upon the Strawberry Banks within the precincts of Elizabeth City, "east upon the land of Lieutenant Edward Waters, west along the great river."[13] The great river was the part of Hampton Roads lying between Hampton Creek and Salter Creek.[14] This part of the Virginia Colony on Chesapeake Bay at the mouth of the James River was a favorite destination of London ships because of the many waterways that coursed through the Tidewater area, giving ready access to the trading ships that plied with their wares the isolated communities spread along the rivers' shores.

In 1632, when Master John Neale negotiated his lease in Elizabeth City precinct, the division of the colony into four corporations was still in force, and Elizabeth City was one of the four. Soon thereafter, the Virginia Company of London, proprietor of the colony, abandoned the four corporations, and in 1634, Virginia divided into eight shires or counties, including Elizabeth City as one of the eight.[15] Originally known by its Indian name, Kecoughtan, the English seized the Indian land and renamed it ever after as Elizabeth City Shire.

Elizabeth City Shire lay on the north shore of Hampton Roads, the name given to a body of water that comprised a wide channel into which flowed the James, Nansemond, and Elizabeth Rivers, and several smaller rivers before emptying into Chesapeake Bay and on into the Atlantic Ocean. One of the world's largest natural harbors, British colonists quickly recognized Hampton Roads as a prime location for settlement, shipbuilding, and commerce; and as a defensible location against Indian attacks. Old Point Comfort went up at

Hampton Roads in 1610. Well-traveled sloops kept a steady trade through this port to and from the Colony of Virginia.

Hiden, in her analysis of the movements of the *Tristram and Jane,* described Hampton Roads where Thomas Cardwell went ashore in Elizabeth City Shire at Strawberry Banks. "We would note the 'ports of call' of the *Tristram and Jane.* The first was Kickhowtan or Kecoughtan, the Indian name for Hampton, which settled in 1610." Here stood Fort Field and the great church. "Mr. George C. Mason in *Colonial Churches of Tidewater Virginia* stated that the Fort Field was the site of Forts Henry and Charles built by Sir Thomas Dale in 1610 on the eastern side of the mouth of Hampton Creek. He located the churchyard 'as the east end of College Place.' This was the church built after 1624 and in use in 1636. Mr. Mason described it from its foundations as being fifty-three feet six inches long by twenty-three feet wide."[16]

Hiden followed the ship's route, "After selling servants and commodities, the *Tristram and Jane* left Kecoughtan, passed Old Point, entered Chesapeake Bay, and then turned into Back River, which flows into the Bay. This river lies to the northwest of and "back" of Hampton as implied by its name, and was a well-settled area. It is formed by the union of two branches now styled Northwest and Southwest… Some eight or ten miles to the northwest lies Poquoson River, which in 1636 was known as New Poquoson. It too flows into Chesapeake Bay."[17] Michael Tepper, who republished the Hiden analysis, added, "It might be of interest to explain the use of the adjective 'New' Poquoson. It was not until 1630 that the Council and Governor issued an order for the securing and taking in of a tract of land called 'the forrest [*sic*], bordering upon the chiefe residence of the Pamunkey King, the most dangerous head of the Indian Enemie.' The area lying on York River and along the Poquoson River where patents were quickly taken up was therefore new territory in comparison with Back River, Kecoughtan, and Warwick where land had been cultivated over twenty years."[18]

Hiden continued, "After Back River, the *Tristram and Jane* touched at Old Poquoson and New Poquoson. We can be sure that at both places commodities and servants were sold and hogsheads of tobacco taken on. Turning at New Poquoson the *Tristram and Jane* came down the Bay and headed across to Accomack, as the entire Eastern Shore of Virginia was then called. It seems likely that after leaving Accomack, the boat sailed back through Hampton Roads and across James River into Chuckatuck Creek and Nansemond River. She may also have gone up the James River to its junction with the

Appomattox." Hiden's basis for this conjecture is the place of residence of the purchasers of the ship's wares. They lived mainly in Elizabeth City, Warwick, York, Accomack, Isle of Wight, and Nansemond Counties, though a few were of James City and Charles City Counties.[19] It is likely that Thomas Cardwell the Immigrant landed at Strawberry Banks. On the other hand, he could have put ashore at any of the several ports of call visited by the *Tristram and Jane*. Some speculate that he landed at Yorktown or Jamestown.[20] However, the majority of researchers agree on Strawberry Banks, perhaps because of its historic connections. Captain John Smith landed at Strawberry Banks on his first voyage up the James River in 1607.

According to Pendergraft, Thomas the Immigrant resided on the south side of the Mattaponi River in York County; the original Charles City Shire established in 1634 and renamed York in 1643 that covered territory on both sides of the Mattaponi.[21] That area became King William County. The rapidly changing geography of Tidewater Virginia appears to identify Thomas the Immigrant as a transient settler, when actually changing county placenames was more the result of evolving geography than movement on his part. For example, New Kent County, in which he once resided, formed in 1654 out of York County; King and Queen County grew out of New Kent in 1691, and King William out of King and Queen in 1702, all locations associated with Thomas the Immigrant. Moreover, he is likewise associated with Goochland County, which formed in 1728 from Henrico County, another of the eight original shires of Colonial Virginia first formed in 1634. The association of Thomas the Immigrant with the named counties of Goochland, King and Queen, and King William are prerogatives of transcribers because Thomas predated all of them. Court transactions executed in York County, for example, became associated with subsequent counties carved out of York. Nevertheless, later generations associated with the same places lend circumstantial credence to the identities of his descendants clustered in the same counties.

Thomas the immigrant married and raised a family. Despite efforts by genealogists to arrive at conclusions about his personal life, records are insufficient to document a reliable biography. Official records say only that his wife's name was Mary. Some claim that he married twice, first to Mary Grace Spencer of Shropshire, England, and secondly to Mary Elizabeth Collyer, in Middlesex County, Virginia.[22] Claims that he married her in 1638 and that she was the mother of his children are erroneous and unsupported by documented evidence because the marriage of Thomas Cordwell [*sic*] to Mary Elizabeth Collyer occurred in 1662, according to the *Christ Church Parish Register*. Moreover, his indenture servant status raises questions regarding his early marriage. While it is possible that he secured a release from his indenture contract, a term of service was normally for at least five years during which time a servant could not marry without a master's consent. However, Thomas the Immigrant and progenitor of later generations apparently had a son about 1639. Either this was a different Thomas, or Thomas the Immigrant found a way to shorten his indenture service. Genealogists working to put the puzzle together suggest that Thomas had children first by Mary Grace Spencer; she died about 1660, he married Mary Elizabeth (Carey) Collyer in 1662, and had additional children by her.[23]

The Virginia Colony expanded into the Tidewater, across the Coastal Plain, and westward toward the Piedmont. In the spring of 1644, the Powhatan Indian confederacy launched another assault on the English, determined to drive them out of Indian Territory. Five hundred whites died in the massacre that followed before a determined resistance by the colonists killed the warring leader and ended the uprising. The role of Thomas the Immigrant in this event has no historic relevance, except that he survived as the likely progenitor of Cardwell generations that followed.

Family tradition holds that Thomas Cardwell the Immigrant first settled in King William County, paid off his indenture, bought land in what became Goochland County, Virginia, and engaged in tobacco farming.[24] Speculation about his possible London roots connects him to his alleged farm called Farrington, located on Church Hill, in Richmond, Virginia. Farrington was also the name of a suburb of London.[25] However, this claim is not widely supported. Most agree that Thomas the Immigrant settled first on the south bank of the Mattaponi River in King William County and then moved later to the northern side of the Mattaponi.

The public record documents his presence in Lancaster (later Middlesex) County, Virginia. In January 1666, he purchased 300 acres from Robert Chowning on the south side of Sunderland Creek, later called Burnham's Creek, in Lancaster County, in what became Middlesex County in 1669.[26] Middlesex County formed from Lancaster County, which formed from York in 1651. Originally, the region was the Indian District of Chickacoan. A persistent family tradition is that an early Cardwell ancestor married an Indian girl;

Pendergraft mused that she may have entered the line from the Indian District of Chickacoan. In 1667, Thomas bought an additional tract of land from Joane Chowning.[27]

In a 1673 Middlesex County Deed, Thomas Cardwell the Immigrant and Mary his wife sold land to Thomas Fenney.[28] His association with the Northern Neck of Virginia is of particular historical interest. His land purchase of 300 acres on Sunderland, or Burnham's Creek (present LeGrange Creek), and the 1673 transaction placed him in the Upper precinct of the fabled Christ Church Parish of Middlesex County.[29] Here adjacent to the great Dragon Swamp in "Jamaica Land" was some of the best tobacco farming in Virginia. His neighbors were the Meacham, Daniel, and Bristow families, to name a few.[30] William Daniel purchased 115 acres on Indian Bridge Creek on Dragon Swamp in 1672.[31] The indefatigable English cavalier Henry Corbin built his manor house here to escape the politics of England. The estate of Ralph Wormeley towered over the village of Urbana a few miles to the south. Urbanna, destined to be the county seat, was the only town of any size in all of Middlesex County. The Wormeley family was arguably the richest family in Virginia, behind only the Carter dynasty of John Carter and his son "King" Carter on the other side of the Rappahannock River, seated in old Lancaster County. The record is relatively silent on the activities of Thomas the Immigrant in Middlesex County, despite Middlesex being one of the most documented counties in Virginia. The Middlesex County Order Book makes one mention of him in October 1679 when he personally appeared in court; "Thomas Cardwell, Attorney of John Burford."[32]

Thomas the Immigrant wrote his will on May 12, 1687, in Middlesex County.[33] In it, he left his plantation to his wife, Mary, and two minor daughters, Ann and Nora. He mentioned Thomas and John Baskett, named Raleigh Massey as executor, and named Thomas Cardwell, [Sr.] and Job Richards as overseers of his estate. An unnamed daughter may have been Elizabeth, wife of John Baskett named in the *Christ Church Parish Register*.[34] The interpretation of his somewhat cryptic will has led some to assume also that he had another daughter who married Raleigh Massey. Others speculate that the reference to Thomas, [Sr.] as overseer may have been his son who would have been about age 30 at the time but was not specifically named as an heir in the will. Meanwhile, one of the witnesses to his will was William Daniel, Jr., of the close-knit Meacham, Daniel, Bristow, and Cardwell community.[35] John Bristow had but a few years earlier witnessed the will of William Daniel, Jr.'s father.[36] These transactions are of interest to the present genealogy because William Daniel, Sr. the immigrant and contemporary of Thomas Cardwell the Immigrant was also a close friend of John Bristow, immigrant and progenitor of the Bristow family in America.[37] Bristow descendants trace to Peyton Bristow of Kentucky and Missouri, whose daughter Martha Bristow married Joseph Burchett and settled in St. Clair County, Missouri, in 1846. Their great grandson Willis Burchett married Beatrice Cardwell, whose ancestors potentially trace back to Thomas Cardwell the Immigrant of Middlesex County, Virginia.

Thomas Cardwell the Immigrant died in 1689, based on the proving of his will by the Middlesex County Court July 6, 1689.[38] His burial was allegedly in the Old Christ Church Parish Churchyard in Middlesex County.[39] After the death of Thomas, his widow Mary Elizabeth married secondly John Williams on October 10, 1696, in Christ Church Parish, Middlesex County.[40] Mary died in 1698.[41]

Pendergraft speculated that Thomas the Immigrant and Mary (maiden name unidentified) had at least six children: William Cardwell, Richard Cardwell, Nathaniel Cardwell, Thomas Cardwell, Sr., Ann (Cardwell) Brooks, and Nora Carey (Cardwell) Massey. An alternative interpretation to Pendergraft centers on his known children named in his will, viz., his two minor daughters, and supposed son Thomas, Sr. who the elder Thomas the Immigrant named as overseer of his will but not his heir. Based on the estimated age of 65 of Thomas the Immigrant at the time of his death, his minor daughters were likely of his second marriage to Mary Elizabeth Collyer. Meanwhile, in the case of his son, Thomas, Sr., it was common for the heir-apparent to receive his inheritance early and not appear by name in the will. A parsing of the language of the will also infers that there were two daughters and two in-laws or grandsons named Thomas and John Baskett. An Elizabeth Cardwell married John Basket prior to 1679 in Middlesex County, which suggests that she was an older daughter not previously identified in Pendergraft's pedigree list. Genealogists believe also that Thomas Cardwell, Sr. married a woman named Baskett.

The continuity of the Cardwell genealogy does not reliably link Thomas Cardwell the Immigrant of 1636 or his offspring to the known ancestors of the Cardwell family of Cedar County, Missouri. Despite well-intentioned efforts by many historians to connect him to later generations of the Cardwell name, the record does not support an association except in theory and tenuous assumptions based on circumstantial evidence. Nevertheless, he occupies a substantial place in Cardwell genealogy dating from the earliest genealogies of the Cardwell family in America.[42] The following genealogical summaries represent the best consensus of his descendants, with the caveat that they are admittedly unproven in many instances. Nevertheless, they are of interest for their longstanding claims and because nothing better promises to replace them in the near future. Whether the individuals in the summaries were direct descendants of Thomas the Immigrant or kin to him in other ways, they were all of the larger Cardwell family that eventually surfaced in the person of Thomas Cardwell of Granville, North Carolina, who is the earliest proven ancestor of the Cardwell family of Cedar County, Missouri, dating to the year 1760.

Opposite page. Virginia Geography. Thomas Cardwell the Immigrant appeared at different times at (A) Hampton Roads, Virginia, (B) on the Mattaponi River in New Kent County, Virginia, and (C) Middlesex County, Virginia.

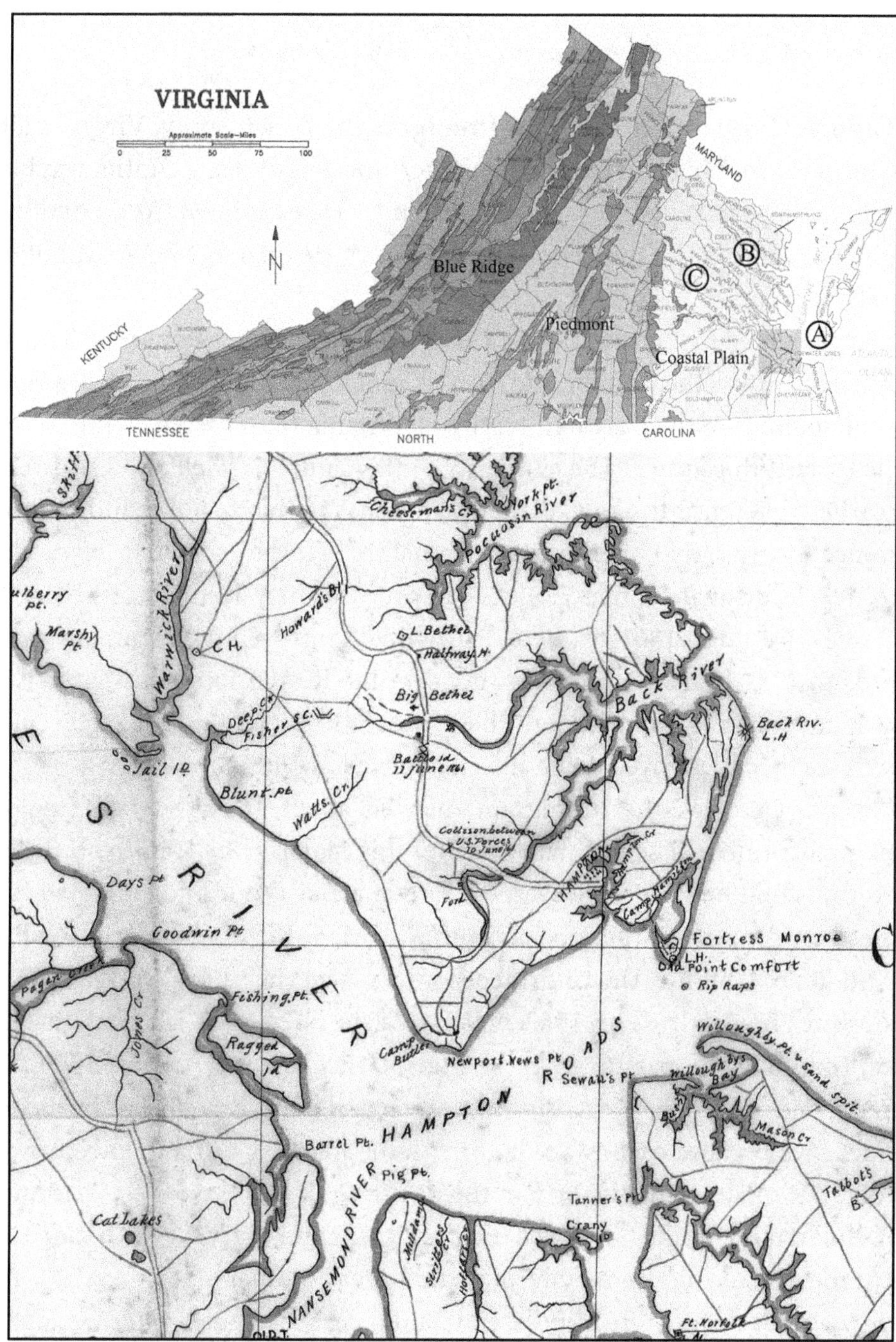

Hampton Roads. Thomas Cardwell the Immigrant came to America in 1636 on board the English Ship *Tristram and Jane.* The ship docked at Strawberry Banks on the north shore of Hampton Roads, northeast of Newport News at the mouth of the James River, in the Colony of Virginia. Map modified from Hove, *Southeastern Part of Virginia*, 1862. U.S. Department of Agriculture. Library of Congress.

Cardwell First Generation Family Group

Thomas (Cordell) Cardwell the Immigrant of York County, Virginia, later of King William, King and Queen, Lancaster, and Middlesex Counties was born in 1614 perhaps in Wiltshire County, England.[43] He emigrated from London to Virginia in 1636 on the ship *Tristram and Jane.*[44] He died in 1689 in Middlesex County, Virginia.

The presumed first generation of Cardwells in America begins with Thomas (Cordell) Cardwell the Immigrant. *Tyler's Cyclopedia of Virginia Families* wrote that the founder of the Cardwell family of Virginia immigrated to the Colony in the early 17th century. The similarity of the names Cordell and Cardwell is the earliest reference to the Cardwell name in Virginia history, and the only reference to any early emigrant of a like name.[45] However, further research is ongoing. Unfortunately, many of the early records of Virginia perished in the wars of 1776-81 and 1861-65. Benedict Arnold destroyed the Henrico County records in 1781 in his raid on Richmond in the Revolution. During the Civil War, many outlying counties sent their records to Richmond for safekeeping, only to see them destroyed when the city burned in 1865.[46]

Thomas Cardwell the Immigrant married about 1638 to Mary (maiden name unidentified). The estimated date of this marriage is from the birthdate of his first child in 1639. However, the only marriage so far documented for a Thomas Cardwell in this period was in 1662 to **Mary Elizabeth (Carey) Collyer** in Middlesex County. Unconfirmed sources have her born about 1615 in Shropshire, England.[47] The 1662 marriage date infers that Thomas married twice, first to Mary, presumed to be **Mary Grace Spencer**, before 1660. The shared name of Mary between his first and second wives renders family records inconclusive because each Mary had the same married surname of Cardwell. Pendergraft made no distinction in the offspring of the two wives, attributing their children to Thomas Cardwell the Immigrant and Mary but with the caveat that some of the children may have had different mothers. Meanwhile, *Christ Church Parish Register* in Middlesex County recorded the 1696 marriage of Mary Cardwell of Shropshire, England, to John Williams of Oxfordshire, England.[48] Although unproven, genealogists interpret her as the widow of Thomas Cardwell the Immigrant. According to Pendergraft, Thomas and Mary had the following children.[49] The Pendergraft pedigree is a list of possible and probable descendants but not necessarily proven reliably accurate.

1. **William Cardwell, Sr.** was born about 1639 in Lancaster County, Va. William married Margaret (maiden name unidentified).[50] His birthdate of c.1639 derives from the size of his family recorded in a 1664 Stafford County land grant to William Cordwell [*sic*], Sr., Margaret Cordwell [wife], William Cordwell, Jr. [son]; Grace Cordwell [daughter], Henry Saynes, John Ozzet, and John Twiggs [presumed in-laws].[51] Another land grant in 1691 to William Cardwell and William Fenney placed William, Sr. in New Kent County, later King and Queen County. Also in 1691, William Cardwell and William Fenney received a land grant in what became Drysdale Parish on the Mattaponi River in Caroline County, Virginia.[52] Neither Caroline County nor Drysdale Parish formed until 1728 from Essex, King and Queen, and King William Counties. The 1691 property on the Mattaponi was therefore likely in what first became King and Queen County. Genealogists who claim that William, Sr. and his family were descendants of Thomas the Immigrant appear to confuse him with the later immigrants William, Sr., William Jr., Margaret, and Grace Cardwell, all of whom came to Virginia in 1664, meaning they could not have been the descendants of Thomas the Immigrant of 1636.[53] Nevertheless, his association or the association of another William Cardwell with the Cardwells of Stafford County, Virginia, makes him a likely candidate for kin to Thomas the Immigrant.

2. **Richard Cardwell, Sr.** was born about 1643 in Middlesex County, Virginia.[54] He died in 1715/16 in Westmoreland County, Virginia.[55] Richard married Mary (maiden name unidentified). A Richard Cardwell moved to Rockingham County, North Carolina, in the early 1700s and settled on the Dan River, near Madison, North Carolina. If this was Richard, Sr., he also held property in the Fairfax Grant in Westmoreland County, Virginia, which infers Richard Cardwell of Westmoreland and Richard of North Carolina were two different men.[56] The relationship of Richard Cardwell to Thomas the Immigrant lacks significant proof beyond their joint presence in Middlesex County. The elder Thomas the Immigrant did not name him in his will. His appearance or that of another Richard Cardwell in North Carolina in the early 1700s invites consideration of him as a possible connection to the Cardwells of North Carolina. However, no one to date has convincingly disputed him as the son of Thomas the Immigrant. Richard and Mary Cardwell had the following chil-

dren: Richard Cardwell, Jr., Margaret Cardwell, and Winifred Cardwell.[57] Richard Cardwell, Jr., a minor when his father died, inherited his estate. He died in 1726,[58]

3. **Nathaniel Cardwell** was born in 1648 in Middlesex County, Virginia.[59] (Pendergraft concluded that Nathaniel died without issue).

\+ 4. **Thomas Cardwell, Sr.** of Henrico County was born in 1660 in New Kent County or Lancaster County, Virginia. He died in 1717 in Henrico County, Virginia.[60] The name Thomas Cardwell, Sr. is a reference to a 1713 Henrico County deed in which he appeared as Thomas, Sr., suggesting that his father, Thomas the Immigrant, no longer lived, and that Thomas, Sr. had a son named Thomas, Jr.[61]

5. **Ann Cardwell** was born after 1666 (c.1669) in Lancaster County, Va. She was a minor when her father wrote his will in 1687. She married **William Brooks** on 8 Nov 1687 in Christ Church Parish, Middlesex County, Virginia.[62]

6. **Nora Carey Cardwell** was born after 1666 in Lancaster County, Virginia. She was an unidentified minor named in her father's will in 1687.[63] Competing sources identify her as Margaret Cardwell who married Raleigh (or Ralph) Massey.

Not named in the genealogies of Pendergraft and Boddie was **Elizabeth Cardwell,** probable child of Thomas the Immigrant. She was born about 1663 in Christ Church Parish, Middlesex County. She married John Baskett prior to 1679. The name John Baskett appeared in the will of Thomas the Immigrant as a son-in-law or possible grandson, along with Thomas Baskett, also named in his will. John and Elizabeth (Cardwell) Baskett had at least three children born in Middlesex County: Elizabeth in 1679, Henry in 1680, and Thomas Baskett in 1682.[64] The elder John Baskett died in 1686, and his Widow Elizabeth (Cardwell) Baskett married John Guthrie or Guttery of Scotland, on 6 Feb 1687, in Christ Church, Middlesex County, Va.[65] Their first child, Ann, was born in October of the same year. Three other children followed; viz., John in 1689, Richard in 1691, and Massey in 1692.[66] Elizabeth died in 1700 in King and Queen County. Her burial was in the Upper Church of Stratton Major Parish Cemetery, King and Queen County.[67] Her probable son, John Baskett died in 1720, in Middlesex County. Four members of the Basket family died within months of each other in 1720. John Guthrie, probably her son by her marriage to John Guthrie [Sr.], died in Middlesex County in 1733.[68]

16

Thomas Cardwell, Sr.

Cursory overview of public records suggests that Thomas Cardwell, Sr., presumed son of Thomas Cardwell the Immigrant, was born about 1660 in Kent County, Virginia; moved with his parents to Middlesex County, Virginia; married in Middlesex County between 1681 and 1684; and settled in Henrico County, Virginia, where he died in 1717. His movements generally parallel those of Thomas the Immigrant in the same period. However, the relationship of Thomas the Immigrant and Thomas, Sr. as father and son remains tentative. Consequently, family historians often begin the Cardwell lineage in America with the proven ancestry of Thomas Cardwell, Sr. and his descendants.[1] In any event, his presence in the Tidewater of Virginia lends insight into the region that was the undeniable seat of early Cardwell family history.

The 1660-estimated birthdate of Thomas Cardwell, Sr. comes from a 1690 deposition in Henrico County in which he was then age 30. His birthdate of 1660 occurred before the known marriage date of Thomas the Immigrant to Mary Collyer in 1662.[2] This reinforces the claim that Thomas, Sr. was born in New Kent County, Virginia, or Lancaster County before it became Middlesex County in 1669, and that he was the offspring of a previous marriage, generally thought to be the union between Thomas Cardwell the Immigrant and Mary Spencer.

Thomas, Sr. married Ann "Little Flower" Baskett between 1681 and 1684 in Middlesex County, Virginia.[3] Historians believe she was of Native American descent. Middlesex County was originally part of the Indian District of Chickacoan. Ann was born about 1662 in Chickacoan District, known to the English as Lancaster County, and later Middlesex County.[4] His marriage to Ann

Baskett aligns with the Middlesex County Baskett family of Thomas and John Baskett mentioned in the will of Thomas Cardwell the Immigrant, and presumed to be his grandsons or in-laws. The *Christ Church Parish Register* of Middlesex County recorded the Baskett family on multiple occasions, including the marriage of John Baskett to Elizabeth Cardwell, presumed daughter of Thomas the Immigrant and sister to Thomas, Sr. who married Ann Baskett.[5]

Thomas, Sr. and Ann removed from Middlesex County to Henrico County, Virginia, settling on the upper James River near the future location of Richmond. The first mention of Thomas, Sr. in the public record was in Henrico County in the spring of 1686, as a planter. He paid 1,000 pounds of tobacco for a tract of ground owned by the carpenter Samuel Bridgewater of Varina Parish in Henrico, situated "at [the] head of [the] land of Gilly Grove Malliga [*sic*] [probably Gilly Gromarrin] on [the] south side of little run, sometimes called Crawl's and now Gillys Creek," and dated April 11, 1686.[6] The following year, the elder Thomas Cardwell the Immigrant wrote his Last Will and Testament in 1687 but did not name a legacy for Thomas, Sr., suggesting that the 1,000 pounds of tobacco used to buy the Henrico County land possibly came courtesy of Thomas the Immigrant as an early token of his son's inheritance. On the other hand, Thomas, Sr. may have borrowed the tobacco he used as payment because in December 1687, he confessed in open court that he owed 700 pounds of tobacco and cask, which he agreed to repay out of the current year's crop. He owed another 400 pounds payable next year, according to the judgment of the court. This scenario has him acquiring the Henrico land on credit from the seller, and the 1,100 pounds of tobacco in the court settlement represented the amount due plus interest.[7]

The 1687 tobacco judgment marked a series of court appearances for Thomas, Sr. in Henrico County. In February of 1688, the court dismissed a case he brought, and in the fall of the same year, appointed him, Daniel Johnson, John Bayly, and Gilly Gromarrin (the Gilly of Gilly's Creek) to appraise the estate of Barth Burrows.[8] He was in court again in the spring of 1689/90 answering another judgment against him, and in the same month of February was in a tiff with John Bayly who had been his colleague in the appraisal of the Burrows estate. Bayly retracted his unspecified complaint, and the court closed the suit.[9]

In the spring of 1689, in a land grant dated April 20, Nathaniel Bacon gave to Thomas Cardwell, planter, 550 acres on the north side of the James River in

Henrico County for transporting eleven persons into the colony.[10] The land grant lay in Varina Parish near the Thomas, Sr. existing tract, beginning at Samuel Bridgewater's property between the north and south branches of Gilley's Creek.[11] Three things are of particular interest about this transaction. First, where did the financing come from to pay for the transport of eleven persons into the colony? Only two years before, he was in court trying to arrange payment of a debt. No answer is in the Henrico records, except to suppose that he was an entrepreneur who knew how to finance a business deal.

The second item of interest about the Henrico grant was its location. Thomas, Sr. settled in a part of Virginia known for its historic setting and storied past. Gilly's Creek was in Henrico Parish, once called Varina Parish, an 18-by-25-mile region that took its name from Varina Farm, the home of the famous tobacco farmer John Rolfe and his Indian bride Pocahontas. In 1620, when Rolfe was in route to Virginia, he landed in Bermuda and took an interest in a type of tobacco grown there. He crossed it with an Indian tobacco grown in Virginia, and thus was born a species of tobacco that resembled a mild strain grown in Span called Varinas, a strain well suited for cultivation in the Virginia climate. Rolfe named his plantation Varinas. A little town grew up around his manor to become eventually the first county seat and courthouse of Henrico County. In time, the town of Varina became Henrico City, relegating the name Varina to refer to the original site of Rolfe's farm. The location of the Thomas, Sr. land on Gilly's (present Gillies) Creek—a tributary of the James River—was about five miles north of Varina, and about a mile east of what became Richmond, Virginia, on the fall line of the James, and once a village of the mighty Powhatan Confederacy.

Finally, in the Gilly-Creek transaction, Nathaniel Bacon, the grantor of the land, was a name infamous in Virginia for an unsuccessful rebellion led against British occupation, which forced then Governor Sir William Berkeley to flee Virginia. Bacon burned Jamestown and reaped havoc across a broad swath of the Tidewater before his sudden death ended the uprising. However, the Nathaniel Bacon who granted 550 acres to Thomas Cardwell, Sr. was not the Nathaniel Bacon who died in 1676, but rather his distinguished cousin of the same name. A member of the House of Burgesses, member of the governor's Council, and fierce loyalist of Governor Berkeley, Nathaniel Bacon (the elder) served as president and acting governor of the Colony on multiple occasions. It was on one such brief occasion between governors that Bacon in his acting governor capacity awarded the land grant to Thomas Cardwell, Sr.

The annals of the Henrico County Court contain many entries on the activities of Thomas, Sr. The court ordered a judgment against him on April 1, 1689, for 460 pounds of tobacco and cask.[12] His repeated court appearances did not seem to impugn his respected service to Henrico County because in October 1690, the court impaneled him to sit on a jury.[13] In February 1691, the court dismissed a case he filed against George Cogbill because neither he nor Cogbill showed up for the court hearing.[14] In another case involving Thomas, Sr. and John Bayly in 1692, Thomas sought an attachment against the estate of Bayly; the court dismissed it, too, because neither party showed up.[15] These suits were often amicable writs meant to settle disputes over boundaries and debts that went to court as a kind of arbitration. It was common for neighbors to sue each other and then join together to sue someone else. This happened multiply times in Bayly's case. In one instance in 1691, Thomas, Sr. filed a lien against Bayly for 800 pounds of tobacco and cask, and when Bayly failed to appear in court, the justices ordered an attachment of Bayly's property. This was similar to another legal tiff in 1690 when Thomas failed to show up for a claim Henry Trent made against him for 245 pounds of tobacco. However, in that debacle, the sheriff failed to bond the appearance of Thomas, Sr. When he did not produce "the body of said Thomas," the court ordered a judgment against the sheriff for the amount due from Cardwell, subject to the sheriff's subsequent attachment of Cardwell property "repleviable according to law."[16]

Thomas, Sr. stayed active in the real estate business. On December 19, 1691, he sold half of his 550-acre land grant to Robert Green "for valuable consideration." Ann Cardwell relinquished her dower right to permit the sale to go forward, as required by colonial law. George Cogbill, a sometime adversary in court, witnessed the sale.[17] Meanwhile, in the spring of 1694, Thomas paid 1,000 pounds of tobacco for 100 acres next to what he already owned on the north side of James River. Curiously, and perhaps begrudgingly the remittance for the sale went to John Bayly on behalf of Giles Webb. Mr. Webb had lately bought the land from Bayly apparently on credit; therefore, the sale to Cardwell benefitted Bayly.[18]

On October 1, 1696, Thomas, Sr. and Ann sold the other half their property on Gilly's Creek to George Fairfax. "Thomas Cardwell of County and Parish of Henrico, planter, to George Fairfax of same, planter, for 2,500 lbs. of tobacco land on north side of James River, bounded by Gilly's Creek, Robert Green, and said Cardwell, 275 acres; being half of 550 acres by patent 20 April 1689 to said Cardwell."[19] An exception to the sale held out 50 acres "which is to be laid out for my Godson Thomas Wood, son of Thomas Wood [Sr.]." In this transaction, Ann Cardwell again relinquished her dower right.[20] The original Cardwell land grant of 550 acres continued to be a base reference for land sales in Henrico County well into the eighteenth century. For example, a sale in July 1751 described the location of a tract on "Gilleys Cr. part of a patent of 550 acres granted Thomas Cardwell 20 Apr 1689."[21]

The identification of the children of Thomas, Sr. and Ann (Baskett) Cardwell comes from the interpolation of land deeds. A 1713 deed referred to Thomas, Sr., inferring that he had a son named Thomas, Jr. That deed, made out to his daughter Eleanor Williams, wife of Richard Williams, accounted for a second child named Eleanor Cardwell. Pendergraft believed that a 1706 deed from a Thomas Cardwell (but not proven to be Thomas, Sr.) identified a third child, Mary Cardwell, who married James Franklin.[22] A possible fourth child may have been the wife of Thomas Woods indicated in the 1696 deed in which Thomas, Sr. reserved 50 acres for his "godson," frequently a reference in colonial records to a grandchild.

Thomas, Sr. died sometime after 1729. His name appeared on a Henrico County bond in 1717 and in a deed for property in Goochland County in 1729. (Goochland formed from Henrico County in 1728.) The deed, dated August 19, 1729, showed he paid 42 pounds for 400 acres on the south side of the James River on a branch of Deep Creek.[23] Genealogists divide on whether this sale was to Thomas, Sr. or his son Thomas, Jr. Meanwhile, Ann, wife of Thomas, Sr. died sometime before June 1737, in Henrico County.

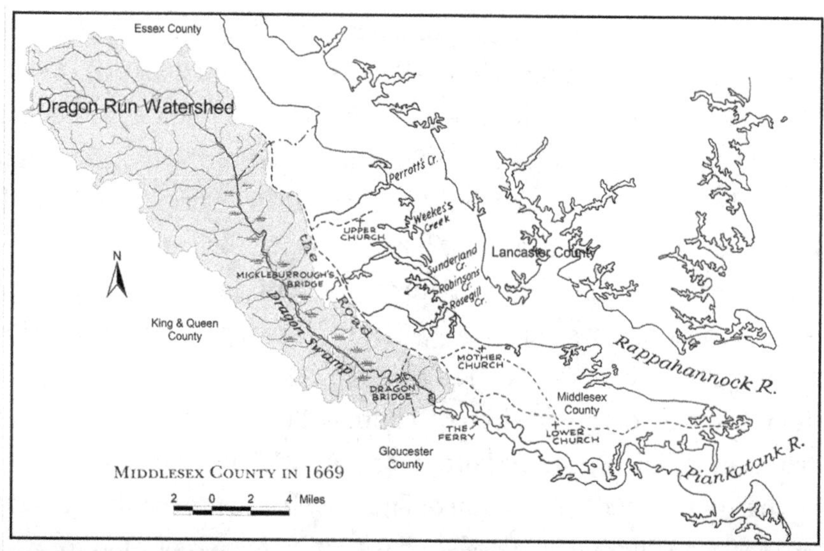

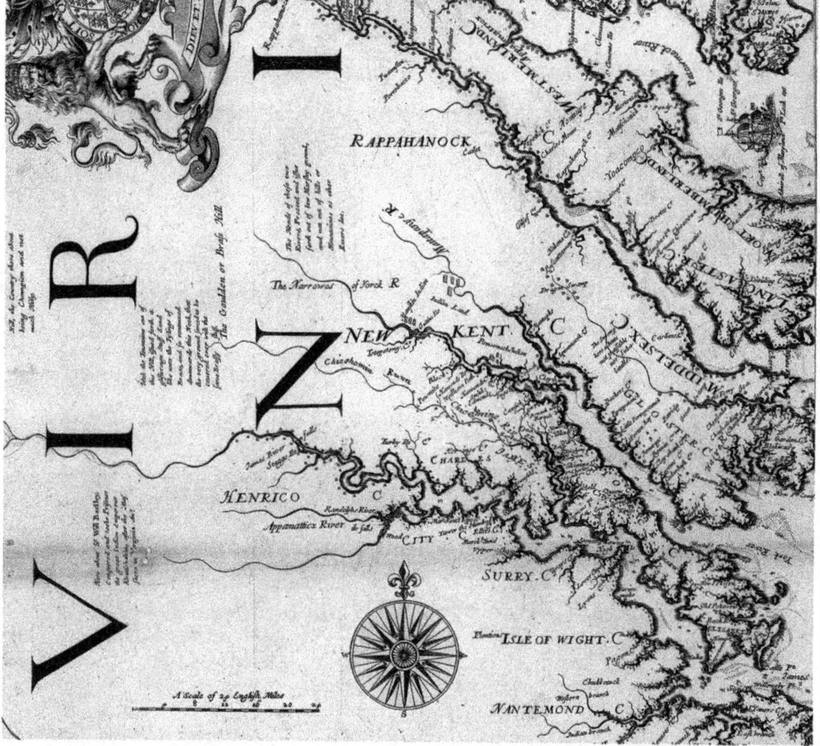

Virginia Tidewater. Thomas Cardwell the Immigrant settled in New Kent County south of the Mattaponi River before moving north to Middlesex County on Sunderland Creek, shown at the center of the top map. Here Thomas Cardwell, Sr. grew to adulthood. An inscription on this original 1670 map reads, "The Land between James River and Roanoke River is for the most part Low Sunken Swampy Land not Well passable but with great difficulty And therein harbours Tygers Bears And other Devouringe Creatures." Middlesex County is at right-center of the map. Modified from Rutman & Rutman, *A Place in Time*; and Herrman, *Virginia and Maryland,* 1673. Library of Congress.

Cardwell Second Generation Family Group

Thomas Cardwell, Sr. was born about 1660 probably in Lancaster County (later Middlesex County), Virginia, based on a deposition taken in 1690 citing his age at the time as about age 30.[24] He may have been born in New Kent, County, which formed in 1654 from York County. He died after 1729 in Henrico County, Virginia.[25] He was the probable son of **Thomas (Cordell) Cardwell the Immigrant**. A 1713 Henrico County Deed to Eleanor Cardwell Williams referred to him as Thomas Cardwell, Sr.

Thomas married **Ann "Little Flower" Baskett** in 1681 in Middlesex County, Virginia.[26] Ann was born about 1662 in Chickacoan District, Lancaster County (later Middlesex County), Virginia.[27] She died before June 1737 in Henrico County, Virginia.[28] Her marriage to Thomas Cardwell, Sr. is probable but unproven. Likewise, according to Cardwell historian Allen Pendergraft writing in 1973, the relationship between Thomas the Immigrant and Thomas Sr. is unproven. Professional genealogist J.U. Stucki of Salt Lake City, Utah, researched and authenticated the names and dates of the first Cardwell generation but provided little additional data on subsequent generations.

Pendergraft listed only three children for Thomas Cardwell, Sr.: Thomas, Jr., Eleanor, and Mary. However, he cited a number of contemporary persons for this family taken from Christ Church Parish Records, Middlesex County, Virginia. Listed among them were William Cardwell born in 1695; Elizabeth Cardwell who married William Brooks in 1708; William Cardwell who died December 19, 1744; and the children of William and Jane Cardwell, viz., Mary baptized December 4, 1721, Thomas, baptized in 1726, and William, baptized in 1728, all in Middlesex County. Meanwhile, unverified sources list additional children of Thomas, Sr. and Ann as William Cardwell born in 1684, in Henrico County, Edward Cardwell born in 1687, John Thomas Cardwell born in 1687, an unidentified Cardwell born in 1693, an unidentified Cardwell born about 1702, Martha Ann Cardwell born in 1698, and Mathew Cardwell born in 1700, all born in Henrico County. Martha Ann died after Apr 1736 in Henrico County; Matthew died before June 19, 1744, in Middlesex County. The contemporaneous existence of these individuals in Middlesex and Henrico Counties suggest that they were separate branches of the Cardwell family. However, association with Middlesex County where Thomas the Immigrant owned land on Sunderland Creek allows for the Henrico branch and the

Middlesex branch to be the offspring of the patriarch Thomas. A logical conclusion is that Thomas Cardwell, Sr., son of Thomas the Immigrant, married in Middlesex County, and then removed to Henrico County. His genealogy requires additional research to clarify and identify his movements and better explain his association with New Kent and Middlesex Counties.

Thomas Cardwell, Sr. and Ann (Baskett) Cardwell had the following children, all presumably born in New Kent County, Virginia.[29]

\+ 1. **Thomas R. Cardwell, Jr.** was born c.1686 in New Kent County, Virginia. He died before 29 May 1751 in Cumberland County, Virginia.[30]

2. **Eleanor Cardwell** was born in 1692 in New Kent County. She married Richard Williams by 1713.[31] Eleanor and Richard had Richard Williams, Jr. In a deed dated July 1713, Thomas Cardwell, Sr. gave to his daughter Eleanor and husband Richard Williams 50 acres on the north side of James River.[32]

3. **Mary Ann Cardwell** was born in New Kent County. A 1706 deed from Thomas Cardwell named his daughter Mary.[33] She died in 1756. Mary married James Franklin in 1713.[34] They had a daughter Ann Franklin.

17

Thomas Cardwell, Jr.

Family historian and descendant of Thomas Cardwell, Sr., Allen Pendergraft, summarized his branch of the Cardwell line. "Thomas Cardwell [the Immigrant] crossed the Mattaponi to the north into the area of the Middle Neck, which became King and Queen County and Middlesex County… Thomas, Sr. moved to Henrico County on the north side of the James River near Richmond… The third generation crossed to the south side of the James and moved west of the river about 15 miles to the area adjoining Henrico on the southwest, now divided among the counties of Goochland, Powhatan, Amelia, and Dinwiddie. Cumberland County formed from Goochland in 1748-49. Some Cardwells moved to adjoining Prince Edward County. Led by Richard A. Cardwell, the fourth generation moved into adjoining Charlotte County and settled along both sides of the Roanoke River, the boundary between Charlotte and Halifax counties."[1] The descendant of immediate interest in Pendergraft's summary is Thomas Cardwell, Jr., presumed son of Thomas, Sr. and grandson of Thomas the Immigrant, styled in Pendergraft's summary as the third generation.

There is no documentation of the early life of Thomas, Jr. Even his birthplace is in question. Pendergraft claimed he was born about 1690. Other sources placed his date of birth closer to 1686, or as early as 1683, in New Kent County before part of New Kent became King and Queen County. This appears to place his location at odds with the known activities of his father Thomas, Sr. in Henrico County. The discrepancy is of little consequence; however, because either Henrico or New Kent Counties placed him in approximately the same geographic location as Thomas, Sr. In the spring of 1705, Thomas Cardwell, Jr. paid taxes on 350 acres of land in Henrico County.[2] Records identified him as a blacksmith; however, other documents clearly identify him as a planter.[3] His association with the Perrin family of Henrico County further confirms his roots in Henrico. Moreover, useful insight into his life comes from the history of the Perrin family, which enjoys extensive research among genealogists. The name Perrin is a common Cardwell name found repeatedly in different generations and among numerous descendants of the Cardwell family.[4]

Thomas, Jr. married Martha Perrin, granddaughter of the immigrant Richard Perrin [I], of Sussex, England. Richard came to Henrico County in June 1637 transported by Thomas Osborne.[5] According to family tradition, Richard Perrin [I] the immigrant had two sons, Richard [II] and Thomas who both acquired land on James River from 1670 to 1710.[6] Each patented 740 acres on the "north side of the James."[7] Richard [II] (identified in records as Richard, Sr.) married Katherine Royall, and Thomas married Ann Porter. Richard Sr.'s only son, Richard, [III] Jr. predeceased his father, and his descendants did not continue through the male line. Meanwhile, John, only son of Thomas and Ann (Porter) Perrin, likewise died young about 1706, and the Perrin name went extinct in his line as well, because Thomas Perrin himself died without heir in Henrico County soon after 1689.[8] Following Thomas' death, his Widow Ann (Porter) Perrin continued to acquire land. She patented 200 acres in 1703, claiming four persons transported to the colony as headrights. By 1704, the Henrico County rent roll showed her with 500 acres. When her son John died without an heir, and absent any male heir, the original 740-acre Perrin patents lapsed. Deeds to subsequent owners of the property described the lands as "deserted."[9] Nevertheless, the acreage in Ann (Porter) Perrin's hands was still considerable. When she died in 1711, her will directed her administrators to divide the total acreage of her land between her four daughters: Ann, Elizabeth, Jane, and Martha. She noted in her will modest property holdings of "my horse, five sheep, one cow with calf, one hog that is now in the pen, [and] one steer three years old."[10] At about the same time that Ann Perrin died and willed her property to her four daughters, Thomas Cardwell, Jr. married her daughter Martha Perrin, heir to her brother John Perrin and her mother Ann (Porter) Perrin.[11] The date of the Cardwell-Perrin marriage variously appears in marriage indexes from 1710 to 1712.[12] Pendergraft opted for a date of 1711 based on his assumption that Thomas Cardwell, Jr. was born in 1690, and 1711 would make him of age to marry at age 21. Martha Perrin was born about 1694, which infers she married at about age 16. Age restrictions on marriage did not apply to females with a guardian's consent for anyone under age 18.[13]

A land sale recorded on January 7, 1716, in Henrico County mentioned Thomas R. Cardwell, the initial "R" being perhaps in deference to an alleged Uncle Richard A. Cardwell. The following year, on April 1, 1717, a bond recorded in Henrico County placed Thomas, Jr. and Martha Cardwell in Henrico. They bound themselves to pay 50 pounds for a parcel of land consisting of 239 acres descended from the late John Perrin deceased, part of the land from the estate of John to his four sisters, which included Martha (Perrin) Cardwell.[14]

In the summer of 1729, Thomas Cardwell, Jr. bought 400 acres in Goochland County (Goochland formed from Henrico County in 1728), recorded in a sale dated August 19, 1729, from Warsham Easley of Goochland. Thomas paid 42 pounds for the parcel of land on the south side of the James River on a branch of Deep Creek.[15] Conflicting claims assign this land purchase to Thomas Cardwell, Sr., which then passed on to Thomas, Jr.

The Goochland property may have been an investment. On the other hand, Thomas, Jr. may have removed to the south side of the James River temporarily; temporarily because in 1735 he and Martha witnessed the will of Martha Wilkinson in Henrico County north of the James. Mrs. Wilkinson wrote her will on September 21, 1735, and the court proved it on April 5, 1736. This document is of interest because not only did it record Thomas, Jr. and Martha in Henrico County, it named George Cardwell as their probable son: "To Godson George Cardwell a heifer."[16] The other witness to the Wilkinson will besides Thomas and Martha Cardwell was Matthew Bridgeman, a familiar surname of Henrico County. The Bridgeman family lived next door to the Thomas Cardwell, Sr. property in Henrico. Cardwell and Bridgeman witnessed the proving of the Wilkinson will. One may reasonable infer from this that Thomas, Jr. remained on the family farm on Gilley's Creek after his father's death. It is possible that Thomas Cardwell of Goochland County was a different Thomas because Thomas of Goochland appeared again in 1745, named in a land transaction involving John Phelps, in which Phelps bought 54 acres in Goochland south of the James River on a branch of Deep Creek adjoining the land of Thomas Cardwell.[17] However, on July 20, 1745, by deed of gift, Thomas Cardwell, Jr. of Henrico gave each of his four sons; viz., Richard, Thomas Perrin, John, and George 100 acres of land on Deep Creek. These were the four sons named later in the will of Thomas, Jr. of Henrico County, suggesting that Thomas, Jr. had property interests on both sides of the river in both Henrico and Goochland Counties.[18]

Martha (Perrin) Cardwell died around the year 1751.[19] Thomas Cardwell, Jr. (aka Thomas R. Cardwell) wrote his Last Will and Testament December 2, 1772. He died in Henrico County.[20] Family researchers over the years accumulated a list of some twelve children allegedly born of this marriage.[21] However, credible sources—including his will—limit the list to seven provable children: Lucy (Cardwell) Breazeale, Thomas Perrin Cardwell, Richard Ambrose Cardwell, George Cardwell, John Cardwell, Martha Perrin (Cardwell) Epperson, and Elizabeth (Cardwell) Bandy.[22]

Meanwhile, a question lingers over the ancestral ties of Thomas, Jr. to other branches of the Cardwell family. There remains the unanswered question of whether he was a descendant of Thomas the Immigrant of Middlesex County. One notable characteristic deserves analysis. Thomas Cardwell, Jr. was a large slave owner. Slave ownership among the Cardwell branches was usually modest but common in many Cardwell families of later generations. Slave labor was a common practice on the cotton plantations of Virginia. It supplanted and then replaced the headright, indentured slave system of the colony. Thomas, Jr. owned at least 15 slaves in 1772. His will exclusively listed legacies of slaves to each of his five surviving children and two of his grandchildren. He freed his elderly slave Hannah, and loaned two others named Absalom and James to his eldest daughter Lucy for three years. He wrote in his will, "The rest of my Negroes named as followeth, Judith, Lucy, Bob, Napper, and Janney to gather with all the rest of my estate not mentioned to be sold to paye my debts. At the expiration of the three years within mentioned then these two Negroes Absalom and James to be sold and all my debts to be paid, and if any balance overpaying my debts then it is to be equally divided amongst all my sons and daughters"[23] A family squabble over slave ownership surfaced in 1780. Richard A. Cardwell, son of Thomas, Jr., died, leading to a lawsuit in 1783 in Henrico County Chancery Court, brought by Richard's sons George and Daniel, executors of their father's will. The details of the suit never made it into court records, except to infer in the filing that its purpose was to clarify matters related to slavery in the will of Thomas, Jr. The case was still in court in 1789.[24]

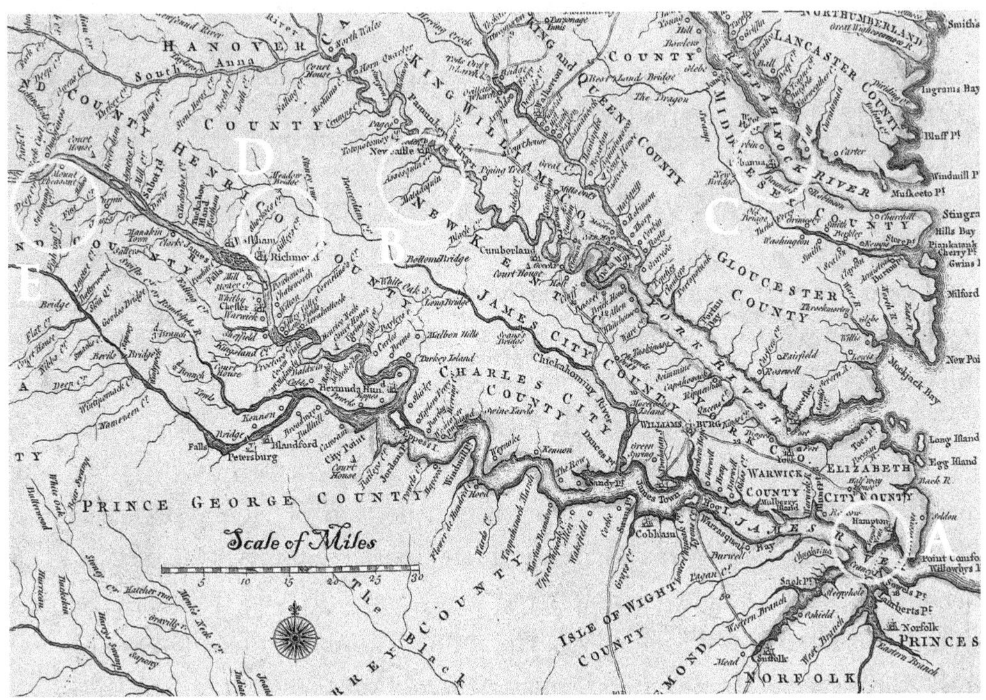

Virginia North of James River. Thomas Cardwell the Immigrant disembarked at Hampton Roads (A) Point Comfort. He settled in Henrico County (later New Kent County) on the south side of the Mattaponi River (B), a tributary of the York River, about 25 miles north of Williamsburg. New Kent County, King William, and King and Queen Counties, shown on this 1775 map, did not exist at that time. He removed east to Middlesex County (C), which formed from Lancaster County in 1669. His presumed son Thomas Cardwell, Sr. left Middlesex County and acquired land on Gilley's Creek on the James River in Henrico County (D), near Richmond. His son, Thomas Cardwell, Jr. in turn, bought land on Deep Creek in Cumberland County south of the upper arm of James River (E). Excerpt from Fry's *Map of the Most Inhabited Part of Virginia*, 1775. Library of Congress.

Cardwell Third Generation Family Group

Thomas R. Cardwell, Jr. was born about 1690, allegedly in New Kent County, Virginia.[25] (New Kent County became King and Queen County in 1691.) A 1713 Deed referred to his father as Thomas, Sr.; hence, the reference to him as Thomas, Jr.[26] He wrote his will 2 Dec 1772 and died soon thereafter in Henrico County. He was the son of **Thomas Cardwell, Sr.** and **Ann "Little Flower" Baskett.**

Thomas married **Martha M. Perrin**, daughter of **Richard Perrin** and **Ann Porter** about 1711 in Henrico County, Virginia. Martha was born about 1694 in Henrico. She died before 1751 in Henrico County.[27]

Thomas, Jr. and Martha had the following children.

1. **Lucy Cardwell** was born about 1712 in Henrico County, Virginia. She died after 1783.[28] She married Drury Breazeale, son of Henry Breazeale and Elizabeth Drury. Drury was born in 1702 in Henrico County.[29] He died in 1778 in Henrico. In 1782, Lucy Brazeal [*sic*], a widow, was on the Tax Roll in Henrico County for the ownership of slaves. Her father Thomas, Jr. listed her in his will in 1772 to receive "one Negroe woman named Phillis"

2. **Thomas Perrin Cardwell** was born on 31 Mar 1716 in Henrico County, Virginia. He died 7 Apr 1751, according to an inventory of his estate 29 May 1751 in Cumberland County, Virginia.[30] (Cumberland County formed in 1748-49 from Goochland County, which formed in 1717 from Henrico County.) Thomas Perrin died intestate.[31]

3. **Richard Ambrose Cardwell** was born on 15 Apr 1719 in Henrico County, Virginia. He died on 8 Mar 1780 in Charlotte Parish, Charlotte County, Virginia.[32] Richard died in Charlotte County in the same year as the death of his son, Thomas Cardwell. After Richard died in 1780, his remaining sons sued in Henrico County Chancery Court over his estate, which included "one Negroe girl named Nancy."[33] Richard married **Susannah LeGrand**, daughter of Jean Pierre (John Peter) LeGrand and Jane Madelaine Micheaux, about 1740 in Cumberland County, Virginia. Susannah was born on 14 Dec 1719 in Goochland County, Virginia. She died on 30 May 1813 in Charlotte County, Virginia. The link of Richard A. Cardwell to Thomas Cardwell, Jr. is in a deed dated 20 July 1745 in which Thomas, Jr. of Henrico County deeded to his son Richard A. Cardwell 100 acres on a branch of Deep Creek in Goochland County (Cumberland County after 1748).[34] Richard Ambrose Cardwell was the ancestor

of Cardwell family historian Alan Pendergraft who wrote a definitive genealogy of Cardwell ancestry.

+ 4. **George Cardwell** was born about 1720 in Henrico County, Virginia. He died on 24 Aug 1767 in Cumberland County, Virginia. George married Letitia (last name unspecified). Family historians disagree on whether she was Letitia Corbin (Ball) Lee or **Letitia Mary Frances Gaines.**

5. **John Cardwell** was born about 1721 in Henrico County, Virginia. He died in July 1795 in Prince Edward County, Virginia. John married **Keziah Lowe**, daughter of Thomas Lowe, about 1742 in Goochland County, Virginia. Keziah was born about 1725 probably in Goochland County. She died in 1810 in Prince Edward County, Virginia. In his will of 1772, Thomas Cardwell, Jr. gave John Cardwell "one Negroe woman named Cloe."[35] A deed dated 17 Oct 1771 from John Cardwell of Charlotte County and his wife Keziah showed they sold 400 acres on Hunting Creek in Halifax County for 80 pounds, which confirmed that at one time they owned land in Halifax County.[36] John Cardwell was in the 1790 census of Prince Edward County where he died in 1795.[37] His branch of the Cardwell family enjoys extensive research.[38]

6. **Martha Perrin Cardwell** was born in 1722 in Henrico County, Virginia. She died after 1783. She married **Francis Epperson** son of John Epperson and Elizabeth Alexander. He was born 20 Dec 1718 in New Kent County, Virginia. In 1786, Francis signed a petition for repeal of an act that allowed the Episcopal Church to collect a tax from everyone regardless of denomination.[39] Several entries for Francis Epperson are in the *New Kent St. Peter's Parish Vestry Book and Register, 1684-1786.*[40] Martha received "one Negro girl" in her father's will in 1772.[41]

7. **Elizabeth Cardwell** was born in Henrico County. She died about 1794 probably in Cumberland County, Virginia. She married **Richard Bandy** (his second wife) son of Richard and Ann (Majors) Bandy of Whitwell, Derbyshire, England. He was born 8 Jul 1722 and died in 1795, in Roanoke County, Virginia.[42] A deed in 1760 for purchase of land placed the couple in Cumberland County in 1760.[43] They were slave owners, including "one Negro woman" left to Elizabeth in her father's will.[44]

The gaps between birthdates of the children of Thomas, Jr. and Martha (Perrin) Cardwell infer that there were probably additional offspring. Some historians have named as many as 12. A few genealogists claim that Thomas, Jr. married secondly **Mary Blackly** on 22 Jun 1716 in Middlesex County, and they had two children.[45] 8) **William Cardwell** was born 7 Jul 1717 in Middlesex County, Virginia.[46] 9) **Anne Cardwell** was born 20 Nov 1719 in Middlesex.[47] Their recorded dates of birth and association with Middlesex County make it unlikely that they were the children of Thomas, Jr. of Henrico and Goochland Counties, although they were probable descendants of Thomas Cardwell the Immigrant of Middlesex County.

18

George Cardwell

George Cardwell was born about 1720 in Henrico County, Virginia, one of several children born to Thomas Cardwell, Jr. and Martha (Perrin) Cardwell. He died on August 24, 1767, in Cumberland County, Virginia, at the early age of 47.[1] The earliest mention of George Cardwell is in Henrico County on September 21, 1735, when his name appeared as a legacy in the will of Martha Wilkinson, "To Godson George Cardwell a heifer." Among the witnesses to her will, proved April 5, 1736, were Thomas and Martha Cardwell, his presumed parents.[2] Around 1741, George married Letitia, her last name unspecified. Some contend that she was Letitia Corbin (Ball) Lee. A competing claim makes her Letitia Mary Frances Gaines of Goochland and Cumberland Counties.[3]

On July 20, 1745, by deed of gift, George received land from his father, Thomas Cardwell, Jr. of Henrico who gave each of his four sons; viz., Richard, Thomas Perrin, John, and George, 100 acres of land on Deep Creek, on the south side of the James River, in Goochland County.[4] The gift divided equally the 400 acres acquired by Thomas, Jr. in 1729 when it was in Henrico County before Henrico split off into Goochland County.[5] The property later was in Cumberland County created out of Goochland in 1749, thus the association of George Cardwell with Cumberland County, Virginia.

By most accounts, George and Letitia had a large family, including five sons: Thomas Cardwell, Perrin Cardwell, John G. Cardwell, Richard Cardwell, and Francis Cardwell.[6] George Cardwell died on August 24, 1767, in Cumberland County, leaving his minor children as wards of the county.[7] Perrin was three years old.[8] The court appointed Thomas Tabb administrator of George's estate with all dower rights laid off for Letitia.[9] Thomas, Perrin, and John Cardwell became wards of the Southam Parish Methodist Episcopal Church of Powhatan County. Southam Parish was originally in Cumberland County. It fell in Powhatan County after the county's creation from Cumberland in 1777. The church contributed to the support of the children from 1771 until January 1779.[10] Records refer to them as orphans, suggesting that Letitia might be deceased. It is possible that sons Francis and Richard Cardwell also became wards of the church; however, they were likely older and of age because their names do not appear in church records. On February 18, 1779, the church assigned Thomas, Perrin, and John Cardwell to John Netherland as apprentices to learn a trade. "It is ordered that the Church wardens of Southam Parish bind out John Cardwell, Perrin Cardwell, and Thomas Cardwell orphans of George Cardwell according to Law." The Southam Parish Vestry showed that John Netherland received an annual amount of 800 pounds of tobacco for support of the children.[11]

The longstanding claim among some genealogists that George and Letitia Cardwell were the ancestors of the Cardwell branch of North Carolina lacks proof. For many years, they were the ancestors of convenience; that is, of the right generation to be a connecting link between Thomas Cardwell the Immigrant and Thomas Cardwell of Granville, North Carolina. However, the research of Rand Cardwell, among others, found that if there is a linkage, it may begin somewhere within previous Cardwell generations. Descendants of George Cardwell appear to be those who seeded the early settlement of Claiborne County, Tennessee. John G. Cardwell, probable son of George, appeared there as early as 1801 with his adult family. Therefore, he could not have been the John who was the son of Thomas Cardwell of Granville, North Carolina, born in 1787; although, yet unresolved is the claim of family historian P.G. Fulkerson who said that John Cardwell of Claiborne, Tennessee, came from North Carolina in 1810 and settled on Lone Mountain in Claiborne County.[12] Meanwhile, Rev. Perrin Cardwell, son of George, settled in Knox County, Tennessee.[13] George Cardwell also had a son named Thomas who was of age to be Thomas Cardwell of Granville. He often receives that distinction in Cardwell genealogies. However, Thomas, son of George Cardwell, was born after 1747 in Cumberland County, Virginia. He was one of the three Cardwell brothers growing up under the welfare of the Episcopal Methodist Church of Cumberland (Powhatan) County. He married Mary A. Freeman on September 11, 1787, in Amelia County, Virginia. His marriage date alone is sufficient to disqualify him as Thomas Cardwell of Granville, North Carolina, because that Thomas married Mary Leonard and had several children before 1787. Nevertheless, family historians persist in identifying Thomas of Cumberland County, Virginia, as Thomas of Granville. Furthermore, efforts to establish Thomas, son of George, as the Thomas who settled with his brother John G. in Claiborne County, Tennessee, are also lacking in convincing proof.[14]

Efforts to identify Thomas Cardwell of Granville, North Carolina, with branches of the Cardwells of Virginia are ongoing. All of the sons of Thomas Cardwell, Jr. had offspring named Thomas. However, reliable records appear to document all of them as other than Thomas of Granville. For example, one failed attempt makes Thomas Cardwell, brother of George and son of Thomas Cardwell, Jr., the Thomas of Granville. The obvious miscalculation of the generational differences renders such an idea unacceptable. Thomas predeceased his father, who died in 1772, well before Thomas of Granville appeared in the 1790 census in Granville.[15]

Another Thomas, nephew of George and son of John and Keziah (Lowe) Cardwell who married Mary Joyce, is a possible candidate. He was born about 1743 in Henrico County, Virginia, and supposedly died in Stokes County, North Carolina, at an advanced age. He acquired 100 acres on Peters Creek in Surry County, North Carolina, in 1789. Surry County became Stokes County in 1789.[16] However, both Thomas of Surry and Thomas of Granville appeared in the 1790 North Carolina census at their respective locations in Granville and Stokes Counties. They may have shared a common ancestry but clearly, they were different individuals.

Looking to other offspring of Thomas, Jr., his son Richard Ambrose Cardwell had a son named Thomas who married Obedience Thweatt.[17] However, that Thomas allegedly died in the Revolutionary War in 1780 in South Carolina, although it is probable that he was the same Thomas of Deep Creek, Goochland County, who died in 1789 in Dinwiddie County.[18] Obedience (Thweatt) Cardwell was executor of his will.[19] In either event, both death dates—1780 and 1789—predate the death of Thomas of Granville County, North Carolina.[20]

None of the Thomas Cardwells known to have descended from Thomas, Jr. appears to be Thomas of Granville. This finding recalls the riddle of Tyler who wrote in 1915, "The first Cardwell of record in this country is believed to have come from Wales in the eighteenth century. He had three sons, one of whom settled in King William county, Virginia, on the Mattaponi River; the other two in Charlotte County, Virginia. One of the latter, Richard Cardwell, moved to North Carolina, locating in Rockingham County, on the Dan River, where he acquired a large landed estate."[21] Records indicate this was probably Richard Perrin Cardwell, son of Richard Ambrose and grandson of Thomas, Jr., who acquired 400 acres in 1782 between Beaver Island Creek and the Mayo River, a tributary of the Dan River.[22] Unfortunately, Tyler began his theory of the origin of the Cardwell family in America two generations after Thomas, Jr. While he was wrong in his conclusions, the origin of the Cardwell family of North Carolina may, as Rand Cardwell has speculated, eventually rest on the discovery of a completely different line of the Cardwell family distantly related or totally unrelated to Thomas Cardwell the Immigrant, Thomas Cardwell, Jr., or to their descendants. Since none of the descendants of Thomas Cardwell, Jr. as identified matches the demographics of Thomas Cardwell of Granville, it becomes necessary to look back past the generations of George Cardwell and Thomas Cardwell, Jr. to connect to the Cardwell families of Virginia. Whether he was from a branch of the descendants of Thomas Cardwell, Sr. of Henrico County or Thomas the Immigrant may yet emerge. Meanwhile, it is enough to know that the generations of Virginia Cardwell families were the ancestral roots of a Cardwell presence that spread across America. While it may prove necessary to reach back across the Atlantic to Wales or England to find a common ancestor, the Cardwell name established itself early as part of the settlement of the Virginia Colony and of the nation.

Historian William Smith Bryan did not yet know the full extent of Cardwell genealogy when he wrote his 1876 passage, "Thomas R. Cardwell, of England, (hereafter referred to as Thomas the Immigrant), came to America in 1636 and settled in present Richmond, Virginia. His children were John, Perrin, and George. John married Keziah Low [*sic*], and they had John, Jr., Thomas, William, James, Wiltshire, George, Elizabeth, Nancy, Martha, Lucy, and Mary. George, son of Thomas Cardwell, Sr. (some name him as the son of John Jr.), married Anna Hamilton, and they had John, Elizabeth, William, Keziah, Martha, Mary, George, Jr., Jane, Rebecca, Wyatt, and James. George, Jr. married Ida Vansdoll and settled in Missouri in 1832. Martha married William Shelley. Wyatt married May Woods and settled in Audrain County in 1834. Jane married William Woods. William married Barbara Sanford and settled in Audrain County in 1837. He was married a second time to Elizabeth Watts."[23]

These early Cardwell descendants of the line described by Bryan settled primarily in Charlotte and Halifax counties, Virginia. Later generations migrated to Stoddard County, Audrain, and Webster Counties, in Missouri.[24] However, nowhere in Bryan's summary of Cardwell descendants did he mention the Cardwell families of Granville, North Carolina, ancestors of Cardwell generations in Tennessee, Kentucky, and Cedar County, Missouri. Nevertheless, the names of the children of Thomas of Granville, North Carolina, share a conspicuous relationship to their Virginia counterparts.

Salt Box Colonial House. Late seventeenth century style Virginia architecture was of medieval origin and featured a steeply pitched side gable roof, and massive end chimney of brick. The familiar colonial weatherboard siding and wooden shingles were the dominant mode of construction, eventually augmented by the log house known as the Virginia House. The English Salt Box was the common style of early housing in colonial Virginia. *Historic American Buildings Survey.* Library of Congress.

Windsor Shades. Known as Waterville, James Ruffin built this manor house about 1750 during the generation of George Cardwell. Its beaded weatherboards, gambrel roof, and massive brick chimneys were typical of Tidewater Virginia colonial plantation architecture of the 18th century. Built in King William County, it overlooked Ruffin's Ferry on the Pamunkey River crossing into New Kent County. The association of the Cardwell family with King William and New Kent Counties infers a likely familiarity with the Pamunkey ferry and Windsor Shades. The house was once a tavern along the Burgess Route to Williamsburg. George Washington was a regular patron. *Historic American Buildings Survey*, c.1933. Library of Congress.

Cardwell Fourth Generation Family Group

George Cardwell was born in 1720 in Henrico County, Virginia. He died on 24 Aug 1767 in Cumberland County, Virginia. He was the son of **Thomas R. Cardwell, Jr.** and **Martha M. Perrin**.

George married Letitia, variously identified as Letitia Corbin (Ball) Lee or **Letitia Mary Frances Gaines.**[25] She died Jan 1788, in Virginia. George and Letitia lived on plantations on the James and Appomattox Rivers with their sons Richard Perrin, John, and Thomas Cardwell who were all in the Revolutionary War.

George and Letitia had the following children.

1. **Rev. Perrin Cardwell** was born in 1743 in Prince Edward County, Virginia. He died in Knox County, Tennessee. His child was John Cardwell, born 17 Jan 1790 in Fauquier County, Virginia, and died on 11 Feb 1876 in Breathitt County, Kentucky. John married Arminta W. Watkins on 12 May 1823 in Jefferson County, Tennessee. Arminta was born on 13 May 1799 in Wilkes County, North Carolina. She died on 13 Mar 1891 in Breathitt County, Kentucky.

2. **John G. Cardwell** was born in 1760. He died before 1824 in Claiborne County, Tennessee. John married Mary Royal. Their children were Francis G. (Frank) Cardwell b. c.1796. He died in 1844. Francis married Judah (Judy) Leabow in 1826 in Claiborne County, Tennessee. Judah was born in 1804. She died in 1867. Other children of John G. and Mary (Royal) Cardwell were Perrin Cardwell, John Cardwell, Jr., Royal Cardwell, William Cardwell, Sarah Cardwell, and Mary Cardwell.

\+ 3. **Thomas Cardwell**. He was born after 1747, in Cumberland County, Virginia. He died on an unknown date probably in Tennessee. He married Mary A. Freeman on September 11, 1787, in Amelia County, Virginia. Genealogists point to him by default as Thomas Cardwell of Granville, North Carolina, because he is of the right generation and plausible descent to link Thomas of Granville and Thomas Cardwell the Immigrant. However, that link is unproven and disputed.

19

Thomas Cardwell of Granville

The proven Cardwell genealogy of Beatrice begins with Thomas Cardwell of Granville who was born about 1744, possibly in Cumberland County, Virginia, and died in 1799, in Granville County, North Carolina. He married Mary Leonard, the daughter of Jonathan Leonard and Martha Nelson, between the years 1765 and 1784. Mary died in 1802, in Granville County.[1] A competing theory that Thomas married Mary Freeman in 1787, in Amelia County, Virginia, is without merit.[2] It is unlikely because records indicate that Thomas and Mary Leonard had children born before 1787, among them their firstborn son Jonathan Leonard named for his maternal grandfather.[3]

It is unknown when Thomas Cardwell arrived in Granville County, North Carolina, but certainly well after the founding of the county in 1746. The birthdates of his first four children born in Virginia suggest he arrived in North Carolina around 1783.

Thomas and Mary settled in the Island Creek District of the greater Hillsboro District of North Carolina, which included the county of Granville. Hillsborough District combined six counties into one district, Granville County being one of the six. The historical seat of the Cardwell family of North Carolina was in the old Island Creek District, which originally was in Granville County, near the Virginia line, and about midway along the northern boundary of North Carolina. Island Creek today lies in Vance County, Tennessee. Island Creek District followed the boundaries laid out in a 1770 description that had the district "bounded by Taylors Road from the County line to Hico Road, by that road up to Grassy Creek, by Grassy Creek down to the county line and by the county line to Taylors Road."

The earliest record of Thomas Cardwell in North Carolina was in 1788. The 1788 Granville County tax list filed with the Granville County Court listed him among the taxpayers assessed in the Island Creek District.[4] He was the only Cardwell of tithable age who appeared on the tax list for Granville County that year.[5] The early records of North Carolina do not say much about the Cardwell family. According to historians, the Island Creek District was part of the Nutbush region that lay immediately east, which became a prosperous area of Granville County in the late 1780s. Visitors to the region described it as a "healthy and pleasant situation, well-watered with cool refreshing springs, also well calculated for an inland manufacturing town." One enthusiast said, "There arose around the area of Williamsboro a society different from the frontier rural environment experienced elsewhere in Granville County. The atmosphere was marked by 'intellectual distinction, social graces,' and the dignity of the large planters that came to congregate there."[6] The region was dependent on slave labor to work the lucrative and labor-intensive cultivation of tobacco. Thomas Cardwell was not a large plantation owner, although he did own slaves. His sons appeared to have engaged in the commerce and manufacturing that characterized the Williamsboro area. However, mostly the Cardwells were farmers.

The 1790 U.S. Census listed Thomas in the Island Creek District.[7] The 1790 document was a reproduction of the 1788 tax list, which substituted for the lost Granville records. Thomas was the only Cardwell in Granville County in the compiled 1790 census.[8] Only two other heads of household of the name Cardwell lived in the entire state of North Carolina. Another of the same name, Thomas Cardwell of Stokes County, North Carolina, lived a few counties west of Granville County.[9] He was a large slave owner who appeared in later censuses in Stokes County as a possible relative of Thomas of Granville County. Meanwhile, Perrin Cordwell [*sic*], thought to be Richard Perrin Cardwell, lived in Wilks County, North Carolina.[10] Wilks County formed from Surry County in 1778. Richard Perrin, grandson of Thomas Cardwell, Jr. of Henrico County, Virginia, was originally from Henrico and Cumberland Counties, Virginia. He settled in Surrey County (later Wilks), and was a probable relative of Thomas of Granville.

Thomas Cardwell of Granville died on May 3, 1799, in Granville County. The head of household then passed to his wife, Mary (Leonard) Cardwell.[11] The 1800 census recorded Mary Cardwell as a widow living in the Hillsborough District of Granville County with 11 members of her household assumed to be her children.[12] She had not yet attained her 44th birthday. The eldest children were already on their own and not enumerated in the census. Thomas and Mary (Leonard) Cardwell had 12 children: Leonard, Thomas [Jr.], William, John, Dudley, Wilson, Caleb, Anderson, and Nelson. Their daughters were Mary, Sally, and Nancy.[13] A fourth daughter, Martha, is likely. Among their offspring were sons Leonard and Nelson named for maternal grandparents, and Thomas [Jr.] and Mary named for their parents, as well as for the obvious linkage of previous generations to the name Thomas. Naming conventions of early ancestors were often reaffirmations of genealogical connections within a family group. For example, a previously unnamed but likely fourth daughter of Thomas and Mary was Martha Patty Cardwell, probable namesake of Martha (Nelson) Leonard her maternal grandmother, or perhaps Martha (Perrin) Cardwell, wife of Thomas Cardwell, Jr. of Henrico County, Virginia. The circumstantial evidence of family connections between the Henrico, Virginia, and Granville, North Carolina, branches of Cardwells is notable but lacks sufficient documented verification to establish a true relationship.

Thomas of Granville died intestate. In May 1800, the Granville County Court probated his estate naming as his "Devisees," or heirs, "Thomas Cardwell, Leonard Cardwell, William Cardwell, John Cardwell, Patti Nance, and Mrs. Thomas Cardwell."[14] A second filing by the court repeated the assignments but named "Patti Nance" separate from the other adult children, raising in the process the question of her identity.[15] Circumstantial evidence suggests that she was Martha Cardwell who married Harwood (aka Howard) Nance on May 9, 1798, in Granville County.[16] It is likely that Patti Nance named in the probate records with the other Cardwell children was the same person as Martha (Cardwell) "Patti" Nance, and the adult daughter of Thomas and Mary Cardwell of Granville.[17]

In 1801, the Granville County Court appointed Leonard and Thomas [Jr.] guardians of their minor siblings.[18] Nine of the children were under the age of 16; the youngest was about four years old. Mary Cardwell was in failing health, leaving the Cardwell children in the care of her two older sons, the only sons with nascent families able to act as guardians for their young siblings.[19] The two older boys married about this time in Granville County. Thomas [Jr.] married Nancy Loyd in 1801, and Leonard married Lucy (Longmire) Strum in 1802,

However, no sooner had the court taken action to administer the late Thomas Cardwell's estate than one of his creditors filed a lawsuit against Mary and the Cardwell children. John Brodie, Esquire, of Orange County, North Carolina, instituted a suit against Thomas Cardwell's executors on January 10, 1801, seeking a judgment of 100 pounds. The sheriff of Granville County received orders "to take the body of Mary Cardwell Executrix of Thomas Cardwell" into custody to appear in court. Mary was very ill at the time and did not appear as ordered. A court verdict set damages of 43 pounds, 4 shillings, and 2 pence, plus court costs. The Granville Court ordered the sheriff to take goods and chattels in the amount to cover the judgment, "if to be found." The sheriff reported back, "no goods and chattels to be found." The court ordered Mary to appear before the court in the next 1802 Term.[20]

Mary died in the summer of 1802 before the next court term convened. Nevertheless, Mr. Brodie pressed his lawsuit against the Cardwell estate, and the Granville Court ordered that the remaining heirs appear to defend the suit, at the same time reaffirming Thomas and Leonard as guardians of their underage siblings now orphans in the wake of Mary's death. The order to the sheriff, filed in August 1802, read, "It hath been reported to us that William, John, Wilson, Caleb, Anderson, Dudley, Nelson, Mary, Sally, and Nancy Cardwell are heirs of the said Thomas Cardwell dec'd who are infants under age. You are therefore commanded to make known to Leonard Cardwell and Thomas Cardwell who is appointed guardians to the said orphans to defend said suit to appear before the justices of our court of pleas and quarter sessions to be held for the county of Granville at the courthouse in Granville on the first Monday of November inst." The order threatened to take the judgment out of Cardwell real estate.

The Cardwell brothers obtained a lawyer. On September 23, 1803, Leonard Cardwell through his attorney filed to have the judgment reversed. Meanwhile, court costs continued to mount. The sheriff returned a list of expenses acknowledged by the court September 26, 1803, for 7 pounds.

The plea of reversal filed in the October Term of 1803 argued, "William Cardwell, John Cardwell, Caleb Cardwell, Anderson Cardwell, Dudley Cardwell, Nelson Cardwell, Mary Cardwell, Wilson Cardwell, Sallie Cardwell, and Nancy Cardwell, heirs of Thomas Cardwell dec'd infants under twenty-one years of age by Leonard Cardwell and Thomas Cardwell their guardians against John Brodie. Alleged error: That there was Manifest Errors. That it does not appear in the record and proceedings that the Executrix Mary Cardwell of Thomas Cardwell had fully administered the estate of her testator or that she had [sufficient ability and means] to satisfy the suit brought against her." The Cardwell legal defense claimed that inasmuch as the estate "had not been fully administered," a suit against the heirs was premature, and that the judgment should be against Brodie for filing a false claim.

On April 6, 1804, the case of *The Heirs of Thomas Cardwell vs. John Brodie* moved to Superior Court. The upper court wasted no time in rendering a judgment. Writing to the Granville County Court, the justices said, "Manifest error irregularity and injustice have intervened to the great damage of the Heirs of the said Thomas Cardwell. We therefore do command you that you certify and send to us in our Superior Court of Law to be held for the District of Hillsborough at the courthouse in Hillsborough on the sixth day of October next the record and judgment aforesaid and all proceedings thereon with all things touching the same, distinctly and plainly under your seal together with the writ to the end that such other further proceedings may be had thereon as to our said Court may seem just and according to law ought to be done, and that you give notice to the said John Brodie that he appear before our said court at the day and place aforesaid to hear judgment thereon." The Superior Court ordered the lower court to "forbear to execute any judgment or writ" in the Granville Court case. The Superior Court heard the case in the October Term of 1804. No transcripts of the arguments exist. However, the case dragged on for more than a year. In the December Term 1805, A Court of Conference issued its verdict. "This court is of opinion that the judgment of the county court be reversed and that the plaintiffs in error be restored to all things they have lost by the same."

Thomas [Jr.] removed with part of the Cardwell family to Sumner County, Tennessee, in 1807.[21] The marriage of Nancy Cardwell, the youngest daughter of Thomas and Mary (Leonard) Cardwell, to Samuel Bradley in Sumner County, Tennessee, in 1811 confirmed that the Cardwell family lived in two different places, some in Tennessee and some in North Carolina, and reaffirmed that part of the family left Granville County consistent with the 1807 date recorded by family tradition.[22]

The Tennessee Cardwells moved north from Granville, crossing Tennessee to a location below the Kentucky border in Sumner County. Sumner County was in Middle Tennessee, one of the three Grand Divisions of East, Middle, and West Tennessee. Formed from Davidson County in 1786, Sumner was the second-oldest county in Middle Tennessee, distinct culturally, economically, and geographically from its East and West counterparts. The county seat of Sumner was Gallatin, established there in 1802.

A parsing of tax rolls and an analysis of early census records suggest that Nelson, Wilson, and the three Cardwell girls went with Thomas [Jr.] to Tennessee. Thomas [Jr.] and Nancy (Loyd) Cardwell raised the youngest Cardwell children as their own.[23] The tax rolls may also suggest a motivation for the move to Sumner County. Listed in the 1809 rolls along with Thomas [Jr.] was a heretofore unaccounted for James Cardwell and a William Cardwell who appeared on the rolls in 1812.[24] It may be relevant to note that Thomas Cardwell, Jr. of Henrico, Virginia, had grandsons named William and James, sons of John Cardwell of Henrico, Goochland, and Prince Edward Counties. However, it is pertinent to the record to acknowledge that Thomas [Jr.] had two brothers, William and James Dudley, who were of taxable ages in 1812. Meanwhile, another brother, Richard Wilson Cardwell, acquired 43 acres of land next to Thomas [Jr.] on Second Creek, in Sumner County. Wilson disappeared from the Sumner County tax rolls in 1817. He resurfaced in Bedford County, Tennessee, became a clergyman in the Episcopal Methodist Church, and lived a long life in Washington County, Arkansas.

Thomas [Jr.] became the surrogate father of the next generation of the present Cardwell lineage, establishing himself in Sumner County where he appeared on the tax rolls from 1809 through 1838. Beginning in 1817, he paid taxes each year on one-hundred-ten and one-fourth acres of land located on Second Creek.[25] He paid $3.00 in county taxes in 1838, mostly poll tax for household members. The head of the household paid a tax on any male in the house deemed able to work in the fields, usually ages 16 to 59. The county placed a value of $700 on the 110 acres that Thomas owned, and taxed him .35 cents, an amount well below the property valuations of most of his neighbors.[26] His name disappeared from the tax rolls after 1838, about the time he moved to Calloway County, Kentucky.[27]

Meanwhile in North Carolina, by the year 1810, the only Cardwells left in Granville County of an age to be included as heads of households in the census were Leonard and William.[28] When the family broke up, Leonard the oldest of the Cardwell siblings, remained in Granville County, raised a family including his younger siblings, became a slave owner, and lived in Granville a number of years as a farmer and manufacturer in the commercial district of Williamsboro, North Carolina.[29] He moved to Smith County, Tennessee, before 1830 and lived to a good age. William Cardwell also remained in Granville County along with Leonard and younger brothers John G., Caleb, James Dudley, and Anderson. William was a farmer who owned slaves, and lived his entire life in Granville County, except for a brief time toward the end of his life when he moved to Smith County, Tennessee, to live with his son. He likewise lived to a good old age. Given the presence of William and James Dudley in Granville County, it seems unlikely that they were the William and James previously noted in the Sumner County tax rolls.

By 1820, Anderson Cardwell, the next to the youngest brother in the Cardwell clan, came of age and appeared on the census as a head of household in Granville County. Nancy G. (Cardwell) Bradley had meanwhile moved from Sumner County, Tennessee, to Smith County, Tennessee, shortly after her marriage in Sumner County in 1811. By the early 1820s, she and Anderson Cardwell had both resettled in Smith County. Their two brothers, John G. and Caleb joined them. John G. remained in Smith County, Tennessee, his entire life. Caleb removed to Montgomery County, Illinois, about 1827.

The Cardwell migration from Granville, North Carolina, to Smith County, Tennessee, corresponds to the movements of Martha "Patti" (Cardwell) Nance, and supports the claim of her as a Cardwell sibling. Harwood Nance her husband appeared in the 1820 Smith County census and again in 1830 living in close proximity to Cardwell siblings Anderson Cardwell, John G. Cardwell, and Leonard Cardwell. Martha Nance was in her fifties in 1830, making her of the correct age to be among the elder Cardwell offspring.[30]

The Cardwells were mainly subsistence farmers, meaning they lived off the land and depended on it for income. Several owned slaves. Goodspeed wrote about the farmers of Smith County. "For many years, including the decade of the twenties, they raised cotton to a considerable extent, and afterward abandoned its cultivation. The cultivation of tobacco was early introduced and this crop has always been, and still continues to be [in 1887], a staple production of the county."[31]

The Cardwells of Granville, North Carolina, eventually dispersed across the country to establish households of Cardwells that produced many of the descendants found in North Carolina, Tennessee, Kentucky, Illinois, Arkansas, and Missouri. However, in the late 1820s, most of the original Thomas Cardwell family of Granville still lived close together. Thomas [Jr.], Wilson, and Nelson were in Sumner County, Tennessee; Leonard, Nancy, John, Caleb, Anderson, and Martha were in Smith County adjacent to Sumner County. Only William remained in Granville County. Three of the Cardwell siblings, Mary, Sallie, and Dudley are unaccounted for in primary source documents but probably resided in Sumner County. A long list of Cardwell marriages in the county from about 1830 until the turn of the twentieth century confirms Sumner County as one of the traditional seats of the Cardwell family in Tennessee.[32]

For a while, the Cardwell brothers lived in near proximity to each other in Sumner County and Smith County, Tennessee. In due time, however, they went separate ways. Leonard remained in Smith County, as did John G. Cardwell. Thomas [Jr.] went to Calloway County, Kentucky; and Nelson resettled in Simpson County, Kentucky. Rev. Richard Wilson moved to Washington County, Arkansas, where he was a clergyman for more than 40 years. Anderson went to Macoupin County, Illinois, and Caleb settled in Montgomery County, Illinois.

The Cardwell genealogy continued from Thomas and Mary (Leonard) Cardwell of Granville, North Carolina, to Nelson Cardwell, of Simpson County, Kentucky.

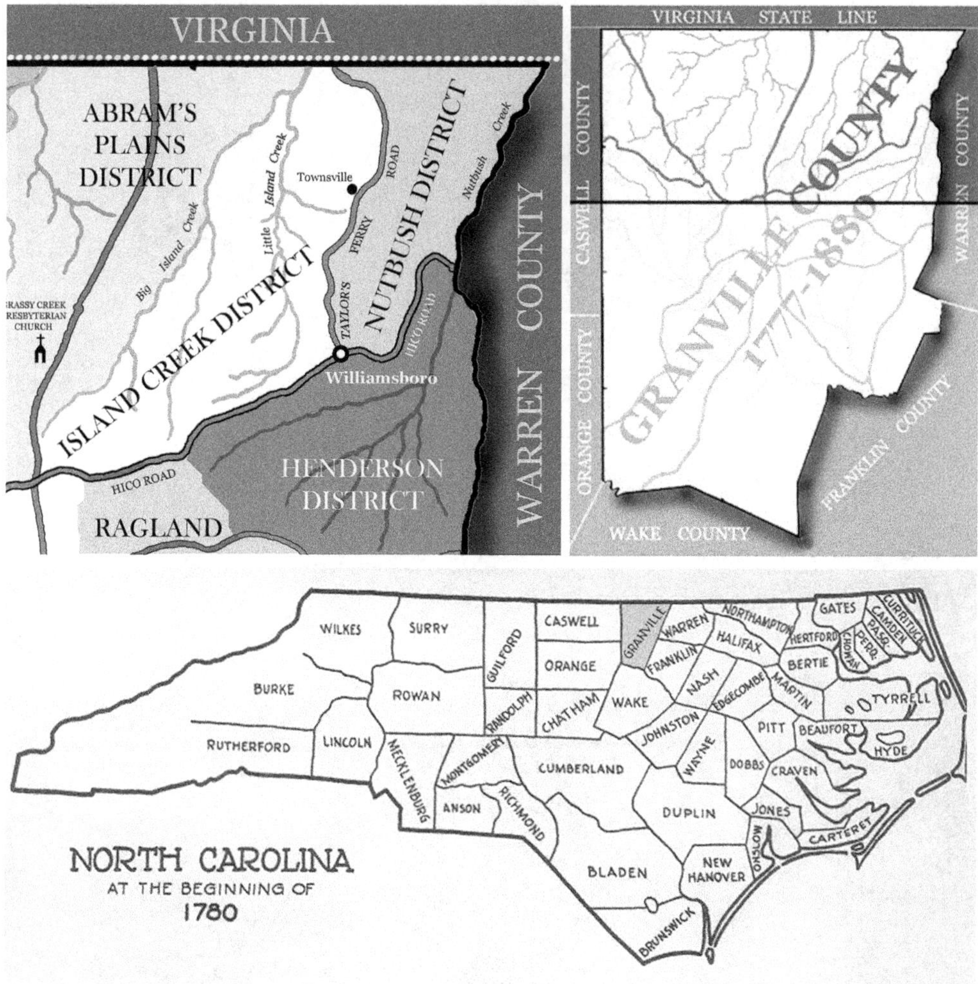

Map of Island Creek District, Granville County, North Carolina. Island Creek District lay in the northeast portion of Granville County, North Carolina, bounded by Taylors Ferry Road down to Hico Road, from Hico Road to Island Creek, up Island Creek to the Virginia state line, along the Virginia state line back to Taylors Ferry Road. Mecklenburg, Virginia, bounded it on the north; Nutbush District bounded it on the east; Henderson District, Ragland District, and Oxford District bounded it on the south; and Abrams Plains District bounded it on the west. By 1872, this irregular shaped district gave way to a square-grid system of townships. Most of Island Creek District assimilated into the Townsville Township. The area that was once the eastern portion of Granville County, which included the old Island Creek District, became Vance County, North Carolina, in 1881.

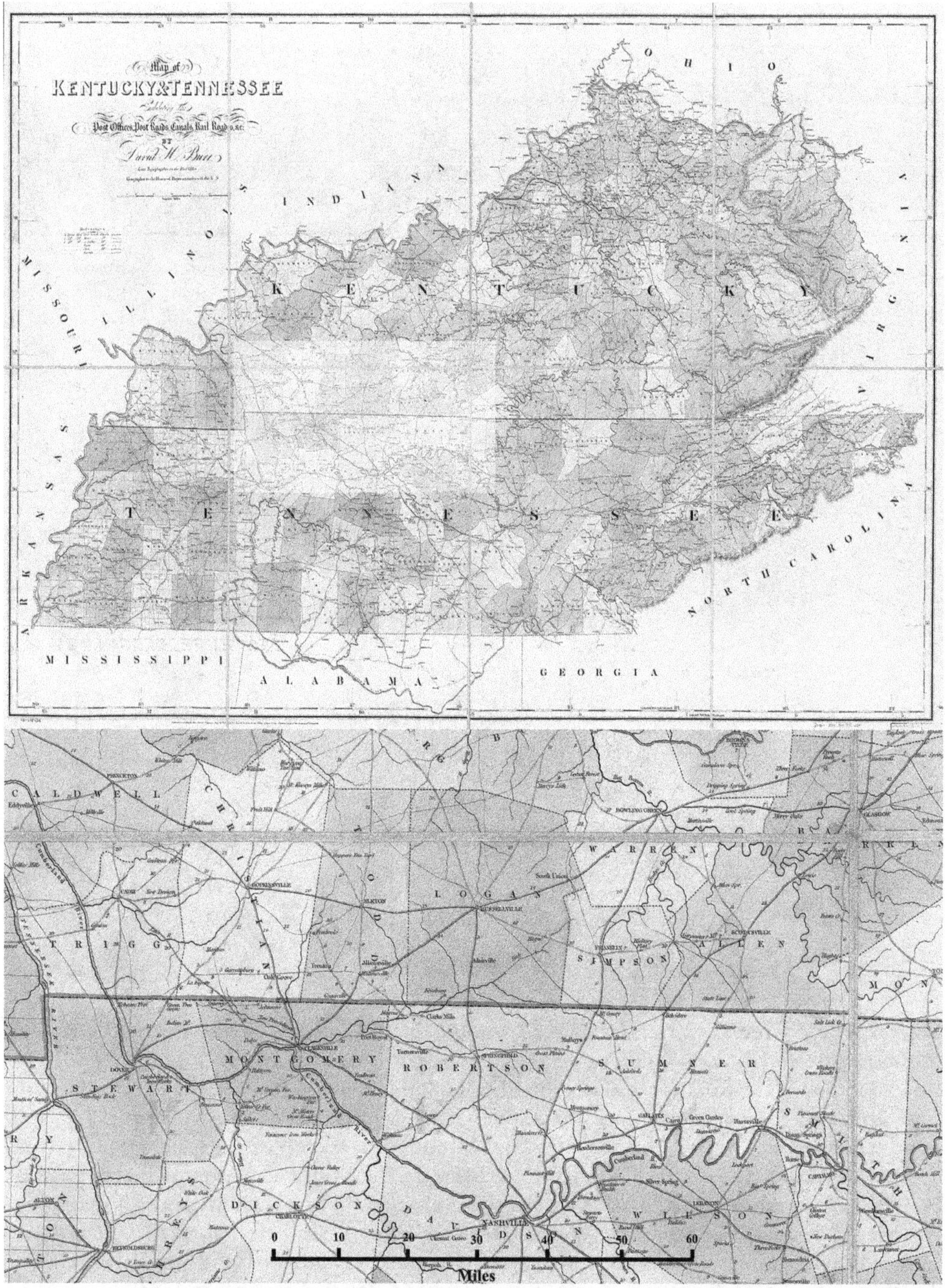

Map of Kentucky and Tennessee. Enlarged inset of a section of approximately 75 by 135 miles that includes the counties of Trigg, Christian, and Simpson, in Kentucky, and Sumner and Smith counties in Tennessee. All were places associated with the Cardwell and Stegall families in the early 19th century. Adapted from a map by David H. Burr from *The American Atlas,* London, J. Arrowsmith, 1839. Library of Congress.

Cardwell Fifth Generation Family Group

Thomas CARDWELL was born about 1744. Some genealogists believe he was the son of **George Cardwell** and **Letitia Mary Frances Gaines**. However, his ancestry is unproven. He died on 3 May 1799 in Granville County, North Carolina.[33]

Thomas married **Mary LEONARD**, daughter of **Jonathan LEONARD** and **Martha NELSON**. Mary died in Aug 1802 in Granville County, North Carolina.[34]

They had the following children.[35]

1. **Jonathan Leonard Jefferson Cardwell** was born before 1774 [genealogists believe 1769], probably in Virginia.[36] He died in 1845 in Smith County, Tennessee. His burial was in Cardwell Cemetery, McClure's Bend, Smith County, Tennessee.[37] Leonard married **Lucy (Longmire) Strum** 18 Dec 1802, in Granville County, North Carolina.[38] Lucy was born before 1790 in Granville County. She died in 1847 in Smith County, Tennessee. Her burial was in Cardwell Cemetery, McClure's Bend, Smith County, Tennessee.[39] Leonard married secondly **Mary Ann Wilson.**[40] Leonard Cardwell was a witness to the will of John Wilson, Sr. in 1802 in Granville County Court.[41] The 1820 census listed him in Capt. Henderson's District of Granville County. The census described a large household of 26 persons, including seven slaves, engaged in multiple enterprises from agriculture (two persons) to commerce (two persons) to manufacturing (four persons).[42] His daughter Lethe married William Summerhill, Jr. 26 Jul 1820 in Granville, North Carolina.[43] Leonard was a witness to the Will of Stephen Sneed in 1821 in Granville County Court, and a witness to the will of William Ragland in 1825.[44] About 1827, Leonard removed to Smith County, Tennessee, where he appeared in the censuses of 1830 and 1840. He was a slave owner. Beginning with two slaves in 1810, he increased his holdings to seven slaves by 1820. However, he had no slaves in 1830 and only one in 1840.[45]

2. **Martha "Patti" Cardwell.** Her estimated birthdate is 1775, in Virginia. She died after 1830 in Smith County, Tennessee.[46] Martha Cardwell married Harwood Nance 9 May 1798 in Granville County, North Carolina. [47] They removed to Smith County, Tennessee, before 1820. Probate records of 1801 mentioned Patti Nance as a "Devisee" of the deceased Thomas Cardwell

presumed to be her father. Patti was likely Martha Cardwell who married Harwood Nance in 1798.

3. **Thomas J. Cardwell [Jr.]**[48] His estimated birth is 1778, in Virginia. He died 29 Sep 1853 in Calloway County, Kentucky.[49] Thomas married **Nancy "Nanni" Loyd** 24 Dec 1801 in Granville County, North Carolina.[50] He married secondly **Mary Westbrook.**[51] A claim of genealogists that he secondly married **Temperance Lemay** 19 Dec 1805 is inaccurate. Temperance Lemay of Granville County, North Carolina, married Gideon Crews on 19 Dec 1805, in Granville County.[52]

The 1820 census found Thomas and his family living in Sumner County, Tennessee, near Gallatin, with a large household of 10 persons. The census enumerated him as above age 45. However, this does not align with enumerations in census records in 1810, 1830, 1840, and 1850, which correspond to an age of 42 and in line with his estimated birthdate of 1778. The 1830 census listed him as Thomas J. Cordwell [*sic*] in Sumner County, Tennessee, engaged in farming with five slaves.[53] His daughter, Nancy Wilson Cardwell, married John Ward on 15 May 1828. They settled in Johnson County, Tennessee.[54] His younger daughter, Thursy G. Cardwell, married her cousin James W. Bradley 22 May 1837, in Sumner County.[55] James W. was the son of Nancy (Cardwell) Bradley.[56] Meanwhile, the presumed son of Thomas, Thomas [III], married B. Lewis in 1838.[57] Around this time, Thomas [Jr.] removed to Calloway County, Kentucky, where the 1840 census found him heavily engaged in farming with his sons and nine slaves.[58] The 1850 census again recorded him in Calloway County, at age 72, with no slaves but still farming and living with his daughter Elizabeth M. Cardwell, age 44.[59] Shortly after his death in 1853, two of his daughters, Mary C. (Cardwell) Bogard and Linda Cardwell died within days of each other in June and July of 1854, in Calloway County, Kentucky.[60]

4. **William W. Cardwell** was born about 1780 in Virginia. He died after 1860, probably in Obion County, Tennessee.[61] He married **Anne Lawrence** on 4 Nov 1806 in Granville County, North Carolina.[62] Probate records of 1802 mentioned him as an heir of Thomas Cardwell, deceased.[63] The U.S. census from 1810 to 1840 listed him in Granville, North Carolina.[64] He owned seven slaves in 1820 engaged in agriculture; in 1840, he had four slaves. In 1850, he was living in Smith County, Tennessee, with his son Daniel J. Cardwell.[65] The family removed to Obion County, Tennessee, where the 1860 census found William at the age of 80 living with his son.[66]

5. **Richard Wilson Cardwell** was born 28 Sep 1785 in Granville County, North Carolina. He died 19 May 1872, in Fayetteville, Washington County, Arkansas.[67] He married **Margaret "Peggy" Loyd** 2 Dec 1806 in Granville County, North Carolina.[68] Probate records mentioned him in 1802 as an heir of Thomas Cardwell.[69] After his parents died, Wilson went to Sumner County, Tennessee, in 1807 with his brother Thomas [Jr.] and a number of younger Cardwell sibling orphans. He disappeared from the Sumner County tax rolls after 1817.[70] He did not appear in the 1820 census but resurfaced in 1830 listed in Bedford County, Tennessee.[71] He became a Methodist Episcopal clergyman and settled in Washington County, Arkansas, around 1835, making his home in Prairie Township, near Fayetteville, Arkansas.[72] The 1840, 1850, and 1870 censuses listed him in Prairie Township.[73] Both he and Margaret lived to be in their eighties.

6. **Sally Cardwell** was born about 1786 in Granville County, North Carolina. It is probably her in the 1800 census of Granville County, North Carolina, listed as female age 10-15 in the household of Mary (Leonard) Cardwell.[74] Probate records mentioned her in 1802 as an heir of Thomas Cardwell.[75]

7. **John G. Cardwell** was born about 1787 in Granville, North Carolina. He died in Feb 1843 in Smith County, Tennessee.[76] John G. married **Sarah (Sally) H. Robinson**. She died after 1843. Probate records confirmed John G. as an heir of Thomas Cardwell in 1802.[77] He grew to adulthood in Granville County and later moved to Smith County, Tennessee, where he raised a large family. The Smith County, Tennessee, census listed him in 1830.[78] His will mentioned a blind grandson.

8. **James Dudley Cardwell** was born about 1788 in Granville County, North Carolina. Records appear to confirm that he settled in Tuscaloosa County, Alabama, living under the name James Cardwell. He married **Elizabeth E. Foster** 26 Apr 1823 in Tuscaloosa County and died in 1851 in Alabama.[79] An unverified source identified him as one of eight brothers of Anderson Cardwell, son of Thomas of Granville.[80] Probate records of 1801-1802 mentioned him as an heir of the deceased Thomas Cardwell. He had a presumed nephew of the same unique name of Dudley.[81] It is probably James Dudley in the 1800 census of Granville County, North Carolina, as male age 10-15 in the household of Mary (Leonard) Cardwell.[82] His estimated birthdate comes from the census enumeration ranked with the known birthdates of his siblings.

9. **Caleb West Cardwell** was born about 1790 in Granville County, North Carolina.[83] He died after 1840. It is possibly him in the 1800 census of Granville County, North Carolina, listed as male age under 10 in the household of Mary (Leonard) Cardwell.[84] Probate records listed him as an heir of the deceased Thomas Cardwell in 1802.[85] He enlisted as a private in the War of 1812, in Captain Harry's Tennessee Militia for which he received land grants in Montgomery County, Illinois.[86] According to Rand Cardwell, Caleb served in the War of 1812 as a Private under Col. James Ralstone, Maj. Gen. William Carroll, and Capt. Edward Robinson, of the Tennessee Infantry. Also listed on the muster rolls for that unit was James Cardwell his presumed older brother James Dudley Cardwell, referred to as Dudley Cardwell in Granville County, North Carolina, court records.[87] Caleb had a daughter born in 1818, later associated with Montgomery County, Illinois.[88] He appeared in the 1820 census in Smith County, Tennessee.[89] However, in the 1830 and 1840 censuses he was in Illinois.[90] He removed to Montgomery County, Illinois, about 1825.

10. **Anderson Nelson Cardwell** was born about 1791 in Granville, North Carolina.[91] He died before 1855, in Macoupin County, Illinois.[92] Anderson married **Elizabeth Robinson**. Granville County probate records named him as an heir of Thomas Cardwell in 1802.[93] He enrolled at the rank of private in the War of 1812, in Captain Blakemore's Tennessee Militia. The muster roll listed him as Anderson Nelson Cardwell.[94] He received a land grant of 160 acres in Palo Alto, County, Iowa, for his service in the war. His widow, Elizabeth (Robinson) Cardwell later assigned the grant to William E. Merrill 2 Nov 1863. This document refers to him as Anderson Nelson Cardwell, "private who served as Nelson Cardwell in Captain Blakemore's Company, Tennessee Militia, War 1812."[95] The 1830 census listed him in Smith County, Tennessee, and again in 1840.[96] Around 1845, he removed to Macoupin County, Illinois, where the census listed him, Elizabeth, and their large family in 1850.[97] Macoupin County, Illinois, is of special interest because Macoupin was the residence of Thomas Lee Baldwin who moved to Cedar County, Missouri, about 1867. His granddaughter Eliza Baldwin married into the Cardwell family.

11. **Mary Cardwell** was born about 1794 in Granville County, North Carolina.[98] It is probably her in the 1800 census of Granville County, North Carolina, listed as female under age 10 in the household of Mary (Leonard) Cardwell.[99] The 1802 probate records named her as an heir of Thomas Cardwell.

12. **Nancy Green Cardwell** was born on 24 May 1797 in Granville County, North Carolina.[100] She died of cancer at the age of 59 on 24 Jun 1856 in Macon County, Tennessee.[101] Nancy was one of 13 children identified in probate records as an heir of Thomas Cardwell of Granville, North Carolina.[102] She moved to Sumner County, Tennessee, in 1807.[103] She married **Samuel Bradley**, Esquire, on 18 March 1811 in Sumner County. She was about age 15 at the time.[104] Samuel was born on 16 July 1785 in Maryland and died 5 April 1886 in Civil District Five, Trousdale County, Tennessee, at the age of 100.[105] He served in the War of 1812 and received a pension. Nancy and Samuel first settled in Smith County, Tennessee, listed there in 1820 and 1830. They returned to Sumner County, Tennessee, appearing in the 1840, 1850 Sumner County censuses.[106] Samuel and Nancy had 13 children.[107] Nancy died in 1856, and Samuel married secondly **Elizabeth Charlton** 19 April 1859 in Sumner County, Tennessee.[108]

+ 13. **Nelson CARDWELL** was born about 1798 in Granville County, North Carolina.[109] He died between 1840 and 1850 in Simpson County, Kentucky.[110] Nelson married **Nancy HUGHS** on 30 Nov 1816 in Sumner County, Tennessee.[111] Nancy was born about 1800. She died before 1834 in Sumner County.[112] Probate records of 1802 named Nelson as an heir of Thomas Cardwell, deceased.[113] The 1820 census placed him in Sumner County, Tennessee.[114] He appeared on the Sumner County tax rolls from 1820 to 1830.[115] Nelson married secondly **Mary Polly Bennett** on 18 Jul 1835 in Sumner County, Tennessee. Mary was born in 1816.[116] They removed to Simpson County, Kentucky, about 1837 where they appeared in the 1840 Simpson County census.[117]

20

Nelson Cardwell

Nelson Cardwell (aka William Nelson and W. Nelson Cardwell) was born in 1798 in Granville County, North Carolina, the youngest of 13 children of Thomas and Mary (Leonard) Cardwell.[1] He died about 1847 in Simpson County, Kentucky.[2] Nelson married Nancy Hughs on 30 Nov 1816 in Sumner County, Tennessee.[3] Nancy was born about 1800. She died before 1834 in Sumner County, Tennessee.[4]

Thomas Cardwell of Granville died when Nelson was not yet four years old, leaving Mary (Leonard) Cardwell in poor health and unable to care for her large family.[5] In 1801, the Granville County Court appointed her oldest sons Leonard and Thomas [Jr.] as guardians of the younger Cardwells.[6] Mary died in the summer of 1802, leaving Nelson and his sibling orphans in the care of their older brothers who assumed adoptive custody of the ten younger Cardwell children, nine of them under the age of 16.[7] The Cardwell children remained at the family home in Granville County for a few years. By the end of 1806, four Cardwell brothers had married, and new Cardwell offspring of the next generation added to the growing Cardwell family. In 1807, the family divided.[8] Thomas Cardwell [Jr], guardian of Nelson and his younger Cardwell siblings, Wilson, Mary, Sarah, and Nancy, moved his part of the family from North Carolina to Tennessee. Nelson was about nine-years-old at the time. Meanwhile, Leonard Cardwell and the other members of Nelson's immediate family: Anderson, Caleb, Dudley, and William, remained in Granville.

Thomas [Jr.] and his contingent of the family traveled more than 400 miles, going from Island Creek in Granville County, North Carolina; westward to Sumner County, Tennessee, for no known purpose except there may have been Cardwell relatives already living in Sumner County.[9] For example, James

Cardwell appeared on the 1809 Tax Rolls for Sumner County alongside the listing of Thomas [Jr.] on the same roll.[10]

Nelson Cardwell grew up in Sumner County, Tennessee, under the guidance of his older brother Thomas [Jr.] who raised him to adulthood. The Cardwells arrived in Sumner County when the western frontier was still an unsettled place. Tennessee Territory was once part of the western lands of North Carolina. Sumner County's creation in 1786 predated Tennessee statehood in 1796, and made it the oldest county in Middle Tennessee. The Cardwells settled north of the Cumberland River along the ridge that extends across the county from southwest to northeast and divides Sumner County into two nearly equal parts. They lived south of "The Ridge," the Highland Rim of the Great Central Basin of Middle Tennessee. The towns of Gallatin, Hendersonville, and Bethpage mentioned in family records placed them about 15 miles south of the Kentucky border, below the Ridge where the land slopes south toward the Cumberland River. The rolling hills and well-watered lands attracted pioneer leaders as well as those of more meager means sometimes at the risk of danger. Tennessee historian Dee Lester wrote, "Native Americans did not passively accept this frontier advance; periodic warfare resulted in the deaths of both Indians and settlers... The opening of wagon roads, the influx of new settlers, and a preemptive strike at the Indian raiders' base village of Nickajack ended the Indian wars by 1795."[11] The Cardwells arrived in the territory less than a decade later at the peak of the county's growth. Sumner County grew rapidly from a population of around 4,500 in the year 1800 to about 20,000 in 1820, growing by a factor of four times in less than 20 years.

Thomas Cardwell [Jr.] acquired 110 acres on Second Branch in what is today Trousdale County, Tennessee; Wilson Cardwell obtained 43 acres nearby and here Nelson and the younger Cardwell children grew to adulthood.[12] With the exception of a two-year agricultural depression (1821-1823), the first half of the nineteenth century was a period of growth and development for Sumner County. Improved roads, a stagecoach line, river trade, and ferry services led to the establishment of some 30 communities and more than 50 manufacturing concerns, mostly distilleries and mills. The Cardwells were farmers. Second Creek where they lived provided handy access to markets. Second Creek, a tributary of the Cumberland River, and many other secondary streams opened early trade and transportation for the area. The Cumberland flowed into the Ohio River to the west, which led to the Mississippi River, and downstream to the major port of New Orleans. Nevertheless, the Cardwells of Tennessee were not entrepreneurs of a type to place business ventures above the common labor of farming.

At least three of the Cardwell brothers served in the War of 1812. War records are unclear about the service of Nelson Cardwell because his brother Anderson Nelson Cardwell also enlisted under the name of Nelson Cardwell. Service documents identify two Nelsons with two different enlistment identifications, suggesting that both Nelson and Anderson Nelson served in the war. Caleb Cardwell also volunteered. The War of 1812 began officially in June 1812 when the U.S. Congress declared war on Britain over maritime rights and British intervention in North American Indian affairs. The Creek Indian War erupted in 1813 between Creek Indian nativists and U.S. troops. The early stages of the War of 1812 were a standoff. By 1814, capable American officers, such as Andrew Jackson, had replaced ineffective veterans from the American Revolution. In the spring of 1814, Jackson defeated the Creeks at the Battle of Horseshoe Bend in Alabama, ending the Creek War, and in December of 1814, the British and Americans signed a treaty ending the war with the British. Unaware of the treaty, British forces attacked New Orleans on January 8, 1815, and were roundly defeated by Jackson's ragtag army, an event that contributed to the idealized notion that the United States won the War of 1812.

Nelson Cardwell—Nelson and or Anderson Nelson—served as a private in the 1st Regiment West Tennessee Militia from June 20, 1814, to February 2, 1815, a total of 7 months and 13 days at the rate of pay of $8 per month, making about $60 during the course of service.[13] It cannot be proven that a Cardwell fought at the Battle of New Orleans, although elements of the First Regiment West Tennessee Militia were part of the left wing of Jackson's army. Nelson would have been about age 16 when he volunteered. His brother Anderson Nelson was 23. The average age of a soldier was between 17 and 25. However, boys as young as 12 years old served as drummers and medics. A youngster enrolled without any promise or expectation of an assignment to the band, or put on drummer's pay. Each state furnished 100,000 militiamen to aid in the war. The Act of April 1812 compelled that no detachment should serve more than six months.[14] Under Tennessee state militia law, a tour of duty was for only three months.[15]

It is unlikely that either of the Nelsons—W. Nelson or Anderson Nelson—was with the First Regiment during the Creek War at the Battle of Talladega, where the regiment sustained heavy casualties, or at the Battle of Horseshoe Bend when Jackson defeated the Creek Indians on March 27, 1814. The First Regiment West Tennessee initially organized in October 1813, reorganized in early January of 1814, and served in Jackson's campaign until May 1814. The name of Nelson Cardwell did not appear on the regiment roll until June 20, 1814, at Fayetteville, Tennessee, in Captain Blakemore's company of Colonel Philip Pipkin's First Regiment.[16] The First Regiment reactivated in June 1814 in response to the Creek troubles, and encamped in the summer and autumn of that year at posts in the Creek country. The Cardwells enrolled after the Creek Indian defeat but was part of the detachment of a thousand men that guarded the Creeks.[17]

The First Regiment West Tennessee under Colonel Pipkin was active from June 1814 to December 1814. [18] Its men were from eight Tennessee counties, including Sumner County, and numbered about 960 men. After the summer of 1814 in Creek territory, the regiment served in various parts of the South, mostly in Mississippi Territory near Mobile, Alabama. Disease took a large toll. The unrest caused by squalid conditions led to a high desertion rate in the regiment. A mutiny ensued, and a court martial levied in December 1814 against alleged deserters led to the execution of six soldiers on February 21, 1815. The case is a story worth retelling. Court convened at Mobile, Alabama, on December 15, 1814. President of the court was Colonel Pipkin, commander of the 1st Regiment West Tennessee Militia, the "mutinous regiment," and the regiment of "Nelson" Cardwell. Fortunately, Nelson was not among those tried as deserters. Two officers and about 200 militiamen of Colonel Pipkin's regiment appeared before the court charged with mutiny, theft of public stores, and desertion.[19] Most of the mutineers had been deluded into a belief that they were about to be wrongfully detained in service past the three months required by Tennessee law. They rebelled to show their displeasure. The large majority of them received clemency or trivial punishment, and the court released them, except for six of the ringleaders; namely, Sergeant David Morrow, Jacob Webb, John Harris, Henry Lewis, David Hunt, and Edward Linsey, privates in the First Regiment West Tennessee. The court found them guilty of deserting while on post and causing a mutiny and ordered them executed.[20]

On February 21, 1815, the condemned men faced a military firing squad. Historian James Parton described the execution scene, "Six coffins were placed in a row, several feet apart, in an open place near the village of Mobile. A large body of troops, perhaps fifteen hundred in number, was drawn up so that a view of the spectacle was afforded to all."[21] A military guard escorted the prisoners to the scene, placing each one next to one of the coffins.[22] Most of the condemned men stood firm and composed, except for John Harris, an illiterate Baptist preacher, the father of nine children, who had enlisted to accompany his son to the war. Unable to control his emotions, he wept bitterly and apologized for what he had done.[23] The night before, David Hunt, another of the condemned, wrote a letter to his wife. "Dear Wife, I wish you to do all you can to keep my children together, if possible… It grieves me hard to part with you all… But, my little sons, you are young, and growing up into life. Be careful of what kind of company you keep, and never bring yourselves to any disgrace."[24] The execution proceeded. Each man knelt blindfolded beside his coffin. Shots rang out, and each prisoner fell dead instantly except for Henry Lewis. Pierced by four balls, he raised his head and asked the colonel in charge, "Have I atoned for my offense?" The colonel agreed and ordered the surgeon to do all he could to save his life. However, Lewis lingered four days and then died.[25]

General Andrew Jackson, commander of the division in which these events transpired, could have intervened to stay the executions but did not, even though he probably knew the war was over. He did not weigh in on the proceedings until January 8, 1815, after his victory at New Orleans and the rout of the British *after* the war had ended.[26] The House Committee on Military Affairs in Washington, outraged by Jackson's conduct, reviewed the court martial.[27] The Congress questioned whether the men were legally tried because the court martial occurred after the third reorganization of the 1st West Tennessee and past its six-month limit of service compelled by Congress.[28] The justices determined that although the regiment served past its legal term, the events on trial occurred before the expiration date.[29] The court of inquiry found that the court acted lawfully and that General Jackson acted properly, exercising the power and discretion vested in him by law when he approved the proceedings. Nelson Cardwell and the other men of Colonel Pipkin's First Regiment likely did not witness the execution of their fellow soldiers. The unit disbanded in January 1815, and Nelson mustered out on February 2, 1815, days before the executions on February 21. He returned home to Sumner County.

On November 30, 1816, Nelson married Nancy Hughs.[30] In 1820, he paid a poll tax in Captain Horsley's District of Sumner County.[31] He did so regularly thereafter, always listed in the same polling district with Thomas [Jr.], suggesting that he never strayed far from the Cardwell farm on Second Creek. The 1820 census found Nelson and Nancy Cardwell in the Gallatin, Tennessee, area with their young son presumed to be Jonathan Duran Cardwell and a baby daughter Cardwell.[32] Thomas Cardwell [Jr.], the surrogate head of the family lived nearby.[33]

Nancy (Hughs) Cardwell died about 1834. An 1834 church roll listed Nelson as a widower.[34] The church roll of 1834 also listed Thomas [Jr.] and his son William, and several other Cardwell offspring, including Nelson's son Dudley Cardwell. The church membership included 12 members of the Cardwell name. They were all members of the Willow Grove Methodist Episcopal Church in Sumner County. It was a large church in 1834 with 151 members, including 23 slaves who were members of the church. Everyone knew Aunt Rose Stovall, a Negro slave member of the church, for her shouting. The Friday preceding each quarterly meeting was a day of fasting and praying.[35] The church was one of the oldest in the county. The present church building, which still stands, now in Trousdale County, is the third church built on the original site. The first was a log cabin built in 1792 with a dirt floor. The second building burned, and Reuben Harris—possible namesake of Nelson Cardwell's son, Reuben—erected the present building.[36] Another Methodist Church at Bethpage, Tennessee, five miles northwest of Willow Grove, could well describe the services at Willow Grove. Located ten miles northeast of Gallatin, on the Scottsville pike, Bethpage was a church noted for being one of the places that held religious revivals, with a store and blacksmith shop nearby.[37]

After Nancy (Hughs) Cardwell died, Nelson married secondly Polly Bennett in Sumner County, Tennessee, on October 3, 1835.[38] With Polly, he had four more children: Peter Lafayette Cardwell, James [Richard] Cardwell, Nancy Cardwell, and Samuel Richard Cardwell.[39] Nelson's name disappeared from the Sumner County tax rolls after 1830. New names of the next Cardwell generation took his place.[40] Sometime after 1835, he removed to Simpson County, Kentucky. His marriage to Polly Bennett in Sumner County and the birth of their first child in Kentucky in 1838 fixed the time of the move at around 1837. The 1840 census found him in Simpson County with his wife and 10 children.[41]

Records of the Cardwells in Simpson County are incomplete. The Simpson County Courthouse burned in May 1882 destroying all wills prior to that time, and few documents survived. Nelson Cardwell died before 1848 because Polly

(Bennett) Cardwell then married Jeremiah Dixon, Jr., and their first child was born in 1849. Nelson's final resting place is unknown. He never benefitted from his military service in the War of 1812. Land grants went to his brothers but not to him, probably because he died prior to the Bounty Land Act of 1855, which authorized the grants.

Nelson and Nancy (Hughs) Cardwell had six children; namely, Jonathan Duran Cardwell, Dudley D. Cardwell, William Cardwell, Thomas G. Cardwell, Reuben Granville Cardwell, and an unidentified daughter Cardwell.[42] The children migrated westward. J.D. Cardwell settled in Arkansas and spent his final years in Washington Territory on the West Coast. Dudley Cardwell lived in Kentucky. Wilson Cardwell lived in different counties but remained in Tennessee. Thomas G. Cardwell migrated from Sumner County, Tennessee, to Simpson County, Kentucky. Reuben Cardwell went first to Missouri and then to California. Of Nelson's second family with Polly (Bennett) Cardwell, Peter Cardwell settled in Muhlenberg, Kentucky. James Cardwell lived mostly in Kentucky, as did his sister Nancy. Samuel Cardwell moved to Chicago.

The genealogy continued from Nelson and Nancy (Hughs) Cardwell to their son Reuben Granville Cardwell and his marriage to Elizabeth Stegall of Kentucky. Their union produced the Cardwell branch of Cedar County, Missouri.

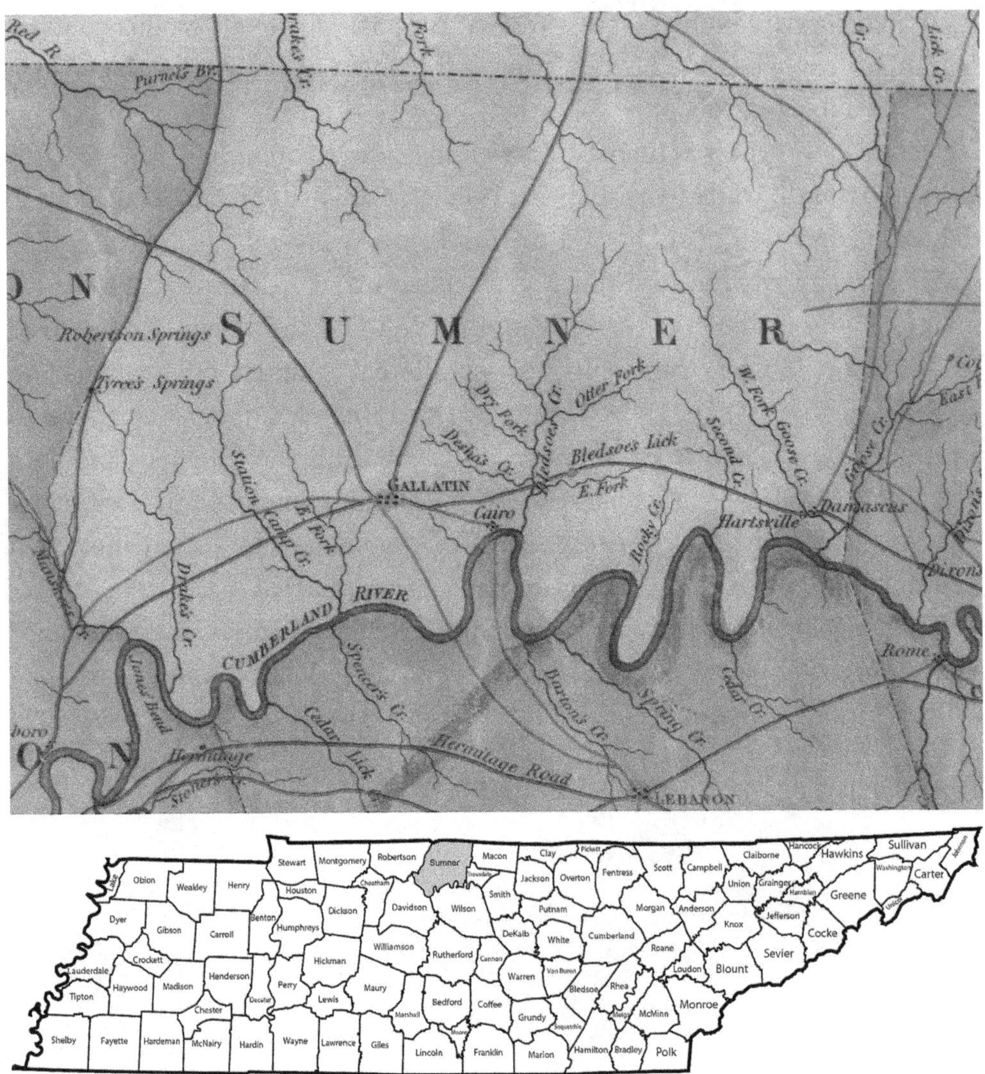

Map of Sumner County, Tennessee, Showing Second Creek. This map from 1832 places Sumner County, Tennessee, between Robertson County to the west, Davidson to the southwest, Wilson to the southeast, and Macon and Trousdale to the east. Northward lies the state of Kentucky where Simpson County borders Sumner County to the southeast. Modified original map by Matthew Rhea, 1832. Library of Congress. Below, modern map of Tennessee depicting present county locations.

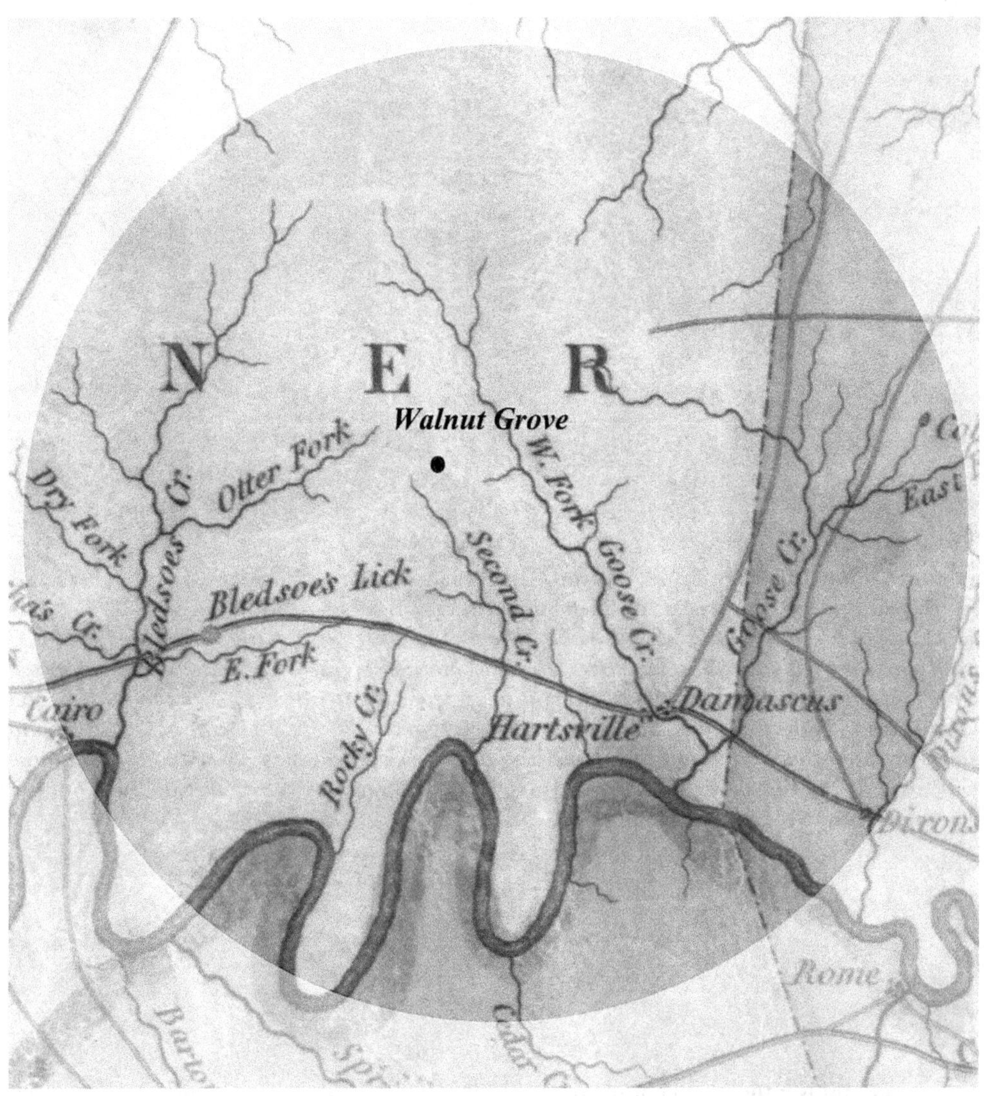

Map Inset of Eastern Sumner County, Tennessee. The circle represents an approximate 5-mile radius around Second Creek showing the location of the Cardwells and Walnut Grove Methodist Church about 4 miles northwest of the towns of Hartsville and Damascus. Second Creek is 2.6 miles west of Hartsville in present Trousdale County. The creek empties into the Cumberland River. The town of Hartville was the Cardwell trading community, which dated to 1797 when a family by the name of Hart settled along the west bank of the West Fork of Goose Creek. Another family named Donoho settled across the creek and built a mill along the creek's east side. Hart purchased the Donoho property in 1800, which in the meantime took the name Damascus. Recognized as a town in 1817, Hartsville merged with Damascus in 1840. Modified from a map of Matthew Rhea published in 1832. Library of Congress.

Sumner County Marriage Bond. Nelson Cardwell and William Stovall pledged $1,250 bond for the impending marriage of Nelson to Nancy Hughs November 30, 1816. "*The condition of the above obligation is such, whereas said Cardwell hath prayed and obtained license to marry Nancy Hughs. Now if the said Nancy Hughs be an actual resident in the aforesaid county, and there shall not hereafter appear any lawful cause why the said Nelson Cardwell and Nancy Hughs should not be joined together in Holy Matrimony, as husband and wife, then this obligation to be void and of no effect, otherwise to remain in full force and virtue.*" The signature of Nelson Cardwell was probably by the clerk who filled out the document. Sumner County Archives.

Tennessee and Kentucky. The roots of the Cardwell family of Cedar County, Missouri, lay along the Middle Tennessee border next to Kentucky. Migrating first from Virginia to Granville County, North Carolina, later generations settled in Sumner County, Tennessee (A) in 1807, followed by members of the same family who moved from Granville to Smith County, Tennessee (B) a few years later. The Cardwells of Sumner County then removed north to Simpson County, Kentucky. Members of the Kentucky family later associated with Simpson, Christian, Trigg, and Calloway Counties, to name some, situated along the southern border of Kentucky. Descendants of the present Cardwell line moved progressively westward, eventually settling in Cedar County, Missouri. Modified Rand McNally Map, c.1882. Library of Congress.

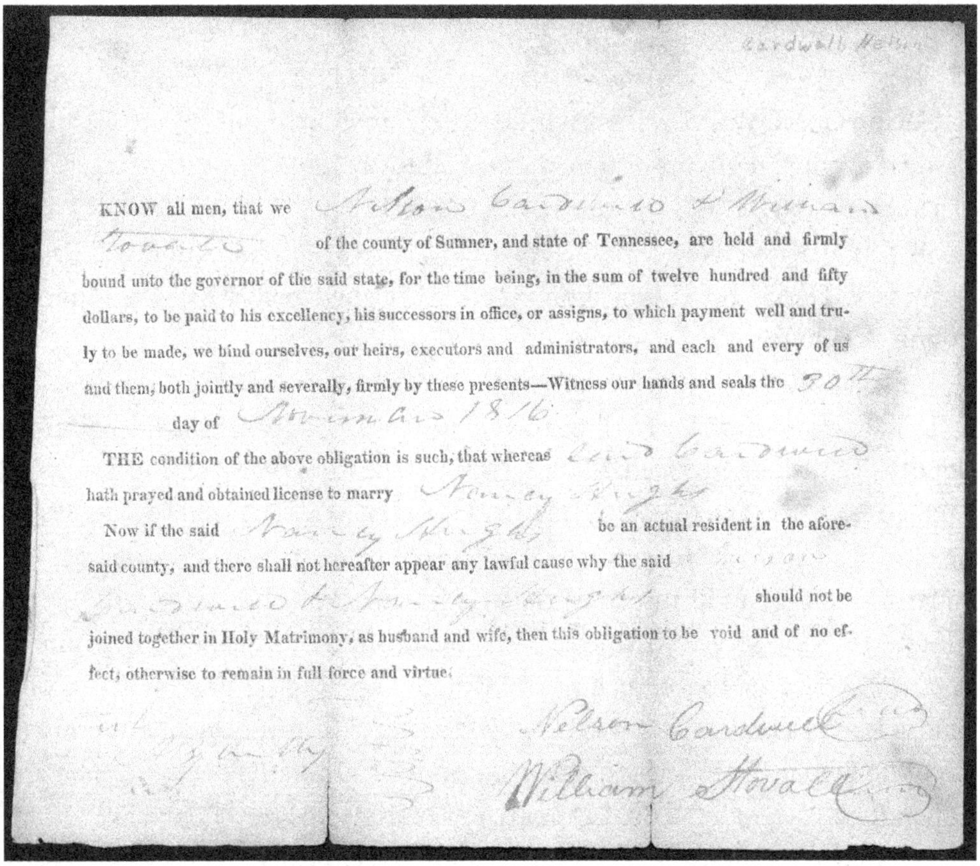

Cardwell Nelson

KNOW all men, that we Nelson Cardwell & William Stovall of the county of Sumner, and state of Tennessee, are held and firmly bound unto the governor of the said state, for the time being, in the sum of twelve hundred and fifty dollars, to be paid to his excellency, his successors in office, or assigns, to which payment well and truly to be made, we bind ourselves, our heirs, executors and administrators, and each and every of us and them, both jointly and severally, firmly by these presents—Witness our hands and seals the 30th day of November 1816

THE condition of the above obligation is such, that whereas said Cardwell hath prayed and obtained license to marry Nancy Hughs

Now if the said Nancy Hughs be an actual resident in the aforesaid county, and there shall not hereafter appear any lawful cause why the said Nelson Cardwell & Nancy Hughs should not be joined together in Holy Matrimony, as husband and wife, then this obligation to be void and of no effect, otherwise to remain in full force and virtue.

Nelson Cardwell (seal)
William Stovall (seal)

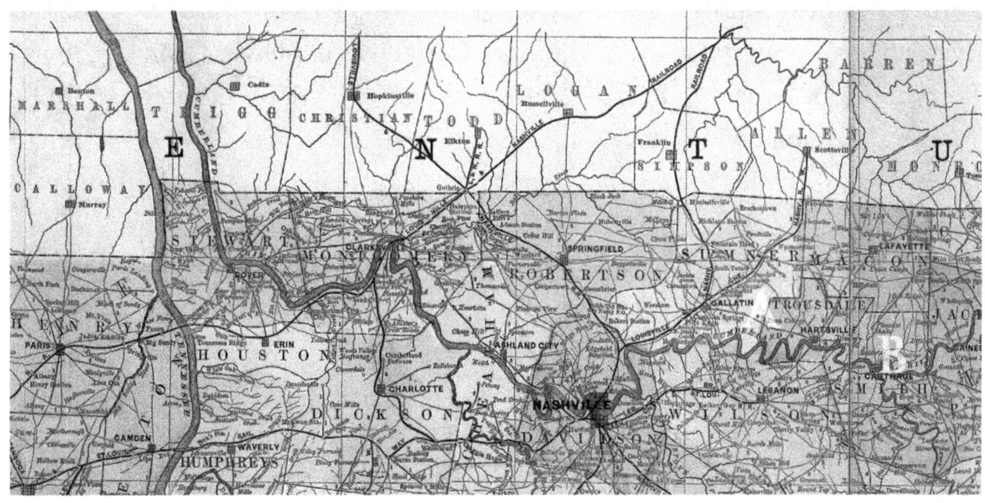

Cardwell Sixth Generation Family Group

Nelson CARDWELL was born in 1798 in Granville County, North Carolina. He died about 1847 in Simpson County, Kentucky.[43] He was the youngest son of **Thomas CARDWELL** and **Mary LEONARD**.

Nelson married **Nancy HUGHS** on 30 Nov 1816 in Sumner County, Tennessee. Nancy was born about 1800.[44] She died before 1834 in Sumner County, Tennessee.[45]

They had the following children.

1. **J.D. (Jonathan Duran) Cardwell** was born 19 Mar 1818 in Sumner County, Tennessee. He died 20 Dec 1900 in Washington State. Burial was in Pataha Flat Cemetery, Pomeroy, Garfield County, Washington.[46] At age 18, he enrolled in the Second Regiment First Brigade of Tennessee Mounted Militia under the command of Brigadier General R. Armstrong. Ordered into service 25 June 1835, he served to 25 Dec 1836. He saw duty in the Second Seminole War in Florida in the company of Captain Josephus Guild.[47] The Second Seminole War (1835–1842) was the result of the U.S. government's attempt to force the Seminoles to leave Florida and move to Indian Territory under the Indian Removal Act of 1830. J.D. married **Harriett Shaver**, 14 January 1840.[48] She was born 8 Jun 1822 in Sumner County, Tennessee.[49] The 1840 census found the couple living in Sumner County.[50] J.D. and Harriett removed to Piney Fork, Lawrence County, Arkansas, about 1845.[51] Harriett died 24 Dec 1861 in Evening Shade, Sharp County, Arkansas. Burial was in Shaver Farm Cemetery, Piney Fork Township, Sharp County, Arkansas.[52] J.D. married secondly **Pernina Webster** 26 Feb 1863 in Lawrence County, Arkansas.[53] By 1870, he had removed to Carrollton, Carroll County, Arkansas, where he lived a few years before he and Pernina moved to Columbia County, Washington Territory when J.D. was about 60 years old.[54] They lived the rest of their lives in Washington.[55]

2. **Unidentified Daughter Cardwell** was born about 1820 in Sumner County, Tennessee. The 1840 census enumerated her in the household of Nelson Cardwell, age 15 to 20.[56] The 1850 Simpson County, Kentucky, census listed a Parthena G. Cardwell, born in 1810, in North Carolina.[57] She appeared on the list of members of the Walnut Grove Methodist Church in Sumner County entered on the list as "moved" and single.[58] Her reported age makes it unlikely; however, that she was the unidentified daughter of Nelson Cardwell.

3. **D.D. (Dudley) Cardwell** was born in 1822 in Sumner County, Tenn. He died after 1880 in Simpson County, Kentucky.[59] Dudley D. Cardwell married **Elizabeth Hinton**, daughter of John Hinton and Margaret Hendricks, on 29 Aug 1842 in Sumner County, Tennessee.[60] Elizabeth was born in 1820 in Sumner County.[61] Dudley moved to Simpson County, Kentucky, about 1842. He divided his time between Simpson County and Sumner County, Tennessee, which joined across the Kentucky-Tennessee line. [62] The 1850 census listed him in Simpson County. Meanwhile, the 1860 census found him back in Sumner County, Tennessee, with Elizabeth and their seven children.[63] He was involved in a lawsuit in Sumner County in June 1860 over a debt owed him by a tobacco dealer.[64] In 1870, he was still in Sumner County but in 1880 had returned to Simpson County, Kentucky. He lived in Franklin, Kentucky, at the city jail where he served as town jailer. Living with him and Elizabeth in 1870 was their youngest son, and their widowed daughter with her two children.[65] Dudley continued as jailor at Franklin for more than a decade.

4. **William Wilson Cardwell** was born 9 Nov 1825 in Sumner County, Tennessee. He died on 11 Nov 1897 in Evansville, Indiana.[66] His burial was in Gallatin Cemetery, Sumner County, Tennessee.[67] Wilson married **Edward Ann Jones** on 23 Dec 1857 in Sumner County.[68] She was born 3 Mar 1828 in Sumner County, and died 16 May 1900.[69] Her burial was in Gallatin Cemetery, Sumner County, Tennessee.[70] Wilson was in Davidson County, Tennessee, in 1860 but spent most of his life in Sumner County.[71] Toward the end of his life, he moved to Indiana where his daughter lived.

5. **Thomas G. Cardwell** was born on 11 Apr 1827 in Sumner County, Tennessee.[72] He died on 13 Feb 1889 in Simpson County, Kentucky. His burial was in Cummings Cemetery, Simpson County, Kentucky.[73] Thomas G. paid taxes in Sumner County in 1834 and intermittently thereafter, attendant to a mobile lifestyle in which he appeared in one place and then another.[74] Thomas married **Margaret (Hinton) McDowell**, daughter of John Hinton and Margaret Hendricks, on 11 Jul 1847 in Sumner County, Tennessee.[75] It was her second marriage.[76] Margaret was born on 11 Mar 1826 in Simpson County, Kentucky. She died on 24 Nov 1907 in Simpson County. Her burial was on 25 Nov 1907, in Simpson County, Kentucky.[77] She was the sister of Elizabeth Hinton wife of Dudley D. Cardwell. In an instance of family intrigue, the bondsman for her first marriage to Henry McDowell was Dudley Cardwell, brother of Thomas G. Cardwell, her second husband. Frontier pedigrees sometimes merged in

curious ways. For example, John Hinton had two daughters, Elizabeth and Margaret. On 29 Aug 1842, Dudley Cardwell, brother of Thomas G., married Elizabeth Hinton. Meanwhile, Margaret Hinton married Henry McDowell 17 Sep 1845. Dudley Cardwell served as his bondsman. It was a brief marriage for unspecified reasons, and in 1847, Thomas G. married Margaret Hinton. Thus, brothers married sisters.[78] Thomas G. and Margaret settled first in Christian County, Kentucky, where their first son Reuben was born.[79] Soon thereafter, they moved to Simpson County, Kentucky, about the time Thomas' father, Nelson, died in Simpson County. His record parallels that of his younger brothers Reuben Granville Cardwell and Dudley Cardwell who the 1850 census appeared in Simpson County, Kentucky. Thomas G. did not remain long in Simpson County. He divided his interests between Simpson County and Sumner County, Tennessee. By 1850, he had resettled in Sumner County.[80] That proved to be short-lived as well, and he returned to Simpson County in 1860.[81] The census of 1870 found him again back in Sumner County.[82] Meanwhile, by 1877, he was once more in Simpson County. There he and Margaret lived out their remaining years.[83] He wrote his will on 17 Mar 1877 and proved 17 Nov 1890.[84]

+ 6. **Reuben Granville CARDWELL** was born in 1829 in Sumner County, Tennessee. He died on 16 Sep 1901 in Los Angeles, California. His burial was in Evergreen Cemetery, Los Angeles, California. Reuben married **Elizabeth STEGALL**, daughter of **Henry STEGALL** and **Irene STRANGE**, on 18 Apr 1851 in Trigg County, Kentucky. Elizabeth was born about 1833, in Virginia. Reuben married secondly **Lydia (Coon) McIntyre** in 1870 in Pueblo De Las Junta, Fresno County, California. Lydia was born in 1852. Her burial was in 1927 in Evergreen Cemetery, Los Angeles, California.

Following the death of Nancy (Hughs) Cardwell c.1834, Nelson Cardwell married secondly **Mary Polly Bennett** on 18 Jul 1835 in Sumner County, Tennessee. Mary was born in 1816.[85] Nelson and Polly (Bennett) Cardwell had the following children.

7. **Peter Lafayette Cardwell** was born 13 Jul 1836 in Simpson County, Kentucky. He died 6 Dec 1911. Burial was in Union Ridge Cemetery, Penrod, Muhlenberg County, Kentucky.[86] He settled in Muhlenberg County, Kentucky, where he was a farmer for more than 40 years.[87] He married first **Elizabeth Mays**. She was born in 1841 in Simpson County, Kentucky.[88] He married secondly **Rachel Ragon** 8 Dec 1880 at Rachel's home in Muhlenberg County.[89]

Rachel was born 30 Mar 1861. She died 18 Mar 1908 in Drakesboro, Muhlenberg County, Kentucky. Her burial was in Union Ridge Cemetery, Penrod, Muhlenberg County.[90] It is probably Peter enumerated in the 1840 census in the household of Nelson Cardwell, age 5 to 10.[91] However, this is unproven.[92]

8. **James Cardwell** was born about 1838, in Kentucky. In 1860, he was living with his widowed mother Mary Polly (Bennett-Cardwell) Dixon and the Cardwell and Dixon children in Simpson County, Kentucky.[93] Following the death of Nelson Cardwell, Polly (Bennett) Cardwell married Jeremiah Dixon, Jr. In 1850, they were living in Macon County, Tennessee.[94] She was a widow in 1860, and living in Simpson County, Kentucky. Jeremiah and Polly had three children: Susan Dixon who was born about 1849, Alsey Dixon born about 1850, and Manda Dixon born about 1854.[95] Living in the Dixon household in 1850 were Richard Dixon age 12 and Samuel Dixon age six believed to be Richard Cardwell and Samuel Cardwell, sons of Mary Polly by Nelson Cardwell. However, missing from the 1850 enumeration were Peter Cardwell age 14, James about age 12, and Nelson and Polly's unidentified daughter.

9. **Nancy Cardwell** was born about 1839, in Kentucky.[96] The 1860 census listed her as age 21 and living with her mother, Mary Polly Dixon, and siblings in Simpson County, Kentucky.

10. **Samuel Richard Cardwell** was born on 23 Nov 1843, in Franklin, Kentucky. He died on 9 Jan 1925 in Chicago, Cook County, Illinois. His burial was in Mount Rose Cemetery.[97] Samuel married **Sarah Elizabeth Malone**. Sarah was born in 1843. She died in 1899. Samuel married secondly **Martha Hampton** on 23 Apr 1899 in Indiana.[98] She was born in Dec 1853 and died before 1925. Samuel settled in Chicago where he worked as a tobacco grader and buyer in the tobacco industry.

21

Cardwells of Cedar County

Edward Cardwell was born on August 15, 1856, in Missouri. He died on April 8, 1884, at the age of 27 and went to his final rest in Gum Springs Cemetery, Cedar County, Missouri. Beyond the scant information engraved on his tombstone and the information contained in the 1880 U.S. Census, no genealogical record previously existed, except that he died very young and his parents were born in Tennessee, according to the 1880 census. Any knowledge of Edward's origin and the names of his parents faded into the past, and he became, in genealogical terms—a "dead end."

Edward married Anna Eliza Baldwin on October 20, 1878, in Madison Township, Cedar County, Missouri. The couple had two children: Laura Frances Cardwell and Thomas Edward Cardwell. Laura was age four and Thomas age three when Edward died, each too young to preserve a memory of their father to pass on to the next generation. No family records survived if any ever existed. Beatrice (Cardwell) Richardson, daughter of Thomas Cardwell, once said that she knew nothing about her grandfather Edward. The only thing she remembered about him was that her dad, Tom Cardwell, Edward's son, told her that Edward "ran off with another woman." She thought also that Edward had a sister. Part of this did not make much sense. If Edward ran off with another woman he did not get very far because he lay buried at Gum Springs not far from the gravesites of his wife Anna Eliza Baldwin, her parents, and members of the Baldwin extended family.

From the time of the rediscovery of Edward's tombstone in the early 1970s, the urge to know more about him led to numerous fruitless attempts to try to uncover his ancestry. Each decade a new effort would dust off the collected files and take another turn at it. After weeks and sometimes months without any success, the files would go back into the cabinet until the urge rekindled a new desire to identify Edward as someone other than a genealogical "dead end." Every clue seemed to lead nowhere. The Cardwell family of Audrain County, Missouri, offered a plausible connection that never materialized. The prominent Cardwell family of Webster County, Missouri, similarly produced no good correlation with the meager information known about Edward Cardwell.

In 2008, the search grew more complicated when a discovery in the 1870 U.S. Census showed an Edward and Laura Cardwell living with George Minix (Minick) in Schuyler County, Missouri. The age of Edward of Schuyler County matched the known age of Edward of Cedar County, he was born in Missouri, and he had a sister named Julia. Unfortunately, the 1870 census did not give the birthplaces of parents, and this particular record was badly marred. Nevertheless, countless hours went into trying to find a plausible explanation as to why Edward and Julia Cardwell might be living with the Minick family far from Cedar County; everything from being stepchildren of George Minick to being visiting relatives, anything that might suggest that their mother either was a Minick or related to the wife of George Minick. None of this achieved anything.

Meanwhile, the 1860 U.S. Census recorded an Elizabeth Cordell [*sic*] age 28, living in Madison Township, Cedar County, Missouri. She had three children, Thomas P. age eight, Edward age four, and Juliany age eight months, all born in Missouri. Elizabeth was born in Virginia, and the census recorded her as a widow. The problem with this record was that the age of Edward did not compute to his known birthdate of 1856, nor to the ages of Edward and Julia in the Minick household in Schuyler County in 1870. Moreover, Elizabeth of the 1860 census was born in Virginia and not Tennessee, as the 1880 census said. Above all, the name Cordell, while a reasonable approximation of Cardwell, obviously was not the same. Nevertheless, a follow up of clues contained in the 1860 census led to a new surge of investigation but with no real success in building any kind of proven genealogical connections.

In 2020, retired and temporarily slowed down by the constraints of the Covid-19 pandemic, the Edward Cardwell files received attention once again. The 1860 U.S. Census record contained a previously overlooked clue. Living with Elizabeth Cordell and her three children in Madison Township was four-month-old John W. Stegall. He turned out to be the gateway to the ancestry of

Edward Cardwell. A search of the 1860 census for Cedar County turned up Sam P. Stegall age 19 and his wife Mary age 23 living in Madison Township, Cedar County. They were of an age to have a four-month-old child like John W. Stegall, and Sam was of the age plausibly to be the brother of Elizabeth Cordell, the assumed nanny to the infant John Stegall of 1860. Could Stegall have been the maiden name of Elizabeth Cordell?

Further investigation proved that Elizabeth was the daughter of Henry Stegall and Irene Strange. Records revealed that Henry and Irene had a son named Samuel and a daughter named Elizabeth, both born in Virginia, and each of the age to correlate with the 1860 census data. Other information later proved that the Stegall family moved to Missouri sometime around 1850. The connection between them and the Cardwells had further merit in the fact that Edward Cardwell and Anna Eliza Baldwin married in the home of Sam P. Stegall in 1878, in Madison Township, Cedar, County, according to their marriage certificate.

On the hunch, that Edward Cardwell's mother was Elizabeth Stegall, the search turned to uncovering the name of her husband, Edward's father. Armed with the details of the ancestry of Elizabeth, the convenience of the internet produced a marriage certificate for Elizabeth Stegall and R.G. Cardwell recorded in 1849, in Sumner County, Tennessee. The parents of Edward Cardwell were R.G. (Reuben Granville) and Elizabeth (Stegall) Cardwell.

Edward had a sister, just as Beatrice (Cardwell) Richardson thought. Her name was Juliann, or Julia, and she married late in life to W.W. Stivers, at Osiris, Cedar County, Missouri, married by Jessie M. Biddey the second husband of Anna Eliza (Baldwin) Cardwell, Julia's onetime sister-in-law. Sufficient proof existed to claim her as the sister of Edward. Records after the 1860 census gave her name as Cardwell and not Cordell as written in the 1860 census. Edward also had a heretofore-unknown older brother, Thomas P. Cardwell. He married Viola Crow and moved to Dade County, Missouri.

The family tradition that Edward ran off with another woman also became credible. It was not Edward who ran off but his father R.G. Cardwell who abandoned his family. Elizabeth was not a widow, as she said in the 1860 census, but rather a deserted wife. Whether there was another woman involved in the episode is unknown. R.G. went to California to pursue mining prospects. He later remarried in 1870 to Lydia (Coon) McIntire and reared a family in California where he died in 1903.

Elizabeth (Stegall) Cardwell remarried to Peter Minick in 1866 in Cedar County. Both of them unfortunately disappeared from the genealogical records after 1866, but not without new questions about Edward and Julia Cardwell in the 1870 census of Schuyler County living in the household of George Minick. Moreover, the union of Reuben Cardwell and Elizabeth Stegall opened the door to several generations of the Cedar County Cardwell lineage beginning with the families of Watts, Strange, and Stegall.

22

Watts, Strange, and Stegall

The families of Watts, Strange, and Stegall were the ancestors of Elizabeth Stegall, who married Reuben Granville Cardwell in the lineage of the present branch of the Cardwell family. The following is a synopsis of their heritage based in part on *To the Tenth Generation: The Watts Family with Roots in Halifax County, Virginia,* by Dawn Watts Westfall, and published in 2015. They were the common ancestors of the descendants born of the union of Reuben and Elizabeth (Stegall) Cardwell.

The history of the Watts family coincides with the history of Halifax County, Virginia, created out of Lunenburg County in 1752. Halifax County was a frontier territory in 1752. Over the decades, it evolved into a tobacco farming community until it was the largest producer of tobacco in the state of Virginia, a largely rural county situated in the Piedmont area of southwestern Virginia. The Watts name appeared in county records from the beginning of Halifax County.[1] Halifax County records mention Samuel Watts, Sr., Thomas Watts, and James Watts as early as 1752.[2] The relationship between the three of them is unknown. Indications are that part of the family migrated from Halifax to South Carolina, except Samuel Watts, Sr. who remained in Virginia.[3] A deed recorded in Halifax County on 20 April 1775 showed he purchased one hundred and twenty-eight acres of land on the branches of Difficult Creek bounded by the property of Mr. Jones, John Legrand, William Nichols, and Thomas Day. Joshua Stone and his wife Mary of Pittsylvania County, Virginia, sold this land to him for thirteen pounds.[4] Compared to other contemporary sales, it was a small amount to pay. Historian Westfall interpreted this to mean a possible relationship with the Stone family later associated with the Watts family.[5]

In April of 1780, Samuel Watts, Sr. appeared in Halifax County Court and made oath that he had been an inhabitant of Virginia for many years. He stated that he enlisted within the same and served as a common soldier in the First Virginia Regiment. He was under Captain Thomas Bullet "in the last war" and he served until discharged by his commanding officer. He further stated that he had never claimed or received any bounty in lands for that service. The court ordered his motion to be certified.[6] The land bounty was for his service in the French and Indian War between the years 1754 to 1763.[7] King George of Great Britain issued a proclamation that granted bounty land to men who served in military units from 1754 until the units disbanded. The proclamation came eight months after the Treaty of Paris in 1763, which ended the war and established the basis for granting bounty land. Samuel Watts, Sr. waited 17 years to apply. In May of 1779, the Virginia Legislature put a time limit of twelve months for anyone to receive such land. To get their land, claimants had to produce a certificate from the county court that established proof of military service. The acreage received depended on the rank held. As a private, Samuel, Sr. obtained a warrant from the Land Office for fifty acres.[8]

Samuel, Sr. was on the Halifax County tax lists for the years 1782 and 1785 with seven persons in his household, presumed to be Samuel, Sr., his wife, and five children. These tax lists replaced the lost 1790 census for Virginia.[9] In February of 1788, he was in court seeking an exemption from the payment of taxes, which the court granted probably due to old age or to some infirmity.[10] In May of 1788, he appeared in court again as a witness for William F. and Henrietta Owen, the administrators of the deceased Byrd Nichols in a suit against Paul Watlington. The court ordered William and Henrietta to pay Samuel, Sr. one hundred and twenty-five pounds of tobacco for five days of court attendance according to law.[11] In December of 1791, Samuel, Sr. and his son Thomas were among the buyers of the estate of Mathew Sims. Court records mentioned both Samuel, Sr. and Samuel, Jr. as creditors in an inventory of the estate of Sims taken in the year 1792.[12]

On 18 September 1810, Samuel, Sr. executed a deed for five shillings paid by James Eastham and John T. Palmer, in which he conveyed his interest in four slaves together with their future increase to his daughter Polly. The deed identified the slaves as a woman named Nancy, a girl named Beckey, a girl named Jane, and a boy named Burwell. The deed stipulated that he—Samuel, Sr.—reserved the use of the four slaves, as long as he lived, and that after his death, Mr. Eastham and Mr. Palmer were to dispose of them for the use and benefit of his daughter Polly, the wife of Joseph Shaw. Upon Polly's death, the said Eastham and Palmer were to divide the property equally amongst the Shaw children.[13] Samuel signed the deed with his mark, although other records indicated he could write his name.[14]

The personal property tax rolls listed Samuel, Sr. for the years 1782 through 1811. He paid taxes on real estate of one hundred acres between the years of 1801-1807; from 1808 to 1811, his taxes were for only forty-five acres.[15] In the year 1812, a previously unknown Sally Watts appeared on the tax list for the first time.[16] She was likely the widow of Samuel, Sr. However, Samuel, Jr. died in 1806, and his widow had the same name of Sally, although she did not pay taxes in the years following her husband's death in 1806, and remarried in April of 1812.[17]

Family historian Dawn Watts Westfall mapped the location of the land owned by Samuel, Sr. in Halifax County. "First, the deed description stated that his land was on Difficult Creek, which was in the northeastern section of the county. A description of a road that ran through his property helps further to pinpoint the location. In October of 1787, a court order reported that the most convenient way to clear a new road was 'from Sims Ferry Road turning out above William Nichols Plantation into Coles Ferry Road near Dunaways.' The road would begin near William Nichols plantation on Sims Ferry Road and run through parts of the said Nichols lands, Michael Roberts, the estate of Bushells [*sic*], Samuel Watts, James Owen, Richard Owen, Walter Bennett, Gunney Wilburn, William Bowman, and Samuel Dunaway.[18] The road thus described was probably a portion of what is now Route 603 starting at about the town of Mount Laurel up to Neal's Corner then running in a northeasterly fashion to the town of Whitesville."[19]

Samuel Watts, Sr. died by the year 1812. There is no record of the administration of his estate. However, evidence of his death is in a Halifax County Court case that arose that year. This controversy was over the slaves he had deeded to his daughter Polly (Watts) Shaw two years earlier. Polly and Joseph Shaw, along with Betsy and Moses Shaw their probable children, found themselves defendants against the other members of the Watts family. Thomas Watts, Joseph Watts, and William Watts, heirs and children of Samuel, Sr. in addition to Sally Watts, widow of Samuel, Jr. sued. The particulars of the complaint did not appear in the record [20] Nevertheless, the case continued in

1819, abated that year because of Thomas Watts' death. The court dismissed the case in 1820.[21]

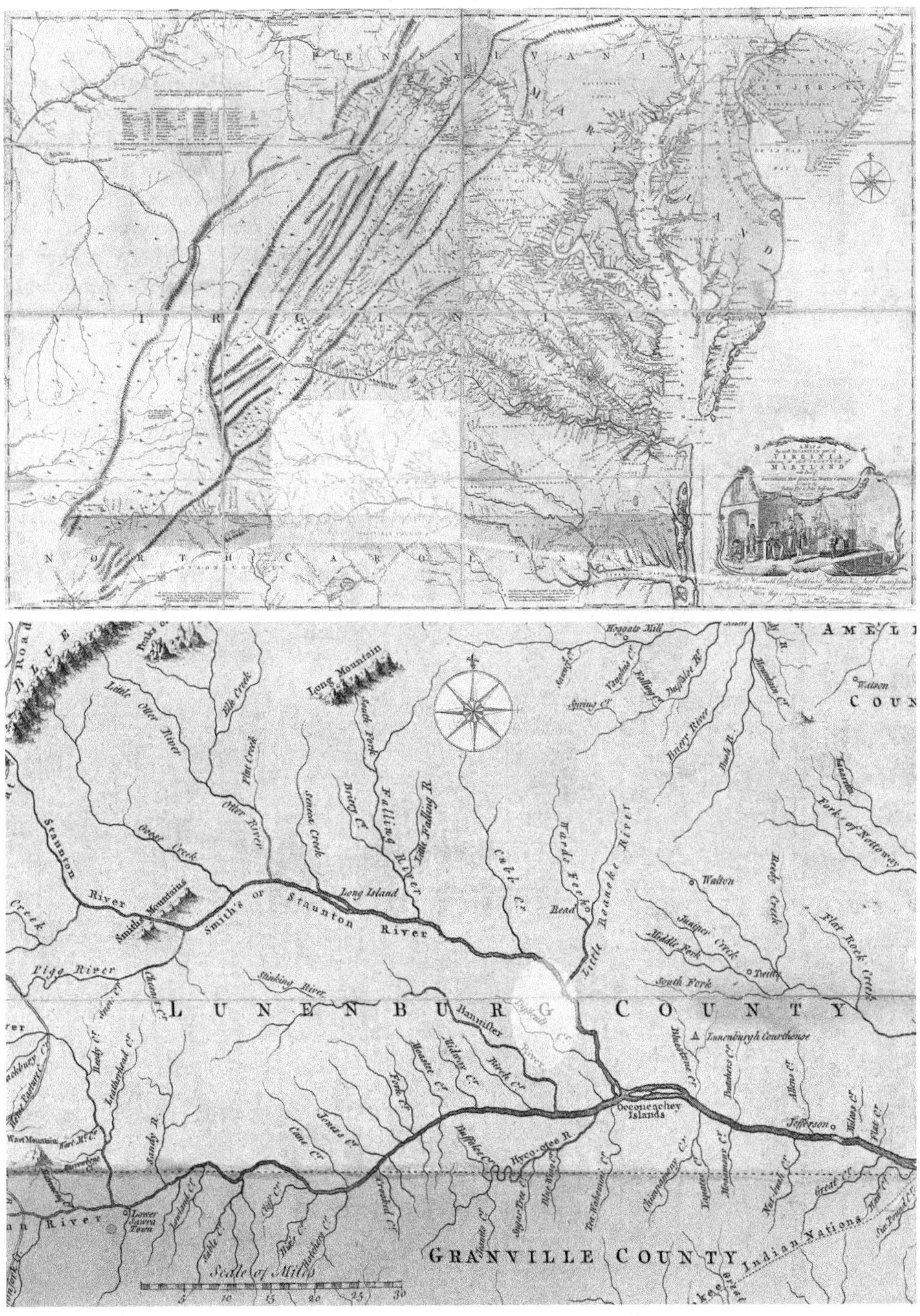

Lunenburg County Virginia. Watts, Strange, and Stegall ancestors came from the Piedmont of Virginia. The white oval shape marks the Watts homestead on Difficult Creek in 1752. Modified map from Fry, et al. *The Most Inhabited Part of Virginia*, 1775. Library of Congress.

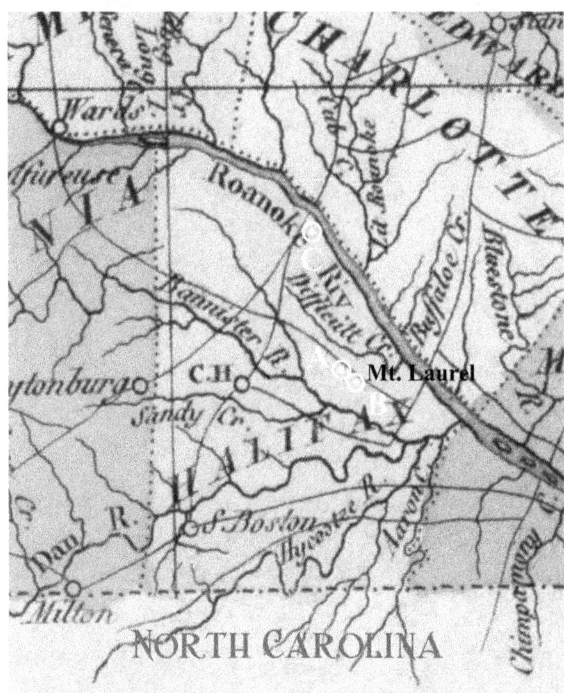

Halifax County Virginia. Small white circles indicate locations of the Watts family on Difficult Creek. (A) The road that ran through the Samuel Watts property in 1750 was Nichols Path (present State Route 603) that paralleled Bannister River. The court ordered a new road cleared in 1787. (B) Land owned by Thomas Watts went for public sale at Mt. Laurel in November 1819. (C) Coles Ferry across Staunton River (Roanoke River) once operated in the area where the Watts owned property. The Staunton River turned into the Roanoke River shown on this 1825 map. Property locations from Dawn Watts Westfall. Modified map of Halifax County from *Carte géographique* by Buchon. Library of Congress.

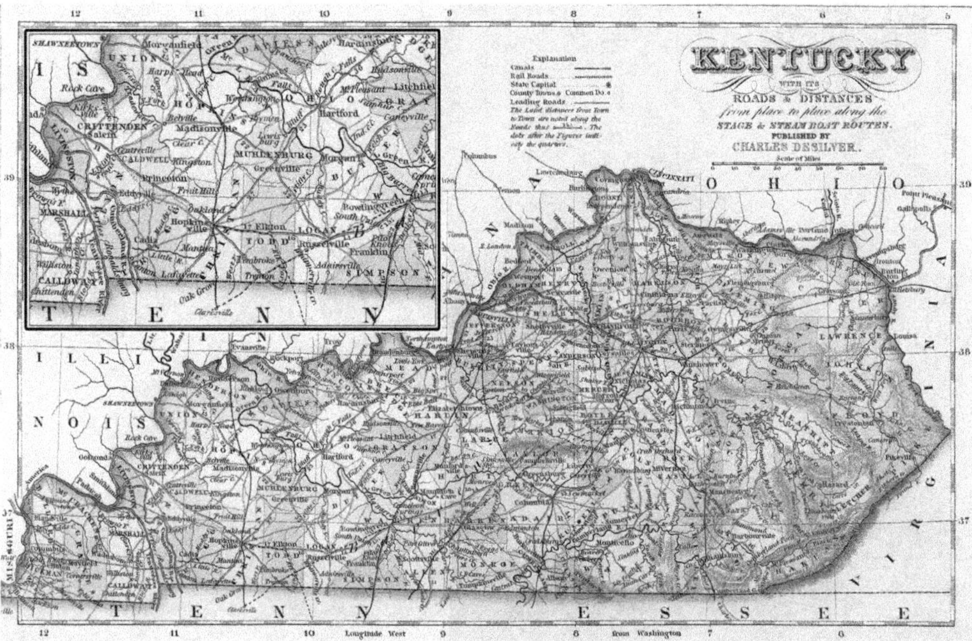

Map of Kentucky. The ancestral lines of the Stegall and Cardwell families united in Kentucky in the counties along the state's southern border (inset). Reuben Cardwell of Simpson County married Elizabeth Stegall of Christian County. They married in Trigg County next to Calloway County, home of Thomas Cardwell, uncle and surrogate grandfather of Reuben. Modified map from *Mitchell's New Universal Atlas*, 1857, Dickinson College.

Watts First Generation Family Group

Samuel WATTS, Sr. was born about 1738 and died around the year 1812 in Halifax County, Virginia.[22] Genealogists speculate that he married Sally Gillum (or Gilliam) based on the appearance of the Gillum name in later generations.[23]

The approximate birthdates of their children are from tax data.[24]

1. **Thomas M. Watts** was born about 1765. He married **Sarah Overton** 15 Nov 1792 in Charlotte County, Virginia.[25] He died between May and September of 1819 in Halifax County, Virginia, at about age 54.[26] Thomas' death in 1819 was untimely. He ran into financial trouble in 1817 and apparently did not recover from it. A depression in the year 1819 may have affected his livelihood as it did several others in Halifax County who mortgaged property for debts owed William Bailey and Company.[27] The 1820 census for Halifax County listed Sally [Sarah Overton], widow of Thomas, as the head of household. Sally O. Watts was again head of household in Halifax County during the 1830 census with five females of various ages and a male aged ten to fifteen.[28] She did not appear in the 1840 census but reappeared in 1850 at age 72, and at age 94 in the census of 1860.[29]

\+ 2. **Samuel WATTS, Jr.** was born about 1767. He married **Sarah "Sally" BURCHETT.**[30] He died in 1805 in Halifax County, Virginia.[31]

3. **William Watts** was born in Virginia about 1773. He married **Martha Patsy (Patty) Lee**, bond 13 May 1795 in Halifax County, Virginia.[32] Patty Lee was the daughter of William Lee, Sr. who gave consent for the marriage.[33] William was probably the same William Watts who was a witness to the will of William Cassada presented in court in Sep 1794.[34] The family lived for a time in Fayette County, Kentucky, before migrating to Missouri, which occurred after 1810 because that was the year of the birth of his youngest son in Virginia.[35] Patty Lee, listed as age 80 in the 1850 census, was living in the household of her son Joseph in Audrain County, Missouri.[36]

4. **Joseph Watts** was born about 1776. He married **Patsey Canaday [Canada]** 29 May 1799 in Halifax County, Virginia.[37] He removed to Scott County, Virginia.[38]

5. **Polly Watts** married **Joseph Shaw** 21 July 1807 in Halifax County, Virginia. Burwell Peak was bondsman and witness to her father's consent. Benjamin Conner gave consent for Joseph.[39] Joseph and Polly had two children: Betsy Shaw and Moses Shaw.[40]

Watts Second Generation Family Group

Samuel WATTS Jr. was born around the year 1767.[41] He died after 29 June 1805. His name appeared on that date in the 1805 tax list in Halifax County, Virginia.[42] Later that year, his widow was administrix of his estate when the court ordered an appraisal of his property.[43] He was the son of **Samuel WATTS, Sr.**

Samuel married **Sarah "Sally" BURCHETT**, a neighbor of the Watts family.[44] **Robert Burchett [Burchate]** was in the 1785 county tax list living four households from Samuel Watts, Sr.[45] The two of them—Robert and Sally—were cousins and contemporaries in Halifax County, Virginia.[46] Both were descendants of **Thomas BURCHETT** of Chatham, Kent County, England. Robert was the son of **Benjamin Hedford Burchett** and **Eveline Young.**[47] Sally was the granddaughter of **Thomas BURCHETT** and great granddaughter of the immigrant **Robert BURCHETT** of Virginia. Her grand uncle Benjamin Hedford Burchett, brother of Thomas Burchett, was the ancestor of the Burchett family of St. Clair County and Cedar County, Missouri. Descendants of the two brothers—Thomas and Benjamin—intermarried as distant cousins. Willis Burchett, 4th great grandson of Benjamin Burchett, married Beatrice Cardwell, 6th great granddaughter of Thomas Burchett, in 1941.

Sally (Burchett) Watts later married James Mayne in 1812.[48] They obtained a marriage bond on 3 Apr 1812 and on 8 Apr entered an agreement recorded at the Halifax County courthouse. The agreement stated that James and Sally "have agreed to be joined together as man and wife" and that said Mayne wished to claim none of the "property belonging to said estate but at her death go to her children." Personal property included three horses, six cattle, sixteen hogs, two sheep, three beds, one cupboard, one pot, one Dutch oven, one dish, four plates, and a spinning wheel lent to **Henry STRANGE.**[49]

Samuel Watts, Jr. and his wife Sally (Burchett) Watts had the following children:[50]

1. **Joseph Watts** was born in 1785. He married **Dorothy "Dolley" Comer**, bond dated 22 Nov 1824 in Halifax County, Virginia. [51] He settled in Bourbon County, Kentucky, and then removed to Audrain County, Missouri.[52] Dolley died in Audrain County on 13 Jan 1874. Her burial was in the Watts-Rickman Cemetery in Audrain County.[53] Joseph was in Audrain County by 1838 when he and his two brothers, Roland and Littleberry, appeared that year on the tax

list. Joseph owned three slaves valued at $800, four horses valued at $120, seven head of cattle valued at $132, and a clock valued at $18. None of the brothers owned land in the county at the time. Joseph's personal property totaled over $1,000.[54] Joseph died in 1879. His burial was in the Watts-Rickman Cemetery in Audrain County. [55]

2. **Rebecca Watts** was born about 1786. She married **Thomas Rickman** on 2 Aug 1810 in Halifax County, Virginia.[56]

3. **Daniel Watts** was born about 1780-1790. He married **Susannah White**, bond dated 5 Dec 1812 in Halifax County, Virginia.[57] He died by Feb 1842 in Halifax County, Virginia.[58]

+ 4. **Lindsey Elizabeth WATTS** was born about 1790. She married **Henry STRANGE** on 20 Dec 1806.[59]

5. **Thomas Gillum Watts** was born about 1792. He married **Rebecca A. White,** bond 9 Jun 1821 in Halifax County, Virginia.[60] He died 17 Apr 1867 in Halifax County, Virginia.[61]

6. **Roland H. Watts** was born between 1795 and 1804 in Halifax County. He died 23 Jan 1845 in Audrain County, Missouri.[62] He married **Mary W. "Polly" Lane** in Halifax County, Virginia, on 3 May 1817.[63] Mary was the daughter of William Lane who left his will in Charlotte County, Virginia, on 26 May 1832, probated 6 August 1834. Polly had brothers and sisters: Benjamin Lane, Sarah M. Lane, Elizabeth Lane, Phillip Lane, Allen Lane, Esther M. (Lane) Toombs, and James B. Lane.[64] Polly died in Dec of 1867 in Audrain County, Missouri. Her tombstone stated she "died in her 75th year," making her birth year around 1792.[65] Roland Watts was in Halifax County, Virginia, during the 1820 census.[66] He migrated west sometime thereafter. The 1830 census listed him in Morgan County, Tennessee.[67] He made his way to Audrain County, Missouri, by 1838 when he appeared on tax lists there.[68]

7. **John W. Watt**s or John Martin Watts married **Catherine** (last name unspecified) before 1850. He died 17 Jan 1887 in Calloway County, Missouri.[69] Although court records that listed the children of Samuel Watts, Jr. made no mention of John Watts, there was a Martin Watts, presumed to be John Martin Watts. However, records in Missouri give his middle initial as "W". The records reveal little about him except that he was allegedly the brother of Roland H. Watts.[70]

8. **Littleberry Watts** or Benjamin Watts was born in 1801. He married **Eliza Throckmorton**, bond dated 19 Dec 1825 in Halifax County, Virginia.[71]

Littleberry moved his family to Audrain County, Missouri, between the years 1834 and 1837 based on the known birthplaces of his children. At the time of the 1850 census, the enumerator listed him as L.B. Watts, in Audrain County, Missouri. His age was forty-nine, and apparently widowed by then.[72]

9. **Sarah Watts** married **John Sadler**; bond dated 2 Jul 1827 in Halifax County, Virginia.[73]

10. **Brackett Barnes Watts** was born 10 Nov 1800. He married **Fatha Overton** 17 Oct 1832 in Halifax County, Virginia.[74] Brackett married secondly **Dicey Clark** 16 Dec 1848 in Warren County, North Carolina.[75]

Watts Third Generation Family Group

Lindsey Elizabeth WATTS was born about 1790 to **Samuel WATTS, Jr.** and his wife **Sally BURCHETT**. Samuel, Jr. her father died in 1805. The following year, she married **Henry STRANGE.**[76] They obtained a marriage bond on 20 Dec 1806. Her mother signed consent for the two to be married, suggesting that Elizabeth was underage at the time.[77] Henry was the son of **Jesse STRANGE** and **Susannah TAYLOR.**[78]

Elizabeth Watts and Henry Strange had the following children:[79]

1. **Samuel Strange** was born in 1802 in Halifax County, Virginia. He died in Marshall County, Kansas. His burial was in the family cemetery on his farm in Marshall County.

2. **Parthena Strange** was born 15 Feb 1810. She married **Robert Rickman** 30 Mar 1829 in Halifax County, Virginia. She died 28 Aug 1877 in Cedar County, Missouri. Her burial was in Lindley Prairie Cemetery in Cedar County, Missouri.

3. **Martin Strange** was born in 1812 in Halifax County, Virginia. He married **Annie** (last name unspecified). Martin died 22 Jul 1898 in Marion County, Alabama. His burial was in the Old Union Baptist Church Cemetery in Marion County.

4. **Benjamin R. Strange** was born in 1814 in Halifax County, Virginia. He married **Rachel** (last name unspecified).

5. **John C. Strange** was born in 1815 in Halifax County, Virginia. He died during the Civil War in 1863.

\+ 6. **Irene STRANGE** was born in 1818 in Halifax County, Virginia. She married first **Henry STEGALL** in Halifax County, Virginia, and secondly **James Hays** in Cedar County, Missouri.

7. **Joseph Strange** was born in 1821 in Halifax County, Virginia. He married first **Elizabeth Wilhite** 6 Apr 1839 in Roane County, Tennessee. He married secondly **Sarah Maguffie** 1 Oct 1843 in Roane County, and thirdly **Jane Mitchell** 4 Apr 1855 in Cedar County, Missouri. Jane was the sister of **Elizabeth Mitchell**, second wife of **Paul H. Strange**, Joseph's brother.

8. **Paul H. Strange** was born 29 Feb 1823 in Halifax County, Virginia. Identification of his first wife is missing. He married secondly **Elizabeth Mitchell**. Paul died 5 Aug 1860 in Cedar County, Missouri.

9. **Calvin Strange** was born in 1825 in Halifax County, Virginia. He married **Nancy Gross**, sister of **Matilda Gross** who married Calvin's brother Rolland Strange on 15 Nov 1846 in Ray County, Missouri. They divorced but remarried. Calvin died 2 Jun 1904 in Waterville, Marshall County, Kansas. His burial was in Marysville, Marshall County.

10. **Rolland Y. Strange** was born 16 Jul 1826 in Halifax County, Virginia. He married first **Matilda Gross** 30 Dec 1846 in Ray County, Missouri, and secondly Mrs. **M.E. Deering** 4 Jul 1886 in Marysville, Marshall County, Kansas. Rolland died in Marshall County.

Strange Fourth Generation Family Group

Irene STRANGE was born in 1818 in Halifax County, Virginia. She was the daughter of **Lindsey Elizabeth WATTS** and **Henry STRANGE**. She married **Henry STEGALL** in Halifax County, Virginia.[80] Henry Stegall was born in 1804 in Virginia. He died in 1860, in Christian County, Kentucky. Irene (Strange) Stegall married secondly **James Hayes** in Cedar County, Missouri.

The Strange family in America dates to the mid-17th century. Early immigrants to Virginia included William Strange in 1635 to Charles City County; Nicholas Strange in 1638 to James City County; William Strange in 1641, also to Charles City County; Benjamin Strange in 1652, to York County; and another Benjamin Strange in 1653, also to York County. The relationship of these immigrants to the patriarch Jesse Strange of Halifax County is yet undetermined.[81] Jesse Strange was in Halifax County before 1782.[82] He was in Meadville, Halifax County, Virginia, in 1820.[83] The 1830 census recorded several members of the Strange and Stegall families living in close proximity in Halifax County.

The Strange and Stegall families migrated west. Henry Stegall and Henry Strange removed to Tennessee at about the same time. Henry Stegall left Virginia between 1833 and 1836 based on birthplaces of his children. His daughter, Elizabeth Stegall future wife of Reuben Cardwell, was born in Virginia around 1833; meanwhile, his son Elvira was born in Tennessee in 1836. The 1840 census found the Strange and Stegall families living near each other in Roane County.[84]

Henry Strange died in Roane County, Tennessee. After the death of Henry Strange, Henry Stegall stayed briefly in Roane County, and then removed to Christian County, Kentucky, about 1849.[85] Elizabeth (Watts) Strange lived as a widow with her daughter Irene and husband, Henry Stegall, in Christian County, Kentucky, during the 1850 census. Elizabeth probably died there because Irene and Henry later appeared in Cedar County, Missouri, living near Irene's brothers, and Elizabeth was not among the family.[86]

Henry Stegall and Irene (Strange) Stegall had the following children.

\+ 1. **Elizabeth STEGALL** was born about 1833 in Virginia. Elizabeth married **Reuben Granville CARDWELL**, son of **Nelson CARDWELL** and **Nancy HUGHS** on 18 Apr 1851 in Trigg County, Kentucky. Reuben was born in Jun

1829 in Sumner County, Tennessee. He died on 16 Sep 1901 in Los Angeles, California. His burial was in Evergreen Cemetery, Los Angeles, California.

2. **Clovira Stegall** was born in 1836 in Tennessee.

3. **Parthenia Stegall** was born in 1837 in Tennessee.

4. **Samuel W. Stegall** was born 4 Aug 1838 in Tennessee. He died 3 Jan 1916 in Corry, Dade County, Missouri, at the age of 77. His burial was in Friends Cemetery, Bona (Cane Hill), Dade County.[87] He married Mary C. Nelson 4 Jan 1857 in Cedar County, Missouri.[88] The marriage record stipulated that both were residents of Cedar County. Mary was the daughter of Jarrett and Carolina "Lina" Nelson, born in 1837 in Roane County, Tennessee. Samuel appeared in Madison Township, Cedar County, Missouri, in the 1860 census living with his wife Mary in the residence of Susan Wilis near Bear Creek.[89] He served 20 months in the Civil War from November 1863 until the end of the war as a Union private, first in Company I of the 7th Provisional Enrolled Missouri Militia, then in Company E of the 6th Missouri Cavalry, and finally in Company I, 15th Missouri Cavalry.[90] He afterwards resided in Greenfield, Dade County, Missouri. In 1889, the government awarded him an invalid pension for his Civil War service. Upon his death in 1916, the pension passed to his second wife Eliza. Mary (Nelson) Stegall died after 1880, and he married secondly Eliza J. (Craft) Casey of Arcola, Dade County, on 28 Jun 1885 at the residence of S.B. Craft in Dade County.[91] Eliza was born 20 Jan 1855 in Missouri. In 1890, Samuel and Eliza were living in Sac Township, Dade County.[92] The 1910 census recorded Samuel Stegall age 70 and Eliza J. age 55 in South Morgan Township, Dade County, Missouri, with their son Floyd H. Stegall.[93] After Samuel's death in 1916, Eliza lived in Kansas with her son Walter, a Wichita police officer.[94] In 1932, then living in Cheney, Kansas, she ordered a Civil War marker to place on Samuel's grave. She had it shipped to her son Floyd at Fair Play, Missouri.[95] Eliza died 3 Sep 1945 at the age of 90. Her burial was in Memorial Gardens, Wichita, Sedgwick County, Kansas, Plot Section 5, Lot 142, and Space 1.[96]

5. **John H. Stegall** was born in 1841 in Tennessee.

6. **Calvin Stegall** was born in 1845 in Tennessee.

7. **Benjamin Stegall** was born in 1848 in Tennessee.

The line of descendants from Watts, Strange, and Stegall continued from Henry Stegall and Irene (Strange) Stegall to their daughter Elizabeth Stegall who married Reuben Granville Cardwell.

23

Reuben Granville Cardwell

Reuben Granville Cardwell was born in June 1829 in Sumner County, Tennessee, in the present county of Trousdale, near Second Creek, a tributary of the Cumberland River. He was the son of Nelson and Nancy (Hughs) Cardwell. His name appears in genealogical records spelled as Reuben and Ruben, although a preference for Reuben is evident in most documents. His mother died in about the year 1833 when he was four. Ironically, his father Nelson was approximately the same age when he lost both of his parents in 1802. The Cardwell children of Granville divided after their parents died. Thomas [Jr.] Cardwell became guardian of Nelson and that part of the family that moved to Sumner County, Tennessee. The eldest sibling Leonard Cardwell became guardian of the other part of the family and remained in Granville before eventually moving the family to Smith County, Tennessee. By 1830, the Cardwell family of Granville had reconstituted itself in Tennessee. The descendants of Thomas [Jr.] and his siblings were the Cardwells of Sumner County. Leonard and the other siblings were the Cardwells of Smith County. Together they represented a sizeable Cardwell presence in Middle Tennessee. Only a few Cardwell descendants remained in Granville County, North Carolina, the original family seat memorialized in the middle name of Reuben Granville Cardwell.

Nelson Cardwell remarried in 1835 to Mary Polly Bennett, giving Reuben a stepmother during his formative years. She became the only mother Reuben knew growing up amid the aunts and uncles of the Cardwell clan. Unlike Nelson Cardwell who lost both of his parents at a very early age, Reuben had the shelter of his father.

No document or source directly identifies Reuben Cardwell as the son of Nelson Cardwell. However, genealogists agree that circumstantial evidence is sufficient to claim that he was the youngest son of Nelson and Nancy (Hughs) Cardwell. Although he did not appear by name in the 1840 census—because the census before 1850 did not contain names of household members—he fit the enumeration of the household of Nelson Cardwell. The 1840 census listed one male 10 to 15 years of age, corresponding to the years 1826 to 1830, which accommodated the known birthdate of Reuben Cardwell in 1829. The birth of Reuben in 1829 made him age 11 in 1840. Other enumerations in the household of Nelson similarly matched his known siblings, including his older brother Dudley D. Cardwell, proven son of Nelson.

Growing up on Second Creek, Reuben would have been a regular visitor to the farms of his Uncles Thomas [Jr.] Cardwell and Wilson Cardwell. He learned the skills of farming. He did not have access to a formal education because there was little schooling on the frontier of Sumner County, Tennessee, in the early 1800s. Illiteracy characterized many frontier settlers in the pioneer generations.[1] According to census records, Reuben could not read and write, although in later life he appeared to correct that shortcoming. We may assume that Reuben grew up on the farm of his father, did chores regularly, and worked the fields to supplement the family livelihood. Weekends might mean a special trip into nearby Hartsville, Tennessee. Sundays would have found him at the Willow Grove Methodist Church where the Cardwells were a plentiful presence among the members of the church.

Sometime around 1837, the Cardwells left Sumner County, Tennessee, and removed to Simpson County, Kentucky. In 1849, Reuben married Elizabeth Stegall, daughter of Henry Stegall and Irene Strange, of Christian County, Kentucky; the county immediately west of Simpson County.[2] Reuben's older brother, Thomas G. Cardwell lived in Christian County in 1848, thus accounting for the happenstance of Reuben meeting Elizabeth in Christian County.[3] We cannot say much about the circumstances of their marriage because the couple married in Trigg County, Kentucky, a county further west of Christian County, on the far southwestern edge of the state, near Calloway County; the home of Reuben's Uncle Thomas [Jr.] Cardwell. His marriage to Elizabeth Stegall uncovered a conundrum of the Stegall family in the census of 1850. There were two Stegall daughters of the similar name of Elizabeth, namely, Elizabeth and Eliza. In 1850, Elizabeth appeared as the wife of Reuben Cardwell living in Simpson County, next door to Reuben's brother, Dudley Cardwell.[4] Meanwhile, the same 1850 census listed Eliza in the household of Henry Stegall of Christian County, effectively appearing to list the same person twice in the 1850 census.[5] However, a parsing of census data showed that Eliza was the younger sister of Elizabeth.

Reuben and Elizabeth (Stegall) Cardwell spent time briefly in Simpson County, Kentucky. About 1850, the couple removed to southwest Missouri to join the Stegall family recently removed from Kentucky to Missouri in the westward migration that caused many pioneer families to relocate out of Kentucky. Samuel Stegall, Elizabeth's younger brother, first settled in Madison Township, Cedar County, Missouri. Reuben and Elizabeth followed and lived nearby. Their first child Thomas P. Cardwell was born in 1851 in Missouri. Two more children followed over the next few years: Edward Cardwell in 1856 and Juliann Cardwell in 1859, each born in Missouri. The Stegall and Cardwell families lived near Paynterville (aka Bearcreek), a small village of about 50 people in 1850. Located in the northeast part of Madison Township, Bearcreek took its name from the nearby stream of Bear Creek that was also the name of the post office, the oldest post office in Cedar County. The name Paynterville honored the Paynter family long prominent there. Paynterville had a hotel kept by Judge C.W. Paynter, a blacksmith shop, a wagon-maker's shop, and two stores. The closest town to Paynterville of any size was Fremont (aka Lancaster and Stockton) about eight miles west northwest of Paynterville. The court of commissioners laid out Lancaster (Stockton) in 1846 as the county seat, the name changed to Fremont in 1848, and remained as such until after the Civil War when for political reasons county leaders dropped the name Fremont in 1868 and reincorporated the town as Stockton.[6] Nevertheless, in 1850, around the time the Cardwells and Stegalls arrived, it was new to the developing geography of southwest Missouri.

Meanwhile, east of Paynterville, the hub of trade and social gatherings was Jerico Springs located conveniently to serve the counties of Cedar, Dade, Barton, and Vernon. It lay in the southwest corner of Benton Township within a day's ride of the towns of Lamar, Sheldon, Nevada, Stockton, and Paynterville. Jerico was famous for its springs and the legendary Indian tales that gave it its reputation as a healing center. The Indians, so the story goes, used the water's curative properties by burying themselves in the mud. The healing virtues of the springs passed to the first white settlers and eventually the reputation of

Jerico reached the East Coast. In 1857, around the time the Stegalls and Cardwells were settling into Madison Township, investors determined to erect a hospital there. However, the Civil War intervened and the project never materialized. Despite its fame, Jerico Springs did not exist as a town until developers laid it out in 1882, after the springs miraculously cured a skeptic of their curative powers of a chronic affliction. The town grew rapidly after 1882. There were soon three hotels, several bath buildings, and a flouring mill. A couple of banks went in, and a host of shops and businesses, not to mention residences that quickly followed. Moreover, Jerico had a reputation for its plethora of fraternities and lodges that at one time numbered in excess of a half dozen, each with a full complement of community-minded members.[7]

Something happened in the Cardwell marriage around 1858. Reuben abandoned Elizabeth and the children. The evidence of a broken marriage first appeared in the 1860 census. Elizabeth "Cordell," sons Thomas P. age nine, Edward age six, and daughter Juliany [*sic*] age eight months, were living alone in Madison Township, Cedar County, near Bearcreek, Missouri. Elizabeth reported herself on the census as a widow. Living with her at the time was four-month-old John Stegall, infant nephew of her brother Samuel Stegall.[8] Where was Reuben? Family tradition said he ran off with another woman. Although possibly true, the story lacked factual verification.

Meanwhile, the 1860 census clarified the mystery of the two Stegall girls similarly named Elizabeth and Eliza. Eliza Stegall, age 26, appeared with Irene Hayes in the 1860 census. Irene (Watts) Strange-Hayes was the mother of Elizabeth (Stegall) Cardwell. Had Eliza Stegall been married to Reuben Cardwell, she would not have been still a Stegall in her mother's household. Elizabeth Cordell [*sic*], age 28, also appeared in the 1860 census next door to Irene Hayes, Eliza Stegall, and other members of the Stegall family.

In 1849, when Elizabeth married Reuben Cardwell, she would have been 18; Eliza her sister was still 16. Henry Stegall had four daughters, two of them of an age in the enumeration of the 1840 census to be Elizabeth and Eliza. The unusual quality of giving to two of his daughters similar names rests with the fact that their maternal grandmother was Elizabeth (Watts) Strange. In any event, Eliza Stegall married William Emberson [Emmerson] on January 30, 1866, in Dade County, Missouri, thus putting an end to the saga of the two daughters.[9] The genealogical record added an additional layer of confusion when Samuel Stegall married Mrs. Eliza Jane (Craft) Casey June 28, 1885, in Dade County, Missouri, to introduce into the record yet another Eliza Stegall.[10]

The circumstances of the life of Elizabeth (Stegall) Cardwell after 1860 are speculative. She apparently continued to live in the Paynterville area. The Poor Farm of Cedar County was in Madison Township near Bear Creek. It consisted of about 160 acres west of Paynterville. Created to serve the indigent and less fortunate residents of the county, clients of the farm worked the fields and cared for livestock to meet the costs of their upkeep in exchange for comfortable housing in log and frame buildings. Although Elizabeth (Stegall) Cardwell, a single mother of three, might easily have fit the definition of an indigent soul, there is no evidence that she worked or resided at the Cedar County Poor Farm.[11]

On September 6, 1866, Elizabeth married Peter Minick in Cedar County.[12] The couple subsequently disappeared from the genealogical record. There were others of the Minick name living in Madison Township. They were the probable kin of Peter Minick but none of them trace specifically to him. The association of the children of Elizabeth with George Minix (Minick) in Schuyler County, Missouri, in 1870 likewise suggests a connection. However, no records verify the placement of Peter and Elizabeth (Stegall) Cardwell-Minick after 1866.

Meanwhile, Reuben Granville Cardwell resurfaced in California in the 1860 census, working as a miner in Nevada County.[13] He worked at the Rough and Ready Mine in Nevada County for more than a decade. Pinpointing his exact movements is difficult because there was another R.G. Cardwell, age 20, recorded in 1860 also living in the mining district and working in Butte Township at the old Sutter mines, in California.[14] Careful comparison of age differences allows separation of the two R.G. Cardwells. There is no doubt that Reuben Granville Cardwell worked at the Rough and Ready. The 1860 census that listed R.G. Cardwell as age 20 was likely an anomaly of census-taking whereby the census counted him twice, once represented by his fellow miners who did not know his true age. In one instance, the census listed R.G. Cardwell, age 30, occupation miner, living with Thomas Hopkins. In the other listing, there were six young men, including R.G. Cardwell, living together in the same household: J.H. Emmerson, P.J. Neal, J. Stigall [*sic*], J.H. Hopkins, and J.H. Brown. Two of the men besides Reuben, namely, J. [John] H. Emmerson and J. [James] H. Brown traced to Cedar County, Missouri, where the 1850 census listed them in District 17 of Cedar County corresponding roughly to Madison

Township. Brown returned to Cedar County, married Eliza Nichols and had a son named Seigal [*sic*] Brown.[15] Emmerson, also from Cedar County but originally from Iowa, returned to Iowa and went into business as a hotelkeeper. Meanwhile, some of the other California mining compatriots of R.G. Cardwell had strong circumstantial ties to Cedar County. J. Stigall was probably John H. Stegall, brother of Samuel Stegall and probable father of John W. Stegall the nephew of Samuel who was in the Elizabeth Cardwell household in 1860. Meanwhile, Hopkins and Neale were prominent surnames in Cedar County before and after the year 1860.

The Rough and Ready Mine dated to the 1849 California Gold Rush. The town had a unique history. It declared its secession from the Union in 1850, largely to avoid mining taxes, but then voted to rejoin the Union three months later when organizers discovered they had nothing to celebrate on the Fourth of July. Congress established a post office there in 1851. The 1850s were boom years in California. Rough-and-Ready was the center of activity in the region. However, the gold slowly gave out in the creeks and on the flats. Fires in 1856 and 1859 nearly obliterated the town, dwindling its once thriving community to just 24 houses. The town declined as fast as it had developed. When Reuben Cardwell arrived there in 1860, it was still a mining town but without much promise for striking it rich. By 1867, Reuben was living in Grass Valley, Nevada County, farming and working the mines.[16]

On November 6, 1870, he married Lydia (Coon) McIntire, a young widow barely half his age.[17] Born in Iowa, Lydia was the daughter of Jacob Coon. She had a baby son named Jacob McIntire from her previous marriage.[18]

During the heydays of California development, officials maintained a strict policy of voter registration. Through these California Great Registers, land claims, marriages, and census records, a reasonable picture emerges of the life and locations of Reuben and Lydia Cardwell. In the summer of 1871, Reuben registered as a miner at Dry Creek and Centerville, east of Fresno, in Fresno County, California, working as a miner at the self-reported age of 37.[19] He was actually age 42. The genealogical records indicate that Reuben did not always give an accurate account of his age. There is no question, however, that this is the correct Reuben. His father-in-law Jacob Coon registered with him.[20]

In 1876, Reuben quit mining and took up farming fulltime, falling back on his Tennessee and Kentucky roots. He homesteaded 160 acres of government land in Tulare County, California.[21] The 1876 voter registration list found him at Mountain View at age 43 engaged in farming to satisfy the conditions of his land grant.[22] The Homestead Act of 1862 promoted the settlement and development of the American West. The Act granted 160 acres of unappropriated public lands to anyone who paid a small filing fee and agreed to work on the land and improve it over a five-year period, including building a residence. Reuben's land lay about two miles north of the Tule River and about 10 miles northeast of the town of Porterville. In 1879, he registered to vote at Porterville. His father-in-law Jacob Coon, now 77 years old, registered with him. In 1880, Reuben, Lydia, and their six children, including Lydia's son Jacob McIntyre, and Lydia's father Jacob Coon, lived on their farm above the Tule River in Tulare County, California.[23] By the year 1882, the five-year residency requirement fulfilled, the government granted a patent for his 160 acres of land in Tulare County under the promise of the Homestead Act of 1862. There is no deed extant in the genealogical record; however, Reuben apparently sold his farm because he quit farming. In 1888, he was in Los Angeles, California, living on North Truman Street and working as a teamster at age 58.[24] However, the following year saw him back in the farming business in the spring of 1889, living in Roberts, Fresno County, California, and then in Oleander, Fresno County.[25]

The stint in Fresno County was short-lived. Sometime between April and October 1892, at age 64, he moved from Oleander back to Los Angeles to work as a laborer.[26] He and Lydia lived at 765 Maple Avenue.[27] The 1892 voter registry added a new requirement, a physical description of the registrant. Reuben Granville Cardwell stood 5' 8 ¾" tall, was light complexioned with blue eyes and gray hair. He had a scar on the back of his right wrist. He registered again for the last time in 1896. Retired at age 67, the difference between him and Lydia became more apparent. She was still a relatively young woman at age 40. The couple had a house at 708 Stephenson in Los Angeles.[28] Their six children were grown. No one knows if there was ever contact between Reuben and his first family in Cedar County, Missouri, or whether he knew that his son Edward had died in 1884. There is evidence of a Thomas P. Cardwell near the places Reuben lived, and of an age to be his firstborn son by Elizabeth (Stegall) Cardwell. However, there is no proof that the two California Cardwell men were father and son.

In 1900, the census recorded Reuben Cardwell renting a place on Burnlynd [*sic* Burlington] Avenue in the North Valley section of Los Angeles (Ward 2) with Lydia, stepson Jacob, and son Lewis.[29] He was working as a laborer at age

70 in the farming community of the San Fernando Valley. Daughter Olive May had married a decade earlier and was on her own. Mattie had married recently and was likewise on her own. So was son Reuben. Conspicuously missing from the 1900 census were twin daughters Lulu and Alice who were age 23 at the time. They reappeared in 1910, both single and still using the surname Cardwell.

The life of Reuben Granville Cardwell ended in double remorse. He died September 16, 1901, in Los Angeles. The following month, on October 31, 1901, his son Lewis Granville Cardwell died. Their burial was in Evergreen Cemetery in Los Angeles. Reuben died of chronic Catarrh—a congestive disorder—at the age of 72. He occupies an unmarked grave in Los Angeles Evergreen Cemetery, Section J, in an area called Side Hill Park, Space 89, laid to rest among the pines and the palms, the willow and the wisteria that characterized the city of Los Angeles. Evergreen Cemetery has the distinction of being the oldest cemetery in Los Angeles, dating to 1877.[30]

Lydia (Coon) McIntire-Cardwell married thirdly William H. Feather a native of West Virginia on October 11, 1902, in Los Angeles.[31] Her son Jacob McIntire and her daughter May (Cardwell) Ingmire were witnesses. William and Lydia were living in Los Angeles in 1920, just the two of them. Mr. Feather died December 14, 1926. Upon Lydia's death in 1927, her burial was next to her husband—William Feather—in Evergreen Memorial Park, Los Angeles. The grave of Reuben Granville Cardwell was in a different section of the cemetery. Lydia's son, and for many years Reuben Cardwell's stepson, Jacob McIntire, died November 26, 1959, in Van Nuys, Los Angeles, California, at the age of 91. He spent much of his life as an oil well driller. His burial was in Forest Lawn Memorial Park, Los Angeles.

The genealogy continued from Reuben Granville Cardwell and Elizabeth (Stegall) Cardwell to their son Edward Cardwell.

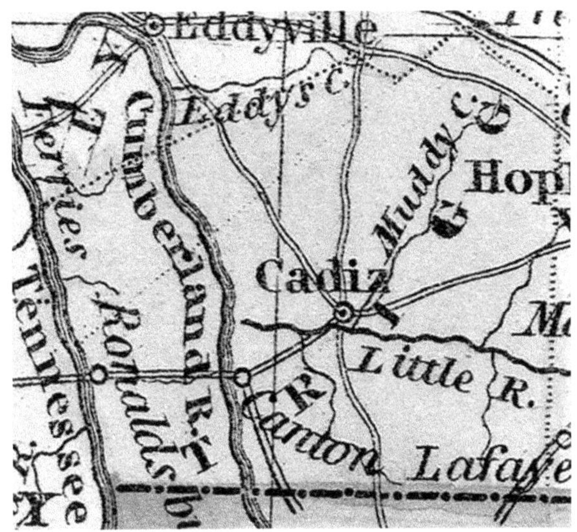

1857 Map of Trigg County, Kentucky. Reuben Cardwell and Elizabeth Stegall obtained their marriage license at the courthouse in Cadiz, the county seat of Trigg County, Kentucky. Trigg County had a population of about 10,000 people in 1850. *Mitchell's New Universal Atlas,* Philadelphia: Charles Desilver, 1857. Dickinson College.

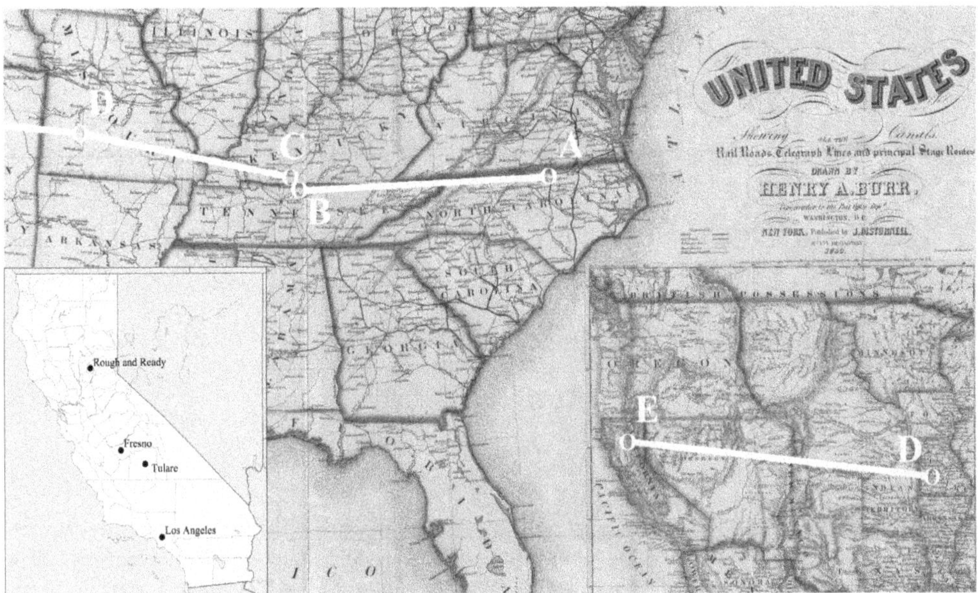

Map of the Westward Migration of Cardwells from c.1788 to 1860, beginning in (A) Granville County, North Carolina, to (B) Sumner County, Tennessee, and (C) Simpson County, Kentucky. Reuben Cardwell and Elizabeth Stegall Cardwell removed to (D) southwest Missouri where Reuben left his family and settled in (E) the mining region of California. Map modified from Disturnell's *New Map of the United States*, 1850. Library of Congress.

Reuben Cardwell and Elizabeth Stegall Marriage Record, Trigg County, Kentucky. Reuben obtained a bond April 19, [1849], filed the marriage license with the county clerk on April 28, and a justice of the peace married them on May 19, 1849. Entry no. 1260 "Reuben Cardwell to Elizabeth Stegall," ***Marriage Docket*****, Vol. 1 1820-1857;** ***Marriage bonds*****, Vols. 2-3 1857-1869;** ***Kentucky County Marriages, 1797-1954*****, Trigg County, Book 1, p. 126.**

124

Feby 21st 1849	1253	Stanley Thomas Jr To Emily Ann Light	16 June 1849
March 9th	1254	Joel D. H. Bristow To Mary Booker	[illegible] 14th 1849
10th	1255	Jonathan M. Rucker To Mary Ann Jones	
14th	1256	John Summers To Teresa Coleman	12 Nov 1849
April 7th	1257	Wiley Johnson To Lucy Ann Harrel	12 Nov 1849
14	1258	Thomas W. Noles To Mary Jane Coleman	3 Sept 1852
16	1259	William H. Ingram To Dicy Rhodes	May 14th 1849
19th	1260	Reuben Cardwell To Elizabeth Stegall	April 28
26	1261	Caudom McKinney To Martha Ann McKinney	April 7th 1851
28	1262	Allen Barnes To Eliza Ann Denson	May 14th 1849

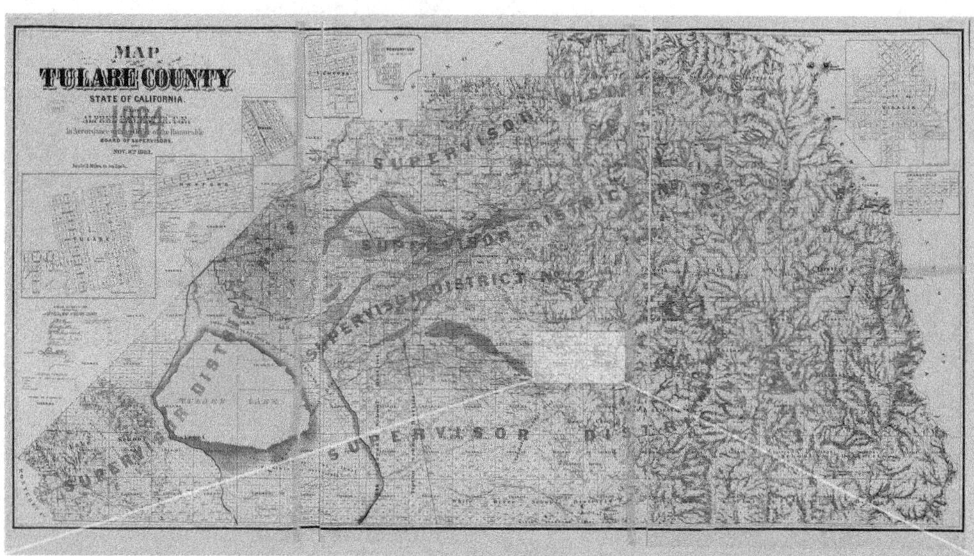

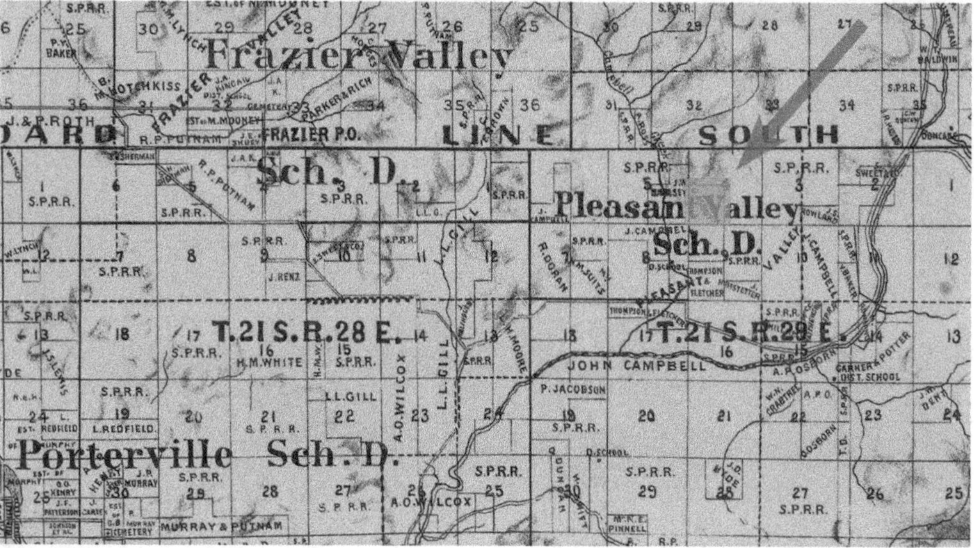

Map of Tulare County, California. Inset shows the quarter section of government land homesteaded by Reuben G. Cardwell in 1882, in Section 4 of the Pleasant Valley School District. *Map of Tulare County, State of California.* Alfred Bannister, San Francisco: Britton & Rey, 1884. Library of Congress.

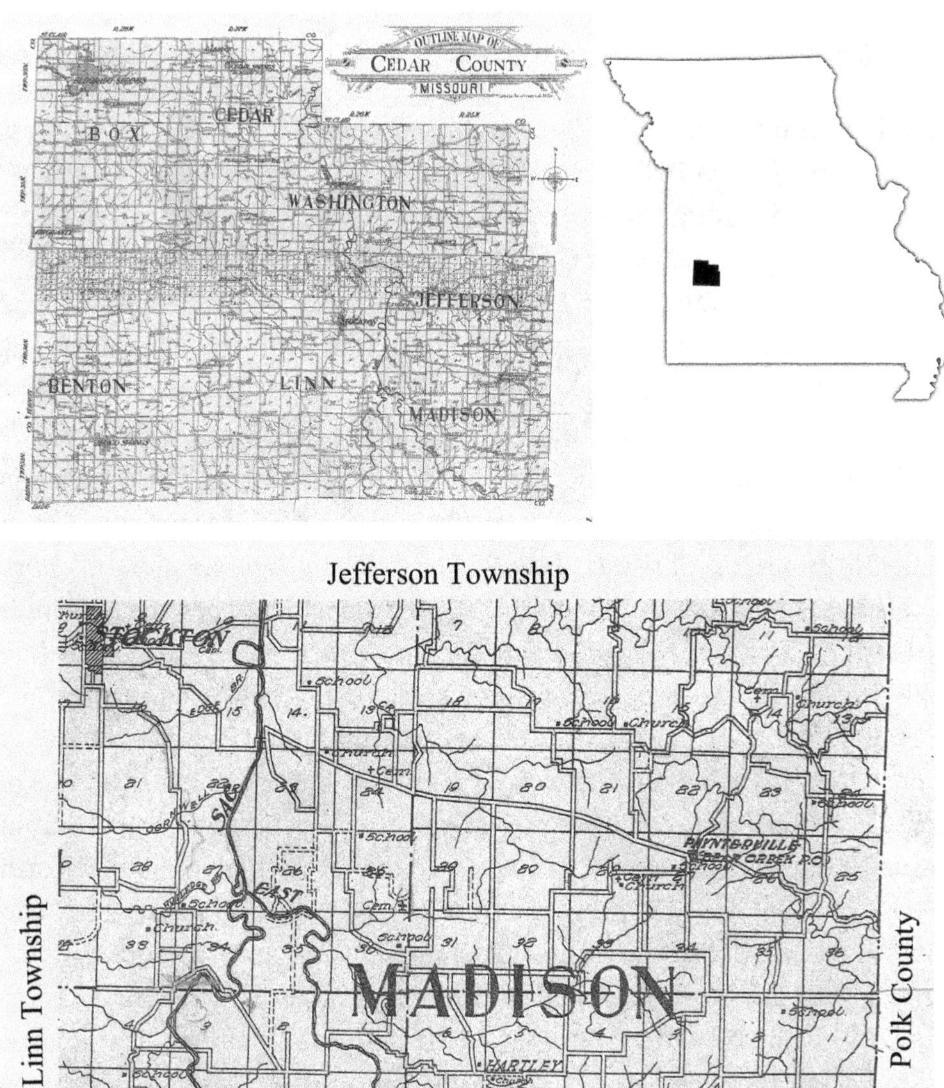

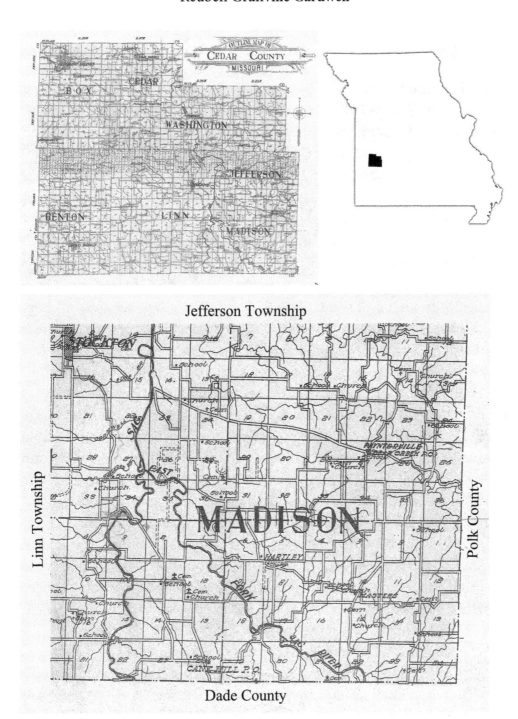

Cedar County, Missouri. Reuben and Elizabeth (Stegall) Cardwell came to Cedar County about 1851. In 1860, Elizabeth and their three children were living in Madison Township, near Paynterville (aka Bearcreek). ***Standard Atlas of Cedar County, Missouri*****, Geo. A. Ogle, 1908. Library of Congress.**

Cardwell Seventh Generation Family Group

Reuben Granville CARDWELL was born in June 1829 in Sumner County, Tennessee. He died on 16 Sep 1901 at the age of 72 in Los Angeles, California.[32] His burial was in Evergreen Memorial Park Cemetery, Los Angeles, California.[33] He was the son of **Nelson CARDWELL** and **Nancy HUGHS**.

Reuben married **Elizabeth STEGALL**, daughter of **Henry STEGALL** and **Irene STRANGE** on 19 May 1849 in Trigg County, Kentucky.[34] Elizabeth was born about 1833 in Virginia.

They had the following children.[35]

1. **Thomas P. Cardwell** was born about 1851 in Missouri.[36] He married **Viola D. Crow** daughter of Isaac and Margaret Crow of Linn Township, Cedar County, Missouri, on Christmas Day, 25 Dec 1872, in Dade County, Missouri. She was born about 1857 in Illinois.[37] Viola moved with her parents to Hannibal, Marion County, Missouri, when she was about three years old before settling in Linn Township, Cedar County, in southwest Missouri, sometime before 1870.[38] She was not yet age 16 when she and Thomas P. married. They obtained their marriage certificate on 23 Mar 1872 and married at the home of George D. White.[39] The couple disappeared from the genealogical record from 1872 to 1901 when on 9 Dec 1901 Viola D. Cardwell married Josiah S. Goforth in Polk County, Arkansas. She was still a relatively young woman at age 44 and living in Baden, Indian Territory [Oklahoma].[40] One may assume that her marriage with Thomas P. Cardwell ended. It appears she married Mr. Goforth before 1901 because the 1900 census listed the couple in Township 13, Cherokee Nation, Indian Territory, with four Goforth children, the oldest age 14 down to the youngest age 3. According to the census, Viola and Mr. Goforth had been married 23 years and had children. Yet, the marriage record gives a marriage date of 1901. They were apparently together since 1877, five years after she married Thomas P. Cardwell. Her last name was Cardwell when she married Mr. Goforth. It is likely that the Cardwells made their home at least for a time in Oklahoma. It is unknown if there were children of the Thomas P. and Viola (Crow) Cardwell marriage. No further record of this Thomas P. Cardwell exists.

Meanwhile, there was another Thomas P. Cardwell living in Oklahoma at the same time.[41] He was the younger Thomas Perrin Cardwell born in 1858 the son of Thomas G. Cardwell, son of Nelson Cardwell, and cousin of Thomas P. of Dade County.[42] Thomas Perrin died in 1829 at the age of 71; the other

Thomas P. of Dade County would have been 78, according to the 1860 census. Whether Thomas P. of Dade County and Baden, Indian Territory, knew Thomas P. of Coal County, Oklahoma, is wholly speculative. However, others of the present genealogical line settled in Arkansas, adjacent to Indian Territory. Jonathan Duran Cardwell, son of Nelson Cardwell and uncle of Thomas P. Cardwell of Dade County and Baden removed to Lawrence County, Arkansas. Their Great Uncle Rev. Richard Wilson Cardwell lived for many years in Washington County, Arkansas.[43] Both Jonathan Duran and Wilson were long-established residents of the region whose offspring made up a large and inviting circle of kinship in Missouri, Arkansas, and Oklahoma.

\+ 2. **Edward CARDWELL** was born on 15 Aug 1856 in Missouri. He died on 8 Apr 1884. His burial was in Gum Springs Cemetery, Linn, Cedar County, Missouri. Edward married **Anna Eliza BALDWIN**, daughter of **John Calvin BALDWIN** and **Frances Pherby (aka Pherba) JACKSON**, on 20 Oct 1878 in Madison Township, Cedar County, Missouri. Anna Eliza was born on 15 Jan 1863 in Ottawa, Waterloo, Breckenridge County, Kansas. She died on 10 Apr 1942 in Jerico Springs, Cedar County, Missouri, from Tuberculosis, or Consumption. She was buried in Gum Springs Cemetery, Linn Township, Cedar County, Missouri.

3. **Juliann (aka Juliany and Julia) W. Cardwell** was born about 1858 in Missouri. The date of her birth varies in the genealogical records between 1858 and 1860. She died in 1935 in Jasper County, Missouri. Her burial was in Fairview Cemetery, Joplin, Jasper County, Missouri.[44] Julia married **W.W. (William Wesley) Stivers**, the son of John and Elizabeth Stivers, on 20 Nov 1903 in Cedar County, Missouri.[45] He was born January 1872 in Missouri. In 1860, Juliany Cordell [*sic*] lived with her mother and two siblings in Madison Township, Cedar County, Missouri, near Paynterville (aka Bearcreek). The census recorded her as age eight months.[46] She next appeared in the 1870 census living with her brother Edward in the household of George Menix [Minick] in Schuyler County, Missouri.[47] No one yet knows why Julia and Edward were in northern Missouri in 1870. They were both youngsters who had not reached their majority ages. Their mother, Elizabeth (Stegall) Cardwell, had married Peter Minick in Cedar County in 1866, but no connection is verifiable between him and the Minick family of Schuyler County.

By 1880, Juleanna [*sic*] was back in Madison Township, Cedar County, Missouri, living in the household of William Montgomery, probably as a housekeeper. He was a 69-year-old farm manager living alone who happened also that year to be the census enumerator. The self-reported age of Julia in 1880 corresponded to a birthdate of 1860 and not 1858 as reported previously on the Schuyler County 1870 census.[48] Julia lived several years at Jerico Springs, Cedar County, Missouri.[49] In 1903, she married William Wesley Stivers of Jerico. He was just shy of his 32nd birthday; she was about age 42. It was his second marriage, her first. He first married Melinda Jane Stegall, 10 Nov 1896 in Dade County, Missouri. Melinda Jane was the daughter of Benjamin Stegall, niece of Elizabeth (Stegall) Cardwell, and cousin of Julia. Malinda Jane died, leaving Wesley a widower with a two-year-old son named John Stivers.[50] Julia never had children of her own, and the infant Stivers appears not to have survived.

Julia and Wesley married at Osiris, Missouri, in a ceremony officiated by J. M. Biddey, Minister of the Gospel.[51] He was also the postmaster at Osiris and the stepbrother-in-law of Julia. He married Anna Eliza (Baldwin) Cardwell, the widow of Edward, Julia's brother. A notice of the marriage of Wes and Julia appeared in the *Stockton Journal* on 26 Nov 1903 noting that the couple was at home in Jerico Springs.[52] By 1910, Julia and Wes had moved to Joplin, in Jasper County, Missouri, living in the East 6th Ward of the city, in the mining region where Wes made a living doing general work as a laborer in the galena mines.[53]

For the next 25 years, Julia made her home in Jasper County. Wes died sometime during the intervening years because in the 1930 census, the census taker listed Julia as a widow living at the Jasper County Poor Farm with other elderly citizens of the county.[54] She died there in 1935, all but forgotten. No one knew her birthday and could only list the birthplaces of her parents as the "United States." Her burial was in Fairview Cemetery, Joplin. A note in the cemetery records said she died at the age of 70, which would have calculated to a birthdate of 1865. Since no birthdate appeared on her death records, her age would have been unknown. She died closer to the age of 75.

Reuben Granville CARDWELL married secondly widow **Lydia (Coon) McIntyre** on 6 Nov 1870 in Pueblo De Las Junta, Fresno County, California.[55] Lydia was born in 1852 in Iowa, the daughter of Jacob Coon.[56] She died in 1927. Her burial was in Evergreen Cemetery, Los Angeles, California.

Reuben and Lydia had the following children.

4. **Olive May Cardwell** was born September 1871 in California. She died 14 Sep 1961 in San Diego, California.[57] She married **Sheridan Ingmire** 6 Nov 1890 in Fresno County, California.[58] Sheridan was born 15 Jan 1865 in Circlemill,

Ohio. A farm boy, he came to California by way of Kansas, the son of Snoden Ingmire and Rachel (Mitchell) Ingmire.[59] Sheridan Ingmire became superintendent of the Los Angeles sewer district. He died 26 Jun 1934.[60] His burial was in Inglewood Cemetery, Los Angeles. In 1892, Olive May and Sheridan settled at Pine Ridge, in Fresno County, California.[61] They had two children but only one survived. A third child, a son Herbert Wilson Ingmire born 5 Oct 1894 in Fresno County was stillborn. Sheridan worked as a railroader in 1896.[62] The couple lived in Los Angeles in 1900 with their daughter Juanita, age nine, born Nov 1891. They lived on Alameda Street. The census noted that Sheridan and May had two children but only one survived.[63] The census did not mention the loss of a third child. The census taker listed Sheridan as a day laborer. The 1910 census confirmed the couple still lived in Los Angeles on Alameda Street. The record noted one child surviving, their only daughter Juanita May Ingmire.[64] Juanita married Henry N. Nelson of Santa Barbara, California, 3 Jun 1914.[65] Meanwhile, Sheridan had a steady job in Los Angeles as city "sewer flusher." By 1930, Sheridan had worked his way up to become superintendent of sewer maintenance for the city of Los Angeles. He and May lived on a small farm at the edge of the city.[66] Sheridan died in 1934. In 1940, May was living in Los Angeles as a widow with her daughter Juanita (Ingmire) Nelson-Snider, age 48, likewise a widow, and her 11-year-old son Bruce Snider. Juanita worked as a "winder" in a knitting factory.[67]

5. **Reuben C. "Dube" Cardwell** was born in 1874 in California. He died 15 Feb 1939 in Amador, Amador County, California. Burial was in Jackson City Cemetery, Jackson, Amador County, California.[68] He went by the nickname Dube, variously transcribed as Darbe and Dealie. He married **Lillie (aka Lily) Ethel Bowen** on 9 Aug 1901. She was a native of Illinois with a fifth grade education.[69] She was born in May 1881, the daughter of Harry and Mary Bowen.[70] Dube and Lillie had an only surviving son named Ralph Granville Cardwell born 13 Dec 1902.[71] They had five children by the year 1908, but only one survived.[72] A child born prematurely in 1907 lived only three days. Infant mortality unfortunately ran high in the Bowen family. Only two of Lillie's five siblings had survived.[73]

In 1896 at the age of 22, Dube Cardwell registered to vote in Los Angeles Precinct 56, Ward 7. The record described him as 5' 10 ¾" tall, light complexion, blue eyes, light hair, with a scar over his right eye, born in California, and working as a laborer. He lived at home in the household of his mother and father at 708 Stephenson Avenue.[74] In 1908, Dube and Ethel lived on 18th Avenue. He worked as a foundry man.[75] The 1910 census showed Dube (Reuben, Jr.) living with his mother and stepfather William Feather in Los Angeles.[76] The census revealed a curious conundrum about census taking because Dube, Lillie, and their son Ralph appeared in the 1910 census also at another location.[77] All of the children of Lydia (Coon) McIntire-Cardwell-Feather except for one deceased son appeared enumerated in the Feather household as if they used the census event to memorialize the entire Cardwell family. All four of Lydia's living children appeared on the list as stepchildren of Mr. Feather; viz., Jacob McIntire [married eight years]; May (Cardwell) Ingmire [married 20 years, two children, one living]; Reuben [Dude] Cardwell [married nine years, one child, one living]; Lulu Cardwell age 33 [single]; Alice Cardwell age 33 [single]; and Mattie (Cardwell) Parker age 29 [married 12 years, one child, one living]. Mr. Feather worked as a carpenter. Jacob McIntire was a teamster for an oil company. No one else listed an occupation. The census listed none of the wives or husbands of the children compounding the mystery of why the family appeared grouped for a family snapshot all well into their adult years and some recorded elsewhere in the 1910 census.[78] In any event, by 1920 Dude (Reuben) and Lillie were in Fresno County, California. He worked as a "boiler washer" and a teamster in the oil fields.[79] Sometime before 1930, they moved to Monterey, Monterey County, California. They paid $16 a month for a rental on English Avenue while Dude worked as a gardener for a private estate.[80]

Reuben C. (Dude) Cardwell died 15 Feb 1939 in Amador, California. He lies buried in an unmarked grave verified by cemetery records in Jackson City Cemetery, Jackson, California.[81] His wife Lillie E. Cardwell and son Ralph Granville Cardwell survived him. In 1940, Lillie was living alone as a roomer in Monterey, California at the age of 58.[82] Meanwhile, things did not turn out well for the Cardwell's son, Ralph Granville Cardwell.[83] In 1930, he was in jail in Bakersfield, Kern County, California, for an unspecified infraction. Divorced at age 27, Ralph G. married multiple times and died on 21 Sep 1984, in Marysville Convalescent Hospital, Yuba County, California, at the age of 81.[84] He spent 32 years in the Yuba-Sutter area, much of the time as a bartender. He was the last of the Cardwell name descended from Reuben Granville Cardwell.[85]

6. **Lewis (aka Louis) Granville Cardwell** was born in 1875 in California.[86] He died on 31 Oct 1901 in Los Angeles, California.[87] His burial was in Evergreen Memorial Park Cemetery, Los Angeles, California.[88] In 1896 at the age of 21, he

registered to vote in Los Angeles Precinct 56, Ward 7. The record described him as six feet tall, light complexion, grey eyes, brown hair, born in California. He lived at home in the household of his mother and father, Reuben and Lydia Cardwell, at 708 Stephenson Avenue.[89] Lewis worked as a barber in Los Angeles. Tragically, he died at the age of about 26 of Pulmonary Phthisis [Tuberculous] and complications of influenza, a condition that claimed the lives of other members of the Cardwell family, including Lewis' half-brother, Edward Cardwell who died at the age of 27 in Missouri.

7. **Lulu G. [C] Cardwell** was born about 1876 in California. She was the twin of Alice Cardwell, and apparently never married.[90] The 1880 census inadvertently omitted her name, and she did not appear in the 1900 census as a Cardwell. However, the 1910 census listed her as stepdaughter Lulu Cardwell, age 33 and single, in the curious conglomerate of the William Feather household. Because no other records of her are in the genealogical record, it may be that the circumstances of her life were unusual.

8. **L. Alice Cardwell** was born about 1876 in California, the probable twin sister of Lulu Cardwell. The 1910 census listed her as the stepdaughter of William H. Feather.[91] She was age 33 and single. She appeared previously in the 1880 census as L.A. Cardwell, age four, living in Tule River Township, Tulare County, California, in the household of her parents, R.G. and Lida [*sic*] Cardwell.[92] A similar genealogical record parallels that of her sister. The censuses of 1890 and 1900 did not list her, but she reappeared in 1910 as stepdaughter Alice Cardwell age 33 and single in the household of William Feather.

9. **Martha "Mattie" Jane Cardwell** was born in January 1879 in California. She died 27 Jan 1927 in Santa Cruz, California. Her burial was at Oakwood Memorial Park, Santa Cruz. Her gravestone recorded her birth as 1880.[93] Mattie married **Alfred Crowder (or Croucher) Parker** 23 Oct 1897 in Los Angeles.[94] He was born 8 Sep 1876, the son of Hiram L. and Elizabeth Parker. He died 11 Feb 1945, at Alameda, California. Announcement of their marriage appeared in the *Los Angeles Times*.[95] The couple generally went by their names A.C. and Mattie. However, their marriage certificate was unique. The record showed that Fred Parker and Martha Cardwell married on the above date. The affidavit for a marriage license bore the signature of A.C. Parker.[96] His Christian name was Alfred, (aka Fred); Martha Cardwell was the formal version of the more familiar Mattie. The couple settled in Lucerne, Kings County, California, where Alfred

worked managing a fruit farm.[97] In 1900, they were living with A.C.'s parents in Lucerne, and had a baby daughter born 28 Jul 1898 who they named Marvel Elizabeth.[98] Marvel would be their only child. The 1910 census confirmed the presence of the Parker family in Lucerne, California.[99] Inexplicably, Mattie's name also appeared in the infamous 1910 listing of the Cardwell children as the daughter of Lydia (Coon) McIntire-Cardwell Feather in the household of William Feather, 175 miles south of Lucerne on virtually the same day the census occurred in Lucerne.

Alfred registered for the WW I draft in 1918. He had a different job at the time, working as a teamster for the Associate Oil Company.[100] Voter registration records placed the family at Hanford, Kings County, California.[101] Sometime after 1920, they moved to Santa Cruz, California, where Alfred worked in the poultry industry nursery.[102] After Mattie's death in 1927, Alfred remarried and continued to live in Santa Cruz until his death in 1945 at Alameda, California. Meanwhile, Marvel Parker married Karl Frederick Henckel about 1917, and had children.[103] They made their home in San Francisco.[104] Sometime after 1926, the couple divorced and Marvel married Ralph Archie Elliott on 7 Dec 1928 at Alameda.[105] Marvel died 30 Mar 1997 in Grass Valley, Nevada County, California, ironically the county her grandfather Reuben Granville Cardwell chose when he first came to California in 1860.[106]

24

Edward Cardwell

Very little documentation exists on the life of Edward Cardwell. He died very young. The genealogical record relies on five data points, none of which conclusively establishes Edward as the son of Reuben Granville Cardwell. However, circumstantial evidence is well within the boundaries ordinarily accepted as proof of relationship. To begin with, the know documentation comprises the census data of 1860, 1870, and 1880, as well as the marriage license of Edward Cardwell and Anna Eliza Baldwin, and cemetery information taken from Edward's tombstone. According to his tombstone, Edward Cardwell was born August 15, 1856, and, according to census records, he was born in the state of Missouri. He died, according to the inscription on his tombstone, April 3, 1884, at the calculated age of 27. Burial was in Gum Springs Cemetery, Cedar County, Missouri. His lone burial near the Baldwin family burial plot, in the same cemetery as his wife and son, and within the county where he lived is, in lieu of documentation of his death, acceptable proof that this is the final resting place of Edward Cardwell.

The earliest record of his presence in Cedar County is the 1860 census enumerated on September 19. At that time, living in Madison Township, near Bearcreek (aka Paynterville), was Elizabeth Cordell [*sic*] and her three children: Thomas P., age nine; Edward, age six; and Juliany, age eight months.[1] In addition, living in the household was an infant named John Stegall, age two months. All the children were born in Missouri, according to the census; Elizabeth was born in Virginia, and the census reported her as a widow.

The surname of "Cordell" does not present a major genealogical hurdle. Names in census records are frequently misspelled. According to contemporary records, many of the people living in Madison Township at the time were illiterate; they could not read and write. Census takers relied on phonetic guesswork to decipher pronunciations often given in unfamiliar southern dialects. Moreover, the evolution of the spelling from Cordell to Cardwell in later records linked to known members of the Elizabeth Cordell household is acceptable theory that this was the family of Edward Cardwell. Further anecdotal data indicates that the name Cordell survived in related branches of the Cardwell ancestry.

The largest hurdle in establishing Edward in the present genealogical line is not in the misspelling of the name Cordell but in the reported ages given in the 1860 census. For example, Edward Cardwell and Julia Cardwell later appeared in the 1870 census, ages 14 and 12 respectively, living in the household of George Minix [*sic*] in Schuyler County, Missouri.[2] Because the names Edward and Julia Cardwell and their approximate ages compare favorably with the 1860 census data from Cedar County, family historians assume Edward and Julia of Schuyler County in north Missouri were the same Edward and Juliany of Cedar County. However, the age differences cannot be satisfactorily resolved. One would assume that Elizabeth Cardwell (aka Cordell) would know the ages of her children in 1860, not to mention her own age, none of which matches ages reported in other documents ascribed to the family. Moreover, no records survive that explain the presence of Edward and Julia in north Missouri in 1870. The difference in reported birthdates persisted in related documents. For example, Juliany, reported as age eight months in 1860 and age 12 in August 1870, was probably the Juliann that later reappeared in Cedar County in 1880 at age 20 living in the home of William Montgomery. Her age of 20 coincided with her reported age in 1860 as the probable daughter of Elizabeth. A computed birthdate of 1860 is consistent with later census data for her. If she was the Julia of Schuyler County, she was age 10 and not 12 as reported in 1870. While her age is inconsequential to subsequent events, it helps to establish the members of the Elizabeth Cordell (Cardwell) family, of which she was unmistakably a part.

Meanwhile, the age of Edward as 14 cited in Schuyler County in 1870 confirmed his recorded birthdate on both his gravestone and in the 1880 census. However, his age in 1870 differs from the 1860 census when he was age six. One plausible theory suggests that the Schuyler County age of 14 instead of 16, as evidenced in 1860, may relate to taxation. The assessment of taxes usually applied to males 16 and above. Nevertheless, the date of his birth of 1856, established by the 1870 census, is the date cited in the 1880 census and on his tombstone. Just as one might assume that Elizabeth would know the ages of her children in 1860, one would likewise assume that Edward would know his own birth year self-reported in 1880 and subsequently memorialized on his grave marker in 1884. Still, it is not without possibility that he did not know his true birth year and adopted 1856 instead of 1854, the latter of which would better establish him as the son of Elizabeth Cordell (Cardwell), according to the 1860 census. Meanwhile, assuming he was the son of Elizabeth, further proof must be forthcoming to establish Edward as the son of Reuben Granville Cardwell. Here, his marriage license, paired with other similar documents, builds a compelling case.

Edward married Anna Eliza Baldwin October 20, 1878, in Madison Township, Cedar County. The couple married at the home of Samuel Stegall. Samuel was the brother of Elizabeth Stegall and the uncle of baby John Stegall identified in the household of Elizabeth Cordell in 1860. The genealogical record of the Stegall family progressed from Virginia—birthplace of Elizabeth, according to the 1860 census—through Tennessee and Kentucky, to Missouri. Elizabeth Stegall married Reuben Cardwell in Kentucky in 1849. Kentucky was at that time the residence of Henry Stegall, progenitor of the Stegall family that settled in Madison Township, Cedar County, Missouri. The date of the marriage of Reuben and Elizabeth accommodates the birth of Thomas P. Cardwell in 1851, reported in the 1860 census of the Elizabeth Cordell household. The linkage is compelling. Reuben Cardwell married Elizabeth Stegall; the Stegall family migrated to Missouri; and records document a relationship between Elizabeth (Stegall) Cardwell and members of the Stegall family, including the documented marriage of her son Edward in the home of her brother, Samuel Stegall. The children listed in the household of Elizabeth Cardwell (Cordell) in 1860 were by association the children of Reuben Cardwell.

Reuben Cardwell abandoned his family in 1858 and settled in California. Elizabeth married Peter Minick in 1866, and then dropped from sight in genealogical records. Speculation is that Peter Minick and George Minix (Minick) of Schuyler County were kin; thus, a possible reason for Edward and Julia Cardwell to be in the George Minix (Minick) household in 1870. The record is silent on Peter Minick other than his marriage to Elizabeth Cardwell. There were two others of the Minick name living in Madison Township, Cedar County, at the time: Henry Minick and William Minick, both from Tennessee, each of an age to be brothers of Peter. There was a George Minick also of Tennessee but apparently not the George of Schuyler County whose roots were in Pennsylvania. Nevertheless, the Minick family was prodigious in northern Missouri. A connection with Peter and Elizabeth (Stegall) Cardwell-Minick is probable. A theory not confirmed by any source suggests that Peter and Elizabeth moved to Schuyler County, or in a worst-case scenario, Elizabeth and Peter died and the care of her children came under the guardianship of George Minix (aka Minick) of Schuyler County.

When Edward Cardwell reappeared in Cedar County in 1878 and married Anna Eliza Baldwin, Anna was age 15.[3] It was a private ceremony at the home of Edward's Uncle Samuel Stegall, in Madison Township, Cedar County.[4] Anna Eliza Baldwin was born January 15, 1863, in Ottawa, Waterloo County, Kansas. She was the oldest of 11 surviving children of John Calvin and Frances Pherby (Jackson) Baldwin. John Calvin and Frances had 13 children but two did not survive infancy. John Calvin Baldwin was the son of Thomas Lee Baldwin, a successful trotting horse breeder of the upper Midwest. In 1858, Thomas Lee sold the Baldwin Horse Ranch in Macoupin County, Illinois, and bought land in Ottawa, Kansas. John Calvin, one of the eight sons of the Baldwin family, moved with his new bride, Frances Jackson, to Ottawa to establish a horse farm in Kansas, which he did. The Kansas Breeding Association listed the Baldwin Horse Ranch under his management. The Civil War interrupted business operations in Kansas, and John Calvin enlisted in the Kansas Militia on the Union side. After the war, the Baldwin family gathered in Cedar County, Missouri. Thomas Lee came first from Illinois with his sons. Soon thereafter, John Calvin joined them out of Ottawa in 1867, settling on a tract of land south of Stockton, Missouri, in Linn Township.[5] An 1879 map of Linn Twonship in southern Cedar County noted substantial land holdings in the names of Thomas Lee Baldwin and his sons, including the parcel where John Calvin reestablished the Baldwin Horse Ranch in Cedar County. Thomas Lee remained with the ranch until his death in 1879.[6]

The 1880 census confirmed the union of Edward and Anna Eliza (Baldwin) Cardwell, listing Edward, age 24, and "Ann E" [Anna Eliza] age 17; and their infant daughter, "Laura F" [Laura Frances], in South Linn Township, Cedar County. Linn Township was the location of the Baldwin family. Edward listed an occupation of farmer in 1880, which likely meant a connection to John Calvin Baldwin—father of Eliza—who lived nearby with his large family, and who along with others of the Baldwin clan maintained a considerable presence in the agricultural life of southwest Missouri.[7] In a quirk of census taking, the census enumerated Laura Cardwell as one month old born in December 1878, apparently ignoring the date of the census as June 9, 1880. Accordingly, Laura would have been 7 months old. The error recalls the census of 1860 when the ages of Edward and his siblings appeared questionable. Meanwhile, Thomas Edward Cardwell, son of Edward and Anna Eliza, was not yet born in 1880. By 1881, Anna Eliza had two children by Edward Cardwell; namely, Laura Frances Cardwell and Thomas Edward Cardwell. An analysis of the 1880 census placed the young couple near Bishop Grove, probably on Baldwin land.

Edward died on April 8, 1884, at the age of 27 of tuberculosis, the same disease that at age 26 claimed the life of Lewis Cardwell, the half-brother that Edward probably never knew, born of the second family of Reuben Cardwell in California.[8] Edward Cardwell's grave stands alone in Gum Springs Cemetery without the companionship of any family members. The grave plot probably came from John Calvin Baldwin, placed adjacent to the Baldwin family section at Gum Springs, perhaps as a gift in response to the premature death of his young son-in-law.[9]

On February 8, 1885, Anna Eliza married Jessie M. Biddey.[10] They both lived at Stockton at the time but chose to be married at Bishop Grove Church about six miles south of Stockton past Gum Springs, and five miles east of White Hare and the Omer Post Office. White Hare was once a thriving community destination for residents of Linn Township. The 1880 census had recorded Edward Cardwell in the voting precinct of White Hare. It was also the location of the Omer Post Office.[11] Consequently, White Hare and Omer became interchangeable names for the same place. White Hare dated to the 1830s; the establishment of the post office at White Hare dated to December 11, 1840. The name White Hare officially changed to Omer in 1883. During its lifetime, Omer had a store, church, schoolhouse, post office, and lodge hall. During the Civil War, White Hare played an important role in local guerrilla activities.

Upon the marriage of Anna Eliza, Jesse Biddey became the stepfather of the Edward Cardwell children and raised Laura and Tom Cardwell from infancy. The three of them—Jesse, Laura, and Tom—shared a common bond because they came from similar family stories. Jesse lost his father at a very early age and grew up himself a stepson never knowing his actual father. Born April 11, 1860, in Georgia, Jesse was the son of Tolbert Biddey and Martha Ann Lovelady of

Cherokee County, Georgia. Martha Lovelady had her own story to tell.[12] She was born in 1840 in Cherokee County; she married first Tolbert Biddy of Cherokee in March of 1859, in Pickens County, Georgia, and then married Francis M. Weaver, a previously married Civil War veteran from Illinois.[13] Martha had two children from her first husband, her son Jesse Biddey being the older of the two. The circumstances of the Lovelady-Biddey marriage are unclear. Martha appeared in the 1860 census living alone, with two-month-old Jesse, and working as a domestic in Pickens County, Georgia.[14] She owned real estate valued at $300 and personal property worth $50. Tolbert did not appear listed; instead, Martha lived with another young mother whose husband was likewise missing. Family tradition said that Tolbert suffered a wound in a battle of the Civil War and died leaving Martha with two children. The tradition further said that her infant daughter died in Nashville, Tennessee, during the war. There were two men of names similar to Tolbert Biddey who served in the confederacy from Georgia. However, their units did not organize for the war until 1861, which begs the question of Tolbert's absence from the census in 1860. In any event, Martha and son Jesse next appeared in Illinois where she married Francis Weaver in 1866.[15] Martha and Francis subsequently had four sons, all stepbrothers of Jesse Biddey. Moreover, Francis Weaver already had a son from his previous marriage, rounding out the Weaver-Biddey blended family.

By 1878, the Weaver family and Jesse Biddey settled into South Linn Township in Cedar County, Missouri.[16] Mr. Weaver acquired property adjacent to Baldwin property, and by association near Edward and Anna Eliza (Baldwin) Cardwell. Members of the Baldwin family owned several parcels of land in Cedar and Dade Counties. The 1880 census for Linn Township, Cedar County listed "Jessey Bailey [*sic*]," age 20, stepson of Francis M. Weaver, working on the Weaver farm with his stepsiblings who were in school and could read and write; Jesse could not. The Weaver farm sat amid a trio of the Baldwin brothers, between Jeremiah Washington Baldwin on one side, Thomas Jackson Baldwin on the other, and near John Calvin Baldwin and the Baldwin Horse Ranch. Nancy (Brizendine) Baldwin, matriarch of the Baldwin family, lived with her son Jeremiah following the recent death of her husband, Thomas Lee Baldwin who had died in November of 1879.[17] Nancy, grandmother of Anna Eliza (Baldwin) Cardwell, died in 1881.

Jesse Biddy grew to manhood in Cedar County, learned the hard work of farming, and took up the service of the gospel. Those who later remembered him always spoke of his "works sake as a minister of the Old Baptist Church."

When Edward Cardwell died in the spring of 1884, he left his young widow Anna Eliza and their two infant children, the oldest five years old. Less than a year passed before Eliza married her neighbor, farmer, and sometimes preacher Jesse Biddey on February 8, 1885.[18] Reverend S.E. Odell married them at Bishop Grove, a small community west of Sac River built around a church and a school, and close to the Cardwell residence and the Weaver farm where Jesse lived. The closest trading villages were at Cane Hill 5.5 miles east across Sac River, and Omer four miles northwest. The young couple—Jesse was age 24; Eliza was 22—set up housekeeping in Linn Township and shouldered the task of raising the Cardwell children. Therefore, it was that the genealogy of the Cardwell family proceeded under the parental stewardship of Anna Eliza (Baldwin) Cardwell and Jesse Biddey, surrogate father and guardian of the Cardwell name. Eliza and Jessie did not have children. Family relationships evolved. Anna Eliza's mother died in 1891, and in December of 1892, her father married Sarah Cordelia O'Connor, a woman of 30, nearly 30 years younger than he was, and only a year older than Anna Eliza was. Together John Calvin Baldwin and Cordelia had seven more children, bringing to 20 the number of children fathered by John Calvin Baldwin. Their offspring resulted in an awkward family relationship in which the grandchildren of John Calvin by his daughter Eliza were considerably older than his children by Cordelia were.

Jesse Biddey homesteaded a piece of government land immediately north of the Dade County line and adjacent to property owned by Eliza's father, and purchased sometime before 1879. It is likely that this was the Biddey home in the early years of their marriage because on November 9, 1896, Jesse Biddey received a government land patent for approximately 55 acres next to the Baldwin property.[19] The property was north and adjacent to a similar plot owned by John Calvin Baldwin. The Biddey tract was some of the last remaining government land in that part of the county. The 1862 Homestead Act gave parcels of land to anyone who agreed to improve the land and build on it, usually within seven years or less, meaning Biddey probably applied for the grant prior to 1896 and completed the requisite work to obtain the patent.

The Cardwell children grew to adulthood in the Biddey household. In the summer of 1900, Tom Cardwell was age 19, worked on the Biddey farm, and lived in the home of his parents in Linn Township. Laura Cardwell was in the household as well.[20] That fall, they sold the farm to Thomas Simmons; Laura married Roy McGuire in December; and Tom, Jesse, and Eliza moved to Osiris, Missouri. Osiris was a country store on present Highway 97, 4.5 miles north and slightly west of Jerico Springs in Benton Township of Cedar County, 12 miles from White Hare, and 17 miles from the Baldwin Horse Farm and the seat of the Cardwell, Weaver, and Biddey families. The year 1900 was the year Jesse Biddey established a post office at Osiris. He opened a store there and petitioned the postal service to call the post office Osiris, which the postal service approved in 1902, naming him its first postmaster retroactive to 1901.[21] In Egyptian mythology, Osiris was the god of the afterlife and symbol of fertility, agriculture, and the religious gateway to life, death, and resurrection, all fitting choices for Jesse's religious nature.[22] Jesse became postmaster at Osiris on May 7, 1901. The pay was $37.25 a year, compared with a salary of $694.60 that John W. Jones made as the postmaster at Jerico Springs.[23] Family tradition said that Jesse Biddey and Tom Cardwell farmed while Eliza ran the post office and operated the Osiris store. A specialty of Osiris was an elaborate display of soap that Eliza kept. It was at Osiris on November 20, 1903, that Jesse united in marriage William Wesley Stivers and Julia Ann Cardwell. Julia was the sister of the deceased Edward Cardwell. The wedding circumstantially reaffirmed the sibling relationship of Edward and Julia Ann. Her marriage was one of Jesse's last deeds at Osiris because on August 9, 1904, Dona A. Snow replaced him as postmaster.[24] It turned out that Jesse was the first of only two postmasters of Osiris. In 1906, the post office at Osiris closed after only five years of operation and mail service moved to Jerico Springs.[25] When Eliza left the Osiris store, she took "enough soap to last ten years," according to her granddaughter.[26]

The twentieth century arrived. Tom Cardwell married in 1904 and moved to his own place, kept on farming, and started a family. His grandfather John Calvin Baldwin died in 1908, and two years later Jesse Biddey died. Jessie Maries Biddey died on March 8, 1910, from Pneumonia and heart failure. He was 49.[27] He contracted Pneumonia and within less than a week, the disease took his life. His burial was at Gum Springs Cemetery near the Baldwin plot, a few paces from the grave of Edward Cardwell whose son he raised to continue the Cardwell name another generation.[28]

Meanwhile, Martha (Lovelady) Biddey-Weaver, esteemed citizen of Cedar County, outlived her son Jesse more than twenty years. She died at the age of 91 on July 19, 1931, at the home of her son Arthur M. Weaver of Jerico Springs. Her burial was in Liberty Cemetery near Bishop Grove beside the grave of her husband and stepfather of Jesse Biddey, Francis M. Weaver.

Anna Eliza (Baldwin) Cardwell-Biddey married thirdly to Austen Andrew McCollom, a Cedar County farmer originally from Scottville, Macoupin County, Illinois, born there January 11, 1864, in the same Illinois county that was the original seat of the Baldwin family, and the origin of the Baldwin Horse Ranch. Austen McCollum—Ott as people knew him—was a colorful character. He kept 17 goats and churned butter made from their milk.[29] Eliza and Ott lived in Jerico Springs, 'off school house road' (present Golden Street), in a house northwest of the school and just west of the road (present East Harwood Street). Their place cornered on the road.

Anna Eliza died on April 10, 1942, at her home in Jerico Springs where she had lived as a homemaker for many years. She died at the age of 79 years 3 months and 25 days of Lobar Pneumonia caused by chronic Tuberculosis, an ailment that plagued her for much of her life.[30] For years, she carried a Prince Albert Tobacco can to contain the discharge of mucus to avoid spreading the disease.[31] Her husband Edward Cardwell had died of Tuberculosis and so had their daughter, Laura. Funeral services for Anna Eliza were at Gum Springs Church at 2 p.m. on Sunday April 12, 1942 with Rev. Tom Scoggin officiating. Burial followed behind the church, near the grave of her husband Jesse Biddey, and a few paces up the hill from the burial site of her parents and the gravesite of Edward Cardwell. Her headstone memorialized her third marriage as the "Wife of A.A. McCollom."[32] Mr. McCollom moved to El Dorado Springs, Missouri, and died at a hospital there on April 7, 1956, at the age of 92. His burial was in Hall Cemetery, Jerico Springs, Missouri.[33]

The genealogy of the Cardwell family continued from Edward Cardwell and Anna Eliza Baldwin to their children, Laura Frances Cardwell and Thomas Edward Cardwell.

Edward Cardwell and Anna Eliza Baldwin. This unidentified and undated photograph came from a collection of Baldwin family pictures. Facial recognition technology identified Anna Eliza at a significant validation level compared with known later photos of her and of family members.[34] Edward's association with Anna Eliza and facial recognition at a high degree of similarity between him and his children suggests that this was probably the wedding portrait of Edward Cardwell and Anna Eliza Baldwin who married October 20, 1878, when Eliza was age 15.

Sis Cardwell. This rare photograph claims to picture Julia Ann Cardwell, daughter of Reuben and Elizabeth (Stegall) Cardwell. The unidentified photo was in a stack of photos attributed to the family of Eliza (Baldwin) Cardwell and labeled simply "Sis Cardwell." Inasmuch as she was the only Cardwell woman associated with Eliza Baldwin, it is reasonable to speculate that this is Julia Ann. Facial recognition technology returned a good verification-of-kin when compared with pictures of Cardwell relatives. While the comparisons were not conclusive, they were high enough to support a likely family relationship.

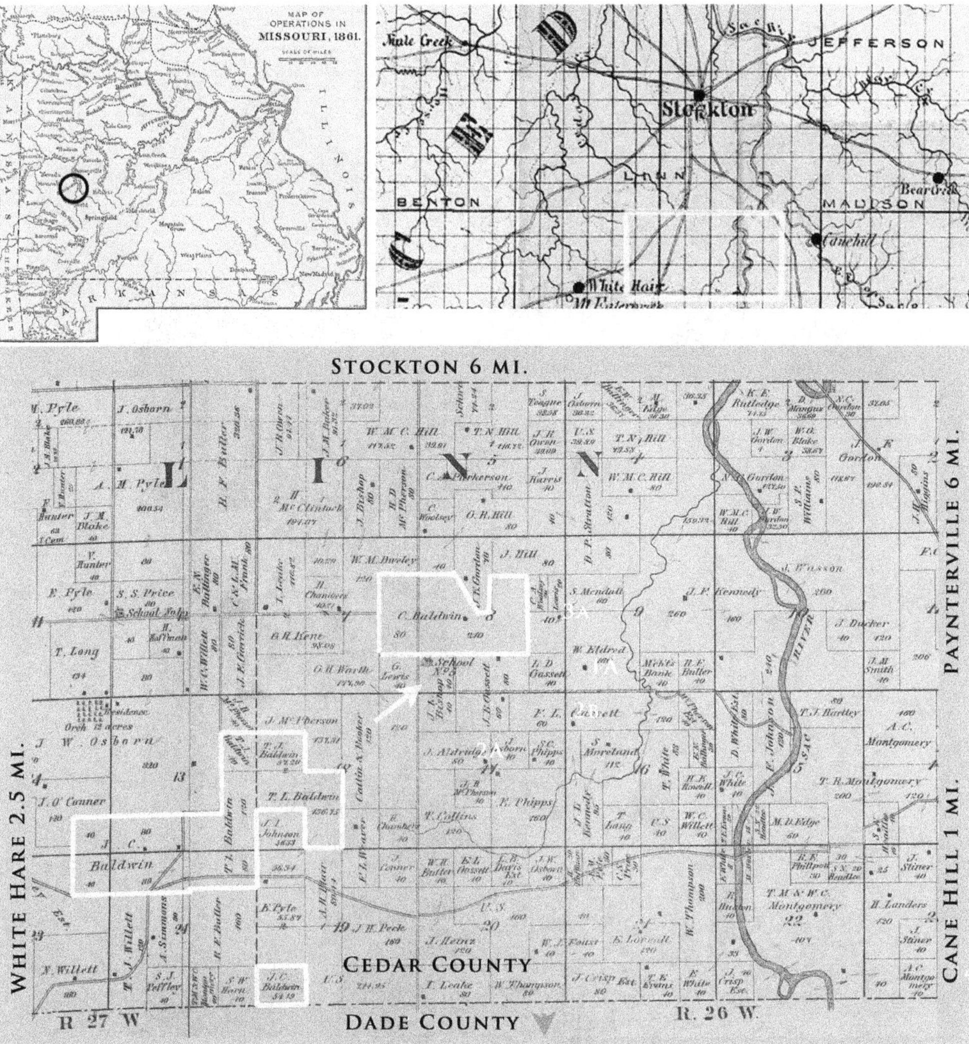

Baldwin Land in Linn Township in 1879. The Baldwin family owned more than 1,000 acres of land west of Sac River in the south part of Cedar County. Analysis of the enumeration of residents in the 1880 census indicated that Edward and Anna Eliza (Baldwin) Cardwell lived close to Caleb Baldwin, probably near Bishop Grove (arrow). They married in Madison Township east of the river at the home of Samuel Stegall who lived near Cane Hill. Stegall was the uncle of Edward and Julia Ann Cardwell. The 1880 census listed Julia in the home of William Montgomery in Madison Township. Town names on the perimeter of the map show the distance from the edge of the map to their locations in Cedar County. Paynterville on the lower 1879 map is Bear Creek on the upper 1874 map. Snead, *The Fight for Missouri*, 1860; *Campbell's New Atlas of Missouri*, 1874; *Map of Cedar County, Missouri*, Reily, 1879. Library of Congress.

Jesse Biddey and Family. Tom Cardwell and his sister Laura stand behind their mother Anna Eliza (Baldwin) Cardwell and her husband Jesse Biddey. Following the death of Edward Cardwell in 1884, Eliza married Jesse Biddey in 1885. He raised the Cardwell children as his own until his death in 1910.

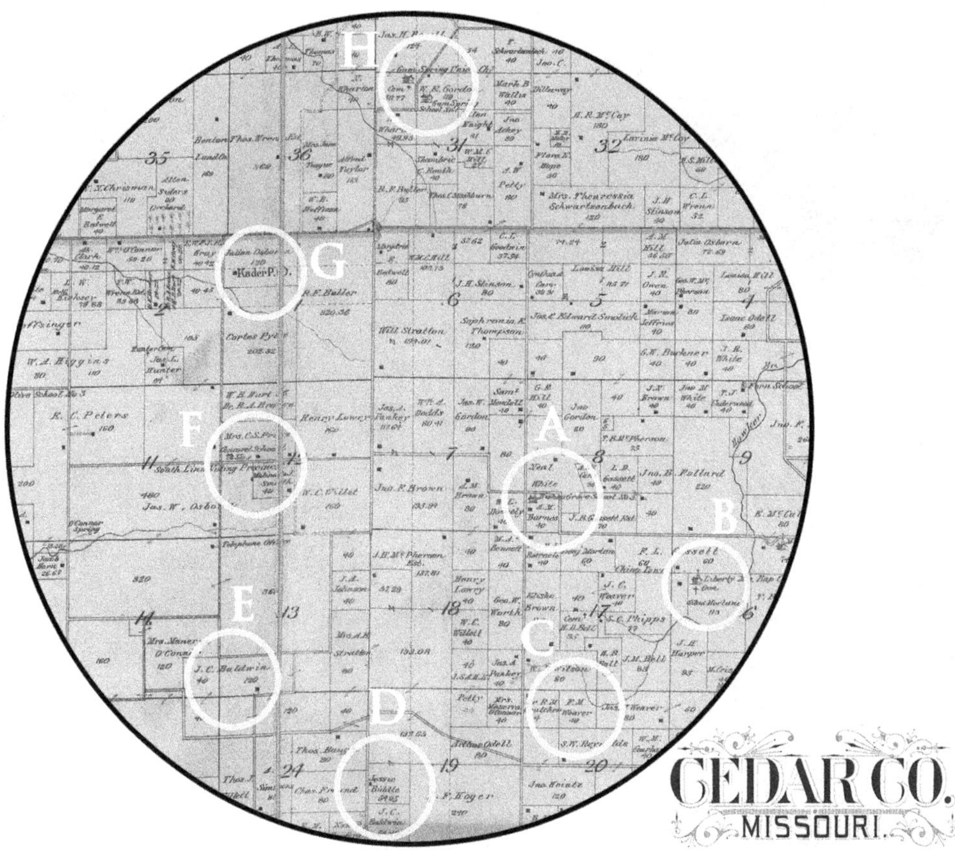

Places of Family Interest. Sites associated with Cardwell, Baldwin, Biddey, and Weaver families in 1897 were within an approximate 5-mile diameter area in South Linn Township, in Cedar County, Missouri. (A) Bishop Grove was where Eliza (Baldwin) Cardwell married Jesse Biddey. (B) Liberty Cemetery was the burial place of Francis M. Weaver, stepfather of Jesse Biddey. (C) this was the home of Mr. Weaver. (D) Jesse Biddey patented 55 acres of land adjacent to J.C. Baldwin on the Dade County line. (E) the Baldwin Horse Ranch operated here. (F) South Linn Voting Precinct at Concord School No. 1 was at this location. (G) Kader Post Office was a country store that dated to about the time of the Civil War. (H) Gum Springs Church and Cemetery served as the burial site of Edward Cardwell, the Baldwin family, Jesse and Eliza (Baldwin) Cardwell-Biddey-McCollom, and Thomas Edward Cardwell. Outside this small circle but within a 12-mile radius of its center, three generations of the Cardwell, Baldwin, and Fellows families spread to other parts of Cedar and Dade Counties. Trading centers were at Stockton 6.5 miles north, Wagner 5.5 miles northwest, Osiris 11 miles west northwest, Jerico Springs 8.5 miles west, White Hare 3 miles southwest, Cane Hill 6.5 miles southeast, and Arcola 5 miles west southwest in Dade County. Map adapted from *New Map of Cedar Co. Missouri*, E.P. Noll, 1897. Library of Congress.

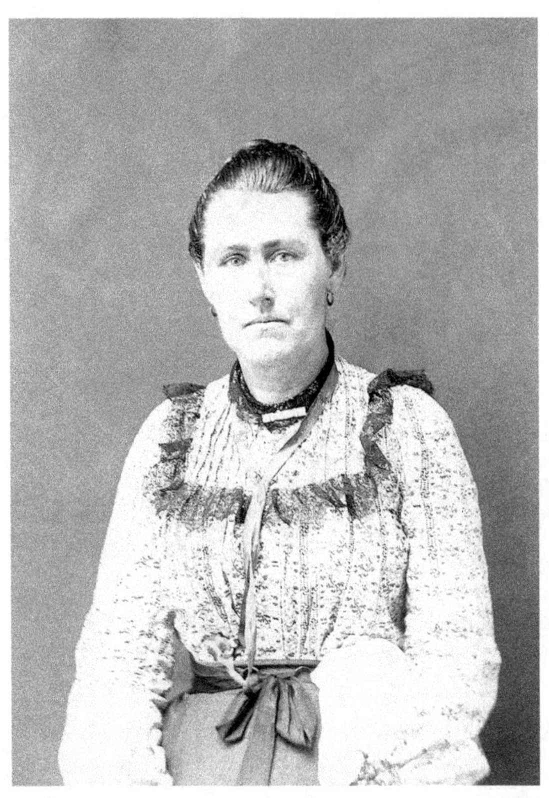

Anna Eliza Baldwin Cardwell Biddey

Jesse Maries Biddey

Mr. and Mrs. Austin Andrew McCollom. This photograph pictured Ott McCollom and Anna Eliza (Baldwin) Cardwell-Biddey taken shortly after their marriage at their home in Jerico Springs.

Cardwell Eighth Generation Family Group

Edward CARDWELL was born on 15 Aug 1856 in Missouri. He died on 8 Apr 1884 in Cedar County, Missouri, from Tuberculosis. His burial was in Gum Springs Cemetery, Linn Township, Cedar County, Missouri. He was the son of **Reuben Granville CARDWELL** and **Elizabeth STEGALL.**

Edward married **Anna Eliza BALDWIN**, daughter of **John Calvin BALDWIN** and **Frances Pherby (aka Pherba) JACKSON**, on 20 Oct 1878 in Madison Township, Cedar County, Missouri.[35] Anna was born on 15 Jan 1863 in Ottawa, Waterloo, Breckenridge County, Kansas. She died on 10 Apr 1942 in Jerico Springs, Cedar County, Missouri, from Tuberculosis or Consumption. Her burial was in Gum Springs Cemetery, Linn Township, Cedar County, Missouri.

They had the following children.[36]

\+ 1. **Laura Frances Cardwell** was born in Dec 1879 in Linn, Cedar County, Missouri. She died 15 Dec 1929, in Wichita, Sedgwick County, Kansas, of Tuberculosis and Pneumonia.[37] Her burial was in Maple Grove Cemetery, Wichita, Sedgwick County, Section O, Lot 246, and Grave 4. Laura married **Royal (Roy) "Irish" Cyrus McGuire,** son of William M. McGuire and Eva Cinderella Green Stenson, on 6 Dec 1900 in Stockton, Cedar County, Missouri. Roy was born 4 Sep 1879 in Republic, Big Bend Township, Republic County, Kansas. He died 22 Nov 1958 in Springfield, Lane County, Oregon, from Cancer. His burial was in Aaron Section, West Lawn Cemetery, Eugene, Lane County, Oregon.

\+ 2. **Thomas Edward CARDWELL** was born in Feb 1881. He died 25 Jan 1944 in Ozark Hospital, Springfield, Greene County, Missouri, from a wood saw accident. He was buried in Gum Springs Cemetery, Linn, Cedar County, Missouri. Thomas married **Mary Belle FELLOWS**, daughter of **Willie (William) Ira FELLOWS** and **Martha Frances CRUTCHFIELD**, on 10 Apr 1904 in Linsa Ward's home, Cedar County, Missouri. The marriage ended in divorce. Belle was born 29 Sep 1885 near Salisbury, Chariton County, Missouri. She died 1 Aug 1958 in the home of Beatrice Richardson, Cedar County, Missouri, from Stroke. Her burial was 4 Aug 1958 in Brasher Cemetery, Cedar County, Missouri.

25

Laura Frances Cardwell

Laura Frances Cardwell was born between December 15 and December 31, 1879, in Linn Township, Cedar County, Missouri, the oldest child of Edward and Anna Eliza (Baldwin) Cardwell. She died December 15, 1929, in Wichita, Sedgwick County, Kansas, of Tuberculosis and Pneumonia at the age of 49.[1] Her burial was in Maple Grove Cemetery, Wichita, Sedgwick County, Kansas, Section O, Lot 246, and Grave 4.

The 1880 census listed Laura Cardwell as the infant daughter of Edward and Ann E. (Baldwin) Cardwell. The census of 1880 was the first to identify relationship to the head of the household.[2]

Laura's father died when she was five, and her mother married Jesse Biddey who raised her to adulthood. She grew up on a farm in southern Linn Township, Cedar County, Missouri, on the Dade County line. She probably went to school at the one-room school at Bishop Grove located a couple of miles north of her stepfather Jesse Biddey's place. She moved with the Biddey family to Osiris, Missouri, around 1900, and helped with the family chores, running the store at Osiris, and tending to the post office that her stepfather founded. She had a plethora of aunts and uncles on the Baldwin side of the family but no known relatives on the Cardwell side except for her brother Thomas Edward Cardwell and Aunt Julia (Cardwell) Stivers, her father's sister. The Weaver family—relatives of Jesse Biddey—occupied land in the same vicinity. When the census taker came around in the spring of 1900, Laura was living in the Biddey household. She was age 20, and single, but not single for long.[3] On December 6, 1900, she married Royal (Roy) Cyrus "Irish" McGuire, a Kansas boy of Irish descent, son of William M. McGuire and Eva Cinderella Green Stenson.[4] Roy was born September 4, 1879, in Republic, Big Bend Township,

Republic County, Kansas. Laura and Roy married at Stockton in Cedar County, Missouri, settled into Cedar County life, and began their family. Roy McGuire and Laura (Cardwell) McGuire had three children: Jessie Ethel "Jack" McGuire, Cecil Edward McGuire, and Albert Ancil McGuire. All the McGuire children were born in Missouri. Roy and Laura moved their young family to Oklahoma and by 1920 lived on Kaw Avenue, next to West First Street in Ward 4 of northwest Bartlesville, Washington County, Oklahoma.[5]

After Laura and Roy [Royal] left Missouri in the early part of the twentieth century, they never returned except for sporadic visits. Although separated by many miles, contact with friends and family was never far away. Karen (Duckworth) Hall, great granddaughter of Laura and Roy, wrote, "In my mother's baby book, my grandmother has written that congratulations were received from a Mr. & Mrs. T.E. [Thomas Edward] Cardwell in Stockton, Missouri. She also mentions a Mr. and Mrs. A.A. McCollom from Jericho, Missouri; she later refers to a 'Grandma McCollom."[6] Grandma McCollom was Anna Eliza (Baldwin) Cardwell-Biddey-McCollum, mother of Thomas Edward and Laura (Cardwell) McGuire. Beatrice Richardson, Laura's niece, recalled of the family, "They would make trips back to Missouri from time to time and take lots of pictures." One picture shows Jessie McGuire about age 12 holding Beatrice on her lap. Cecil McGuire worked in a drugstore at Bartlesville, and Beatrice remembered, "Occasionally he would clear out old merchandise and bring me dolls."[7]

The genealogical record is largely silent about the McGuire family for the next few years. They removed from Bartlesville to Sedgwick County, Kansas, around 1925 where the 1930 census found Roy widowed and living in Wichita on East Harry Street of the First Ward, and working as a molder at a foundry. Living with him were his recently married son Albert and Albert's wife Ester. Laura did not appear in the 1930 census, which started a decades-long search to uncover what happened to her.[8]

The circumstances of Laura's death left genealogists in a quandary for many years, wondering when and where she died. Only hearsay of her demise existed. Some thought she died in Bartlesville, Oklahoma, between 1920 and 1928. Family tradition claimed that she died in Oregon.[9] Others believed she died in Wichita, Kansas. Karen Hall recalled, "As far as Laura is concerned, I had always been under the impression that she had died when my grandmother [Jessie (McGuire) Beebe] was still just a girl; however, I have a picture of my grandparents [Jessie and Bill Beebe] on their way to Oregon in 1929, Royal and Laura are with them. I would assume, therefore, that Laura did die in Oregon."[10] The same family tradition remembered that Jessie took care of her mother before she died and that Royal cut Laura's hair when she was sick. However, the census enumerated Roy as widowed in 1930; therefore, Laura must have died in 1929 or 1930 before Roy moved to Oregon. Photographs usually do not lie. Laura was in the Karen Hall picture, but she did not live long afterwards. If she made the 1,700-mile trip to Oregon in 1929, it was only to stay for a short time. In the fall of 1929, the entire McGuire family converged at Wichita to care for her. Her two sons, Cecil and Albert, returned from Oregon where they worked as truck drivers for the logging camps out of Eugene, Oregon. Her daughter, Jesse Beebe, was in Wichita with her baby daughter Betty Lou, a granddaughter Laura knew only briefly. The family—all five of them—the children with their respective spouses, lived at the same 1832 Salina Avenue address in Wichita. Unfortunately, their care and attention did not improve Laura's health.[11] She died in the winter of 1929, on December 15, at the age of 49, in Wichita, Kansas.[12] The discovery of her gravesite in 2021, in Maple Grove Cemetery in Wichita, solved the mystery of Laura's early death that had so long confounded her descendants.[13] The family buried her in Maple Grove within a few days of her birthday and just shy of Christmas Day. There were no details kept of her passing, only that she died of Pneumonia, probably from complications of Tuberculosis. Her illness was of the same kind that claimed her father and others of the Cardwell line.

The genealogical record does not provide much detail about the life of Laura (Cardwell) McGuire. Mrs. Hall wrote, "Unfortunately, I will be of little help in providing you with any further information about Laura's father, Edward Cardwell. I don't remember my grandmother talking much about her grandfather. All I know is that Laura died relatively young and that my grandmother helped to take care of her for some time. She also had told me that Laura had very long hair which she kept in a braid and that my grandmother's father, Royal, had cut the braid off after Laura had become ill, as the long hair tended to weaken her. Grandma said that her father had kept the braid for years."[14]

After Laura's death, Roy McGuire moved to Oregon in 1930. He and Laura had made trips there before, once in 1926 to see their sons, and to visit relatives. Roy had two brothers, William and Noble McGuire who settled in Lane County, Oregon. Roy eventually made his home in Springfield, Oregon, where he lived out the remaining years of his life.[15] For 16 years, Springfield was his home. On November 1, 1942, he married Lavenia Pearlisita (Edwards) Peerson, recently widowed wife of Julius Peerson. She brought Roy several stepchildren.[16] By 1956, both Roy and Lavenia were in decline. A family member wrote, "Roy McGuire is very poorly so is his wife."[17] Roy died November 22, 1958, in Springfield, Lane County, Oregon, from Cancer, at the age of 79.[18] His burial was in the Aaron Section of West Lawn Cemetery, Eugene, Lane County, Oregon.[19]

Family historian David Bays wrote of the McGuire family, "I have been intrigued with Laura F. Cardwell McGuire for some time. I'm not sure why other than the fact that she was known to be quite a gal and that she died tragically young. I know from stories that Royal was devoted to her and was devastated upon her death. I know she passed on the same qualities to her daughter 'Jack' whom my mother was acquainted with. Jessie Ethel 'Jack' McGuire married a fellow by the name of Ervin Marcellus Beebe. Betty Lou [their daughter] married Calvin Coolidge Duckworth who became the parents of Karen [Karen (Duckworth) Hall]. Betty Lou married another five times so Karen ended up being mostly raised by her grandmother 'Jack.' So, the Cardwell and McGuire line started to disappear."[20]

The genealogy of the Cardwell family continued from Edward and Anna Eliza (Baldwin) Cardwell to Thomas Edward Cardwell, brother of Laura Frances (Cardwell) McGuire.

Laura Frances Cardwell. She was the daughter of Edward and Anna Eliza (Baldwin) Cardwell. Her father died when she was five years old, and she grew up in Cedar County, Missouri, as the stepdaughter of Jesse Biddey. She married in 1900; moved with her husband to Bartlesville, Oklahoma; and then to Wichita, Kansas.

Royal and Laura (Cardwell) McGuire. Laura and Roy married on December 6, 1900, in Stockton, Missouri. They had three children. Laura died in Wichita, Kansas, in 1929. Roy moved to Oregon and lived in Lane County until his death in 1958.

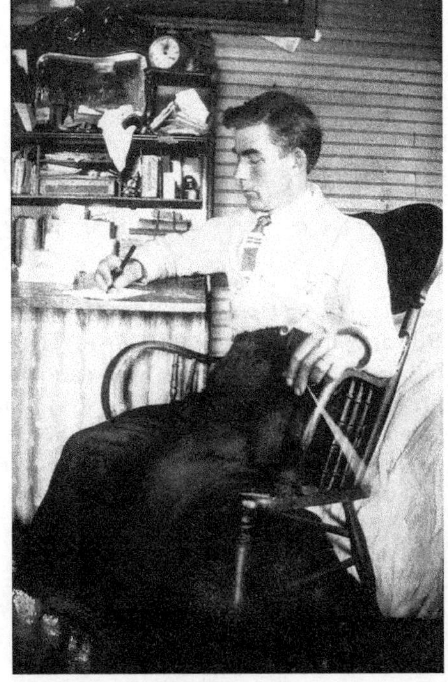

Royal McGuire. He was born in Republic County, Kansas, in 1879. He worked as a moulder in the foundry and ironworks casting trade.

Cardwell Family Portrait. Four decades after the death of Edward Cardwell, his family posed for this portrait, which pictures his daughter, Laura Frances (Cardwell) McGuire, widow Anna Eliza (Baldwin) Cardwell-Biddey-McCollom, and son Thomas Edward Cardwell. This photo dates to the late 1920s when the family probably was together for one of the last times.

Four Generations. Pictured are Betty Lou Beebe, Jessie (McGuire) Beebe, Great Grandmother Anna Eliza (Baldwin) Cardwell-Biddey-McCollom, and Grandmother Laura (Cardwell) McGuire. Laura died in 1929 soon after the date of this photo in 1928. Photo courtesy of Karen (Duckworth) Hall, daughter of Betty Lou Beebe.

The McGuire Children. Albert Ancil, Jessie Ethel "Jack," and Cecil Edward were the children of Roy and Laura (Cardwell) McGuire and grandchildren of Edward Cardwell.

Cardwell Ninth Generation Family Group

Laura Frances Cardwell was born in Dec 1879 in Linn Township, Cedar County, Missouri. She died on 15 Dec 1929 in Wichita, Sedgwick County, Kansas, from Tuberculosis and Pneumonia. Her burial was in Maple Grove Cemetery, Sedgwick County, Kansas. She was the daughter of **Edward CARDWELL** and **Anna Eliza BALDWIN.**

Laura married **Royal (Roy) Cyrus McGuire** known as "rish," son of William M. McGuire and Eva Cinderella Green Stenson, on 6 Dec 1900 in Stockton, Cedar County, Missouri. Irish was born on 4 Sep 1879 in Republic, Big Bend Township, Republic County, Kansas. He died in Springfield, Lane County, Oregon, from Cancer. His burial was on 20 Nov 1958 in the Aaron Section of West Lawn Cemetery, Eugene, Lane County, Oregon.

They had the following children.

1. **Jessie Ethel "Jack" McGuire** was born on 5 Apr 1902 in Jerico Springs, Cedar County, Missouri. She died on 28 Mar 1991 in Lebanon Community Hospital, Lebanon, Linn County, Oregon.[21] Her burial was on 1 Apr 1991 in the Galilee Section of West Lawn Cemetery, Eugene, Lane County, Oregon.[22] Jessie married **William Ervin Marcellus "Bill" Beebe** on 25 Aug 1919 in Bartlesville, Washington County, Oklahoma, when Jessie was age 17.[23] William preferred the name Bill.[24] He was the son of Marcellus Clark Beebe and Martha Ann Hatfield.[25] He was born on 26 Aug 1899 in Cherokee Nation, Indian Territory, Oklahoma. He died on 28 Jun 1970 in Mill City, Linn County, Oregon. His burial was on 3 Jul 1970 in the Galilee Section of West Lawn Memorial Park, Eugene, Lane County, Oregon.[26]

Jessie McGuire's parents called her "Jack".[27] Her childhood friend Mae Kephart remembered, "Royal nicknamed her and always referred to his daughter as Jack. Jack was 8 or 9 years older than I was, but we seemed to enjoy each other despite the age difference."[28] After Jessie and Bill married, they lived with Jessie's parents in Bartlesville for a short time.[29] By 1923, Bill had a job in Wichita, Kansas, working as a laborer, and the couple set up housekeeping in Wichita.[30] Nearly a decade passed after their marriage, and children did not come along. In 1928, they adopted a baby daughter in Wichita and named her Betty Lou. She was born 22 March 1928.[31] During the fateful year of 1929 when Jessie's mother Laura was fighting for her life, Jessie and Bill joined the McGuire family together as one to care for her. After Laura's death, they did not stay long in Wichita. Family tradition claimed that the whole family moved to Oregon in 1929.[32] However, they moved sometime after that because documents show that Bill Beebe still worked as a molder in 1929 in Wichita.[33] At the beginning of 1930, the family was still on Salina Avenue, in Wichita. In the spring of 1930, Jessie and Bill moved to a place on Payne Street in Wichita where they rented a $20 a month apartment.[34] Bill worked at his job as a molder in a foundry while Jessie cared for Betty Lou, their newly adopted daughter who was then age two.[35]

Sometime in the early 1930s, Bill and Jessie, along with Jessie's father Roy McGuire, did move to Lane County, Oregon, near Roy's brothers, William and Noble McGuire. Bill Beebe became a truck driver for a logging camp out of Eugene, Oregon. Meanwhile, Roy opted to remain in Springfield, Oregon, located in the Southern Willamette Valley immediately east of Eugene. In 1940, the Beebes were renting a place in Douglas County, Oregon.[36] The couple moved frequently in their early years in Oregon. In 1942, they moved to Lakeside, in Coos County. Bill registered for the World War II draft at Lakeside.[37] However, there is no indication that he actually served in the war. He had registered also in 1918 for the World War I draft, signing up in September just two months before the war ended. Serendipitously, he missed that war, too.[38] Not everyone who registered for the war received a call to duty. His age of 42 at the time of WW II no doubt played a part in his exemption because in 1942 he was a fit 135 pounds and stood 5 feet 9 inches tall with a deep tan from his outdoor job driving for the South Bay Logging Company in North Bend.

After a few years, the Beebes settled in Coos Bay, Oregon, where they spent much of the remainder of their lives. Coos Bay-North Bend, Coos County, was in the Oregon Bay Area where the Coos River enters the bay and the Pacific Ocean. Coos Bay was home to about 6,000 residents in 1950. By 1955, Jessie and Bill had the maledictions of aging. Jessie broke her ankle, and then she hurt her other foot doing spading in the garden. Bill was "slim as a rail" but still drove a logging truck.[39] Betty Lou had married and started a family. Jessie and Bill busied themselves raising their granddaughters. By 1965, they lived in the Eastside District of Coos Bay.[40]

Betty Lou their daughter died June 10, 1973. Her burial was in the family plot in West Lawn Cemetery, Eugene, Oregon. Betty Lou left two daughters who Jessie and Bill helped to raise.[41] Bill Beebe died in 1979. Jessie, in failing health, moved to Lebanon, Oregon, in 1988 and from there to Sweet Home,

Oregon, a year later.[42] She died in 1991 at the age of 89. She left in addition to her two granddaughters, seven great grandchildren, and five great-great grandchildren.[43] The graves of Jessie "Jack" and Ervin "Bill" Beebe lie next to each other in the garden section of West Lawn Cemetery called Galilee, not far from where Royal McGuire lies buried in the same cemetery in Eugene, Oregon.[44]

2. **Cecil Edward McGuire**, son of Royal and Laura (Cardwell) McGuire, was born on 4 Aug 1903 in Cedar County, Missouri.[45] He died on 12 May 1976 in St. Margaret's Hospital, Fredonia, Wilson County, Kansas. His burial was on 14 May 1976 in a graveside service at Fredonia City Cemetery, Fredonia, Wilson County, Kansas.[46] Cecil married **Miriam Bertha (Bryngelson) Harding** on 19 Feb 1930 in Wichita, Sedgwick County, Kansas.[47] It was her second marriage. Miriam was born on 16 Apr 1910 to Ethriam Bryngelson and Bertha Scott in Wichita, Sedgwick County.[48] Miriam died on 30 Dec 1968 in Parsons, Labette County, Kansas.[49] Her burial was in Fredonia City Cemetery, Grave Lot 2324, and Space 5, next to Cecil McGuire in Fredonia, Wilson County, Kansas.[50]

Cecil McGuire grew up in Bartlesville, Oklahoma, received an eighth grade education, worked as a drugstore delivery boy, and at the age of 21 took a job on the west coast where he and his brother Albert were truck drivers out of Eugene, Oregon.[51] They gave up the venture in Oregon and resettled in Sedgwick County, Kansas, doing foundry work in Wichita. Around 1928, Cecil became acquainted with a young single mother named Miriam (Bryngelson) Harding, working in Wichita, and caring for her baby daughter Georgiana Pauline, born 22 May 1927.[52] Miriam and Cecil married in 1930. The 1930 census found the three of them living in Wichita—Cecil, Miriam, and stepdaughter, Georgiana, age two. Miriam was age 19, Cecil age 26.[53] By 1936, Cecil and Miriam had established themselves in Wichita. Cecil worked as a molder for the Clear Vision Pump Company, later the Sellars Foundry in 1939, and then the Christopher Iron Works. They lived on Osie Street at the same address as Albert and Esther McGuire.[54] By 1940, the McGuire siblings had resettled. Jessie "Jack" (McGuire) Beebe went to Oregon and Albert fell on hard times in Oklahoma. Cecil still worked a foundry job in Wichita. Approaching middle age, Cecil McGuire was small of stature, 120 pounds, standing 5 ft. 4 inches tall, of ruddy complexion with gray eyes and brown hair.[55] He and Miriam owned a house in the Delano neighborhood of Wichita.[56] His father,

Roy McGuire, now age 60, was with them in 1940 and, of course, stepdaughter Georgianna, using the surname McGuire, and not Harding.

Cecil retired and moved to Fredonia, in Wilson County, Kansas. He bought some land and took up farming. In the course of his life, he lived at various places in Kansas, including Buxton, Coyville, LaFontaine, and lastly Fredonia, but mostly in Wichita.[57] Tragedy struck in 1968 when Miriam died in a car wreck. She succumbed 30 Dec 1968 in the Labette County Medical Center at Parsons following injuries sustained in a three-car accident north of Preston, Kansas. She was age 58. Cecil lived on until 1976 when he passed away in Fredonia. Georgiana Pauline married a man named DeSoto. She died 3 February 1990, the only surviving child of Cecil and Miriam, identified on her tombstone as Miriam's daughter.[58] Her burial was in the Fredonia City Cemetery near her parents. At the time, only Jessie (McGuire) Beebe remained of the nuclear McGuire family, and she died the next year. Relatives lost touch. Jessie's granddaughter, Karen Hall, remembered only that, "Uncle Cecil had a farm in Fredonia, Kansas and passed away either in 1974 or '75."[59]

3. **Albert Ancil McGuire** was born on 19 Nov 1906, son of Royal and Laura (Cardwell) McGuire, in Cedar County, Missouri. He died on 13 Jun 1964 at the age of 58 in a local nursing home in Bartlesville, Oklahoma. His burial was on 17 Jun 1964 in White Rose Cemetery, Bartlesville, Oklahoma.[60] Albert married **Esther H. Beebe** of Welch, Craig County, Oklahoma, on 15 Mar 1930 in Wichita, Sedgwick County, Kansas.[61] Albert was age 22; Ester was 18.[62] Esther was born 29 Oct 1911, the daughter of Jeff and Lily B. Beebe of Native American descent. Ester died 3 Sep 2005 in Ketchum, Craig County, Oklahoma. Burial was in Ketchum Cemetery.[63]

Albert McGuire moved with his parents from southwest Missouri to Bartlesville, Oklahoma, as a young child. He received a seventh-grade education in Bartlesville.[64] As a teenager, he adventured with his brother Cecil to Oregon where the two of them worked as truck drivers out of Eugene, Oregon.[65] He later moved to Wichita, Kansas, where he married Ester H. Beebe in the spring of 1930.[66] He worked in a foundry in Wichita at a gasoline pump factory.[67] In 1931, the couple moved back to Welch, Oklahoma, where their daughter Patsy Jean was born 3 January 1932. By 1936, they were back in Wichita living on Osie Street with their new baby.[68] After 1936, the details of their movements are scarce. Albert suffered from mental illness. In 1940, he was an inmate at Eastern Oklahoma Hospital, Vinita, Craig County, Oklahoma. The Eastern Oklahoma

Hospital for the Insane originated in 1912, and continued until its abandonment in the 1990s. Patients worked on the farm in swine, poultry, and dairy operations while receiving treatment for mental illness. Family awareness of Albert's illness remained quiet. Karen Hall, a relative, recalled, "Uncle Albert lived for years in an institution, but [I] never found out exactly where."[69] Most family members knew only that he "farmed." Albert and Esther's marriage ended. Esther remarried multiple times, lastly to Herbert L. Hensley using her maiden name Beebe.[70] She had a second daughter named Bonnie Sue Morrow.[71] When Esther died in 2005, her burial was beside Mr. Hensley.[72]

Albert returned to Bartlesville only two months before his death in 1964, following what his obituary described as "a lengthy illness." His listed survivors were his siblings, Cecil McGuire of Fredonia, Kansas; Mrs. Jessie Beebe of East Side, Oregon; his daughter Mrs. Patsy Jean (McGuire) Hardesty of Collinsville, Oklahoma, and three grandchildren.[73] Patsy Jean married multiple times. She died 8 May 2001 in Las Vegas, Clark County, Nevada.[74]

26

Thomas Edward Cardwell

Thomas Edward Cardwell was born February 26, 1881, in Linn Township, Cedar County, Missouri, the only son of Edward Cardwell and Anna Eliza (Baldwin) Cardwell.[1] His father died when he was three years old; leaving him and his sister Laura, age five, in the care of their widowed mother. He grew up under the guidance of uncles and aunts of the Baldwin family who comprised a large presence in Linn Township. His mother was one of 12 surviving siblings born to Frances (Jackson) and John C. Baldwin, a respected Cedar County farmer and horse breeder. In 1884, Eliza married Jesse Maries Biddey, and together they raised Tom and Laura. Jesse was a farmer, and Tom grew up doing chores and following in the footsteps of his stepfather. Jesse was the only father he ever knew. Tom and Jesse had much in common. The only son of Talbot and Martha (Lovelady) Biddey, Jesse lost his father before he was two months old, and like Tom grew up knowing only the father figure of his own stepfather. Tom once remarked that Jesse Biddey was the "best father a son could ever have."[2] Eliza and Jesse had no children of their own.

Tom was a year behind his sister Laura in school. The nearest school was at Bishop Grove No. 5 northeast of the Biddey farm about two miles. Another school, Concord No. 1, sat north and a little west about the same distance, and Stony Point No. 3 was east about equal distance and slightly more convenient. Nevertheless, Bishop Grove was close to Biddey and Baldwin kin, and No. 5 was near Bishop Grove Church where Jesse and Eliza married. It mattered little in the end because Tom only finished the fourth grade.[3] Nevertheless, both he and Laura could read and write, a quality not always found in many of their ancestors who lived in the pioneer days of rural America. Cedar County,

Missouri, in the latter part of the nineteenth century was still a sparsely settled place. The closest town to the Biddey farm was three miles southwest at Arcola, in Dade County. The Omer Post Office at the village of White Hare was four miles northwest, and Cane Hill was 5.5 miles distant across Sac River to the east. Four or five miles up county from the Biddeys were Jerico Springs and Wagoner. A half-day's ride by horse and buggy reached Stockton the county seat about ten miles northeast.

The 19th century rolled over to the 20th. Tom was age 19, working on the Biddey farm, and living in the household of his parents. The 1900 census found his mother Eliza and stepfather Jesse Biddey in Linn Township, Cedar County, in the summer of 1900. Tom's sister Laura was in the household as well.[4] That fall, they sold the farm to Thomas Simmons; Laura married Roy McGuire in December; and Tom moved with Jesse and Eliza to Osiris. The year 1900 was the year Jesse Biddey established Osiris Post Office on present Highway 97, located 4 1/2 miles northwest of Jerico Springs.[5]

On April 10, 1904, Tom Cardwell married Mary Belle Fellows, a neighbor girl originally from northern Missouri and living on a farm northwest of Osiris with her parents, Willie Ira and Martha Frances (Crutchfield) Fellows. Preacher Charley Stone married Tom and Belle in a private ceremony at the home of Linsa Ward. The wards, Linsa and Eva, were witnesses to the ceremony.[6] In the spring of 1910, Tom and Belle were living with Tom's mother Widow Eliza Biddey. Jesse Biddey had died in March of that year.

They relocated to a place near Baldwin kin in South Linn Township. Eliza's stepmother, the Widow Cordelia S. Baldwin, and her six children lived next door, according to the 1910 census. Several of the Baldwin offspring built houses on the large tract of John Baldwin property, along Connor Branch. Soon thereafter, six years into their marriage, Tom and Belle moved north a few miles, onto the Jesse Biddey "forty" southwest of Wagoner between Wagoner and Jerico Springs. The property had an old house on it where they could live alone and establish themselves as independently engaged in the life of farming. On September 13, 1914, Belle gave birth to a daughter. They named her Maud Beatrice Cardwell. Belle was age 28 when Beatrice was born; Tom was in his early thirties.[7]

It was around this time that a tragic event occurred in the Wagoner community. What happened shook the normally peaceful solitude of rural Cedar County, and was an incident that ultimately involved the Cardwell family. Three murders transpired in a house at Wagoner, a short distance up the road from the Cardwell home. On July 12, 1915, Jim Mingus murdered his wife and mother-in-law and turned the gun on himself. Writing for the Cedar County Historical Society, author Linda Clifford described what happened. She wrote, "Probably the biggest event to happen at Wagoner occurred September 12, 1915. At this time Blanche Wagoner, who had married Jim Mingus, was living at home with her parents and baby, estranged from her husband. On that fateful day, Jim Mingus came to his in-law's home, blaming both Charles and wife Belle for their daughter's separation from him. With a .38 caliber revolver, Mingus shot Belle running down the road and followed Blanche up the stairs of the two-story house with the baby in her arms. Blanche dropped the baby to safety below and was confronted by Mingus on the balcony. As legend has it, Mingus kissed her good-bye, and then shot her. He then went downstairs looking for Charles Wagoner. When Mingus could not find Wagoner, he shot himself."[8]

The details of the shooting reached the national press the next day.

"MURDER FOLLOWED WIFE'S REFUSAL TO PARTAKE OF $6 PIE. Details of Cedar County Double Slaying and Suicide Ascertained Here With Resumption of Wire Service to Stockton.

"SLEW SPOUSE WHILE SHE HELD THEIR BABY IN ARMS. Tragedies Most Startling in the Criminal History of Region of Waggoner, Mo.—Authorities Decide Inquest Is Unnecessary.

"With the resumption yesterday of wire service between Springfield and Stockton, reports were received here giving in detail the tragedy enacted near Wagoner post office, nine miles west of Stockton, at 6 o'clock Monday evening, in which James H. Mingus, 21 years old, shot and killed his wife, 19 years old, and her mother, Mrs. Belle Wagoner, and then killed himself. Mingus, according to the reports spent Sunday at the Wagoner store and returned again Monday. About 5 o'clock, he went to the Wagoner home, but Mrs. Wagoner and her daughter, having seen his approaching, went into the house. Mrs. Wagoner went out another door and Mingus shot four times, all of the bullets taking effect.

"Slain While Holding Baby. Mrs. Mingus, meanwhile, had fled upstairs following the shooting of her mother but the enraged husband followed her. He found her holding their baby in her arms. Mingus shot her in the temple and then turned the gun on himself. C.M. Wagoner, the husband and father, was at work on the farm and had not come to the house. He knew nothing of the tragedy until W.E. Nance informed him. Nance is a storekeeper in the village and he was the only eyewitness to any part of the shooting. Cedar County officials decided no inquest was necessary. James Mingus and Blanche Wagoner were married in April 1913. They spent some time after their marriage in California and then returned and rented the Wagoner farm in 1914. They quarreled and separated last fall. One child was born of the marriage.

"BOUGHT PIE HIS WIFE MADE. It is said that Mingus has since the separation, been trying to induce his wife to return to him. According to reports, on last Thursday night Mingus bid $6 for the pie his wife had placed on sale at a pie supper. She refused to eat with him and had nothing whatever to say to him. The double murder and suicide is one of the worst tragedies in the history of Cedar County. The Wagoners are well-to-do farmers and have long been residents of the locality in which the tragedy occurred. For many years, Mr. Wagoner was a storekeeper and postmaster there. Mingus was reared in that locality. His parents moved to California two years ago."[9]

What the press did not report was that Belle Cardwell took the Mingus baby in the story and cared for it along with Beatrice her own infant daughter until other arrangements were possible. Belle nursed the little girl during that time.

Things returned to normal. Belle pronounced their little house on the Biddey forty as a "shack" unfit as a place to raise a family. Tom moved his young family from the Biddey place near Wagoner to a piece of land in Benton Township in southwest Cedar County. He opened a farm on Horse Creek near the Willie Ira Fellows farm and adjacent to the house where Belle grew up. Tom mortgaged some farmland on Horse Creek where he continued to build his farming operation. They rented a nicer house within walking distance of Osiris, the Methodist Church, Fairview School, and Grandmother and Grandfather Fellows.[10] They set up housekeeping with their now five-year-old daughter Beatrice amid what was, euphemistically speaking, a hub of the Fellows enclave. The 1920 census listed Tom and Belle as family 126; Belle's father Willie I. Fellows lived at family 128 and Belle's brothers Willie Irl and Lee Fellows were at 127 and 137, respectively. By this time, Jesse Biddey had left nearby Osiris, died in the meantime, and Eliza had married A.A. "Ott" McCollom. The McColloms were living in the same Fellows neighborhood at residence 130.[11]

Tom farmed to pay off the mortgage, Belle kept house, and Beatrice began school at Fair View School No. 66. Jean Nipps Swaim wrote, "Beatrice Cardwell started school at Fair View. Her desk mate was Fleeta Dodd. Later, Fleeta and her husband, Arch Walker, ran the Osiris store for 37 years. Fleeta remembered starting to school with a 5-cent tablet, pencils, and a box of crayons."[12]

After a decade of farming on Horse Creek, it was time to move on to other opportunities. Tom and Belle sold the Benton County farm and moved to a place near Wagoner, located at the end of Highway Z about halfway between Stockton and Jerico Springs. Wagoner was an old village that had grown to be a respectable trading center. The store and post office dated to 1882, named for Charles M. Wagoner, the unfortunate husband and father of the Wagoner murder victims. His large house where the shootings took place was on the east side of the village.[13] In 1925, the Cardwells settled on a rented farm on the north side of town. Tom hired a farmhand and continued to build his farming business. Beatrice attended Cedar Bluff School at Wagoner, riding her horse to school, turning him loose, and watching him return home on his own a couple of blocks to the Cardwell farm. In 1928, Tom bought a 1926 Model T Touring Car.[14] Beatrice learned to drive it; however, after she nearly wrecked the car by going too fast, she rarely drove after that. Tom never learned to drive nor did Belle. The hired hand did all the driving.

On February 5, 1930, Beatrice married the hired hand, Elick Beaty, son of Ben F. and Viola Beaty of Greenfield.[15] Elick was a Dade County boy born September 26, 1906 and eight years Beatrice's senior. Bea was age 15 when they married, (much to her mother's regret), and only recently out of school. The couple lived with Tom and Belle.[16] The 1930 census found Tom and Belle renting the farm in Linn Township, and boarding Beatrice and her new husband.[17]

After five or six years at Wagoner, Tom removed his farming operation to Goose Creek on the Dade County line. He rented the old Cobb place from W. Austen Butcher, a well-to-do farmer and stockman in Cedar and Dade Counties. The old Cobb farm was located 4 miles west and 2 miles north of Arcola, 2.5 miles east of Cedarville, and 3 miles southwest of Omer.[18]

The Beatrice and Elick Beaty marriage did not set well in the Cardwell household. Tom had given his consent but Belle was adamantly opposed to the marriage. Beatrice later said, "It was the biggest mistake of my life." Elick wanted to go to California. Bea started with him, stopped midway, and turned around and came home. The couple split up, eventually divorced, and Elick remarried.

Meanwhile, the relationship between Tom and Belle also deteriorated. Whether it was because of Bea's marriage or the consequence of other disagreements, after more than 25 years of marriage, Tom and Belle separated. Belle walked out of the house on Goose Creek, walked across the bridge to the Leonard Moore house, and never returned. The evening walk had an element of daring because Leonard and Nellie Moore had an adult son name Charlie who had an illness that caused him to have fits.[19] The evening passed without incident, and the next day Belle moved to Jerico Springs.

For some time, Tom had been in declining health. Elick and Beatrice kept the farming operation going up until this time. Health reasons and the separation from Bell caused Tom to quit farming. On August 4, 1931, he held an auction at the old Cobb place to sell everything he and Belle owned. The auction bill listed a modest but respectable estate of livestock, farming implements, and household items accumulated over more than three decades.[20] Livestock comprised eight head of cattle, 21 sheep, 14 hogs, and four work-horses with harness, along with Belle's prized flock of 85 Plymouth Rock chickens. Several John Deer, Case, Deering, and Moline brands of farm implements also sold, along with a good Chattanooga walking plow, all horse-drawn because Tom never owned a tractor. He sold the 1926 Ford touring car "in good condition" rarely used by the Beaty family, and never by the Cardwells.[21] The Bradley buggy that comprised the usual means of travel sold with everything else. The sale began at 10 o'clock in the morning and lasted most of the day. The Cedarville Ladies Club came out and served lunch.[22]

Tom and Belle divorced in November 1934.[23] Belle filed for the divorce complaining to the court to be the injured party in the case. The details of her complaint were not part of the record, except that the court agreed and granted the divorce. Tom did not appear at the hearing but consented through his attorney to the verdict trial.[24] Neither Belle nor Tom remarried. They remained amicable the rest of their lives. Beatrice said, "Dad was crazy about her. In later years, they visited together. He would come over to see her at Jerico."[25] After the divorce, Tom faced a downturn in his financial status. After he sold his livestock and property, he and Belle divided the proceeds. They moved into separate houses in Jerico Springs. Belle bought a house on Broadway Street; Tom rented a place on the highway north of town.

In 1938, Tom signed up for Social Security, the new program established by the government in 1935 to address poverty among senior citizens coming out of the Great Depression.[26] He traveled from his home at Jerico Springs to the District Employment Office at Nevada, Missouri, and applied for unemployment. He classified himself as a farmer, and curiously signed his application with "his X mark."[27]

He went to work as a laborer for the Work Progress Administration (W.P.A.), an agency set up by President Franklin Roosevelt as part of his New Deal policy to employ out-of-work Americans still recovering from the Great Depression. The project assignment was the new Cedar County Courthouse begun in 1938. Completed in 1939, officials dedicated the building January 4, 1940. Built of poured concrete, the courthouse was the first monolithic public building made of architectural concrete in the state of Missouri. The job lasted Tom for seven months; the project ended and a reduction in force resulted in his termination from the W.P.A.[28] He went back to work again in August 1939, assigned this time as a laborer on the W.P.A. County Wide Roads project.[29]

People who knew Tom described him as an honest, very likeable person. Those who knew him best said he was a "very religious person."[30] He was of medium physical build and slender in stature. At age 57, he stood 5 feet 10 inches tall and weighed 120 pounds. Photographs often pictured him with a moustache. His health deteriorated in later years, which caused him to suffer from prostrate trouble. His daughter, Beatrice, remembered him sitting on the floor behind the stove on a sheepskin to relieve the pain.[31] Bea was his closest companion and caregiver; the two were never far apart. She married Willis Adley Burchett on New Year's Day 1941, and the couple opened a store at Rowland, in Cedar County. One could usually find Tom at the Burchett household when not doing odd jobs around the county.

It was a custom in those days for neighbors to help neighbors. At the start of each winter, each farmstead collected logs to cut into firewood. Sawing crews went from farm to farm cutting up each neighbor's stock of logs for the winter. It was a dangerous operation. Workers connected a stationary wood saw 24 inches or more in diameter to a power source run by a pulley and belt. The power source was a tractor or the back wheel of a car jacked up off the ground and attached to the pulley belt. The wood crew comprised about a half dozen workmen, each with a job to do whether retrieving logs from the pile, feeding them into the saw to be cut into firewood length, or off-bearing the cut pieces and tossing them into a pile. For some reason, Tom always wanted to be the off-bearer in the wood crew; the most dangerous job because his hands were within a foot or less of the saw blade.

On January 18, 1944, a wood-sawing crew met at the farm of Jesse McGatha. Tom was the off-bearer. In an instant that no one saw, the blade of the saw caught his jacket and pulled him directly into its rotating teeth. It was a ghastly wound. Members of the crew quickly got him into a car and rushed him to a Springfield hospital. They said his wound was so severe, it exposed his heart, which they could see beating. He held on for several days but died January 25, 1944, at about 3:15 in the morning. Doctors amputated his left arm, and he died of shock. He would have been 63 in February.[32] On January 26, the Greene County coroner held an inquest into his death in response to information that supposed him "to have come to his death by violence." An informant relayed information that his body was at Ozark Osteopathic Hospital. The coroner did not convene a jury and concluded that the "deceased was injured in a wood saw on the 18th of January, and died as the result of the accident." [33] The *Cedar County Republican* on January 27, 1944, printed a brief account of the accident. "MAN DIES OF INJURIES—Tom Cardwell, 62, who was injured so badly while working around the wood saw at Jesse McGatha's place south of Stockton on Tuesday of last week, died at Ozark Hospital, Springfield, during Tuesday night of this week. His left arm had been amputated at the shoulder."[34]

His burial was in Gum Springs Cemetery, Cedar County, Missouri, beside his mother, Eliza McCollum who died in 1942, and near the grave of his stepfather Jesse Biddey who preceded each of them in death in 1910.[35] His father Edward Cardwell lay a short distance down the hill in the same cemetery. Tom's gravestone said simply, "Father, Thomas Edward Cardwell 1881-1944."[36]

In due time, Belle deeded her home in Jerico Springs to her son-in-law, Willis Burchett, and took up residence with her brother Claude and his family at the old Fellows home on Horse Creek, site of her childhood. After a few years, living at the Fellows place, she moved back to Jerico Springs to the old Jerico Hotel where she lived alone in a second floor corner apartment overlooking the Jerico town spring. Later, she moved closer to her immediate family, to a house on East Street, in Stockton where she lived out the remainder of her life.[37] Mary Belle Fellows died August 1, 1958, at 12:00 noon at the home of her daughter, Beatrice (Cardwell) Richardson, west of Stockton, in Cedar County.[38] Her obituary, penned by her sister, Maud, poignantly recounted her life and the family she left behind.[39] "Mary Belle Fellows, eldest daughter of W.I. and Martha

Frances (Crutchfield) Fellows, was born September 29, 1885, near Salisbury, in Chariton County, Missouri. She answered the Master's summons to 'come home,' August 1, 1958, being at the time of her passing, 72 years, 10 months and 2 days of age.[40]

"When she was a baby, her parents moved to Ness City in Western Kansas, where they lived 'til Belle was three years old, when the family came to Cedar County and where she lived the remainder of her life—almost 80 years [*sic*]. On April 10, 1904, she was married to Thomas Edward Cardwell who preceded her in death on January 25, 1944. They were the parents of one daughter, Beatrice, now Mrs. Richard Richardson, of Stockton, in whose home she passed away.

"Early in their married life, she and her husband were converted to Christ but it was not until several years later while living at the home of her brother, Claude Fellows, and wife, that she received the sacrament of baptism administered by Rev. Frank Calame pastor of the Jerico Springs Methodist Church, of which she became a member.

"For years, while living in Jerico Springs, Belle cared for many aged and feeble patients, and lucky indeed was the person in need of such care who found refuge with her. She continued in this work as long as her health permitted. The past four years she lived in Stockton. When she became ill just a week before her passing, she was taken to the home of her daughter where all that willing hands and loving hearts could do were not enough and she slipped quietly away into eternity about noon, Friday."[41] One of the aged and feeble persons Belle took care of was Mr. Amos Richardson, father of the son-in-law mentioned in her obituary. Grandma Belle died from a Cerebral Hemorrhage and the complications of Stroke, at the Old Ice Plant apartment where her daughter, Beatrice, and her family lived. After her stroke, Belle lived for a week but could not speak and remained in a persistent semiconscious state. She communicated by responding to questions with a squeeze of her hand.[42]

Traveling from Jerico Springs up Route 97, the highway passes the Brasher Cemetery on the east side of the road. The cemetery is about a mile and a half beyond the big curve in Route 97. Here Mary Belle Fellows entered her final rest beside the graves of her parents, Willie Ira and Martha Fellows. Buried here, too, are Belle's brother, Claud Fellows, and Claud's son, Wayne Fellows, along with their spouses, and Charlie, the infant son of Willie Ira and Martha who died in infancy in 1897, a sad reminder of a time when Belle was but a young girl growing up on the Fellows family farm on Horse Creek.

Thomas Edward Cardwell

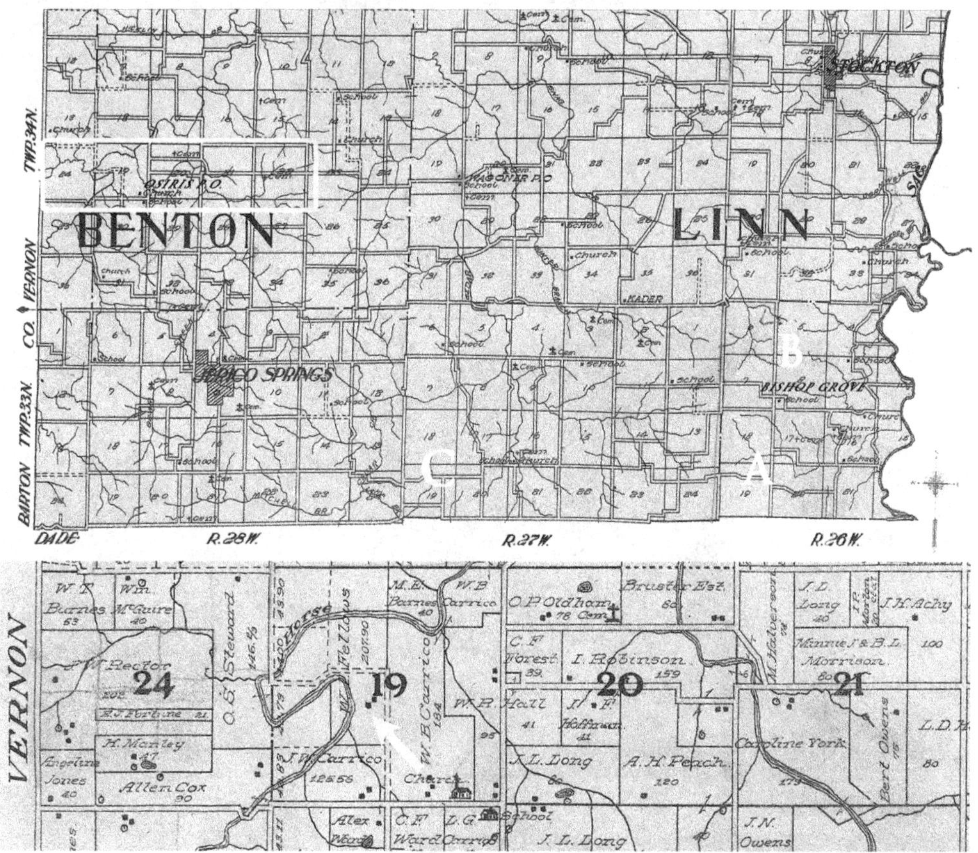

Geography of Tom and Belle (Fellows) Cardwell. Tom Cardwell never ventured much beyond the borders of Cedar County, Missouri. Most of his life he spent at various places in Benton and Linn Townships. The earliest days of his youth were on a farm on the Dade County line in Linn Township (A). He went to school at Bishop Grove (B) mapped in Section 8 of Linn Township. Later, he lived on Goose Creek (C). Other addresses over the course of his life were at Osiris, Wagoner, Rowland, and Jerico Springs. After their divorce, Belle Fellows lived at Jerico Springs, Osiris, and at Stockton. The strip map below shows a close-up of Section 19 and the W.I. Fellows farm on Horse Creek where Belle grew up. Fairview Church and School were directly across present Highway 97 from Osiris Store and Post Office. The large stream on the right in Section 20 and 21 is Bear Creek. Modified maps adapted from *Standard Atlas of Cedar County*, Geo. A. Ogle, 1908. Library of Congress.

Tom and Mary Belle (Fellows) Cardwell. Photo taken about 1915 at the Fellows farm in Cedar County, Missouri.

Tom Cardwell and Laura (Cardwell) McGuire. This photograph pictures the last generations of the Cardwell surname. Shown left to right are Belle (Fellows) Cardwell, Tom Cardwell, and on his lap Beatrice Cardwell. Laura (Cardwell) McGuire is on the right, next to her is her daughter Jessie McGuire. Seated are Roy McGuire and his sons, Cecil and Albert. Tom, Laura, and Beatrice were the last of the Cardwell name in the line of the Cardwell family descending from Edward Cardwell. Photo dates to 1915.

Thomas Edward Cardwell. Tom sat for this portrait about the time of his tragic death in 1944. He lived one month short of 63 years.

Belle and Beatrice. This snapshot of Belle Fellows and her daughter Beatrice (Cardwell) Beaty dates to about 1940.

Belle Fellows and Grandchildren. Left to right are Gladys Sharleen Burchett, Kenneth Eugene Burchett, and Sharron Kay Burchett. The photo dates to about 1955. Belle died in 1958.

The Park Hotel in Jerico Springs. Mary Belle Fellows lived in a second-floor corner apartment seen next to the large tree pictured in this photo, which shows the old hotel as it appeared in the 1950s. The map dates to 1897 and includes the Park Hotel and another hotel on Broadway Street across from the M.E. Church. Belle regularly attended the Methodist Church seen at the center-right of the diagram. Her funeral was in this church. Map inset *New map of Cedar Co. Missouri*, E. P. Noll, 1897.

Cardwell Ninth Generation Family Group

Thomas Edward CARDWELL was born in Feb 1881. He died on 25 Jan 1944 in Ozark Hospital, Springfield, Greene County, Missouri, from injuries sustained in a wood saw accident. His burial was in Gum Springs Cemetery, Linn Township, Cedar County, Missouri. He was the son of **Edward CARDWELL** and **Anna Eliza BALDWIN**.

Thomas married **Mary Belle FELLOWS**, daughter of **Willie (William) Ira FELLOWS** and **Martha Frances CRUTCHFIELD**, on 10 Apr 1904 in the home of Linsa Ward, Cedar County, Missouri. The marriage ended in divorce. Belle was born on 29 Sep 1885 near Salisbury, Chariton County, Missouri. She died on 1 Aug 1958 at the home of Beatrice Richardson, Cedar County, Missouri, from Stroke. Her burial was on 4 Aug 1958 in Brasher Cemetery, Cedar County, Missouri.

Thomas Edward and Mary Belle (Fellows) Cardwell had one child.

\+ 1. **Maud "Maudie" Beatrice "Bea" Cardwell** was born on 13 Sep 1914 in Benton Township, Cedar County, Missouri. She died on 9 Mar 2005 in Citizens Memorial Hospital, Bolivar, Polk County, Missouri. Her burial was on 13 Mar 2005 in Anna Edna Cemetery near Jerico Springs, Cedar County, Missouri. Bea married **Elick T. Beaty**, son of Ben Franklin Beaty and Viola Mable Huggins, on 5 Feb 1930 in Stockton, Cedar County, Missouri.[43] The marriage ended in divorce. Elick was born on 26 Sep 1906 in Polk County, Missouri. He died on 30 Jun 1991 in California. His burial was in Hillcrest Cemetery, Porterville, Tulare County, California.[44] No children were born of this union. Bea married secondly **Willis Adley Burchett**, son of **George Emmett Burchett** and **Pearl May (Mae) Brock**, on 1 Jan 1941 in Dade County, Missouri.[45] The marriage ended in divorce. Willis was born on 21 Sep 1902 near Rookins, Cedar County, Missouri. He died on 21 Feb 1996 in Stockton Nursing Home, Cedar County, Missouri. His burial was on 24 Feb 1996 in Alder Cemetery, Jefferson Township, Cedar County, Missouri.[46] Beatrice and Willis had three children. Bea married Thirdly **Richard Hayden Richardson**, son of Amos Richardson and Rebecca E. McGowen, on 2 Feb 1952 in Methodist Parsonage, Jerico Springs, Cedar County, Missouri. Richard was born on 15 Dec 1909 in Bucyrus, Texas County, Missouri. He died on 26 Aug 1985 in Stockton, Cedar County, Missouri. His burial was in Anna Edna Cemetery, Jerico Springs, beside the grave of Beatrice. No children were born of this union.

27

Beatrice Cardwell Early Years

Maud "Maudie" Beatrice "Bea" Cardwell was born at 8:20 a.m. on September 13, 1914, to Thomas Edward and Mary Belle (Fellows) Cardwell. Dr. A.J. Mynatt, a Jerico Springs physician, attended her birth.[1] Bea came along rather late in life, a decade after the Cardwell-Fellows marriage in 1904. When she was born, Tom was 32 years old and Belle was just short of her twenty-ninth birthday. Beatrice would be their only child. Bea, as everyone called her, was born in a one-room "shack," in Benton Township, in Cedar County, Missouri, situated on a patch of hardscrabble land southwest of Wagoner, in the rural countryside between Wagoner and Jerico Springs.[2] The old house sat on 40 acres that belonged to Jesse Biddey as late as 1908. Tom likely inherited it when Jesse died in 1910. The farm once occupied a place on a well-travelled road from Jerico to Wagoner but long since abandoned for routes that were more direct to Wagoner.

Wagoner drew national attention when Bea was an infant. The little village of Wagoner was about two miles from where they lived. A family named Wagoner had a daughter who married and had a baby. In a fit of rage, the husband shot and killed his young wife and her mother, and then turned the gun on himself, leaving the couple's newborn daughter alone. Bea's mother took the baby and nursed it with Bea until the Wagoner family found a home for the orphaned infant. The horrific murders happened long before Bea could remember. Nevertheless, the story of the Wagoner infant lived on as part of Bea's early life that touched the Cardwell family often told about the good character of Tom and Belle Cardwell.

Around 1917, when Bea was about three years old, the Cardwells moved to a place on Cedar Creek near the Barrow farm. One of Bea's earliest memories was of men roofing a building there. She remembered a hammer falling and mashing her finger. She also remembered as a toddler getting a whipping from her dad with a razor strop for cussing him, the only corporal punishment she ever received.[3] They were at Cedar Creek but a short time when they removed to Fairview in Benton Township in 1919, to a "nice place" situated near her Grandfather Willie Ira Fellows on Horse Creek.[4] Tom Cardwell took up farming on a small piece of land adjoining the Fellows Farm, tended crops, and raised livestock. Bea usually tagged along to the fields with her father, occupying herself with the child's play of a five-year-old in the woods and streams along Horse Creek. She would frequently accompany her dad to play in the fields while he worked during the day. She drank from the springs that fed the streams until one day she started to get a drink, and a snake looked back at her coiled at the water's edge. In the springtime, Horse Creek often flooded, sometimes covering the fields in large areas. A flood one time washed the planks off the Horse Creek Bridge that spanned the creek near the Cardwell farm.

The Cardwells lived south of the Fellows Farm, conveniently within walking distance of Bea's grandparents, Willie Ira and Martha (Crutchfield) Fellows who farmed 200 acres on Horse Creek. To reach the Fellows Farm, and the Tom Cardwell place, travelers took Route 97 west out of Jerico Springs. The highway turned 90 degrees sharply to the north and ran approximately four and one-half miles to Osiris, home of Bea's paternal Grandmother Eliza (Baldwin) Cardwell-Biddey. From Osiris, a left turn west off Route 97 onto a dirt road went past Fairview School on the immediate left.[5] One-half mile on this dirt road, past the Fairview Community Church on the right, a narrow lane went north. A right turn onto this lane took the traveler about one-half mile to where the lane dead-ended at the Fellows home. In the distance rose the tree line of Horse Creek. To reach the Cardwell farm, one went past the Fellows lane turnoff and continued west on the dirt road from Osiris, across the branch where Bea played, to a point about one-half mile from the Horse Creek Bridge, situated in the bottoms where Tom Cardwell farmed for six years. Along the way to the Horse Creek Bridge was the Cardwell home on the north side of the road.

Bea started school at Fairview School—Fairview District 66. The one-room school faced Route 97 across from Osiris Store. Her first teacher was Miss Lena Jones, then Mr. Cecil Casey, followed by Mr. Oral Walker, and Miss Elizabeth Kappenhauer.[6] Her desk mate was Fleeta Dodd. Like her classmates, she started school with a 5-cent tablet, pencils, and a box of crayons. Fairview School was a white frame schoolhouse of the "boxcar" style built with two front doors and four windows along a sidewall. Concrete steps led to the entry. Historian Jean Nipps Swaim described Fairview in its heyday. "In the early days, the road in front of the school was still gravel and mud, and the school was close enough to the road that the children who played in the front yard, often had to jump the ditch to retrieve a ball. The dug well was also in the front yard with bucket and rope and a big rock on the cover. Inside, the teacher sat on a raised stage between the front doors and the children either faced her, or lined up along the side walls facing to the center, leaving an aisle down the middle."[7] Bea attended school at Fairview until age 11, and then the Cardwell family moved again. In 1925, they removed to a place south of Wagoner. Bea recalled that the family moved during the winter with a team and wagon when ice was on the ground. The house they rented was near Cedar Bluff School, and was not a very good one, "a little run down," she said. They arrived at Wagoner sometime around February, late in the school year, and Bea did not start school there until fall. Although she was not in class that year, she would go to the school to play with the other children.

The house they moved to sat just west of Wagoner, next to the cemetery—east and a little south. To occupy her time, she played in the cemetery among the tombstones, one of which was for an African American buried in the cemetery, near the old cemetery gate. It made an impression on Bea because in her time, there were few African Americans living in Cedar County.[8] Tom Cardwell soon moved his family to a better location, to a little pink house 0.3 miles north of the intersection of Highway Z and present County Road 825, about one-half mile north of Wagoner on the east side of Wagoner Road, and a ways south of English Branch. Compared to other places she had lived, it was a nice house. A porch went halfway around the house. It was closer to Stockton, the county seat. Wagoner lay between Jerico Springs and Stockton, about seven miles to either place.[9] Every week they would take eggs and produce to the Farmer's Store in Stockton.[10]

In the fall of 1925, Bea enrolled in Cedar Bluff School, at Wagoner. Because she had arrived late in the school year, her mother made her repeat the fifth grade. Bea remembered this as a good thing because she was able to learn math by taking fifth grade twice. She had three teachers at Cedar Bluff. Bernard Mitchell taught her for two years, another teacher whose name she did not recall

("She didn't amount to anything as a teacher," Bea said), a teacher whose first name was Miss Ruth, and Vivian Stevens.[11] The white frame schoolhouse at Cedar Bluff School—District 63 (aka Wagoner School)—sat on the southeast corner of the crossroads in the center of town, facing east. A new church built in 1912 stood next door. Residences lined either side of the road leading south to the cemetery.[12]

Jean Swaim wrote, "Students could stand in the front yard of the school, which faced east, look to the right, and see the church, almost next door, and the residences on either side of the road leading south to the cemetery. If they looked to the north, they could see a store on either side of the road. Farther north of the store on the west side, where the post office was until 1916, was a feed and chicken storage house, an oil house, and the blacksmith's shop. Close to the store on the east side of the road was the historic Wagoner house where a succession of families lived who ran the store or 'kept' the teachers."[13] Historians remember the house unfortunately as the scene of the grisly murder of Blanche and Belle Wagoner, and the suicide of their killer.

It was at Wagoner that the tale of the joint snake originated. Bea vividly remembered seeing such a "snake" for the first time. A joint snake allegedly breaks into sections capable of reassembling. Modern biology considers the snake a myth, probably confused with a species of legless lizard that can regenerate its tail. Nevertheless, Benjamin Franklin used a cartoon of the joint snake in 1754 to illustrate the fate of the separate colonies, inferring that the colonies could come together as one nation. Whether Bea imagined the snake that she saw, it was one of her strongest childhood memories, and other tales of such creatures persisted for many years, particular in southern culture.

The village of Wagoner when the Cardwells arrived consisted of two stores—one on both sides of the road—Cedar Bluff School, a church, and a few houses.[14] The Wagoner Post Office had closed in 1916, the feed and chicken storage house, oil house, and the blacksmith shop went out of business shortly thereafter, and Wagoner was never again the thriving place that it once was beginning in the 1890s. On the edge of town stood the historic Wagoner house on the northeast where the tragic shooting occurred in 1915, and where generations of the Wagoner family ran the Wagoner store and boarded teachers from Cedar Bluff School.[15] From time to time, the Cardwells traveled by horse and buggy west to another little store called Tingely, originally located at the intersection of present Highway O and County Road 1550 some distance from

Wagoner. There at Tingely, the adults would trade and visit while the kids played. The storeowners had a daughter named Velma who was a little older than Bea was. Each time they went to Tingely, the two young "girlfriends" would sit on the porch of the store; share a bag of coconut, and talk. One of these pleasure trips resulted in an event at school that Bea remembered in detail. She was a very good speller in school. Her mother gave her a dollar for each month that she correctly spelled all her words. She studied diligently. However, one time she went to Tingely instead of studying. As a result, she misspelled the word "alright," spelling it "allright." It was the only word she ever recalled misspelling.[16] She said. "It nearly broke my heart." (She might have been pleased to know that modern usage of the word prefers her spelling, in the form "all right" in preference to the nineteenth century spelling of "alright.")

Bea walked to school or rode a horse. She was the only one who rode a horse to school because there was no place for kids to keep them while they were in class. Since she lived close, she would ride to school, turn her horse loose, and it would find its way back home, eating its fill of grass along the way. Sometimes she would walk to school, usually when it rained and the road was muddy; she walked up the fencerow in the grass. Bea graduated from the eighth grade at Wagoner Cedar Bluff School in 1928, at age 14. She did not attend high school. There were five in her graduating class. There had been six through most of her grades at Wagoner, but one student moved away and graduated elsewhere. She tried to keep up with the lives of her classmates. Leona and Nadine Whistance, daughters of Bill Whistance, went to California; she lost track of Jessie Spencer; Lester Boeher and Vivian Stevens stayed in Cedar County.[17] Vivian was an excellent teacher and friend who often stayed overnight at the Cardwell house and walked to school with Bea in the morning. Bea had disparaging words for the girl that moved away. Blanche Oldham, sister of Alfred Oldham, future Cedar County sheriff, chose not to graduate with them "because she thought she was too good," in Bea's words.[18] Blanche graduated instead with the class at Cherry Valley School.

Tom owned a Ford Model T Touring Car in 1928, a 1926 model equipped with cloth and Isinglass curtains all around, the very popular and affordable "tin lizzie." No one in the family knew how to drive it except the hired hand. Bea tried to drive it. Coming home from Wagoner Store one day, she turned into the driveway so fast she almost hit a tree. She never tried to drive it again, and she seldom drove even in later adult life. Her dad, Tom, never learned to drive either, nor did her mother, Mary Belle. They eventually got rid of the car. Bea often wondered where the money came from to buy that new car, "I never knew where he [Tom] got his money," she said.[19]

On February 5, 1930, Bea married Elick Thomas Beaty, the hired hand on the Cardwell farm. The ceremony was at Stockton; she was fifteen years old. Elick was almost eight years her senior.[20] He came from a large family recently settled in Greenfield from Polk County, Missouri. Tom depended on Elick for help with the farm. One day, so the story goes, Elick threatened to quit and leave but said he would stay if Bea could marry him. Finally, her dad agreed, although her mother strongly opposed the marriage. The reason for Belle's opposition never became part of the record. Perhaps her objection was because of Elick and Bea's age differences of 23 and 15, although Tom and Belle themselves had married at ages 23 and 17, respectively. In any event, as spring came on in 1930, the 1930 census found Bea and Elick living with Tom and Belle at Wagoner, on the rented farm in Linn Township.[21]

The Cardwell family, including Bea and Elick Beaty, left Wagoner after Bea graduated, and moved to a remote location on the Dade County line, near Cedarville, Missouri, situated on Goose Creek. To get there, Route 97 went south out of Jerico Springs, made a sharp turn to the left about three miles out, and continued east a mile and a half to the village of Cedarville.[22] Further on east out of Cedarville about two miles, a sharp left turn off Route 97 turned on to a dirt road going north (present State Road 279/725). About two-thirds of a mile up this road, a one-lane bridge crossed Goose Creek. Immediately across this bridge on the right and going east was the farm lane that led to the old William Cobb farm that the Cardwells rented from Mr. W. Austin Butcher.[23] Butcher was a big stock farmer in the region. He and his wife Hattie owned almost 1,800 acres in Cedar and Dade Counties, on both sides of the county line, mostly in Dade County.[24] He rented his land to other sock farmers who accounted for a sizeable farming presence in the area.[25] Like Wagoner, there were few choices nearby for socializing and shopping; none that was much more than a country store anchored in a small rural community. Arcola in Dade County was four miles southeast of the Cobb place. The closest village in Cedar County was three miles northeast at Omer (formerly White Hare).[26] The closest settlement to where they lived was at Cedarville, about two and one-half miles west on the Dade County line. This had been a thriving little town at one time. It had had a store, a hotel, a church, and a population in 1874 of about 50 people.

However, the post office discontinued in 1905 when Rural Free Delivery became available, beginning a slow exodus out of the Cedarville community. Nevertheless, the Cardwells were not hopelessly isolated because they had a telephone, a convenience seldom used because it required skill to turn a crank to signal the long and short rings necessary to call anyone.[27]

Soon, Bea and Elick moved to Greenfield to live with Elick's parents. That experiment proved unsatisfactory, and they removed to their own place in Greenfield. Before long, they were back at Cedarville helping Tom on the farm. They boarded nearby at the Ralph and Lora Evans place, south of the Butcher Farm.[28] The Evans home was a popular gathering location for local inhabitants. Mr. Evans liked to play cards, which attracted a steady stream of visitors much to the chagrin Mrs. Evans. The families—Cardwell, Elick, and Evans—became good neighbors. Mr. and Mrs. Evans had a little girl about age six, named Mildred. She liked to go to the Cardwell home where Belle would cut her hair.[29]

Bea was still in her teens when she lived on Goose Creek, recently married but still a child in some respects. Her friends would come out from Cedarville to swim in the big swimming hole on Goose Greek. The big swimming hole was what locals called "Big Lake," a body of water about a quarter of a mile up Goose Creek from the Cobb place where the creek widened into a large pool. Locals called it the Blue hole.[30] Further up the creek was a second pool not quite as large called "Little Lake." Early maps of the area recorded Goose Creek as Lake Branch. Bea could not swim. She had a large inner tube she slipped into to float out into deep water, as much as 17-feet deep in places.[31] Goose Creek was a wilderness. Bea once described it as the "snakiest place I ever saw." Snakes would fall out of the cedar trees. When she swam in the creek, there were always snakes in the water with her. She learned how snakes behaved. A blue racer snake chased after her one time; when she ran, it chased her; when she stopped, it stopped. A blue racer is an agile snake, capable of climbing trees, that moves rapidly with its head raised in a threatening manner. Whether they chase people, the opinions of herpetologists divide on such a claim.[32]

Unfortunately, while living on Goose Creek, the relationship of Belle and Tom deteriorated, and they separated in 1931.[33] Belle, who never favored the marriage of Bea and Elick, continued to be unhappy, walked out one evening, and went to a neighbor's house. She walked across the bridge to the home of Charlie Moore and stayed the night. She never returned and moved to a house in Jerico Springs. Bea and Elick moved in with Tom at the Cobb place on the hill west of the Evans farm. Elick helped with haymaking and took care of the farm.[34] Tom continued to live at Goose Creek. However, he was in poor health, and Elick kept the farm going up to this time.[35]

Belle had an interest in their shared property; Tom auctioned off their assets on August 4, 1931, on a Tuesday. Memories of the sale remained with Bea the rest of her life. There were personal things collected over the 27 years of the Cardwell marriage. There were two loom-made carpets, a stand table that Bea purchased with five one-gallon jars of pickles, and a Wisconsin brand incubator that her mother used to "hatch off chickens every year," to name a few items. She remembered that Belle would set the incubator, and "they would turn the eggs every day." Belle kept 76 pure-breed Plymouth Rock hens, the only kind she would have. The chickens sold at the sale, too, along with several horses. (Tom never owned a tractor.) One item Bea did not mind seeing sold was the Primrose No. 2 cream separator. "I hated it. Every day I had to wash that thing all the time. It was a dirty, hard job. Had to take it apart and put it back together." An item that did not sell was an iron bedstead; the one that sat under the phone that the lightening ran in on. There was also a poignant moment at the sale. Throughout her life, Bea had a superb ability to sew clothing. The daughter of a neighbor was at the sale; Bea recognized that she had made the little girl's dress.[36]

With her part of the money from the sale, Belle purchased a home on Broadway Street in Jerico Springs across the street from Widow Nancy Jones.[37] She lived there for many years and never reconciled with Tom. She earned income keeping lodgers and caring for infirm patients in her home, oftentimes without pay. After the sale, Tom, Elick, and Bea lived for a short time in the Lon Sortor house on Sac River. Lon had married Bea's Aunt Lizzie Baldwin and they had a daughter, Zula, who became one of Bea's best friends. Campouts on Sac Rive were a favorite pastime. On one such outing, they camped out on a gravel bar surrounded by hogs that made threatening noises all night.[38]

After the sale, Tom never had anything. In his later life, he never owned land and always rented from other landowners. The three of them—Bea, Elick, and Tom—removed to Greenfield where Elick's family worked for the Kings, a successful family of farmers and merchants in Dade County. In 1934, when Bea was about twenty, the three of them moved back to Cedar County. They lived there in three different houses. First, they settled into a place west of Cedarville on Highway 97, which Bea remembered as "the big house," and then to locations closer to Jerico Springs.[39] They moved to Jerico and rented a place across the road from Frank Bannister, near Belle's house. Soon after they had settled in Jerico Springs, Bea contracted a serious case of measles. There was fear that she would not recover, but she did.[40] All of this occurred over the course of a couple of years. Tom did farm labor, and they managed to scrape out a living. He was in poor health, suffering from prostrate problems most of his life.[41]

By 1935, Elick had grown restless. He wanted to move to California. However, Tom had become ill, and Bea was reluctant to leave him.[42] Nevertheless, she and Elick started for the West Coast. They got as far as Kansas, stayed overnight on the porch of a charitable Kansan, and spent a sleepless night in a terrible storm. The next morning, Bea refused to go any further, and the couple returned home.[43] Soon afterward, Elick moved anyway without her, and that ended their marriage. Bea remembered it was the right decision for her. She called the marriage "a big mistake." After Elick left, Belle arranged the divorce proceedings.[44] "She got our divorce," Bea said of her mother.[45] They officially divorced on January 13, 1939, in a divorce decree filed in Weld, Colorado.[46] Unbeknownst to Bea or Belle, Elick had married again on November 9, 1938, to nineteen-year-old Luella Marie Cowan, in Brighton, Adams County, Colorado.[47] By state law, he was guilty of bigamy and subject to criminal and civil penalties for marrying before being legally divorced. His second marriage was void because it legally could not exist and was subject to annulment. However, by that time, no one cared and nothing came of it. Elick returned to Missouri only once after he left. Years later, Bea heard that he had remarried and raised a family in California.[48] He died in 1991 in Tulare County, California.[49]

Beatrice and Jessie. This early photograph of Beatrice Cardwell, taken in 1915, pictures her sitting on the lap of her cousin, Jessie Ethel "Jack" McGuire, daughter of Laura (Cardwell) McGuire.

Beatrice Cardwell. Taken at about age 7, this view pictured her on the Cardwell farm near the home of her Grandfather Willie Ira Fellows on Horse Creek. The iron-wheeled tricycle was similar to models manufactured by the Colson Company in the early 1900s, made commonly of steel rather than wood because of the more indestructible properties of steel. Bea never owned a bicycle. She never saw a movie growing up, and did not see her first television until 1956.

Beatrice Cardwell Cedar Bluff School 8th Grade Graduation. Bea Cardwell sits front right in the picture. Row 1 is Jessie Spencer, Nadine Whistance, and Beatrice Cardwell; back row is Lester Boeher, Vivian Stevens (teacher), and Leona Whistance. The number 63 seen in the photo was the number of the Cedar Bluff School District; the significance of the number 92 may allude to the year 1892, which was about the year the new school building opened at Wagoner. Copy of a 1928 photograph probably taken by Stevens Photography Studio in Bolivar, Missouri. Stevens was the brother of Vivian Stevens seen in the picture.

Photo courtesy of the Wagoner Community Association.

Cedar Bluff School. Beatrice attended this one-room school at Wagoner, Missouri. Originally painted white, the "boxcar" style featured a row of windows on the side and concrete steps that led to double entry doors. A wood stove at the center of the classroom heated the building in winter. Bea graduated from eighth grade at this school in 1928; she first attended a school of the same "boxcar" style at Fairview, near Osiris.

Locator Map of the Birthplace of Beatrice Cardwell. The house was on 40 acres in Township 34N Range 28W Section 25, on a spur of English Branch, about two miles southwest of Wagoner. The property sat 2/3 of a mile west of present Farm Road South 725 but is no longer accessible by road. The family moved next to a farm on Horse Creek adjoining the W.I. Fellows property in Benton Towship north of Jerico Springs and not pictured on this map. Modified map adapted from *Standard Atlas of Cedar County*, Geo. A. Ogle, 1908. Library of Congress.

The Tom Cardwell Family. Identified from left to right are Belle (Fellows) Cardwell, Beatrice Cardwell, Laura (Cardwell) McGuire, Eliza (Baldwin) McCollum, and Tom Cardwell. Eliza was the mother of Laura and Tom and grandmother of Beatrice. She previously married Edward Cardwell and Jessie Biddey, both deceased. This photo dates to about 1928 when the Cardwells lived at Wagoner.

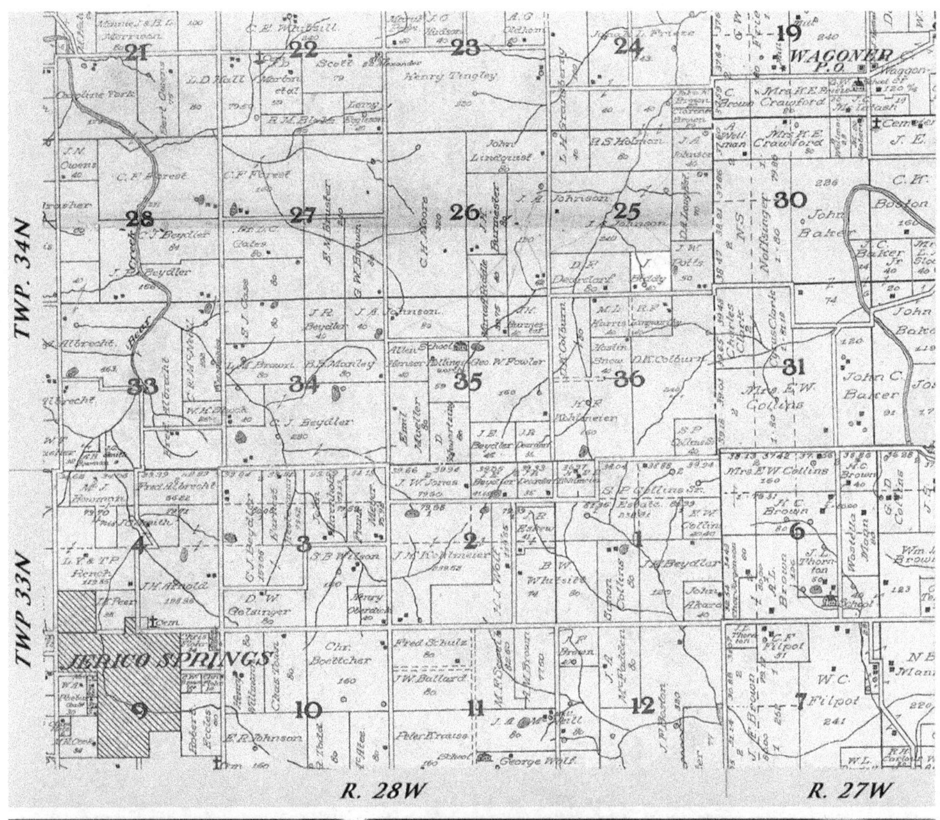
TWP. 34N
TWP 33N
R. 28W
R. 27W
JERICO SPRINGS
WAGONER
P.O.
21
22
23
24
19
28
27
26
25
30
33
34
35
36
31
4
3
2
1
6
9
10
11
12
7

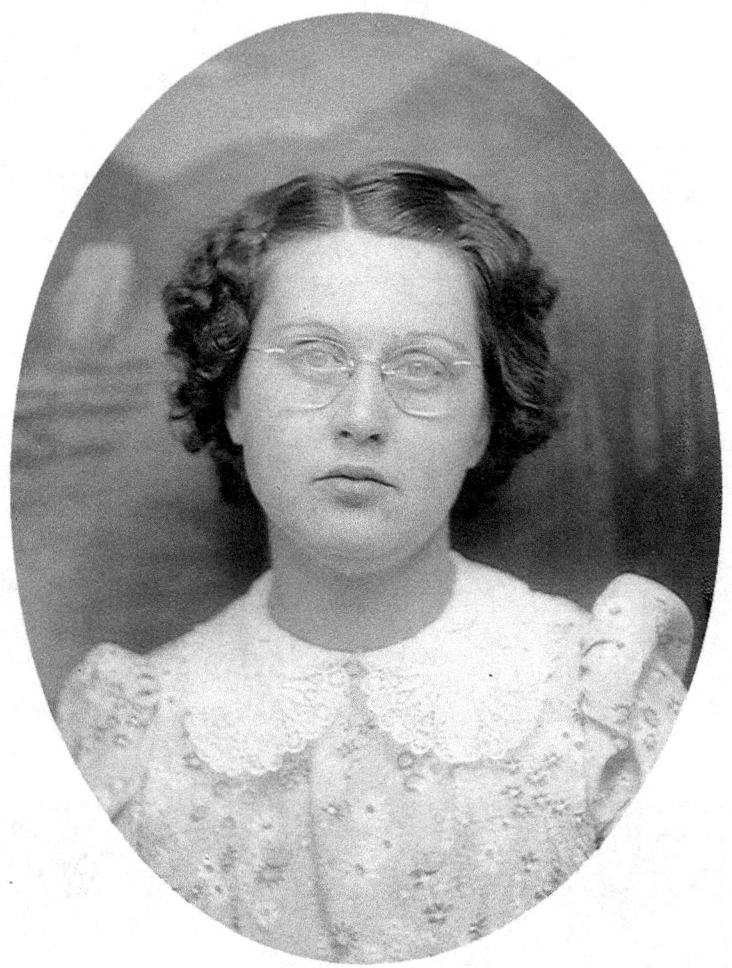

Beatrice (Cardwell) Beaty. Beatrice married Elick Beaty in 1930. Her parents divorced in 1934, and this photo pictures her soon after her separation from Elick in 1935. The couple legally divorced in 1939.

FORD MOTOR COMPANY DETROIT

All-steel bodies
Closed cars in color

THE TOURING
Black. All-steel body. One-man top. Weather-proof side curtains opening with all four doors. Four cord tires, nickeled head lamp rims, windshield wiper. Starter and demountable rims $85 extra. Balloon tires $25 extra. *Price f. o. b. Detroit.*
$290

1926 Ford Touring Car. Tom and Belle Cardwell owned a car like this one. Ford advertised it in *The American Magazine* for $290 as "Today's High Peak in Motor Car Value." For the price, the buyer received a Model T with kerosene cowl lamps, a windshield wiper, non–demountable 30 X 3 ½ inch tires on "clincher" rims, and no spare wheel, or tire. The model the Cardwells owned came with Isinglass curtains.

National Automotive History Collection, Detroit Public Library.

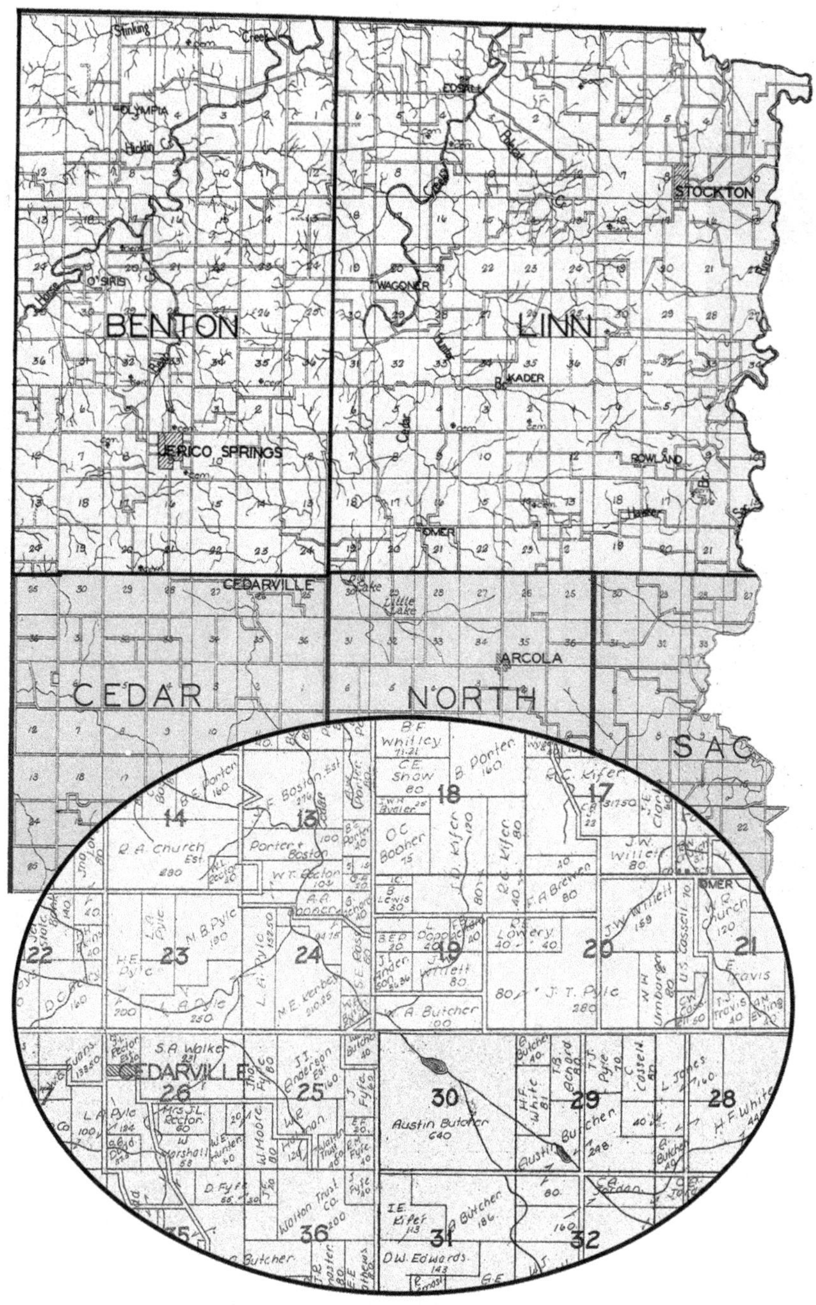

Cedar and Dade Counties. On this map are places Bea lived in the first 25 years of her life. In Benton Township are the Fellows Farm on Horse Creek near Osiris and Jerico Springs. In Linn Township are Wagoner, Goose Creek near Omer, Rowland, and Amity near Stockton. At the center of the enlarged inset east of Cedarville in Section 30 is the Swimming Hole in North Township of Dade County. Across from it in Cedar County in Section 19 was the Cardwell home, located on Goose Creek on part of the Butcher 100 acres. *Plat Books of Cedar and Dade Counties, Missouri*, W.W. Hixson, 1930, University of Missouri.

28

Beatrice Cardwell Later Years

Bea and her dad Tom rented a home on Route B (present Ridge Street) on the outskirts of Jerico Springs. They took in boarders to help pay the rent. One of the qualities that Bea inherited from her mother was caring for the needy. She cared for Milton Maphis in the Cardwell home for a long time. Mr. Maphis was a retired farm laborer from Virginia. Widowed for many years after his wife Sarah died, he lived with his son who then moved to Montana, leaving Mr. Maphis alone. After Milton died in 1938, Bea purchased out of her own pocket a headstone for his grave.[1] She also cared for Uncle Tom Barnes until he died, again opening her home where she and Tom lived.[2]

She was living in Jerico Springs when she met and married Willis Burchett, on New Year's Day 1941. They obtained their marriage license on December 31, 1940 in Dade County and married the next day in Jerico Springs, Cedar County, at the home of Elder A.A. McCollum and Anna Eliza (Baldwin) McCollum, grandmother of Bea.[3] Mr. McCollum was a colorful character.[4] He was a Methodist preacher who lived on Broadway Street in Jerico, next door west of Belle's house. Willis Adley Burchett was almost 12 years Bea's elder when they married. He was born September 21, 1902, near Rookins, Missouri, a country store that served a sizeable Burchett family in St. Clair County. It was his second marriage. He divorced his first wife after five children, and had been divorced for about a year when he met Bea. Bea was age 26 at the time. A decade had passed since her failed first marriage to Elick Beaty. The newly wed couple spent their first night at the Phipps home located "up the hill" from Rowland, Missouri. Friends found them there and celebrated their marriage with the customary chivaree.[5]

Willis rented and operated the store at Rowland, a little trading-point in the southern part of Cedar County about seven miles south of Stockton. Rowland got its name from R.P. Rowland who opened the post office there in 1908. As late as 1930, he still owned the property.[6] After they married, Willis built a long shed on the side of the store where the family lived. Soon he decided to build a new store and constructed a second Rowland on Mr. Phipps' land at the crossroads not far north of the original store.[7] The building stood at the intersection of State Highway H and a gravel lane that ran east (present County Road 2074). A church was a short distance north on Highway H and along with a school filled out the Rowland community.[8] The store had a dug well, and the building sat on the east side of the highway just north of the intersection, facing west. The terrain was low at this intersection. After a heavy rain, water would come into the store from a little branch than ran past it.[9]

Rowland was a family affair. Tom Cardwell stayed with Willis and Bea, and helped in the store, along with Willis' elder son, Joe, and Willis' two youngest sisters, Edith and Elsie Burchett. Meanwhile, his other children by his first marriage: Neta, Neva (Bunny), Dennis, and Willis, Jr.—who was about three years old at the time—lived with their mother.[10]

Bea's Grandmother Eliza (Baldwin) McCollum died on April 2, 1942, at Jerico Springs, of tuberculosis at the age of 79. Bea always lived in fear she would contract the disease. It had been the main reason she did not live with her grandmother to attend high school at Jerico. Bea did not attend high school because she would have had to stay with her Grandmother Eliza at Jerico to attend the new high school there. She sometimes did laundry for Eliza and often wondered how she managed not to become ill. Eliza's first husband, Edward Cardwell, and their daughter Laura (Cardwell) McGuire also died of tuberculosis. Eliza died when Bea was bedfast awaiting the birth of her first child, and unable to attend Eliza's funeral. She cared deeply for her grandmother, sometimes correcting people who would refer to her as "Lizzy." Eliza did not go by the name Lizzy; that was her younger sister, Lzzie Alice Baldwin who married Lon Sortor.[11]

On April 26, 1942, Bea gave birth to a son.

On January 21, 1944, Tom Cardwell died in a tragic wood saw accident working in a wooded area near Rowland. In those days of wood-fired heating, communities gathered to cut cordwood for each other. Sawing crews went from place to place with a large wood saw usually tractor mounted, and cut up large piles of timber collected at one place. A saw crew could make short work of a substantial pile of logs. Tom always insisted on being the "off-bearer" for the crew, a job that placed him closest to the saw blade, a very sharp tool usually about 18-24 inches in diameter and turning at a high speed with no kind of safety shield around it. As the "feeder" crew fed a length of log into the saw, it was the job of the "off-bearer" to take the cut-off piece of wood and pitch it away from the saw into a pile. While doing this, Tom's jacket caught in the machinery, and pulled him into the saw. It was a mortal wound. Lee Price drove him to a hospital in Springfield, where he hung on for a few days but did not recover. Bea never saw her father alive again. Discouraged from seeing him in the hospital, she was pregnant with her second child, and the doctor feared that the stress would be too dangerous for her; and, so, she never saw him again. She did not go to the funeral for the same reason.[12] Tom went to rest in Gum Springs Cemetery, Cedar County, Missouri, next to his mother, Eliza, who had died only two years before. A short distance down the hill in Gum Springs Cemetery lay his father, Edward Cardwell. Tom Cardwell died at age 62, too young, his neighbors thought.

The Burchett family—Willis, Bea, and their toddler son—left Rowland. Life became a whirlwind of nomadic existence. She and Willis lived in seven different places before their son was age seven. They removed first to Claud Store in the northeast corner of Cedar County. Claud stood on State Highway N, about 5 miles northeast of Caplinger Mills and 8 miles west of Humansville, Missouri. Charles E. Eliston put up the first store at Claud and named the trading post for his nephew.[13] It passed into the hands of the Burchett family and was for many years in the proprietorship of Alexander Burchett, grandfather of Willis. George Burchett, son of Alexander and father of Willis, married Pearl Brock at Claud Store in 1901. Willis rented the store from his Uncle Henry Burchett, brother of George and youngest son of Alexander. Willis moved his family into a room in the back of the store that Bea once described as a "shed."[14] Pregnant with her second child, Bea temporarily moved in with her mother Belle in Jerico Springs closer to medical care to give birth to her daughter on March 17, 1944.

From Claud Store, the family moved to the old Alexander Burchett place near Orville Burchett, the brother of Willis.[15] Alexander Burchett died the year before Bea was born; his wife Elizabeth died in 1926 leaving the old Burchett house abandoned. The house had no electricity and none of the simple comforts of home. Willis had a sawmill set up on the property and was frequently away from home. Bea entertained by sitting on the floor across from her young son rolling a half gallon of cream back and forth to churn butter. Willis decided to build a new house. He moved the family into a tiny trailer across the road from the house site. They lived there only a short while because Willis sold the house without ever finishing it.[16] Their next stop was Jerico Springs. They moved into the Jones house on Broadway Street, across from Belle's house. Another daughter came along on September 4, 1945.

For reasons never disclosed, Belle moved out of her Jerico Springs house to stay with her brother Claud Fellows and his wife Hope on the old Fellows Farm where Bea spent her childhood on Horse Creek.[17] Willis, Bea, and their three children moved into Belle's house and lived there until 1949. By this time, Willis had a well-drilling business in addition to his sawmill, and was away for extended periods. Willis sold the Jerico Springs house and allegedly never gave any of the money to Belle or Bea.[18] Instead, he used the proceeds to buy an 80-acre farm located four miles west of Stockton, Missouri, on present Farm Road 1350, and about the same distance southwest to Wagoner. There was a small house on the property. Willis built a new barn, bought a few milk cows, and took on the role of farmer. Bea kept a large garden that included an array of flowerbeds, canned an extraordinary stock of foodstuffs kept in a new rock cellar, and tended to a large share of farm chores. Still, things did not go well. Their marriage fell apart, and in 1951, they divorced. Bea won custody of the children and an arrangement to have the farm assigned jointly to their three kids. Its purchase was in part with money from the sale of Belle's house in Jerico Springs. They split the costs of the divorce proceedings, Willis acquired 20 acres of land directly across the road, set up a mobile home, built some outbuildings, and that was the arrangement.

On February 2, 1952, Bea married Richard Hayden Richardson at the Methodist Parsonage in Jerico Springs. Rich—everyone called him Rich—was a World War II veteran who styled himself as a farmer and coal miner in his younger days in the mines in Kansas but lately a carpenter and laborer in and around Jerico Springs and Stockton. Born on December 15, 1909, he was the son of Amos and Rebecca Richardson. He rose to the rank of staff sergeant in the army in charge of a 12-man anti-tank crew of the 159th Infantry. He served for the duration of the war, spending 22 months overseas in the Pacific Theater of Operations, seeing action in the Aleutian Islands and the Philippines for which he received the Philippine Liberation Ribbon.[19]

Bea was a religious person. Never one to wear her faith on her sleeve, she harbored a quiet dignity of Christian belief that sustained her through difficult periods in her life. In February 1958, at the invitation of the Brothers Clyde Bough and Web Foster at the Old Amity School House, she joined the Hopewell Baptist Church that became one of the many objects of her community service.[20] She had a way of always thinking of others. She served as a 4-H Club leader and became a second mother to many. If a child in the community needed help and a little extra love, especially little girls, she would attend to it, often inviting a neighbor's youngster over to the house where she would doll them up and send them home in a clean new, homemade dress. It happened many times. Her special empathy was not only for people. If a baby animal needed attention, she brought it into the house, made a palette behind the stove, and nursed it until it could stand on its own. It happened many times, almost like a continuation of her childhood when she would put aside her dolls (which she did not care for) to spend time with her live animal friends.[21] Remembering all the good times in the Amity community, she organized the Amity Reunion, working each year to make it a huge success, and garnering the gratitude of the children that had so often benefitted from her generosity of time and caring.

She delighted in visiting neighbors and having the pleasure of return visits. A regular social gathering was the taffy pull that always brought neighbors together. She was a ringleader in organizing pie suppers and holiday celebrations at the Amity School. However, what most set her apart as a caring person, and perhaps least known about her, was her insistence on always sending flowers to funerals. She never hesitated to solicit acquaintances to send a floral arrangement in memory of a departed friend, always including the names of the contributors, sometimes even if they did not contribute but should have. This went on for her entire life.[22]

Bea and Rich left the Amity farm in the summer of 1958 to operate and manage the Old Ice Plant Service Station west of Stockton on Highway 32, moving into the living quarters above the store. For the next fifteen years, they worked in the retail grocery and gas business. Health concerns arose when doctors diagnosed Bea with a pre-cancerous thyroid condition. She checked in to the Ellis Fischel Cancer Center in Columbia, Missouri, a state-operated cancer hospital devoted to the treatment of needy patients suffering from cancer and related diseases.[23] Doctors proposed removal of her Thyroid. Such invasive surgery required lifelong medication with possible side effects and further compromise of her health. She was still a relatively young woman in her mid-forties. Her son, who accompanied her to Columbia, opposed the surgery, and Bea rejected it. She came home, recovered from her condition, and lived a normal life.

Bea and Rich retired in 1972. The Old Home Place at Amity had burned several years before when a renter tried to stoke a fire with a rubber tire jammed into the old wood stove. Rich started to rebuild the house but gave up on that project after pouring the foundation. Instead, they bought a larger farm more accessible to Stockton from Ted D. and Christine Vance. It had a small house on it located off Highway 39 about three miles northwest of Stockton, on present Farm Road 1120.[24] Buying the farm was a complicated process because to finance the purchase they had to take out a loan on the old 80, which legally belonged to Bea's three children who had collateral ownership.[25] The kids signed off on the deal, and the bank loaned $17,500 at 8-percent interest to buy the Vance property.[26] Bea and Rich created a life-estate in the Vance property for the duration of their natural lives with the remainder to Bea's children. [27] They sold the old 80-acre Amity farm to Ed and Blanche Farmer in 1973. The Farmers agreed to make payments on the Vance property, and the bank released the lien obligations. The bank arranged it all. A story goes that the bank manager wanted to charge Bea $10 to handle the paperwork; she got so mad they waived the fee. [28] By fall of 1978, Bea and rich had paid off the mortgage on the Vance farm. [29] It was their home for more than a dozen years. Bea busied herself in retirement with gardening, entertaining grandchildren, and her favorite pastime of fishing in the small pond west of the house. Bea was a proud homemaker who always had her door open for family and friends. She always had Sunday meals available for her children and their families. She was an excellent cook to go with her superb sewing skills, gardening ability, husbandry, and other domestic qualities that helped to shape her deeply felt attachment to nature.

Tragedy came to the Richardson household on August 16, 1985. Rich had developed terminal cancer. He took his own life about 2:30 in the afternoon in the small shed that stood a few feet south of the house. Sheriff C.A. LaRew determined he died from a self-inflicted gunshot wound. People remembered Rich as "a quiet man of few words, but always ready to be of help in any way he could to his family, friends, and neighbors."[30] His burial was near his parents at Anna Edna Cemetery, near Jerico Springs, with full military honors.

Bea held on to her independence as long as her health permitted, living several years alone on the Vance farm, then moving into Stockton at an apartment at the top of the hill, at the intersection of Davis and North Streets, a picturesque setting above Stockton City Park and the cave-fed spring and branch that flowed through it. Her last days were at the Stockton Nursing Home on Owen Mill Road, northeast of town. Here, she survived the great tornado of the spring of 2003 that destroyed the town of Stockton. She lived a sedentary life broken up by occasional appointments to the doctor and welcome visits from friends and family, plus special outings when a family member took her for a drive, usually stopping at one of her favorite fast food establishments for a burger and fries.[31]

Bea died March 5, 2005, at the age of 90 years, five months, and 24 days. Her long life exceeded that of any of her Fellows or Cardwell forbearers. Her burial was at Anna Edna Cemetery at Jerico Springs, beside the grave of Rich. One of her last requests for her funeral was a reading of her favorite poem, paraphrased from the nineteenth century poet, George Linnaeus Banks. "*Live for those who love you, For those whose hearts are true, For the heaven that smiles above you, And for the good that you can do.*"[32]

Bea and the Amity Farmhouse. The house sat on 80 acres of land located four miles west of Stockton, Missouri, in the Amity community on present Farm Road 1350. The house burned to the ground. Bea posed for this photo before leaving for Ellis Fischel Cancer Center in Columbia, Missouri.

Beatrice Cardwell Richardson
1914 - 2005

GENERATIONAL LIFE SPANS

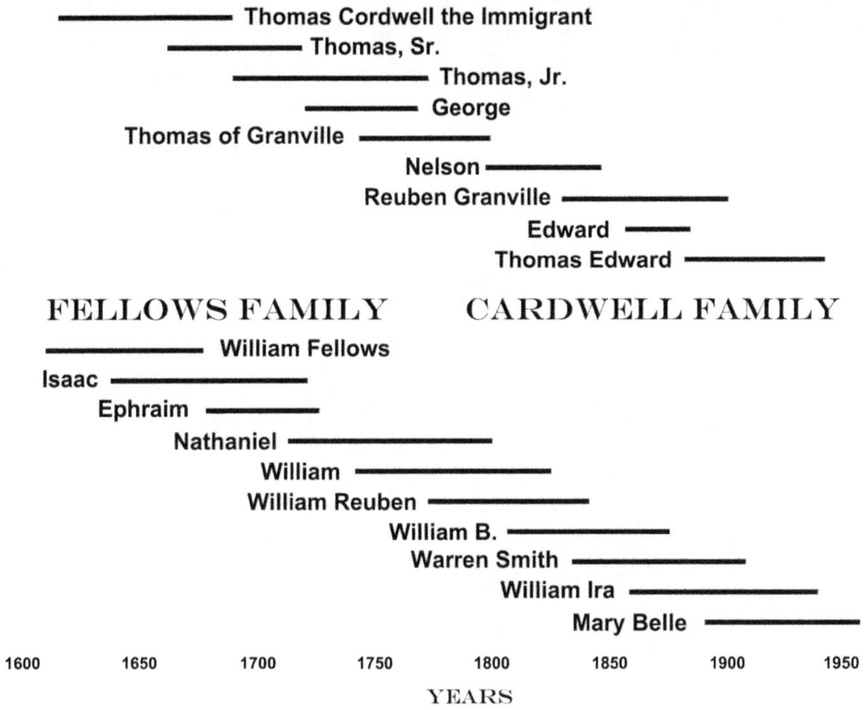

THE FELLOWS GENEALOGY COVERS 349 YEARS IN TEN GENERATIONS FROM 1609 TO 1958. THE CARDWELL GENEALOGY COMPRISES A SIMILAR PERIOD OF 330 YEARS IN 9 GENERATIONS FROM 1614 TO 1944. THE AVERAGE LIFESPAN OF A CARDWELL GENERATIONS WAS 57 YEARS; THE YOUNGEST WAS EDWARD CARDWELL WHO DIED IN 1884 AT AGE 27; THE OLDEST WAS THOMAS CARDWELL, JR. OF VIRGINIA WHO DIED IN 1772 AT THE AGE OF 82. THE AVERAGE LIFESPAN OF A FELLOWS GENERATION WAS 73 YEARS; THE YOUNGEST TO DIE WAS EPHRAIM FELLOWS WHO DIED IN 1725 AT THE AGE OF 45; THE OLDEST WAS HIS SON NATHANIEL WHO DIED IN 1800 AT AGE 87.

Notes

Chapter 1 Fellows Genealogy Introduction

[1] Henry A. Baker, ed., *History of Montville, Connecticut, Formerly the North Parish of New London from 1640 to 1896,* Hartford, Conn.: Press of Case, Lockwood, and Brainard, 1896, p. 346.

[2] Mark D. Fellows, *Descendants of William Fellows of Ipswich, Massachusetts 1635*, eBook, accessed 2009.

[3] LDS Pedigree Resource File, Disk 24, 6695562; See also Disk 8, 403049, Disk 19, 170526, and Disk 27, 64103; boards.ancestry.com, Apr 2000. Mara Childers replied to an inquiry by Oren Cobb on "William Fellows of England." Childers and her father did extensive research on the Fellows family. The city of Ipswich, Massachusetts, sponsors a website on the Founding Fathers of Ipswich that includes William Fellows.

[4] Fellows, *Descendants of William Fellows of Ipswich.*

[5] *Biographical Review Containing Life Sketches of Leading Citizens of Essex County, Massachusetts* (Vol. 28). Boston: Biographical Review Publishing, 1898, p. 376.

[6] Willie Ira Fellows, *A Short History of W.I. Fellows and the Fellows Family as Far Back as He Can Remember.* Unpublished Autobiography, c.1940.

[7] Columbus, *History of the Fellows Family*, 1997.

[8] Fellows, *Descendants of William Fellows of Ipswich.* Two of the descendants of William Fellows became the forty-first president of the United States, George Herbert Walker Bush and his son George W. Bush, forty-third president.

[9] Fellows, *Descendants of William Fellows of Ipswich.*

Chapter 2 The Great Migration

[1] Robert Charles Anderson, *The Great Migration Begins: Immigrants to New England, 1620-1633, Volumes 1-3; The Great Migration: Immigrants to New England, 1634-1635, Volumes 1-6*. Boston: New England Historical and Genealogical Society, 1996-2011.

[2] Robert Charles Anderson, "A Note on the Pace of the Great Migration," *The New England Quarterly* 59 (1986): 406-407.

[3] Columbus, *History of the Fellows Family*, 1997.

[4] Charles Edwards Banks, *Topographical Dictionary of 2,885 English Emigrants to New England,* edited by Elijah Ellsworth Brownell, Baltimore: Southern Book, 1957, p, 92; LDS Pedigree Resource File, Disk 24, 6695562; See also Disk 8, 403049, Disk 19, 170526, and Disk 27, 64103; boards.ancestry.com, accessed Apr 2000.

[5] Frank R. Holmes, *Directory of the Ancestral Heads of New England Families: 1620-1700* (reprint ed),. Baltimore: Genealogical Publishing, 1923 1980, p. lxxxi.

[6] Anderson, et al., *The Great Migration*, p. 507, citing Ipswich Land Records, 1:1, & *The Probate Records of Essex County, Massachusetts, 1635-1681,* 1:11.

[7] Meredith B. Colket, Jr., *Founders of Early American Families: Emigrants from Europe, 1607-1657.* "Fellows, William, came on the *Planter* 1635, Ipswich (Mass.) 1641, d. there by 27 Mar 1676/77, citing Herder, (Tag 17:159) (son Isaac); Fellows-Craig, 1919; David W. Hoyt, *Old Families of Salisbury and Amesburg*, 1897; Myrtle M. Morris, *Joseph and Philena (Elton) Fellows*, 1940; *Fellows of Shelburne*, 1957. Colket also lists a brother of William Fellows, Samuel Fellows of Salisbury, Mass. 1641, d. there 6 Mar 1657/58.

[8] Fellows, *Descendants of William Fellows of Ipswich;* Anne Pillsbury, ancestry.com message boards, posted under Fellows England to Massachusetts, May 2002. "My mother and I started working on the fellows Family History fourteen or more years ago;" Larraby Fellows reply to Pillsbury, "I have done one complete branch of the Fellows family history starting with William Fellows (b. 1558) in Nottinghamshire, including his grandson William Fellows (b. 1609) who came to Ipswich, Massachusetts, in 1635 and ending with Robert Fellows (b. 1924) who is my grandfather. My mother began this research in the Dartmouth College Baker Library in the 1970s. Our branch of the family ended up in Hanover, New Hampshire, and my family now lives in Vermont." Neither the Pillsbury nor Fellows messages contained supporting sources. However, both support the family tradition about the three Fellows brothers who migrated from England to American about 1635.

[9] *England, Select Births and Christenings, 1538-1975*; Dennis Fellows, *William Fellows (1609-1676)*, geocities.com/Heartland/Meadows/5445/william_fellows. The narrative of William Fellows of Ipswich written by Dennis Fellows is a generally accurate summary of genealogical information gathered through 2003. He points out that alternate interpretations exist regarding his ancestors, including that he may have descended from the Fellows of the village of Foxton, Lincolnshire, England, instead of Nottinghamshire.

[10] LDS Pedigree Resource File, Disk 24, 6695562; See also Disk 8, 403049, Disk 19, 170526, and Disk 27, 64103; boards.ancestry.com, Apr 2000.

[11] LDS Pedigree Resource File, Disk 11, 402279. See also Disk 1 and Disk 25, 717541; LDS International Genealogical Index Family History Library; LDS Ancestral File (R), AFN-MBZS-G2LDS Pedigree Resource File, Disk 24, 6695562; See also Disk 8, 403049, Disk 19, 170526, and Disk 27, 64103; boards.ancestry.com, Apr 2000.

[12] *England & Wales Christening Records, 1530-1906*; London Metropolitan Archives; London, England; Reference Number: DRO/051/001; *England, Select Essex Parish Registers, 1538-1900.*

[13] Anderson, et al., *The Great Migration*, p. 511, citing Suffolk County, Massachusetts, Probate Records, 1:494-495.

[14] Anderson, et al., *The Great Migration*, p. 511, citing *New England Historical and Genealogical Register,* 138:17-24.

[15] Anderson, et al., *The Great Migration*, p. 511, citing *New England Historical and Genealogical Register,* 138:22.

[16] Anderson, et al., *The Great Migration*, p. 511, citing "Early Hartford Vital Records" in *Collections of the Connecticut Historical Society,* 577.

[17] Anderson, et al., *The Great Migration*, p. 511, citing *Records and Files of the Quarterly Courts of Essex County, Massachusetts, 1636-1686,* 7:279.

[18] Anderson, et al., *The Great Migration*, p. 511, citing *Records of the Particular Court of Connecticut, 1639-1663,* 23, and *The Public Records of the Colony of Connecticut, 1626-1776,* 1:92.

[19] Anderson, et al., *The Great Migration*, p. 512, citing *New England Historical and Genealogical Register,* 138:17-23.

[20] Clarence Almon Torrey, *New England Marriages Prior to 1700,* Baltimore: Genealogical Publishing, 1997, p. 26; Fellows, *William Fellows (1609-1676),* geocities.com/Heartland/Meadows/5445/william_fellows; Ralph Arthur Watson, *Ancestors and Descendants of John and Hannah (Goodwin) Watson of Hartford, Connecticut, and Associated Families,* Baltimore: Gateway Press, 1985, p. 205. Watson appears to confuse Selston, Nottinghamshire, with Selsten Walk, Northants, or Northamptonshire.

[21] Hammatt, *The Hammatt Papers; Early Inhabitants of Ipswich, Massachusetts, 1633-1700,* Baltimore: Genealogical Publishing, [1880-1899] 1980, 1991, p. 100.

[22] Banks, *Topographical Dictionary*, p. 70; Anderson, et al., *The Great Migration*, p. 509, citing Hotten, *The Original Lists of Persons of Quality,* 45; Hoyt, *Old Families of Salisbury and Amesbury, Massachusetts,* (Vol. 1), Providence, Rhode Island: Snow & Farnham, 1897, p. 155; Mitch Vander Vorst, *Benedict [Vander Vorst/Fellows] Family Genealogy,* Springfield, Ore., freepages.genealogy.rootsweb.com/~mitchvv/ webcards/benedict/INDEX. Banks copied a transcription that gave the age of William in 1635 as age 27.

[23] Anderson, et al., *The Great Migration*, p. 509, citing *Records and Files of the Quarterly Courts of Essex County,* 2:170; Louis Dow Sisco, *Fellows, Fallowes, Fellow and Like Names, Fellows Ancestry in New England and Old England,* New York: Tobias A. Wright, 1926, p. 13, citing *Recs. Essex Quart. Ct.*, ii, 170; Vorst, *Benedict [Vander Vorst/Fellows].*

[24] Anderson, et al., *The Great Migration*, p.509.

[25] W.H. Whitmore, *The Ayres and Ayer Families* (NEGHS 1863), Vol. 17, pp. 307-310.

[26] Vorst, *Benedict [Vander Vorst/Fellows];* Hoyt, *Old Families of Salisbury and Amesbury,* p. 155.

[27] Fellows, *Descendants of William Fellows of Ipswich*; LDS Pedigree Resource File, Disk 24, 669551. See also Disk 8, 403052 and Disk 27, 642539.

[28] Anderson, et al., *The Great Migration*, p. 512, citing *The Probate Records of Essex County, Massachusetts, 1635-1681,* 2:282-184, and *Records and Files of the Quarterly Courts of Essex County, Massachusetts, 1636-1686,* 2:334; *Salem, Massachusetts Quarterly Court Records*, Vol 4:81 & 4:334, 29 Mar 1659. This document states, "Whereas our Brother William Lampson late of Ipswich dyed intestate and Administration granted by the Honered Court at Ipswich at his widow our Sister Sarah Lampson and divided the estate about halfe to her & halfe to the children being eight in number and whereas she being about to change her estate to one Thomas Harteshorne of Redding, it was agreed before the marriage he should signe and seale a wrighting to give our sayd sister power & liberty to dispose of the one halfe she brought to him by way of will (of wch there is sufisient wittnes besydes ourselves) but by evidence that wrighting being neglected to be finished before marriage (though then promised it should be done after) but it is now refused and thereby the children of or Brother William Lampson like to suffer and whereas the estate in the Inventory delivered into court was underprised especially the Land wch now appeareth to be worth eightye pounds wch was then prised but forty foure pound. Our Humble request to this Honered Court is that the children of our brother may Inioy a part of the advance of their fathers estate and do humbly intreat (if this Honered Court shall thinke fitt) that the Land may be to pay the childrens portions, it being prised in the Inventory as before exprest & there portions fiftye foure pounds & soe there portions will be advanced twentye six pound & the widow still have about halfe the estate and that it would please the court that those children that are put out [apprenticed] may be have their portions improved for their use & Benifitt [that]| when they come to age to receive the same, that being all (as the case now stands) that they are like to have their Father's estate.".

[29] Ancestors of Hugh Rutherford, Internet.

[30] Fellows, *William Fellows (1609-1676).*

[31] Fellows, *Fellows Families of Onondaga County,* p. 9.

[32] *Biographical Review Containing Life Sketches of Leading Citizens of Essex County, Massachusetts* 28, p. 376.

[33] LDS Pedigree Resource File, Disk 24, 6695562; See also Disk 8, 403049, Disk 19, 170526, and Disk 27, 64103; boards.ancestry.com, accessed Apr 2000.

[34] Banks, *Topographical Dictionary*, p. 70; Fellows, *Descendants of William Fellows of Ipswich,* 262.

[35] Anderson, et al., *The Great Migration*, p. 507, citing Hotten, *The Original Lists of Persons of Quality,* 45.

[36] Vorst, *Benedict [Vander Vorst/Fellows]*, citing Fellows, *Descendants of William Fellows of Ipswich*; Fellows, *William Fellows (1609-1676)*; *Biographical Review Containing Life Sketches of Leading Citizens of Essex County, Massachusetts,* 28, p. 376; LDS Pedigree Resource File, Disk 24, 6695562; See also Disk 8, 403049, Disk 19, 170526, and Disk 27, 64103; boards.ancestry.com, Apr 2000.

[37] Fellows, *William Fellows (1609-1676.*

[38] Fellows, *Descendants of William Fellows of Ipswich.*

[39] Hoyt, *Old Families of Salisbury and Amesbury,* p. 155.

[40] Watson, *Ancestors and Descendants of John and Hannah (Goodwin) Watson of Hartford, Connecticut,* p. 205.

[41] Thomas Franklin Waters, *Candlewood, an Ancient Neighborhood in Ipswich: with Genealogies of John Brown, William Fellows, Robert Kinsman* (reprint ed.). Newburyport, Mass.: Parker River Researchers, [1909] 1986, pp. 50-53.

[42] Fellows, *Descendants of William Fellows of Ipswich.*

[43] Waters, *Candlewood,* pp. 50-53.

[44] Waters, *Candlewood,* pp. 50-53.

[45] Waters, *Candlewood,* pp. 50-53.

[46] Waters, *Candlewood,* p. 71; Laraby Fellows posted on boards.ancestry.com, May 2002; Fellows, *William Fellows (1609-1676).*

Chapter 3 Candlewood

[1] Thomas Franklin Waters, *Candlewood, an Ancient Neighborhood in Ipswich: with Genealogies of John Brown, William Fellows, Robert Kinsman* (reprint ed.), Newburyport, Mass.: Parker River Researchers, [1909] 1986, pp. 50-53.

[2] Waters, *Candlewood,* pp. 50-53. Waters described some of the aristocracy who owned black Negro slaves. His description did not extend to William Fellows who was not among the aristocracy, and there is no evidence that he or any of his descendants owned slave.

[3] Waters, *Candlewood,* pp. 50-52.

[4] The historical society named by Waters was the Ipswich Historical Society, which published the first edition of *Candlewood* in 1909.

Chapter 4 William Fellows of Ipswich

[1] *Biographical Review Containing Life Sketches of Leading Citizens of Essex County, Massachusetts* 28, p. 376; Fellows, *Descendants of William Fellows of Ipswich.* The full name William Israel Fellows comes from information supplied by the Ipswich Historical Commission, Historic Ipswich. Sources generally refer to him only as William Fellows.

[2] Fellows, *William Fellows (1609-1676).*

[3] John Farmer, *A Genealogical Register of the First Settlers of New England,* Lancaster, Mass., 1829; edited and reprinted by Samuel G. Drake, Baltimore: Genealogical Publishing, 1976. Farmer placed William fellows in Ipswich in 1648; however, other scholars have since updated his research to account for William in Ipswich by 1639.

[4] Fellows, *Descendants of William Fellows of Ipswich.*

[5] Waters, *Candlewood,* p. 71.

[6] Vorst, *Benedict [Vander Vorst/Fellows]*; Hoyt, *Old Families of Salisbury and Amesbury,* 1897, p. 155; Waters, *Candlewood;* Fellows, *Descendants of William Fellows of Ipswich;* Fellows, *William Fellows (1609-1676).*

[7] Fellows, *Descendants of William Fellows of Ipswich;* Hoyt, *Old Families of Salisbury and Amesbury*, p. 155; Vorst, *Benedict [Vander Vorst/Fellows]*, citing *New England Historical and Genealogical Reg.* Vol. 3, p. 9.

[8] Fellows, *William Fellows (1609-1676).*

[9] Fellows, *Descendants of William Fellows of Ipswich*; Vorst, *Benedict [Vander Vorst/Fellows].*

[10] Anderson, et al., *The Great Migration*, p. 508, citing *Records and Files of the Quarterly Courts of Essex County, Massachusetts, 1636-1686,* 1:3361.

[11] Fellows, *William Fellows (1609-1676).*

[12] W.H. Whitmore, "The Ayres and Ayer Families," in *The New England Historical and Genealogical Society Register*, 1863,17:307-310; Vorst, *Benedict [Vander Vorst/Fellows];* Fellows, *Descendants of William Fellows of Ipswich,* LDS Pedigree Resource File, Disk 24, 669551. See also Disk 8, 403052 and Disk 27, 642539.

[13] Fellows, *William Fellows (1609-1676).*

[14] Fellows, *William Fellows (1609-1676).*

[15] Fellows, *Descendants of William Fellows of Ipswich.*

[16] Waters, *Candlewood,* p. 71.

[17] Waters, *Candlewood,* pp. 50-53. The brief history of Ipswich comes from *Massachusetts, A Guide to Its Places and People,* (Federal Writer's Project). Boston: Houghton Mifflin Company, 1937, p. 417; Fellows, *Descendants of William Fellows of Ipswich*; Fellows, *William Fellows (1609-1676)*; Vorst, *Benedict [Vander Vorst/Fellows].* The name Candlewood came from the trees of the local pine forests. Inhabitants used the clear grain and pitch to light their homes.

[18] Anderson, et al., *The Great Migration*, p. 509, citing Ipswich Land Records, 1:237, and *Records and Files of the Quarterly Courts of Essex County, Massachusetts, 1636-1686,* 7:88-89, 84-85, 87-89, 120-121, 218-221, and *Ipswich Land Records*, 4:242. After the death of William Fellows, this land became the object of a lawsuit.

[19] Waters, *Candlewood,* p. 71. In 1909, the heirs of Asa P. Stone in Argilla owned this farm.

[20] Anderson, et al., *The Great Migration*, p. 508, citing *Ipswich Land Records*, 4:75-76.

[21] Waters, *Candlewood,* p. 71; Fellows, *William Fellows (1609-1676).*

[22] Waters, *Ipswich the Massachusetts Bay Colony*, 1:335-336.

[23] Anderson, et al., *The Great Migration*, p. 507, citing *Records and Files of the Quarterly Courts of Essex County, Massachusetts, 1636-1686,* 1:210, 414, 3:182, 4:178.

[24] Vorst, *Benedict [Vander Vorst/Fellows]*; Fellows, *Descendants of William Fellows of Ipswich.*

[25] Anderson, et al., *The Great Migration*, p. 508, citing *Records and Files of the Quarterly Courts of Essex County, Massachusetts, 1636-1686,* 4:337; Fellows, *Descendants of William Fellows of Ipswich*; Vorst, *Benedict [Vander Vorst/Fellows]*; Fellows, *William Fellows (1609-1676).*

[26] Anderson, et al., *The Great Migration*, p. 508, citing *Records and Files of the Quarterly Courts of Essex County, Massachusetts, 1636-1686,* 3:436, 5:79.

[27] Waters, *Candlewood,* pp. 50-53.

[28] *Probate Records of Essex County, Massachusetts, 1635-1681,* originally published by Essex Institute, Salem, 1920, Vol. 3, pp. 128-129; Anderson, et al., *The Great Migration*, p. 509, citing *Ipswich Land Records*, 4:88 & *The Probate Records of Essex County,* 3:128-129. The Will of William Fellows did not name an executor. The court granted administration to his sons in Ipswich Court, 27 March 1677.

[29] Fellows, *William Fellows (1609-1676).*

[30] Fellows, *William Fellows (1609-1676)*; Waters, *Candlewood,* p. 71; Vorst, *Benedict [Vander Vorst/Fellows];* Fellows, *Descendants of William Fellows of Ipswich.* In addition to an introduction to his genealogy and notes, Mark Fellows posted the Will of William Fellows, published originally by the Essex Institute.

[31] Anderson, et al., *The Great Migration*, p. 508, citing Ipswich Land Records, 4:75-7; Fellows, *William Fellows (1609-1676)*; Fellows, *Descendants of William Fellows of Ipswich.* Mark Fellows claimed that William Fellows died November 19, 1676. However, this date predates his will dated November 27, 1676; Watson, *Ancestors and Descendants of John and Hannah (Goodwin) Watson of Hartford,* p. 205; Sisco, *Fellows, Fallowes, Fellow and Like Names, Fellows Ancestry in New England and Old England,* p. 12; Vorst, *Benedict [Vander Vorst/Fellows].* Comments by genealogist Vorst of Springfield, Oregon. He also posted a copy of William Fellows' will on this website; See also LDS Family Search Data Base, Batch 8424490, sheet 10, call 1395854.

[32] Anderson, et al., *The Great Migration*, p. 507, citing *Records of the Suffolk County Court, 1671-1680*, 1:3361, and *Records and Files of the Quarterly Courts of Essex County, Massachusetts, 1636-1686*, 4:77.

[33] Anderson, et al., *The Great Migration*, p. 508.

[34] Anderson, et al., *The Great Migration*, p. 509, citing *Ipswich Land Records*, 4:100, and *The Probate Records of Essex County, Massachusetts, 1635-1681,* Case #9367.

[35] Anderson, et al., *The Great Migration*, p. 509, citing *Ipswich Land Records*, 4:88, and *The Probate Records of Essex County, Massachusetts, 1635-1681,* 3:129.

[36] Anderson, et al., *The Great Migration*, p. 509, citing *Essex County, Massachusetts, Deeds*, 15:151.

[37] Anderson, et al., *The Great Migration*, p. 512.

[38] Waters, *Candlewood,* pp. 50-53.

[39] Waters, *Candlewood,* p. 71.

[40] Fellows, *William Fellows (1609-1676)*; Vorst, *Benedict [Vander Vorst/Fellows];* LDS Pedigree Resource File, Disk 24, 6695562; See also Disk 8, 403049, Disk 19, 170526, and Disk 27, 64103; boards.ancestry.com, Apr 2000.

[41] *Probate Records of Essex County* (Vol. 3, 1675-1681), originally published Salem, Mass.: Essex Institute, 1920, pp. 128-132. Estate of William Fellows of Ipswich, The last Will of William Fellows, probate November 29, 1676. "I hauing my perfit memory I commit my soull to god and my body to ye graue and bequea my earthly goods as followeth my will is yt my wif shall haue one rome in my house to her self and for her uese dewring her life yt is to say ye parler and to haue twelve pounds yearly paid her in good marchantable pay by my three Sons Ephram Samul Joseph and likewis it is my will yt my wif should haue two of my best Cowes and to be kept by my sonns winter and Somer for my wifs uese and my wif shall haue liberty to keep two swine and like wise my sons shall maintain her with conuenient fiering winter and somer as long as she lius a widow and like wise tis my will yt my wife shall haue a conueanant peice of land for a gearding and a quarter of a acker of good land yearly to sow flaxe on and it is my will yt my wif shall haue all ye houshould goods at her dispoasel tis my will yt my sonne Isack shall haue my march lote at hog Iland adid to that which I haue giuing him allredy and my will is yt my other three sonns yt is Ephram Samuel and Joseph shall haue ye other half of my farme and ye rest of my sault march with ye buildings and stock and corn upon ye farme to be posest of it after my deseas only to fullfill to thr mother what is aboue menchoned and to pay all my depts and legisis as foloweth tis my will yt my daughter mary shall haue ten pounds paid her within two yeare after my deseas and ten pounds after my wifes deseas and it is my will yt my othr three daughters Elisebeth Abegill Sary shall haue tewenty pounds a peice one half paid them two years after my deseas ore one thr day or mariag and ye othr half two years after yt and after my depts are all paid my will is yt my daughters should be maid equale with ther three brothers Ephram Samuele Joseph only fifty pounds yt my Sonne Isack is to pay after my wifs deseas shall be deuided equaly amongst my three daughters Elisebeth Abigil Sary and then to be equallised with thr brothrs aboue menshnd. /s/ Willaim Fellowes Witness: William (his X mark) Story, Senear, Thomas Burnon, Senier, Samuel Ingals, Seanir." This writing, produced in Ipswich Court 27 Mar 1676 as the will of William. Fellows, but no executor being named, administration was granted to the three sons, Ephraim, Samuell and Joseph, and they were to order the division of the estate: according to the mind of the father as expressed in this will. Inventory taken 27 Dec 1676 , by Henry Benet, William Story, Senior and Thomas Burnum, Senior. Values li.=pounds, s.=shillings, d.=pence: "his wearing Apparrell, 9li. 4s.; paire of Oxen, 12li.; Three Cowes, 10li. 10s.; five Heifers, 14li. 10s.; Two yearelings, 4li.; Three Calves, 3li. 10s.; Horse kind, 12li. 10s.; Sheep, 21li.; Swine, 5li.; Timber Chaine, Draft Chains, Carts, wheeles, hoops, boxes, Spanshackle, Plowe, Plowe Irons, Beetle, wedges, slead & sum other small things, two Axes & Muck forke, 13li. 1s. 10d.; 15 bushells of wheat, 3li. 15s.; Rie, lli. 18s.; Three scoare & ten bushells of Barly, 14li.; 4 bushells of pease, 16s.; flax, 12s.; Ten bushells of Indian corne, 2 bush. of oates, lli. 15s.; Sixty bushells of Indian Corne in ye Barne, 9li.; 38. Acres of upland at home and 26 Acres of Marsh, 250li.; all the Howsinge, 100li.; hookes & Ringes, 2s. 6d.; Cart roape, Traisses & Coller, 15s.; oard & other small things with a hamer, 6li. 11s. 6d., bridle & Saddle, lli.; Sythes with their taceling, 11s.; one piece of old Iron & 2 pr. sheepe sheers, 3s. 4d.;

one dore Lock & yoake hookes, 6s. 6d.; fowre Rod of Ground on the meting house hill where ye old house stood. A pair of Stillyards, lli. 5s.; beefe, pork, Chese, Apples & butter, 11li. 2s. 6d.; Bedd & bed Cloathes with the boulster & pillow in the Parlor Chamber, 6li. 10s.; three bedds, 12li.; flax teere, 16s.; Sheeps wooll, 5li.; one Chest, 12li. of Cotton wooll, tooe old wheeles, sacks, lli. 15s.; Sheets & one table Cloath, 9li.; other small Lening, lli. 11s.; tooe Chests, lli. 48.; one Cupbord, 2li.; one bedd in the Parlor, 10li.; Chairs & one basket, lli.; Table & Forme, 14s.; for Cushens, 4s.; warming pan, glasses & earthen potts, lli. 3s. 6d.; Tubs, keel ers, panns, pewter & tinn, 3li. 9s.; woodden ware, 4li.; Table & a meale trough, 14s.; Iron potts & Kettles, lli. 18s.; Brass Kettles & Skillets, 6li. 2s. 6d.; Tramells, Spitts, slice & other small things, 2li. 1s. 6d.; Bookes, pillion & Riding cloth, lli. 7s.; 2 Cowes, 8li.; 2 Swine, 24s.; a Lead, 30s ; hive of bees, 10s.; total, 581li, 17s. 11d. Debts due to the estate, 8li. 5s. 3d. Debts to be deducted out of the estate, 83li. 11s. Yd.; total remaining, 498li. 6s. 4d." Attested in Ipswich Court 27 Mar 1677 by the administrators. Bond of Jonathan Fellows, yeoman , with James Brown, yeoman, and Isaac Knowlton , cordwainer, all of Ipswich, as sureties, for the sum of 300li., dated 13 Feb 1722-23, for administration on estate not already administered upon belonging to his grandfather William Fellows. Witness: Robert Holmes, Daniell Appleton, Reg. "These ar The undersigned to segnefi we desire Cosen Jonathan Fellows to administer on the intestate estate of our father William Fellows." Signed Abigel (her X mark) Fellows, Sara (her + mark) Fellows. *Essex County Probate Files*, Docket 9,367. "Whereas an agreement hath been made Mar. 27, 1702, among Isaac Fellowes, Ephraim Fellowes, Ruth Fellowes widow and administratrix to the estate of her husband Joseph Fellowes, all of Ipswich , and Samuell Ayres of Newbury attorney to Samuell Fellowes of the same town, to settle and divide the real estate of their father William Fellowes formerly of Ipswich, according to his donation in his will, Ephraim, & Ruth Fellowes and Samuell Ayres do by these presents quit claim to their brother Isaac Fellowes the land as now divided and set out by these bounds following: westerly upon a stake by the river north east side upon Samuell Ayres about sixty nine rods to a stake with stones about it & then westerly fourteen Rods upon Samuell Ayres land to a stake with stones about it which is Ephraim Fellowes corner & then northeasterly by Ephraim's land Till it comes to a stake with stones about it at the common & easterly by the common & southerly by the land that was Quartermaster Kinsman and south westerly by the common with all the priviledges thereunto belonging." Signed and sealed 30 Mar 1702. Witness : Thomas Manning, William Fel lowes, Jarvas Ringe, Acknowledged 24 Jul 1702 by Ephraim Fellowes, Samuell Ayres , Ruth Fellowes. The widow Ruth Fellowes signed to all except eight acres of land conveyed to her husband per Ephraim Fellowes by a deed dated Feb. 1697. Also, signed and sealed 30 Mar 1702. Witness: Thomas Manning, William Fellowes, Jarvas Ringe. Acknowledged 24 Jul 1702 by Isaac Fellowes, Samuell Ayres, Ruth Fellowes. *Essex County Probate Records*, Vol. 308, pp. 24-26. "Administration on a common right or rights of William Fellows, late of Ipswich, which have not been already administered upon, was granted Feb. 11, 1722/23, to his grand son William Fellows (son of ___ Fellows, late of Ipswich), - having renounced their right of administration, he giving bond to administer according to law."

[42] Anderson, et al., *The Great Migration*, p. 510, citing *Records and Files of the Quarterly Courts of Essex County, Massachusetts*, 1636-1686, 4:151 & 5:312.

[43] Watson, *Ancestors and Descendants of John and Hannah (Goodwin) Watson*, p. 206; LDS International Genealogical Index, Film 184708, Ref: 13310, p. 382.

[44] Sisco, *Fellows, Fallowes, Fellow and Like Names, Fellows Ancestry in New England and Old England*, p. 21; Watson, *Ancestors and Descendants of John and Hannah (Goodwin) Watson*, p. 206.

[45] Hammatt, *The Hammatt Papers; Early Inhabitants of Ipswich, Massachusetts, 1633-1700*, p. 100.

[46] Waters, *Candlewood*, p. 71. Waters refers to Ephraim's wife as Mary. Hammatt agrees, as does Jerry Fellows, who cites "American Genealogist," *Genealogical Periodical Magazine*, No. 67, Vol 17, no. 3, Jan 1941.

[47] Fellows, *Descendants of William Fellows of Ipswich.*

[48] Vorst, *Benedict [Vander Vorst/Fellows]*; Fellows, *Descendants of William Fellows of Ipswich.*

[49] Vorst, *Benedict [Vander Vorst/Fellows]*; Fellows, *Descendants of William Fellows of Ipswich.*

[50] Vorst, *Benedict [Vander Vorst/Fellows]*; Fellows, *Descendants of William Fellows of Ipswich.*

[51] Vorst, *Benedict [Vander Vorst/Fellows]*; Fellows, *Descendants of William Fellows of Ipswich.*

[52] Vorst, *Benedict [Vander Vorst/Fellows]*; Fellows, *Descendants of William Fellows of Ipswich.*

[53] Vorst, *Benedict [Vander Vorst/Fellows]*; Fellows, *Descendants of William Fellows of Ipswich.*

[54] Waters, *Ipswich the Massachusetts Bay Colony*, 1:23.

[55] Hammatt, *The Hammatt Papers*, p. 100; Sisco, *Fellows, Fallowes, Fellow and Like Names, Fellows Ancestry*, p. 21. Sisco confirmed the death of Mary, but for her death year only; Vorst, *Benedict [Vander Vorst/Fellows]*; Fellows, *Descendants of William Fellows of Ipswich*. Fellows included extensive notes and sources in his genealogy of Ephraim Fellows.

[56] Vorst, *Benedict [Vander Vorst/Fellows]*; Fellows, *Descendants of William Fellows of Ipswich.*

[57] Vorst, *Benedict [Vander Vorst/Fellows]*; Fellows, *Descendants of William Fellows of Ipswich.*

[58] Waters, *Ipswich the Massachusetts Bay Colony*, 1:335-336.

[59] Vorst, *Benedict [Vander Vorst/Fellows]*; Fellows, *Descendants of William Fellows of Ipswich.*

[60] Vorst, *Benedict [Vander Vorst/Fellows]*; Fellows, *Descendants of William Fellows of Ipswich.*

[61] *The Records and Files of the Quarterly Courts of Essex County, Massachusetts*, Vol. 6, p 425.

[62] *The Records and Files of the Quarterly Courts of Essex County, Massachusetts*, Vol. 6, p 425.

[63] Fellows, *Descendants of William Fellows of Ipswich.* Mark Fellows gives a conflicting date of the marriage of Ephraim and Anna as 30 Dec 1690. However, this cannot be accurate if their first child was born in 1685, as claimed by multiple sources. He also listed only three children by her, instead of five: namely, Ephraim, Elizabeth, and Anna.

[64] Torrey, *New England Marriages Prior to 1700.* References to Anna Cross as the wife of Ephraim Fellows also appear in Hammatt, p. 40, and Waters p. 72.

[65] Anderson, et al., *The Great Migration*, p. 510,

[66] Anderson, et al., *The Great Migration*, p. 510, citing *Records and Files of the Quarterly Courts of Essex County, Massachusetts, 1636-1686*, 9:172.

[67] Vorst, *Benedict [Vander Vorst/Fellows].*

[68] Vorst, *Benedict [Vander Vorst/Fellows];* Fellows, *Descendants of William Fellows of Ipswich.*

[69] *Biographical Review Containing Life Sketches of Leading Citizens of Essex County, Massachusetts* 28; Torrey, *New England Marriages Prior to 1700*, p. 261; Hoyt, *Old Families of Salisbury and Amesbury*, Vol. 1, p. 155.

[70] Vorst, *Benedict [Vander Vorst/Fellows];* Fellows, *Descendants of William Fellows of Ipswich.*

[71] Vorst, *Benedict [Vander Vorst/Fellows];* Fellows, *Descendants of William Fellows of Ipswich.*

[72] Torrey, *New England Marriages Prior to 1700.*

[73] *Mass. and Maine Families in the Ancestry of Walter Goodwin Davis.*

[74] Fellows, *Descendants of William Fellows of Ipswich.*

[75] Fellows, *Descendants of William Fellows of Ipswich.* Amye and Mary Fellows are questionable as children of Ephraim Fellows and Anna Cross.

[76] Fellows, *Descendants of William Fellows of Ipswich.*

[77] Anderson, et al., *The Great Migration*, p. 510.

[78] Waters, *Ipswich the Massachusetts Bay Colony*, 1:335-336.

[79] Fellows, *Descendants of William Fellows of Ipswich.*

[80] Fellows, *Descendants of William Fellows of Ipswich;* LDS International Genealogical Index, Film 184708, Ref: 13311, p. 382; LDS Ancestral File, 3VRT-83.

[81] Waters, *Candlewood*, pp. 39-40.

[82] Anderson, et al., *The Great Migration*, p. 509, citing *Essex County, Massachusetts, Deeds*, 15:151.

[83] *Biographical Review Containing Life Sketches of Leading Citizens of Essex County, Massachusetts;* Hoyt, *Old Families of Salisbury and Amesbury,* Vol. 1, p. 156; Myrtle M. Morris, *Joseph and Philena (Elton) Fellows,* p. 39; Mable Fellows Murphy, *The Fellows Family in America.*

[84] Anderson, et al., *The Great Migration,* p. 510, citing *The Probate Records of Essex County, Massachusetts,* 1635-1681, 311:58-59.

[85] Anderson, et al., *The Great Migration,* p. 510, citing *Essex County, Massachusetts, Deeds,* 311:581.

[86] David Pane-Joyce, *Massachusetts Bay Colony, Genealogy.* This is an extensive genealogy, covering many of the immigrant families in the Massachusetts Bay area.

[87] Anderson, et al., *The Great Migration,* p. 510; Myrtle M. Morris, *Joseph and Philena (Elton) Fellows,* p. 42. A conflicting source claimed that Josiah Browne was born in Malford, Worcestershire, England, the son of Thomas Browne.

[88] David Pane-Joyce, *Massachusetts Bay Colony, Genealogy.*

[89] LDS International Genealogical Index, Film 184708, Ref: 13313, p. 382; Torrey, *New England Marriages Prior to 1700,* p. 108; Thomas Baldwin, *Vital Records, Reading, Middlesex Co., Massachusetts to the Year 1850,* Boston, 1912, p. 296, Compact Disk, Search and ReSearch Publishing Corporation, Wheat Ridge, Colorado, 1998.

[90] Fellows, *Descendants of William Fellows of Ipswich.* Sources cited by Mark Fellows show a marriage date for Mary Fellows and Josiah Browne of 23 Feb 1665/66 in Reading, Middlesex County, Massachusetts. Other sources cite a date of 23 Nov 1667.

[91] Sisco, citing Fellows, *Descendants of William Fellows of Ipswich.*

[92] Fellows, *Descendants of William Fellows of Ipswich.* Mark Fellows has Josiah Brown born in Reading, Middlesex County, Massachusetts. He died in 1691.

[93] Vorst, *Benedict [Vander Vorst/Fellows].*

[94] Fellows, *Descendants of William Fellows of Ipswich.*

[95] Fellows, *Descendants of William Fellows of Ipswich.*

[96] Anderson, et al., *The Great Migration,* p. 510; LDS Ancestral File 3JVN-11; LDS International Genealogical Index Film 184708, Ref: 13312, p. 382; Waters, *Candlewood,* p. 73. Waters claimed Joseph Fellows died before 1693. Mark Fellows cites several sources in his genealogy of William Fellows. Note. Jerry Fellows shows Joseph's death as 7 Nov 1693, Ipswich, Mass.

[97] Waters, *Ipswich in the Massachusetts Bay Colony,* 2:259.

[98] Waters, *Candlewood,* p. 73; Fellows, *Descendants of William Fellows of Ipswich.* Mark Fellows recorded the marriage of Joseph and Ruth as 19 Aug 1676.

[99] Fellows, *Descendants of William Fellows of Ipswich.*

[100] *Biographical Review Containing Life Sketches of Leading Citizens of Essex County, Massachusetts*, Vol. 28, p. 376; The Essex Institute, *Vital Records, Ipswich, Essex Co., Massachusetts to the End of the Year 1849*, (Vol. 2), p. 161; Waters, *Candlewood*, p. 73.

[101] Fellows, *Descendants of William Fellows of Ipswich.*

[102] George Madison Bodge, *Soldiers in King Philip's War*, (3rd ed. reprint). Baltimore: Genealogical Publishing, [1891, 1906].

[103] Waters, *Candlewood*, p. 73.

[104] Fellows, *Descendants of William Fellows of Ipswich.*

[105] Waters, *Candlewood*, p. 73.

[106] Fellows, *Descendants of William Fellows of Ipswich.*

[107] Waters, *Ipswich the Massachusetts Bay Colony*, 1:335-336.

[108] *Biographical Review Containing Life Sketches of Leading Citizens of Essex County, Massachusetts* 28; Fellows, *Descendants of William Fellows of Ipswich.* Records refer to the son of Joseph and Ruth as William the "Mariner."

[109] Bodge, *Soldiers in King Philip's War;* Fellows, *Descendants of William Fellows of Ipswich.*

[110] Anderson, et al., *The Great Migration*, p. 510. Some claim an alternate birthdate of 14 Jul 1644 in Ipswich, Essex County, Massachusetts,

[111]. LDS International Genealogical Index, Film 184708, Ref: 13314, p. 382.

[112] Fellows, *Descendants of William Fellows of Ipswich.*

[113] Anderson, et al., *The Great Migration*, p. 509, citing *Ipswich Land Records*, 4:88, and *The Probate Records of Essex County, Massachusetts, 1635-1681,* 3:128-129; Vorst, *Benedict [Vander Vorst/Fellows]*; Anderson, et al., *The Great Migration*, p. 510.

[114] Anderson, et al., *The Great Migration*, p. 509, citing *Essex County, Massachusetts, Deeds*, 15:151.

[115] Fellows, *Descendants of William Fellows of Ipswich.*

[116] Anderson, et al., *The Great Migration*, p. 511; Fellows, *Descendants of William Fellows of Ipswich*; LDS Ancestral File 4DL8-KT; LDS International Genealogical Index, Film 184708, Ref: 13315, p. 382.

[117] "American Genealogist," *Genealogical Periodical Magazine*, Vol. 17, Jan 1941.

[118] Fellows, *Descendants of William Fellows of Ipswich*; George Brainard Lodgette, *Early Settlers of Rowley, Massachusetts,* Rowley, Mass.: n. p., 1933, citing *Essex Probate Records and Essex Deeds.*

[119] Vorst, *Benedict [Vander Vorst/Fellows].*

[120] Fellows, *Descendants of William Fellows of Ipswich.*

[121] William Henry Whitmore, *Descendants of Capt. John Ayers of Brookfield, Massachusetts.* Boston: T.R. Marvin & Son, 1870. pp. 12-13; Lodgette, *Early Settlers of Rowley,*

Massachusetts, p. 5; The Essex Institute, *Vital Records, Ipswich, Essex Co., Massachusetts to the End of the Year 1849, Vol. II, 1634-1892*, p. 33, cited by David Fellows in *Descendants of William Fellows*;. Waters, *Candlewood,* p. 72.

[122] Lodgette, *Early Settlers of Rowley, Massachusetts*, citing *Essex Probate Records* and *Essex Deeds* 18:35.

[123] Fellows, *Descendants of William Fellows of Ipswich,* citing The *Hammett Papers* and other sources on Samuel Ayres.

[124] Lodgette, *Early Settlers of Rowley, Massachusetts*, citing *Essex Probate Records and Essex Deeds.*

[125] Anderson, et al., *The Great Migration*, p. 509, citing *Essex County, Massachusetts, Deeds*, 3:130.

[126] LDS International Genealogical Index Film 184708, Ref: 13316, p. 382; LDS Ancestral File 1G0Q-SFT.

[127] Fellows, *Descendants of William Fellows of Ipswich.*

[128] Fellows, *Descendants of William Fellows of Ipswich.*

[129] Torrey, *New England Marriages Prior to 1700*, p. 596. "married about 1661."

[130] Vorst, *Benedict [Vander Vorst/Fellows]*; Anderson, et al., *The Great Migration*, p. 511, citing *The Probate Records of Essex County, Massachusetts*, 1635-1681.

[131] "American Genealogist", *Genealogical Periodical Magazine*, p. 22; Sisco, *Fellows, Fallowes, Fellow and Like Names.*

[132] Anderson, et al., *The Great Migration*, p. 511, citing Cooke, *The Driver Family*, p. 382, citing *Essex County, Massachusetts, Deeds* (microfilm copies), 14:103.

[133] Anderson, et al., *The Great Migration*, p. 509, citing *Essex County, Massachusetts, Deeds*, 3:130.

[134] Vorst, *Benedict [Vander Vorst/Fellows]*; Anderson, et al., *The Great Migration*, p. 511, citing *The Probate Records of Essex County, Massachusetts*, 1635-1681.

[135] Fellows, *Descendants of William Fellows of Ipswich.*

Chapter 5 Isaac Fellows and King Philip's War

[1] Waters, *Candlewood*, pp. 50-53.

[2] The Essex Institute, *Vital Records, Ipswich, Essex Co., Massachusetts to the End of the Year 1849,* (Vol. 2), Salem, Massachusetts, 1910, p. 553; Compact Disk, Search and ReSearch Publishing Corporation, Wheat Ridge, Colorado, 1998; Torrey, *New England Marriages Prior to 1700,* Baltimore: Genealogical Publishing, 1997, p. 261. Both Essex Institute and Torrey characterized the date of birth of Isaac Fellows as "bef. 1637."

[3] LDS Ancestral File, Film 184708, Ref 13309, p. 382, and Film 458388; *Biographical Review Containing Life Sketches of Leading Citizens of Essex County, Massachusetts,* Boston,

1898, p, 376. They [William and Mary Fellows] had eight children, the eldest of whom, a son, Isaac, some believe, was born in England.

[4] LDS Pedigree Resource File, Disk 24, 669550.

[5] Waters, *Candlewood,* p. 71. In 1909, the heirs of Asa P. Stone in Argilla owned this farm.

[6] Hammatt, *The Hammatt Papers,* pp. 100-101, cited by Mark D. Fellows; Fellows, *Fellows Families of Onondaga County, New York and Their Ancestry,* published by the author, 1991, p. 79, cited by Mark D. Fellows; LDS Pedigree Resource File, Disk 24, 669551; The Essex Institute, *Vital Records, Ipswich, Essex Co., Massachusetts* p. 160.

[7] Waters, *Candlewood,* p. 72; Baker, *History of Montville, Connecticut,* p. 346. Baker claimed that Isaac, son of William Fellowes, married Joanna Brown [*sic*], 29 Jan 1672. See also Hoyt, *Old Families of Salisbury and Amesbury, Massachusetts,* Providence, Rhode Island, 1897, p. 155; *Biographical Review Containing Life Sketches of Leading Citizens of Essex County, Massachusetts,* 28, p. 376; *American Genealogist, Genealogical Periodical Magazine,* Vol. 27 (Jan 1941); *Vital Records, Ipswich, Massachusetts, 1634-1892,* p. 160. Both the *American Genealogist* and *Vial Records* listed the wife of Isaac Fellows as Joanna Bourne.

[8] Anderson, et al., *The Great Migration,* p. 510, citing *Early Hartford Vital Records,* 2:50, 160.

[9] Anderson, et al., *The Great Migration,* p. 510; LDS Ancestral File 35KM-V9.

[10] Hammatt, cited by Fellows, *Descendants of William Fellows of Ipswich.*

[11] Anderson, et al., *The Great Migration,* p. 510, citing *The Probate Records of Essex County, Massachusetts, 1635-1681,* 3:350; Vorst, *Benedict [Vander Vorst/Fellows];* Fellows, *Descendants of William Fellows of Ipswich.*

[12] Charles Hudson, *History of the Town of Marlborough,* Boston, 1862, p. 80.

[13] Albert Bushnell Hart, ed., *American History Told by Contemporaries* (Vol. 1), New York, 1898, pp. 458-60.

[14] Fellows, *Descendants of William Fellows of Ipswich*; Vorst, *Benedict [Vander Vorst/Fellows].*

[15] Henry William Elson, "Colonial New England Affairs: King Philip's War," *History of the United States of America.* New York: MacMillan, 1904; Robert E. Cray, Jr, "Weltering in Their Own Blood:" *Puritan Casualties in King Philip's War,* 2009.

[16] Bodge, *Soldiers in King Philip's War,* pp. 406, 414. "Narragansett Township No. 1, now the Town of Buxton, Maine. Soldier Grantee: Fellows, Isaac. Claimant: Jonathan Fellows, son. Soldier Grantee: Fellows, Joseph. Claimant: Joseph Fellows, son."

[17] Bodge, *Soldiers in King Philip's War,* (3rd ed.). Boston, [1891] 1906; reprinted Baltimore: Genealogical Publishing, 1976, pp. 73, 126 & 367. This lengthy volume includes an introductory overview of King Philip's War as well as muster rolls of soldiers under various officers' commands.

[18] Waters, *Ipswich the Massachusetts Bay Colony,* 1:220.

[19] Bodge, *Soldiers in King Philip's War*, pp. 406, 414.

[20] Fellows, *Descendants of William Fellows of Ipswich*; Vorst, *Benedict [Vander Vorst/Fellows]*.

[21] Burnham, *Birthplace of American Independence*, 440-452.

[22] Waters, *Candlewood*, pp. 50-53, 71. This book contains valuable information about William Fellows of Ipswich and some of his descendants, particularly in tracing early real estate transactions. However, the author does, not trace grandson Ephraim Fellows. Ephraim Fellows was the line of descendency to William Ira Fellows and the Missouri branch of the family.

[23] Waters, *Ipswich the Massachusetts Bay Colony*, 1:101. A tabulation of the male inhabitants of Ipswich in 1678 listed Isaac, Ephraim, Samuel, and Joseph Fellows.

[24] Waters, *Ipswich in the Massachusetts Bay Colony*, 2:739.

[25] Waters, *Candlewood*, p. 71-72.

[26] Waters, *Ipswich in the Massachusetts Bay Colony*, 2:713, 721.

[27] Waters, *Ipswich in the Massachusetts Bay Colony*, 2:6-9.

[28] Hammatt, *The Hammatt Papers*, 1880-1899, pp. 100-101, cited by Mark D. Fellows; Waters, *Candlewood*, pp. 71-72; *Vital Records, Ipswich, Massachusetts, 1634-1892*. "Joanna Boreman Fellows died Mar 20, 1731/32."

[29] Find A Grave 157776422 "Corp. Isaac Fellows, Sr." and Find a Grave 157776253 "Joanna Boreman Fellows."

[30] Fellows, *Descendants of William Fellows of Ipswich.*

[31] Fellows, *Descendants of William Fellows of Ipswich.*

[32] Vorst, *Benedict [Vander Vorst/Fellows]*. Vorst presents a well-documented genealogy site with over 135 sources, many of them pertaining to the Fellows lineage.

[33] Fellows, *Descendants of William Fellows of Ipswich*, citing *Massachusetts Soldiers and Sailors in the Revolutionary War* (Vol. 14), p. 476. Fellows included a copy of the will of Jonathan Fellows.

[34] Hoyt, *Old Families of Salisbury and Amesbury*, p. 155. "Isaac-2 b. abt. 1637; m. Jan. 29 1672 (Ipswich), Joanna (Bourne?) (Boardman?); residence Ipswich; served in King Philip's war, Aug. 1676; d. Apr 6. 1721. 6 children of whom Ephraim presented, May 3, 1708, prob. the Sam Fellows of Hampton who m. Nov. 15, 1698, Deborah Sanborn and had several children, the youngest, Sam. b. Oct 1707 was son of Isaac-2. Jonathan Fellows of Ipswich appointed guardian of Sam. Fellows, age 15, son of Sam. Fellows, late of hm. "saddler," June 14, 1723; inv. est. bro. Isaac-3, Jr. b. Nov. 27, 1673 (Ipswich);" See also Waters, *Candlewood*, p. 71-72; *Family Bible of Isaac Fellows 1637-1721, New England Historical Genealogical Register*, No. 127, p. 127. The Family Bible lists a number of vital statistics for the descendants of Isaac Fellows. Mark D. Fellows cites entries from 1764-1826, indicating that descendants continued to keep records in the Isaac Fellows Bible.

[35] Fellows, *Descendants of William Fellows of Ipswich*, citing Waters and Erwin Wilcox Fellows, *Fellows Families of Onondaga County, New York and Their Ancestry*. Zephyrhills, Fla.: Author, 1984, 1991.

[36] Fellows, *Descendants of William Fellows of Ipswich*, citing Waters, Dick Pence, and Audrey Kinezian.

[37] Fellows, *Descendants of William Fellows of Ipswich*.

[38] Fellows, *Descendants of William Fellows of Ipswich*, citing Audrey Kinezian.

[39] Fellows, *Descendants of William Fellows of Ipswich*.

[40] Fellows, *Descendants of William Fellows of Ipswich*, citing Waters, *Candlewood*.

[41] Fellows, *Descendants of William Fellows of Ipswich*, citing Erwin W. Fellows.

[42] Fellows, *Descendants of William Fellows of Ipswich*, citing Erwin W. Fellows.

[43] Fellows, *Descendants of William Fellows of Ipswich*, citing *Massachusetts Soldiers and Sailors in the Revolutionary War* (Vol. 14), p. 476.

[44] Fellows, *Descendants of William Fellows of Ipswich*.

[45] Fellows, *Descendants of William Fellows of Ipswich*.

[46] Fellows, *Descendants of William Fellows of Ipswich*.

[47] Fellows, *Descendants of William Fellows of Ipswich*.

[48] Fellows, *Descendants of William Fellows of Ipswich*.

[49] Fellows, *Descendants of William Fellows of Ipswich*, citing *Massachusetts Soldiers and Sailors in the Revolutionary War* (Vol. 14), p. 476.

[50] Fellows, *Descendants of William Fellows of Ipswich*.

Chapter 6 Ephraim Fellows

[1] *Vital Records, Ipswich, Massachusetts, 1634-1892*, p. 135, cited by Mark D. Fellows; LDS International Genealogical Index, Film 456288. LDS erroneously gave Ephraim's date of birth as 3 Feb 1679.

[2] Baker, *History of Montville, Connecticut*, p. 346. "Ephraim b. 3 Sept [*sic*] 1679, son of Isaac Fellowes and Joanna Brown [*sic*]; married Hannah Warner, 18 [*sic*] May 1703." Baker transcribed the surname of Joanna Boreman as Brown.

[3] *Vital Records, Stonington, New London County, Connecticut* , transcribed by Coralynn Brown, from Barbour Collection, 1668-1852 (Vol. 2), pp. 6, 93.

[4] Find A Grave 157776866.

[5] Hammatt, *The Hammatt Papers; Early Inhabitants of Ipswich, Massachusetts, 1633-1700*, p. 101, 398, cited in Mark D. Fellows; Waters, *Candlewood*, pp. 50-53, 71-73.

[6] Fellows, *Family Chronicles; Fellows Family Saga*, unpublished genealogy, 1996.

[7] Hoyt, *Old Families of Salisbury and Amesbury*, p. 341; LDS Pedigree Resource File, Disk 24, 669549; LDS International Genealogical Index, Film 178089, pp. 211, 219-237; LDS

International Genealogical Index, Film 0178100, Ref: 33041, p. 949; LDS Ancestral File ZDFN-ZW.

[8] Find A Grave 157781557.

[9] Baker, *History of Montville, Connecticut,* p. 346; Fellows, *Descendants of William Fellows of Ipswich.*

[10] Wheeler, *History of the Town of Stonington,* 3.

[11] Wheeler, *History of the Town of Stonington,* 11.

[12] Wheeler, *History of the Town of Stonington,* 13.

[13] Wheeler, *History of the Town of Stonington,* 17.

[14] Ellen D. Larned, *History of Windham County, Connecticut,* Westminister, Md.: Heritage Books, 2008, p. 182.

[15] Waters, *Candlewood,* p. 72.

[16] Richard Anson Wheeler. *History of the First Congregational Church, Stonington, Conn., 1674-1874.* Salem, Mass.: Higginson Book, 1997, p 228.

[17] Wheeler, *History of the First Congregational Church,* 64-65.

[18] Frederic W. Bailey, *Early Connecticut Marriages as Found on Ancient Church Records Prior to 1800* (7 vols.), New Haven, Conn.: Bureau of American Ancestry, 1896-1906.

[19] *Vital Records, Stonington, New London County, Connecticut,* transcribed by Coralynn Brown, from Barbour Collection, 1668-1852 (Vol. 2), pp. 6, 93.

[20] Fellows, *Descendants of William Fellows of Ipswich.*

[21] Fellows, *Descendants of William Fellows of Ipswich.*

[22] Ephraim Fellows Probate Records, Case 1985, *Wills and Probate Records, 1609-1999,* Connecticut State Library, Hartford, Connecticut.

[23] Charles J. Hoardly, *Public Records of the Colony of Connecticut,* Hartford, Conn.: Lockwood & Brainard, 1868, p. 156.

[24] Homer de Lois Sweet, *The Averys of Groton,* Syracuse, N.Y.: n. d., 1888, p. 407.

[25] Find A Grave 157781557; Wheeler, *History of the Town of Stonington, Connecticut,* Baltimore: Genealogical Publishing, 1977, p. 367, cited by Mark D. Fellows.

[26] Baker, *History of Montville, Connecticut,* p. 346. Baker claimed that Ephraim, Jr. was born in Ipswich and not Stonington.

[27] Find A Grave 157776866.

[28] Find A Grave 157781557.

[29] Find A Grave 157781557.

[30] LDS International Genealogical Index, Film 456288,

[25.] Waters, *Candlewood,* p. 73.

[31] Waters, *Candlewood,* p. 73.

[32] Wheeler, *History of the First Congregational Church,* p. 232.

[33] Fellows, *Descendants of William Fellows of Ipswich*, citing *Candlewood,* p. 73.

[34] Wheeler, *History of the First Congregational Church.*

[35] Fellows, *Descendants of William Fellows of Ipswich.*

[36] LDS International Genealogical Index. Film 456288,

[37] Find A Grave 20784507; Cemetery, Great Plain Cemetery, copied by Charles R. Hale, 1932. Located northwest of Town Hall 3/4 miles. Ephraim Fellows, died 28 Apr 1786, age 75.

[38] Wheeler, *History of the Town of Stonington*, p. 368; *Vital Records, Stonington, New London County, Connecticut.* "Ephraim, m. Prudence Plumbe, May 13, 1731, by Rev. Ebenezer Russell. Witnesses: Samuel Holdredge & Sarah Fellows." Sarah Fellows was Ephraim's sister. She would marry Samuel Holdredge in Sept. of the same year (1731).

[39] Cemetery, Great Plain Cemetery. "Prudence Fellows, wife of Ephraim Fellows, died June 11, 1796, age 86."

[40] Find A Grave 20784518.

[41] Wheeler, *History of the First Congregational Church, Stonington, Connecticut.*

[42] Fellows, *Descendants of William Fellows of Ipswich.*

[43] Find A Grave 20784512.

[44] Bailey, *Early Connecticut Marriages,* 60.

[45] Wheeler, *History of the Town of Stonington,* 77.

[46] Bailey, *Early Connecticut Marriages,* 60.

[47] Bailey, *Early Connecticut Marriages,* 62.

[48] Fellows, *Descendants of William Fellows of Ipswich.*

[49] LDS International Genealogical Index, Film 456288,

[50] Richard Wheeler, *History of the First Congregational Church, Stonington,* p. 209. "Sarah Fellows, daughter of Ephraim Fellows. Baptized 19 Mar 1711 by Rev. James Noyes."

[51] *Vital Records, Stonington, New London County, Connecticut,* (Vols. 1 & 3), pp. 31, 93, 96, 128. "Samuel, m. Sarah Fellows, Sept. 23, 1731, by Rev. Ebenezer Rosseter; Sarah, dau. Ephraim b. Jan 3, 1710/11."

[52] Wheeler, *History of the First Congregational Church, Stonington.* "Samuel Holdredge & Sarah Fellows. Married 23 Sep 1731 by Rev. Ebenezer Rosseter." Other sources record that the marriage was by Rev. James Noyes.

[53] *Vital Records, Stonington, New London County, Connecticut,* Vols. 3 & 4, Book C, p. 13. "Samuel married Sarah Fellows, daughter of Ephraim Fellows and Hannah Warner, on 23 Sep 1731 in Stonington, New London Co., Connecticut, by Rev. Ebenezer Rossiter. Sarah was born 3 Jan 1710/1711 in Stonington, New London Co., Connecticut, and was christened 19 Mar 1711 in 1st Church of Stonington, Stonington, New London Co., Connecticut. She died 17 May 1803 in Stonington, New London Co., Connecticut."

[54] Fellows, *Descendants of William Fellows of Ipswich.*

[55] Wheeler, *History of the First Congregational Church,* 210.

[56] Bailey, *Early Connecticut Marriages,* 53.

[57] *Vital Records, Stonington, New London County, Connecticut.* "Isaac, son Ephraim b. Feb 19, 1719;" Wheeler, *History of the First Congregational Church, Stonington.* "Isaac Fellows, son of Ephraim Fellows. Baptized 16 Aug 1719 by Rev. James Noye."

[58] LDS International Genealogical Index, Film 456288; Wheeler, *History of the First Congregational Church, Stonington,* 214. "Isaac Fellows - parents: [mother not given] & Ephraim Fellows - bapt. 16 Aug 1719 - by Rev. James Noyes."

[59] Fellows, *Descendants of William Fellows of Ipswich.*

[60] Fellows, *Descendants of William Fellows of Ipswich.*

[61] LDS International Genealogical Index, Film 456288; *Vital Records, Stonington, New London County, Connecticut.* "John, son Ephraim b. Oct 8, 1722; died Apr 22 (year unspecified);" Fellows, *Descendants of William Fellows of Ipswich.* Fellows claimed that John Fellows died young at one year of age.

[62] *Vital Records, Stonington, New London County, Connecticut.* "Joanna, dau. Ephraim b. Apr 4, 1724."

[63] LDS International Genealogical Index, Film 456288; Wheeler, *History of the First Congregational Church, Stonington,* p. 217.

[64] Wheeler, *History of the First Congregational Church, Stonington,* p. 252. "William Brown & Joanna Fellows. Married 2 Jul 1742 by Rev. Nathaniel Eells."

[65] Fellows, *Descendants of William Fellows of Ipswich.* The birthdate given by Fellows for Euphrasia was likely in error, since the birth year is the same as her brother, Isaac, unless they were twins.

[66] LDS International Genealogical Index, Film 456288; *Vital Records, Stonington, New London County, Connecticut.* "Mary, dau. Ephraim b. Aug 16, 1726; died Sept 16, (year unspecified);" Fellows, *Descendants of William Fellows of Ipswich.* Mark D. Fellows said she died in infancy.

Chapter 7 Deacon Nathaniel Fellows

[1] Wheeler, *History of the First Congregational Church,* 210; Frederick Martner, *The Refugees of 1776 from Long Island to Connecticut,* Albany, N. Y.: J.B. Lyon, 1913. Nathaniel Fellows was born 22 Jun 1713 in Stonington, New London County, Connecticut; *Vital Records, Stonington, New London County, Connecticut.* "Nathan, son Ephraim b. June 22, 1714;" LDS Ancestral File 1K3S-DRM, 1987; LDS International Genealogical Index, Film 456288.

[2] Wheeler, *History of the First Congregational Church, Stonington, Connecticut 1674-1874,* Norwich, 1875. The Congregational Church organized in 1727, being then the second church of Stonington. Records complete to 1781. "Nathaniel Fellows-parents [mother not given] &

Ephraim Fellows-bapt. 6 Sep 1713 by Rev. James Noyes;" *Vital Records, Stonington, New London County, Connecticut.* "Nathan, son Ephraim b. June 22, 1714," Church records show Nathaniel baptized in 1713.

[3] Connecticut Church Record Abstracts, 1630-1920 Index, pp. 161, 162, Vol. 3 p. 118; Wheeler, *History of the First Congregational Church,* 221.

[4] Connecticut Church Record Abstracts, 1630-1920 Index, pp. 161, 162, Vol. 2 p. 7; Wheeler, *History of the First Congregational Church,* 230.

[5] Martner, *Refugees from 1776 from Long Island to Connecticut.* Martner gives marriage of Nathaniel Fellows and Hopestill Holdredge as 2 Mar 1736/37; Fellows, *Fellows Families of Onondaga County.* Nathaniel Fellows died 25 Aug 1800 in Stonington, New London County, Connecticut. Hopestill Holdredge was the daughter of William Holdredge and Deborah Elliott. She was born 18 Feb 1719/20 in Stonington, New London County, Connecticut, and died 3 Jul 1765 in Stonington; *Vital Records, Stonington, New London County, Connecticut,* Barbour Col. p. 128, Vol. 2 p. 18, also p. 93, Vol. 3, p. 172. "Hopestill, wife Nathaniel, died July 3, 1765."

[6] *Vital Records, Stonington, New London County, Connecticut,* citing Barbour Collection, 1668-1852, p. 128, Vol. 3, p. 57. "Hopestill, m. Nathaniel Fellows, 2 Mar 1736/37 by Rev. Joseph Fish;" see also Disk 31, pin 797645; Disk 32 pin 329404; Disk 14, pin 39554, and 587210; Disk 44, 429090; Disk 38, pin 897385; Disk 19, pin 147925; *Early Connecticut Marriages, 1733-1781.* Also recorded in *The Congregational Church, North Stonington,* New London County, Connecticut.

[7] *Vital Records, Stonington, New London County, Connecticut,* from Barbour Collection, 1668-1852, p. 128, Vol. 3, p. 57.

[8] Frederick W. Bailey, *Early Connecticut Marriages as found on Ancient Church Records Prior to 1800,* New Haven, [in 7 volumes, 1896-1906], First Book, p. 53; see also Vol. 2, p. 7, *First Church,* New London, New London County, Connecticut. "Nathaniel Fellows & Hopestill Holdridge [*sic*], March 2, 1737," North Stonington, New Haven Second Church; *Vital Records, Stonington, New London County, Connecticut,* p. 128, Vol. 3, pp. 18, 93, 172. "Hopestill, dau. William b. Feb. 18, 1719/20" and "Hopestil[l], wid. Nath[anie]l, d. July 3, 1765."

[9] Wheeler, *History of the First Congregational Church,* 281.

[10] Wheeler, *Homes of Our Ancestors in Stonington,* 271.

[11] Wheeler, *Homes of Our Ancestors in Stonington,* 161-162.

[12] *Vital Records, Stonington, New London County, Connecticut,* p. 128, Vol. 3, pp. 18, 93, 172.

[13] Find A Grave 65268851. "Thomas Miner."

[14] Wheeler, *History of the Town of Stonington,* 138.

[15] Wheeler, *Homes of Our Ancestors in Stonington,* 160-161.

[16] Wheeler, *History of the Town of Stonington,* 138.

[17] Anna Chesebrough Wildey, *Genealogy of the Descendants of William Chesebrough,* New York: Press of T.A. Wright, 1903, pp. 540-541, dated 14 Oct 1776, recorded in the Capitol Building, Hartford, Connecticut. See *Revolutionary War*, 4, Document 400 and Hurd's *History of New London County*, p. 629.

[18] Hurd, *History of New London County,* 629.

[19] Wheeler, *History of the Town of Stonington*, 46.

[20] Daughters of the American Revolution, *Lineage Book,* 243.

[21] Wheeler, *History of the Town of Stonington*, 37.

[22] *Collections of the Connecticut Historical Society,* 137.

[23] *Connecticut Wills and Probate Records, 1609-1999,* Connecticut State Library, Hartford, Connecticut, Case 1266.

[24] *Connecticut Church Record Abstracts*, 1630-1920 Index, pp. 161, 162, Vol. 4 p. 87.

[25] Wheeler, *Homes of Our Ancestors in Stonington*, 106; Fellows, *Descendants of William Fellows of Ipswich.*

[26] 1790 US Census, Unidentified Town, New London, Connecticut M637 Roll 1, pp. 116, 117, 118 & 128, National Archives and Records Administration. See also p. 48, Image 38; Family History Library Film 0568141. Enumeration for Nath'l Fellows: age 16 and over 1, females 2.

[27] *Connecticut Church Record Abstracts*, 1630-1920 Index, pp. 161, 162, Vol. 4 p. 87; Fellows, *Fellows Families of Onondaga County.*

[28] 1800 US Census, New London, New London County, Connecticut; Series M32 Roll 3, p. 627, Image 176; Family History Library Film 205620. "Sarah Watson."

[29] Find A Grave 65268580. "Sarah Watson Fellows."

[30] Fellows, *Descendants of William Fellows of Ipswich*; Wheeler, *History of the First Congregational Church, Stonington, Connecticut, 1674-1874.* Information found in Wheeler's *Stonington*, pp. 367-368. "Hopestill Holdredge born 18 Feb 1719/20, Stonington, New London Co., Conn., married 2 Mar 1737, Nathaniel Fellows, Fellows children: [partial list] Nathaniel, 1734; Warner, 1741; William, 1743; Lydia, 1747; Hopestill, 1737; Mercy, 1749; Elnathan, 1754."

[31] *Vital Records, Stonington, New London County, Connecticut.* "Hopestill, wife Nathaniel, died 3 July 1765."

[32] Fellows, *Fellows Families of Onondaga County,* p. 82. Erwin Wilcox confirms the marriage of Nathaniel Fellows to Sarah Watson, his first wife.

[33] Fellows, *Descendants of William Fellows of Ipswich.*

[34] Jerry Fellows, *Family Chronicles; Fellows Family Saga,* unpublished genealogy, 1996, cited by Mark D. Fellows. Jerry Fellows states that Sarah Watson died 17 May 1803 in Stonington, Connecticut.

[35] Fellows, *Descendants of William Fellows of Ipswich.* Mark D. Fellows noted that Deborah died in infancy.

[36] *Vital Records, Stonington, New London County, Connecticut,* Barbour Collection p. 93, Vol 3, p. 172. "Deborah, dau. Nathaniel b. 4 Apr 1738, d. 11 Apr 1738."

[37] Wheeler, *History of the First Congregational Church, Stonington, Connecticut, 1674-1874.* "Nathaniel Fellows - parents: [mother not given] & Nathaniel Fellows - bapt. 25 Mar 1739 - by Rev. Ebenezer Rosseter;" *Vital Records, Stonington, New London County, Connecticut.* "Nathaniel, son Nathaniel b. 4 Feb 1738/39."

[38] *Connecticut Church Record Abstracts, 1630-1920 Index,* pp. 161, 162, Vol. 2 p. 46, Vol. 3 p. 128; Wheeler, *History of the First Congregational Church, Stonington, Connecticut, 1674-1874,* p. 223. "Nathaniel Fellows, son of Nathaniel Fellows. Baptized 24 Mar 1739 by Rev. Ebenezer Rosseter."

[39] Fellows, *Descendants of William Fellows of Ipswich.*

[40] Fellows, *Descendants of William Fellows of Ipswich.*

[41] 1790 US Census, Unidentified Town, New London, Connecticut M637-1, p. 117.

[42] Wheeler, *History of the Town of Stonington,* pp. 301, 307. "Zebulon Ward b 3 May 1779 son of Zerviah Chesebrough and Jonathan Ward, m. Hopestill Fellows, daughter of Nathaniel Fellows, she b. 16 May 1776, d. 1 Jul 1868, he d. 28 Feb 1851.

[43] *Vital Records, Stonington, New London County, Connecticut.* "Warner, son Nathaniel b. 15 Feb 1740/41."

[44] *Connecticut Church Record Abstracts, 1630-1920,* Vol 2 p. 46, Vol. 3 p. 124; Wheeler, *History of the First Congregational Church, Stonington,* p. 224. "Wardner [*sic*] Fellows, son of Nathaniel Fellows. Baptized 5 Apr 1741 by Rev. Ebenezer Rosseter."

[45] Wheeler, *History of the Town of Stonington,* p. 368; Bailey, *Early Connecticut Marriages,* p. 59; *Congregational Church,* North Stonington, New London, Connecticut. *Early Connecticut Marriages, 1733-1781.* "Fellows, Warner and Hall, Eunice 25 Nov 1762;" *Vital Records, Stonington, New London County, Connecticut.* "Warner, m. Eunice Hall, both of Stonington, 25 Nov 1762, by Rev Joseph Fish;" Fellows, *Descendants of William Fellows of Ipswich.* Wheeler gives a marriage date of 22 Nov 1762.

[46] Fellows, *Descendants of William Fellows of Ipswich.*

[47] Fellows, *Descendants of William Fellows of Ipswich.*

[48] Wheeler, *History of the First Congregational Church,* 226.

[49] Wheeler, *History of the First Congregational Church,* 255. Rathbone spelled "Rathbun" in the record.

[50] *Vital Records, Stonington, New London County, Connecticut,* Barbour Collection, p. 93, Vol 3 p. 172. "Hopestill, dau. Nathaniel b. Feb. 8, 1745."

[51] Wheeler, *History of the First Congregational Church, Stonington, Connecticut, 1674-1874,* p. 226. "Hopestill Fellows - parents: [mother not given] & Nathaniel Fellows - bapt. 7

Apr 1745 - by Rev. Ebenezer Rosseter;" Wheeler, *History of the First Congregational Church, Stonington, Connecticut, 1674-1874.* "Hopestill Fellows, daughter of Nathaniel Fellows. Baptized 7 Apr 1745 by Rev. Ebenezer Rosseter."

[52] Wheeler, *History of the First Congregational Church,* 254.

[53] Wheeler, *History of the First Congregational Church, Stonington, Connecticut, 1674-1874.* "John Belcher & Hopestill Fellows marriage 1 May 1763, married by Rev. Nathaniel Eells."

[54] *Vital Records, Stonington, New London County, Connecticut,* Barbour Collection, p. 93, Vol 3 p. 172. "Lydia, dau. Nathaniel b. 20 Feb 1747."

[55] Wheeler, *History of the First Congregational Church, Stonington, Connecticut ,1674-1874,* 227. "Lydia Fellows - parents: [mother not given] & Nathaniel Fellows - bapt. 10 May 1747 - by Rev. Ebenezer Rosseter;" Wheeler, *History of the First Congregational Church, Stonington, Connecticut, 1674-1874.* "Lydia Fellows, daughter of Nathaniel Fellows. Baptized 10 May 1747 by Ebenezer Rosseter."

[56] Wheeler, *History of the First Congregational Church, Stonington, Connecticut, 1674-1874,* pp. 256, 492. "Nathan Noyes & Lydia Fellows married 23 Sep 1770 by Rev. Nathaniel Eells."

[57] Fellows, *Descendants of William Fellows of Ipswich.*

[58] Fellows, *Descendants of William Fellows of Ipswich.* "Mercy and Mary listed as daughters of Nathaniel may be the same person."

[59] Wheeler, *History of the First Congregational Church,* p. 227.

[60] *Vital Records, Stonington, New London County, Connecticut,* Barbour Collection, p. 93, Vol 3 p. 172. "Mercy, dau. Nathaniel b. 10 Aug 1749."

[61] *Vital Records, Stonington, New London County, Connecticut,* Barbour Collection, p. 93, Vol 3 p. 172. "Elnathan, son of Nathaniel b. 18 Aug 1751."

[62] Wheeler, *History of the First Congregational Church, Stonington, Connecticut, 1674-1874,* 227. "Elnathan Fellows, child of Nathaniel Fellows. Baptized 29 Sep 1751 by Rev. Ebenezer Rosseter;" Wheeler, *History of the First Congregational Church, Stonington, Connecticut, 1674-1874.* "Elnathan Fellows- parents: [mother not given] & Nathaniel Fellows - bapt. 29 Sep 1751 - by Rev. Ebenezer Rosseter."

[63] 1790 US Census, Unidentified Town Town, New London, Connecticut M637-1, p. 116. The enumeration for Elnathan was 2 males age 16 and up, 2 under 16, and 4 females. Elnathan was living in the same community as brothers Nathaniel, Ephraim, and Joseph.

[64] Find A Grave 69165056. "Elnathan Fellowes [*sic*]."

[65] Cemetery, Robinson Burying Ground (Connecticut: The Stonington Historical Society), Personal Correspondence, 28 Apr 2003, The Richard W. Woolworth Library, Stonington, Conn., Mary M. Thacher, Archivist. Photocopy of a page with the Fellows/Brewster inscriptions of graves identified as (77)-Hannah, wife of Capt. Stephen Brewster, died 10 Apr 1829, aged 53 years. "Nor pain, nor grief, nor anxious care invades thy bounds nor mortal

woes can reach the peaceful sleeper here, while angels watch the soft repose." (78)-Deacon Elnathan Fellowes, died 31 Jan 1837, aged 85. "So Jesus slept, God's dying Son, passed through the grave and blest the bed, rest here blest saint, 'till from His throne the morning breaks and pierce the shade." (79)-Hannah, consort of Deacon Elnathan Fellowes, died 16 Aug 1845, aged 87 years. "Thou hast gone to meet the loved one who arose before thee there, now thou sit'est no more alone, in thy home of widowed care, bright in glory, thou thy promised crown dost wear." (80)-L.F.C. (Lydia Fellowes Chesebro 1790-1882, newer granite grave marker). Epitaph is located on the Fellowes Monument #83. (81)-C.O.B. (Charles O. Brewster 1808-1884, newer granite grave marker) Epitaph is located on the Fellowes Monument #83. (82)-M.E.B. (Mary E. Brewster Fellowes 1806-1897, newer granite grave marker) Epitaph is located on the Fellowes Monument #83. Fellowes - Brewster Monument: (83)-On the north side: George S. Brewster, 1811-1882, his wife, Mary L. Clark, 1812-1894. Their children: Helen Mary, 1836-1848. George, 1834-1840. Three infants, 1846-1849. (A hand pointing down to the words) "Till he comes." (83)-South side of monument: Charles O. Brewster, 1808-1884, his wife, Mary E. Forsyth, 1806-1897. Their children: Mary Hannah, 1833-1842; Charles Henry, 1838-1838; Alice Brewster, adopted daughter, 1858-1884. (83)-East side of monument: Our father and mother, Stephen Brewster 1775-1807, Hannah Fellowes, 1778-1829. (83)-West side of monument: In emporium of Elnathan Fellowes, Deacon of the First Baptist Church of Stonington over fifty years, 1752-1837. His wife, Hannah Packer, 1758-1845. Their children: Nathan, 1779-1810; Betsey Grant, 1781-1818; Joseph, 1784-1803; Mary, 1786-1813; Lydia F. Chesebro, 1790-1882. (84 to 93)-various other gravestones, mostly Brewsters. (94)-Abby Jane, Dau. of Stephen & Hannah Brewster, died 6 Sep 1805, aged 1 year & 11 months. (95)-Unknown. (96)-Benjamin S. Brewster, son of Stephen & Hannah Brewster, died 15 Aug 1801, aged 1 year and 3 months. (97)-In memory of Content, daughter of Mr. William & Mrs. Susanna Fellowes, who died 17 Jan 1770. (100)-In memory of Thomas Hall who died 20 Feb 1777, possibly the husband of Hannah Fellows, daughter of Ephraim.

[66] Find A Grave 80594639. "Hannah Packer Fellowes."

[67] Fellows, *Descendants of William Fellows of Ipswich.*

[68] Wheeler, *Homes of Our Ancestors in Stonington*, p. 115.

[69] Fellows, *Descendants of William Fellows of Ipswich.*

[70] Wheeler, *History of the First Congregational Church,* p. 265.

[71] Find A Grave 163279212. "Nathan Fellowes."

[72] Find A Grave 132835569. "Betsey Grant Fellowes."

[73] Find A Grave 132835570. "Joseph Fellowes."

[74] Find A Grave 132835571. "Mary Fellowes."

[75] Find A Grave 132835572. "Lydia F. Fellowes Chesebro."

[76] Elnathan Fellows supposedly had thirteen children. Mark D. Fellows listed only seven. Five children listed on the Fellowes-Brewster Monument in the Robinson Buying Ground, Stonington, Connecticut: (1). Nathan, 1779-1810, (2). Betsey Grant, 1781-1818, (3). Joseph, 1784-1803, (4). Mary, 1786-1813, (5). Lydia F. Chesebro 1790-1882.

[77] *Vital Records, Stonington, New London County, Connecticut* , Barbour Collection, p. 93, Vol 3 p. 172. "Ephraim, son of Nathaniel b. 19 Nov 1753, d. 22 Dec 1753."

[78] 1790 US Census, Unidentified Town, New London, Connecticut M637-1, p. 116. The enumerations for Ephraim was 2 males age 16 and up and 6 females; Ephraim is living in the same community as brothers Elnathan, Nathaniel, Jr, and Joseph, as well as his father Nathaniel, Sr.

[79] Wheeler, *History of the Town of Stonington*, pp. 368, 409. Wheeler gives the date of the marriage of Pricilla Fellows to John Devol as 1 Dec 1771.

[80] *Vital Records, Stonington, New London County, Connecticut*, Barbour Collection, p. 93, Vol 3 p. 172. "Pricilla [*sic*], dau. Nath'l b. 14 Apr 1755."

[81] Wheeler, *History of the First Congregational Church,* p. 257.

[82] Wheeler, *History of the First Congregational Church, Stonington, Connecticut, 1674-1874*. "John Devol & Priscilla Fellows. Married 15 Dec 1774 by Rev. Nathaniel Eells."

[83] Wheeler, *History of the Town of Stonington*, p. 409.

[84] Fellows, *Descendants of William Fellows of Ipswich*. Mercy and Mary listed as daughters of Nathaniel may be the same person. Note also that the birthdate of Mary Fellows of 1757 conflicts with that of her sibling, Joseph Fellows, also allegedly born in 1757.

[85] *Vital Records, Stonington, New London County, Connecticut*, Barbour Collection, p. 93, Vol 3 p. 184. "Mary dau. Nath'l b. 16 May 1757.

[86] Wheeler, *History of the First Congregational Church,* p. 257; *Vital Records, Stonington, New London County, Connecticut*, Barbour Collection, p. 93, Vol 3 p. 184. "Joseph, son of Nath'l & Hopestill b. 29 Sep 1757." Other sources have Joseph born in 1759. His sister was also born, according to sources in 1757. Other transcriptions show Mary's death in 1757.

[87] Wheeler, *History of the First Congregational Church, Stonington, Connecticut, 1674-1874*. "Joseph Fellows & Mary Hewitt married 11 May 1777 by Rev. Nathaniel Eells."

[88] *Public Records of the Colony of Connecticut 1780-81*, p. 419.

[89] Fellows, *Descendants of William Fellows of Ipswich.*

[90] *Vital Records, Stonington, New London County, Connecticut*, Barbour Collection, p. 93, Vol 3 p. 184. "David, son of Nath'l & Hopestill b. 16 Mar 1760."

[91] George Marshall Fellows, *A Genealogy and Partial History of Fellows Families in America*, personal manuscripts, 6 vols. c.1910.

Chapter 8 William Fellows of Stonington

[1] *Vital Records, Stonington, New London County, Connecticut,* transcribed by Coralynn Brown, from Barbour Collection, 1668-1852, p. 93, Vol. 3 p. 172, "William, son Nathaniel, b Jan 19, 1742/43;" Fellows, *Fellows Families of Onondaga County*, pp. 82-83. "William Fellows b. 19 Jan 1743 d. 24 Jul 1827;" David Pane-Joyce, *Massachusetts Bay Colony Genealogy*, April 2002. "Susannah Rathbone. Born on 1 May 1748. On 8 Nov 1767 when Susannah was 19, she married William Fellows, born on 28 Feb 1743." Notwithstanding the incorrect dates, this is

an extensive genealogy, covering many of the immigrant families in the Massachusetts Bay area.

[2] *Vital Records, Stonington, New London County, Connecticut,* transcribed by Coralynn Brown, from Barbour Collection, 1668-1852, p. 93, Vol. 3 p. 172.

[3] *Connecticut Church Record Abstracts, 1630-1920,* Vol. 2 p. 47, Vol. 3 p. 133; Wheeler, *History of the First Congregational Church, Stonington, Connecticut,* 1674-1874, Norwich, 1875, p. 226. The Congregational Church in 1727, then the second church of Stonington, records complete to 1781. "William Fellows, son of Nathaniel Fellows, baptized 12 Jun 1743 by Rev. Ebenezer Rosseter."

[4] Find A Grave 62773077; "William Fellows;" LDS Ancestral File KLSD-T8; LDS International Genealogical Index, Film 456288; LDS Pedigree Resource File, Disk #50 PIN 10034.

[5] Rensselaer County, New York GenWeb project, Cemetery, Fellows, Rensselaer County, New York; Grave Stone: Fellows Cemetery, Stephentown, Rensselaer County, New York. "Fellows, Susannah b. 15 May 1748 d. 15 Jul 1825 Age, 77. Husband, William Fellows; Mother, Tabitha Brown Rathbone, Father, Valentine Rathbone." Buried beside her husband, William Fellows; LDS Pedigree Resource File, Disk #50 PIN 10024; LDS International Genealogical Index, Film 458671; LDS Ancestral File J1PL-TK.

[6] *Vital Records, Stonington, New London County, Connecticut,* transcribed by Coralynn Brown, from Barbour Collection, 1668-1852, "Susannah, dau. Valentine b. May 5, 1748." The gravestone of Susannah Rathbone Fellows in Stephentown, New York, confirms date of birth as 15 May 1748.

[7] *Connecticut Church Record Abstracts, 1630-1920,* Vol. 4 p. 47; Wheeler, *History of the First Congregational Church, Stonington, Connecticut,* 1674-1874, Norwich, 1875, p. 255. "William Fellows & Susanna Rathbun [*sic*] married 8 Nov 1767 by Rev Nathaniel Eells;" *Vital Records, Stonington, New London County, Connecticut.* "William Fellows & Susanna Rathbun m. 8 Nov 1767 - by Rev. Nathaniel Eells."

[8] John C. Cooley, *Rathbone Genealogy: A complete History of the Rathbone Family Dating from 1574 to Date* (Vol. 1). Syracuse, NY: Currier Job Press, 1808, p. 329.

[9] Find A Grave 62773086. "Susannah Rathbun Fellows;" Cornwell, *Cornwell* (Sep 2002), Source incorrectly gives the birthdate of Susannah as 1 May 1748, not 15 May, and death date of 25 Jul 1825, not 15 Jul. A record of their marriage in 1767 is on file at the First Congregational Church.

[10] Cooley, *Rathbone Genealogy*, pp. 13, 161.

[11] Fellows, *Descendants of William Fellows of Ipswich.*

[12] *Compiled Revolutionary War Military Service Records, 1775-1783.*

[13] Find A Grave 28165612.

[14] *Valley Forge Muster Roll Project* ID Ct15481.

[15] *Connecticut Revolutionary War Military Lists, 1775-83*, p. 138.

[16] *Connecticut Men in the Revolutionary War, Record of Service of Connecticut Men in the I-War of the Revolution, II-War of 1812, III-Mexican War, IV State Troops of Levies, 1776, Regiments for Various Service*, pp. 61, 396.

[17] *Records from the War Department Collection of Revolutionary War*, Record Group 93, Compiled Service Records of Soldiers Who Served in the American Army during the Revolutionary War [microform] Reel 314, 1972; *American Revolutionary War Service Records; Soldier Registers, Connecticut*, Seventh Regiment: E-F Images 506-572.

[18] *Connecticut Town Birth Records, pre-1870* (Barbour Collection) Canaan, Conn., Vol. LR1 p. 424, Vol. A p. 6.

[19] *Connecticut Wills and Probate Records, 1609-1999*, Cases 1242 & 1243.

[20] Cooley, *Rathbone Genealogy*, p. 326.

[21] Nancy Thomson, *First Thomsons and the Fourth Baptist Church of Bellingham, Massachusetts.*

[22] David Benedict, *A General History of the Baptist Denomination in America, and Other Parts of the World*, London: Lincoln & Edmands, 1813.

[23] Dwight H. Bruce, ed., *Onondaga's Centennial* (Vol. 1), Boston History, 1896, Vol 1, pp. 631-658.

[24] Thomson, *First Thomsons and the Fourth Baptist Church of Bellingham, Massachusetts.*

[25] J.E.A. Smith, *History of Pittsfield, Berkshire County, Massachusetts 1800-1876*, Springfield: C.W. Bryan, 1876, p. 37.

[26] Bruce, *Onondaga's Centennial*, Vol. 1 pp. 142, 631-658.

[27] Instructions from the Town of Pittsfield to their Representative, Mr˙ Valentine Rathbun, for Independence, dated 31 May 1776, Northern Illinois University Archives S4-V6-P02-sp01-D0562.

[28] Cooley, *Rathbone Genealogy*, p. 326.

[29] Smith, *History of Pittsfield, Berkshire County, Massachusetts 1800-1876*, p. 94.

[30] Find A Grave 62776357.

[31] Article published in the *Rathbun Family Historian* Oct 1981 & Jan 1982.

[32] Cooley, *Rathbone Genealogy*, p. 326.

[33] *A brief account of a religious scheme, taught and propagated by a number of Europeans, who lately lived in a place called Nisqueunia, in the state of New-York, but now residing in Harvard, Commonwealth of Massachusetts, commonly called, Shaking Quakers.* Evans Early American Imprint Collection, 1780.

[34] Cooley, *Rathbone Genealogy*, p. 329; Columbus, *History of the Fellows Family*, p. 3.

[35] Cemetery, Robinson Burying Ground. Connecticut: The Stonington Historical Society, Personal Correspondence, 28 Apr 2003, The Richard W. Woolworth Library, "In memory of Content, daughter of Mr. William & Mrs. Susanna Fellowes, who died Jan. 17, 1770."

[36] Columbus, *History of the Fellows Family*, p. 3.

[37] Wheeler, *History of the Town of Stonington*, 129.

[38] Columbus, *History of the Fellows Family*, p. 4.

[39] 1790 US Census, New York, Albany, Stephentown, Roll M637 6, p. 49, National Archives and Records Administration. "Willm Fellowes of Stephen Town, Albany County, New York." See also 1790 US Census, Stephen Town, Albany, New York; Series M637 Roll 6, p. 289; Image 291; Family History Library Film 0568146. "Willm Fellows." Under 16-2, 16 and over-3, Females-5.

[40] Anderson, *Landmarks of Rensselaer County, New York*, Syracuse, NY: D. Mason, 1897.

[41] *New York Tax Assessment Rolls of Real and Personal Estates, 1799-1804.*

[42] 1800 US Census, Stephentown, Rensselaer, New York; Series M32 Roll 26, p. 110, Image 111; Family History Library Film 193714. "William Fellers." [*sic*], Males 10-15, 1; Males 16-25, 1; Males 45 and over, 1; Females 10-15, 2; Females 16-25, 1; Females 26-44, 1.

[43] 1810 US Census, Stephentown, Rensselaer, New York, National Archives and Records Administration. The enumeration categories for the 1810 census were the same as the census of 1800. The official enumeration day of the 1810 census was 6 Aug 1810. "Wm. Fellows," Males: age 0 to 10 - 2, 10 to 16 - 0, 16 to 26 - 1, 26 to 45 - 0, above age 45 - 1; Females: 0 to 10 - 0, 10 to 16 - 0, 16 to 26 - 0, 26 to 45 - 1, above age 45 - 1.

[44] 1820 US Census, Stephentown, Rensselaer, New York, NARA Roll M33 68, p. 37, Image 258. "William Fellows," Males 10-15,1; Males 45 and over, 1; Females 10-15, 1; females 26-44, 1; Females 45 and over, 1; Persons engaged in agriculture, 2.

[45] Will of William Fellows, New York, Rensselaer County, Stephentown, Liber [Book] 9, p. 64, recorded in Rensselaer County, New York Surrogate Court Records.

[46] *Rensselaer County Probate, Surrogate Abstracts,* abstracted & and compiled by Barbara Jeffries. "Fellows, William of Stephentown, 8 Oct 1825-23 Aug 1827. Heirs: children, William, Joshua, Isaac, Jeremiah, & David Fellows; Susannah w/o William Hunt; Parmela w/o Moses Cowl, Jr.; Ruby w/o Dan Wright; and Polly Fellows; Grand-daughter, Eliza Ann Fellows. Exec.: David and Polly Fellows."

[47] Stephentown Historical Society's *Bicentennial Album (1784-1984)*; Interments in Rensselaer County, New York, Cemeteries, Rensselaer County, New York, GenWeb project , Grave Stone: Fellows Cemetery, Stephentown, Rensselaer County, New York. "Fellows, William b. 19 Jan 1743 d. 24 Jul 1827, age 84y. Wife, Susannah; Mother, Hopestill Hodge [*sic*] Fellows; Father, Nathaniel Fellows." William's burial was beside his wife, Susannah. The name of his mother, Hopestill "Hodge" was a transcribed abbreviation for Hopestill Holdredge. The Fellows Cemetery served from 1813-1904 and contains 26 gravesites. It can be located as follows: .5 mile from South Stephentown Road on Hager Road, there is a roadway leading to the left. Follow this until it starts to turn to the right. Park and walking, turn to the left, cross the field ahead, at an angle and up the hillock.

[48] Will of William Fellows, New York, Rensselaer County, Stephentown, Liber [Book] 9, p. 64, recorded in Rensselaer County, New York Surrogate Court Records. The clerk copied the

original Will into the court records by hand. The clerk's handwriting is legible and in good penmanship. No original signatures appear on this document, except the "X' mark of the subscribing witness, Meshack Strait. Transcribed by K. Burchett. "The last Will and Testament of William Fellows with the probate thereof, Recorded 23d Aug 1827. "The last Will and Testament of William Fellows of the Town of Stephentown, County of Rensselaer and State of New York [illegible mark]. I [mark] William Fellows considering the uncertainty of this mortal life and being of sound mind and memory blessed be Almighty God for the same do make and publish this my last Will and Testament in manner and form following, that is to say, I give and bequeath to my beloved sons William Fellows, Joshua Fellows, Isaac Fellows and Jeremiah Fellows the sum of seven dollars each [to] be paid out of my Estate. I also give and bequeath to my beloved daughters Susannah the wife of William Hunt, Parmela, the wife of Moses Cowl Junr and Ruby the wife of Dan Wright the equal undivided half of all my household furniture to be equally divided among them excepting such articles as is herein otherwise disposed of. I also give and bequeath to my beloved daughter Polly Fellows her maintenance out of the share of my son David Fellows so long as she shall remain unmarried– or should be unable to support herself. I also give and bequeath to my Grand Daughter Eliza Ann Fellows one bed and bedding. I give and bequeath and demise unto my beloved son David Fellows all my lands and tenements situate in the Town of Stephentown aforesaid to have and to hold unto the said David Fellows his heirs and assigns forever. And as to the rest and remainder of my estate, both real and personal I give and bequeath to my son David Fellows. And I do hereby constitute and appoint David Fellows the Executor and Polly Fellows the Executrix of this my last Will and Testament hereby revoking all former wills by me made. In Witness whereof I have hereunto set my hand and seal this eighth day of October in the year one thousand and eight hundred and twenty five." Signed, sealed, published and declared /William Fellows/ S.S. by the above named William Fellows to be his last Will and Testament in the presence of us who have subscribed our names as witnesses in the presence of the Testator. Meshack Strait, John Chapman, Wanlow Chapman, Joseph Tayer. (Will delivered to [illegible name] Order Executor 21 Sept 1827). State of New York. "Rensselaer County: Be it Remembered That on the twenty third day of August in the year of our Lord one thousand, eight hundred and twenty seven personally appeared before me, Philipe Viele Esquire Surrogate of the said County of Rensselaer, Meshack Strait one of the subscribing witnesses of the will of William Fellows late of the town of Stephentown in said county deceased, who being duly sworn declared that he did see the said William Fellows seal and execute the annexed written instrument purporting to be the last will and testament of the said William Fellows bearing date the eighth day of October in the year of our Lord one thousand eight hundred and twenty five and heard him publish and declare the same as and for his last Will and Testament, that at the time thereof, he the said William Fellows was of sound disposing mind and memory to the best of the knowledge and belief of the said Meshack Strait and that he the said Meshack together with John Chapman, Wanlow Chapman and Joseph Tayer the other witnesses of the said will, severally subscribed their hands and names to the said will as witnesses thereto in the presence of the Testator and each other. In Testimony whereof the said Surrogate has hereto set his hand and affixed the /X mark/ S.S.Seal of his office at the City of Troy the day and year aforesaid. Philip Viele."

[49] *Connecticut Church Record Abstracts, 1630-1920,* Vol. 2 p. 47, Vol. 3 p. 133; Wheeler, *History of the First Congregational Church,* 226. "William, son [of] Nathaniel, baptized June 12, 1743."

[50] *Connecticut Church Record Abstracts, 1630-1920,* Vol. 4 p. 47; Wheeler, *History of the First Congregational Church,* p. 255. "William m. Susanna Rathbun Nov 8, 1767;" see also Cooley, *Rathbone Genealogy,* p 329.

[51] Cooley, *Rathbone Genealogy,* p. 329.

[52] Cooley, *Rathbone Genealogy,* p. 329. Rathbone omitted Warner and Content Fellows and misdated the birthdate of Pamela Fellows. Otherwise, *Rathbone Genealogy* is the standard reference on the Rathbone family.

[53] LDS International Genealogical Index, Film 107504, Ref 47715, p. 876.

[54] Find A Grave 17248080. "Susanna Fellows Hunt."

[55] Fellows, *Descendants of William Fellows of Ipswich.*

[56] Find A Grave 17248056. "William Hunt."

[57] Fellows, *Descendants of William Fellows of Ipswich.* Content Fellows listed by this source as a child of William Fellows and Susannah Rathbone. Some genealogy sources omit her, perhaps because she died in infancy. Content died, according to this source, 19 Jul 1770 in Stonington, New London.

[58] Cemetery, Robinson Burial Ground (Connecticut: The Stonington Historical Society), Richard W. Woolworth Library, Mary M. Thacher, Archivist. "(97)-In memory of Content, daughter of Mr. William & Mrs. Susanna Fellowes, who died Jan. 17, 1770."

[59] LDS International Genealogical Index, Film 107504, Ref 47717, p. 876.

[60] Fellows, *Descendants of William Fellows of Ipswich,* citing *World Family Tree,* Vol 2, Broderbund Software. Fellows said that Warner Fellows died in Westfield, Chautauqua, New York. However, it is more likely that he died in Westford, Otsego, New York, which was his longtime home.

[61] Find A Grave 161191453. "Warner Fellows."

[62] Fellows, *Descendants of William Fellows of Ipswich,* citing *World Family Tree,* Vol 2. Warner Fellows married Lucinda Winslow Nov 08, 1797, in New Lebanon, New York. She was the daughter of Job Winslow. The dates of her birth and death are lost.

[63] Find A Grave 61191453. "Warner Fellows."

[64] Fellows, *Descendants of William Fellows of Ipswich*; Hurd, *History of Otsego County New York, 1740-1878,* pp. 353, 355. "Warner Fellows was a post-rider. He lived in this town [Westford] and carried the mail from Westford to Cherry Valley."

[65] *Two Centuries in Westford 1787-1987,* Westford Community Association, Westford, N.Y., 1987, p. 24.

[66] Hurd, *History of Otsego County New York, 1740-1878,* pp. 353, 355.

[67] 1800 US Federal Census, Worcester, Otsego, New York, M32-25, p. 44. "Warner Fellows," Males: age 0 to 10 – 0, 10 to 16 - 0, 16 to 26 - 0, 26 - 45 - 1, above age 45 - 0; Females: age 0 to 10 - 2, 10 to 16 - 0, 16 to 26 - 1, 26 to 45 – 0, above age 45 - 0. No slaves recorded. Warner Fellows was age 27 in 1800. His wife, Lucinda, was 20. The identities of his two daughters under age 10 are unknown, although one is probably Mary.

[68] 1810 US Census, Westford, Otsego, New York M252-34, p. 241. "W. Fellows," Males: age 0 to 10 - 4, 10 to 16 - 0, 16 to 26 - 0, 26 to 45 - 1, above age 45 - 0; Females: age 0 to 10 - 2, 10 to 16 - 1, 16 to 26 - 0, 26 to 45 - 1, above age 45 - 0. No slaves listed. The enumeration includes Warner, age 37 in 1810, wife, Luicinda, age 30, and members of his family: 4 males under age 10, 2 females under age 10, and one female age 10 to 16.

[69] 1820 US Census, Westford, Otsego, New York, M33 74, p. 41. "Warner Fellows," Males: age 0 to 10 - 2, 10 to 16 - 2, 16 to 18 - 1, 16 to 26 - 2, 16 to 45 - 0, above age 45 - 1; Females: age 0 to 10 - 0, 10 to 16 - 1, 16 to 26 - 1, 26 to 45 - 1, above age 45 - 1. Three members of the household were engaged in Agriculture. The 1820 census for the first time asked additionally for the number of males 16 to 18. Therefore, the enumeration for the age category 16 to 26 may include the same person twice.

[70] *Two Centuries in Westford 1787-1987*, Westford Community Association, Westford, N.Y., 1987, p. 71.

[71] 1850 US Census, Westford, Otsego, New York M432-579, p. 202, National Archives and Records Administration.

[72] Fellows, *Descendants of William Fellows of Ipswich*; Profile by Joan Stewart Smith, Warner Fellows' 3rd great granddaughter, on his Find A Grave Memorial 161191453.

[73] Fellows, *Fellows Families of Onondaga County,* p. 89, cited by Mark D. Fellows. This source does not give the location of Warner Cemetery, but it was probably in Lysander, Onondaga County, New York.

[74] Fellows, *Descendants of William Fellows of Ipswich.*

[75] Fellows, *Descendants of William Fellows of Ipswich.*

[76] LDS International Genealogical Index, Film 107504, Ref 47718, p. 876.

[77] LDS International Genealogical Index, Film 107504, Ref 47719, p. 876.

[78] Rensselaer County Deaths 1850-1860-1870-1880 (Federal Mortality Schedules). "Stephentown, May 1860 Jeremiah Fellows, age 80."

[79] Find A Grave 62773112. "Jeremiah Fellows;" Rensselaer County, New York GenWeb project, Cemetery, Fellows, Rensselaer County, New York. "Fellows, Jeremiah b. 3 Dec 1777 d. May 1860, 82y. Fellows Cemetery, Stephentown, New York."

[80] *War of 1812* - miscellaneous records, New York Sate Archives. "1750 Fellows, Jeremiah; Stephentown, $58.00."

[81] LDS International Genealogical Index, Film 107504, Ref 47720, p. 876; Fellows, *Descendants of William Fellows of Ipswich*, citing the 1800 Connecticut Census, which showed

Isaac Fellows living in New London County, Connecticut. The census did not list any other individuals in the household, Roll No 3, p. 625.

[82] LDS International Genealogical Index, Film 107504, Ref 47721, p. 876.

[83] LDS International Genealogical Index, Film 107504, Ref 47722, p. 876.

[84] *Rensselaer County Probate/ Surrogate Abstracts.* "Fellows, David of Stephentown, Will 5 Feb 1855, Recorded 23 Nov 1855. Heirs: widow, Chloe; sons, Lorenzo & David H. Fellows; daughters: Chloe, Jane, Catherine S., Mary L., and Amanda Melvina Fellows."

[85] Erwin W. Fellows, *Fellows Families of Onondaga County*, p. 85; Find A Grave 62773060. "David Fellows;" Rensselaer County, New York GenWeb project, Cemetery, Fellows, Rensselaer County, New York. "Monument, right side. Fellows, David b. 16 Mar 1785 d. 19 May 1865, 70y 2m 3d. h/o Chloe turner. Fellows Cemetery, Stephentown, New York." Erwin Fellows suggested David was born in Stonington, Connecticut. His information was incomplete based on "sketchy information on this family from George B. Anderson, *Landmarks of Rensselaer County, New York*, 1897."

[86] Marriages, Reformed Protestant Dutch Church at Nassau, Rensselaer County, New York, transcribed and compiled by Barbara Jeffries, New York State Library. "Oct 8, 1812 - David Fellows - Chloe Turner."

[87] Find A Grave 62773072. "Chloe Turner Fellows;" Rensselaer County, New York GenWeb project, Cemetery, Fellows, Rensselaer County, New York, Inscription "Chloe Turner Fellows 13 May 1878, 83y 11m. Katherine Turner [mother], John Turner [father]."

[88] 1880 US Federal Census for Stephentown, Rensselaer, New York, Roll T9-0922, p. 604D; Fellows Cemetery, Stephentown, Rensselaer County, New York, GenWeb, rootsweb.com/~nyrensse/cemf2.txt), accessed 2003.

[89] 1850 US Stephentown, Rensselaer, New York M432-586, p 243. Family No. 1199. The 1850 US Census described David Fellows as age 64, value of real estate $6,000, born in Connecticut; Chloe Fellows, age 50, born in New York; Lorenzo, age 23, David [H.?], 28, [Mabring?], 30, Chloe J., 20, Catharine, 16, Laurietta, 19, and Jeremiah, age 32, a Farmer, born in Connecticut. The census listed all others as born in New York. Catharine and Laurietta attended school within the year. Tombstone inscriptions for Chloe Fellows, David's wife, and son, Lorenzo, differ from the census data. Chloe was about 56, Lorenzo age 27.

[90] Fellows, *Descendants of William Fellows of Ipswich.* Fellows presented an alternate list of the children of David Fellows and Chloe Turner: (1). Nathaniel Fellows b. 1818, m. Susan M. Snyder 1862. Nathaniel was from West Lebanon, New York,(2). John T. Fellows b. 19 Jul 1820 in Stephentown, New York, (3). Lorenzo Fellows b. 02 Dec 1822 in Stephentown, Rensselaer County, New York, (4). Mary Laurietta Fellows b. 1836 in New York, d. 1906, m. 1st Daniel M. Beers, 2nd David Beers, (5). David Harvey Fellows b. abt.1822, d. Aug 1903, (6). J.N. Fellows b. Unknown in Stephentown, New York, d. 26 Nov 1887 in West Point, Wisconsin.

[91] LDS International Genealogical Index, Film 107504, Ref 47723, p. 876.

[92] LDS International Genealogical Index, Film 107504, Ref 47724, p. 876. This source gives an alternate burial site of Lyons, Walworth County, Wisconsin.

[93] Find A Grave 69342316. "Parmela Fellows Cowles."

[94] Find A Grave 63411989. "Moses Cowles, Jr."

Chapter 9 William Reuben Fellows

[1] LDS International Genealogical Index, Film 107504, Ref 47716, p. 876; LDS International Genealogical Index, Film 170521, Ref 21121.

[2] Fellows, *Fellows Families of Onondaga County,* p. 84.

[3] Find A Grave 85105786. "William Fellows."

[4] Columbus, *History of the Fellows Family*, p. 2.

[5] Hamilton Child, *Gazetteer and Business Directory of Otego County, N.Y. for 1872-73,* Syracuse, NY: Journal Office, 1872, p. 112.

[6] Columbus, *History of the Fellows Family*, p. 4.

[7] Child, *Gazetteer and Business Directory of Otsego County, NY*, pp. 61-63, 81.

[8] 1860 US Census, Geneva, Walworth, Wisconsin, p. 236. "G.E.S. Fellows;" Fellows, *Fellows Families of Onondaga County,* p. 85. Erwin Fellows gives an alternate marriage date of 22 Dec 1796 in Stephentown, New York, p. 85. See also Western Michigan Historical Society for Erwin Fellows genealogy reference, Family Group Sheets F68450 & F34002.

[9] *New York Tax Assessment Rolls of Real and Personal Estates, 1799-1804*; Find A Grave 159162866. "Ebenezer Smith." See also Find A Grave 141210614.

[10] 1790 US Census of New York State, Washington, D.C.: Government Printing Office, 1908, p. 49, "Gideon Smith."

[11] 1820 US Census, Stephentown, Rensselaer, New York, Roll M33 68, p. 40, Image: 261, NARA. "Gedion Smith" [*sic*]; 1830 US Census, Unadilla, Otsego, New York, Series M19, Roll 102, p. 211; Family History Library Film 0017162. "Gideon Smith."

[12] Fellows, *Descendants of William Fellows of Ipswich.* In his notes for William Fellows, Mark Fellows says, William lived with his family in Stephenton [*sic*], New York.

[13] 1800 US Census, Worcester, Otsego, New York, Roll M32 25, p. 44, National Archives and Records Administration. The enumeration for Reuben Fellow: 1 male age 26 to 45 correlates with William's age of 29 in 1800, living with Reuben is 1 female age 16 to 26, which correlates with the age of William's wife, Martha, age 20 in 1800.

[14] Hurd, *History of New London County,* p. 356.

[15] *Biographical Review Biographies of the Leading Citizens of Otsego Co., NY,* c.1893.

[16] 1800 US Census, Worcester, Otsego, New York; Series M32 Roll 25, p. 669, Image: 94; Family History Library, Film 193713. "Warner Fellows."

[17] Worcester, Otsego County, *New York, Tax Assessment Rolls of Real and Personal Estates, 1799-1804*

[18] 1790 US Census, National Archives and Records Administration.

[19] *New York Tax Assessment Rolls of Real and Personal Estates, 1799-1804.*

[20] Hurd, *History of Otsego County New York,* p. 23. This is an unindexed work of 378 pages with illustrations and biographical sketches of some of the prominent men and pioneers of Otsego County, New York.

[21] Child, *Gazetteer and Business Directory of Otsego County, NY,* pp. 61-63, 81.

[22] Columbus, *History of the Fellows Family,* p. 4.

[23] Columbus, *History of the Fellows Family,* p. 4.

[24] Columbus, *History of the Fellows Family,* p. 4.

[25] Cooley, *Rathbone Genealogy,* p. 330.

[26] 1810 US Census, Westford, Otsego, New York, Roll M252 34, p. 241, National Archives and Records Administration. The enumeration categories for the 1810 census were the same as the census of 1800. The official enumeration day of the 1810 census was 6 Aug 1810. "W. Fellows." The enumerations for W[illiam] Fellows is 1 male age 26 to 45, 1 female age 26 to 45, 4 males age 0 to 10, and 1 female age 0 to 10.

[27] Columbus, *History of the Fellows Family,* p. 4.

[28] 1820 US Census, Maryland, Otsego, New York, M33_74, p. 80, National Archives and Records Administration. "William Fellows." The enumerations for William Fellows is 1 male above age 45, 1 female age 26 to 45, 1 male age under 10, 2 males age 10 to 16, and 1 female age under 10. Enumerations in these age categories correspond to William, age 49; Martha, age 40; sons: William, 13; Gideon, 12; David, 10; and daughter, Affia, age 8. Two members of the household reported as engaged in Agriculture, one is engaged in Manufacturing. William's eldest son, Reuben, would have been 19 in 1820. No one of his age listed in William's household. Enumerators possibly counted him in the household of Warner Fellows.

[29] 1830 US Census, Maryland, Otsego, New York, Roll M19 102, p. 120, National Archives and Records Administration. The official enumeration day of the 1830 census was 1 June 1830. "William Fellows." The enumeration for William Fellows was 1 male age 15 to 20, 4 males age 20 to 30, 1 male age 50 to 60, 1 male age 60 to 70, 1 female age 15 to 20, 1 female age 20 to 30, and 1 female age 50 to 60. The male age 60 to 70 was possibly Martha's father. William's parents died in 1825 and 1827 before the 1830 census.

[30] 1840 US Federal Census, Maryland, Otsego, New York, Roll M704 329, p. 266, National Archives and Records Administration, "Wm Fellows," Males 60-69 – 1, Females 59-59 – 1, person in Agriculture - 1.

[31] Find A Grave 85105786; *New York, US, Wills and Probate Records, 1659-1999,* Petitions, Box 8, 1844-1845. "Petition: proving the last will & testament of William Fellows deceased, Date: 27 May 1845, Petition to: Schuyler Crippen, Surrogate of the County of Otsego, New York, Petitioners: William Fellows and Gideon E.S. Fellows of Maryland, Otsego County, Death Info.: William Fellows 6th of December 1843 died at Maryland in said county, Heirs in Will: The following persons are heirs at law and next of kin of the said deceased to wit: Martha Fellows, widow of said deceased residing in the town of Maryland in the County of Otsego, Reuben Fellows, William Fellows, Gideon .S. Fellows, Affia Sperry, wife of Matthew Sperry, all of the town of Maryland in the County, and David Fellows of the town of Van

Buren in the County of Onondaga, New York. Signed Gideon E.S. Fellows and William Fellows, Cooperstown, Otsego County, New York, 27 May 1845. Some genealogists include Amos as a possible son of William Fellows who died young. However, most records of his children do not include a child named Amos. The name of Amos did not appear on the above petition. Family historian Joan Stewart Smith claimed Amos was the son of William's brother [or cousin], Warner Fellows and Lucinda Winslow.

[32] Columbus, *History of the Fellows Family*, p. 5.

[33] Columbus, *History of the Fellows Family*, p. 5.

[34] 1860 US Census, Geneva, Walworth, Wisconsin, p. 236. "G.E.S. Fellows."

[35] 1850 US Census, Van Buren, Onondaga, New York, Roll 570, p. 421b. "Martha Fellows."

[36] 1860 US Census, Geneva, Walworth, Wisconsin, p. 236; Family History Library Film 805434. "Martha Fellows;" Biographical sketch by Joan Stewart Smith, GGG grandniece of Martha Smith's husband, William Fellows, and a descendant of his brother Warner Fellows.

[37] Cooley, *Rathbone Genealogy*, p. 330. Fellows, *Fellows Families of Onondaga County*, p. 5. She was born 3 Mar 1780 in Stephentown, New York, and died 12 Apr 1864 in Schenevus, Maryland [Otsego, New York].

[38] Columbus, *History of the Fellows Family*, p. 4; Find A Grave 85105810. "Martha Smith Fellows."

[39] Cooley, *Rathbone Genealogy*, p. 330; Columbus, *History of the Fellows Family*, p. 4.

[40] Cooley, *Rathbone Genealogy*, p. 330. Cooley's *Rathbone Genealogy* makes mistakes in the listing of the children of William and Martha Fellows. He incorrectly cited the birthdate of William B. Fellows as 7 Sep 1808 and omitted Gideon E.S. Fellows as the son of William and Martha.

[41] Find A Grave 85105786. "William Fellows."

[42] Cooley, *Rathbone Genealogy*, p. 330.

[43] Find A Grave 85105810. "Martha Smith Fellows."

[44] Erwin W. Fellows, *Fellows Families of Onondaga County*, p. 85; Cooley, *Rathbone Genealogy*, p. 330. Fellows recorded a son named Amos (b. about 1804) with the caveat that he was not included in William's Will and may not have been his son. Cooley omitted mention of Amos.

[45] LDS International Genealogical Index, Film 107504, Ref 47688, p. 875.

[46] Find A Grave 92619463. "Reuben R. Fellows."

[47] *Cherry Valley Gazette* (October 8, 1818 - September 19, 1826), CV 3-1-25, p. 3 c. 2. "Fellows-Goddard Marriage. At Maryland, the 17th inst. Reuben R. Fellows and Miss Betsy Goddard, dau. of Edward Goddard Esq."

[48] Find A Grave 92619638. "Betsy Goddard Fellows."

[49] Fellows, *Descendants of William Fellows of Ipswich*. Ruben identified in his father's will as "eldest son."

[50] *Biographical Review Biographies of the Leading Citizens of Otsego Co., NY*. This abstract of a larger biography covers several members of the Fellows, Goddard, and Dunham families.

[51] 1840 US Census, Maryland, Otsego County, New York.

[52] Hurd, *History of Otsego County New York, 1740-1878*. Township Sections of Mini-Biographies.

[53] 1850 US Census, Town of Maryland, Otsego, New York, National Archives and Records Administration. Fellows, Betsey 52y; w/ Hubbard; Fellows, Diana 24y (could be 29y?); Fellows, Mary 20y; Fellows Affia M. 19y; Fellows, William E.R. 14y; Hubbard, Samuel 20y; w/ Fellows.

[54] Cemetery, Schenevus Cemetery, Maryland, Otsego County, New York. Schenevus Cemetery is the site of the 1861 Civil War Soldiers Memorial and Fellows family burials. "Betsy Goddard, wife of Ruben R. Fellows, d. Aug 10 1881 in the 84th year of her age (buried right next to Diana E. Fellows [her daughter] in Section A)."

[55] Schenevus Cemetery Records. Gravestone "Diana E. Fellows, wife of W.R. Cooke, d. June 20, 1891 at 65 y 6 m."

[56] genforum.genealogy.com/fellows/messages/340.

[57] www.interment.net/data/us/ny/otsego/schenevus_cemetery. Gravestone "S.H. Dunham b. Dec 22 1823, d. March 24 190?, Mary Fellows, his wife b. July 3 1829, d. May 26 1905 (looks like 1901 or 1904) Grave is located in far right court up the hill, Wicken Restaurant side. S.H. Dunham mentioned in this memorial was her son-in-law, husband of Mary {Fellows] Dunham."

[58] Fellows, *Descendants of William Fellows of Ipswich*.

[59] LDS International Genealogical Index, Film 107504, Ref 47690, p. 875.

[60] Find A Grave 8977239. "Gideon Ebenezer Smith Fellows."

[61] Fellows, *Descendants of William Fellows of Ipswich*.

[62] Fellows, *Descendants of William Fellows of Ipswich*, citing Erwin Wilcox Fellows and George Marshall Fellows.

[63] Find A Grave 131454707. "Rachel Cook Fellows."

[64] Fellows, *Fellows Families of Onondaga County*, p. 90. Gideon E.S. Fellows married Laura Benson Aug 1863.

[65] Fellows, *Descendants of William Fellows of Ipswich*.

[66] Find A Grave. 152676683. "Laura Benson Martin Fellows."

[67] 1840 US Census, Maryland, Otsego, New York. "G.E.S. [Gideon] Fellows."

[68] 1850 US Census, Town of Maryland, Otsego, New York. Fellows, Gideon E.S. 41y; with Rachel 42y; w/ Sperry; Fellows, Susanna 14y; Fellows, Betsey 12y; Fellows, Clarissa 10y; Fellows, Elnathan 9y; Fellows, Amos 7y; Fellows, Arthur 3y; Sperry, Jabez 16y; w/ Fellows.

[69] Obituary of Betsy (Fellows) Bright, *Jefferson County Union*, Friday, 7 Sep 1923, citing Mark D. Fellows.

[70] 1860 US Census, Geneva, Walworth, Wisconsin, p. 236. "G.E.S. Fellows."

[71] Adapted from *The History of Racine and Kenosha Counties, Wisconsin*, Chicago: Western Historical Company, 1879.

[72] 1880 US Census, Burlington, Racine, Wisconsin T9-1443, p. 224A. "Gideon, age 72, Laura, age 59, stepson, Fred Martin, age 28."

[73] Fellows, *Descendants of William Fellows of Ipswich.*

[74] Fellows, *Descendants of William Fellows of Ipswich.*

[75] Fellows, *Descendants of William Fellows of Ipswich.*

[76] LDS International Genealogical Index, Film 107504, Ref 47691, p. 875.

[77] Find A Grave 22823781. "David Fellows."

[78] Find A Grave 22823798. "Harriet Lobdell Fellows."

[79] Fellows, *Descendants of William Fellows of Ipswich.*

[80] 1880 US Census.

[81] Fellows, *Descendants of William Fellows of Ipswich.*

[82] Find A Grave 85105922. "Affia M. Fellows Sperry;" LDS International Genealogical Index, Film 457914; LDS International Genealogical Index, Film 107504, Ref 47692, p. 875.

[83] Find A Grave 85105972. "Matthew Sperry."

[84] 1850 US Census, Town of Maryland, Otsego, New York. "Sperry, Mathew 42y with Affia M. 37y; Sperry, Gideon F. 17y; Sperry, Henrietta E. 11y; Sperry, Betsey A. 4y; Sperry, Olive 60y Olive b. Mass.; Sperry, Naomi V. 22y

[85] Fellows, *Descendants of William Fellows of Ipswich.*

Chapter 10 William B. Fellows

[1] Fellows, *Fellows Families of Onondaga County,* cited by Mark D. Fellows, p. 85; LDS International Genealogical Index, Film 107504, Ref 47689, p. 875; LDS International Genealogical Index, Film 457677.

[2] The middle initial B in the name of William B. Fellows has no substantiated origin. Although it appears as part of his name in some documents, its origin is unclear. The only possible ancestor with a surname beginning with B traces back five generations to Joanna Boreman, wife of Isaac Fellows in 1672. The long span of time makes it unlikely that the B stood for Boreman.

[3] Hurd, *History of Otsego County New York, 1740-1878*, p. 354. This is an unindexed work of 378 pages with illustrations and biographical sketches of some of the prominent men and pioneers of Otsego County, New York. Hurd refers to William B. Fellows and William, Jr.

[4] Fellows, *Descendants of William Fellows of Ipswich*, citing Eleanor R. Eckert for date of marriage, not place; LDS International Genealogical Index, Film 457951.

[5] 1840 U.S. Federal Census, Maryland, Otsego, New York, Roll M704 329, page 266, National Archives and Records Administration. The enumeration 1 Jun 1840 for "Wm.

Fellows" was 1 male age 0 to 5, 2 males age 5 to 10, 1 male age 30 to 40, 1 female age 5 to 10, 1 female age 15 to 20, and 1 female age 30 to 40, The order of enumeration in the 1840 census listed Wm. Fellows (Jr.), G.E.S. (Gideon) Fellows, and Wm. Fellows (Sr.) living next to each other in that order. William (Jr.) was 33 years old, his wife, Nancy, 31. The enumeration age categories also corresponded to sons, Russell S., age 3, Wm. Ansel, 7, Warren S., 5, and daughter, Amanda, who was age 9. An unknown female 15 to 20 listed but not identified. She did not appear in the 1830 census and was probably not a household member. Enumerations of the 1840 census were the same categories as those of the 1830 census. Additionally, the 1840 census asked for the first time the ages of revolutionary war pensioners, as well as the number of persons attending school.

[6] 1850 US Census, Town of Maryland, Otsego, New York. The official enumeration day of the 1850 census was 1 June 1850. "Fellows, William 43y; Nancy 41y, Nancy born in Massachusetts" William and Nancy (Sperry) Fellows are recorded in the Town of Maryland, along with children William A. age 17, Warren S. 14, Russell S. 12, Austin M. 7, and Aaron O. age 3. (A daughter, Nancy, died in infancy in 1841). Their oldest daughter, Amanda, married Dow Webster and lived in the house next door. William's brother, Gideon, was also living in the same neighborhood with his wife and family of 6 children. William and Gideon's sister, Affia, is living nearby with her husband, Matthew Sperry, their three children, and Affia's grandmother, Olive Sperry, and her daughter, Naomi. Naomi was Nancy Sperry Fellows' youngest sister. In the Town of Maryland also in 1850 is Samuel J. Thompson, his wife Sarah, and their 4 children, including Roxanna, age 11, who will become the wife of Warren S. Fellows. It was common to find families living together in the same household or clustered in close-knit communities. There are several other Sperry and Thompson households in the town of Maryland. Reuben Fellows, the oldest brother of William, died in 1847. However, his widow, Betsey, age 52, was living in the same Maryland community as William and the other Fellows family members. The only family member not accounted for was David Fellows and mother Martha. William (Sr.) Fellows died in 1843.

[7] 1850 US Census, Maryland, Otsego, New York, Roll 579, p 148b. "Wm Fellows."

[8] Columbus, *History of the Fellows Family*, p. 5.

[9] 1860 US Census, Maryland, Otsego, New York, p. 446; Family History Library Film 803841. "Warren S Fellows."

[10] 1860 US Census, Maryland, Otsego, New York, p. 452; Family History Library Film 803841. "Wm Fellows."

[11] Hurd, *History of Otsego County New York, 1740-1878,* pp. 23, 34. This is an unindexed work of 378 pages with illustrations and biographical sketches of some of the prominent men and pioneers of Otsego County, New York.

[12] Columbus, *History of the Fellows Family*, 6.

[13] *New York State Census, 1865,* Maryland, Otsego, p. 13. "William Fellows."

[14] 1870 US Census, New York, Otsego, Maryland, image 21 of 48; citing NARA microfilm publication M593 Roll 1075, p. 35, National Archives and Records Administration. William Fellows, age 63, Nancy, age 61, and son Olen [sic], age 23, were living at dwelling 289, family

number 326 on their farm near Elk Creek. William listed as a Farmer, Nancy as Keeping House, and Olen as a Farm Laborer. All gave birthplaces of New York. Value of real estate was $2,000; value of personal property was $3,000. Before the next census in 1880, both William and Nancy would die, and Olen would move to Missouri to live with his brother, Warren S. Fellows.

[15] Columbus, *History of the Fellows Family*, p. 6, citing *Biographical Review* published in 1893; Child, *Gazetteer and Business Directory of Otego County, N.Y. for 1872-3*, p. 185. Figures placed after the listed occupation of a farmer indicated the number of acres of land owned or leased by the individual.

[16] 1870 US, Census Non-Population Schedules, New York, 1850-1880, Otsego, Maryland, pp. 7-8.

[17] Hurd, *History of Otsego County New York, 1740-1878.*

[18] Hurd, *History of Otsego County New York, 1740-1878.*

[19] *New York Wills and Probate Records, 1659-1999*, Otsego, Record of Wills, Book 0021-0022, 1873-1875, pp. 163-171, image beginning 419.

[20] Fellows, *Descendants of William Fellows of Ipswich*, citing Erwin W. Fellows. William's Will, dated 13 Jun 1874, indicated six children. The petition on the estate referred to Olin Fellows as legal heir and next of kin, proven the same person as Aaron O. in the list of children. The burials of both William and his wife Nancy were at Elk Creek Cemetery, Maryland, New York. This source mentions six children. There were, in fact, seven children. Nancy Caroline died in infancy, buried near her parents at Elk Creek Cemetery.

[21] *New York Wills and Probate Records, 1659-1999*, Otsego, Record of Wills, Book 0021-0022, 1873-1875, p. 165,

[22] Columbus, *History of the Fellows Family*, p. 10.

[23] Cemetery Records, Elk Creek, Town of Maryland, Otsego County, New York (Gravemarkers read by Glenn Aspinwall and Lealah Smith 24 Sep 1960). "William Fellows d. 9 Jan 1875 age 67y 8m 16d; Nancy [Sperry] Fellows d. 1 Mar 1879 age 69y 9m 0d [William's wife]; Nancy C. Fellows d. 23 Feb 1841 age 7m 17d dau./o William & Nancy; Carrie Fellows d. 1 Apr 1867 age 6m 4d dau./o Russell Sylvester (or Samuel & Mary Fellows); and Ira S. Webster d. 14 Sep 1856 age 1y 2m 7d son/o Dow & Amanda." Ira Webster was a grandchild of William and Nancy Fellows, son of Dow and Amanda Webster. These five members of the Fellows family lie buried next to each other.

[24] Columbus, *History of the Fellows Family*, p. 2; Fellows, *Short History of W.I. Fellows.* Their grandson, Willie Ira Fellows, in his autobiography, remembered William and Nancy. He described the countryside and told stories he remembered from his childhood in Otsego County, New York.

[25] Willie Ira Fellows, *A Short History of W.I. Fellows and the Fellows Family as Far Back as He Can Remember.* Unpublished Autobiography, c. 1940.

[26] Find A Grave 64856676. "William B. Fellows;" Fellows, *Descendants of William Fellows of Ipswich*, citing primarily Erwin Wilcox Fellows and George Marshall Fellows, who give birthdates and locations of the various families; Cornwell, *Cornwell* (Sep 2002),

[27] Find A Grave 64856676. "William B. Fellows."

[28] Find A Grave 64856880. "Nancy Sperry Fellows."

[29] Find A Grave 100759776. "Amanda Rosetta Fellows Webster."

[30] Fellows, *A Genealogy and Partial History of Fellows Families in America*, cited by Mark D. Fellows. This source has Amanda married to "David" Webster on 4 Aug 1831. Her husband's name was Dow Webster and they married in 1846. The 1831 date was the birthdate of Amanda.

[31] Cemetery Records, Elk Creek Cemetery, Otsego County, New York; Find A Grave 85095794. "Dow M. Squires Webster."

[32] 1850 US Census, Town of Maryland, Otsego, New York. "Webster, Dow M. 23y with Amanda R. 19y, Elener [*sic*] A. 6 mo."

[33] Fellows, *Short History of W.I. Fellows.*

[34] *Civil War Soldiers and Sailors System,* National Park Service, M551 Roll 148.

[35] Hurd, *History of Otsego County New York, 1740-1878.*

[36] Child, *Gazetteer and Business Directory of Otego County, N.Y. for 1872-73.*

[37] 1880 US Census. Maryland, Otsego, New York. "Amanda R. Fellows Webster, age 48, with husband Dow M. Webster, transcribed as Don [*sic*]."

[38] *The Otsego Farmer* (Cooperstown, NY), 4 Mar 1910, p. 7.

[39] Cemetery Records, Elk Creek Cemetery, Otsego County, New York. "Ira S. Webster d. 14 Sep 1856 age 1y2m7d son/o Dow & Amanda."

[40] Find A Grave 78081013.

[41] *Civil War Soldiers and Sailors System.*

[42] Columbus, *History of the Fellows Family*, p. 8.

[43] Fellows, *Short History of W.I. Fellows.*

[44] 1880 US Federal Census, Newark Valley, Tioga, New York. "Wm. A. Fellows and Mary Fellows, he was age 46 and she age 44. A son, Willis [*sic*], age 21 lived with them."

[45] Fellows, *A Genealogy and Partial History of Fellows Families in America,* cited by Fellows *Descendants of William Fellows of Ipswich.*

[46] Find A Grave 111027988.

[47] Find A Grave 78081012.

[48] *New York Death Index, 1852-1956* for Russell F Fellows, New York State Department of Health, 1905, No 3967, p. 267.

[49] Find A Grave 78081011.

[50] Fellows, *Descendants of William Fellows of Ipswich.*

[51] Fellows, *Short History of W.I. Fellows.*

[52] 1880 US Census, Newark Valley, Tioga, New York. "R. S. Fellows, age 42."

[53] Cemetery Records, Elk Creek, Town of Maryland, Otsego County, New York. "Nancy C. Fellows d. 23 Feb 1841 age 7m 17d dau./o William & Nancy;" Find A Grave. 64857043. "Nancy C. Fellows."

[54] Find A Grave 68707319. "Austin Morrell Fellows."

[55] Find A Grave 80057506. "Kate Wilson Fellows."

[56] Find A Grave 68710951. "Roxanna J. Pipes Fellows."

[57] *Civil War Soldiers and Sailors System.* Film Number M551 Roll 45. "Fellows, Austin M., Union, Infantry, 121st Regiment, New York Infantry."

[58] Columbus, *History of the Fellows Family*, p. 8.

[59] *Civil War* - Miscellaneous Records, rootsweb.com/~nyotsego/cof121. "Muster-In Roll of Captain Nelson O. Wendell's Company F, in the 121st Regiment of New York State Volunteers, commanded by Colonel B. Franchot, called into service of the United States by Proclamation of the President, from the twenty-third day of August 1862 (date of muster), for the term of three years, unless sooner discharged. "Name: Fellows, Austin M., Rank: Private, Age: 19, When: Aug 7, Where: Maryland. Credited to the regiment by the War Department: Maryland Campaign September 6-22, 1862. Duty at Sharpsburg, Md., 'til October 30. Movement to Falmouth, Va., October 30-November 19. Battle of Fredericksburg, Va., December 12-15. At Falmouth 'till April, 1863. "Mud March" January 20-24. Chancellorsville Campaign April 27-May 6. Operations at Franklin's Crossing April 29-May 2. Battle of Maryes Heights, Fredericksburg, May 3. Salem Heights May 3-4. Banks' Ford May 4. Gettysburg (Pa.) Campaign June 14-July 24. Battle of Gettysburg July 2-4. Pursuit of Lee to Manassas Gap, Va., July 5-24. Duty on line of the Rappahannock and Rapidan 'til October. Bristoe Campaign October 9-22. Advance to line of the Rappahannock November 7-8. Rappahannock Station November 7. Mine Run Campaign November 26-December 2. Campaign from the Rapidan to the James May 3-June 15, 1864. Battles of the Wilderness May 5-7; Spotsylvania May 8-12; Spotsylvania Court House May 12-21. Assault on the Salient, "Bloody Angle," May 12. North Anna River May 23-26. On line of the Pamunkey May 26-28. Totopotomoy May 28-31. Cold Harbor June 1-12. Before Petersburg June 17-18. Siege of Petersburg to July 9. Jerusalem Plank Road June 22-23. Moved to Washington, D.C., July 9-11. Repulse of Early's attack on Fort Stevens and the Northern Defences of Washington July 11-12. Expedition to Snicker's Gap July 14-23. Sheridan's Shenandoah Valley Campaign August 7-November 28. Near Charleston August 21-22. Battle of Winchester September 19. Fisher's Hill September 22. Mt. Jackson September 23-24. Battle of Cedar Creek October 19. Duty in the Shenandoah Valley 'til December. Moved to Petersburg, Va., December 9-12. Siege of Petersburg December 12, 1864, to April 2, 1865. Dabney's Mills, Hatcher's Run, February 5-7, 1865. Appomattox Campaign March 28-April 9. Assault on and fall of Petersburg April 2. Sailor's Creek April 6. Appomattox Court House April 9. Surrender of Lee and his army. At Farmville and Burkesville 'til April 23. March to Danville April 23-27 and

duty there 'til May 24. March to Richmond, thence to Washington, D.C., May 24-June 3. Corps Review June 8. Mustered out June 25, 1865. Veterans and Recruits transferred to 65th New York Infantry."

[60] Cemetery Records, Schenevus Cemetery, Maryland, Otsego County, New York.

[61] Fellows, *Short History of W.I. Fellows.*

[62] Fellows, *Descendants of William Fellows of Ipswich.*

[63] 1880 US Census, Missouri, Howard County, Boons Lick, T9-0691, p. 313A0. "Austin Fellows, age 33."

[64] Find A Grave 14452915. "Aaron Olin Fellows."

[65] 1880 US Federal Census, Salisbury, Chariton, Missouri, T9-0680, p. 412D. "Olin A. Fellows."

[66] Fellows, *Short History of W.I. Fellows.*

Chapter 11. Warren Smith Fellows Early Years

[1] Fellows, *Fellows Families of Onondaga County,* cited by Mark D. Fellows, p. 90.

[2] Columbus, *History of the Fellows Family* (written in June 1997), 12-page biography of Fellows ancestry of Warren S.Fellows, Willie Ira Fellows, and Belle Fellows; LDS International Genealogical Index, Film 457677,

[3] Columbus, *History of the Fellows Family,* p. 7.

[4] 1850 U.S. Federal Census, Town of Maryland, Otsego, New York, National Archives and Records Administration.

[5] Hurd, *History of Otsego County New York, 1740-1878.*

[6] Hurd, *History of Otsego County New York, 1740-1878,* p. 178.

[7] Hurd, *History of Otsego County New York, 1740-1878,* p. 179.

[8] Hurd, *History of Otsego County New York, 1740-1878,* p. 34. This is an unindexed work of 378 pages with illustrations and biographical sketches of some of the prominent men and pioneers of Otsego County, New York. The Fellows section begins on page 23.

[9] Columbus, *History of the Fellows Family,* p. 7.

[10] 1850 US Census, Maryland, Otsego, New York, Roll 579, p. 148b. "Warren S. Fellows." For the first time enumerators of the 1850 census had instructions to record the names of every person in the household. Added to this, enumerators had printed instructions, which account for the greater degree of accuracy compared with earlier censuses. The official enumeration day of the 1850 census was 1 June 1850. Warren Fellows was listed in the 1850 census living with his parents in the town of Maryland, Otsego County, New York.

[11] Columbus, *History of the Fellows Family,* p. 7.

[12] Columbus, *History of the Fellows Family,* p. 7, citing his "Volunteer Enlistment" paper, dated 24 Aug 1864, on file in the National Archives, Washington, D.C.

[13] Documents spell Roxanne's name variously as Roxanne, Roxanna, and Roxana. The name on her gravestone is Roxanne.

[14] George Marshall Fellows, *A Genealogy and Partial History of Fellows Families in America* (Personal manuscripts, 6 volumes, c.1900), cited by Mark D. Fellows.

[15] New York, US, State Census, 1865, for Samuel Thompson, Otsego, Maryland, p. 57. The 1865 New York census contained numerous errors for the ages of members of the Thompson household. The census listed Roxanne and Warren as 22 and 24 respectively. They were actually 27 and 30, according to their birthdates.

[16] *The Freeman's Journal* (Cooperstown, NY), May 25, 1893, p. 5.

[17] Fellows, *Short History of W.I. Fellows*, p. 8.

[18] 1860 US Census, New York, Otsego, Maryland, Schenevus P.O., NARA Series M653 Roll 841, p. 23.

[19] Columbus, *History of the Fellows Family*, p. 7.

[20] Columbus, *History of the Fellows Family*, p. 7.

[21] Columbus, *History of the Fellows Family*, p. 8.

[22] Fellows, *Short History of W.I. Fellows*, p. 8; *Civil War Soldiers and Sailors System* (National Park Service), Film Number M551 Roll 45. "Fellows, Warren S., Union, Cavalry, 3rd Regiment, New York Cavalry;" Warren S. Fellows served on the Union side of the Civil War in Company D of the Third New York Cavalry. He served in the rank of Private. Two of his brothers, Austen and William Ansel, one of his wife's brothers, Beckwith Thompson, and a cousin, Edward R. Fellows(Reuben's son)—all from Maryland, Otsego County, New York—also served. Columbus, *History of the Fellows Family*, p. 8, citing the autobiography of Warren Fellows. Willie Ira Fellows wrote in his autobiography that his father served three years in the car. However, his service lasted only a year.

[23] Columbus, *History of the Fellows Family*, p. 8.

[24] Columbus, *History of the Fellows Family*, p. 8, citing Warren Fellows autobiography.

[25] Columbus, *History of the Fellows Family*, p. 8, citing Warren Fellows autobiography and War Department records. "On roll for Sept & Oct. '64, present Nov & Dec. '64, absent sick in Regtl hospl since Dec. 25, '64. Jan & Feb. '65 present same to Apr 30, '65. Mustered out on detachment muster out roll June 7, 1865 at Norfolk Va. Name not borne on Return for Nov. 1864 as absent. Company Morning Report Book shows him as follows: December 25th 1864 "from pres D to abs S in Hosp Ports. Va." January 6th 1865 "from abs S pres S. per Orders" February 1st 1865 "sick," March 1st 1865 "sick," March 26th 1865 "from S to D."

[26] Columbus, *History of the Fellows Family*, p. 9.

[27] Columbus, *History of the Fellows Family*, p. 9.

[28] Columbus, *History of the Fellows Family*, p. 8. Mrs. Daum tried unsuccessfully to locate the pictures mentioned in Willie Ira's autobiography.

[29] Fellows, *Short History of W.I. Fellows*, p. 1-2.

[30] Fellows, *Short History of W.I. Fellows*, p. 10; Columbus, *History of the Fellows Family*, p. 9.

[31] Columbus, *History of the Fellows Family*, p. 9.

[32] Cemetery, Schenevus Cemetery, Maryland, Otsego County, New York, interment.net/data/us/ny/otsego/schenevus_cemetery; 1861 Civil War. Soldiers Memorial, Schenevus Cemetery, Town of Maryland, Otsego County, NY. Schenevus Cemetery is the site of the 1861 Civil War Soldiers Memorial and Fellows family burials including Austin M. Fellows, Wm. Ansel Fellows, and Warren Fellows. Other Fellows listed on the memorial are: Edward R. Fellows, Beckwith Thompson [This is Warren's brother-in-law, Roxanne's brother]. Other Thompsons on the memorial are: Augustus G. Thompson, and John Thompson. The Schenevus Cemetery War Memorial honors Warren S. Fellows and all who served in the Civil War from Otsego County, New York. Warren S. Fellows was not buried in Schenevus Cemetery but in Neosho, Missouri.

[33] Hurd, *History of Otsego County New York, 1740-1878*, p. 183. "The following is a partial record of those who enlisted from Maryland during the late Rebellion, completed by James Thompson in 1865. Austin M. Fellows, enl. in Co F, 121st Regt., Aug. 11, 1862; in battles of the Wilderness, Fredericksburg, Gettysburg, and Shenandoah Valley; wounded at Wilderness. D.M. Webster, enl. in Co E. 1st Eng., 1864; dis. 13 June 1865. Warren S. Fellows, enl. in Co D, 3rd Cav, Aug 1864; dis. 1865 (credited to Westford). William Ansel Fellows, enl. 1st Eng. Aug 1864; dis. July 1, 1865 (credited to Westford). Beckwith Thompson, enl. Co I, 51st Regt, Sept 5, 1862; in battles of Fredericksburg, Petersburg, Wilderness, and Jackson; dis. June, 1865. Edward R. Fellows, Sergt. Enl. Co D, 3rd Cav, Aug 5, 1861; in battles of Little Washington, Kingston, Goldsboro', Reams' Station; dis. Aug 12, 1864."

[34] Census of the State of New York, for 1865. (Microfilm), New York State Archives, Albany, New York, p. 57. "Warner [*sic*] Fellows."

[35] Fellows, *Short History of W.I. Fellows*, p. 10. New York Land Records, 1630-1975, Schoharie, Grantor index 1859-1875, Vol. 4-5, p. 398. "Warren S. Fellows and wife Grantors to Grantee Mary A. Strail, Land Assessment, 17 Apr 1866."

[36] Columbus, *History of the Fellows Family*, p. 7.

[37] Fellows, *Short History of W.I. Fellows*, p. 2; Columbus, *History of the Fellows Family*, p. 7.

[38] Fellows, *Short History of W.I. Fellows*, p. 2.

[39] Fellows, *Short History of W.I. Fellows*, p. 2.

[40] *New York Land Records, 1630-1975, Schoharie, Grantor Index 1859-1875*, Vol. 4-5, pp. 153-154, Image 126. "Warren S. Fellows and wife Grantors to Grantees Peter J. Strail and Mary Ann Strail, Land Assessment, 10 Oct 1867, Schoharie, New York." Records of Land Assessments in Schoharie County suggest that Warren and Roxanne may have lived on the Strail property from April 1866 to October 1867, and that the move to Missouri took place a year later than previously believed.

[41] Columbus, *History of the Fellows Family*, p. 10.

[42] Fellows, *Short History of W.I. Fellows,* p. 3.

[43] Fellows, *Short History of W.I. Fellows,* p. 5. The Willie Ira Fellows' autobiography is devoted primarily to memories of his parents, the family's early days in Otsego County, New York, and later travels to Missouri and Kansas.

[44] Fellows, *Short History of W.I. Fellows,* p. 7.

Chapter 12 Warren Smith Fellows Later Years

[1] Missouri State Census Collection, 1844-1881, 1876, Township 50-N, Range 17-W, Howard County, Missouri, Roll MOSC 2817, p. 6. "W. S. Fellows." The location of the Fellows farm in 1870 was the same location set forth in the Missouri census of 1876.

[2] 1870 US Census, Chariton Township, Howard County, Missouri M593 780 p. 298, National Archives and Records Administration. W. S. Fellows was listed as family No. 302 in the 1870 US Census, Chariton Township, Howard County, Missouri, Post Office, Fayette. The census listed him age 35, a Farmer with land valued at $5,000, and property of $800. He was born in New York. His wife, Roxana [*sic*] listed as age 32 and Keeping House. She was also born in New York. Three children: Flora, age 13; Willie, 11; and Isabel [*sic*] age 9 shown as attending school in the census year. Roset [*sic*], age 4 was at home. These five children were born in New York. The youngest child listed, Ernest, age 1, was born in Missouri. Living with Warren and Roxanne in 1870 was Warren's brother Austin J. [*sic*], age 28, a Farmer, also born in New York. Not listed on the 1870 census was daughter, Katie Caldonia, who was born in 1870 after the census occurred. Warren S. Fellows came to Howard County, Missouri, in 1868 following a year in Linn County, Missouri, in 1867. Austin accompanied Roxanne and children from New York to Missouri in 1867

[3] Fellows, *Short History of W.I. Fellows,* p. 9.

[4] Fellows, *Short History of W.I. Fellows,* p. 10.

[5] Fellows, *Short History of W.I. Fellows,* p. 7

[6] Fellows, *Short History of W.I. Fellows,* p. 5. Willie Ira Fellows was slightly incorrect in his characterization of Boones-borough. Daniel Boone was not a settler of Boones-borough, although he did visit his sons Nathan and Daniel Morgan Boone there who were early pioneers of the Boonslick region.

[7] Fellows, *Short History of W.I. Fellows,* p. 5.

[8] Fellows, *Short History of W.I. Fellows,* p. 5.

[9] Missouri State Census Collection, 1844-1881, 1876, Township 50-N, Range 17-W, Howard County, Missouri, Roll MOSC 2817, p. 6. "W.S. Fellows." For unknown reasons, the 1876 Missouri census did not list Katie Caldonia Fellows who was born in 1872. Austin Fellows lived in the same Township 50, Range 17.

[10] Fellows, *Short History of W.I. Fellows,* p. 7; Columbus, *History of the Fellows Family*, p. 11. Mrs. Columbus claimed that Warren sold the Howard County property in 1881 and not 1778, as others claimed. She cites a Warranty Deed from Chariton County, in which Warren bought land from William and Josephine Thomas, according to a deed signed August 6, 1881.

[11] 1880 US Census, Salisbury, Chariton, Missouri T9-0680, p. 412D, National Archives and Records Administration. Warren S. Fellows, age 44 b. N.Y., Farmer, father b. Conn., mother b. Mass.; Roxinia Fellows, wife, age 42 b. N.Y., Keeps House, father b. N.Y., mother b. N.Y.; Flora A. Fellows, dau, single, age 22 b. N.Y., Teacher; William L.[*sic*] Fellows, single, age 20 b. N.Y., Works on Farm; Bell S. Fellows, dau, single, age 18 b. N.Y.; Ernest S. Fellows, son, age 10 b. N.Y., Works On Farm; Katie C. Fellows, dau, age 10 b. Mo.; Olin A. Fellows, son [*sic*], single, age 32 b. N.Y.; Rose Fellows, dau, age 12 b. N.Y. Warren S. Fellows was listed in the 1880 US Census as living in Salisbury, Chariton, Missouri, with his wife Roxinia [*sic*] and 6 children—ranging in age from 22 to 12 (4 daughters and 2 sons) and his brother, Olin A. Fellows. In the previous 1870 census, Olin was living with his parents in Elk Creek, New York. Warren's occupation in 1880 listed as Farmer; Roxanne listed as Keeps House. Flora A. Fellows, a daughter age 22, listed as a schoolteacher. Children William L. [*sic*], Bell S. Ernest S. Katie C., and Rose listed, but ages and birthplaces were incorrectly recorded, as was Olin Fellows as a son instead of brother. There appear to be several problems with the LDS transcription.

[12] 1880 US Census, Salisbury, Chariton, Missouri T9-0680, p. 412D, National Archives and Records Administration. "Warren S. Fellows, age 44."

[13] Columbus, *History of the Fellows Family*, p. 10.

[14] *Civil War Pension Index*. 14 Aug 1883 Invalid application 492.616 Certificate 506.607. Cavalry Company/regiment D/3.

[15] Columbus, *History of the Fellows Family*, p. 11.

[16] Columbus, *History of the Fellows Family*, p. 11.

[17] Fellows, *Short History of W.I. Fellows and the Fellows Family as Far Back as He Can Remember*, Unpublished Autobiography, 1940; Columbus, *History of the Fellows Family*, p. 11. Columbus claimed the move to Ness City, Kansas, occurred in 1889.

[18] Fellows, *Short History of W.I. Fellows*, p. 8.

[19] 1900 US Census, Kansas, Ness, Center Township (Ness City) Dist. 160, sheet 5, p. 217A, National Archives and Records Administration. Warren S. Fellows and wife, Roxana [*sic*], were living in Ness City, Kansas, dwelling number 104, census family 110. Living with them was a boarder, the "Clerk of the Court," Frank H. Gelmon, age 32. Warren S. age 64, birthday recorded as June 1835; Roxanne age 61, birthday recorded as October 1838. In 1900, they had been married for 45 years. Roxana is listed as the mother of 6 children, 6 of these children living. On the census report, Roxanne and her parents listed as born in New York. Warren S. was born in New York, his father in Massachusetts, and mother born in Connecticut. [These were backwards; his mother was born in Massachusetts, father in Connecticut.] Under the heading of education, both indicated they could read and write. In 1900, they owned their home free of mortgage. The census noted that they were living in a house, rather than on a farm.

[20] Columbus, *History of the Fellows Family*, p. 11.

[21] 1895 Kansas State Census, Ness, Kansas. "W.S. Fellows, age 59."

[22] Columbus, *History of the Fellows Family*, p. 11.

[23] Columbus, *History of the Fellows Family*, p. 12; 1905 Kansas State Census, Ness, Kansas, p. 3. "W. S. Fellows, age 69."

[24] Fellows, *Short History of W.I. Fellows.*

[25] Roxane and Warren bought Lot 8, Block 3, of Wheelers Addition to Neosho on May 21, 1906. Their street address was 314 Grant Street, citing Marjorie Daum Columbus, *History of the Fellows Family*, p. 12; see also 1910 US Census.

[26] Columbus, *History of the Fellows Family*, p. 13.

[27] Warrend S. Fellows, *US Veterans Administration Pension Payment Cards*, Military Unit Army Invalid NARA Roll 717. $15 per month certificate approved 19 Apr 1907 effective from 18 Feb 1907. Warren Fellows died 4 Apr 1909.

[28] Find A Grave 22869486. "Warren Smith Fellows;" Cemetery Records, International Order of Odd Fellows, Neosho, Newton, Missouri. "Fellows, W.S., d. 4/4/1909, Age 73 yrs, Cancer, attending physician Dr. Lamson, Neosho, Missouri."

[29] Warrend S. Fellows, *US Veterans Administration Pension Payment Cards*, Military Unit Army Invalid NARA Roll 717. Roxanna Fellows Army Widow Certificate approved 25 Jun 1909 effective 23 Apr 1909. Widow application 918,469 Certificate 684,227.

[30] 1910 US Census, Missouri, Newton, Neosho, 2-Ward, Dist. 125, T624 802 p. 202, National Archives and Records Administration. In 1910, Roxanne [spelled Rohana in census transcriptions] was living alone in Neosho, Missouri. Warren died in 1909 a year and a month before the census was recorded on 3 & 4 May 1910, and Roxanne is listed as the head of the household. She is living on Somerset [or Summit] Street, house number 314, dwelling number 654, family number 666; age is 71, and widowed. She was recorded as the mother of 6 children, 4 of them surviving in 1910. Her birth and that of her parents was New York. She listed an occupation but it is illegible on the census form, possibly "own support." She owned the house she was living in free of mortgage. Her son, William Ira in his autobiography said his parents retired to a nice place in Neosho.

[31] Find A Grave 22869485. "Roxanne Thompson Fellows."

[32] Roxana [sic] Fellows Death Certificate 42147-1, Missouri State Board of Health Vital Statistics.

[33] Cemetery, International Order of Odd Fellows, Neosho, Newton, Missouri. "Fellows, R., d.12/6/1917."

[34] Find A Grave 22869486; Cornwell, *Cornwell* (Sep 2002), Source gives the birth dates and locations of the children of Warren Smith and Roxanna.

[35] Columbus, *History of the Fellows Family*, p. 13. Mrs. Columbus noted in her account of Roxanne' funeral that Nicholas Daum, Roxanne's son-in-law, did not attend, nor did any of the Daum family, nor did the Cowles family.

[36] Find A Grave 86476270. "Flora Amanda Fellows Rutledge."

[37] Find A Grave 86476302. "Rev. Johnson Keith Rutledge."

[38] Motta/Fulmer Family Tree 2011.

[39] Find A Grave 29701095. "William Ira Fellows."

[40] Find A Grave 107790746. "Isabel S 'Belle' Fellows Reid."

[41] Find A Grave 107790865. "Arthur W. Reid."

[42] Columbus, *History of the Fellows Family*, p.8; Missouri, US, State Census Collection, 1844-1881, 1876, Howard County, Missouri, Roll MOSC 2817. Rosetta Fellows was the great grandmother of Marjorie (Daum) Columbus. Rosetta's name appears three ways in various documents. Her brother referred to her as Rosett, but also as Rosie in his autobiography. The newspaper called her Mrs. Rose Daum in her death notice; the cemetery record calls her Rosett Ella Daum. Included with the cemetery record is a photograph from Rose Coventry, Rosie's granddaughter, daughter of Verna Daum. A typed note says, "Rose Fellows Daum, for whom you were named."

[43] Find A Grave 34321870. "Rosett Ella Daum."

[44] Find A Grave 34321766. "Nicholas Freeland Daum."

[45] Columbus, *History of the Fellows Family*, p. 13.

[46] 1900 US Census, Lawrence, Ward 2, Douglas, Kansas, Enumeration District 0060, FHL microfilm 1240479, p. 10.

[47] *Ness County News*, 27 Apr 1901.

[48] Find A Grave. 41238878. "Ernest Samuel Fellows."

[49] Find A Grave. 41238903. "Jacqueline Barnd."

[50] Obituary of William Ira Fellows, *Cedar County Republican*.

Chapter 13 Willie Ira Fellows

[1] State Board of Health of Missouri Standard Certificate of Death No.13104; Find A Grave 29701095. Documents consistently refer to him as Willie Ira, the name he used in his autobiography, and the name recorded on his death certificate. The 1880 census and subsequent census records recorded him as William. The name carved on his gravestone was William. Neighbors also knew him locally as Will Fellows.

[2] Willie Ira Fellows, *A Short History of W.I. Fellows and the Fellows Family as Far Back as He Can Remember*, Unpublished Autobiography, 1940, p. 2. The Fellows autobiography is devoted primarily to memories of his parents, the family's early days in Otsego County, New York, and later travels to Missouri and Kansas. According to Willie Ira, Warren S. Fellows moved to Missouri in 1866; his wife and family followed a year later in 1867. Warren settled originally in Linn County, near Brookfield, Missouri, before moving to Howard County, six miles from Glasgow, Missouri. He later moved in 1889 to Ness City, Kansas, before coming to Neosho, Missouri, in 1907 where he spent his last years.

[3] Fellows, *Short History of W.I. Fellows*, p. 4.

[4] Fellows, *Short History of W.I. Fellows*, p. 4.

[5] Fellows, *Short History of W.I. Fellows*, p. 4.

[6] Fellows, *Short History of W.I. Fellows*, p. 5.

[7] Fellows, *Short History of W.I. Fellows*, p. 7.

[8] 1870 US Census, Chariton, Howard, Missouri, National Archives and Records Administration, 700 Pennsylvania Avenue NW, Washington, DC 20408. The official enumeration day of the 1870 census was 27 Jul 1870.

[9] Fellows, *Short History of W.I. Fellows*, p. 6.

[10] 1880 US Census, Salisbury, Chariton, Missouri, National Archives and Records Administration; Ready, *History of Willie Ira Fellows* (written about 1983). Family history by Aunt Effie (Fellows) Ready who wrote it for her son, Archie Ready. "Fellow's father, Warren Smith Fellows was born June 22, 1835, in Otsego County, New York. He married Roxana Thompson, born October 6, 1839, in Otsego County, New York, March 17, 1855. They had two sons and two daughters, Willie Ira, Ernest, Mary and Roxana. They came to Salisbury, Missouri in 1866. The town was called Brookfield then. My father, [Willie Ira] Fellows, was seven years old then. They also lived at Moberly, Clifton Hill, and Glasgow, Missouri. Father used to go down to Booneslick Park and gather Hickory nuts. This park is where Daniel Boone used to be at one time. My father's uncle, Austin Fellows and his second wife, Roxana Pipes Fellows, are put away in Salisbury Cemetery." Effie's recollection of Warren and Roxanne's children was somewhat inaccurate.

[11] 1880 US Census, Salisbury, Chariton, Missouri, Roll 680, p. 412D, Enumeration District 162. The 1880 census incorrectly listed Olin Fellows, age 32, as the son of Warren and Roxanne. Olin would die later that year in December 1880 from the scourge of alcoholism.

[12] Ready, *History of Willie Ira Fellows*. Effie has Willie Ira Fellows and Martha [Crutchfield] married 27 Dec 1881 by Rev. Pope Bond. However, Willie Ira confirmed in his autobiography the 1882 date.

[13] Ready, *History of Willie Ira Fellows*. "Martha's father, John James (Jack) Crutchfield was born June 1, 1840, in Randolph County, Missouri. He passed away July 23, 1928. He married Frances Henderson, Chariton County, Mo. She was born about 1845. They had two daughters, Mary Barbara, born in 1862 and died July 7, 1940. Martha Frances was born March 27, 1865 and died January 22, 1943. My mother's father, John (Jack) Crutchfield and his wife, Frances Henderson Crutchfield are put away in Salisbury Missouri Cemetery. My two great uncles Taylor and Logan Henderson are buried in Salisbury Cemetery."

[14] "Be It Known and Remembered," *Bible of William B. Crutchfield,* Louisiana Genealogical and Historical Society, 1961. Vol. 2, Bible Records, pp. 61-113. Record submitted to the [Louisiana Genealogical and Historical] Society through DAR by Mrs. Paul Stinson, Jonesboro, La. certified to be a true copy of the data contained in the Crutchfield Bible as copied for her from the original by Gladys Crutchfield Ferguson. William B. Crutchfield and Barbara Mathlock were married 24 May 1837 by Peter Doupt, in Caswell County, North Carolina, and came to Missouri in 1838. See also *Caswell County, North Carolina, Marriage Bonds, 1741-1868,* An Index to Marriage Bonds Filed in the North Carolina State Archives, Raleigh, N.C., North Carolina Division of Archives and History, 1977. Bride: Barbara

Matlock, Groom: William B. Crutchfield, Bond Date: 08 May 1837. The date recorded is the bond date and may or may not be the date of actual marriage.

[15] "Be It Known and Remembered," *Bible of William B. Crutchfield.* Births: William B. Crutchfield was born April 15, 1814; Barbara Matlock was born March 12, 1818; Thomas Gunn Crutchfield was born May 24, 1838; John James Crutchfield was born June 1, 1840; Martha Elizabeth Crutchfield was born Feb. 10, 1842; William Alexander Crutchfield was born Sept. 19, 1843; George Washington Crutchfield was born Apr. 3, 1845; Sarah Ann Crutchfield was born Feb. 4, 1847; Leander Asbury Crutchfield was born May 15, 1849; Mary Susan Crutchfield was born Mar. 23, 1851; Nicholas Andrew Crutchfield was born Jan. 4, 1853; Stapleton Terrisha Crutchfield was born Nov. 21, 1855. Births recorded in the Crutchfield Bible are for William B. Crutchfield and Barbara Matlock, and their 10 children. William Blane Crutchfield married two times. After the death of Barbara Matlock, William married Sallie [*sic*] Bentley, 21 Feb 1870. They had no children. Barbara Matlock was the daughter of James and Martha Hooper (Gunn) Matlock. Email message from Don Crutchfield.

[16] Bureau of Land Management, Department of the Interior, Accession No. KS3070-064, Certificate No. 9459 dated 13 Dec 1889. "Willie I. Fellows NW ¼ Twp-Rng 0175-24 W, Section 26, 160 acres in Ness County, Kansas." Willie Ira erred slightly in his recollection of the dates associated with Ness County, Kansas. He said he sold out and returned to Missouri in 1888. However, the Bureau of Land Management did not issue the patent for his 160 acres until 13 Dec 1889.

[17] Fellows, *Short History of W.I. Fellows*, p. 7.

[18] 1900 US Census, Benton, Cedar, Missouri, p. 3, Enumeration District 0044, FHL microfilm 1240847. "William I. Fellows." The 1900 census recorded Martha as "Martha M." and not Martha F. Fellows.

[19] 1910 US Census, Missouri, Cedar County, Benton Township, T624-768, p. 114, 19 Apr 1910, National Archives and Records Administration. "William I. Fellows;" 1920 US Census, Missouri, Cedar County, Benton Township, 51-08b, enumerated 13 Apr 1920, National Archives and Records Administration. "Willie I. Fellows."

[20] Fellows, *Short History of W.I. Fellows*, p. 10.

[21] 1920 US Census, Missouri, Cedar County, Benton Township, 51-08b, 13 Apr 1920, National Archives and Records Administration.

[22] Fellows, *Short History of W.I. Fellows*, pp. 7-8.

[23] Beatrice Memory Book. Beatrice provided brief answers to a series of questions in a memory book completed at the request of her granddaughter.

[24] Fellows, *Short History of W.I. Fellows*, p. 9.

[25] Fellows, *Short History of W.I. Fellows*, p. 10.

[26] Robert Lee Meyers, *Place Names in the Southwest Counties of Missouri*, M.A. thesis, University of Missouri-Columbia, 1930; Joseph Thomas, ed., *Lippincott's Gazetteer of the World: A Complete Pronouncing Gazetteer*. Philadelphia: J.B. Lippincott, 1902. Doylesport was

a township of Barton County, Missouri, 20 miles south-southeast of Nevada, Missouri, with a population of 385 in 1902.

[27] Martha Frances Fellows Death Certificate No. 5729, Missouri State Board of Health; Effie Fellows Ready, *History of Willie Ira Fellows,* citing Obituary of Martha Frances Crutchfield. Her obituary read, in part, "Services were in charge of Mr. Beeney of Sheldon, who delivered a fitting tribute to one whom he had known well for so many years. 'Sunset and evening star, And one clear call for me, And may there be no moaning at the bar, When I put out to sea, But such a tide as moving seems asleep, Too full for sound and foam, When that which drew from out the boundless deep, Turns again home. For though from out bourne [*sic*] of Time and Place, The flood may bear me far, I hope to see my Pilot face to face, When I have crossed the bar!'." The followsin Card of Thanks followed the obituary: "We wish to thank everyone for their kindness and sympathy shown during our hour of bereavement. Especially do we thank the singers, and those who helped prepare the final resting place for our dear one. W.I. Fellows and Family;" Cemetery, Brasher, Cedar, Missouri, Grave Stone Inscription: "Fellows, Martha 1865-1943." Single headstone with husband, William I. Fellows, inscribed on the left side.

[28] Find A Grave 29701093. "Martha Frances (Crutchfield) Fellows."

[29] Willie Ira Fellows Death Certificate No.13104, Missouri State Board of Health Vital Statistics. Rumors that Willie Ira died from the complications of Gangrene are unconfirmed as contributing to cause of death, according to the medical report on his death certificate.

[30] Find A Grave 29701095 & 29701093. "William Ira Fellows, Martha Frances Crutchfield Fellows." Cemetery, Brasher, Cedar, Missouri: Grave Stone Inscription (personally viewed and copied), Brasher Cemetery, Cedar County, Missouri. Inscription:

Fellows
Martha William I.
1865 - 1943 1859 - 1945

[31] Obituary of William Ira Fellows, *Cedar County Republican.* The obituary read, in part, "Last rites were conducted in Brasher Cemetery Friday afternoon, March 2nd by Rev. B. O. Brooks. Church & Neale in charge." A Card of Thanks followed the obituary. "We wish to express our heartfelt thanks to our friends and neighbors who were so kind and thoughtful during our recent bereavement, the passing of our father, W.I. Fellows. The many acts of kindness shown to us at this time, the words of consolation, and everything done to assuage our grief will never be forgotten. May God bless you all. The Fellows Family."

[32] Fellows, *Short History of W.I. Fellows.*

[33] Obituary, William Ira Fellows, *Cedar County Republican.*

[34] Merle Fellows Family, *W.I. Fellows Genealogy.* In December 1977, the Merle D. Fellows family received a copy of the Fellows Family History compiled by his grandfather, W.I. Fellows. In an effort to bring it to the present date [1977], the family updated the Wayne Fellows information concerning the tradition of carrying the testament through wartime. Wayne Fellows kept the Bible at his home east of Stockton, Missouri. He died 6 Jun 1979, and

the Bible was last in the possession of his wife, Ellen Fellows. Wayne and Ellen did not have children. When Ellen died in 2003, the Bible apparently passed into unknown hands.

[35] Cornwell, *Cornwell* (Sep 2002), Internet, Source lists the children of William Ira and Martha Crutchfield Fellows, along with their life dates and places.

[36] Find A Grave 29701095. "William Ira Fellows."

[37] State Board of Health of Missouri Standard Certificate of Death No. 13104. "Willie Ira Fellows."

[38] Death Certificate No. 26295, *Missouri Death Certificates*. Missouri Secretary of State.

[39] Obituary of Claud Arthur Fellows. "Claude Arthur Fellows, son of W.I. and Martha Frances Fellows was born in Chariton County, Missouri, September 30, 1884. Departed this life at his home near Jerico Springs, August 11, 1956, at the age of 71 years, 10 months and 11 days. He came with his parents to Cedar county, Missouri when about four years old and spent the remainder of his life here on the farm of his father except for about eight years in Oklahoma. He was converted to Christ some thirty or thirty-five years ago and was baptized by the Rev. Porter. He was never too busy to leave his own work to go to help someone else and even when his health was failing and he was not physically able he would still go and help. He remained cheerful to the end and his kind deeds will be long remembered by his many friends. Surviving are his wife, Hope, of the home; two sons and their wives, Wayne of Neosho and Elmo of De Queen, Ark.; one grandson, Raymond Elmo, Jr. and a great-grandson, Raymond E. III, of Bartlesville, Okla.; three brothers, Lee of Nevada, Mo.; Earl of Lamar; Mo.; and Lester of Milford, Mo.; three sisters, Mrs. Belle Cardwell of Stockton, Mo., Mrs. Maud Potter of Montevallo, Mo., and Mrs. Effie Ready of Kansas City, Mo., and three nieces and six nephews. Funeral services were conducted Monday afternoon at 2 o'clock, August 13, 1956, at the Jerico Springs Methodist Church by Rev. W. H. Jones officiating, assisted by Rev. Frank Nickel. Songs: 'In the Garden,' 'It Is Well with My soul,' and 'No Night There' were sung by Wanonia Skaggs, Gladys Morrison, Buenta Long, Rev. Frank Nickel, Rev. W.H. Jones. The accompanist was Mrs. Lutie Brasher. Interment in the Brasher Cemetery under the direction of Long Funeral Home, Jerico springs, Mo."

[40] Cemetery, Brasher, Cedar, Missouri, Grave Stone Inscription, personally viewed. "Claude Fellows and Hope Lester, 21 Oct 1941." The marriage date of Claud and Hope Fellows is inscribed on their joint tombstone; Ready, *History of Willie Ira Fellows*. "Married by Rev. W.B. Carrico."

[41] Obituary of Hope Fellows. "Gladys Hope Fellows, 73, died October 11 at the Medi-Center in Springfield after a long illness. The daughter of Joseph and Flora Lester, she was born in Kingston, Mo. She taught school for two years and then entered the business world as a private secretary. She moved to Jerico Springs from Caldwell County in 1937. In 1941, she married Claude Fellows, who died in 1956. She was a member of the Fairview Community Church, the Jerusalem Club, and Greenridge WPFA Club. Survivors include two sisters, Mrs. Elma Shadduck, Peculiar, Mo., Mrs. Joy Chase, El Dorado Springs; two brothers, Charles Lester, Manson, Wash., and Jesse Lester, Conway, Ark.; 21 nieces and nephews and other relatives. Rites were conducted at 2:00 p. m, October 13 at the Jerico Springs United

Methodist Church, Rev. Frank Nickel officiating. Burial was in Brasher Cemetery under direction of Long Funeral Home;" Newspaper Clipping, Hope Fellows. "Mrs. Hope Fellows, 73, Jerico Springs, died at 12:15 a.m. Monday at Medi-Center, Springfield, after a long illness. The daughter of Joseph and Flora Lester, Mrs. Fellows was born March 3, 1903, in Caldwell County in North Missouri She moved to Jerico Springs in 1937. She married Claude Fellows in October 1941. He died in August 1956. She made her home on a farm near Jerico Springs until 1974 and moved to town in 1974. She held memberships in the Fairview Community Church, Jerusalem Club of Jerico Springs, and Green Ridge WPFA. Burial will be in Brasher Cemetery near Jerico Springs under direction of Long Funeral Home."

[42] 1910 U.S. Federal Census, T624 Roll 768, p. 120,

[43] 1930 US Census, Benton, Cedar, Missouri, p. 6A, Enumeration District 0003, FHL microfilm 2340917.

[44] *World War II Draft Cards (Fourth Registration) for the State of Missouri, Records of the Selective Service System*; Record Group Number 147; Box or Roll Number 865, National Archives at St. Louis; St. Louis, Missouri,

[45] Cemetery, Brasher, Cedar, Missouri: Grave Stone Inscription: Claude A. Fellows 30 Sep 1884 – 11 Aug 1956, Hope Lester Fellows 3 Mar 1903 – 11 Oct , Wayne A. Fellows 4 Oct 1911 – 6 Jun1979 married 24 Dec 1972, Inscribed "Sarge," Ellen L. Fellows 23 Apr 1912 [she died in 2003 but her tombstone does not include a death date]. Claud and Hope share a gravestone. The single stone of son Wayne and his wife, Ellen, is nearby in the same Fellows plot, along with William Ira and Martha Fellows and their daughter, Belle Fellows Cardwell. William and Martha's infant son, Charlie, also is buried in this plot.

[46] Funeral Memorial Book of Jack Fellows. "John Roscoe Fellows b. June 28, 1887, Ness County, Kansas. d. April 25, 1947, Vernon County, Missouri, age 59 years 9 months 27 days."

[47] 1910 US Census,

[48] Newspaper Clipping, Jack Fellows, Apr 1947. "Milford Man Drowns. Body of Jack Fellows Found in the Well on the Place North of Milford Friday Morning—Snapped Well Rope and Broken Well Platform Told the Fatal Story—Deceased Batched with His Brother on the Farm—Funeral Service at Sheldon Saturday Afternoon...The deceased was born at Ness, Kansas, June 28, 1887. He had never married. He leaves the bachelor brother with whom he made his home along with four other brothers and three sisters. They are Claude Fellows of Jerico, Lee of Idaho, Willie of Sheldon, Lester of Milford, Mrs. Mary Bell Cardwell of Jerico Springs, Mrs. Maude Potter of Montevallo and Mrs. Effie Ready of Kansas City. The body was taken to the Beeny Funeral Home in Sheldon to be prepared for burial. Funeral services were announced to take place at the Beeny Chapel at 2:30 Saturday."

[49] Merle Fellows Family, *W.I. Fellows Genealogy*. Sources disagree about the birthplace of Lee Fellows. This source says that Lee was born in Chariton County, Missouri. Others give Sheridan County, Missouri. Since there is no Sheridan County, Missouri, he may have been born in Kansas during the brief time that the family lived there. Sheridan, Missouri, is in Worth County, which is in the far northwest corner of Missouri and not known to be a place where the Fellows family lived. There was no township or city in Chariton County of the

name Sheridan. Find A Grave research gives his birthplace as Salisbury, Chariton County. On his WW I Draft Registration card, he entered Salisbury.

[50] Sharron Burchett O'Connor Genealogies.

[51] Find A Grave 190527850. "Lee Crutchfield Fellows."

[52] Cornwell, *Cornwell.* Source gives her birth date as 1902; other sources say 1892.

[53] Ready, *History of Willie Ira Fellows.* "Lee Crutchfield Fellows died Nov. 22, 1970 at 10:15 a.m. at Eldorado Springs, Missouri. Put away at Dunnegan Grove, Cemetery, close to Sheldon, Missouri;" Find A Grave 190528026. "Pauline Richey Fellows Hale."

[54] Obituary, William Ira Fellows, *Cedar County Republican.*

[55] *World War I Draft Registration Cards, 1917-1918.*

[56] 1920 US Census, Missouri, Cedar County, Benton Township, 51-08b.

[57] Obituary of Lee Fellows. Obituary 1: Lee Fellows. "Lee Fellows, eighty-two, long time resident of Jerico Springs, died at his home at 10:15 a.m., Sunday. He leaves two sons, Everett Fellows of Anchorage, Alaska, Merle Fellows of Nevada, one daughter, Mrs. Frances Cross of Nevada, two sisters, Mrs. Maude Potter of Eldorado Springs, Mrs. Effie Ready of Fulton, two brothers, Irl Fellows of Kansas City, Lester Fellows of Milford, and six grandchildren. The body was taken to the Long funeral home at Jerico Springs to be prepared for burial. The last rites were announced for 2:00 p.m. Tuesday at the United Methodist church at Jerico Springs. Interment follows in Dunnegan Grove cemetery." Obituary 2: "Lee Fellows El Dorado Springs. Funeral services for Lee Fellows, 82, of El Dorado Springs, were at 2 p.m. Tuesday in the Jerico Springs United Methodist Church with the Rev. Lloyd Wasson officiating. Burial was in Dunnegan Grove Cemetery with military rites conducted at the graveside. Funeral arrangements were under the direction of Long of Jerico Springs. He was a native of Chariton County, Mo., and a World War I veteran. Survivors include his wife, Pauline; two sons, Everett of Anchorage, Alaska, and Merle of Nevada; one daughter, Mrs. Frances Cross of Nevada; two sisters, Mrs. Maude Potter of El Dorado Springs, and Mrs. Essie [*sic*] Ready of Fulton; two brothers, Irl of Kansas City, and Lester of Milford, Mo.; and six grandchildren." These two obituaries appeared in the local newspaper, one before the funeral, the other after. The first obituary does not name his wife, Pauline from whom he divorced. The obituary clippings were undated and unidentified by newspaper names. Newspaper Clipping for Lee Fellows. "Fellows Last Rites. The last rites in memory of Lee Fellows were conducted at the United Methodist Church at Jerico Springs by the Rev. Lloyd Wasson, at 2:00 p.m., Tuesday. Florence Posson and Callie Achord sang two duets, 'Have Thine Own Way Lord' and 'In the Garden.' Violet Sitton accompanied the singers at the organ. The casket bearers were Woodford Wilson, Rich Richardson, Preston Potter, Charles Cross, John Higgins, and Oscar Higgins. Following the service in the church the remains were escorted to Dunnegan Grove Cemetery for interment under the direction of the Long Funeral Home." Funeral Announcement, Lee Fellows. "Lee C. Fellows b. October 26, 1888, Sheridan County, MO. d. November 22, 1970, Community Nursing Home, El Dorado Springs, MO. Services 2:00 P.M. Tuesday November 24, 1970, Jerico Springs Methodist Church; Clergy Rev. Lloyd Wasson; Ministry of Music Jerico Choir, Violet Sitton Accompanist; Interment Dunnegan Grove

Cemetery." Obituary of Lee Fellows, *Nevada Daily Mail*, 23 Nov 1970. "Lee Fellows, 82, a longtime resident of Nevada, died Sunday morning at a nursing home in El Dorado Springs. His birth was in Sheridan County on October 26, 1988. He married Pauline Richey in 1920. He was a veteran of World War I. Survivors include three children, Everett W. Fellows of Anchorage, Alaska, Merle D. Fellows and Mrs. Norman (Frances) Cross, both of Nevada; two sisters, Mrs. Maude Potter of El Dorado Springs and Mrs. Effie Ready of Fulton, Mo.; two brothers, Irl Fellows of Kansas City and Lester Fellows of Milford; six grandchildren... Interment will be in Dunnegan Grove Cemetery with military rites." This obituary is slightly at variance with other published accounts of his death.

[58] Obituary of Pauline Fellows Hale. "Mrs. Pauline Fellows Hale, 72, 726 N. Adams, died Wednesday evening at Nevada City Hospital, following an illness of several months. She was born Feb. 17, 1902 at Bona, Mo., the daughter of William Bert and Louisa Hall Richey. She made her home in Vernon County most of her lifetime, and was employed for 15 years prior to retirement at Nevada State Hospital as a Psychiatric Aide, LPN. Two sons, William Everett Fellows and Charles Warren Fellows, preceded her in death. Survivors include one son, Merle Fellows, Nevada; one daughter, Mrs. Frances M. Cross, Nevada; one stepbrother, Paul Perkins, Bona, Mo.; one half-brother, Floyd Perkins, Nevada; one half-sister, Floy Lucetta, Lamar; 6 grandchildren. Funeral services will be held 10 a.m. Saturday at Beeny Funeral Home, with the Rev. Charles Layman officiating. Interment will be in Dunnegan Grove Cemetery. The body will lie in state until 10 p.m. Friday at Ferry Funeral Chapel, where friends may call;" Newspaper Clipping, Pauline Fellows Hale, 4 Aug 1974. "Funeral services for Mrs. Pauline Fellows Hale, 72, 726 N. Adams, who died Wednesday evening at Nevada City Hospital were held Saturday morning at Beeny Funeral Home, Sheldon. The Rev. Charles Layman officiated. Mrs. Juanita Cooper, soloist, sang 'In the Garden' and 'Haven of Rest,' accompanied by Mrs. LaVerne Leininger, Organist. Interment was in Dunnegan Grove Cemetery."

[59] Obituary of Katie M. Potter. "Katie Maude Potter was born December 12, 1890, in Cedar County the daughter of W.I. and Martha (Crutchfield) Fellows and departed this life January 5, 1983, in the Community Nursing Home at age 92 years. She lived most of her lifetime in the Olympia neighborhood. She is survived by one son, Preston Potter, El Dorado Springs, one sister, Mrs. Effie Jane Ready, Fulton, Mo., five grandchildren, nine great-grandchildren and other relatives. Memorial services were Saturday, January 8, at 2 p.m. with Rev. G.H. Sublett officiating at the Janssens-Brown Chapel. Ray Sublett sang 'Rock of Ages' and 'In the Garden' with Lovell Beydler as organist. Interment was in Waggoner Cemetery." Funeral Announcement, Katie Maude Potter. "Katie Maude Potter b. Dec. 12, 1890, d. Jan. 5, 1983. Service: Janssens-Brown Chapel, El Dorado springs, Mo., Jan. 8, 1983, 2:09 P.M. officiating Rev. G.H. Sublett, soloist Rev. G. H. Sublett, organist Lovell Beydler; Selections: 'Rock of Ages, 'In the Garden.' Interment Waggoner Cemetery."

[60] Find A Grave 34141648. "Kathryn (Katie) Maude Fellows."

[61] Obituary of Ray Potter. "El Dorado Springs—Services for Ray Potter, 85, El Dorado Springs, will be at 2 p.m. today at the Jerico Springs United Methodist Church, with the Rev. G.H. Sublett officiating. Burial will be in the Wagner Cemetery under direction of Long of

Jerico Springs. Mr. Potter died at 10 a.m. Monday in the Cedar County Memorial Hospital after a short illness. He was a native of Cedar County and a life-long resident of the Olympia vicinity. Survivors include his wife, Maude, one son, Preston, El Dorado Springs; three sisters, Mrs. Cora Hoerning and Mrs. Effie Schramm, both of Eldorado Springs, and Mrs. Myrtle Johnson, Gentry, Ark.; six grandchildren and eight great-grandchildren." Funeral Announcements, Ray Potter. "Ray Potter b. December 14, 1893, Cedar County; d. September 3, 1979, El Dorado Springs, Mo. Services 2:00 p.m. Wednesday September 5, 1979, Jerico Springs United Methodist Church. Clergy: Rev. G.H. Sublett; Ministry of Music, Crystal Cantrell, Vera Albrecht, Pete Vest, Bernice Beckley, Acc.; Escorts: Berlin Collins, Robert Potter, Donald Potter, Lloyd Hoerning, Carl Hoerning, Lloyd Potter. Interment Waggoner Cemetery."

[62] Find A Grave 34141733. "Ray Potter."

[63] Find A Grave 114286074. "Willie Irl Fellows."

[64] *Missouri Marriage Records* (microfilm), Missouri State Archives, Jefferson City, Mo.

[65] 1920 US Census, Missouri, Cedar County, Benton Township, p. 51-08b,

[66] Obituary, W. Irl Fellows. "Willie Irl Fellows, 79, Kansas City, formerly of the Milford area, died early Monday morning at Lakeside Hospital, Kansas City, following an illness of six months. He was born Sept. 7, 1893, in Cedar County, the son of Ira W. and Martha Jane Crutchfield Fellows. He had made his home with his daughter in Kansas City the past five years. Prior to that time, he had lived and farmed near Milford most of his adult life. He was a member of the United Methodist Church. Survivors include one daughter, Mrs. Lila Halterman, Kansas City; two sisters, Mrs. Effie Ready, Fulton, and Mrs. Maudie Potter, Montevallo; one brother, Lester Fellows, Milford; two grandchildren and three great-grandchildren. Funeral services will be held 2 p.m. Saturday at Beeny Funeral Chapel, Sheldon, Rev. Arthur Daughtery will officiate. Interment will be in Sheldon Cemetery under the direction of Beeny Funeral Home." Funeral Announcement, Willie Irl Fellows. "Willie Irl Fellows b. September 7, 1893, d. January 22, 1973. Service Beeny Funeral Chapel January 27, 1973 2:00 p.m. officiant Rev. Arthur Daughtery, soloist Rev. R.B. Shook, selections 'Rock of Ages, The Old rugged Cross,' Mrs. LaVerne Leininger, organist. Interment in the Sheldon Cemetery."

[67] Sharron Burchett O'Connor Genealogies.

[68] Cemetery, Brasher, Cedar County, Missouri: Grave Stone Inscription: "Fellows Charlie P. son of W.I. & M. F. Sep 5 1896 Jan 29 1897." Charlie P. Fellows died of Catarrh, an inflammation of mucous membranes in the nose and throat, according to Beatrice Richardson (2003).

[69] Find A Grave 29701089. "Charlie P. Fellows."

[70] Cornwell, *Cornwell*. This source has Effie born in Jerico Springs, Cedar County, Missouri. The source has complete information on Effie and Joseph Ready.

[71] Obituary of Effie Jane Ready. "Effie Jane Ready, 90, of Fulton, died April 15, 1988, at the Heartland Nursing Home in Fulton. She was born Feb. 13, 1898, the daughter of the late

Willie and Francis Crutchfield Fellows at Jerico Springs in Cedar County, Mo. She married Joseph P. Ready and he preceded her in death Aug. 10, 1971. Mrs. Ready is survived by two sons, Cleve Ready of Mokane and Archie of Cheyenne, Wyo.; seven grandchildren; 9 great-grandchildren and several nieces and nephews. One son, Delbert Ready of Tacoma, Wash., two sisters and six brothers, also preceded her in death. Mrs. Ready joined the Christian Church in Kansas City in 1962. She moved to Fulton in 1966. Graveside services will be held at 2 p.m. Sunday, April 17 at the Hillcrest Cemetery with the Rev. Peter Soens officiating." Funeral Announcement, Mrs. Effie Jane Ready. "Effie Jane Ready b. February 13, 1898, d. April 15, 1988. Visitation at Debo Chapel April 17, 1988, 12:00-2:00 p.m. Graveside Services held at Hillcrest Cemetery April 17, 1988, 2:00 p.m., officiating Rev. Peter Soens."

[72] Find A Grave 37151036. "Effie Jane Fellows Ready."

[73] Ready, *History of Willie Ira Fellows.* Married by Rev. Chambers.

[74] Find A Grave 37150732. "Joseph Pearl Ready."

[75] Cornwell, *Cornwell.* Source gives information on Lester and Etta Crites Fellows.

[76] Find A Grave 72026231. "Mary Etta Crites Fellows."

[77] Find A Grave 72027997. "Lester Fellows;" Obituary of Lester Fellows. "Lester Fellows, 73, Milford, Mo. died Saturday at Barton County Memorial Hospital, Lamar, following a long illness. Born April 26, 1901, at Jerico Springs, he was the son of William and Martha Fellows. He was married to Mary Etta Crites in 1944 and lived more than 30 years at Milford. Surviving is his wife of the home: two sisters, Mrs. Maude Potter, Route 3, El Dorado Springs, and Mrs. Effie Ready, Fulton. Services will be 2 p.m., Tuesday at Milford Christian Church. The Rev. Ed Marshall will officiate. Interment will be Howell Cemetery near Milford. Funeral arrangements are under the direction of Long Funeral Home, Jerico Springs." Funeral Announcement, Lester Fellows. "Lester Fellows b. April 26, 1901, Jerico Springs, Mo., d. February 15, 1975, Lamar, Missouri. Services 2:00 p.m. Tuesday, February 18, 1975, Milford Christian Church; Clergy Rev. Ed Marshall; Ministry of Music Helen Gardner, Fontella Chapman, H.C. Hooper, Zelma Hooper accompanist. Interment Howell Cemetery."

[78] Ready, *History of Willie Ira Fellows.* "Lester Smith Fellows died Feb. 15, 1975, at 8:00 PM at Lamar, Mo. Put away at Howell Cemetery close to Milford, Missouri."

[79] Merle Fellows Family, *W.I. Fellows Genealogy.*

Chapter 14 Cardwell Genealogy Introduction

[1] Michael Cardwell, *Cardwell Genealogy,* WaybackMachine, Internet Archive May 6, 2004.

[2] Cardwell, *Cardwell Genealogy,* WaybackMachine, Internet Archive.

[3] *US and Canada, Passenger and Immigration Lists Index, 1500s-1900s,* citing Nell M. Nugent, *Cavaliers and Pioneers: Abstracts of Virginia Land Patents and Grants, 1623-1666* (Vol. 1). Richmond, Va.: Dietz, 1934, reprinted by Genealogical Publishing, Baltimore, 1983.

[4] William P. Filby and Mary K. Meyer. *Passenger and Immigration lists index a guide to published arrival records of about 500,000 passengers who came to the United States and*

Canada in the Seventeenth, eighteenth, and nineteenth centuries. 1982-1985 Cumulated Supplements in Four Volumes. Detroit, Mich.: Gale Research, 1985.

[5] Cardwell, *Cardwell Genealogy,* WaybackMachine, Internet Archive.

Chapter 15 Thomas Cardwell the Immigrant

[1] William Smith Bryan, et al. *A History of the Pioneer Families of Missouri: with Numerous Sketches, Anecdotes, Adventures, etc., Relating to Early Days in Missouri. Also the Lives of Daniel Boone and the Celebrated Indian Chief, Black Hawk, with Numerous Biographies and Histories of Primitive Institutions.* St. Louis: Bryan, Brand, 1876, p. 172.

[2] Bryan, *History of the Pioneer Families of Missouri,* p. 424.

[3] Allen Pendergraft, *The Cardwells of Virginia: Thomas Cardwell of Henrico County, His Descendants and Allied Families: Osborne, Farrar, Spencer, Worsham, Royal, Perrine, Lockett, Thweat, Hankley, Crews, West, and Butler*, Professional Research by J. U. Stucki, Sedona, Az.: Author, 1973

[4] Pendergraft, *Cardwells of Virginia.*

[5] RootsWeb.com, Nancy, 2000. Rand Cardwell is the foremost authority on Cardwell family history.

[6] RootsWeb.com, Nancy, 2000.

[7] Martha W. Hiden, "Accompts of the Tristram and Jane," *The Virginia Magazine of History and Biography* 62, no. 4 (1954): 424-47, citing "A Booke of Accounts for the Shippe called the *Tristram and Jeane,* Exhibit 26th Aprilis 1637. An abstract of the Cargazoune [cargo] of goods laden aboard the good shipped called the *Tristram and Jane* of London, Daniell Hopkinson, Merchant, and Joseph Blowe, Master, bount for Virginia, and what Tobacco was received for the said goods by Joseph Clifton Executor of the said Hopkinson this 22th of April 1637." This 1637 account was after the ship had landed at Virginia in 1636 and returned to England in April 1637. Daniell Hopkinson, merchant and one of eight partners who sponsored the voyage, died in Virginia. He had an interest in the ship, and named the seamen in his will. He also had a brother, Abraham, on the trip. Ms. Hiden based her estimate of the arrival of the *Tristram and Jane* in London on the Will of Daniell Hopkinson's, ship's merchant who died in Virginia, which was probated April 8, 1637.

[8] Hiden. "Accompts of the *Tristram and Jane,*" p. 435.

[9] Hiden. "Accompts of the *Tristram and Jane,*" pp. 433, 435-436; Will probated in London (P.C.C. (52) Goare 1636 in the *Principal Probate Registry*, Somerset House, London; Tepper, *New World Immigrants*, p. 96. From the ship log, "Tobacco Creditors Vizt, Shipt aboard the shippe called the Tristram and Jane of London at severall times and from severall places as Kickhowtan, Backe river, Ould Pocoson, New Pocoson, Accamach, etc. in Virginia 99 hogsheads of Tobacco, Content nett tare of Caske Deducted" 31,800 lbs. of tobacco."

[10] Hiden. "Accompts of the *Tristram and Jane,*" p. 428-429. "The Names of the Servants and to what Masters they were turn'd over unto in Virginia." Thomas Cordell [*sic*] was entry

No. 19, 1,000 lbs. of tobacco turned over to Master John Neale. Of the 74 Servants, at least 17 were maids.

[11] Hiden. "Accompts of the *Tristram and Jane*," p. 437.

[12] Hiden. "Accompts of the *Tristram and Jane*," p. 428-429.

[13] Hiden, p. 439, citing Nugent, *Cavaliers and Pioneers*, p. 18.

[14] Hiden. "Accompts of the *Tristram and Jane*," p. 439.

[15] Hiden. "Accompts of the *Tristram and Jane*," p. 441.

[16] Hiden. "Accompts of the *Tristram and Jane*," p. 446.

[17] Hiden. "Accompts of the *Tristram and Jane*," p. 446; Tepper, *New World Immigrants*, p. 107.

[18] Tepper, *New World Immigrants*, p. 107, citing Nugent, *Cavaliers and Pioneers*, p. 44.

[19] Hiden. "Accompts of the *Tristram and Jane*," pp. 446-447.

[20] Charfee Isaac, Ancestry World Tree Project: Cardwells of Virginia and Tennessee.

[21] Pendergraft, *The Cardwells of Virginia*, citing *Tyler's Cyclopedia of Virginia History*, Vol. 4, pp. 103-04.

[22] *Christ Church Middlesex Co., Va. Parrish Register, 1653-1812*, p. 11; see also *US and International Marriage Records, 1560-1900*, source number: 12848.000. This source has Thomas the Immigrant married to Mary in 1636. However, this database is not widely relied upon because records come from a variety of sources including family group sheets and electronic databases originally derived from an array of materials including pedigree charts, family history articles, and online queries.

[23] Find A Grave Memorial 171711382, maintained by Dale Lee Lane; *US and International Marriage Records, 1560-1900*. "Thomas Cardwell b. England 1614 m. Mary 1636."

[24] Charfee Isaac, Ancestry World Tree Project: Cardwells of Virginia and Tennessee.

[25] Charfee Isaac, Ancestry World Tree Project: Cardwells of Virginia and Tennessee.

[26] Mrs. John Bennett Boddie, "Cardwell of Virginia," *Historical Southern Families* (Vol. 19), Baltimore: Genealogical Publishing, 1974, p. 8; Pendergraft, *The Cardwells of Virginia*, citing *Lancaster County Deed Book* 4, p. 12. "Robert Chowning of Lancaster County, planter, sold to Tho. Cordwell [*sic*] of same, 300 acres on s. s. of Sunderlands Creek 8 January 1666."

[27] Boddie, "Cardwell of Virginia," p. 8, citing *Lancaster County Deed Book* 4, p. 2, "Joane Chowning sold Thomas Cordwell, 9 April, 1667. Wit: Tho. Chatwyn and Cliz. Chatwyn. Recog. 10 April 1667."

[28] Pendergraft, *The Cardwells of Virginia*, citing 1673 Deed, p. 11. "In a 1673 Middlesex County deed, Thomas Cardwell and Mary his wife sell land to Thomas Fenney 5 Aug 1673."

[29] Dan Gill, *Pleasant Living* (January - February 2013).

[30] *Christ Church Parish Register*, p. 80.

[31] Charles Brunk Heinemann, *Daniel families of the Southern States, a Compilation of 2 Volumes Covering Numerous Daniel Families*. Washington, D.C.: C.B. Heinemann, 1949, p. 1/5 generation 1.

[32] Boddie, "Cardwell of Virginia," p. 5, citing *Middlesex County Order Book, 1674-1780*, pp. 193-94.

[33] Pendergraft, *The Cardwells of Virginia*, citing*Will Record Book for Middlesex County (1673-1800)*. The year date on the Will is illegible. Transcribers variously transcribe it as 1680, 1682, and 1687. Sources claim he wrote his Will 12 May 1680, etc. Others claim the May 12 date was when the Will was proved while still others set a date of Oct 1700 when the court proved his will.

[34] *Christ Church Parish Register*, pp. 19, 37, 177.

[35] Heinemann, *Daniel families of the Southern States*, p. 1/9 generation 2, citing *Will Record Book for Middlesex County 1673-1800*. William Daniel, Jr. did not appear to prove the will of Thomas Cardwell in 1689, although he was undersheriff in Middlesex County at the time. His signature as witness to Thomas' will was the first public record of note for him in Middlesex County.

[36] From abstract of Will of William Daniel, recorded Book S, proved 2 Jul 1723, p. 267. See also Will of Christopher Robinson, 1693, p. 22.

[37] Heinemann, *Daniel Families of the Southern States*, p. 1; Teetor, *Early History of the Daniel and Daniels Family in Europe and America*.

[38] Pendergraft, *The Cardwells of Virginia*, citing Will of 1687 proved in Middlesex County; *Christ Church Parish Register in Middlesex County*, p. 11. Internet genealogies that claim he died in King & Queen County are without merit. See Ancestry World Tree Project: Cardwells of Virginia and Tennessee.

[39] Find A Grave 119394050, memorial page for Thomas Cardwell, Sr. (1614–12 May 1687); see also Christ Church Cemetery, Christchurch, Middlesex County, Virginia, maintained by Dale Lee Lane. "Thomas Cardwell Sr."

[40] *The Parish Register of Christ Church, Middlesex County, Va., from 1653 to 1812*. Richmond, Va.: National Society of the Colonial Dames of America, 1897, p 29. "John Williams & Mary Cordwell both of y' parish married 10th of Octob. 1686".

[41] Find A Grave 119401029. "Mary Elizabeth (Collier) Cardwell."

[42] Last Will and Testament of Thomas Cardwell, transcribed by W. Rand Cardwell, 2007.

[43] Allen Pendergraft, *Cardwells of Virginia: Thomas Cardwell of Henrico County, His Descendants and Allied Families*. Researched by I. U. Stucki, 1973, pp. 11-18 and genealogical charts.

[44] Pendergraft, *The Cardwells of Virginia*, p. 11, citing *Virginia Magazine of History*, pp. 424-29.

[45] Pendergraft, *The Cardwells of Virginia*, citing *Tyler's Cyclopedia of Virginia Families*, pp. 103-04.

[46] Pendergraft, *Cardwells of Virginia,* p. 12.

[47] *Christ Church Parish Register,* p. 11. "Thomas Cordwell [*sic*] and Elizabeth Collyer [no date]," probably about April 11 or 12, 1662 because their entry in the registry is between two marriages of those dates. See also *US and International Marriage Records, 1560-1900* "Thomas Cardwell b. England 1614 m. Mary 1636."

[48] *Christ Church Parish Register,* pp. 29, 33. "John Williams & Mary Cordwell both of ye parish married 10th of Octob 1686 p. 29, and John Williams of Oxfordshire & Mary Cordwell of Shropshire In England married 10 Octob 1686 p. 33." The church clerk recorded their marriage twice with the same date but slightly different descriptions.

[49] Pendergraft, *Cardwells of Virginia,* p. 12. Until recently, Pendergraft was the authority on the Cardwell family of Thomas the Immigrant. Research that is more recent corrects some of his work. However, many genealogists persist in applying his findings.

[50] Pendergraft, *The Cardwells of Virginia,* citing 1691 Land Grant to William Cardwell and William Penney in New Kent County, later King and Queen County. Also in 1691, William Cardwell and William Penney received Land Grant in Drysdale Parish on the Mattaponi River, in Caroline County.

[51] Pendergraft, *The Cardwells of Virginia,* p. 12, citing 1664 Stafford County Land Grant, Nugent, *Cavaliers and Pioneers,* p. 432. To William Cordwell, Sr. and Margaret Cordwell (presumed wife], William Cordwell, Jr. [son], Grace Cordwell [daughter], Henry Saynes, John Ozzet, and John Twiggs [probably in-laws].

[52] Boddie, "Cardwell of Virginia," p. 4, citing Campbell, *Colonial Caroline,* p. 305; Pendergraft, p. 12.

[53] *US and Canada, Passenger and Immigration Lists Index, 1500s-1900s,* citing Nugent, *Cavaliers and Pioneers.*

[54] Pendergraft, *The Cardwells of Virginia,* citing Westmoreland County Inventory, p. 12.

[55] Pendergraft, *The Cardwells of Virginia,* citing Westmoreland County Wills, p. 56.

[56] Boddie, "Cardwell of Virginia," p. 7; Pendergraft, *The Cardwells of Virginia,* p. 12.

[57] Pendergraft, "The Cardwells of Virginia," citing Westmoreland County Inventory, p. 12.

[58] Boddie, "Cardwell of Virginia," p. 10, citing Westmoreland County Inventory.

[59] Pendergraft, *The Cardwells of Virginia,* citing 1690 Henrico County Deposition, aged 42, p. 12.

[60] Pendergraft, *The Cardwells of Virginia,* citing 1673 Deed and 1687 Will, p. 13.

[61] Pendergraft, *The Cardwells of Virginia,* citing 1713 Henrico Deed that refers to her father as Thomas Cardwell, Sr., p. 13.

[62] *Christ Church Parish Register,* p. 35. "William Brooks & Ann Cardwell both of this pish marryed 8th of Novemb. 1687."

[63] Pendergraft, *The Cardwells of Virginia,* citing 1687 Will, p. 12.

[64] *Christ Church Parish Register,* pp. 15, 19, 25, 37, 177. "Elizabeth dau. of John and Eliz Basket bapt. 14 Mar 1679; Henry Basket y' sone of Jno. & Eliz Baskett bapt. 23rd March 1681. Thomas Basket sone of John and Eliz Basket was bapt. 16th of April 1682."

[65] *Christ Church Parish Register,* pp. 33, 296.

[66] *Christ Church Parish Register,* pp. 34, 40, 50, 51.

[67] Find A Grave 134779705, citing Upper Church of Stratton Major Parish Cemetery, King and Queen County, Virginia. "Elizabeth Cordwell Guthrie."

[68] *Christ Church Parish Register,* p. 189. "John Baskett dyed Novem' y' 28 & was buried Novem' y' 30, 1720."

Chapter 16 Thomas Cardwell, Sr.

[1] Boddie, "Cardwell of Virginia," p. 9.

[2] Boddie, "Cardwell of Virginia," p. 11.

[3] Pendergraft, Allen. *The Cardwells of Virginia: Thomas Cardwell of Henrico County, His Descendants and Allied Families.* Researched by I. U. Stucki. 1973, pp. 11-13, and genealogical chart, citing 1696 Deed, p. 13; Ancestral File 1996 Version, submission of Mel and Janet Bowers. Their cousin Oveda Meier lived in Salt Lake and did all of the research. See also Kenneth D. Smith, DMUB77A@prodigy.com. Ann [Baskett] was a Powhatan Indian. She is sometimes identified as Anne Marten. See also *US and International Marriage Records, 1560-1900* listing for the marriage of Thomas Cardwell b. 1660 to Ann (maiden name unspecified).

[4] Pendergraft, *The Cardwells of Virginia,* citing 1696 Deed, p. 13.

[5] *Christ Church Parish Register,* pp. 19, 37, 177. "Henry Basket y' sone of Jno. & Eliz' Baskett bapt. 23rd March 1681, Thomas Basket sone of John and Eliz Basket was bapt. 16th of April 1682. John Baskett dyed Novem' y' 28 & was buried Novem' y' 30. 1720."

[6] *Henrico County Virginia Deeds 1677-1705.*

[7] *Virginia Genealogical Society Quarterly* Vol. 35 No. 4, Nov 1997, p. 304.

[8] *Virginia Genealogical Society Quarterly* Vol. 31 No. 4, Nov 1993, pp. 295, 313.

[9] *Virginia Genealogical Society Quarterly* Vol. 32 No. 1, Feb 1994, p. 12 and Vol. 32 No. 2, May 1994, pp. 134-135.

[10] William A. Crozier, *Virginia County Records.* Baltimore: Genealogical Publishing, 1905-1913, p. 128, citing Henrico County Book 7, 1589, 550 acres, p 716.

[11] *Henrico County Patent Book 8,* p. 716, cited in Foley, *Early Virginia Families along the James River.*

[12] *Magazine of Virginia Genealogy,* Vol. 33 No. 2, May 1995, p. 123.

[13] *Virginia Genealogical Society Quarterly* Vol. 32 No. 3, Jul 1979, p. 220.

[14] *Magazine of Virginia Genealogy,* Vol. 33 No. 2, May 1995, p. 136.

[15] *Virginia Genealogical Society Quarterly* Vol. 33 No. 4, Nov 1995, p. 284.

[16] *Virginia Genealogical Society Quarterly* Vol. 32 No. 4, Nov 1994, p. 303.

[17] *Henrico County Deed Book*, recorded 1 Feb 1691.

[18] *Henrico County Deed Book*, recorded 1 Dec 1694.

[19] *Henrico County Deed Book 5, 1689-1702*. "Oct. 1, 1689, Thomas Cardwell and wife Ann sell 2,500 lbs. of good tobacco to George Fairfax, 50 acres of the north side of James River on the south branch of Gilley's Creek."

[20] *Henrico Deed Book 5, 1689-1702*, 1 Oct 1696. This land joined the land of Samuel Bridgewater. Witnesses to the deed of sale were John Field and John Robinson, signed by Thomas Cardwell and Ann his wife.

[21] *Virginia Genealogical Society Quarterly* Vol, 31 No. 1, Feb 1993, p. 81, citing *Virginia Land Patent Book 30*, pp 457, 459, with reference to the original Cardwell patent of 1689, *Patent Book 7*, p. 716.

[22] Pendergraft, *The Cardwells of Virginia*, citing 1706 Deed from Thomas Cardwell to daughter. Mary, p. 13.

[23] Boddie, "Cardwell of Virginia," p. 12, citing Deed dated 19 Aug 1729. "Warham Easeley of Gooch County sells 400 acres to Thomas Cardwell Sr. of Henrico County for 42 pounds, on south side of James River on a branch of Deep Creek, in the possession of William Moseley."

[24] Pendergraft, *The Cardwells of Virginia*, citing a 1688 Land Grant in Henrico County, and a 1690 Henrico Deposition when he was age 30, p. 13. Pendergraft alternately lists the birthplace of Thomas, Sr. as New Kent County, Virginia. (New Kent County formed from York County in 1654.)

[25] Pendergraft, *The Cardwells of Virginia*, citing Henrico County Bond; 1696 Deed, Henrico; 1703 Quit Rent Rolls, Goochland County; and 1729 Deed, p 13. The rent rolls do not include the Northern Neck, the counties between the Rappahannock and the Potomac rivers: Stafford, King George, Westmoreland, Northumberland, Richmond, and Lancaster.

[26] Pendergraft, *The Cardwells of Virginia*, pp. 11-13 and genealogical chart, citing 1696 Deed, p. 13.

[27] Pendergraft, *The Cardwells of Virginia*, citing 1696 Deed, p. 13.

[28] Pendergraft, *The Cardwells of Virginia*, citing 1696 Deed, p. 13. Pendergraft does not mention her Indian name, nor does he speculate about the date of her death. He gives an alternate marriage date of c.1684.

[29] Pendergraft, *Cardwells of Virginia*, p. 13.

[30] Boddie, "Cardwell of Virginia," p. 12, citing Pendergraft, *The Cardwells of Virginia*, Cumberland County Inventory, p. 13;

[31] Pendergraft, *The Cardwells of Virginia*, citing 1713 Henrico County Deed that referred to her father as Thomas Cardwell, Sr., p. 13.

[32] Boddie, "Cardwell of Virginia," p. 12.

[33] Boddie, "Cardwell of Virginia," p. 12.

[34] Pendergraft, *The Cardwells of Virginia*, citing 1706 Deed from Thomas Cardwell to daughter Mary, p. 13.

Chapter 17 Thomas Cardwell, Jr.

[1] Pendergraft, *Cardwells of Virginia*, p. 11.

[2] *Virginia Magazine of History and Biography*, p. 210. "A True and Perfect Rent Roll of all the Lands held of her Majesty in Henrico County, April 1705."

[3] Boddie, "Cardwell of Virginia."

[4] Thomas Perrin Harrison, "Early Perrin Families of Virginia," *Virginia Genealogical Society Quarterly* 20 pp. 68, 118, citing Pendergraft for the marriage date of Martha Perrin to Thomas Cardwell.

[5] Nugent, *Cavaliers and Pioneers*, Vol. 1, p. 78. Between 1637 and 1657, a Richard Perrine appears as immigrant five times: twice in 1637, others in 1653, 1654, and 1657, possibly the same person sent to London as tobacco agent.

[6] Harrison, "Early Perrin families on the James River," *Virginia Genealogist*, 21 (1977), pp. 243-247.

[7] Nugent, *Cavaliers and Pioneers*, Vol. 2, pp. 123, 325.

[8] Harrison. "Early Perrin Families of Virginia," *Virginia Genealogical Society Quarterly* 20 (April-June 1982), p. 115.

[9] Harrison, "Early Perrin Families of Virginia," *Virginia Genealogical Society Quarterly* 20 (April - June), 1982, pp. 61-67.

[10] Harrison, "Early Perrin Families of Virginia" *Virginia Genealogical Society Quarterly* 20 (April - June, 1982), p. 69.

[11] Helen E. H. Peyton, *Some Early Pioneers of Western Kentucky: Their Ancestors and Descendants* (2nd ed.). Charleston, S.C.: H. E. H. Peyton, 1990, p 216; Pendergraft, *The Cardwells of Virginia.*

[12] *US and International Marriage Records, 1560-1900.* Unfortunately, many genealogical indexes glean data from unverified sources, further damaging the reliability obtained from original source documents.

[13] Find A Grave 148535691. Unsourced and unverified.

[14] *Goochland County [Virginia] Deed Book 5*, p. 7; Peyton, *Some Early Pioneers of Western Kentucky*, 296; Boddie, "Cardwell of Virginia," p. 13.

[15] Boddie, "Cardwell of Virginia," p. 12.

[16] Beverley Fleet, *Virginia Colonial Abstracts, Henrico County-Southside 1736* (Vol. 21). Baltimore: Genealogical Publishing, 1961, p. 75; Boddie, "Cardwell of Virginia," p. 12, citing Henrico County Records, p. 533.

[17] *Virginia Genealogical Society Quarterly* Vol. 27 No. 4, Nov 1989, p. 295, citing *Virginia Land Patent Book 24, 1745-1746.*

[18] Boddie, "Cardwell of Virginia," citing *Goochland County Deed Book 5*, p. 7.

[19] Find A Grave 148535691. Her date of death is unverified.

[20] Thomas Cardwell, Jr. of Henrico County had a son named Thomas of Cumberland County, Virginia, who died in 1751. Genealogists sometimes confuse him with Thomas, Jr. citing an inventory for Thomas Cardwell dated 29 May 1751 in *Virginia Wills and Administrations for Cumberland County*. Thomas of Cumberland died intestate and with a modest amount of property, suggesting that he died young and was not Thomas, Jr. who died in 1772.

[21] WaybackMachine, Internet Archive, May 6, 2004.

[22] Henrico County Chancery Court, Cardwell Chancery Case 1783-9, and Henrico Chancery Court file 1780-2; Boddie, "Cardwell of Virginia," pp. 13-16; Find A Grave 148535691.

[23] Last Will and Testament of Thomas Cardwell, Jr. transcribed by W. Rand Cardwell, 2007. "In the name of God Amen this 2nd day of December one thousand seven hundred and seventy-two (2 Dec 1772) I Thomas Cardwell of the Parrish and County of Henrico Being very weak in Body but of perfect mind and memory do make and confirm this my last Will and Testament as Followeth the First I give and forfeit my soul to the Almighty God that made it and my Body to the Grave to be Buried in a Christian decent like manner the maker and to my worldly goods I give in manner and form as followeth. Item I give to my son Richard Cardwell one negroe girl named Nancy to him and her heirs forever. Item I give to my daughter Martha Epperson one negro girl name ____ to her and heirs forever. Item I give to my son John Cardwell one negroe woman named Cloe to him and his heirs forever. Item I give to my daughter Elizabeth Bandy one negro woman named _____ to her and her heirs forever. Item I give to my daughter Lucy Brazeel one negroe woman named Phillis to her and her heirs forever. Item I give my grandson John Henry Brazeel one mullato boy Jack to him and his heirs forever. Item I give to my grand daughter Polly Peron Brazeel one negro girl named Hanah to her and her heirs forever. Item it is my will and desire that my old negro woman Hanah may after my decease have her Liberty as a free woman also I lend my daughter Lucy Brazeel two fellows named Absalom and James to the space of three years _______________leave the rest of my negroes named as followeth Judith Lucy Bob Napper and Janney to gather with all the rest of my estate not mentioned to be sold to paye my debts and at the expiration of the three years within mentioned then these two negroes Absolom and James to be sold and all my debts to be paid and if any balance overpaying my debts then it is to be equally divided amongst all my sons and daughters I do wise appoint Charles Lewis and Daniel Marwood and my daughter Lucy Brazeel to be executors and executrix of this my Last Will and Testament as above mentioned in Witness whereof I have ___ unto set my hand and seal the day and year above. To the Worshipful the Justices of Henrico County Court sitting in Chancery showeth to your worshipsome orators and oratines George Cardwell and Daniel Cardwell executors of Richard Cardwell deceased. John Cardwell Francis Epperson and Martha his wife, Richard Bandy and Elizabeth his wife that Thomas Cardwell late of the County of Henrico being possessed of a number of negroes and other personal estate and having a son Richard Cardwell the Testator of your orators Daniel Cardwell and Richard

Cardwell a son John Cardwell and three daughters your oratines Martha and Elizabeth intermarried with your orators Francis Epperson and Richard Bandy and Lucy Brazeel widow and relict of Drury Brazeel deceased and make and publish his last Will and Testament in writing bearing date the second day of December in the year of our God one thousand seven hundred and seventy two (1772) and shortly after departed this life without reworking or altering the same by which said will after devising a negroe to each of his children and one negroe to each of his two grand children John Henry Brazeel and Polly Peron Brazeel children of the said Lucy Brazeel should have the use of two negroe men slaves named Absolom and James for the term of three [years]." See also Henrico County Chancery Court, Cardwell Chancery Case 1783-9 & Henrico Chancery Court file 1780-2

[24] Henrico County Chancery Court, Cardwell Chancery Case 1783-9 and Henrico Chancery Court file 1780-2.

[25] Pendergraft, *The Cardwells of Virginia,* citing Henrico County Bond dated 1717, Goochland County Deeds dated 1729 and 1745, and Cumberland County Inventory dated 1751. Pendergraft gives a birthdate as about 1690 probably in New Kent County, p. 13.

[26] Pendergraft, *The Cardwells of Virginia,* citing 1713 Henrico Deed that refers to her father as Thomas Cardwell, Sr., p. 13.

[27] Pendergraft, *The Cardwells of Virginia,* citing property mentioned in a 1717 Bond, p. 13.

[28] Henrico County Chancery Court, Cardwell Chancery Case 1783-9 and Henrico Chancery Court file 1780-2.

[29] *US and International Marriage Records, 1560-1900.*

[30] Pendergraft, *The Cardwells of Virginia,* citing Cumberland County inventory of his estate, p. 13.

[31] Boddie, "Cardwell of Virginia," citing Cumberland County Inventory dated 29 May 1751.

[32] Pendergraft, *The Cardwells of Virginia*, pp. 11-13 and genealogical charts.

[33] Henrico County Chancery Court, Cardwell Chancery Case 1783-9 and Henrico Chancery Court file 1780-2.

[34] Boddie, "Cardwell of Virginia," p. 13.

[35] Henrico County Chancery Court, Cardwell Chancery Case 1783-9 and Henrico Chancery Court file 1780-2.

[36] Boddie, "Cardwell of Virginia," p. 13.

[37] Boddie, "Cardwell of Virginia," citing Will in Prince Edward County dated 18 Jul 1795.

[38] Thomas Cardwell Bible of Missouri. Owner: Mrs. Jennie Clark Hawkins. "Samuel Clark b. 10/1740, Thomas Cardwell b. 9/1/1745 (father), Mary Cardwell b. 8/21/1747(mother), John Cardwell b. 3/15/1777, Sarah Cardwell 8/10/1780, Elizabeth Cardwell b. 4/8/1787, Perrin Cardwell b. 4/11/1791, Joel Clark b. 9/5/1783 m. Elizabeth Cardwell, George Clark m. Sarah Cardwell. Brothers married sisters Deaths: Samuel Clark 6/7/1832, Thomas Cardwell 10/24/1828 (father), Mary Cardwell 5/15/1824 (mother), Perrin Cardwell 9/26/1826, Mary

Clark 7/18/1828, George Clark 5/1840, St. Charles, Mo., Elizabeth Clark 10/5/1855, Wilshire Clark 6/19/1854, Sarah Clark 5/1863.

[39] William Waller Hening, *Statutes at Large* (1823), Vol. 11, pp. 532-537.

[40] *William Epperson Collection*, New Kent County, Virginia, *St. Peter's Parish Vestry Book and Register, 1684-1786.*

[41] Henrico County Chancery Court, Cardwell Chancery Case 1783-9 and Henrico Chancery Court file 1780-2.

[42] Find A Grave 110544819.

[43] *Magazine of Virginia Genealogy*, Vol. 33 No. 1, Feb 1995, p. 66, citing *Virginia Land Patent Book 33*, p. 899.

[44] Henrico County Chancery Court, Cardwell Chancery Case 1783-9 and Henrico Chancery Court file 1780-2.

[45] *Christ Church Parish Register,* p. 162. "Thomas Cardwell & Mary Blackly Married June ye 22, 1716."

[46] *Christ Church Parish Register*, p. 97. "William Son of Thomas & Mary Cardwell born July ye 7th baptized August ye 4, 1717."

[47] *Christ Church Parish Register,* p. 103. "Anne daughter of Thomas & Mary Cardwell born Novem 20 baptized Dec 20 1719."

Chapter 18 George Cardwell.

[1] Rand Cardwell on Thomas Cardwell - 17 Nov 2003, updated 5 Dec 2006.

[2] Fleet, *Virginia Colonial Abstracts, Henrico County-Southside 1736,* Vol. 21: p. 75; Boddie, "Cardwell of Virginia," p. 12, citing Henrico County Records, p. 533.

[3] Rand Cardwell on Thomas Cardwell - 17 Nov 2003, updated 5 Dec 2006; Cardwell Genealogy (2004), Internet, http://www.geocities.com/cardwellhistory/.

[4] Boddie, "Cardwell of Virginia," citing *Goochland County Deed Book 5*, p. 7.

[5] Boddie, "Cardwell of Virginia," p. 12.

[6] WaybackMachine, Internet Archive, May 6, 2004.

[7] Rand Cardwell on Thomas Cardwell - 17 Nov 2003, updated 5 Dec 2006; Cardwell Genealogy (2004), Internet, http://www.geocities.com/cardwellhistory/.

[8] Boddie, "Cardwell of Virginia," citing Daughters of American Revolution Application No. 84813.

[9] *Powhatan County Virginia Order Book 1*, p. 80, "Feb 18, 1779;" Rand Cardwell on Thomas Cardwell - 17 Nov 2003, updated 5 Dec 2006.

[10] Rand Cardwell on Thomas Cardwell - 17 Nov 2003 updated 5 Dec 2006; Cardwell Genealogy (2004), Internet, http://www.geocities.com/cardwellhistory/.

[11] *Powhatan County Virginia Order Book 1*, p. 80, "Feb 18, 1779."

[12] Rand Cardwell on Thomas Cardwell - 17 Nov 2003, updated 5 Dec 2006.

[13] Boddie, "Cardwell of Virginia," citing Daughters of American Revolution Application No. 84813. Perrin Cardwell enlisted in the Revolutionary War in 1781, cavalry, married 4 Sep 1785 Amelia Elizabeth Warsham in Amelia County, listed in the 1790 census of Amelia County, and died in 1854 in Knox County, Tennessee.

[14] Rand Cardwell on Thomas Cardwell - 17 Nov 2003, updated 5 Dec 2006; Cardwell Genealogy (2004), Internet, http://www.geocities.com/cardwellhistory/.

[15] Henrico County Chancery Court, Cardwell Chancery Case 1783-9 and Henrico Chancery Court file 1780-2.

[16] *North Carolina Land Grant Files, 1693-1960* for Thomas Cardwell, Surry County, 952-1258. No. 1134. Grant 1157, Book 70, p. 97, 18 May 1789. "100 acres on Peters Creek, assignee of Archelous Foxe."

[17] Boddie, "Cardwell of Virginia," p. 19.

[18] *Virginia Genealogical Society Quarterly* Volume 25 Number 4 Nov 1987, pp. 23, 119, 121, 123; Boddie, "Cardwell of Virginia," p. 20, citing *William and Mary Quarterly*, Vol. 23, Series 1, p. 216.

[19] Will of Richard Cardwell, Charlotte County, Virginia, 27 Feb 1780. Thomas was still living in 1780 when Richard wrote his will.

[20] *Dinwiddie County, Virginia, Court Order Book 1789-1791*; *Virginia Genealogical Society Quarterly*, Vol. 3, No. 4, p. 81. Order Book, p. 9–16 March 1780–William Cardwell, Henry Cardwell, Jane Cardwell, Thomas Cardwell, and Elizabeth Cardwell, infant orphans of Thomas Cardwell deceased, against Henry Thweatt and Obedience Cardwell, executors of Thomas Cardwell, deceased. OR p. 9 -Henry Cardwell and Thomas Cardwell, Orphans of Thomas Cardwell, deceased, made choice of Henry Thweatt for their guardian.

[21] Lyon Gardiner Tyler, Ed, *Encyclopedia of Virginia Biography*, Vol. 4, Baltimore: Genealogical Publishing, 1915, pp. 103-105.

[22] *North Carolina Land Grant Files, 1693-1960*, Guilford County, 404-885, No. 549. "Richard Perrin Cardwell, 400 acres Grnt no. 540, 22 Oct 1782, Entry No. 1313, Entered 23 Feb 1779," Book 48, p. 97. Guilford County, North Carolina, "On between Mayo River and Beaver Island Creek." [Mayo is a tributary of the Dan River.]

[23] Bryan. *A History of the Pioneer Families of Missouri*, p. 394; *History of Audrain County, Missouri*, p. 172.

[24] Pendergraft, *The Cardwells of Virginia* pp. 11-13 and genealogical charts.

[25] Records do not reveal exactly this woman's name. It could be Letitia Corbin Lee born 1709 died 1778 or Mary Frances Perrin Gaines. There is no proof either way except family tradition remembered her first name was Letitia.

Chapter 19 Thomas Cardwell of Granville

[1] Ancestry Message Boards, Lorrie, 19 Jan 2000, citing a "prof. genealogist" [probably Alan Pendergraft] claimed Thomas Cardwell and Mary Leonard had 5 children. She placed the death of Thomas as April 1800, Granville, N.C. Thomas and Mary actually had 12 children, unless there was a heretofore unknown first marriage.

[2] Elizabeth Petty Bentley. *Virginia Marriage Records: From the Virginia Magazine of History and Biography, the William and Mary College Quarterly, and Tyler's Quarterly.* Genealogical Publishing, 1982, p. 25. "Sept. 11, 1787, Cardwell, Thos., & Mary Freeman."

[3] 1790 US Census, Granville, North Carolina, Series M637 Roll 7, p. 90, Family History Library Film 0568147; 1800 US Census, Hillsboro, Granville, North Carolina, Series M32 Roll: 31, p. 564; Image: 522, Family History Library Film 337907.

[4] *List of Taxpayers in Granville County in 1788/1790*, Vol. 26, p. 1282.

[5] "Granville Connections," *Journal of the Granville County Genealogical Society 1746*, Vol. 5, No. 3, Summer 1999, p. 48.

[6] Lewis Shapard, *Island Creek District - Granville County, North Carolina 1790–1795*, Chap. 3, accessed 2 Dec 2020.

[7] 1790 US Census, Granville, North Carolina; Series M637 Roll 7, p. 90, Family History Library Film 0568147. Granville County census records for 1790 did not survive. The 1788 Granville County tax lists substituted as census counts. The census listed only the head of household and did not enumerate persons in the household.

[8] S.N.D. North, *Heads of Families at the First Census of the United States Taken in the Year 1790: North Carolina,* Washington [D.C.]: G.P.O., 1908. A computerized search of North's digitized book returned only the name of Thomas Cardwell in Granville County, North Carolina.

[9] 1790 US Census, Stokes, North Carolina, Series M637 Roll 7, p. 541, Image 313, Family History Library Film 0568147.

[10] 1790 US Census, North Carolina, Wilkes County, p. 151.

[11] 1800 US Census, Hillsboro, Granville, North Carolina; Series M32 Roll 31, p. 564, Image 522, Family History Library Film 337907. The Hillsboro District of the 1800 census was the district of Thomas Cardwell in the 1790 cennsus. This suggests that Thomas died between 1790 and 1800. Other sources place the date more precisely at 3 May 1799 or April 1800.

[12] 1800 US Census, Hillsboro, Granville, North Carolina; Series M32 Roll 31, p. 564, Image 522, Family History Library Film 337907.

[13] Ancestry Message Boards, Karen Edwards Henderson, 23 Jul 2000, "Anderson was the son of Thomas Cardwell of Granville, N.C. His brothers were Wm, John, Wilson, Caleb, Dudley, and Nelson. Sisters were Mary, Sally, and Nancy. Leonard and Thomas, brothers, appointed Guardians of minor children according to court records in 1801, Granville, N.C."

[14] *North Carolina Wills and Probate Records, 1665-1998* for Thomas Cardwell, Granville, General Index Vol. 1. 1749-1875, Book 4, p. 48, Image 64. "Devisor: Thomas Cardwell To Devisees: Thomas Cardwell, Leonard Cardwell, William Cardwell, John Cardwell, Pattey Nance, Mrs. Thomas Cardwell." Probated May Court 1800.

[15] *North Carolina Wills and Probate Records, 1665-1998* for Thomas Cardwell, Granville, General Index, Vol 1, 1749-1875, Book 5, p. 48, Image 65. "Devisees: Thomas, Leonard, William, John, & Mrs. Thomas From Devisor Thomas Cardwell [to each] Probated May Court 1800; *North Carolina Wills and Probate Records, 1665-1998* for Thomas Cardwell, Granville, General Index, Vol 1, 1749-1875, Book 5, p. 48, Image 241. "Devisee: Pattti Nance From Devisor: Thomas Cardwell," Probated May Court 1800.

[16] *North Carolina Marriage Index, 1741-2004*, p 114; see also 1790 US Census, North Carolina, Granville. "Harwood Nance;" *Marriage Bonds (1763 - 1869)*; *North Carolina Marriage Records, 1741-2011*; *North Carolina County Registers of Deeds*, (microfilm), Record Group 048, North Carolina State Archives, Raleigh, N.C.

[17] Find A Grave 216980444.

[18] Ancestry Message Boards, Karen Edwards Henderson, 23 Jul 2000, citing Granville County, N.C, court records.

[19] *North Carolina, County Marriages, 1762-1979, Granville Marriage bond abstracts, 1749-1868*, p. 26. "Thomas Cardwell to Nanni Floyd," 24 Dec 1801, Granville, North Carolina." Differences of opinion weigh whether Nancy was a Loyd or a Floyd. Both family names existed in the Hillsboro District of Granville County. The last name is illegible on the original marriage record. Transcribers of the record wrote it in marriage indexes as both Floyd and Loyd. Peggy Loyd married Richard W. Cardwell. She appeared on the same marriage register as Nanni Floyd. So did Leonard Cardwell and his bride Lucy Strum, along with W.M. Cardwell who married Annie Lawrence. The four Cardwell brothers married within five years of each other from 1801 to 1806. Genealogists prefer the Name Nancy Loyd, opting for a probable relationship with Peggy Loyd.

[20] *North Carolina Wills and Probate Records, 1665-1998*; *Orange County, Wills, 1663-1978*; *Estate Papers, 1754-1944*, Images 3590-3609.

[21] Jonathan K.T. Smith, "Genealogical Abstracts from Reported Deaths," *The Nashville Christian Advocate 1857-1860,* 1997, p. 6, "Nancy G. Bradley w/o Samuel Bradley, Esq.; d/o Thomas and Mary Cardwell; born Granville Co., N.C., May 24, 1797; moved to Sumner Co., Tenn. 1807."

[22] *Marriage Bond, Sumner County Court.* "Samuel Bradley to Nancy G. Cardwell 18 Mar 1811, Benjamin Clary bondsman." When planning to marry, the prospective groom took out a bond from the clerk of the court in the county where the bride had her usual residence as surety that there was no legal obstacle to the proposed marriage. On file in the North Carolina State Archives are 170,000 marriage bonds, covering the years 1741-1868. The Works Progress Administration abstracted these records. The date recorded is the bond date and may or may not be the date of actual marriage.

[23] 1820 US Census, Tennessee, Sumner, Gallatin, citing NARA microfilm publication M33, Image 16 of 57, pp 282, 283, National Archives and Records Administration.

[24] Correspondence from Beth Cavanaugh, 11 Dec 2020. Research on the earliest establishment of Cardwells in Tennessee is ongoing. A search of records by the Tennessee State Library and Archive failed to produce any land transactions. See *Tennessee Land Grants*

by Barbara Byron and Samuel Sistler, and *Earliest Tennessee Land Records and Earliest Tennessee Land History* by Irene M. Griffey.

[25] *Sumner County [Tenn.] Tax Lists 1802-1870*; Record of the Taxable Property in Sumner County for the years 1817 and 1819.

[26] *Early Tax Lists of Tennessee*, (microfilm) 12 rolls. The Tennessee State Library and Archives, Nashville, Tennessee; "Thomas Cardwell, 1838, Sumner, Tennessee."

[27] *Sumner County [Tenn.] Tax Lists 1802-1870*;1830 US Census, South Regiment, Granville, North Carolina, Series M19 Roll 121, p. 44, Family History Library Film 0018087; 1820 US Census, Granville, North Carolina, Roll M33 85, Image 20, p. 17, NARA. William N. Cardwell, son of Thomas [Jr.] appeared on the Sumner County tax rolls beginning in 1825 through 1834 causing minor confusion with his uncle in Granville County, North Carolina, whose name was identical.

[28] 1810 US Census, Granville, North Carolina, Roll 40, p. 886, Image 00256 and p. 890 Image 00261, Family History Library Film 0337913.

[29] 1810 US Census, Granville, North Carolina, Roll 40, p. 886, Image 00256, Family History Library Film 0337913; 1820 US Census, Capt. Henderson's District Granville, North Carolina, Roll M33 85, Image 14, p. 5, NARA.

[30] 1820, 1830 US Census, Tennessee, Smith, p. 33. In the 1830 census, Harwood Nance and [Martha] (1 male 60 to 70; b. 1760-1770 and 1 female 50 to 60 b. 1770-1780) are living in close proximity to Anderson Cardwell, John G. Cardwell, Leonard Cardwell, and Fenelon Cardwell in Smith County, Tennessee.

[31] "Smith County History," *History of Tennessee from the Earliest Time to the Present*, Nashville, Tenn.: Goodspeed Publishing, 1887.

[32] Sumner County Archives, 1828-1899.

[33] Ancestry Message Boards, Lorrie, 19 Jan 2000, citing a "prof. genealogist" [probably Alan Pendergraft]. Records an alternate date of death of Thomas as April 1800, Granville, N.C.

[34] Ancestry Message Boards, Lorrie, 19 Jan 2000, citing a "prof. genealogist" [probably Alan Pendergraft] claimed Thomas Cardwell and Mary Leonard had 5 children.

[35] The compiled list of children of Thomas and Mary Cardwell comes from census records, marriage documents, family histories, genealogies, wills, death records, cemetery records, and other sources.

[36] 1790 US Census, Granville, North Carolina, Series M637 Roll 7, p. 90, Family History Library Film 0568147; Ancestry Message Boards, Chad, 16 Jan 2000, citing "father's records" claimed Leonard Cardwell married twice, secondly to Lucy Strum and had "many" children, among them: Susan, Buckner S., Leonard J., and Alvin P. The 1790 census appears to confirm his birth before 1774. The birthdate of 1769 does not appear to match census records from 1790 to 1850 that compute a birthdate closer to 1774, which also closes the gap between Leonard and his brother Thomas [Jr.] born about 1778. Email correspondence from John Waggoner 15 Dec 2020 said, "The people who submitted the other [Find A Grave] memorials

are not local to this area and I do not know them." Mr. Waggoner's firsthand canvass of the site did not mention Leonard or Lucy but gave information on their son and his wife, Lockey. Find A Grave acknowledged that Leonard's plot is unmarked, which questions the validity of his 1769 birthdate without obtainable information supporting the claim,

[37] Find A Grave Leonard Cardwell 147082386, Lucy (Strum) Cardwell 147082409. This cemetery is located on the farm of the late Alfred Robinson in McClure's Bend. The cemetery is three-tenths mile from the road near the Corps of Engineer boundary fence for Cordell Hull Lake Reservoir. Leonard reportedly lies buried in an unmarked grave next to his wife Lucy. Several graves marked by fieldstones. See *Goodspeed's Smith County History*. 1987; *Smith County TN Homecoming '86 Heritage Committee,* p. 430; and *Smith County TN Cemeteries-North of the Cumberland River,* 1983, p. 187.

[38] *North Carolina County Marriages, 1762-1979,* Granville Marriage bonds, 1758-1868, box 19-22, "Strum, Lucy to Cardwell, Leonard 18 Dec 1802."

[39] Find A Grave 147082409. "Lucy Strum Cardwell."

[40] Ancestry Message Boards, Lorrie, 19 Jan 2000, citing Alan Pendergraft "Jonathan Leonard Jefferson Cardwell b. 1769 Granville co N.C. was 1st m. to Lucy (Longmire) Strum, a widow, 2nd wife Mary Ann Wilson. Leonard and Lucy had: William S., Susannah, John, Buckner S., Leonard Jefferson, Alvin Perrin, daughter Margaret M., Daniel J., son possibly J. W., and a daughter. Leonard was the son of Thomas Cardwell of Granville Co N.C. and Mary Leonard."

[41] *Granville County Wills, Book 5*, pp. 247-252.

[42] 1820 US Census, Capt. Henderson's District Granville, North Carolina, Series M33 Roll 85, Image 14, p. 5, NARA.

[43] *North Carolina County Marriages*, Granville."Cardwell, Lethe to Summerhill, William Jr. 26 Jul 1820."

[44] *Granville County Wills, Will Book 9*, pp. 1, 397.

[45] 1810, 1820, 1830 US Census: 1810 Granville, North Carolina, Roll 40, p. 886, Image 00256, Family History Library Film 0337913; 1820 US Census, Capt. Henderson's District Granville, North Carolina, NARA Roll: M33 85, p. 5, Image 14; 1830 Smith County Tenn. (Shelby, Smith, Sumner, Stewart, Tipton, and Warren Counties), NARA Series M19 Roll 181, p. 33.

[46] 1830 US Census, Tennessee, Smith, p 33.

[47] *North Carolina Marriage Records, 1741-2011.*

[48] GedCom, citing Ancestry.Com 1790 US Census, Granville, North Carolina; *Virginia Marriages 1740-1850*; Dodd, et al, *Early American Marriages to 1850.* Source names Thomas Cardwell born 1744 in Cumberland County, Virginia, and Mary Freeman 15 Feb 1769 in Schenectady, Schenectady County, New York, deceased 1 October 1827 - Cincinnati, Hamilton County, Ohio, as parents of Thomas Jr. and Nancy Cardwell. However, this does not comport with other sources that claim Thomas Cardwell married Mary Leonard.

[49] GedCom "Cardwell Family Tree," citing Rootsweb.Com. Source claims Thomas Cardwell [Jr.] was born in 1778 in Virginia and died 29 Sep 1853 in Calloway County, Kentucky. He married Nancy Lloyd [Floyd] 24 Dec 1801 in Granville County, North Carolina.

[50] *North Carolina, County Marriages, 1762-1979; Granville Marriage bonds, 1758-1868*, box 12-15, FamilySearch, North Carolina State Archives Division of Archives and History. Transcribed as "Loyd [*sic*], Nancy to Cardwell, Thomas 24 Dec 1801."

[51] Ancestry Message Boards, Lorrie, 19 Jan 2000, citing a "prof. genealogist" [probably Alan Pendergraft].

[52] Find A Grave 79993727.

[53] 1830 US Census, Shelby, Smith, Sumner, Stewart, Tipton, and Warren Counties, NARA Series M19 Roll 181, p. 33.

[54] *Tennessee Marriages, 1796-1950*, "Nancy W. Cardwell in entry for John Ward, 1828;" 1850 US Census, "John Ward," Johnson County, Tennessee, citing family 71, NARA microfilm publication M432; Marriage Bond, Sumner County Archives. "John Ward to Nancy W. Cardwell 15 May 1828, John W. Franklin bondsman."

[55] *Tennessee, County Marriages, 1790-1950, Sumner Marriage records, 1787-1838*, Image 149 of 341, citing Tennessee State Library and Archives, Nashville and county clerk offices from various counties. "John Ward & Nancy W. Cardwell, John W. Franklin bondsman, 15 May 1828;" *Tennessee, County Marriages, 1790-1950, Sumner Marriage records, 1787-1838*, Image 326 of 341, citing Tennessee State Library and Archives, Nashville and county clerk offices from various counties. "J.W. Bradley & T. [Thursy] G. Cardwell, by C.G. Browning, 22 May 1837." See also Marriage License, Sumner County Court Archives. J.W. Bradley to T.G. Cardwell 22 May 1837.

[56] *Sumner County [Tennessee] Marriage Records 1787-1838*;1850 US Census, District 14, Sumner, Tennessee, Roll 897, p. 183a. "James W. Bradley."

[57] *Tennessee, County Marriages, 1790-1950, Sumner Marriage records, 1787-1838*, Image 149 of 341, citing Tennessee State Library and Archives, Nashville and county clerk offices from various counties. "Thos. Cardwell & B. Lewis, by J.A. Browning, 25 Jun 1838."

[58] Find A Grave 9758359; 1830 US Census, Tennessee: Shelby, Smith, Sumner, Stewart, Tipton, and Warren counties, NARA Series M19 Roll 181, p. 33; 1840 US Census, Calloway, Kentucky, Roll 106, p. 61, Family History Library Film 0007824; 1850 US Census, District 1, Calloway, Kentucky, Roll 194, p. 467b; 1860 US Census, Township 39 Range 22, Benton, Missouri, p. 265, Family History Library Film 803607; Sumner County [Tenn.] *Tax Lists 1802-1870-C*. Genealogists sometimes confuse Thomas [Jr.]'s son William N. [Nimrod] Cardwell of Sumner County, Tennessee, and Calloway County, Kentucky, with his uncle William Cardwell of Granville County, North Carolina, and Smith County, Tennessee. A William Cardwell appeared on the Sumner County tax rolls in 1812, too old to be the William N. Cardwell who traces to the 1850 census that listed him as age 48. In 1825, William N. appeared on the Sumner County tax list when he reached his age of majority, and remained on the list until at least 1834, He was in Calloway County in 1850 at age 48 with his wife S.

[Sidney "Synda"] N. Cardwell. William N. married Sydney N. Langford. Her name appeared as Synda and S.M. Cardwell in the 1850 and 1860 censuses. In 1860, he removed to Benton County, Missouri, where he died 28 Jan 1862.

[59] 1850 US Census, District 1, Calloway, Kentucky, Roll 194, p. 473b.

[60] *Kentucky Death Records, 1852-1965* for Thos Cardwell, Death Records, 1852-1910, Film 994030, Calloway.

[61] 1850 US Census, South Division, Smith, Tennessee, Roll 896, p. 374a.

[62] *North Carolina, County Marriages, 1762-1979, Granville Marriage bonds, 1758-1868*, box 12-15. "Lawrence, Annie to Cardwell, William M 4 Nov 1806." The marriages of four Cardwell brothers appeared as indexed by hand on the same page of the Granville County marriage register: Thomas Cardwell to "Nanni" [Nancy] Floyd (24 Dec 1801), Leonard Cardwell to Lucy Strum (18 Dec 1802), William M. Cardwell to Annie Lawrence (4 Nov 1806), and Rich. W. Cardwell to Peggy Loyd [*sic*] (12 Dec 1806).

[63] *North Carolina Wills and Probate Records, 1665-1998* for Thomas Cardwell, Granville, General Index, Vol 1, 1749-1875, Book 5, p. 48.

[64] 1810 US Census, Granville, North Carolina, Roll 40, p. 890, Image 00261, Family History Library Film 0337913; 1820 U S Census, Granville, North Carolina, NARA Roll M33 85, p. 17, Image 20; 1830 US Census, South Regiment, Granville, North Carolina, Series M19 Roll 121, p. 44; Family History Library Film 0018087; 1840 US Census, Granville, North Carolina, Roll 360, p. 118, Family History Library Film 0018094.

[65] 1850 US Census, South Division, Smith, Tennessee, Roll 896, p. 374a.

[66] 1860 US Census, Tennessee, Obion, Civil District No. 7, Image 7 of 22, citing NARA microfilm publication M653 (Washington, D.C.: National Archives and Records Administration).

[67] Find A Grave 33636333.

[68] *North Carolina County Marriages, 1762-1979, Granville Marriage bond abstracts, 1758-1868*, "Loyd [*sic*], Peggy to Cardwell, Richard Wilson 02 Dec 1806."

[69] *North Carolina Wills and Probate Records, 1665-1998* for Thomas Cardwell, Granville, General Index, Vol 1, 1749-1875, Book 5, p. 48.

[70] *Sumner County [Tenn.] Tax Lists 1802-1870-C.*

[71] 1830 US Census, Bedford, Tennessee; Series M19 Roll 174, p. 63, Family History Library Film 0024532.

[72] Find A Grave 33636333; *Fayetteville Democrat,* 31 Jan 1880.

[73] 1840 US Census, Prairie, Washington, Arkansas, Roll 20, p. 276, Family History Library Film 0002474; 1850 US Census, Prairie, Washington, Arkansas, Roll 31, p. 383b; 1870 US Census, Prairie, Washington, Arkansas, Roll M593 66, p. 196B, Family History Library Film 545565.

[74] 1800 US Census, Hillsboro, Granville, North Carolina, Series M3 Roll 31, p. 564, Image 522, Family History Library Film 337907,

[75] *North Carolina Wills and Probate Records, 1665-1998* for Thomas Cardwell, Granville, General Index, Vol 1, 1749-1875, Book 5, p. 48.

[76] *Tennessee Wills and Probate Records, 1779-2008*, Smith Will Records, Vol 1-3, 7-8, 1803-1896; Ancestry Message Boards, Carmelita Walker, 28 Dec 1999, edited: 31 Dec 2003; Lorrie, 19 Jan 2000, citing a "prof. genealogist" [probably Alan Pendergraft]; CK0764, 10 Apr 2000, edited: 09 Jul 2004.

[77] *North Carolina Wills and Probate Records, 1665-1998* for Thomas Cardwell, Granville, General Index, Vol 1, 1749-1875, Book 5, p. 48.

[78] 1830 US Census, Shelby, Smith, Sumner, Stewart, Tipton, and Warren counties, NARA Series M19 Roll 181, p. 33.

[79] *Alabama, US, Marriage Index, 1800-1969.*

[80] Ancestry Message Boards, Karen Edwards Henderson, 23 Jul 2000, "Anderson was the son of Thomas Cardwell of Granville, N.C. His brothers were Wm, John, Wilson, Caleb, Dudley, and Nelson. Sisters were Mary, Sally, and Nancy. Leonard and Thomas, also brothers, appointed Guardians of minor children according to court records in 1801 Granville, N.C.

[81] *North Carolina Wills and Probate Records, 1665-1998* for Thomas Cardwell, Granville, General Index, Vol 1, 1749-1875, Book 5, p. 48.

[82] 1800 US Census, Hillsboro, Granville, North Carolina, Series M32 Roll: 31, p. 564, Image: 522, Family History Library Film 337907.

[83] Ancestry Message Boards, Karen Edwards Henderson, 23 Jul 2000.

[84] 1800 US Census, Hillsboro, Granville, North Carolina, Series M32 Roll 31, p. 564, Image: 522, Family History Library Film 337907.

[85] *North CarolinaWills and Probate Records, 1665-1998* for Thomas Cardwell, Granville, General Index, Vol 1, 1749-1875, Book 5, p. 48.

[86] *Bounty-Land Warrant Applications Index*, Index of approved and disapproved bounty-land applications for soldiers who served post-Revolutionary War, 1790-1855, Warrant Number: 55-132154. National Archives; Bureau of Land Management, Department of the Interior, Document No. 5982, Accession No. IL0230 016.

[87] Caleb Cardwell, United States War of 1812 *Index to Service Records, 1812-1815.*

[88] Anonymous online post, "Martha Cardwell who married Isaac Kelly. From what I have found online, Martha Cardwell was born abt. 1818 in Tenn., the daughter of Caleb W. Cardwell. She married Isaac Kelly in Montgomery Co. Ill."

[89] 1820 US Census, Smith, Tennessee, NARA Roll M33 125, p. 49, Image 63.

[90] 1830 US Census, 1830, Tazewell, Illinois, NARA Series M19 Roll 23, FHL microfilm 7,648, "Caleb W. Cardwell;" 1830 US Census, Montgomery, Illinois, Series M19 Roll 23, p. 189, Family History Library Film 0007648; 1840 US Census, Montgomery, Illinois, Roll 66, p. 368, Family History Library Film 0007643.

[91] 1850 US Census, Macoupin, Macoupin, Illinois, Roll 118, p. 190a. Age 65 does not match previous census records in 1810, 1830 and 1840. Also listed as born in Virginia and not North Carolina.

[92] Ancestry Message Boards, Karen Edwards Henderson, 23 Jul 2000, "Anderson was the son of Thomas Cardwell of Granville, N.C. I think Anderson was married before Elizabeth and may have had children by 1st wife. Anderson was on the 1820, 1830, 1840 census in Smith Co. Tenn. He was in Macoupin Co. Illinois census 1850 with wife Elizabeth and some of his children. He died before the 1855 census in Macoupin co. Ill. as Elizabeth was listed as a widow."

[93] *North Carolina Wills and Probate Records, 1665-1998* for Thomas Cardwell, Granville, General Index, Vol 1, 1749-1875, Book 5, p. 48.

[94] *Bounty-Land Warrant Applications Index*, Index of approved and disapproved bounty-land applications for soldiers who served post-Revolutionary War, 1790-1855, Warrant Number 55-160-100153. National Archives.

[95] Bureau of Land Management, US Department of the Interior Military Warrant 0079-104, Patent No. 100153 for 160 acres. "NE1/4 of Section 28 Township 95N of Range 32W."

[96] 1830 US Census, Shelby, Smith, Sumner, Stewart, Tipton, and Warren Counties, NARA Series M19 Roll 181, p. 33; 1840 US Census, Smith, Tennessee, Roll 534, p. 240, Family History Library Film 0024549.

[97] 1850 US Census, Macoupin, Macoupin, Illinois, Roll 118, p. 190a [121b]. Anderson Cardwell's age of 65 does not match previous census records in 1810, 1830, and 1840. The census enumeration of 1850 listed an age of 65, which does not comport with previous census entries in 1830 and 1840 that placed him in younger age categories closer to age 59. Nevertheless, his older children were all born in Tennessee and his wife's first name was Elizabeth in the 1850 census.

[98] Ancestry Message Boards, Karen Edwards Henderson, 23 Jul 2000.

[99] 1800 US Census, Hillsboro, Granville, North Carolina, Series M32 Roll 31, p. 564, Image 522, Family History Library Film 337907.

[100] Smith, "Genealogical Abstracts from Reported Deaths," *The Nashville Christian Advocate 1857-1860*, p. 6; "Nancy G. Bradley w/o Samuel Bradley, esq., d/o Thomas and Mary Cardwell; born Granville Co., N.C., May 24, 1797, moved to Sumner Co., Tenn. 1807, m. 1811, died Macon Co., Tenn., June 24, 1856, cancer; GedCom, citing Ancestry.Com 1790 US Census, Granville, North Carolina; *Virginia Marriages 1740-1850*; Dodd, et al, *Early American Marriages to 1850*. Source names "Thomas Cardwell born 1744 in Cumberland County, Virginia, and Mary Freeman 15 Feb 1769 in Schenectady, Schenectady County, New York, deceased 1 October 1827 - Cincinnati, Hamilton County, Ohio, as parents of Thomas Jr. and Nancy Cardwell." The source confuses Mary Freeman with Mary Leonard, wife of Thomas Cardwell.

[101] Smith, "Genealogical Abstracts from Reported Deaths," *The Nashville Christian Advocate 1857-1860*, p. 6.

[102] *North CarolinaWills and Probate Records, 1665-1998* for Thomas Cardwell, Granville, General Index, Vol 1, 1749-1875, Book 5, p. 48.

[103] Smith, "Genealogical Abstracts from Reported Deaths," *The Nashville Christian Advocate,* March 12, 1857, p. 2.

[104] *Sumner County [Tennessee] Marriage Records 1787-1838* "Bradley, Samuel to Cardwell, Nancy G. Mar. 18, 1811, Benjamin Clary, bndsman." See also Smith, "Genealogical Abstracts from Reported Deaths," *The Nashville Christian Advocate* , March 12, 1857, p. 2; *Granville County, North Carolina Marriages,* "Cardwell, Nancy [to] Stem, Asa 30 Dec 1813." Some genealogists have attempted to tie Nancy Cardwell to Asa L. Stern 20 Dec 1813 in Granville County, North Carolina. However, that appears to be incorrect. The Sterns settled in Bedford County, Tennessee. See "Many Mini Biographies" http://www.teachergenealogist007.com/2009/12/bell-112-113.html. Nevertheless, the claim has credibility because Richard Wilson Cardwell, brother of Nancy, was in Bedford County, Tennessee, in 1830, according to the 1830 census. Moreover, the Nancy Cardwell who married Asa Stern was age 16 or 17 rather than about 15 as attributed to the Nancy Cardwell who married Samuel Bradley. The question remains open: who was the second Nancy Cardwell? Primary source documents support the marriage of Nancy to Samuel Bradley. See Smith, "Genealogical Abstracts from Reported Deaths," *The Nashville Christian Advocate 1857-1860,* p. 6.

[105] Find A Grave 103014711.

[106] 1820 US Census, Smith, Tennessee, NARA Roll: M33 125, p. 44, Image: 58; 1830 US Census, Smith, Tennessee, Series M19 Roll 181, p. 124, Family History Library Film 0024539; 1840 US Census, Sumner, Tennessee, Roll 534, p. 354, Family History Library Film 0024549; 1850 US Census, District 14, Sumner, Tennessee, Roll 897, p. 183a. The enumeration of Nancy's age in 1820 does not comport with other census years.

[107] Nathan Lorance, Thomas Cardwell of Granville Co., N.C, 19 May 2008, https://www.genealogy.com/forum/surnames/topics/cardwell/1644/, accessed 12/3/2020, citing US Census 1820 to 1910 and military pension file.

[108] *The History of Gibson County, Tennessee,* published by Goodspeed in 1887. "William M. [Marion] Bradley is a son of Samuel and Nancy G. [Green] (Cardwell) Bradley, and was born in Gibson [born in Smith] County, Tenn., in 1825. The father was born in Maryland, and the mother in North Carolina. They came to Tennessee when young, and settled in Smith County [later moved to Sumner in the 1830's]. Here Samuel Bradley followed farming the greater part of his life, although a wheelwright and blacksmith by trade. He served in the War of 1812, and was at New Orleans. He was pilot on a boat taking troops from Nashville to that city, and made the entire run without sleep. For services rendered during this time, he received a pension up to the time of his death. He served as justice of the peace about forty years, and supported a family of fifteen children. His wife, who died in 1854 [died 24 June 1856 in Macon Co., Tenn.], bore him thirteen children. His second wife, Martha E. (Charlton) Bradley, became the mother of two children. He died in Trousdale County, Tenn., April 5, 1886, being one hundred years, eight months and twenty days old [born 16 July 1785] at the time of his death."

[109] Ancestry Message Boards, Karen Edwards Henderson, 23 Jul 2000.

[110] MyHeritage, https://www.myheritage.com/names/nelson_cardwell, accessed 12/4/2020.

[111] Marriage Bond, Sumner County Archives, $1,250 Nelson Cardwell to Nancy Hughs 30 Nov 1816, William Stovall bondsman. See also Marriage License, Sumner Archives, Nelson Cardwell to Nancy Hughs 30 Nov 1816.

[112] *Tennessee County Marriages, 1790-1950, Sumner Marriage records, 1787-1838*, Image 163 of 341, citing Tennessee State Library and Archives, Nashville and county clerk offices from various counties. "Nelson Cardwell & Nancy Hughs, by C. Ballard, William Stovall, bondsman, 30 Nov 1816."

[113] *North CarolinaWills and Probate Records, 1665-1998* for Thomas Cardwell, Granville, General Index, Vol 1, 1749-1875, Book 5, p. 48.

[114] 1820 US Census, Tennessee, Sumner, Gallatin, NARA Series M33, Image 16 of 57, microfilm publication National Archives and Records Administration.

[115] *Sumner County [TN] Tax Lists 1802-1870-C.*

[116] *Tennessee, County Marriages, 1790-1950, Sumner, Marriage records, 1787-1838*, Image 163 of 341, Tennessee State Library and Archives, "Nelson Cardwell to Polly Bennett 3 Oct 1835 (second marriage) Sumner County, Tennessee."

[117] 1840 US Census, Simpson, Kentucky, Roll 124, p. 185, Family History Library Film 0007832. "Nelson Caldwell".

Chapter 20 Nelson Cardwell

[1] 1820 US Census, Tennessee, Sumner, Gallatin, Image 16 of 57, NARA microfilm publication M33.

[2] MyHeritage, https://www.myheritage.com/names/nelson_cardwell, accessed 12/4/2020. Nelson Cardwell's date of death estimated from the birth of his son Samuel Cardwell in 1843 and the marriage of his widow Polly about 1848.

[3] Marriage Bond, Sumner County Archives. $1,250, Nelson Cardwell to Nancy Hughs 30 Nov 1816, William Stovall bondsman; Marriage License, Sumner County Archives. Nelson Cardwell to Nancy Hughs 30 Nov 1816.

[4] MyHeritage, https://www.myheritage.com/names/nelson_cardwell, accessed 12/4/2020.

[5] 1800 US Census, Hillsboro, Granville, North Carolina, Series M32 Roll 31, p. 564, Image 522, Family History Library Film 337907. The Hillsboro District of the 1800 census was the district of Thomas Cardwell in 1790 Heads of Families census. This suggests that Thomas died between 1790 and 1800. Other sources place the date more precisely at 3 May 1799 or April 1800. See also Ancestry Message Boards, Lorrie, 19 Jan 2000, citing a "prof. genealogist" [probably Alan Pendergraft] who claimed Thomas Cardwell and Mary Leonard had 5 children. She placed the death of Thomas as April 1800, Granville, NC. Thomas and Mary actually had 12 children, unless there was a heretofore-unknown first marriage.

[6] Ancestry Message Boards, Karen Edwards Henderson, 23 Jul 2000, citing Granville County, N.C, court records.

[7] 1800 US Census, Hillsboro, Granville, North Carolina, Series M32 Roll 31, p. 564, Image 522, Family History Library Film 337907.

[8] Jonathan K.T. Smith, "Genealogical Abstracts from Reported Deaths," *The Nashville Christian Advocate 1857-1860,* 1997, p. 6. "Nancy G. Bradley w/o Samuel Bradley, Esq.; d/o Thomas and Mary Cardwell; born Granville Co., N.C., May 24, 1797; moved to Sumner Co., Tenn. 1807."

[9] *Sumner County [Tenn.] Tax Lists 1802-1870-C.*

[10] Correspondence from Beth Cavanaugh, 11 Dec 2020. Research on the earliest establishment of Cardwells in Tennessee is ongoing. A search of records by the Tennessee State Library and Archives failed to produce any land transactions. See also *Tennessee Land Grants* by Barbara Byron and Samuel Sistler, and *Earliest Tennessee Land Records and Earliest Tennessee Land History* by Irene M. Griffey.

[11] Dee G. Lester, "Sumner County," *Tennessee Encyclopedia,* Tennessee Historical Society, October 8, 2017.

[12] Record of the Taxable Property, 1817, rootsweb.com.

[13] Congress, *American State Papers*, pp. 694, 734-735, 738.

[14] Congress, *American State Papers*, p. 693.

[15] Congress, *American State Papers*, p. 696.

[16] Congress, *American State Papers*, pp. 734, 739. Nelson Cardwell's six-month enlistment in Blakemore's regiment technically ended 20 Dec 1814 but he appears to have continued with Colonel Pipkin until January 27, 1815, mustering out on Feb 2, 1815.

[17] Fold3 File 307330122, citing *Indexes to the Carded Records of Soldiers Who Served in Volunteer Organizations during the War of 1812*, compiled 1899 – 1927, Record Group 94: Records of the Adjutant General's Office, 1762 – 1984, ID 70926294. National Archives. Under Colonel Richard C. Napier, a detachment of the 1st Regiment fought in the Battle of Horseshoe Bend on March 27, 1814. The regiment numbered about 500 men.

[18] Fold3 File 307330123, citing *Indexes to the Carded Records of Soldiers Who Served in Volunteer Organizations during the War of 1812*, compiled 1899 - 1927, Record Group: 94, Roll M6020034, Catalog ID 654501, ID 70926297. National Archives. Records list Nelson Cardwell under two different file IDs. Land records show that Anderson Nelson Cardwell served under the name Nelson, thus accounting for the two IDs. See also Bureau of Land Management, US Department of the Interior Military Warrant 0079-104, Patent No. 100153.

[19] Congress, *American State Papers*, p. 694.

[20] Congress, *American State Papers*, p. 694.

[21] Parton, *Life of Andrew Jackson*, p. 277.

[22] Parton, *Life of Andrew Jackson*, p. 277.

[23] Parton, *Life of Andrew Jackson,* p. 278.

[24] Parton, *Life of Andrew Jackson,* p. 279.

[25] Parton, *Life of Andrew Jackson,* p. 280

[26] Congress, *American State Papers,* p. 695.

[27] Congress, *American State Papers,* pp. 693, 739; *Regimental Histories of Tennessee Units during the War of 1812,* Tennessee Secretary of State. "On the Proceedings of a Court-Martial Ordered for the Trial of Certain Tennessee Militiamen in 1814."

[28] Congress, *American State Papers,* p. 694.

[29] Congress, *American State Papers,* p. 695.

[30] *Tennessee, County Marriages, 1790-1950,* Sumner Marriage records, 1787-1838, Image 163 of 341, citing Tennessee State Library and Archives, Nashville and county clerk offices from various counties. "Nelson Cardwell & Nancy Hughs, by C. Ballard, William Stovall, bondsman, 30 Nov 1816."

[31] *Sumner County [TN] Tax Lists 1802-1870-C.*

[32] 1820 US Census, Tennessee, Sumner, Gallatin, Image 16 of 57, NARA microfilm publication M33.

[33] 1820 US Census, Gallatin, Sumner, Tennessee, p. 283, NARA Roll M33 124, Image 168.

[34] *Class Book for the Willow Grove Society.* March 8, 1834.

[35] *Class Book for the Willow Grove Society.* March 8, 1834.

[36] "Willow Grove Methodist Church History," *Hartsville Vidette Newspaper,* 20 Oct 1955.

[37] *Rural Sun,* Nashville, Tennessee, Vol. 1, No. 37, June 19, 1873. A concise account of the Bethpage church is in "The Early Times in Middle Tennessee," by John Carr who lived and died near this place.

[38] Marriage Bond, Sumner County Archives. $1,250 Nelson Cardwell to Polly Bennett 3 Oct 1835 R.M. Bayers bondsman; *Tennessee, County Marriages, 1790-1950,* Sumner, Marriage Records, 1787-1838, Image 163 of 341, citing Tennessee State Library and Archives. "Nelson Cardwell to Polly Bennett 3 Oct 1835 (second marriage) Sumner County, Tennessee."

[39] https://www.myheritage.com/names/peter_cardwell, accesssed 21 Dec 2020.

[40] *Sumner County [TN] Tax Lists 1802-1870-C.*

[41] 1840 US Census, Simpson, Kentucky, Roll 124, p. 185, Family History Library Film 0007832.

[42] MyHeritage, https://www.myheritage.com/names/nelson_cardwell, accessed 4 Dec 2020.

[43] 1850 US Census, District 4, Macon, Tennessee, Roll 888, p. 185b. Nelson's death date derives from the birthdate of his youngest son by Polly (Bennett) Cardwell in 1843 and the birth of her oldest child by Jeremiah Dixon, her second husband, in 1849.

[44] *Tennessee, County Marriages, 1790-1950*, Sumner, Marriage Records, 1787-1838, Image 163 of 341, citing Tennessee State Library and Archives. "Nelson Cardwell to Nancy Hughes [*sic*], 30 Nov 1816, Sumner County, Tenn., William Stovall bondsman."

[45] *Class Book for the Willow Grove Society*. March 8, 1834.

[46] Find A Grave 38957152.

[47] Seminole War, 1836, Muster Rolls from the companies organized in Sumner County, from *Old Sumner, A History of Sumner County, TN, From 1805-1861* by Walter T. Durham.

[48] Marriage Bond, Sumner County Archives. J.D. Cardwell to Harriett Shaver 14 Jan 1840 James Padgett bondsman; Marriage License, Sumner County Archives. J.D. Cardwell and Harriett Shaver 14 Jan 1840. J.D. Cardwell, aka Jonathan Duran Cardwell, married a second time in 1862 in Arkansas.

[49] 1850 US Census, Piney Fork, Lawrence, Arkansas, Roll 27, p. 192a.

[50] 1840 US Census, Tennessee, Sumner, NARA Series M704, Rolls 533-535, Image 11 of 168.

[51] 1850 US Census, Piney Fork, Lawrence, Arkansas, Roll 27, p. 192a.

[52] Find A Grave 198911128.

[53] *Arkansas, County Marriages, 1837-1957*, Image 19 of 664, county offices [Lawrence County], Arkansas.

[54] 1870 US Census, Arkansas, Carrollton, Carroll County, NARA microfilm publication M593, Image 3 of 21. "John [*sic*] Cardwell."

[55] 1880 US Census, Washington, Columbia, District 3, ED 53, NARA microfilm publication T9, Image 17 of 36.

[56] 1840 US Census, Simpson, Kentucky, Roll 124, p. 185, Family History Library Film 0007832.

[57] 1850 US Census, Tennessee, Sumner, Sumner County, NARA microfilm publication, Roll 218, p. 12a, Image 347 of 356.

[58] *Class Book for the Willow Grove Society*, March 8, 1834.

[59] *Tennessee Marriages, 1796-1950*, "D. D. Dudley Cardwell to Elizabeth Hinton, 29 Aug 1842, Sumner County, Tenn."

[60] Marriage Bond, Sumner County Court Archives. Dudley Cardwell to Elizabeth Hinton 29 Aug 1842, William Cardwell bondsman; Marriage License, Sumner County Court Archives. Dudley Cardwell to Elizabeth Hinton 29 Aug 1842.

[61] *Tennessee Marriages, 1796-1950*, D.D. Dudley Cardwell to Elizabeth Hinton, 29 Aug 1842, Sumner County, Tenn." The 1850 census recorded Elizabeth as born in Kentucky.

[62] 1850 US Census, Kentucky, Simpson County, NARA microfilm publication M432 Roll 218, Image 23 of 142

[63] 1860 US Census, District 19, Sumner, Tennessee, p. 40, Family History Library Film 805275, and M653, p. 202, transcribed as "V. S. Cardwell." In various sources

[64] Sumner County Chancery Court 1860, Case 12478. "D.D. Cardwell, et al. vs. Isaac Groves."

[65] 1870 US Census, District 19, Sumner, Tennessee, Roll M593 1566, p.846A, Family History Library Film 553065; 1880 US Census, Franklin, Simpson, Kentucky, Enumeration District 214, Roll 442, p. 357C.

[66] *Indiana Death Index, 1882-1920*, "Wm W. Cardwell, 11 Nov 1897, Evansville, Indiana," citing the book CSS-2 on page 113 within the series produced by the Indiana Works Progress Administration, City Health Office, Evansville.

[67] Find A Grave 98414684.

[68] Marriage Bond, Sumner County Court Archives. Wm. M. Cardwell to E.A. Jones 23 Dec 1851 Thomas Sneed bondsman; Marriage License, Sumner County Court. Wm. M. Cardwell to Edward Ann Jones 23 Dec 1851; *Tennessee Marriages, 1796-1950*. "William W. Cardwell to E.A. Jones 23 Dec 1851;" *Tennessee Deaths, 1914-1966*, Image 32 & 280, Tennessee State Library and Archives.

[69] *Illinois, County Marriages, 1810-1940*, Image 1; county offices, Illinois. William and Edward Anne Cardwell listed as parents of Tabitha Cardwell on the marriage register in Anna, Union County, Illinois, in 1904, at the Methodist Episcopal Church.

[70] Find A Grave 98414653.

[71] 1860 US Census, Tennessee, Davidson, 2nd District NARA microfilm publication M653, Image 18 of. "Wm Cardwell, 1860;" 1870 US Census, Tennessee, Sumner, District 06, NARA microfilm publication M593, Image 13 of 24; 1880 US Census, Sumner, Tennessee, Enumeration District (ED) 212, NARA microfilm publication T9, sheet 66D. "W.W. Cardwell."

[72] 1830 US Census, Shelby, Smith, Sumner, Stewart, Tipton, and Warren Counties, NARA Series M19, Roll 181.

[73] Find A Grave 51890240.

[74] *Sumner County [Tenn.] Tax Lists 1802-1870-C.*

[75] Marriage Bond, Sumner County Court Archives. Thomas Cardwell to Margaret McDowell 11 Jul 1847. Feneman Fenton, Jr. bondsman; Marriage License, Sumner County Court Archives. Thomas Cardwell to Margaret McDowell 11 Jul 1847. *Tennessee Marriage Records, 1780-2002*, Marriage License for Margaret McDaniel [McDowell] and Thomas Cardwell 4 Jul 1847, Sumner, Jan 1845-Jun 1854. The 4 Jul 1847 date on this record is incorrect; *Kentucky Death Records, 1911-1965*, Image 1 of 1, Office of Vital Statistics, Frankfort.

[76] *TennesseeMarriage Records, 1780-2002.* Margaret Hinton, Sumner, 1840-1849 Marriages (Loose Rec) A-P. Margaret Hinton first married Henry McDowell 17 Sep 1845 in Sumner County, Tennessee. Margaret and Henry divorced. See Find A Grave 91175452.

[77] Descendants of John Hinton Family Album Entry (rootsweb.com).

[78] *Sumner County Marriage Records, Selected Marriages from 1791-1925*, compiled and transcribed by Sherry Wilson from Sumner County Archives in Gallatin, Tenn.

[79] Commonwealth of Kentucky Certificate of Death 34680, State Board of Health. "Ruben Cardwell, son of Tommy Cardwell and Margaret Hinton, born 13 Aug 1848, Christian County, Kentucky."

[80] 1850 US Census, Tennessee, Sumner, Sumner County, NARA microfilm publication M432, Image 347 of 356.

[81] 1860 U.S. Census, Kentucky: Shelby, Simpson, and Spencer Counties, NARA Series M653, Roll 395, p 59, "Thomas G Cardwell."

[82] 1870 US Census, District 19, Sumner, Tennessee, Roll M593 1566, p. 855B, Family History Library Film 553065.

[83] 1880 US Census, Simpson, Kentucky, Enumeration District 215, Roll 442, p. 71A, NARA.

[84] Will of Thomas G. Cardwell, son of Nelson Cardwell. Made at the August Term of the Simpson County Court. "Witness my hand this the 17th day of November 1890. J.H. Covington, C.S.C.C. [Clerk, Simpson County Court]. In the name of God amen, I Thomas G. Cardwell now of the county of Simpson and state of Kentucky being of sound mind but in bad health knowing the uncertainty of life make this my last will and testament. First. I want my wife Margaret who helped me make all I have, after all my just debts are paid, to have all the property I may be in possession of at the time of my death to have and hold the same during her life time and to dispose of as she please when she dies. Second. I will except this much of my personal property, which each one of my boys who are under age, Thomas T. and William E. Cardwell both have a good horse saddle and bridle. In testimony I have set my hand this 17th day of March 1877. Thomas G. Cardwell [his mark]. Attest: R.B. Piper & John Gregory." Simpson County Court. December Term December 15th, 1890. "The foregoing instrument of writing purporting to be the last will and testament of Thomas Cardwell deceased was this day produced in open court and proved to be such by good and sufficient evidence. It is therefore ordered by the court to be recorded as the last will and testament of the said Thomas G. Cardwell deceased, which is done accordingly. Witness my hand this the 15th day of December 1890. J.H. Covington, C.S.C.C." *Kentucky Wills and Probate Records, 1774-1989*, Simpson, Wills, Vol 1-4, 1882-1962, p 152.

[85] *Tennessee, County Marriages, 1790-1950*, Sumner Marriage Records, 1787-1838, Image 311 of 341, citing Tennessee State Library and Archives, Nashville, and county clerk offices from various counties. "Nelson Cardwell & Polly Bennett, R.M. Boyers, bondsman, no date," confirmed as 3 Oct 1835 (second marriage) Sumner County, Tennessee.

[86] Find A Grave 7293968.

[87] 1910 US Census, Lafayette Cardwell, Drakesboro, Muhlenberg, Kentucky, Enumeration District (ED) 78, NARA microfilm publication T624, Roll 496, sheet 7A, family 132.

[88] *Kentucky Births and Christenings, 1839-1960*. "Lafayette Cardwell and Elizabeth Mays in entry for Kitty Cardwell, 1874 [daughter]."

[89] *Kentucky County Marriages, 1797-1954*, citing multiple county clerks, county courts, and historical societies, Kentucky; 1900 US Census, Magisterial District 4, Rosewood Precinct

Dumor Town, Muhlenberg, Kentucky, Enumeration District (ED) 64, NARA microfilm publication T623, sheet 3B, family. "Peter L Cardwell."

[90] Find A Grave 7293930.

[91] 1840 US Census, Simpson, Kentucky. Roll 124, p. 185, Family History Library Film 0007832.

[92] Genealogists Rand Cardwell wrote in 2008, "Peter Lafayette Cardwell was born in Simpson County, KY. Research has not proven his parents 100%, but he might be the son of Nelson Cardwell. He married Elizabeth [Mays]. They are listed in the 1870 census of Allen County, KY."

[93] 1860 US Census, Kentucky, Simpson, NARA microfilm publication M653, Image 63 of 140.

[94] 1850 US Census, District 4, Macon, Tennessee, Roll 888, p. 185b.

[95] 1860 US Census, Simpson, Kentucky, p. 63, Family History Library Film 803395.

[96] 1860 US Census, Kentucky, Simpson, Image 63 of 140.

[97] *Illinois Deaths and Stillbirths, 1916-1947,* Nelson Cardwell in entry for Samuel Cardwell, 9 Jan 1925, Public Board of Health, Archives, Springfield, Illinois, FHL microfilm 1877617; *Illinois, Cook County Deaths, 1871-1998*, Nelson Cardwell in entry for Samuel Cardwell, 9 Jan 1925, citing Chicago, Cook, Illinois, Cook County Courthouse, Chicago.

[98] *Indiana Marriages, 1810-2001*. "Martha Hampton."

Chapter 21 Cedar County Cardwells

(No Endnotes)

Chapter 22 Watts, Strange, and Stegall

[1] Wirt Johnson Carrington, *A History of Halifax County, Virginia*, Richmond, Va.: Appeals Press, 1924, reprinted 1994 Southern Historical Press, p. 15. Genealogists have tried to connect the Watts family of Halifax County to Samuel Watts, allegedly born in Somerset, England, the son of Thomas Watts and Mary Hayden. However, there is insufficient proof that Samuel Watts of Halifax County was the Samuel Watts born in Somerset.

[2] *Halifax County, Virginia, Index to Court Records*-Defendant, microfilm of original housed at the Virginia State Archives, Richmond, Va. There were numerous cases for Samuel Watts in these court records beginning in 1752. It is unclear whether or not this was the same Samuel of this study.

[3] *Halifax County, Virginia Pleas No. 10*, p. 211 (microfilm of original). An entry on this page dated September 1781 shows a Susannah Watts "late inhabitant of South Carolina" delivering a schedule of slaves brought to Virginia in August.

[4] *Halifax County, Virginia Deed Book 9*, p. 424 (microfilm of original).

[5] *Halifax County, Virginia Deed Book 11*, p. 9 (microfilm of original); "Joshua Stone to Mary Hoskins 15 July 1769;" *Marriage Bonds Register of Halifax County*, Virginia (microfilm

of original); US Bureau of the Census, *Heads of families at the first census of the United States taken in the year 1790*, Virginia, Genealogical Publishing, 1976, 1790 Census of Virginia. A Richard Wyatts listed in Halifax County, Virginia, in 1785, p. 89.

[6] *Halifax County, Virginia Pleas No. 10*, p. 130 (microfilm of original). It may be worth noting that Samuel did not say he was born in Virginia nor did he say that he had been a resident of Virginia all of his life.

[7] H.J. Eckenrode, *Virginia State Library, List of the Colonial Soldiers of Virginia, Special Report of the Department of Archives and History for 1913*, Genealogical Publishing, 1978, p. 87. According to this book, Samuel was listed in the French and Indian Bounty Warrants; two manuscript volumes copied from the loose applications for land bounties in the Virginia land office (in the Virginia Historical Society Library).

[8] Lloyd DeWitt Bockstruck, *Virginia's Colonial Soldiers*, Genealogical Publishing [1988] 1990, p. 267.

[9] 1790 Census of Virginia, pp. 24, 88.

[10] *Halifax County, Virginia Court Orders, Plea Book 12*, p. 311 (microfilm from the Virginia State Archives).

[11] *Halifax County, Virginia Court Orders, Plea Book 12*, p. 393.

[12] *Halifax County, Virginia Wills 1792-1797*, T.L.C. Genealogy, 1991, p. 261 "Estate of Mathew Sims dec'd in account current 1792," and p. 267 "account of the sales of the estate of Mathew Sims dec'd December 1791 and January 1792."

[13] *Halifax County, Virginia Deeds*, Book 22, p. 340.

[14] Samuel, Sr. signed the consent for his daughter Polly to be married to Joseph Shaw (photocopy of marriage bond and consent, *Marriage Register Book 1*, p. 66, obtained from Halifax County courthouse. He also signed the consent for his son Thomas M. to marry Sally Overton (photocopy of Marriage Bond and consent, p. 173, obtained from Charlotte County courthouse).

[15] *Halifax County, Virginia Land Tax Books 1800B-1817B* (microfilm from the Virginia State Archives).

[16] *Halifax County, Virginia Personal Property Tax Lists 1782-1821* (microfilm, Virginia State Archives).

[17] *Marriage Bonds Register of Halifax County, Virginia*. "James Mayne to Sally Watts, 3 April 1812."

[18] *Halifax County, Virginia Pleas No. 12*, p. 268.

[19] Map of Halifax County, Virginia by M. French, 1899. Copy found in the vertical files of the Orange County Public Library, Orlando, Florida. Copies available from the Virginia State Library. See alsotranscript of cemetery inscriptions at Ellis Creek Baptist Church, Halifax County, Virginia at Va. GenWeb Archives, accessed 25 Jan 2015. http://files.usgwarchives.net/va/halifax/cemeteries/elliscre.txt, surveyed and submitted by H. Mark Saunders in 1998. The church is located "on Buckskin Trail (present Rte. 695) off Coles

Ferry Road (present Rte. 624); Halifax County, Ludwig Bucholtz Map, 1859, Map Collection of the Virginia Library and Archives; Pocahontas Wight Edmunds, *History of Halifax County, Virginia*, Vols. 1 & 2, Virginia Book, [1977]); William Mulford, *Banister Lodge: A History of Unbaffled Virginians*, self-published, 1982, p. 9. See also transcript of Will of John Clark on p. 276, citing Will Book 14, p. 258 in Carrington's book, *A History of Halifax County, Virginia*. Well into the twentieth century, Watts's descendants had land in the area of Neal's Corner. A map drawn by M. French in 1899 showed Coles Ferry on Staunton River between Ellis Creek and Buckskin Creek. Present Route 624 is currently Coles Ferry Road. Sims Ferry was not located on French's map or on an 1859 area map. There was a Clarks Ferry listed on those maps where Watkins Bridge is now located. According to a county history book, Mathew Sims had a large plantation "near the town of Clover which encompassed the Crystal Hill area" and he received a license for a ferry in 1779. Was Priscilla Sims his daughter who possibly inherited the land that included the ferry? Priscilla married John Clark (his second marriage) in 1801, and so it may be that Sims Ferry became Clarks Ferry. John Clark had a substantial interest in a mercantile firm called William Bailey and Company, which later figured prominently in the life of Samuel's son Thomas Watts.

[20] *Halifax County, Virginia Court Records*, Plea Book 29, pp. 388, 398; Plea Book 30, pp. 1, 8; Plea Book 35, pp. 380, 551, (microfilm, Virginia State Archives).

[21] *Halifax County, Virginia Index to Court Records*-Plaintiff, microfilm, Virginia State Archives.

[22] *Halifax County, Virginia Court Records*, Plea Book 29, pp. 388, 398, microfilm from the Virginia State Archives, Richmond, Virginia. "Watts vs. Shaw."

[23] Samuel Watts Jr. named a son Thomas Gillum Watts who had a grandson named Rufus Gilliam Watts.Thomas M. Watts had a daughter named Charity G. Watts and possibly a son named Samuel G. Watts. Another son James Watts may have been the same as Gilly Watts.

[24] *Halifax County, Virginia Personal Property Tax Lists 1782-1821*. Thomas was the first of Samuel's sons to appear on the tax lists in 1786; so he apparently was born around 1765. There was a male age 16-21 in Samuel Sr.'s household that year, which would appear to be Samuel Jr. Samuel Jr. listed by name on the tax list in his father's household for the years 1788 and 1789 and then charged with tax himself in 1789. William Watts appears on the tax lists in 1795.

[25] Catherine Lindsay Knorr, *Marriage Bonds and Minister's Returns of Charlotte County, Virginia 1764-1815*, (1951), p. 88. A photocopy of marriage bond and consent, p. 173, also obtained from the courthouse.

[26] *Halifax County, Virginia Plea Book 35*, pp. 183, 365. In September 1819, Richard High appointed administrator of the estate of Thomas M. Watts. Thomas listed as the plaintiff in a case against Lewis Hardwick in May of 1819.

[27] *Halifax County, Virginia Deed Book 12*, pp. 42, 72 "Joseph Ashby," pp. 38, 69. "James Owen," and Deed Book 22, p. 36 "LeGrand".

[28] 1830 U. S. Census, Halifax County, Virginia, p. 446;

[29] 1850 U S Census, Halifax County, Virginia, p. 8, dwelling 110, family 111; 1860 US Census, Halifax County, Virginia, dwelling 666, family 646.She was not listed in the 1870 US Census and assumed to have died by that time.

[30] Letter from Mildred Miller of Missouri, 1996, which included a photocopy of a biographical sketch of the Samuel Watts family, cited as from the book, *History of Audrain County*.

[31] *Halifax County, Virginia, Court Orders, Book 24*, p. 122, microfilm from the Virginia State Archives, Richmond, Virginia. His widow Sally Watts was appointed administrix of his estate along with John Haskins (or Hawkins) and William Hall.

[32] *Marriage Bonds Register of Halifax County, Virginia, Book 1*, p. 31, (microfilm of original) "William Watts to Patty Lee;"Marriage Records 1750-1800 in Halifax County, Va., from Wirt Johnson Carrington, *A History of Halifax County, Virginia*, 1924, "William Watts to Patty Lee 13 May 1795." William disappeared from Halifax County, Virginia, records in 1807. Stuart Butler's *Virginia Soldiers 1800-1815* shows a William Watts a soldier in the 5th infantry, enlisted in June of 1808 aged 31, discharged at Fort Claiborne, La., in May of 1815. This may have been this William, though no proof at this time.

[33] *Marriage Bonds Register of Halifax County, Virginia, Book 1*, p. 31 (microfilm of original) "William Watts to Patty Lee;" Eunice M. White, *Sand Through Our Fingers: The White Family and its Related Families, England, Maryland, Virginia, Kentucky, Missouri and Points Beyond*, Joplin Mo., privately printed, 1980, p. 67.

[34] Will of William Cassady, September Court 1794, Halifax County, Virginia http://files.usgwarchives.net/va/halifax/wills/cassady1.txt, submitted by Ray Parker, accessed 25 Jan2015.

[35] White, *Sand Through Our Fingers*, 1980; *Halifax County, Virginia Personal Property Tax Lists 1782 – 1821*, (microfilm, Virginia State Archives). Ages for William and his siblings have been calculated based on when they first appeared in these tax lists. For instance, William's birthdate had long been calculated to about 1773 since he first appeared on the tax lists in 1795. Later a record of his wife's age was located placing her birth date at around 1770. The estimation of his birth date is likely close to that time as well.

[36] Don and Carley Worth, www.bishir.org, accessed 12 Jan 2014. The Bisher Scrapbook online provides information on the Lee family and Watts connections and provides sources.

[37] *Marriage Bonds Register of Halifax County, Virginia, Book 1*, p. 41 (microfilm of original) "Joseph Watts to Patsey Canaday;" Marriage Records 1750-1800 in Halifax County, Va., from Carrington, *A History of Halifax County, Virginia*, 1924. "Joseph Watts to Patsey Canaday 29 May 1799." Joseph Watts is listed in the 1820 US Census in Halifax County, Virginia; *Halifax County, Virginia Index to Deeds*- Grantor (microfilm of original), Joseph sold his land in 1821, and was listed in the 1820 US Census in Halifax as aged 26-44, which calculates his birth date between 1776 and 1794.

[38] See the biographies of Granville H. Watts and his nephew Henry Watts at the online transcription of *History of Greene County, Missouri*, 1883 by R.I. Holcombe, Editing Historian, Chapter 21, Center Township, Part 2 "Biographies of Old Settlers and Prominent

Citizens" http://thelibrary.org/lochist/history/holcombe/grch21pt2.html, accessed 25 Jan 2015.

[39] *Marriage Bonds Register Book 1*, p. 66, of Halifax County, Virginia (photocopy obtained from courthouse). "Joseph Shaw to Polly Watts."

[40] These two listed as plaintiffs along with Joseph and Polly in the dispute over slaves Samuel conveyed to Polly in 1810. See also *Halifax County, Virginia, Court Records*, Plea Book 29, pp. 388, 398; Plea Book 30, pp. 1, 8; and Plea Book 35, pp. 380, 551.

[41] Letter from Mildred Miller of Missouri, 1996, which included a photocopy of a biographical sketch of the Samuel Watts family cited from the book, *History of Audrain County, Missouri.* According to this biographical sketch, Samuel, Jr. was born in England. This was probably inaccurate, although that may have been his father or grandfather's birthplace.

[42] *Halifax County, Virginia Personal Property Tax Lists 1782-1821.*

[43] *Halifax County, Virginia Court Orders, Book 24*, p. 122.

[44] Miller letter, citing *History of Audrain County, Missouri.*

[45] 1790 Census of Virginia. The 1782 and 1785 tax lists were used in place of the 1790 US Census for the state of Virginia because the census records were destroyed.

[46] Marriage Records 1750-1800, in Halifax County, Va., from Carrington, *A History of Halifax County, Virginia*, Richmond, 1924. "Robert Burchett married Martha Sikes 18 Feb 1789."

[47] Descendants of Thomas Burchett shared by William S. Burchett found online at http://homepages.rootsweb.com/~burchett/burctomdesc2.html, accessed 13 Apr 2001.

[48] *Marriage Bonds Register of Halifax County*, Virginia (microfilm of original). "James Mayne to Sally Watts, 3 April 1812."

[49] *Halifax County, Virginia Deed Book 12*, p. 4 "Watts with Mayne agreement"

[50] Miller letter, citing *History of Audrain County, Missouri; Halifax County, Virginia Court Orders, Book 29*, p. 398 and *Book 30*, p. 1 (microfilm from the Virginia State Archives, Richmond, Virginia). Court records verify the names of most of these children, though there were some discrepancies. For instance, court records did not show a John but showed a Martin; perhaps he was John Martin. Gillum was in those court records as Thomas Gillum. There was no mention of Brackett in the court records.

[51] *Marriage Bonds Register of Halifax County, Virginia, Book 1*, p. 117.

[52] Wm. S. Bryan and Robert Rose, *A History of the Pioneer Families of Missouri*, John B. Swift, 1876; 1850 Audrain County Census *Index*, p. 174. Source also stated that Joseph Watts came to Calloway County from Bourbon, Kentucky, in 1824 and was the brother of Roland Watts. Additional documentation included a transcript dated 1975 of the Watts - Rickman Cemetery in Audrain County, Missouri.

[53] Copy of a transcript dated 1975 of the Watts - Rickman Cemetery in Audrain County, Missouri, courtesy Mildred Miller of Missouri.

[54] Copy of computerized printout of 1838 tax assessment in Audrain County, Missouri, p. 6, dated October 1989, courtesy Mildred Miller of Missouri.

[55] Copy of a transcript dated 1975 of the Watts-Rickman Cemetery in Audrain County, Missouri, courtesy Mildred Miller of Missouri, 1996.

[56] *Marriage Bonds Register of Halifax County, Virginia, Book 1*, p. 74.

[57] *Marriage Bonds Register of Halifax County, Virginia, Book 1*, p. 80.

[58] *Halifax County, Virginia Minute Book 9*, p. 256, 258 (microfilm of original). James H. Watts appointed administrator of Daniel's estate.

[59] *Marriage Bonds Register, Book 1*, p. 64.

[60] *Marriage Bonds Register, Book 1*, p. 104, 208.

[61] *Halifax County, Virginia Register of Births and Deaths 1853 - 1871, Book 1*, p. 23.

[62] Information taken from a family group sheet compiled by Mildred Miller, 1996, a Watts descendant.

[63] *Marriage Bonds Register, Book 1*, p. 95. Edmunds, *History of Halifax County, Virginia*, Vol. 1. The bond dated 30 April. Her brother Phillip Lane was bondsman.

[64] Will of William Lane, Charlotte County, Virginia, 1832/1834, contributed online at rootsweb archives http://www.vagenweb.org charlotte/w0wlane.htm, submitted by Judi Gleason 15 Mar 1999, accessed 11 Jan 2014.

[65] Information from a family group sheet compiled by Mildred Miller, 1996.

[66] 1820 US Census, Halifax County, Virginia, p. 74. Roland had two females under age ten.

[67] *Tennessee Census Index.*

[68] Copy of computerized printout of 1838 tax assessment in Audrain County, Missouri, p. 6, dated October 1989, courtesy Mildred Miller of Missouri.

[69] Copy of computerized printout of 1838 tax assessment in Audrain County, Missouri, p. 6.

[70] Information taken from a family group sheet compiled by Mildred Miller, 1996.

[71] *Marriage Bonds Register, Book 1*, p. 1. Littleberry appears to have been a nickname for Benjamin.

[72] 1850 US Census, Audrain County, Missouri, family 40, from a typewritten copy courtesy Mildred Miller of Missouri.

[73] *Marriage Bonds Register, Book 1*, p. 126.

[74] *Marriage Bonds Register, Book 1*, p. 142. Although this marriage record listed his middle initial as "T", a message posted online from a descendant, Becky Cartwright, stated his full names as Brackett Barnes Watts.

[75] See USGenWeb for Warren County, North Carolina. No other Watts appear listed in these marriage records through 1868.

[76] *Virginia Marriages, 1785-1940.* "Henry Strange to Elizabeth Watts, 20 Dec 1806, Halifax, Virginia; spouse's mother's name Sarah Wats [*sic*]."

[77] *Halifax County, Virginia Marriage Bonds Register, Book 1*, p. 64.

[78] The information on this family supplied by descendant William Gaulding.

[79] The information on this family supplied by descendant William Gaulding.

[80] 1830 US Census, Halifax, Virginia, Series M19, Roll 192, p. 433; Family History Library Film 0029671. "Henry Steagall, Henry Strange," counted as neighbors living four households apart.

[81] George Cabell Greer, *Early Virginia Immigrants,* Richmond, Va.: W.C. Hill, 1912.

[82] United States. Bureau of the Census. *Heads of Families at the First Census of the United States Taken in the Year 1790: Records of the State Enumerations, 1782 to 1785, Virginia* (Reprint). Washington: Government Printing Office, 1961. First Census of the United States, Heads of Families-Virginia 1785, Halifax County, List of Joseph Haynes. Jesse Strange 5 white souls [listed with three other men of the Strange surname: Benjamin, Julius, Dick] p. 89. See also First Census of the United States, Heads of Families-Virginia 1782 & 1785, Halifax County. Littlebury [*sic*] Strange in Halifax County 9 white souls, pp. 24, 88. The name Littleberry recurs as Littleberry Watts in 1801.

[83] 1820 US Census, Virginia, Halifax, Series M33, Roll 131, NARA. The 1820 census for Meadville, Halifax County, Virginia, pp. 77-79, listed Henry Strange and his family next door to Sarah Strange and a small child. Enumerated nearby were the families of Nancy Steagall [*sic*], Claiborne, Elizabeth, and Frederick Steagall.

[84] 1840 US Census, Roane, Tennessee, Roll 535, p. 75, Family History Library Film 00245491840.

[85] 1850 US Census, District 1, Christian, Kentucky, Roll 196, p. 463b. The census incorrectly listed Elizabeth (Watts) Strange as Elizabeth Stegall in the household of Henry Stegall, her son-in-law.

[86] 1820 US Census, Virginia, Halifax, Series M33, Roll 131, NARA.

[87] Find A Grave 141566142.

[88] *1857 Missouri Marriages.*

[89] 1860 US Census, Madison, Cedar, Missouri, p. 138.

[90] *Civil War Pension Index: General Index to Pension Files, 1861-1934* for Samuel W Stigall [*sic*], Certificate 664098, Widow's Certificate A-8-10-32.

[91] 1870 US Census, Madison, Cedar, Missouri, Roll M593 768, p. 100Al; 1880 US Census, Madison, Cedar, Missouri, Roll 680, Enumeration District 253, p. 368B. In the 1880 census, John Stegall age 20 listed as Samuel Stegall's nephew, suggesting that he was the John Stegall in the household of Elizabeth Cardwell in 1860. Samuel and Eliza do not appear to have had children. John W. Stegall b. 18 May 1860, allegedly was the son of James B. and Nellie Stegall of the South Carolina Stegall family that settled in Vernon County, Missouri. However, this contradicts the 1860 census that identified him as the "nephew" of Samuel Stegall of Cedar

and Dade Counties. He married Mary Brown of Madison Township in Cedar County. Birth records show a son William Alfred born 22 Feb 1886 in Madison. John died in California in 1942.

[92] *Special Schedules of the Eleventh Census (1890) Enumerating Union Veterans and Widows of Union Veterans of the Civil War*, Series M123, National Archives.

[93] 1910 US Census, South Morgan, Dade, Missouri, Enumeration District 0077, Roll T624 778, p. 9A.

[94] *1927 Wichita, Kansas, City Directory.*

[95] Headstone Applications for Military Veterans, 1925-1970 for Samuel W Stigall [*sic*] 1925-1941.

[96] Find A Grave 120830549.

Chapter 23 Reuben Granville Cardwell

[1] 1850 US Census, District 1, Christian, Kentucky, Series M432 Roll 196, p. 463b, National Archives. 10 Sep 1850 "Henry Stegall, 46, [1804] b. Virginia; Juna [Irene], 37 [1813] b. Virginia; Eliza 17 [1833] b. Virginia; Elvira (f) 14 [1836] b. Tennessee; Pathenia (f) 13 [1837] b. Tennessee; Saml 12 [1838] b. Tennessee; William H. 9 [1841] b. Tennessee; Benj C. 2 [1848] b. Tennessee; Elizabeth Strange 61 [1789] b. Virginia [mother-in-law]

[2] *Kentucky, County Marriages, 1797-1954, Book 1*, p. 126, "Reuben Cardwell and Elizabeth Stegall, 19 May 1849," citing *Marriages, Trigg County, Kentucky*, various county clerks and county courts, Kentucky, FHL microfilm 321335, Image 164. "Reuben Cardwell to Elizabeth Stegall." Record entered 18 April, returned to office and noted 28 April, executed and entered in the record May 19, 1849. The transcribed marriage date of 19 May 1849 comes from an interpretation of the record beginning with an entry of license and bond 19 April. The Trigg County Clerk posted it in the office on 28 April, and a justice of the peace certified the marriage as of 19 May 1849, hence the date of their wedding as 19 May 1849, in Trigg County, Kentucky. When planning to marry, the prospective groom took out a bond from the clerk of the court in the county where the bride had her usual residence as surety that there was no legal obstacle to the proposed marriage. The date recorded is the bond date and may or may not be the date of actual marriage. Noted of Interest also in this record, p 81, was John W. Burchett 3 Mar 1841 to Jcy. F. M. Cameron.

[3] Commonwealth of Kentucky Certificate of Death 34680, State Board of Health. "Ruben Cardwell, son of Tommy Cardwell and Margaret Hinton, born 13 Aug 1848, Christian County, Kentucky."

[4] 1850 US Census, Simpson County, Simpson, Kentucky, family 141, NARA microfilm publication M432, Image 23, Enumerated 7 Aug 1850. "R.G. Cardwell 21 b. [1829] Tenn., E. Cardwell b. Va., No Children; Living next door to: D. Cardwell 28 b. [1822] Tenn., E. Cardwell 30 b. [1820] Ky., Wm. D. male 7, J.N. male 6, M.E. f 4, S.J. f 3, L.M. f 2, N.D. f 0 all b. Ky., [Not in 1860 Simpson, Ky. US Census]."

[5] 1850 US Census, District 1, Christian, Kentucky, Series M432 Roll 196, p. 463b, National Archives. "Henry Stegall." No one in the Stegall family had the benefit of education, and like

the Cardwells could neither read nor write, enumerated 10 Sep 1850, "Henry Stegall, 46, [1804] b. Virginia, Juna [Irene], 37 [1813] b. Virginia; Eliza 17 [1833] b. Virginia; Elvira (f) 14 [1836] b. Tennessee; Pathenia (f) 13 [1837] b. Tennessee; Saml 12 [1838] Tennessee; William H. 9 [1841] b. Tennessee; Benj C. 2 [1848] b. Tennesseee; Elizabeth Strange 61 [1789] b. Virginia [mother-in-law]." Genealogical Note: Data match for Eliza and Samuel Stegall who migrated to Missouri and appeared there in the 1860 census and subsequent census records.

[6] Goodspeed Publishing. *History of Hickory, Polk, Cedar, Dade, and Barton Counties, Missouri.* Chicago: Goodspeed, 1889, pp. 409, 421.

[7] Goodspeed, *History of Hickory, Polk, Cedar, Dade, and Barton Counties,* pp. 413-416.

[8] 1860 US Census, Madison, Cedar, Missouri, p. 127, Family History Library Film 803613. "Elizabeth Cordell [Cardwell]." Assuming Juliann's age of 8 months on 19 Sep 1860 [date of the census] to be correct, Reuben could not have left before the spring of 1859. The infant John Stegall appeared again in the 1880 census, age 20, living in the household of Samuel Stegall as Stegall's nephew. His parents are unidentified. Samuel Stegall had a brother named John H. Stegall who was of age to be the father of John W. but their relationship is unproven.

[9] *Missouri, County Marriage, Naturalization, and Court Records, 1800-1991.* "William Emberson, 30 Jan 1866," citing Marriages, Dade, Missouri, United States, Missouri State Archives, Jefferson City, FHL microfilm 007424391.

[10] Find A Grave 141566142. *Missouri, County Marriage, Naturalization, and Court Records, 1800-1991,* "Samuel W. Stegall, 28 Jun 1885," citing Marriages, Dade, Missouri, United States, Missouri State Archives, Jefferson City, FHL microfilm 007424392. Samuel Stegall first married Mary Nelson cited in *1857 Missouri Marriages,* "Samuel W. Stegall m. Mary C. Nelson 4 Jan 1857, Cedar, Missouri." He married a second time to Eliza Casey and moved to Dade County. "Samuel W. Stegall of Greenfield m. Mrs. Eliza J. [Craft] Casey of Arcola 28 Jun 1885, at the residence of S.B. Craft Dade County, Missouri." Eliza's maiden name was Craft. Samuel Stegall was a Civil War Veteran. An unidentified personal source has him born 4 Aug 1842, Roane County, Tennessee.

[11] Goodspeed, *History of Hickory, Polk, Cedar, Dade, and Barton Counties,* p. 407.

[12] *Missouri Marriage Records,* microfilm, Missouri State Archives; Jefferson City, Mo. "Peter Minick and Elizabeth Cordwell [*sic*]."

[13] 1860 US Census, Rough and Ready, Nevada, California, p. 406, Family History Library Film 803061. 1860 Rough and Ready Township, Nevada, California Census [mining district], Data match: "R.G. Cardwell 30 b. [1830] Tenn., occupation miner, living with Thos. Hopkins 19 b. Mo. [age possibly 49] occupation miner, Hopkins returned to Mo., counted in 1870 census." [See also 1860 Sutter, California, for second R.G. Cardwell listing].

[14] 1860 US Census, California, Sutter, Butte Township. "R.G. Cardwell." Different census takers enumerated the two R.G. Cardwells that appeared in the 1860 census on approximately the same day in June 1860. Therefore, they had to be two different persons unless one household represented Reuben in his absence. See also the research of Rand Cardwell.

[15] 1850 US Census, District 17, Cedar, Missouri, Roll 395, p. 159a.

[16] *1867 California Great Registers, 1850-1920,* Voter Registration. "Reuben Granville Cardwell, 37, [1830] b. Tennessee, Local Residence, Grass Valley Twp., Nevada, California, occupation miner."

[17] 1880 US Census, Tule River, Tulare, California, Roll 85, p. 112C, Enumeration District 102, 15 Jun 1880. "R.G. Cardwell;" *California, County Marriages, 1850-1952,* FHL microfilm 004666548, Image 488 of 778, multiple county courthouses, California. The marriage certificate of Ruben and Lydia affirmed that Lydia was a widow above the age of 18. See also *1870 United States Western States Marriage Index,* Vol. A, p. 95. "Reuben Granville Cardwell m. Lydia McIntyre," listed as a widow, age 18, Pueblo de las Juntas, Fresno, California.

[18] *California Marriages, 1850-1945,* "Reuben Granville Cardwell, 6 Nov 1870;" *California, County Marriages, 1850-1952,* "Reuben Granville Cardwell and Lydia Mcintyre [*sic*], 06 Nov 1870;" citing Fresno, California, county courthouses, California, FHL microfilm 1548472.

[19] *California Great Registers, 1850-1920, 1872,* Film 005028141, Image 22 & 55 of 511. "Centerville. Jacob Coon age 69 born Virginia, farmer, registered at Centerville, Fresno County, California, April 1871."

[20] *California Great Registers, 1850-1920,* 12 Jun 1871. "Reuben Granville Cardwell, 37 [1834?] b. Tenn., miner, Dry Creek, Fresno County, Calif."

[21] Bureau of Land Management, Department of the Interior, Certificate No. 1420, Accession No. CA1560-408. "The southwest quarter of Section 3, Township 21, Range 29."

[22] California Great Registers, 1850-*1920,* "Reuben Granville Cardwell, 1877," citing Voter Registration, Mountain View, Tulare, California, county clerk offices, California, FHL microfilm 1434237; California Great Registers, Tulare County, California, 3 Nov 1876, "Reuben Granville Cardwell, 43 b. Tenn., Farmer, Mountain View Calif."

[23] 1880 US Census, Tule River, Tulare, California, Roll 85, p.112C, Enumeration District 102, 15 Jun 1880. "R.G. Cardwell." The census listed Jacob Cardwell, age 12 [b. 1868] as the son of Reuben Cardwell. Jacob was his stepson, Jacob McIntyre. The census also listed all the Cardwell children as born in Iowa, when in fact Jacob was the only one of the children born in Iowa. All the others were born in California. "Tule River Township, Tulare, Calif. Census 15 Jun 1880, R.G. Cardwell 46 [? 50] b. Tenn. parents b. Tenn., Farmer, Lida 27 [1843] b. Iowa; Jacob 12 son b. Iowa, O.M. 8 dau., R.C. 6 son, L. [Louis]. G. 4 son, L.A. 4 dau, M.J. 1 dau. All b. in Iowa"

[24] *California Great Registers, 1850-1920,* 1888, Film 005030133, Image 15 of 308. "Reuben G. Cardwell 58 b. [1830] Tenn., Teamster lived on North Truman St., Los Angeles."

[25] *California Great Registers, 1850-1920,* Voter Registration. 8 Apr 1889. "Reuben Granville Cardwell, 59 b. [1830] Tenn., Farmer, Local Residence Roberts, Fresno, Calif.,"

[26] *California Great Registers, 1850-1920,* 1894, FHL Film 005028142, Image 149 of 769.

[27] *California Great Registers, 1850-1920,* 1894, Film 005028152, Image 642 of 676, 22 Oct 1892, "Reuben G. Cardwell 64, 5'9" light complexion, blue eyes gray hair, laborer b. [1828] Tenn., living at 765 Maple Avenue, Los Angeles."

[28] *California Great Registers, 1850-1920,* 22 June 1896. "Reuben Granville Cardwell, 67 Retired, 5'9", light complexion, blue eyes, brown hair, scar on right wrist b. [1829] Tenn., 708 Stephenson Ave., Los Angeles, able to read and write."

[29] 1900 US Census, Los Angeles Ward 2, Los Angeles, California, p. 6, Enumeration District 0019, FHL microFilm 1240089, "R.G. Cardwell," residence given as Burnlynd, probably Burlington Avenue where the lived at 136 Burlington in the 1900 *Los Angeles Directory*, p. 196; 1900 Los Angeles, California Census, "R.G. Cardwell 70 b. 1829 Tenn. m. 30 years [from date of m. in 1870] 2nd marriage, Lida 48 b. 1852 Iowa, 6 children, 5 children living, son Jacob 32 b. 1868 Iowa, Louis 24 b. 1875 California." The 1880 census had previously listed L.G. Cardwell as a son, probably Lewis Granville, age 4. However, the 1880 census did not list him or Lulu Cardwell but listed Alice also as age 4. Lewis should have been 5 or 6 years old in the census. It appears through an enumerator's error that he was left off the 1880 census. Neither Lewis nor Alice appeared in the 1900 census, and neither Alice nor Lulu appeared in the census after 1910.

[30] Correspondence from Evergreen Cemetery, 7 Dec 2020.

[31] *California, County Birth, Marriage, and Death Records, 1830-1980,* California Department of Public Health.

[32] *California, County Birth and Death Records, 1800-1994*, Los Angeles, Deaths 1901, Image 1442 of 2109; California State Archives, Sacramento. "Reuben Granvell [*sic*] Cardwell, 1901"

[33] *Evergreen Memorial Park Cemetery, Los Angeles, Records 1877-1988 and Indexes 1877-1989*; Correspondence from Evergreen Cemetery, 7 Dec 2020.

[34] *Kentucky, County Marriages, 1797-1954, Book 1*, p. 126, "Reuben Cardwell and Elizabeth Stigall [*sic*], 19 May 1849," citing Marriage, Trigg, Kentucky, United States, various county clerks and county courts, Kentucky, FHL microfilm 321, 335. Image 164.

[35] 1860 US Census, Missouri, Cedar, Madison, Bear Creek, p. 127. "Elizabeth Cordell."

[36] Correspondence from Rand Cardwell, 6 Aug 2010. The name Thomas P. Cardwell is common within Cardwell lineage. The 'P' is often for the name of Perrin in the majority of cases. This was the maiden name of Martha Perrin. She married Thomas Cardwell, Jr. in the early 1700's, in Virginia. Perrin was a given name among both male and female descendants. No verification that the 'P' in Thomas P. stands for Perrin.

[37] 1870 US Census, Linn, Cedar, Missouri, Roll M593 768, p. 81A, Family History Library Film 552267.

[38] 1860 US Census, Hannibal, Marion, Missouri, p. 822; Family History Library Film 803632; 1870 US Census, Linn, Cedar, Missouri, Roll M593 768, p. 81A, Family History Library Film 552267.

[39] *Missouri Marriages, 1750-1920,* "Thomas P. Cardwell, 1871." The spelling of Cardwell on the marriage license of Thomas P. corrected the Cardwell spelling of Cordell, or Cordwell, which appeared on the 1860 census and earlier documents.

[40] *Arkansas, County Marriages Index, 1837-1957*, FHL Film Number 1009386. See also 1900 US Census, Township 13, Cherokee Nation, Indian Territory, Enumeration District 0044, FHL Film 1241846, p. 8. "Viola D. Goforth."

[41] 1920 US Census, Coalgate, Coal, Oklahoma, Roll T625 1457, p. 5B; Enumeration District 7. "Thomas P. Cardwell."

[42] Find A Grave 77402862.

[43] 1840 US Census, Prairie, Washington, Arkansas, Roll 20, p. 276, Family History Library Film 0002474; 1850 US Census, Prairie, Washington, Arkansas, Roll 31, p. 383b; 1870 US Census, Prairie, Washington, Arkansas, Roll M593 66, p. 196B, Family History Library Film 545565.

[44] Find A Grave 8649248.

[45] *Missouri, County Marriage, Court Records, 1800-1991, Cedar Marriage Records Index 1884-1929, Book H*, pp. 14 & 15; *Missouri, County Marriage, Naturalization, and Court Records, 1800-1991*, "W.W. Stivers, 18 Nov 1903," citing Marriages, Cedar, Missouri, United States, Missouri State Archives, Jefferson City, FHL Film 007424389.

[46] 1860 US Census, Missouri, Cedar, Madison, Bear Creek, p. 127. "Elizabeth Cordell."

[47] 1870 US Census, Salt River, Schuyler, Missouri, Roll M593 804, p. 387A, Family History Library Film 552303. "George Menix [*sic*]."

[48] 1880 US Census, Madison, Cedar, Missouri, Roll 680, p. 368B, Enumeration District 253. "Wm. Montgomery."

[49] *Missouri, County Marriage, Naturalization, and Court Records, 1800-1991*, "W. W. Stivers and Julia Cardwell, 18 Nov 1903," citing Marriages, Cedar, Missouri, United States, Missouri State Archives, Jefferson City, FHL Film 007211704.

[50] 1900 US Census, Missouri, Dade County, Sac Township, District 68, p. 3B.

[51] *Missouri, County Marriage, Naturalization, and Court Records, 1800-1991*, "W.W. Stivers and Julia Cardwell, 20 Nov 1903," citing Marriages, Cedar, Missouri, United States, Missouri State Archives, Jefferson City, FHL microfilm 007255169.

[52] *Stockton Journal* (Stockton, Missouri), 26 Nov 1903, Thursday, p. 5.

[53] 1910 US Census, Missouri, Jasper, Galena Township, Joplin, Ward 6, p. 12A. "Wes Stivers."

[54] 1930 US Census, Missouri, Jasper, Jackson Township, Jasper County Poor Farm, p. 16B.

[55] *California Marriages, 1850-1945*, "Reuben Granville Cardwell, 6 Nov 1870."

[56] 1860 US Census, Van Buren, Lee, Iowa, p. 507, Family History Library Film 803330. "Lydia Coon". The 1860 census listed Jacob Coon age 58 b. Ohio, Lydia Coon age 8, and Rebecca Coon age 6. It did not list the mother.

[57] California Death Index, 1940-1997, "Olive M Ingmire, 14 Sep 1961," Department of Public Health Services, Sacramento.

[58] *California, County Marriages, 1850-1952*, Film 004666549, Image 364 of 770.

[59] 1900 US Census, California, Los Angeles, Enumeration District 58, Precinct 46, Los Angeles city, Ward 6; 1880 US Census, "Sheridan Ingmire in household of Snoden Ingmire, Neodesha, Wilson, Kansas," citing Enumeration District 184, sheet 99B, NARA microfilm publication T9, FHL Film 1254399.

[60] Find A Grave 140886678; *California, County Birth-Death Records, 1800-1994*, Los Angeles, Los Angeles Death Certificates 1934 No. 5740-7832. "Sheridan Ingemire [*sic*]."

[61] *California Great Registers, 1850-1920*, "Sheridan Inquire, 7 Jul 1892," citing Voter Registration, Pine Ridge, Fresno, California, United States, county clerk offices, California, FHL Film 976462.

[62] *California Great Registers, 1850-1920*, "Sheridan Ingmire, 17 Jun 1896," citing Voter Registration, "Leonard between Henry and Chdeeney, Los Angeles, California," county clerk offices, California, FHL Film 976930.

[63] 1900 US Census, Precinct 46 Los Angeles city Ward 6, Los Angeles, California, "Junita Ingmire in household of Sheridan Ingmire," citing Enumeration District 58, sheet 20A, family 493, NARA microfilm publication T623, Washington, D.C.: National Archives and Records Administration, 1972, FHL Film 1240090.

[64] 1910 US Census, "Sheridan Ingmire," Los Angeles, Los Angeles, California," citing Enumeration District 254, sheet 8B, family 211, NARA microfilm publication T624 Roll 81, FHL Film 1374094.

[65] *California Marriages, 1850-1945*, "May Cardwell in entry for Henry N Nelson, 1914."

[66] 1930 US Census, Los Angeles (Districts 0501-0750), Los Angeles, California, "May Ingmire in household of Sheridan Ingmire," citing Enumeration District 623, sheet 35A, line 28, family 11, NARA microfilm publication T626 Roll 158, FHL Film 2339893.

[67] 1940 US Census, California, Los Angeles, Los Angelis County, Councilmanic District 1 60-5 Los Angeles Township in Assembly District 42. "May Ingmire."

[68] Find A Grave 161793958.

[69] *California Marriages, 1850-1945*, "Dube Cardwell, 1901;" Find A Grave 161793958.

[70] 1900 US Census, Raritan, Henderson, Illinois; p. 7; Enumeration District 0048, FHL Film 1240305. "Lily Ethel Bowen."

[71] 1920 US Census, Township 6, Fresno, California, Roll T625 97, p. 10A, Enumeration District 57. "Darbe C. Cardwell;" BillionGraves Index, "Ralph G. Cardwell, died 21 Sep 1984, [in Marysville, Yuba County, California]," citing BillionGraves, Burial at Sutter Cemetery, Sutter Town, Sutter, California; Find A Grave 100057503.

[72] *California, County Birth and Death Records, 1800-1994*, "Dube Cardwell in entry for Cardwell, 30 Jul 1907," citing Births, Los Angeles, Los Angeles, California, California State Archives, Sacramento.

[73] 1900 US Census, Raritan, Henderson, Illinois, p. 7, Enumeration District 0048, FHL Film 1240305, "Lily Ethel Bowen."

[74] *California Great Registers, 1850-1920*, [1896].

[75] *California, County Birth and Death Records, 1800-1994*, "Dube Cardwell in entry for Cardwell, 25 Dec 1908," citing Birth, Los Angeles, Los Angeles, California, United States, California State Archives, Sacramento.

[76] 1910 US Census, Los Angeles Assembly District 70, Los Angeles, California, Roll T624 81, p. 2A, Enumeration District 0244, FHL Film 1374094.

[77] 1910 US Census, Los Angeles, Los Angeles, California, "Duke [*sic*] Cardwell," citing Enumeration District 82, sheet 16B, family 298, NARA microfilm publication T624 Roll 84, FHL Film 1374097.

[78] 1910 US Census, Los Angeles, Los Angeles, California, "Alice Cardwell in household of Wm. H. Feather," citing Enumeration District 244, sheet 2A, family 34, NARA microfilm publication T624 Roll 81, FHL Film 1374094.

[79] 1920 US Census, Township 6, Fresno, California, Roll T625 97, p. 10A, Enumeration District 57. "Darbe C. Cardwell."

[80] 1930 US Census, Monterey, Monterey, California, "Dube Cardwell," citing Enumeration District 28, sheet 4B, line 99, family 114, NARA microfilm publication T626, Roll 179, FHL Film 2339914.

[81] Find A Grave 161793958.

[82] 1940 US Census, Monterey, Monterey, California, Roll m-t0627-00268 [*sic*], p. 62B, Enumeration District 27-30. "Lillie Cordwell [*sic*]."

[83] 1920 US Census, Township 6, Fresno, California, Roll T625 97, p. 10A, Enumeration District 57 "R. G. Cardwell;" 1930 US Census, Bakersfield, Kern, California, p. 7A; Enumeration District 14, FHL Film 2339856. "Ralph G. Cardwell."

[84] Find A Grave 100057503; *California, County Marriages, 1850-1952*, "Ralph G. Cardwell in entry for Jim Golden and Barbara Jane Cardwell, 26 Aug 1943," citing Los Angeles, California, county courthouses, California, FHL Film 2135397.

[85] *Marysville (California) Appeal Democrat*, 22 Sep 1984. A stepson, Elmer Brown of Reno, Nevada; a stepdaughter Carolyn Wright of Sacramento; a mother-in-law Phoebe Hatch of Marysville; and a sister-in-law Norma Longwell of Marysville survived Ralph G. Cardwell. His cremation and interment was in Sutter Cemetery.

[86] 1880 US Census, Tule River, Tulare, California, Roll 85, p. 112C, Enumeration District 102, 15 Jun 1880. "R.G. Cardwell."

[87] *California, County Birth and Death Records, 1800-1994*, Los Angeles; *Los Angeles, Death Index 1900-1902* Vol. 5, A-K, Image 70 of 224, California State Archives, Sacramento. California, "Lewis Granvill [*sic*] Cardwell, 1901."

[88] *California Death Index, 1905-1939*, Image 282 of 819, p. 1030, Vital Statistics Department, Sacramento; California, Los Angelesl *Evergreen Memorial Park Cemetery, Deceased Card File Index, 1877-1989*. "Louis G. Cardwell, 1901." He lived at 135 N. Bonnie Brea, Los Angeles.

[89] *California Great Registers, 1850-1920*, [1896].

[90] 1910 US Census, Los Angeles, Los Angeles, California, "Lulu Cardwell in household of Wm. H. Feather," citing Enumeration District 244, sheet 2A, family 34, NARA microfilm publication T624 Roll 81, FHL Film 1374094.

[91] 1910 US Census, Los Angeles, Los Angeles, California, "Alice Cardwell in household of Wm. H. Feather," citing Enumeration District 244, sheet 2A, family 34, NARA microfilm publication T624 Roll 81, FHL Film 1374094.

[92] 1880 US Census, Tule River, Tulare, California, Roll 85, p. 112C, Enumeration District 102. "L.A. Cardwell."

[93] Find A Grave 26516983.

[94] *California, County Marriages, 1850-1952,* "Fred C Parker and Martha Cardwell, 23 Oct 1897," citing Los Angeles, California, United States, county courthouses, California, FHL Film 2579; 1910 US Census, Los Angeles, Los Angeles, California, "Mattie Parker in household of Wm. H. Feather," citing Enumeration District 244, sheet 2A, family 34, NARA microfilm publication T624, Roll 81, FHL Film 1374094.

[95] *The Los Angeles Times,* Sunday, October 24, 1897, p. 12.

[96] *California, County Marriages, 1850-1952,* "Fred C Parker and Martha Cardwell, 23 Oct 1897," citing Los Angeles, California, county courthouses, California, FHL Film 2579.

[97] 1910 US Census, Lucerne, Kings, California, Roll T624 79, p. 2B, Enumeration District 79, FHL Film 1374092. "Martha Parker."

[98] 1900 US Census, Lucerne, Kings, California; p. 1, Enumeration District 36, FHL Film 1240087. "Martha J. Parker;" *California County Birth, Marriage, and Death Records, 1849-1980.*

[99] 1910 US Census, Lucerne, Kings, California, Roll T624 79, p. 2B, Enumeration District 79, FHL Film 1374092. "Martha Parker wife of Alfred Parker."

[100] *US World War I Draft Registration Cards, 1917-1918,* California; Registration County: Kings County; 1920; US Census, Hanford, Kings, California, Roll T625 101, p. 1A, Enumeration District 131.

[101] California State Library; Sacramento, California; *Great Register of Voters, 1900-1968.*

[102] 1930 US Census, Santa Cruz, Santa Cruz, California, p. 16A, Enumeration District 19, FHL Film 2339950.

[103] 1920 US Census, Hanford, Kings, California, Roll T625 101, p. 9B, Enumeration District 133.

[104] California State Library; Sacramento, California; Great Register of Voters, 1900-1968.

[105] California, Marriage Records from Select Counties, 1850-1941.

[106] *Social Security Death Index,* Master File, Social Security Administration, Washington D.C.

Chapter 24 Edward Cardwell

[1] 1860 US Census, Madison, Cedar, Missouri, p. 127, Family History Library Film 803613. "Elizabeth Cordell."

[2] 1870 US Census, Salt River, Schuyler, Missouri, Roll M593 804, p. 387A, Family History Library Film 552303. "Edward Cardwell."

[3] 1880 US Census, Linn, Cedar, Missouri, Roll 680, p. 337A, Enumeration District 251. "Edward Cardwell." In the 1870 census Anna E. Baldwin, Age 7, listed at home as the daughter of John C. Baldwin. She was born in Kansas. On 28 June 1870, she was living in Linn Township, Cedar County, Missouri. Anna E. not listed at the Baldwin home in the 1880 census, but rather with Edward Cardwell, her husband, and daughter, Laura F. They, too, were living in Linn Township, Cedar County Missouri, in 1880. She was 17 in 1880. Meanwhile, marriage records show her married 20 October 1878, meaning she was 15 or 16 years old when she married. Thomas Edward Cardwell, their son, was not born until 1881. Therefore, he did not appear in the 1880 census.

[4] *Missouri Marriage Records* (microfilm), Missouri State Archives, Jefferson City, Mo. "Edward Cardwell to Ann E. Baldwin."

[5] 1870 US Census, Missouri, Cedar County, Lynn, 28 Jun 1870. Family 397, Baldwin, Thos L., age 74 b. N.C, farmer, personal property $1,000, real estate $4,770; Baldwin, Nancy, age 69 b. Va.; Baldwin, Joshua, age 38 b. Ind., Martha J. James domestic servant, Stockton P.O. Joshua Baldwin, son of Thomas Lee, was living with Thomas Lee Baldwin in 1870. Son T.J. Baldwin (Thomas Jackson), age 43 b. Va., listed in the 1870 census living at Family 395 with wife Sarah, age 31 b. Ill., and their children.

[6] Cemetery, Gum Springs, Cedar County, Missouri. Tombstone inscription: b. 12 Mar 1796 d. 26 Nov 1879 at age 83 yrs. 8 mos. and 19 days of paralysis. From a series of articles written by Jimmy O. Baldwin, in "History of Cedar County," bet. 1991 & 1998, pp. 145-146, Greene County Archives and Records Center, 1126 Boonville Ave., Springfield, Mo.

[7] 1880 US Census, Linn, Cedar, Missouri, Roll 680, p. 337A, Enumeration District 251. "Edward Cardwell."

[8] Jimmy O. Baldwin, in "History of Cedar County.

[9] Find A Grave 28958811. Cemetery, Gum Springs, Cedar County, Missouri (personally viewed and recorded), Gum Springs Cemetery is located in Linn Township, Cedar County, Missouri, 3.5 miles south of Stockton on Highway 39, just south of the 39 and 215 junction. The cemetery is on the west side of the highway. The old church was still standing in 2003. "Edward Cardwell - Aug. 15, 1856 - July 8, 1884." Find-a-Grave transcription shows this as "15 Aug 1856 - 8 Apr 1884." The Edward Cardwell grave is located in the far southwest corner of the cemetery, the last grave in row two, counting from the west. He is buried in the Baldwin cemetery plot, near the graves of John C. and Frances Baldwin, parents of Edward's wife, Eliza Baldwin. There is no proof that this is Edward's grave; however, given that the dates match dates recorded for him in census records and the fact that he is buried with the family of his wife makes a strong circumstantial case for this being his final resting place.

[10] *Missouri Marriage Records, 1805-2002*, Missouri State Archives, Jefferson City, Mo. "Anna E. Cordwell[*sic*]."

[11] The location of Omer-White Hare was off Highway Y in Cedar County. Take Highway 39 south to Y, then right on Y 2.5 miles.

[12] Lovelady Obituary, *Cedar County Republican*, 30 Jul 1931, Stockton, Missouri.

[13] *Georgia Marriage Records from Select Counties, 1828-1978* for Tolbert Biddy, Pickens County, Record of Marriages, 1854-1878, p. 107; 1850 US Census, Division 15, Cherokee, Georgia, Roll 65, p. 539a; *Civil War Pension Index: General Index to Pension Files, 1861-1934* for Francis M. Weaver, National Archives; *Special Schedules of the Eleventh Census* Enumerating Union Veterans and Widows of Union Veterans of the Civil War, Series No. M123, Record Group No. 15 Records of the Department of Veterans Affairs, Census Year: 1890, p. 6. Tolbert Biddy served briefly in the Civil War with the Company A of the 131st Illinois Infantry.

[14] 1860 US Census, Dug Road, Pickens, Georgia, p. 887, Family History Library Film 803133. "Martha Biddy."

[15] *US Marriage Index, 1860-1920.* "Martha Bidda [*sic*]."

[16] They removed to Missouri between 1867 and 1870 between the birth of their first child in Illinois in 1867 and the second in Missouri in 1870. The estimate of 1878 as the time of their arrival in Cedar County, Missouri, comes from an 1879 plat map of Linn Township showing a tract of land for F.M. Weaver.

[17] 1880 US Census for Francis M. Weever [*sic*], Missouri, Cedar, Linn, District 251, NARA, p. 16.

[18] *US Marriage Records, 1805-2002* for Anna E Cordwell [*sic*], Cedar County 1845-1893, p. 259.

[19] General Land Office Records, 1776-2015, Bureau of Land Management Certificate No. 10617, Application 17481, 9 Nov 1896, Accession Nr: MO6020-157, p. 157. "North half of the Lot numbered two of the South West quarter of Section 19 in Township thirty-three North, of Range twenty-six West of the Fifth Principal Meridian, containing fifty-four acres and ninety-five hundredths of an acre, for Jesse M. Biddey, Missouri, Cedar."

[20] 1900 US Census, Missouri, Cedar, Linn, District 51, p. 6B, NARA. "Jessie M Biddey." Birthdate for Biddy differs in the census from his death certificate. Likewise, the 1900 census recorded Tom Cardwell's birthdate as Feb 1880; his gravestone recorded 1881. Similarly, the birthdate of Anna Eliza appeared as Nov 1859, a substantial difference from the birthdate on her death certificate of November 1863.

[21] Walter Williams, *State of Missouri in 1904.*

[22] Meyers, *Place Names of the Southwest Counties of Missouri.* Osiris store was still open and operated by Mr. Arch Walker in 1974. Located at Section 20, Township 34, Range 28.

[23] *US Register of Civil, Military, and Naval Service, 1863-1959* for Jessie M. Biddey, 1903, Vol. 2, pp. 210, 213.

[24] *Appointments of US Postmasters, 1832-1971*, Missouri, Cedar, p. 118.

[25] Linda Clifford, *Historical Tours of Cedar County, Missouri.*

[26] Beatrice Interview 17 Oct 2004. Shortly before her death in 2005, Beatrice accompanied her son to various places that she had lived, and spoke of her life growing up. Two of these interviews date from 17 Oct 2004 and 19 Feb 2005.

[27] Death Certificate 4608, Missouri State Board of Health Bureau of Vital Statistics. "Jesse Maries Biddey b. 22 Apr 1860, d. 8 Mar 1910, age 49 when he died, farmer, died of Pneumonia b. Pickens County, Geo[rgia], son of Tolbert Biddey."

[28] Find A Grave 85106508. "11 Apr 1860-3 Mar 1910."

[29] Beatrice Interview 17 Oct 2004.

[30] Death Certificate 13998 Standard Certificate of Death, Missouri State Board of Health. "Anna Eliza McCollum."

[31] Beatrice Interview 17 Oct 2004.

[32] Memorial Services Announcement for Anna Eliza McCollom. Anna Eliza's funeral announcement carelessly listed her date of birth as 1883 instead of 1863.

[33] Find A Grave 5481942; Death Certificate 12641 Standard Certificate of Death, Division of Health of Missouri. "Austin A. McCollom."

[34] There are multiple methods by which facial recognition systems work. However, in general, they work by analyzing selected facial features from compared facial images. Accuracy may depend on pose variations, age, quality of the photograph, and a variety of other technical challenges. The photograph believed to be the wedding portrait of Edward Cardwell and Anna Eliza Baldwin underwent facial analysis using three different facial recognition systems. Analysis of pictures of her in later life along with photos of her siblings and her children identified her at a verification accuracy above 80 percent. Her identity compared with images of her children Thomas and Laura at a similar age ranged from 82 percent to 100 percent, in the case of her daughter. Compared to photos of herself after she had aged, verification accuracy ranged from 84 to 88 percent. Comparison with other family members was less significant but expected because siblings may present facial features from both parents. Nevertheless, these results were still in the 70 to 80 percent range, and sufficiently high when taken with the overall results to substantiate Eliza's identity in the photograph. Meanwhile, Edward Cardwell, aside from his identification by association with Ann Eliza in the photograph, returned facial recognition identification at the 85 percent verification level when compared with photographs of his children Laura and Tom. While the vicissitudes of facial recognition make conclusions about identity conditional on a number of variables, the results of the analysis nevertheless suggested a high probability that the unidentified portrait is Edward and Eliza (Baldwin) Cardwell.

[35] *Missouri Marriage Records*, (microfilm), Missouri State Archives; Jefferson City, Mo. "Edward Cardwell to Ann E. Baldwin."

[36] 1880 US Census, Linn, Cedar, Missouri, Roll 680, p. 337A, Enumeration District 251. "Edward Cardwell."

[37] Find A Grave 33264414. Correspondence with Hal George, Maple Grove Cemetery, 4 Jan 2021.

Chapter 25 Laura Frances Cardwell

[1] Find A Grave 33264414. Correspondence with Hal George, Maple Grove Cemetery, 4 Jan 2021.

[2] 1880 US Census, Linn Township, Cedar County, Missouri, National Archives and Records Administration. Listed with her parents, Edward and Ann E. Cardwell. Laura F. listed as 1-month-old b. Mo., father b. Mo., mother b. Kan.

[3] 1900 US Census, National Archives and Records Administration. Laura Cardwell, oldest child of Edward Cardwell and Eliza Baldwin listed in the 1900 census living in Linn Township, Cedar County, Missouri, with her mother Eliza A. Biddey, her stepfather Jessie Biddey, and her brother Thomas Cardwell as family 127. Laura Cardwell was born Dec 1879, age 20 in 1900, listed as single, born in Missouri. Jessie Biddey married Eliza about 1885 when Laura was about age 5 and Thomas was age 4.

[4] Correspondence with Karen (Duckworth) Hall wife of Jesse Hall 20 Jan 2006. "Everyone called my grandfather Bill as tha"s the name he preferred. He and my grandmother were very special people; as I said before, he and my grandmother mostly raised my sister and me.

[5] 1920 US Census, Oklahoma, Washington, 4-WD, Bartlesville, Series T625 Roll 1490, p.137, National Archives and Records Administration. The 1920 Census showed Royal McGuire as family 715. His daughter Jessie and her husband Ervin Beebe lived in the same residence as family 716. Roy's half-Brother William M. McGuire and family lived on the same block. "Roy McGuire -Age 40 b. Kan., father b. Mo., mother b. Ill., Occupation Molder Foundry; Laura-Age 40 b. Mo., father b. Kan,. mother b. Mo. no occupation; Cecil-Aged 16 b. Mo. Occupation delivery drugstore; Albert-Aged 13 b. Mo. no occupation. Jesse 'Jack' McGuire Age 17 b. Mo. and husband Irwin Beebe Age 20 b. Okla."

[6] Correspondence from Karen Hall 30 Jul 2004.

[7] Beatrice Interview Jul 2003.

[8] 1930 US Census, Wichita, Sedgwick, Kansas, p. 46B, Enumeration District 45, FHL Film 2340455. "Roy G. McGuire."

[9] Interview of Beatrice (Cardwell) Richardson, grandniece of Laura (Cardwell) McGuire, 2004.

[10] Correspondence with Karen (Duckworth) Hall 29 Oct 2004. "Royal is buried at West Lawn Cemetery in Eugene, Oregon. Laura may be buried there as well. We would travel to West Lawn every year on Memorial Day to put flowers on a number of graves, but I don't remember which graves we put flowers on. As a kid, you don't pay as much attention to those kinds of details." [Laura's burial was in Wichita, Kansas.]

[11] *US, City Directories, 1822-1995*, Wichita, Kansas, 1930, p. 430. The 1930 Wichita City Directory shed light on the year of Laura's death. The directory listed the McGuire family living in Wichita: Albert, Cecil, Roy and Lura [*sic*]. They all lived at the same address at 1832 Salina Avenue and all worked as molders in the foundry business. Jessie and Ervin (aka Bill) Beebe lived there, too.

[12] Correspondence with Hal George, Maple Grove Cemetery, 4 Jan 2021. "Date of death: Dec. 15, 1929, died of pneumonia. Maiden name was Cardwell, born in Missouri after the 15th of December 1879 (because they told us she was 49 at death). Lived at 1832 N. Salina in Wichita. Married at the time of death. Middle initial was F.; husband was Roy S.[*sic*]; they had lived at 108 S. Edwards a few years ago, and he was working at Clear Vision Pump Co. as a "mldr" - this sentence is all based on the 1928 City Directory. Roy is not buried here, and the only other McGuire is an infant from 1901, but from another family, not hers."

[13] Using computerized search triangulation, Laura's great grandnephew, K.E. Burchett, discovered her gravesite in Wichita, Kansas, 2 Jan 2021.

[14] Correspondence with Karen (Duckworth) Hall 1 Aug 2004 to 30 Jul 2004.

[15] Find A Grave 65373791.

[16] Find A Grave 65373791 and 65366062.

[17] Correspondence from Lulu McGuire to Belle Cardwell 3 June 1956. Lulu was the wife of Noble McGuire, the brother of Royal McGuire. She lived in Eugene, Oregon, in 1956.

[18] Find A Grave 65373791.

[19] Correspondence with Karen (Duckworth) Hall wife of Jesse Hall 20 Jan 2006. "Everyone called my grandfather Bill as that's the name he preferred. He and my grandmother were very special people; as I said before, he and my grandmother mostly raised my sister and me.

[20] Correspondence from David Bays of Prescott, Wis., Jul 2004. Bays descended from the line of Cardwells dating to 1796 from Rockingham County, North Carolina. They migrated to Indiana, Iowa, and Kansas. Any relationship between Bay's Cardwell family and the Cardwells of Missouri is remote. Bays said, "As far as I know Missouri only allowed one Cardwell Jayhawker into their state around 1885 but we've lost track of him."

[21] *Social Security Death Index*. "Jessie Beebe b. 5 Apr 1902 d. 28 Mar 1991, Social Security No. 552-08-3686, issued in California.

[22] Elona Hardnack, Research Our Roots, Jan 2003, ID 14087; see also http://worldconnect.rootsweb.com ID: 13565. Genealogy of Laura Frances Cardwell and Royal C. McGuire. Names children of the couple. Gives birth, marriage, death, and burial information as well as children and information on husband, Ervin Marcellous Beebe. See also Find A Grave 60229667.

[23] The Cameron and Paige Report/Patricia A. (Wren-Simon) LaPlante http://wc.rootsweb.com/~laplante. "Karen (Duckworth) Hall informed me on 30 Oct 2003 that Ervin went by the name Bill—"Just call me Bill." Mrs. Hall discovered her grandfather's mother's bible record of all of her children's births and their full names; "in that we discovered that she had actually spelled his name as 'Ervin', spelled with an 'E' not an 'I'." See also *Idaho Death Records, 1890-1967* for Marcellus Clark Beebe 1967; Death Certificate of Martin Earl Beebe, son of Marcellus and Martha Beebe.

[24] Correspondence with Karen (Duckworth) Hall 1 Aug 2004 to 4 Sep 2004.

[25] 1900 US Census, Indian Territory, Cherokee Nation, Township 29 Range 20 E, Series T623, National Archives and Records Administration.

[26] *Social Security Death Index.* "Ervin Beebe b. 26 Aug 1899 d. Jun 1970, Social Security No. 542-14-6461, issued in Oregon, Death Residence Mill City, Linn, Oregon; Find A Grave 60229445. See also Find A Grave 60229445.

[27] Paul Sigler, worldconnect.rootsweb.com ID: I528986404 & ID: 1528986406. (Jul 2003), Laura Frances Cardwell and Royal C. McGuire. This genealogy gives causes of death and information on children and grandchildren. Includes the nickname of daughter Jessie as "Jack" McGuire. Also gives information on husband Beebe and adopted daughter Betty Lou Beebe. Beebe's name appears as William by this source, not Ervin Marcellous Beebe. See also Correspondence with David E. Bays 16 Jul 2004. "Sure wish I did not lose track of Karen. She would be excited that your mother [Beatrice Richardson] remembers 'Jack.' She would also be anxious to learn if your mother knows anything about her adoptive mother, Betty Lou. My mother also knew 'Jack' and I recall her mentioning to me that Betty was adopted. No one ever bothered to ask the details at the time. Sure hope you are able to hook up with Karen [Duckworth Hall] and Jess [Hall]."

[28] Opal Mae Kephart, Bays-Kephart-McGuire, Rootsweb.com ID: 1542551135; David Bays, McGuire-Kephart-Bays ID: 131531263 (Aug 2001); worldconnect.rootsweb.com. "Laura Frances Cardwell and Royal C. McGuire."

[29] 1920 US Census, Oklahoma, Washington, 4-WD, Bartlesville, Series T625 Roll 1490, p. 137. "Roy McGuire."

[30] *US, City Directories, 1822-1995*, Wichita, Kansas, 1923, p. 79.

[31] Find A Grave 65643469; Correspondence from Karen Hall 30 Jul 2004. "My grandparents adopted my mother in Wichita, Kansas in 1928;" Atwood-Bays-Mahurin-McGuire-Kephart-Wilkerson: http://wc.rootsweb.ancestry.com ID: 584337791. "Jack and Ervin adopted a daughter, Betty Lou. She had three children Karen, Sharon, and Kevin. Betty Lou married several times. Among her husbands were McCall and Duckworth."

[32] Correspondence from Karen Hall 30 Jul 2004. "In 1929, they [the McGuire and Beebe families] moved to Oregon." Note. This proved to be slightly incorrect. They did not move until 1930, after Laura's death in Wichita.

[33] *US, City Directories, 1822-1995*, Wichita, Kansas, 1929, p. 120.

[34] 1930 US Census, Wichita, Sedgwick, Kansas, p. 46A, Enumeration District 47, FHL Film 2340455. "Isack [*sic*] M. Beebe." The census in Wichita was enumerated 29 April 1930,

[35] 1930 US Census, Kansas, Sedgwick County, Wichita Township, Wichita City-part of Ward 2, Sheet 46A, p. 250, National Archives and Records Administration.

[36] 1940 US Census, Empire, Coos, Oregon, Roll m-t0627-03358, p. 3A, Enumeration District 6-16. "Ervin M. Beebe."

[37] *WWII Draft Registration Cards for Oregon*, 16 Oct 1940-31 Mar 1947, Record Group: Records of the Selective Service System, 147, Box 7, National Archives in St. Louis, Missouri.

[38] *US World War I Draft Registration Cards, 1917-1918* for Ervin Beebe, Kansas, Wichita City, 2, Draft Card B, SN 1818, 12 Sep 1918.

[39] Correspondence from Lulu McGuire to Belle Cardwell 3 June 1956. Lulu was the wife of Noble McGuire, the brother of Royal McGuire. She lived in Eugene, Oregon, in 1956.

[40] *Bartlesville Examiner Enterprise* 16 Jun 1964, p. 10.

[41] Correspondence from Karen Hall 30 Jul 2004. "She [Jessie Beebe] and my grandfather [Bill Beebe] raised my sister and me;" Find A Grave 65643469.

[42] Correspondence from Karen Hall 30 Jul 2004. "My grandfather [Bill Beebe] died in 1970, my mother [Betty Lou Duckworth] in 1973 and my grandmother [Jessie (McGurie) Beebe in 1991."

[43] 8. Obituary, Jessie E. Beebe. Huston-Jost Funeral Home, Aug 2004. "Jessie E. Beebe, 89, a resident of Sweet Home died at the Lebanon Community Hospital Thursday, March 28th. She was born in Jericho Springs, Missouri, the daughter of Royal Cyrus and Laura Cardwell McGuire. On April 5, 1902, she married Ervin M. Beebe on August 25, 1919 in Bartlesville, Oklahoma, and he preceded her in death in 1970. Jessie lived in Kansas prior to living in Coos Bay for 50 years. She lived in Lebanon for 2 years and has lived in Sweet Home for 1 year. She was a homemaker. She is survived by her granddaughters, Sharen Milliken of Sweet Home and Karen Hall of Benicia, California, along with 7 great grandchildren and 5 great-great grandchildren. She was preceded in death by her daughter, Betty Lou McCall, in 1973." Karen Hall who the obituary mentions as living in Benicia, California, removed to Placerville, California.

[44] Correspondence from Kathleen Berry West Lawn Memorial Park and Funeral Home, 29 Jun 2004. "McGuire, Roy, int. no 4546, block 54, lot 5, section A, Garden of Aaron, date 22 Nov 1958 box reg, age [not given], undertaker Buell, Deeded to Roy McGuire 8/29/49 deed #1376. Beebe, Jessie Ethel, int. no 10400, contract #4035, block 72, lot 4, section Galilee. b. 5 Apr 1902 d. 28 Mar 1991 age 88 buried 1 Apr 1991, box W.L. Liner, funeral director Jost Funeral Home, Lebanon, Oregon, deeded to Jessie E. Beebe deed #4323, date 29 May 1975, interment fees $355. Beebe, Ervin M., int. no 6813, W.L. no. 4347, block 73 lot 1 section Galilee date 3 Jul 1970 box St. Lin, age 70, undertaker Weedle, deeded to Jessie E. Beebe date 29 Jul 1970 deed #3830."

[45] 1910 US Census, Jackson, Washington, Oklahoma, Roll T624 1276, p. 9A, Enumeration District 256, FHL Film 1375289. "Royal C. McGuire."

[46] Correspondence with Lorrie Stewart of Timmons Funeral Home, Fredonia, Kansas, from 6 May 2020 to 26 May 2020. This source, which managed services for Cecil McGuire, did not know the name of his mother.

[47] *Sedgwick County Marriage Book HH*, p. 189. Sedgwick County, Kansas, Marriage Index: Midwest Historical and Genealogical Society. "McGuire, Cecil E. to Harding, Miriam B. 19 Feb 1930."

[48] Marriage Certificate, File 71354, 19 Feb 1930. "Cecil E. McGuire herewith files application and affidavit for Marriage License to be issued to Cecil E. McGuire and Miriam B. Harding. Office of the Probate Jude of Sedgwick County, Kansas, 19 Feb 1930, license issued #71354 dated same."

[49] Find A Grave 62881907.

[50] Miriam McGuire Obituary, *Fredonia Herald,* Dec. 30, 1968.

[51] *US City Directories, 1822-1995*, Eugene, Oregon Directory, 1925, p. 194.

[52] Miriam McGuire Obituary, *Fredonia Herald,* Dec. 30, 1968; *US City Directories, 1822-1995*, Wichita, Kansas, 1929 p. 291, 1930 p. 325. "Living as Mrs. Miriam Harding."

[53] 1930 US Census, Wichita, Sedgwick, Kansas, p. 2B, Enumeration District 45, FHL Film 2340455. "Cecil E. McGuire."

[54] *US City Directories, 1822-1995*, Wichita, Kansas, 1930 p. 460, 1936 p. 384, 1939 p. 357.

[55] *WWII Draft Registration Cards for Kansas*, 16 Oct 1940-31 Mar 1947, Records of the Selective Service System, Record Group 147, Box: 253, National Archives in St. Louis, Missouri.

[56] 1940 US Census, Delano, Sedgwick, Kansas, Roll m-t0627-01258, p. 7A, Enumeration District 87-6. "Acil C. McGaire [*sic*]." The 1940 census transcribed the famly as "Acil C McGaire, Ronal Mcgaria."

[57] *Social Security Death Index.* "Cecil McGuire b. 4 Aug 1903 d. May 1976, Social Security No. 511-07-1225 issued in Kansas, Death Residence ZIP Code 66736, Localities: Buxton, Coyville, Fredonia, and Lafontaine, Wilson County, Kansas.

[58] 1930 US Census, Wichita, Sedgwick, Kansas, p. 2B, Enumeration District 45, FHL Film 2340455. "Cecil E. McGuire;" *Wichita Eagle,* 4 Feb 1990; Find A Grave 63945576.

[59] Correspondence from Karen Hall 30 Jul 2004.

[60] Find A Grave 157242238, Block 2 Lot 55A Space 1; Correspondence with Carol Goughler Bartlesville Public Library, Bartlesville, Oklahoma, from 3 May 2010 to 6 May 2010, citing obituary in *Bartlesville Examiner Entrprise,* 16 Jun 1964, p. 10.

[61] *Sedgwick County, Kansas, Marriage Affidavits, Book HH,* p 225. "McGuire, Albert to Beebe, Esther 15 Mar 1930."

[62] *Sedgwick County Marriage Book HH*, p. 225, Sedgwick County, Kansas, Marriage Index, Midwest Historical and Genealogical Society. "McGuire, Albert to Beebe, Esther 15 Mar 1930;" Marriage Certificate, 13 Mar 1930, License 71427. "Albert McGuire herewith files application and affidavit for Marriage License to be issued to Albert McGuire and Esther Beebe. Office of the Probate Judge of Sedgwick County, Kansas, 13 Mar 1930, license isssued #71427."

[63] Find A Grave 161609318.

[64] 1940 US Census, Craig, Oklahoma, Roll m-t0627-03287, p. 23A, Enumeration District 18-14. "Albert McGuire."

[65] *US City Directories, 1822-1995*, Eugene, Oregon, 1925, p. 194.

[66] *Sedgwick County, Kansas, Marriage Affidavits, Book HH,* p 225. "McGuire, Albert to Beebe, Esther 15 Mar 1930."

[67] 1930 US Census, Wichita, Sedgwick, Kansas, p. 46B, Enumeration District 45, FHL Film 2340455. "Albert McGuire."

[68] *US City Directories, 1822-1995*, Wichita, Kansas, p. 384.

[69] Correspondence from Karen Hall 30 Jul 2004.

[70] *US Social Security Applications and Claims Index, 1936-2007.*

[71] Find A Grave 161609267.

[72] Find A Grave 161609318.

[73] *Bartlesville Examiner Enterprise,* 16 Jun 1964, p. 10.

[74] Find A Grave 17312923.

Chapter 26 Thomas Edward Cardwell

[1] Death Certificate 2835, Missouri State Board of Health Bureau of Vital Statistics. "Thomas Edward Cardwell."

[2] Beatrice Interview 17 Nov 2004.

[3] 1940 US Census, Benton, Cedar, Missouri, Series T627, Roll m-t0627-02095, p. 9B; Enumeration District 20-3, NARA. "Tom Cardwell."

[4] 1900 US Census, National Archives and Records Administration. The 1900 census recorded Tom's birthdate as Feb 1880; his gravestone recorded 1881. In 1900, Thomas Cardwell was living in Linn Township, Cedar County, Missouri, with his mother, Eliza A. Biddey, his sister Laura Cardwell, and stepfather Jessie M. Biddey as census family 127. Thomas' month and year of birth was Feb 1880, age 19 at the time of the census, born in Missouri. All members of the family were able to read and write. Jessie Biddey was a Farmer. [Thomas' year of birth as 1880 differs from that on his gravestone of 1881.]

[5] Walter Williams, *State of Missouri in 1904.*

[6] Marriage Certificate, Tom Cardwell and Belle Fellows, "This certifies that Thomas E. Cardwell of Osiris, State of Mo. and Belle Fellows of Osiris, State of Mo. were United in Holy Matrimony at Linsa Wards on the 10th day of Apr. A.D. 1904 by authority of a license bearing date the 9th day of Apr. A.D. 1904 and issued by the recorder of deeds of Cedar Co., Mo. Witness my signature: Charley Stone, Preacher of the gospel. Witnesses: Mr. Linsa Ward, Mrs. Eva Ward."

[7] Birth Certificate 048884-14. County of Cedar, Township of Benton. "Maud Beatrice Cardwell, Female, legitimate b. Sept 13, 1914, father: Thomas Edward Cardwell, Jerico Springs, Mo, white, age 32, birthplace: Missouri, occupation: Farmer; mother: Mary Bell [*sic*] Fellows, Jerico Springs, Mo., white, age 28, birthplace Missouri, occupation: Housewife; no. of children of this mother-1, number of children of this mother now living-1, Born at full term-yes. Certificate of Attending Physician or Midwife. I hereby certify that I attended the birth of this child, and that it occurred on Sept 13, 1914 at 8:20 a.m. /s/A.J. Mynatt, MD, Physician, Jerico Springs, Mo. Filed Sept 20, 1914, A.J. Mynatt, MD, Registrar."

[8] Linda Clifford, *Historical Tours of Cedar County, Missouri,* Stockton, Missouri: Cedar County Historical Society, 1977, Tour 3, Southwest Cedar County, Ozarks Genealogical Society, Springfield, Missouri.

[9] *Springfield Missouri Republican Newspaper*, Vol 24 No. 168, p. 1, column 4, 15 Jul 1915, Springfield Library Center, Springfield, Missouri. "Burial of Belle and Blanche Wagoner was in a common grave in Wagoner Cemetery. The burial of Jim Mingus reportedly was in Brashears Cemetery."

[10] 1910 US Federal Census, Missouri, Cedar County, Linn Township, 57-04B, 26 Apr 1910, National Archives and Records Administration. The 1910 census contained several errors in the birthplaces of both Tom's and Belle's parents. In 1910, Thomas E. Cardwell and Belle M. Cardwell listed as family 75, living in Linn Township, Cedar County, Missouri, with Thomas' mother, Eliza Biddy. Eliza's stepmother, Widow Cordelia S. Baldwin, and her six children listed as family 76. Thomas, age 29, born in Missouri; father and mother both born in Missouri. [This is an error because Eliza was born in Kansas as she noted on the census]. Belle M. Cardwell, age 24, born in Missouri; father and mother born in Missouri. [This, too, is an error. Her father was born in New York.] Thomas E. lists an occupation of Farmer, owning his farm with a mortgage. In 1910, the census listed the number of years a couple had been married. Thomas and Belle had been married six years in 1910.

[11] 1920 US Federal Census, Missouri, Cedar County, Benton Township, 51-08b, 13 Apr 1920, National Archives and Records Administration. Thomas Cardwell listed as family 126 in the 1920 census. He is living in Benton Township, Cedar County, Missouri, near family members of his wife, Mary B. [Fellows]. Father-in-law, Willie I. Fellows, was family 128. Brothers-in-law, Willie I. and Lee were families 127 and 137 respectively, and his mother Anna E. and husband Aurthur Mccollom were family 130. Thomas Cardwell, age 39, owned his farm under a mortgage. His occupation listed as Farmer. He was born in Missouri, as were both of his parents, according to the census. [This is in error because his mother was born in Kansas.] His wife, Mary B[elle Fellows], age 36. Daughter, Maudie B[eatrice], age 5, placing her birth in 1914. Thomas and Mary Belle were married about 1904, married approximately 10 years before the birth of their only daughter, Beatrice.

[12] Swaim, *Era of the One-Room Rural Schools of Cedar County, Missouri,* 1988, p. 163. The Old Fair View School building still stood in 1988. A lean-to shed built on one side came from a later renovation when the building no longer served as a school.

[13] Meyers, *Place Names of the Southwest Counties of Missouri.*

[14] Beatrice Interview Sep. 2004.

[15] Sharron Burchett O'Connor Genealogies. "Elick Beaty of Stockton, Mo. married Beatrice Cardwell of Stockton, Mo. at Stockton, Mo. on 5 Feb 1930."

[16] 1930 US Census, Cedar County, Linn Township, District 10, Dwelling 49 Family 51.

[17] 1930 US Federal Census, Cedar County, Linn Township, District 20, Roll T6261182, p. 3A, National Archives and Records Administration. Dwelling 49 Family 50. "Cardwell, Thomas E., Head, Rented, lived on a farm, age 49, married, age 23 at first marriage, can read

& write b. Missouri, Belle, Wife, age 43, married, age 17 at first marriage, can read & write b. Missouri. Also living in Dwelling 49 as Family 51 was Beatrice M. and husband Elick Beaty.

[18] Beatrice Interview 11 Feb 2005.

[19] Beatrice Interview 11 Feb 2005.

[20] Beatrice Interview 11 Feb 2005.

[21] Beatrice Interview 11 Feb 2005.

[22] T.E. Cardwell Sale Bill, Tuesday, 4 Aug 1931.

[23] Divorce Decree, Belle and Tom Cardwell, Nov 1934. "Belle Cardwell, Plaintiff; vs. T.E. Cardwell, Defendant; Divorce. Decree: Now at this day comes the plaintiff herein by his attorney, Lewis B. Hoff, and also comes the defendant herein and files his entry of appearance, his waiver of service and consents to the trial of the issues of said cause. The cause now coming on for hearing, plaintiff submits same upon the pleadings and the proof to the court and the court after hearing the evidence, being satisfied that the plaintiff is the innocent injured party and entitled to the relief prayed for in her petition, the court doth order, adjudge and decree that the plaintiff be absolutely and forever divorced from the bonds of matrimony existing between the plaintiff and defendant and that this plaintiff be restored to all the rights and privileges of an unmarried person and that the plaintiff pay the costs of this addition and that execution issue therefore. State of Missouri, County of Cedar, In the Circuit Court of Cedar County, Missouri, to its November 1934 Term At Stockton, Missouri.".

[24] State of Missouri, County of Cedar, In the Circuit Court of Cedar County, Missouri, to its November 1934 Term At Stockton, Missouri. "Belle Cardwell, Plaintiff; vs. T E. Cardwell, Defendant; Divorce."

[25] Beatrice Interview 11 Nov 2005.

[26] *Social Security Death Index*, No. 49314-3448. "Thomas Edward Cardwell. Date of issue 24 Oct 1938. Reverse of card: 493-14-3448 Thomas Edward Cardwell, Jerico Springs, Mo." Tom Cardwell's Social Security Card in the possession of Sharron Burchett O'Connor confirms the above information. The card was not signed,

[27] US Dept. of Labor Employment Service, 20 Oct 1938. Applicant's Identification Card. (postcard size) ID No. 2920-2404; Registrations date(s) 30 Oct 1938, 12 Jan 1940 to be renewed by 12 Mar 1940, Reverse of card: No. 2920-2404 District Missouri State Employment Service, Nevada, Missouri. Applicant's signature "his X mark", Interviewer Ervin T. Baldwin. "Cardwell, Thomas Edward, Jerico Spgs, Mo. Age 57, Height 5 ft. 10 in. Weight 120 lbs., Classification P, farmer 5-1705."

[28] Federal Works Agency W. P. A. Form 403, 28 Mar 1940. Notice of Termination of Employment. ID No. 2920-2404, Time effective cob Date effective 31 Mar 1940 On Project No. 1-411. Reason for Termination, Reduction of Force. Thomas E. Cardwell, Jerico Springs, Mo. Case No. IC 222, Date Issued 28 Mar 1940, Certified-Yes. Occupation-Laborer." Order issued by Fred Hug, Division of Employment Official.

[29] W P A Form 402, 23 Aug 1939. "You are asked to report ready for work at 8 a.m. on 8-27-39 at County Wide Roads as Laborer, Wage class U, Location of project Cedar County /s/

"Thomas Edward Cardwell. Date employee begins work 28 Aug 1939 /s/ Project Foreman." Notice to Report for Work on Project. Cardwell, Thomas Edward ID No. 2930-2404-W, Jerico Springs, Mo. Case No. IC-222, Date 23 Aug 1939. From Project No. File [no entry] to Project No. 1-411. Although his signature appears on this form, a later form is marked with an X. he probably did not sign this form. The writing looks much like the supervisor's signature that appears on the same form.

[30] Sharron Burchett O'Connor Genealogies.

[31] Beatrice Interview 2003.

[32] Death Certificate 2835. Missouri State Board of Health Bureau of Vital Statistics. "Thomas Edward Cardwell."

[33] *Coroner's Record Books of Greene County, Mo.; Book 13*, p. 71, 26 Jan 1944. "In the matter of view upon the body of Tom Cardwell before Murry C. Stone, Coroner of Greene County, Missouri. Be it remembered, that on the 26th day of January, A.D. 1944, information having been given to the Coroner of Greene County that the dead body of Tom Cardwell of Stockton, Mo, supposed to have come to his death by violence, had been found at "Ozark Osteopathic Hospital on the 26th day of January, A.D., 1944 [remainder of the form/page is blank; no jury was convened] Deceased was injured in a wood saw on the 18th of January, and died as the result of the accident. $5.32 Coroner costs." Tom Cardwell was hurt 18 Jan 1944, died 25 Jan, and the inquest occurred 26 Jan 1944.

[34] Newspaper Clipping, *Cedar County Republican*, 27 Jan 1944.

[35] Cemetery Information, (personally viewed and recorded) "Father, Thomas Edward, Cardwell, 1881-1944."

[36] Gum Springs Cemetery is located in Linn Township, Cedar County, Missouri, 3.5 miles south of Stockton on Highway 39, just south of the 39 and 215 junction. The cemetery is on the west side of the highway. The old church was still standing in 2021. Tom's grave is located near the cemetery road and next to Eliza McCollum, his mother, situated behind the church near the back of the cemetery. His father Edward lies a short distance west of his grave.

[37] Beatrice Interview 11 Feb 2005. There were two houses on East Street that looked identical located on the north side of Highway 32 [East Street]. The city tore down the one where Belle lived after she died to make way for a new post office. The tornado of 2003 destroyed both the post office and the remaining house.[37]

[38] Ready. *History of Willie Ira Fellows* (written Abt 1983). This is a history that Aunt Effie (Fellows) Ready for her son Archie Ready. She titled it "History of Willie Ira Fellows and his wife, Martha Frances (Crutchfield) Fellows."

[39] Obituary of Belle (Fellows) Cardwell. "Mary Belle Fellows, eldest daughter of W.I. and Martha Francis (Crutchfield) Fellows, was born September 29, 1885, near Salisbury, in Chariton County, Missouri. She answered the Master's summons to 'come home,' August 1, 1958, being at the time of her passing, 72 years, 10 months and 2 days of age. When she was a baby, her parents moved to Ness City in Western Kansas, where they lived 'til Belle was three years old, when the family came to Cedar county and where she lived the remainder of her

life—almost 80 years [*sic*]. On April 10, 1904, she was married to Thomas Edward Cardwell who preceded her in death on January 26, 1944. They were the parents of one daughter, Beatrice, now Mrs. Richard Richardson, of Stockton, in whose home she passed away. Early in their married life, she and her husband were converted to Christ but it was not until several years later while living at the home of her brother, Claude Fellows, and wife, that she received the sacrament of baptism administered by Rev. Frank Calame pastor of the Jerico Springs Methodist church, of which she became a member. For years, while living in Jerico Springs, Belle cared for may aged and feeble patients and lucky indeed was the person in need of such care who found refuge with her. She continued in this work as long as her health permitted. The past four years she lived in Stockton. When she became ill just a week before her passing, she was taken to the home of her daughter where all that willing hands and loving hearts could do were not enough and she slipped quietly away into eternity about noon, Friday. Besides her daughter, Bea, she is survived by a devoted son-in-law, three grandchildren, Kenneth, Sharron and Sharleen Burchett who loved her dearly and to whom she was deeply attached; also, three brothers, Lee, of Nevada, Mo., Irl and Lester of Milford, Mo.; two sisters, Maudie Potter of Montevallo, and Effie Ready of Kansas City; three sisters-in-law, one brother-in-law and a number of nieces and nephews. Funeral services at the Jerico Springs Methodist Church on Monday afternoon, August 4, were conducted by Rev. Bill Maggi. Interment was in Brasher cemetery by the side of her father, under direction of the Cantlon Funeral Home of Stockton;" A second obituary that identified her as Mrs. Belle Cardwell appeared in the local newspaper. "Obituary of Mrs. Belle Cardwell. Mary Belle Cardwell b. September 30, 1885, d. 1 Aug 1958. Services Jerico Springs Methodist Church 2:00 p.m., Monday, August 4. Minister; Funeral Announcement, "Mary Belle Cardwell. Mary Belle Cardwell b. 30 Sep 1885, d. 1 Aug 1958. Services Jerico Springs Methodist Church 2:00 p.m., Monday, August 4. Minister Rev. Bill Maggi, Interment Brasher Cemetery, Cantlon Funeral Home, Stockton, Missouri. Pallbearers A.C. Swisher, Walter Albrecht, Guy Todd, Ernest Smith, Myron Smith, Fred Wolf;" Memorial Book for Belle Fellows [*sic*]. Song selections at her funeral were sung by Gracie Thornton, Mr. and Mrs. Myron Smith, and Edna Borrks, pianist Lutie Brasher. Interment in Brasher Cemetery August 4, 1958 at 3:30 p.m. Relatives attending her funeral were Mrs. Beatrice Richardson, Mr. Richard Richardson, (one of the persons Belle took care of was Amos Richardson, the father of the son-in-law mentioned in the obituary), Gladys Sharleen Burchett, Sharron Kay Burchett, Kenneth Eugene Burchett, Maudie and Ray Potter, Lester and Etta Fellows, Earl Fellows, Hope Fellows, Pauline Fellows, Lee Fellows, Luella and Merl Fellows, Linda Fellows, Maxine and Preston Potter. Announcements of Belle's death and funeral referred to her both as Mrs. Belle Cardwell and as Belle Fellows. She was legally Belle Fellows after her divorce.

[40] Death Certificate 58-024889, Standard Certification of Death, Division of Health of Missouri. "Mary Belle Cardwell." The attending physician for Belle was Dr. Lepere. Funeral arrangements were under the direction of Cantlon Funeral Home of Stockton.

[41] Memorial Book for Belle Fellows. "The dawn is not distant, nor is the night starless, Love is eternal! God is still God and his faith shall not fail us. Christ is eternal!" Belle's friends sang three of her favorite songs, *Whispering Hope*, *Beyond the Sunset*, and *Where We'll Never Grow Old*.

[42] Belle's grandson, Kenneth Burchett, was present when she took her last breath, and remembered the men coming to remove her body to the funeral home.

[43] 1920 US Census, Missouri, Polk County, Campbell Township, p. 2B; Find A Grave 78697827, *Missouri Marriage Records, 1805-2002*, Missouri State Archives; Jefferson City, Mo.

[44] Find A Grave 189872649. "Elick T. Beaty."

[45] *Missouri Marriage Records, 1805-2002* for "Willie [*sic*] A. Burchett," Dade County 1926-1941, p. 373.

[46] Find A Grave 89856253. "Willis Adley Burchett."

Chapter 27 Beatrice Cardwell Early Years

[1] Birth Certificate 048884-14. County of Cedar, Township of Benton. "Maud Beatrice Cardwell, Female, legitimate b. Sept 13, 1914, father: Thomas Edward Cardwell, Jerico Springs, Mo, white, age 32, birthplace: Missouri, occupation: Farmer; mother: Mary Bell [*sic*] Fellows, Jerico Springs, Mo, white, age 28, birthplace Missouri, occupation: Housewife; no. of children of this mother-1, number of children of this mother now living-1, Born at full term-yes. Certificate of Attending Physician or Midwife: I hereby certify that I attended the birth of this child, and that it occurred on Sept 13, 1914 at 8:20 a.m. /s/A.J. Mynatt, MD, Physician, Jerico Springs, Mo. Filed Sept 20, 1914, A.J. Mynatt, MD, Registrar."

[2] Beatrice Interview 17 Nov 2004; Beatrice Memory Book. Bea called the little house a "shack."

[3] Beatrice Memory Book.

[4] Beatrice Memory Book.

[5] Fairview School still stood across from Osiris in 2003. Owners built on to the structure and converted it to a storage building. Osiris Store was still open for business, and the Fairview Community Church had undergone restoration and remained in use. However, the original buildings of the Cardwell home and many of the buildings of the Fellows farmstead mostly disappeared. The Horse Creek Bridge (present State Road 1600) was still standing in 2003. One of W.I. Fellow's neighbors who knew him was still living at age 95, at her place south of the old Fellows Farm on the lane directly across from fellows lane. See the location of Cardwell Farm at GPS 37° 40' 08.3 N 94° 02' 49.1 W.

[6] Beatrice Memory Book.

[7] Swaim, *Era of the One-Room Rural Schools of Cedar County, Missouri*, p. 163. Fleeta (Dodd) Walker and her husband, Arch Walker, later ran the Osiris Store for 37 years.

[8] Beatrice Interview 17 Oct 2004. Shortly before her death in 2005, Beatrice accompanied her son to various places that she had lived, and spoke of her life growing up. Two of these interviews date from 17 Oct 2004 and 19 Feb 2005. Beatrice died 9 Mar 2005.

[9] Beatrice Interview 17 Oct 2004. There were two stores at Wagoner at the time. One of her classmates was Imogene Ruth, sister of Elzie Ruth. Imogene married Finis Cowen.

[10] Beatrice Interview 17 Oct 2004. The pink house burned after the Cardwells left.

[11] Swaim, *Era of the One-Room Rural Schools of Cedar County, Missouri*, p. 76. J.B. Mitchell taught at Wagoner from 1926 to 1928. He went on to become superintendent of schools in Cedar County in 1939. In 1955, he became superintendent of the newly reorganized El Dorado Springs R-2 school district.

[12] Swaim, *Era of the One-Room Rural Schools of Cedar County, Missouri*, p. 76. Cedar Bluff took its name from a previous school of that name located near the cemetery. The people of Wagoner built the new Cedar Bluff School after 1897. In 1954, busses began taking schoolchildren to Stockton. Cedar Bluff still stands; the community bought the schoolhouse and restored it.

[13] Swaim, *Era of the One-Room Rural Schools of Cedar County, Missouri*, p. 76. "Cedar Bluff District No. 63."

[14] In 2003, Cedar Bluff School, church, a house, and one of the stores were still standing. The other store, called Hyder's, that stood "catty-cornered" across the road east of Wagoner Store, was no longer there.

[15] Swaim, *The Era of the One-Room Rural Schools of Cedar County, Missouri*, p. 76; Beatrice Interview 17 Oct 2004. Robert Cross lived in the Wagoner house after the shooting.

[16] Beatrice Memory Book.

[17] Find A Grave 29306389. Jessie Stevens, the classmate that Beatrice lost touch with, became a truck driver, married Virginia Mallory in Stockton, moved to Iowa, and died in 1999, in Kansas. His burial was at Anna Edna Cemetery near Jerico Springs, Missouri.

[18] The story of Bea's graduation comes from an interview on 23 Jan 2005.

[19] Beatrice Interview 17 Oct 2004.

[20] Marriage License. "Elick Beaty of Stockton, Mo. and Beatrice Cardwell of Stockton, Mo. At Stockton, Mo. on Feb. 5, 1930. G.W. Elliston, Justice of Peace, Linn Twp., Cedar Co., Mo. Witnesses: E.W. Bright, Lillian Moomaw."

[21] 1930 US Census, Missouri, Cedar, Linn, Roll T626-1182, p. 3A, National Archives and Records Administration, Enumeration District 20, Supervisor's District 10, recorded 10 April 1930. Family 51 Beaty, Elick, head of household, and Beatrice M. his Wife. The listing showed them as renting and living on a farm. Elick was age 23, Beatrice 15. Age at first marriage: Elick age 23, Beatrice age 15. Beatrice attended school within the census year; Elick did not. Both were able to read and write. Both were born in Missouri, as were their respective parents. Elick was a Farm Laborer. They were living with Thomas E. and Belle Cardwell at family 50 on the census.

[22] Arthur Paul Moser, *A Directory of Towns, Villages, and Hamlets Past and Present of Cedar County, Missouri*, Springfield, Mo.: Library Center, n. d, citing *Campbell's Gazetteer of Missouri*, 1874, pp 181-182, quoting Mr. & Mrs. Allen D. Hughes. "In 1971, Cedarville had only a vacant store building. There was an active Community Church, with a full time pastor." Nothing remained of Cedarville in 2003, except a church.

[23] Beatrice Interview 17 Oct 2004. The lane to the Cardwell home was fenced off in 2003 and grown up but still clearly visible. Rockwork used to raise the roadbed was still in place. GPS 37° 34' 52.5 N 93° 56' 47.3 W.

[24] *Plat Books of Cedar and Dade Counties, Missouri*, Rockford, Ill.: W.W. Hixson, 1930, available University of Missouri.

[25] 1930 US Census, Cedar Twp, Dade, Missouri, Series T626, p. 8B, NARA. "W.A. Butcher."

[26] Beatrice Interview 11 Feb 2005.

[27] Beatrice Interview 11 Feb 2005; Beatrice Memory Book.

[28] 1940 US Census, Cedar Twp. Dade, Missouri Series T627, p. 6B. "Ralph Evans."

[29] Beatrice Interview 17 Oct 2004.

[30] Beatrice Memory Book.

[31] Beatrice Interview 17 Oct 2004.

[32] Beatrice Interview 17 Oct 2004.

[33] Beatrice Interview 11 Feb 2005.

[34] Beatrice Interview 17 Oct 2004.

[35] Beatrice Interview 11 Feb 2005.

[36] Beatrice Interview 11 Feb 2004. The little girl in the dress mentioned by Beatrice was the daughter of Lily Baldwin.

[37] Beatrice Interviews 17 Oct 2004, 11 Feb 2005.

[38] Beatrice Interview 11 Feb 2005.

[39] Beatrice Interview 11 Feb 2005.

[40] Beatrice Interview 17 Oct 2004.

[41] Beatrice Interview 17 Oct 2004.

[42] Beatrice Interview 11 Feb 2005.

[43] Correspondence with Sharleen Hobson 27 Jul 2018.

[44] Beatrice Interview 17 Oct 2004.

[45] Beatrice Interview 11 Feb 2005.

[46] Correspondence with Sharleen Hobson 12 Aug 2018.

[47] Marriage Record Report 2364, State of Colorado, Division of Vital Statistics.

[48] 1940 US Census, Colorado, Weld, Precinct 11, p. 7A. Elick was working as a farm laborer near Easton, Colorado. He and Louella had an eight-month-old son.

[49] Find A Grave 189872649.

Chapter 28 Beatrice Cardwell Later Years

[1] Beatrice Interview 17 Oct 2004. The obituary of Milton Maphies mentions Beatrice Beaty and Tom Cardwell.

[2] Beatrice Interview 11 Feb 2005. Uncle Tom Barnes was William T. Barnes who died in 1935. His wife Julia died in 1930.

[3] Willis Adley Burchett Marriage, Missouri, *US Marriage Records, 1805-2002* for Willis A Burchett, Dade County 1926-1941, p. 373, Missouri State Archives; Jefferson City, Mo.

[4] Beatrice Interview 17 Oct 2004.

[5] Beatrice Interview 11 Feb 2005.

[6] Moser, *Directory of Towns.*

[7] 1940 US Census for T. Stanford Phipps, Missouri, Cedar, Linn, 20-10, p. 4-B, NARA.

[8] Moser, *Directory of Towns.* According to local resident Mrs. A.D. Hughes, as of 1974, the Rowland store and school were gone. "The last I knew the church building was still standing."

[9] The intersection at Rowland has since built up over the years. A culvert diverts the branch flowing underneath Highway H.

[10] Beatrice Interview 11 Feb 2005.

[11] Beatrice Interview 11 Feb 2005.

[12] Beatrice Interview 11 Feb 2005. Beatrice thought she did not go to her Grandmother Eliza's funeral because she was pregnant. She was not sure but thought she did attend Tom's funeral. She could not remember.

[13] Moser, *Directory of Towns.*

[14] Beatrice Interview 11 Feb 2005. The Claud Store still stands but has not operated for many years. Don Burchett, grandson of George Burchett, purchased the property and restored it. He died in 1991, and the property eventually passed out of the Burchett family.

[15] Beatrice Interview 11 Feb 2005.

[16] Beatrice Interview 11 Feb 2005.

[17] Beatrice Interviews 17 Oct 2004, 11 Feb 2005.

[18] Beatrice Interviews 17 Oct 2004, 11 Feb 2005.

[19] R.H. Richardson Military Record, Battles, and Campaigns: GO 33 WD 45 Aleutian Islands; Records and Citations: Good Conduct Medal, Philippine Liberation Ribbon; Enlisted Record and Report of Separation, Honorable Discharge. Richard H. Richardson, Army Serial No. 37 181 975.

[20] Correspondence with Sharleen Hobson, 27 & 30 Jul 2018.

[21] Beatrice Memory Book.

[22] Correspondence with Sharlee Hobson, 11 Mar 2021.

[23] Correspondence from Beatrice Richardson, Columbia, Missouri to Richard Richardson, Sharl, and Sharron 30 Dec 1960.

[24] *Cedar County Record Book 169,* p. 541, Warranty Deed 31 May 1972.

[25] *Cedar County Recorder of Deeds Book 97*, p. 101,Deed of Trust, 31 May 1972.

[26] *Cedar County Recorder of Deeds Book 97*, p. 100, 31 May 1972,

[27] *Cedar County Record Book 169*, p. 546, 5 Jun 1972.

[28] Correspondence with Sharleen Hobson, 27 & 30 Jul 2018.

[29] *Deed Book Book 97*, p. 100, 14 Feb 1973.

[30] Newspaper Clipping, [newspaper unidentified], 26 Aug 1985.

[31] Correspondence with Sharlee Hobson, 11 Mar 2021.

[32] George Linnaeus Banks. "What I Live For," in *The World's Best Poetry* (Vol. 4), edited by Bliss Carman, et al., Philadelphia: John D. Morris, 1904, pp. 186-187.

Bibliography

A Guide to Its Places and People, (Federal Writer's Project). Boston: Houghton Mifflin, 1937.

Anderson, George Baker. *Landmarks of Rensselaer County, New York.* Syracuse, N.Y.: D. Mason, 1897.

Anderson, Robert Charles, George F. Sanborn, Jr., and Melinde Lutz Sanborn. *The Great Migration: Immigrants to New England 1634-1635* (Vol. 2). Boston: New England Historic Genealogical Society, 2001.

Bailey, Frederic W. *Early Connecticut Marriages as Found on Ancient Church Records Prior to 1800* (7 vols.). New Haven, Conn.: Bureau of American Ancestry, 1896-1906.

Baker, Henry A., Ed. *History of Montville, Connecticut, Formerly the North Parish of New London from 1640 to 1896.* Hartford, Conn.: Press of Case, Lockwood, and Brainard, 1896.

Banks, Charles Edwards. *Topographical Dictionary of 2,885 English Emigrants to New England.* Edited by Elijah Ellsworth Brownell. Baltimore: Southern Book, 1957.

Barbour Collection. *Vital Records, Stonington, New London County, Connecticut* (Vol. 40). Edited by Lorraine Cook White. Baltimore: Genealogical Publishing, 1994.

Bates, Albert C., Ed. *Rolls of Connecticut Men in the French and Indian War, 1755-1762* (Vol. 2). Hartford, Conn.: Connecticut Historical Society, 1903, 1905.

Benedict, David. *A General History of the Baptist Denomination in America, and Other Parts of the World.* London: Lincoln & Edmands, 1813.

Bicentennial Album (1784-1984). Stephentown, N.Y.: Stephentown Historical Society, 1984.

Biographical Review, Containing Life Sketches of Leading Citizens of Essex County, Massachusetts (Vol. 28). Boston: Biographical Review Publishing, 1898.

Boddie, Mrs. John Bennett. "Cardwell of Virginia." *Historical Southern Families* (Vol. 19). Baltimore: Genealogical Publishing, 1974.

Bodge, George Madison. *Soldiers in King Philip's War*, (3rd ed. reprint). Baltimore: Genealogical Publishing, [1891, 1906] 1976.

Bruce, Dwight H., Ed. *Onondaga's Centennial* (Vol. 1). Boston: Boston History, 1896.

Bryan, William Smith, Robert Rose, and William Wilson Elwang. *A History of the Pioneer Families of Missouri: With Numerous Sketches, Anecdotes, Adventures, etc., Relating to Early Days in Missouri. Also the Lives of Daniel Boone and the Celebrated Indian Chief, Black Hawk, with Numerous Biographies and Histories of Primitive Institutions*. St. Louis: Bryan Brand, 1876.

Burnham, J.H. "The Birthplace of American Independence." *Journal of American History* 9 (no. 3, 1915): 440-452.

Campbell, Thomas E. *Colonial Caroline: A History of Caroline County, Virginia*. Richmond, Va.: Diezt, 1989.

Carrington, Wirt Johnson. *A History of Halifax County, Virginia*. Richmond, 1924.

Child, Hamilton. *Gazetteer and Business Directory of Otego County, N.Y. for 1872-3*. Syracuse, N.Y.: Journal Office, 1872.

Church, Benjamin. *The Entertaining History of King Philip's War, which began in the Month of June 1675* (2 ed. 1772 reprint). Boston: Solomon Southwick, [1716] 1983.

Colket, Meredith B., Jr. *Founders of Early American Families: Emigrants from Europe, 1607-1657*. Cleveland, Ohio: The Ohio Society, 2002.

Collections of the Connecticut Historical Society (Vol. 15). Hartford, Conn.: The Society, 1914.

Columbus, Marjorie Daum. *A History of the Fellows Family.* Unpublished Genealogy, 1997.

Congress of the United States. *American State Papers, Class V: Military Affairs* (Vol. 3). Edited by Asbury Dickins and John W. Forney. Washington D.C.: Gales & Seaton, 1860.

Connecticut Wills and Probate Records, 1609-1999. Connecticut State Library, Hartford, Connecticut.

Cooke, Harriet Ruth (Waters). *The Driver Family: A Genealogical Memoir of the Descendants of Robert and Phebe Driver of Lynn, Mass. With an Appendix, Containing Twenty-three Allied Families, 1592-1887.* New York: J. Wilson & Son, 1889.

Cooley, John C. *Rathbone Genealogy: A Complete History of the Rathbone Family Dating from 1574 to Date* (Vol. 1). Syracuse, N.Y.: Currier Job Press, 1808.

Cray, Robert E., Jr. "Weltering in Their Own Blood: Puritan Casualties in King Philip's War." *Historical Journal of Massachusetts* 2 (2009): 106.

Crozier, William A. *Virginia County Records.* Baltimore: Genealogical Publishing, 1905-1913.

Daughters of the American Revolution. *Lineage Book* (Vol. 14). Harrisburg, Pa.: The Society, 1902.

Early Hartford Vital Records. In *Collections of the Connecticut Historical Society* (Vol. 14, reprint). Hartford, Conn.: Connecticut Historical Society, 1860-1967.

Elson, Henry William. "Colonial New England Affairs: King Philip's War." In *History of the United States of America.* New York: MacMillan, 1904.

Essex Institute. *Vital Records, Ipswich, Essex Co., Massachusetts to the End of the Year 1849* (Vol. 2 1634-1892). Salem, Massachusetts: Essex Institute, 1910.

Family Bible of Isaac Fellows 1637-1721. New England Historical Genealogical Register, No. 127.

Fellows, David. *Descendants of William Fellows*. Internet accessed 2007.

Fellows, Dennis. *William Fellows (1609-1676)*. Internet accessed 2003.

Fellows, Erwin Wilcox, *Fellows Families of Onondaga County, New York, and Their Ancestry*. Zephyrhills, Fla.: Author, 1984, 1991.

Fellows, George Marshall. *A Genealogy and Partial History of Fellows Families in America* (6 vols.) Manuscript M. 55, New England Historical and Genealogical Society Library, c.1910.

Fellows, Jerry, *Family Chronicles; Fellows Family Saga*. Unpublished Genealogy, 1996.

Fellows, Mark D. *Descendants of William Fellows of Ipswich, Massachusetts, 1635* (eBook edition). San Diego, Calif.: Author, 2021.

Fellows, Willie [William] Ira. *A Short History of W.I. Fellows and the Fellows Family as Far Back as He Can Remember*. Unpublished Autobiography, c.1940.

Fleet, Beverley. *Virginia Colonial Abstracts, Henrico County-Southside, 1736* (Vol. 21). Baltimore: Genealogical Publishing, 1961.

Foley, Louise P.H. *Early Virginia Families along the James River: Their Deep Roots and Tangled Branches* (Vol. 1). Baltimore: Genealogical Publishing, 2003.

Goodspeed Publishing. *History of Hickory, Polk, Cedar, Dade, and Barton Counties, Missouri*. Chicago: Goodspeed, 1889.

Gray, George Carrington. *Gray's New Book of Roads*. London: Sherwood, Jones, 1824.

Greer, George Cabell. *Early Virginia Immigrants 1623-1666*. Richmond, Va.: W.C. Hill, 1912.

Hammatt, Abraham. *The Hammatt Papers; Early Inhabitants of Ipswich, Massachusetts, 1633-1700*. Baltimore: Genealogical Publishing, [1888-1899] 1980, 1991.

Harrison, Thomas Perrin. "Early Perrin Families of Virginia." *Virginia Genealogical Society Quarterly* 20 (April-June 1982):1-69, & (July-September 1982):113-119.

Hart, Albert Bushnell, Ed. *American History Told by Contemporaries* (Vol. 1). New York: Macmillan, 1898.

Heinemann, Charles Brunk. *Daniel Families of the Southern States, a Compilation of 2 Volumes Covering Numerous Daniel Families.* Washington, D.C.: C.B. Heinemann, 1949.

Herrman, Augustine, Henry Faithorne, and Thomas Withinbrook. *Virginia and Maryland as It Is Planted and Inhabited This Present Year.* London: Authors, 1673.

Hiden, Martha W. "Accompts of the Tristram and Jane." *The Virginia Magazine of History and Biography* 62 (no. 4 1954): 424-447.

History of Audrain County, Missouri. St. Louis: National Historical, 1884.

History of the Connecticut Valley in Massachusetts (Vol. 2). Philadelphia: Louis H. Everts, 1879.

Hoardly, Charles J. *The Public Records of the Colony of Connecticut.* Hartford, Conn.: Lockwood & Brainard, 1868.

Holmes, Frank R. *Directory of the Ancestral Heads of New England Families: 1620-1700* (reprint ed.). Baltimore: Genealogical Publishing, [1923] 1980.

Hotten, John Camden, Ed. *The Original Lists of Persons of Quality* (reprint ed.). [1874] Baltimore: Genealogical Publishing, 1974.

Hoyt, David W. *Old Families of Salisbury and Amesbury, Massachusetts* (Vol. 1). Providence, R.I.: Snow & Farnham, 1897.

Hubbard, William. *The History of the Indian Wars in New England: From the First Settlement to the Termination of the War with King Philip in 1677* (Vol. 1). Notation by Samuel G. Drake. Roxbury, Mass.: W.E. Woodward, [1677] 1865.

Hudson, Charles. *History of the Town of Marlborough.* Boston: n.p., 1862.

Hurd, Duane Hamilton. *History of New London County*. Lebanon, Conn.: J.W. Lewis, 1882.

Ipswich Land Records. Salem, Mass.: Essex County Courthouse.

Johnston, Henry P., and Iris Rose Guertin, Eds. *Collections of the Connecticut Historical Society Revolution Rolls and Lists, 1775-1783*. Hartford, Conn.: Connecticut Historical Society, 1901, 1999.

Larned, Ellen D. *History of Windham County, Connecticut*. Westminister, Md.: Heritage Books, 2008.

Lodgette, George Brainard. *Early Settlers of Rowley, Massachusetts*. Rowley, Mass.: n.p., 1933.

Martner, Frederick. *The Refugees of 1776 from Long Island to Connecticut*. Albany, N.Y.: J.B. Lyon, 1913.

Massachusetts and Maine Families in the Ancestry of Walter Goodwin Davis (3 vols.). Baltimore: Genealogical Publishing, 1996.

Morris, Myrtle Melona. *Joseph and Philena (Elton) Fellows, and Their Ancestry and Descendants: Also the Ancestry of Reuben Fairchild, John and Dorothy (Waldorf) Turner and George Morris*. Washington, D.C.: R.H. Darby, 1940.

Moser, Arthur Paul. *A Directory of Towns, Villages, and Hamlets Past and Present of Cedar County, Missouri*. Springfield, Mo.: Library Center, n.d.

Murphy, Mable Fellows. *The Fellows Family in America*. Worcester, Mass.: M.F. Murphy, 1940.

New England Historical and Genealogical Register (Vol. 1). Edited by New England Genealogical Society. Salem, Mass.: Higginson Book, [1847] 2004.

Pane-Joyce, David. "Massachusetts Bay Colony, Genealogy." *Pane-Joyce Report*. Internet accessed 2015.

Parton, James. *Life of Andrew Jackson* (Vol. 2). Boston: Houghton, Mifflin, 1860.

Pendergraft, Allen. *The Cardwells of Virginia: Thomas Cardwell of Henrico County, His Descendants, and Allied Families.* Researched by I.U. Stucki. Sedona, Az.: Author, 1973.

Peyton, Helen E.H. *Some Early Pioneers of Western Kentucky: Their Ancestors and Descendants* (2nd ed.). Charleston, S.C.: H.E.H. Peyton, 1990.

Plat Books of Cedar and Dade Counties, Missouri. Rockford, Ill.: W.W. Hixson, 1930.

Probate Records of Essex County, Massachusetts, 1635-1681 (3 vols., reprint ed.). Newburyport, Mass.: Parker River Researchers, [1916-1920] 1988.

Public Records of the Colony of Connecticut, 1626-1776 (15 vols.). Edited by J. Hammond Trumbull and Charles J. Hoadly. Hartford, Conn.: Press of Case, Lockwood & Brainard, 1850-1890.

Ready, Effie Fellows. *History of Willie Ira Fellows and His Wife, Martha Frances (Crutchfield) Fellows.* Unpublished Genealogy, c.1983.

Records and Files of the Quarterly Courts of Essex County, Massachusetts, 1636-1686 (9 vols.). Salem, Mass.: Essex Institute, 1911-1075.

Records of the Particular Court of Connecticut, 1639-1663 (Collections of the Connecticut Historical Society, Vol. 22, reprint ed.). Bowie, Md.: Heritage Books, [1928] 1987.

Records of the Suffolk County Court, 1671-1680 (2 vols.). In *Publications of The Colonial Society of Massachusetts* (Vols. 29 & 30). Boston: The Society, 1933.

Rutman, Darrett B., and Anita Rutman. *A Place in Time: Middlesex County, Virginia 1650-1750.* New York: W.W. Norton, 1984.

Sisco, Louis Dow. *Fellows, Fallowes, Fellow and Like Names, Fellows Ancestry in New England and Old England.* New York: Tobias A. Wright, 1926.

Smith, J.E.A. *The History of Pittsfield (Berkshire County,) Massachusetts 1800-1876.* Springfield, Mass.: C.W. Bryan, 1876.

Swaim, Jean Nipps. *The Era of the One-Room Rural Schools of Cedar County, Missouri.* Springfield, Mo.: Barnabas Publishing Service, 1988.

Sweet, Homer de Lois. *The Averys of Groton*. Syracuse, N.Y.: n.d., 1888.

Tepper, Michael, Ed. *New World Immigrants* (Vol. 1). Baltimore: Clearfield, Genealogical Publishing, 1979.

The History of Racine and Kenosha Counties, Wisconsin. Chicago: Western Historical, 1879.

The Parish Register of Christ Church, Middlesex County, Va., from 1653 to 1812. Richmond, Va.: National Society of the Colonial Dames of America. 1897.

Thomson, Nancy. *The First Thomsons and the Fourth Baptist Church of Bellingham, Massachusetts*. Internet accessed 1998.

Torrey, Clarence Almon. *New England Marriages Prior to 1700*. Baltimore: Genealogical Publishing, 1997.

Two Centuries in Westford 1787-1987. Westford, N.Y.: Westford Community Association, 1987.

Tyler, Lyon Gardiner. *Encyclopedia of Virginia Biography*. Baltimore, Md.: Genealogical Publishing, [1915] 2012.

Virginia Magazine of History and Biography, Richmond, Va.: Virginia Historical Society, 1893.

Vorst, Mitch Vander. *Benedict [Vander Vorst/Fellows] Family Genealogy*. Springfield, Ore.: Internet accessed 2015.

Waters, Thomas Franklin. *Candlewood, An Ancient Neighborhood in Ipswich: with Genealogies of John Brown, William Fellows, Robert Kinsman* (reprint ed.). Newburyport, Mass.: Parker River Researchers, [1909] 1986,

Waters, Thomas Franklin. *Ipswich in the Massachusetts Bay Colony; A History of the Town from 1700 to 1917* (Vol. 2). Ipswich, Mass.: Ipswich Historical Society, 1917.

Watson, Ralph Arthur. *Ancestors and Descendants of John and Hannah (Goodwin) Watson of Hartford, Connecticut, and Associated Families*. Baltimore: Gateway, 1985.

Westfall, Dawn Watts. *To the Tenth Generation: The Watts Family with Roots in Halifax County, Virginia* (2nd ed.). Independently published by the author, 2015.

Wheeler, Grace Denison. *The Homes of Our Ancestors in Stonington.* Salem, Mass.: Newcomb & Gauss, 1903.

Wheeler, Richard A. *History of Stonington, Connecticut.* Baltimore: Genealogical Publishing, 1977.

Wheeler, Richard A. *History of the First Congregational Church, Stonington, Connecticut, 1674-1874.* Salem, Mass.: Higginson Book, 1997.

Whitmore, William Henry. *The Descendants of Capt. John Ayers of Brookfield, Massachusetts.* Boston: T.R. Marvin & Son, 1870.

Wildey, Anna Chesebrough. *Genealogy of the Descendants of William Chesebrough.* New York: Press of T.A. Wright 1903.

Index

Surnames in all capital letters represent proven direct ancestors of Beatrice. Information in parentheses: S denotes a spouse who married a Fellows or Cardwell; b. or m. is birthdate or marriage. Example, (S - m.1820) refers to a spouse in a family group who married a Fellows or Cardwell in 1820.

CPSIA information can be obtained
at www.ICGtesting.com
Printed in the USA
BVHW090721220721
612428BV00004B/261